W9-DGG-324

CONCEPTS AND CHALLENGES IN

Earth Science

Revised Third Edition

Leonard Bernstein • Martin Schachter • Alan Winkler • Stanley Wolfe

STANLEY WOLFE

Project Coordinator

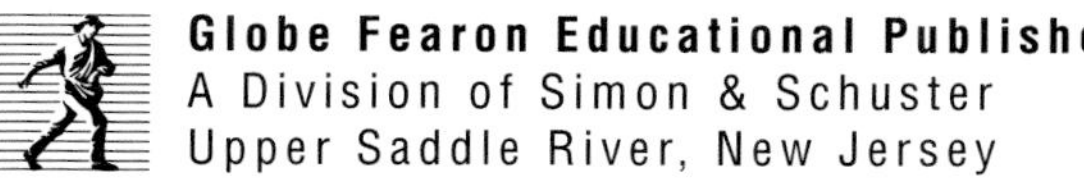

Globe Fearon Educational Publisher
A Division of Simon & Schuster
Upper Saddle River, New Jersey

AUTHORS

Leonard Bernstein

Martin Schachter

Alan Winkler

Stanley Wolfe

Project Coordinator

ABOUT THE COVER

Background: Sand dunes *(M. Fiala, Natural Selection)*
Sand dunes form from sand blown by wind. When wind speed decreases, sand particles drop to the ground. Sand dunes are found in environments such as deserts and beaches. North America's tallest sand dunes are 700 feet tall.

Inset: Iceberg *(E. Hummel, Natural Selection)*
An iceberg forms when a piece of ice breaks off a glacier and falls into the ocean. Icebergs are most often found in the Arctic and Antarctic Oceans. They can be as small as a car or as large as a city.

Printed in the United States of America
1 2 3 4 5 6 7 8 9 10 01 00 99 98 97

ISBN 0-835-92241-3

Globe Fearon Educational Publisher
A Division of Simon & Schuster
Upper Saddle River, New Jersey

Contents

UNIT 4

ROCKS AND HOW THEY FORM *59–78*

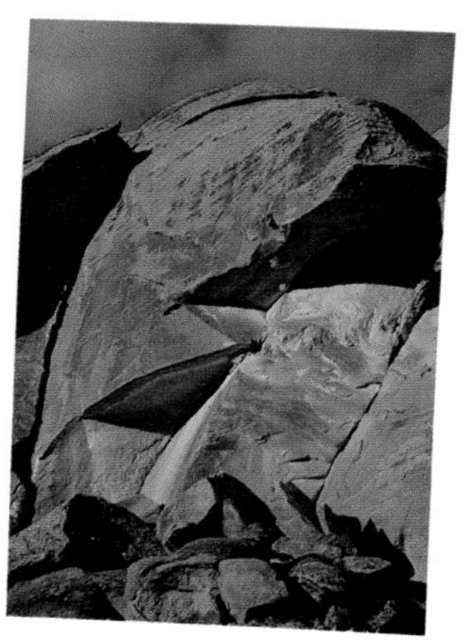

UNIT 5

WEARING DOWN THE EARTH *79–98*

UNIT 6

AGENTS OF EROSION *99–124*

UNIT 7

BUILDING UP THE EARTH *125–148*

UNIT 8
PLATE TECTONICS 149–164

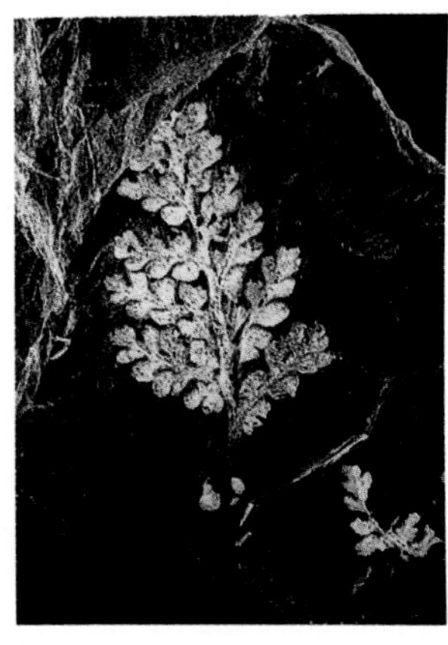

UNIT 9
THE ROCK RECORD 165–182

UNIT 10
THE HYDROSPHERE 183–210

UNIT 15
EXPLORING SPACE

UNIT 16
THE SOLAR SYSTEM

UNIT 17
MOTIONS OF THE EARTH

UNIT 18

STARS *373–400*

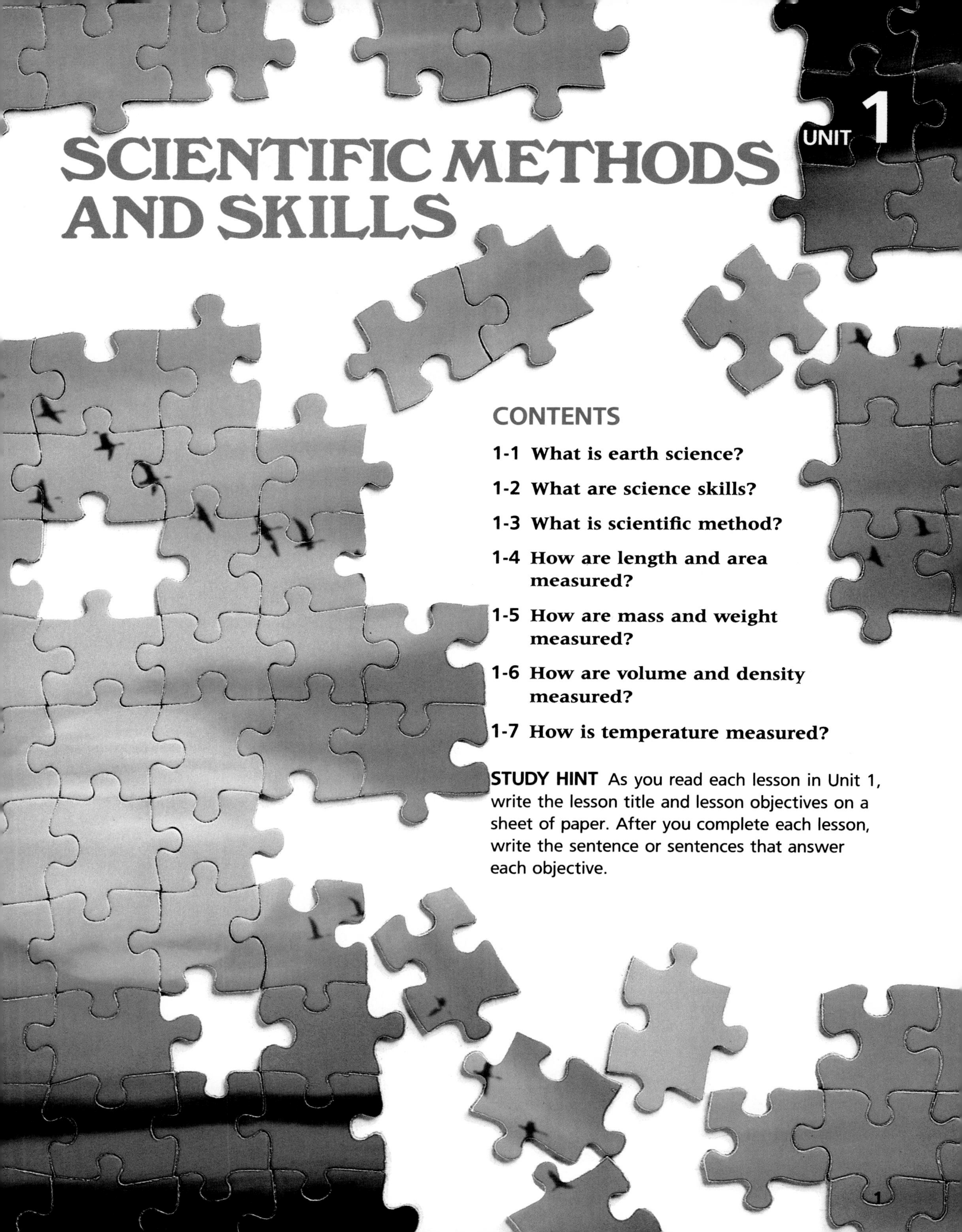

SCIENTIFIC METHODS AND SKILLS

CONTENTS

STUDY HINT As you read each lesson in Unit 1, write the lesson title and lesson objectives on a sheet of paper. After you complete each lesson, write the sentence or sentences that answer each objective.

1-1 What is earth science?

Objective ▸ Identify and describe the main branches of earth science.

TechTerm

▸ **specialization** (SPESH-uh-lih-zay-shun): studying or working in only one part of a subject

Studying Earth Science Earth science is one of the major fields of science. It is the study of the earth and its history. Earth science is also the study of changes on the earth and the earth's place in space.

Earth science is like a jigsaw puzzle made up of four pieces. Each piece is a main branch of earth science. The four main branches are listed in Table 1. Together, they make up the field of earth science.

Analyze: Use Table 1. What are the four main branches of earth science?

Specialization Have you ever heard someone called a specialist (SPESH-ul-ist)? A specialist is a person who studies, or works in, only one part of a subject. This is called **specialization** (SPESH-uh-lih-zay-shun). There are many earth science specialists. Most earth scientists study only one part of earth science. For example, some oceanographers study only waves and tides. Others study the makeup of ocean water. Still others study the ocean bottom.

Describe: What is meant by specialization?

Importance of Earth Science Earth science is part of your everyday life. Did you see a television weather report today? The weather information was reported by an earth scientist. Weather forecasters are meteorologists. Weather forecasters give early warnings about storms. Storm warnings can help save lives and lower property damage.

You are affected by the discoveries of earth scientists. Geologists help locate oil and coal supplies. These fuels (FEWLS) are used to heat homes, run cars, and make electricity. Oceanographers warn people when ocean water is too polluted for swimming. Some oceanographers look for ways to clean polluted water. Experiments carried out in space have helped specialists make new medicines. Space exploration also has led to improvements in radio, television, and telephones.

Explain: Why is the weather important to people?

Table 1 Branches of Earth Science

BRANCH	WHAT IS STUDIED	CAREERS
Geology (jee-AHL-uh-jee)	Earth's structure; formation of the earth; changes on the earth	Surveyor Lapidary
Oceanography (oh-shun-OG-ruh-fee)	Earth's oceans including the living things in the oceans	Underwater photographer Marine chemist
Meteorology (mee-tee-uh-RAHL-uh-jee)	Earth's air, weather, and climate	Weather forecaster Air analyst
Space science	Stars, planets, and other objects in space (astronomy); rockets, satellites, and probes	Astronaut Planetarium technician

LESSON SUMMARY

- Earth science is a major field of science.
- Specialization is the study of only one part of a subject.
- Earth science is part of everyday life.
- People are affected by the discoveries of earth scientists.

CHECK *Complete the following.*

1. The study of the earth's surface and how it changes is ______ .
2. A weather forecaster needs to study the branch of earth science called ______ .
3. The study of the earth's oceans is called ______ .
4. Astronomy is part of the branch of earth science called ______ .
5. Any earth scientist who studies only one small part of earth science is a ______ .
6. Another name for a weather forecaster is a ______ .

APPLY *Complete the following.*

7. **Classify:** In which field of earth science would you study each of these subjects?
   a. whales and fishes **b.** the Grand Canyon **c.** hurricanes **d.** Jupiter
8. What are two ways in which you were affected by or used earth science today?

Ideas in Action

IDEA: People specialize in many areas other than science.

ACTION: List different areas in which people you know, or with whom you come in contact, specialize.

Skill Builder

Building Vocabulary Look at the list of careers in Table 1 on page 2. Use reference materials to find out what the people in each of these careers study or do.

CAREER IN EARTH SCIENCE

SCIENCE TEACHER

You may be surprised to find out that your teacher has homework, too. Science teachers must write lesson plans for each day. They try to find interesting ways to present information to their students. All of this work is done at home. Teachers also correct homework and test papers. They must make up tests and quizzes.

Keeping good records is also important. Attendance and student progress reports must be kept. Science teachers also must keep up-to-date on new science developments. They may attend workshops, meetings, and conferences. Often, teachers will take science and education courses at a university or a college.

For more information about science teaching, you may want to talk to your teacher, guidance counselor, or parents.

1-2 What are science skills?

Objective ▸ Identify and use science skills to solve problems and answer questions.

TechTerm

▸ **hypothesis** (hy-PAHTH-uh-sis): suggested solution to a problem

Science Skills Scientists use many skills to gather information. These skills are sometimes called science skills. You use science skills, too. You probably used some science skills today. When you use most science skills, you use five senses. Your senses are seeing, hearing, touching, smelling, and tasting.

Nine science skills are used in this book. You will even see skills symbols. The symbols will let you know when you are using a skill. Soon, you will be thinking like a scientist.

▸ ***Name:*** What are your five senses?

Researching Do you know what the word "research" means? The prefix "re-" means again. "Search" means to look for or to find out. So when you do research, you look for something again. You study or investigate. You can do research by reading books, magazines, and newspapers. You can also do experiments. Experimenting is a kind of research.

▸ ***Identify:*** What are two ways to do research?

Communicating When you talk to your best friend, you are communicating, or sharing information. If you write a letter, you are communicating. Scientists communicate all the time. They write books and magazine or newspaper articles about their work. Sharing information is very important to scientists.

▸ ***Describe:*** What are you doing when you communicate with someone?

Observing When you observe, you use your senses. You must pay close attention to everything that happens.

Measuring When you measure, you compare an unknown value to a known value. Measuring makes observations more exact.

Inferring When you infer, you form a conclusion based upon facts without making observations.

Classifying When you classify, you group things based upon how they are alike.

Organizing When you organize, you work in an orderly way. You put your information in order.

Predicting When you predict, you state ahead of time what will happen based upon what you already know.

Hypothesizing When you hypothesize, you state or suggest a solution to a problem. A **hypothesis** (hy-PAHTH-uh-sis) is a suggested solution to a problem based upon what is already known or observed.

Modeling When you model, you use a copy of what you are studying to help explain it. A model can be a three-dimensional copy, a drawing, or a diagram.

Analyzing When you analyze, you study information carefully.

LESSON SUMMARY

- Scientists use science skills to gather information.
- Ten science skills are used in this book.
- Researching includes reading and experimenting.
- Communicating means sharing information.
- Other science skills are observing, measuring, inferring, classifying, organizing, predicting, hypothesizing, modeling, and analyzing.

CHECK *Complete the following.*

1. Your five senses are seeing, hearing, touching, _______, and tasting.
2. Skill _______ let you know when you are using a science skill.
3. Research includes reading and _______ .
4. When you communicate with someone, you share _______ .
5. When you _______, you compare an unknown value with a known value.
6. When you _______, you put information in order.
7. A suggested solution to a problem is a _______ .
8. When you _______, you group things based on how they are alike.

APPLY *Complete the following.*

9. **Describe:** Describe two ways in which you used science skills today. What skills did you use? How did they help you to solve a problem?
10. Match each sense to the correct sense organ. A sense organ is part of your body that picks up changes in your surroundings.

1. Nose	a. Hearing
2. Tongue	b. Seeing
3. Eye	c. Smelling
4. Skin	d. Touching
5. Ear	e. Tasting

11. Why do you think observing is an important skill?

Ideas in Action

IDEA: Weather forecasters predict what the weather will be like each day during the week.
ACTION: Predict what you think the weather will be like tomorrow. Then check your prediction to see if it was correct.

ACTIVITY

USING SCIENCE SKILLS

You will need a shoebox with a lid, a rubber band, and several small objects. You will need a partner to do this activity.

1. Place several small objects into the shoebox. Do not let your partner see what you put into the shoebox.
2. Cover the shoebox with its lid.
3. Put the rubber band around the shoebox to keep the lid on.
4. Exchange shoeboxes with your partner.
5. Gently shake, turn, and rattle the shoebox.
6. Try to describe what is in the shoebox without opening it. Write your descriptions on a sheet of paper.

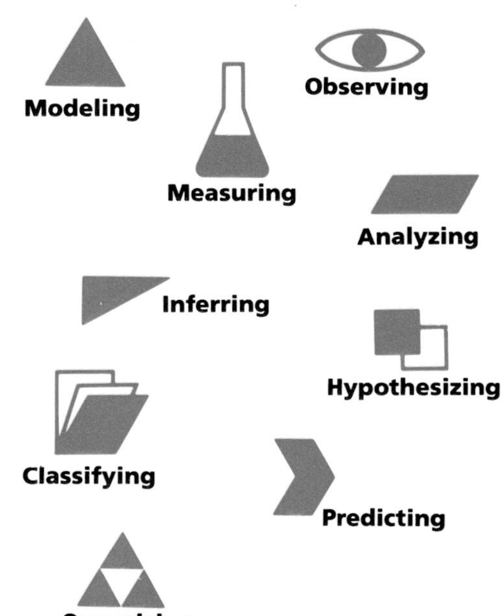

Questions

1. What science skills did you use?
2. Which of your senses was most important to you?
3. Define direct and indirect observations. Which kind of observations did you use?

1-3 What is scientific method?

Objective ▶ Describe how to use scientific method to solve a problem.

TechTerms

- ▶ **data** (DAY-tuh): information
- ▶ **hypothesis** (hy-PAHTH-uh-sis): suggested answer to a problem
- ▶ **scientific method:** model, or guide, used to solve problems and to get information

Scientific Method Scientists solve problems a lot like you do. Suppose you turn on a radio and nothing happens. What would you do? You might look to see if the radio is plugged in. You might check the station by turning the dial. If you did one of these things, you started to use **scientific method.** Scientific method is a model, or guide, used to solve problems.

Scientists do not have one scientific method. They combine some or all of the science skills to solve different problems. Scientists also follow certain steps. Because each problem is different, the steps may be used in any order. You can write a laboratory report using these steps.

▶ ***Define:*** What is scientific method?

- ▶ **Identify and State the Problem** Scientists often state a problem as a question.
- ▶ **Gather Information** Scientists read and communicate with one another. In this way, they can learn about work that has already been done.
- ▶ **State a Hypothesis** Scientists state clearly what they expect to find out. They state a **hypothesis** (hy-PAHTH-uh-sis), or a suggested answer to a problem.
- ▶ **Design an Experiment** To test a hypothesis, scientists design an experiment.
- ▶ **Make Observations and Record Data** During an experiment, scientists make careful observations. The information that they get is their **data** (DAY-tuh).
- ▶ **Organize and Analyze Data** Scientists organize their data. Graphs, tables, charts, and diagrams are ways to organize data. Then the data can be analyzed, or studied.
- ▶ **State a Conclusion** A conclusion is a summary that explains the data. It states whether or not the data support the hypothesis. The conclusion answers the question stated in the problem.

LESSON SUMMARY

- Scientists use a model, or guide, called scientific method to solve problems.
- Scientists use different science skills, and different steps of scientific method, to solve different problems.
- The steps of scientific method are: Identify and state the problem; Gather information; State a hypothesis; Design an experiment; Make observations and record data; Organize and analyze data; State a conclusion.

CHECK *Complete the following.*

1. A model used to solve problems is called scientific ______ .
2. Scientists often state a problem as a ______ .
3. When scientists state what they expect to find out, they are stating a ______ .
4. Scientists design ______ to test hypotheses.
5. During an experiment, scientists gather information, or ______ .
6. Data must be organized and ______ , or studied.
7. A ______ is a summary that explains the data.
8. Tables, graphs, diagrams, and ______ are ways to organize data.

APPLY *Complete the following.*

9. **Explain:** How are a hypothesis and a conclusion related?
10. List the steps in scientific method.
11. Why do you think it is important for scientists to gather information before they begin work on a problem?

Skill Builder

Writing a Laboratory Report Write a laboratory report describing the following experiment. Be sure to include the steps of scientific method in your report.

Fill a glass with water. Place a piece of cardboard over the top of the glass. Hold the glass over a sink with one hand. With the other hand, hold the cardboard tightly against the top of the glass. Turn the glass upside down. Take your hand away from the cardboard. The piece of cardboard stays in place. The water stays in the glass. This happens because air pressure pushes upward. Air pressure keeps the cardboard from falling.

ACTIVITY

ORGANIZING DATA

You will need a sheet of graph paper, lined paper, and a pencil.

1. Study each set of data.
2. Decide the best way to organize each set of data.
3. Be sure to give each table, graph, or diagram a title. Tables should have headings for each column.

Questions

1. How did you organize each set of data?
2. Compare the way you organized the data with the ways two classmates organized the data.

Data 1: Weather Symbols

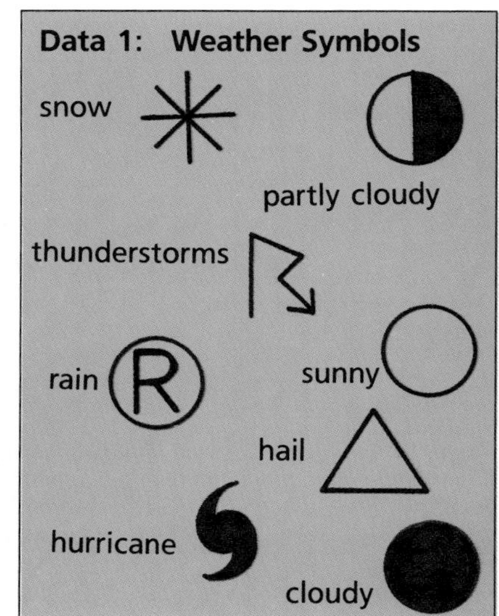

Data 2: Earth's Water Supply

97%	Oceans (salt water)
0.02%	Lakes, rivers, and streams
0.63%	Underground water
2.15%	Ice and snow

Data 3: Uses of Coal

Heating homes; Mothballs; Paint thinners; Detergents; Making electricity; Perfumes; Welding; Dyes; Medicines; Fertilizers; Ink; Plastics

1-4 How are length and area measured?

Objective ▸ Identify the SI and metric units used to measure length and area.

TechTerms

- ▸ **meter** (MEE-tur): basic SI and metric unit of length
- ▸ **unit** (YOU-nit): amount used to measure something

Scientific Measurements The metric system is an international system of measurement. It is used in most countries. Everyday measurements are given in metric **units** (YOU-nits). A unit is an amount used to measure something. In the United States, the English system and the metric system are used.

Since 1960, scientists have used a more modern form of the metric system. This measurement system is called SI. The letters "SI" stand for **S**ystems **I**nternational. Many of the units in SI are the same as in the metric system.

▸ *Name:* What are two internationally used measurement systems?

Changing Size The metric system is based on units of 10. This makes it easy to use. Each unit in the metric system is ten times greater or smaller than the next unit. To change the size of a unit, you add a prefix to the unit. The prefix makes the unit larger or smaller.

Table 1 Prefixes and Meanings

PREFIX	MEANING
kilo- (KILL-uh)	one thousand (1000)
hecto- (HEC-tuh)	one hundred (100)
deca- (DEC-uh)	ten (10)
deci- (DESS-ih)	one tenth (1/10)
centi- (SEN-tih)	one hundredth (1/100)
milli- (MILL-ih)	one thousandth (1/1000)

▸ *Describe:* How do you change the size of a metric unit?

Units of Length In the metric system, length and distance are measured by a unit called the **meter** (MEE-tur). The meter is the basic unit of length. You use prefixes to make larger or smaller units of length. A kilometer (KIL-uh-mee-tur) is 1000 meters. A centimeter (SEN-tih-mee-tur) is 1/100 of a meter. Table 2 compares units of length. The table also shows the symbols for each unit.

Table 2 Units of Length

1000 millimeters (mm)	=	1 meter (m)
100 centimeters (cm)	=	1 meter
10 decimeters (dm)	=	1 meter
10 millimeters	=	1 centimeter
1000 meters	=	1 kilometer (km)

▸ *Compare:* How many centimeters are there in one meter?

Measuring Length and Area A meter stick is used to measure length. A meter stick is divided into 100 equal parts by numbered lines. The distance between two numbered lines is equal to one centimeter (1 cm). Each centimeter is divided into 10 equal parts. Each of these parts is one millimeter (1 mm). One millimeter is 1/1000 of a meter.

Do you know how people find the right size rug for a room? They find the area of the room. You can find the area of any rectangle by multiplying its length by its width. Area is expressed in square units, such as square meters (m^2) or square centimeters (cm^2).

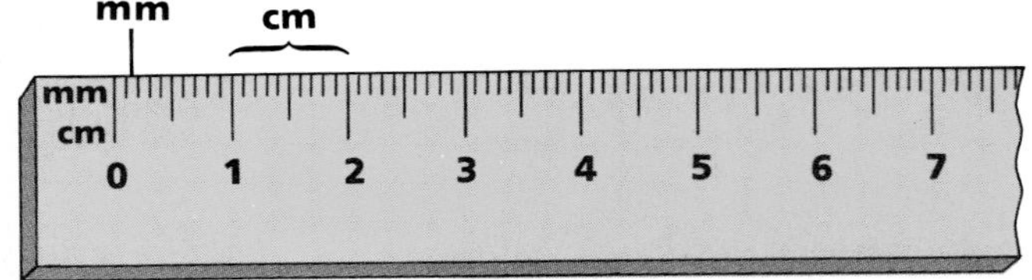

▸ *Calculate:* How many millimeters are there in one meter?

LESSON SUMMARY

- The metric system is an international system of measurement.
- Scientists use a more modern form of the metric system called SI.
- Prefixes are used to change the size of a metric or SI unit.
- The meter is the basic metric and SI unit of length.
- A meter stick is used to measure length.
- The area of a rectangle is found by multiplying the length by the width.

CHECK *Complete the following.*

1. The ______ system of measurement is used in most countries.
2. A ______ is an amount used to measure something.
3. A modern form of the metric system is called ______ .
4. The metric system and SI are based on units of ______ .
5. A ______ added to a unit changes the size of the unit.
6. One centimeter is ______ of a meter.
7. The ______ is the basic metric unit of length.
8. A ______ stick is used to measure length.
9. The area of a rectangle is found by multiplying its length by its ______ .

APPLY *Use the tables on page 8 to complete the following.*

10. **Calculate:** A rug is 4 m wide. How much is this in centimeters?
11. **Calculate:** Two towns are 15 km apart. What is the distance in meters?
12. **Analyze:** What is the symbol for a centimeter?

Skill Builder

Calculating Use a metric ruler to find the length and width of your desk, this book, and a sheet of notebook paper. Find the area of each object. Organize your data in a table.

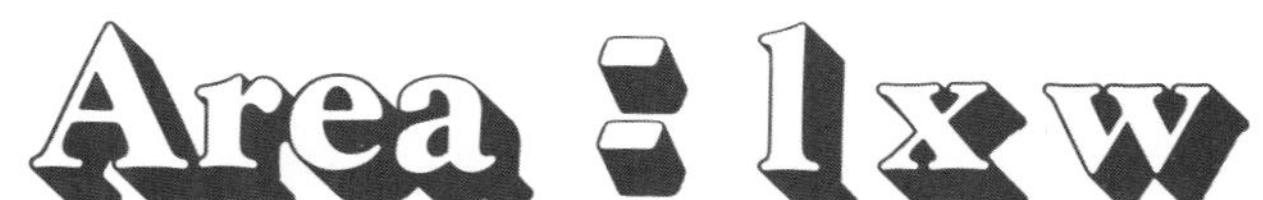

LOOKING BACK IN SCIENCE

LENGTH MEASUREMENTS OF THE PAST

In the past, people used many different units for measuring things. Many ancient civilizations had measurement systems based on units that were the lengths of a man's thumb, hand, arm, and foot. Some of these units are still in use. For example, the height of a horse is still measured in hands.

The ancient Egyptians used a unit of length called a cubit (KYOO-bit). A cubit was the length of a man's forearm from his elbow to the end of his middle finger. The Romans used the width of a man's thumb as a unit of length. This unit was called a unicea. Twelve unicea equalled one foot. As you can probably guess from its name, a foot was the length of a man's foot. A yard was the distance from a man's nose to the end of his middle finger.

In England, these same measurements were used. The measurements were based on the lengths of the king's thumb, foot, and arm. Imagine the problems when another man became king. All the measurements would change.

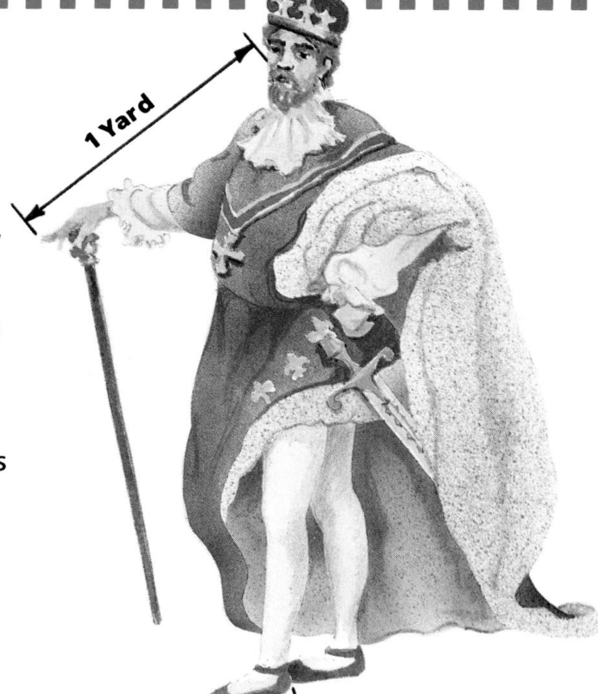

1-5 How are mass and weight measured?

Objectives ▸ Identify the SI unit of mass. ▸ Compare mass and weight.

TechTerms

- **kilogram** (KIL-uh-gram): basic SI unit of mass
- **mass:** amount of matter in an object
- **weight:** measure of the pull of gravity on an object

Mass The amount of matter in an object is its **mass.** There is more matter in a car than in a bicycle. The car has more mass than the bicycle.

The basic unit of mass in SI is the **kilogram** (KIL-uh-gram) (kg). The gram (g) is sometimes used as a smaller unit of mass. Remember that the prefix "kilo-" means 1000. There are 1000 g in a kilogram.

▸ *Identify:* What is the basic SI unit of mass?

Mass and Weight Mass and **weight** are related, but they are not the same. Weight is a measure of the pull of gravity on an object. Gravity is a force that acts between all objects. The strength of the pull of gravity depends on the mass of the objects and how far apart they are. On Earth, gravity pulls all objects toward the center of the earth. Your weight can change because the pull of gravity is not the same everywhere on Earth. You would weigh slightly less on top of a high mountain than at sea level. As an astronaut moves farther away from the earth, the pull of the earth's gravity becomes weaker. The astronaut weighs less in space than on Earth. However, the astronaut's mass stays the same.

▸ *Apply:* Explain why an astronaut's mass would be the same on the moon as on the earth.

Measuring Mass Mass is measured with an instrument called a balance. A balance works like a seesaw. It compares an unknown mass with a known mass. One kind of balance that is commonly used to measure mass is a triple-beam balance. A triple-beam balance has a pan on which the object being measured is placed. It also has three beams. Weights, or riders, are moved along each beam until the object on the pan is balanced. Each rider gives a reading in grams. The mass of the object is equal to the total readings of all three riders.

▸ *Name:* What is an instrument used to measure mass?

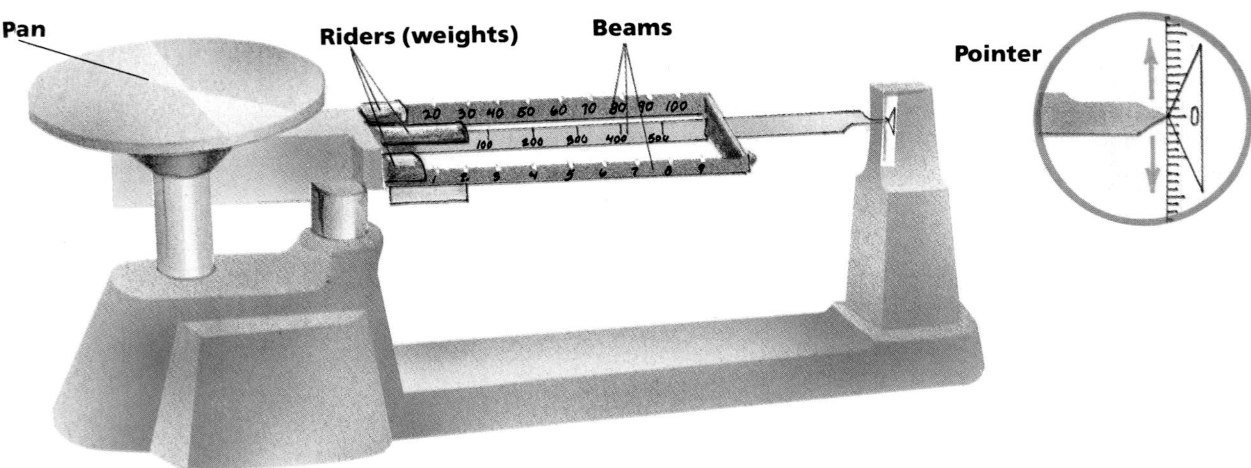

LESSON SUMMARY

- Mass is the amount of matter in an object.
- The basic SI unit of mass is the kilogram.
- Weight is a measure of the pull of gravity on an object.
- A balance is used to measure mass.

CHECK *Complete the following.*

1. The amount of matter in an object is its ______ .
2. A bicycle has ______ mass than a car.
3. The ______ is the basic SI unit of mass.
4. There are ______ grams in one kilogram.
5. The pull of gravity on an object is its ______.
6. Gravity pulls you toward the ______ of the earth.
7. You would weigh ______ at sea level that on top of a mountain.
8. An astronaut's ______ is the same in space and on Earth.
9. An instrument used to measure mass in a ______ .

APPLY *Complete the following.*

10. **Hypothesize:** What force do you think holds you on the surface of the earth?
11. **Infer:** Why does the pull of gravity on an astronaut get weaker as the astronaut moves farther from the earth?
12. How many kilograms is object A? Object B?

Ideas in Action

IDEA: Astronauts in space are "weightless."
ACTION: Pretend that you are an astronaut on a spacecraft. Describe how some of your everyday activities would be affected by weightlessness.

SCIENCE CONNECTION

COMPARATIVE SHOPPING

When you shop, you want to get the most for your money. How can you be sure that you are getting the best value for your money? By reading labels and comparing prices.

Different brands of items come in containers of different sizes. This makes the job of comparative shopping hard. For example, canned green beans may come in at least three sizes. There also are many different brands of canned green beans.

Which can of green beans is the best value? The easiest way to find out is to look at the price tag under the item on the shelf. The price tag usually is divided into two parts. One part lists the price and weight of the item. The other part gives the price per unit of weight. By comparing the price per unit of weight of different cans of green beans, you can determine the best value.

If price tags are not available, you can use a simple formula to determine the price per unit of weight. To figure this out, divide the price of the container by the total weight of the container (ounces or grams). This will give you the price per unit of weight (ounces or grams). Do this for both items and compare the price per unit. Which is the better value? The better value is the item you would buy. By comparing prices, you can get the best value for your money.

How are volume and density measured?

Objective ▸ Explain how volume and density are measured.

TechTerms

- **density** (DEN-suh-tee): amount of mass in a given volume
- **liter** (LEE-tur): basic metric unit of volume
- **volume:** amount of space something takes up

Measuring Volume The amount of space something takes up is its **volume.** The volume of a liquid is often measured in **liters** (LEE-turs). The liter (L) is the basic unit of volume in the metric system. Smaller volumes can be measured in milliliters (MILL-ih-lee-turs). There are 1000 milliliters (mL) in a liter.

▸ ***Define:*** What is a liter?

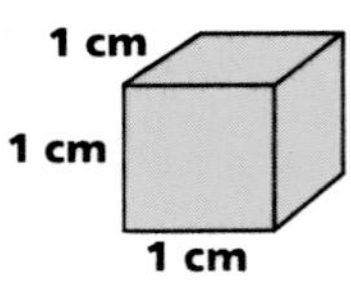

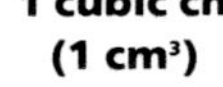
1 cubic cm ($1\ cm^3$)

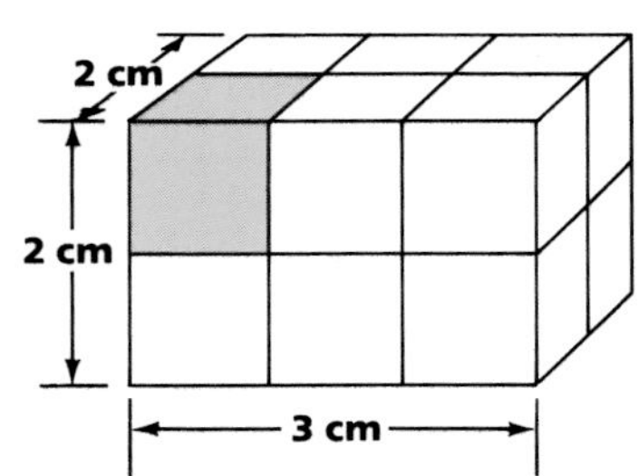

Cubic Centimeters Volume can be measured in cubic centimeters. Look at the drawing of the cube. Each side is 1 cm long. The volume of the cube is 1 cubic centimeter (cm^3). One cubic centimeter is the same as 1 milliliter. Now look at the drawing of the box. Its length is 3 cm. Its width is 2 cm. Its height is 2 cm. The volume of the box can be found by multiplying its length by its width by its height. The volume of the box is 12 cm^3.

If you have a box that is 10 cm on each side, its volume would be 1000 cm^3. A liter is the same as 1000 cm3. One liter of liquid will fill the box exactly.

▸ ***Analyze:*** How many milliliters of water would fill a 12-cm^3 box?

Density Did you ever pick up a large object and find that it was not as heavy as you thought? Did you ever pick up a small object that was very heavy? This happens because objects are made of different materials. Different materials have different **densities** (DEN-suh-teez). Density is a measurement of how much mass is in a given volume. For example, the density of iron is 8 grams per cubic centimeter (8 g/cm^3). This means that a piece of iron with a volume of 1 cm^3 has a mass of 8 g. Gold has a density of 19 g/cm^3. It is more than twice as dense as iron. If a piece of gold and a piece of iron are the same size, the gold will have a weight and mass more than twice iron.

The density of a material does not depend on the amount of material you have. A large piece of iron has the same density as a small piece. If you cut a copper tube in half, each piece has the same density as the whole tube.

▸ ***Analyze:*** What is the mass of 1 cm^3 of a metal if its density is 11 g/cm^3?

Finding Density You can find the density of any material. You need a piece of the material. You need to find the volume and mass of the piece. Mass divided by the volume gives density.

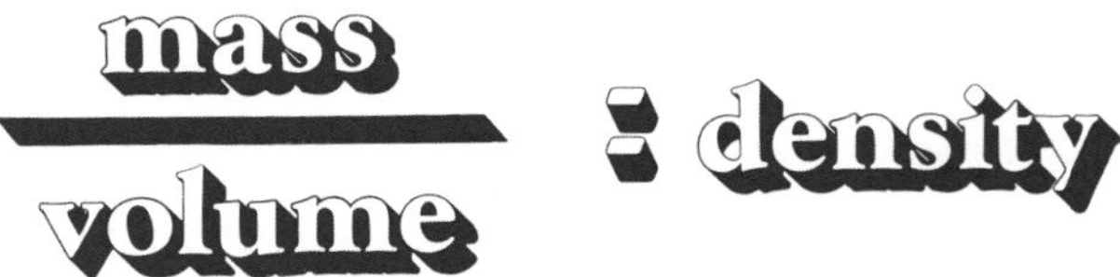

▸ ***Calculate:*** A piece of lead has a mass of 72 g. Its volume is 6 cm^3. What is its density?

LESSON SUMMARY

- The volume of a liquid is often measured in liters.
- Volume also can be measured in cubic centimeters.
- Density is a measure of the amount of mass in a given volume.
- The density of a material does not depend on the size or amount of material you have.
- Density equals mass divided by volume.

CHECK *Complete the following.*

1. The basic metric unit of volume is the ______ .
2. One liter of liquid is equal to ______ cubic centimeters.
3. The symbol for cubic centimeter is ______ .
4. Density = ______/volume.
5. If the density of gold is 19 g/cm^3, the mass of 1 cm^3 of gold is ______ .

APPLY *Use table 1 to complete the following.*

6. **Analyze:** An object has a volume of 10 cm^3 and a mass of 27 g. What is the object made of?
7. Which material has the greatest density?
8. Is lead or iron more dense?

Skill Builder

Calculating The density of all materials is compared with the density of water. Materials that are less dense than water float on water. Materials that are more dense than water sink. Which of the materials in the table will float in water? Which will sink?

Table 1 Densities

MATERIAL	DENSITY	MATERIAL	DENSITY
Cork	0.2 g/cm^3	Iron	7.9 g/cm^3
Alcohol	0.8 g/cm^3	Lead	11.3 g/cm^3
Water	1.0 g/cm^3	Mercury	13.6 g/cm^3
Aluminum	2.7 g/cm^3	Gold	19.3 g/cm^3

ACTIVITY

CALCULATING VOLUME

You will need 3 boxes of different sizes, paper, and a metric ruler.

1. Copy Table 2 on a sheet of paper.

Table 2 Box Measurements

BOX	LENGTH	WIDTH	HEIGHT	VOLUME
1				
2				
3				

2. Measure the length, width, and height of each box in centimeters. Record each measurement in your table.
3. Calculate the volume of each box. Record each volume in the table.

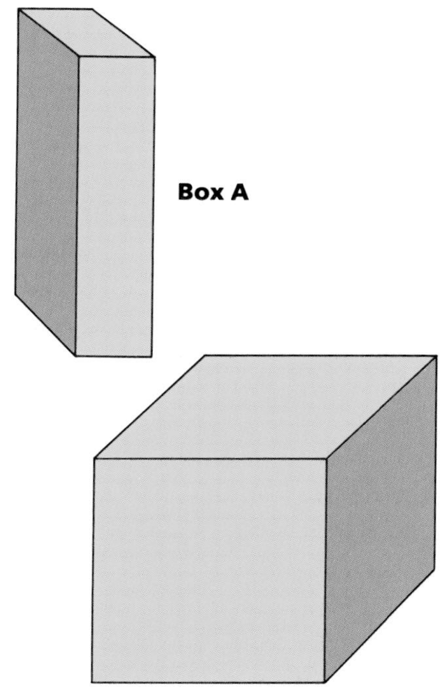

Questions

1. Which of your three boxes has the largest volume?
2. Which box in the diagram has the smaller volume?
3. How many milliliters of liquid would exactly fill each box?

1-7 How is temperature measured?

Objective ▶ Explain how temperature is measured.

TechTerms

- ▶ **degree Celsius** (SEL-see-us): metric unit of temperature
- ▶ **temperature:** measure of how hot or cold something is

Temperature The **temperature** of anything is a measure of how hot or cold it is. You also can say it is the amount of heat energy something contains. For example, warm water has more heat than the same mass of ice.

▶ ***Define:*** What is temperature?

The Thermometer Temperature is measured with an instrument called a thermometer. A thermometer is a glass tube. At the bottom of the tube is a wider part called the bulb. The bulb is filled with a liquid. Some liquids that are often used are mercury, colored alcohol, or colored water. The liquid can rise or fall in the tube. When heat is added, the liquid expands, or gets larger. It rises in the glass tube. When heat is taken away, the liquid contracts, or gets smaller. The liquid falls in the tube. On the side of the tube are a series of marks. You read the thermometer by looking at the mark on the tube where the liquid stops.

▶ ***Name:*** What instrument is used to measure temperature?

Measuring Temperature Temperature is usually measured on one of two scales. They are the Fahrenheit (FAHR-uhn-hyt) scale and the Celsius (SEL-see-us) scale. The Fahrenheit (F) scale is used in the United States. Most other countries use the Celsius (C) scale. The Celsius scale is usually used in science. Each unit on the Celsius scale is a **degree Celsius** (°C). The degree Celsius is the metric unit of temperature.

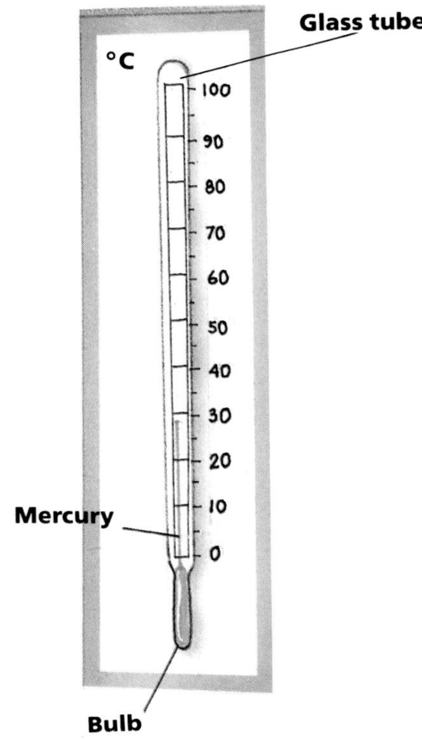

Scientists working with very low temperatures use another temperature scale. It is the Kelvin (K) scale. The Kelvin scale is a part of SI. The Kelvin scale begins at absolute zero, or 0 K. There is no heat energy at absolute zero.

Table 1 Comparing Temperatures

	°C	K	°F
Absolute zero	−273	0	−459
Freezing Point (Water)	0	273	32
Room Temperature	22	295	72
Human Body Temperature	37	310	98.6
Boiling Point (Water)	100	373	212

Observe: What is the freezing point of water on the Celsius scale?

LESSON SUMMARY

- Temperature is a measure of how hot or cold something is.
- Temperature is measured with a thermometer.
- Two commonly used temperature scales are the Fahrenheit scale and the Celsius scale.
- The Kelvin scale is an SI temperature scale.

CHECK *Complete the following.*

1. The _______ of something is how hot or cold it is.
2. Temperature is the amount of _______ energy in something.
3. An instrument used to measure temperature is a _______ .
4. The two parts that make up a thermometer are a glass tube and a _______ .
5. The bulb of a thermometer contains a _______, such as mercury.
6. When heat is taken away, the mercury in a thermometer _______ in the tube.
7. The _______ is the metric unit of temperature.
8. Three temperature scales are the _______ scale, the Celsius scale, and the Kelvin scale.
9. The _______ scale begins at absolute zero.

APPLY *Use the table on page 14 to complete the following.*

10. **Compare:** What is the boiling point of water on each temperature scale?
11. **Compare:** What is absolute zero on the Fahrenheit scale? On the Celsius scale?
12. Read the thermometer on page 14. What temperature is shown on the thermometer?

Health and Safety Tip

Mercury is poisonous if you inhale it. It also can be absorbed through the skin. If you break a thermometer, tell your teacher or your parents immediately. Never clean up a broken thermometer with your hands. Contact your local poison control center. Find out how to clean up mercury properly. Find out the symptoms of mercury poisoning.

PEOPLE IN SCIENCE

WILLIAM THOMSON, LORD KELVIN (1824–1907)

William Thomson was an English engineer, mathematician, and physicist. Thomson entered the University of Glasgow at the age of 10. In 1866, a cable was placed on the floor of the Atlantic Ocean. It was the first successful transatlantic cable. Messages could be sent between Europe and the United States using this cable. William Thomson was the engineer for the transatlantic cable project. Queen Victoria of England knighted him for this work. In 1892, Thomson became Lord Kelvin.

Lord Kelvin had more than 70 inventions patented. One of his inventions was the galvanometer (gal-vuh-NAHM-uh-tur). This instrument improved the way messages on a cable were received. Kelvin also invented the first ship's compass that was not affected by the iron in a ship.

Kelvin is most famous for his work on temperature measurement. He was the first person to suggest using a gas-filled thermometer to make accurate temperature readings. The Kelvin scale is named after him. The Kelvin scale is most often used to measure very cold temperatures near absolute zero.

UNIT 1 Challenges

STUDY HINT Before you begin the Unit Challenges, review the TechTerms and Lesson Summary for each lesson in this unit.

TechTerms

data (6)
degree Celsius (14)
density (12)
hypothesis (4)
kilogram (10)
liter (12)
mass (10)
meter (8)
scientific method (6)
specialization (2)
temperature (14)
unit (8)
volume (12)
weight (10)

TechTerm Challenges

Matching *Write the TechTerm that best matches each description.*

1. amount of mass in a given volume
2. measure of the pull of gravity on an object
3. amount used to measure something
4. studying or working in only one part of a subject
5. measure of how hot or cold something is
6. basic metric unit of length

Identifying Word Relationships *Explain how the words in each pair are related. Write your answers in complete sentences.*

1. meter, length
2. kilogram, mass
3. liter, volume
4. degree Celsius, temperature
5. data, experiment
6. hypothesis, scientific method

Content Challenges

Completion *Write the term or phrase that best completes each statement.*

1. The branch of earth science in which weather is studied is ______ .
2. Reading and experimenting are two kinds of ______ .
3. Using a copy of something to help explain it is called ______ .
4. The grouping of things that are alike in some way is called ______ .
5. Scientific method is a ______, or guide, used to solve problems.
6. An experiment is a test of a ______ .
7. Graphs, tables, charts, and diagrams are ways to ______ information.
8. A conclusion is a summary that explains ______ .
9. Weight is a measure of the pull of ______ on an object.
10. Hearing, smelling, tasting, touching, and seeing are the five ______ .
11. A millimeter is ______ of a meter.
12. The formula for density is ______ .

Multiple Choice *Write the letter of the term or phrase that best completes each statement.*

1. One cubic centimeter is equal to
   a. 1 liter. **b.** 1000 liters. **c.** 1000 mL. **d.** 1 mL.
2. Density is measured in
   a. g/cm^2. **b.** m/cm^2. **c.** g/cm^3. **d.** cm^2.
3. The prefix centi- means
   a. 1/100. **b.** 100. **c.** 1/10. **d.** 1000.
4. The prefix kilo- means
   a. 1/100. **b.** 100. **c.** 1/10. **d.** 1000.
5. The metric system is based on units of
   a. 1. **b.** 10. **c.** 100. **d.** 1000.
6. Temperature is measured with a
   a. balance. **b.** thermometer. **c.** metric ruler. **d.** meter stick.
7. Mass is measured with a
   a. balance. **b.** thermometer. **c.** metric ruler. **d.** meter stick.
8. The basic metric unit of mass is the
   a. meter. **b.** liter. **c.** gram. **d.** kilogram.
9. The SI unit of temperature is the
   a. °F. **b.** °G. **c.** °C. **d.** Kelvin.
10. The temperature scale most often used in the United States is the
    a. Fahrenheit scale. **b.** Celsius scale. **c.** SI scale. **d.** Kelvin scale.
11. In the metric system, the prefix meaning 10 is
    a. kilo-. **b.** hecto-. **c.** deca-. **d.** deci-.
12. The symbol for milliliters is
    a. mg. **b.** ml. **c.** mL. **d.** mm.

Understanding the Features

Reading Critically *Use the feature reading selections to answer the following. Page numbers for the features are shown in parentheses.*

1. **Infer:** Why do you think science teachers often take science and education courses? (3)
2. How is the height of a horse measured? (9)
3. What is a cubit? (9)
4. What kind of information is listed on each part of a price tag? (11)
5. **Measure:** Which is a better value, a 16-ounce can of corn for $ .89 or a 12-ounce can of corn for $ .69? Explain your answer. (11)
6. Identify three things for which Lord Kelvin is responsible. (15)
7. What is the Kelvin scale usually used to measure? (15)

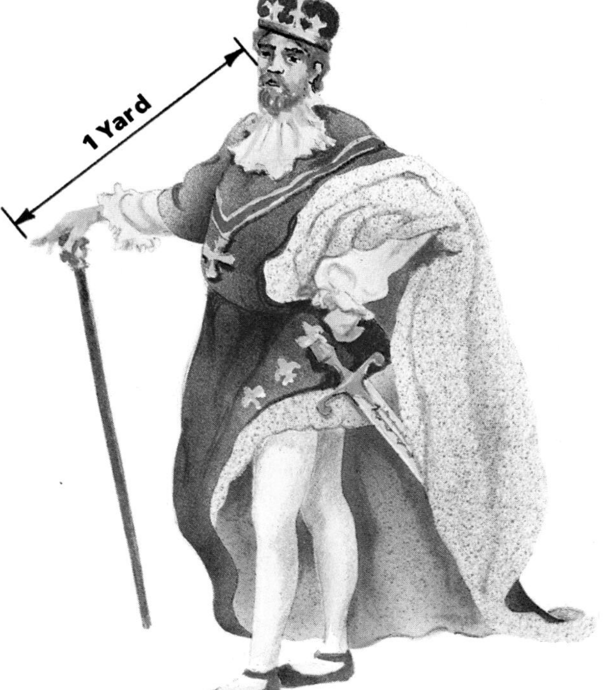

Concept Challenges

Critical Thinking *Answer the following in complete sentences.*

1. **Relate:** Explain why classifying is a way to organize information.
2. How does mass differ from weight?
3. Choose three science skills. Explain how you use each skill in your daily life.
4. How does a hypothesis differ from a prediction?
5. How could you use density to tell the difference between a piece of iron and a piece of lead?

Interpreting a Table *Use the table to help you to answer the following.*

Table 1 Air Temperature in Atlantic City (°C)

	JAN	FEB	MAR	APR	MAY	JUNE
High	6	6	9	13	18	28
Low	−2	−2	2	6	12	22
	JULY	**AUG**	**SEP**	**OCT**	**NOV**	**DEC**
High	?	30	23	18	13	5
Low	?	26	16	11	5	−2

1. Which temperature scale is used in the table?
2. What instrument would you use to find the information in the table?
3. Choose the terms that describe how the data is organized.
   a. By year **b.** By month **c.** High and low temperature **d.** Average weekly temperature **e.** By week
4. What two science skills are you using when you find temperature?
5. What science skill would you use to fill in the temperatures for July?
6. What other way would you organize the information?
7. What branch of earth science would you be studying to find the information in the table?

Finding Out More

1. Many of the products you use everyday use metric measurements. Prepare an illustrated poster that shows examples of metric units used in daily life.
2. Cut pictures from newspapers and magazines of people who work in earth science. Divide a bulletin board into four sections with the headings: Geology, Oceanography, Meteorology, and Space Science. Mount each of your pictures under the head to which it relates. On an index card, explain how the job of the person in the picture relates to earth science.
3. Use library references to research the work of Fahrenheit and Celsius. Find out how each of these men developed his temperature scale. Present your findings in a written report.

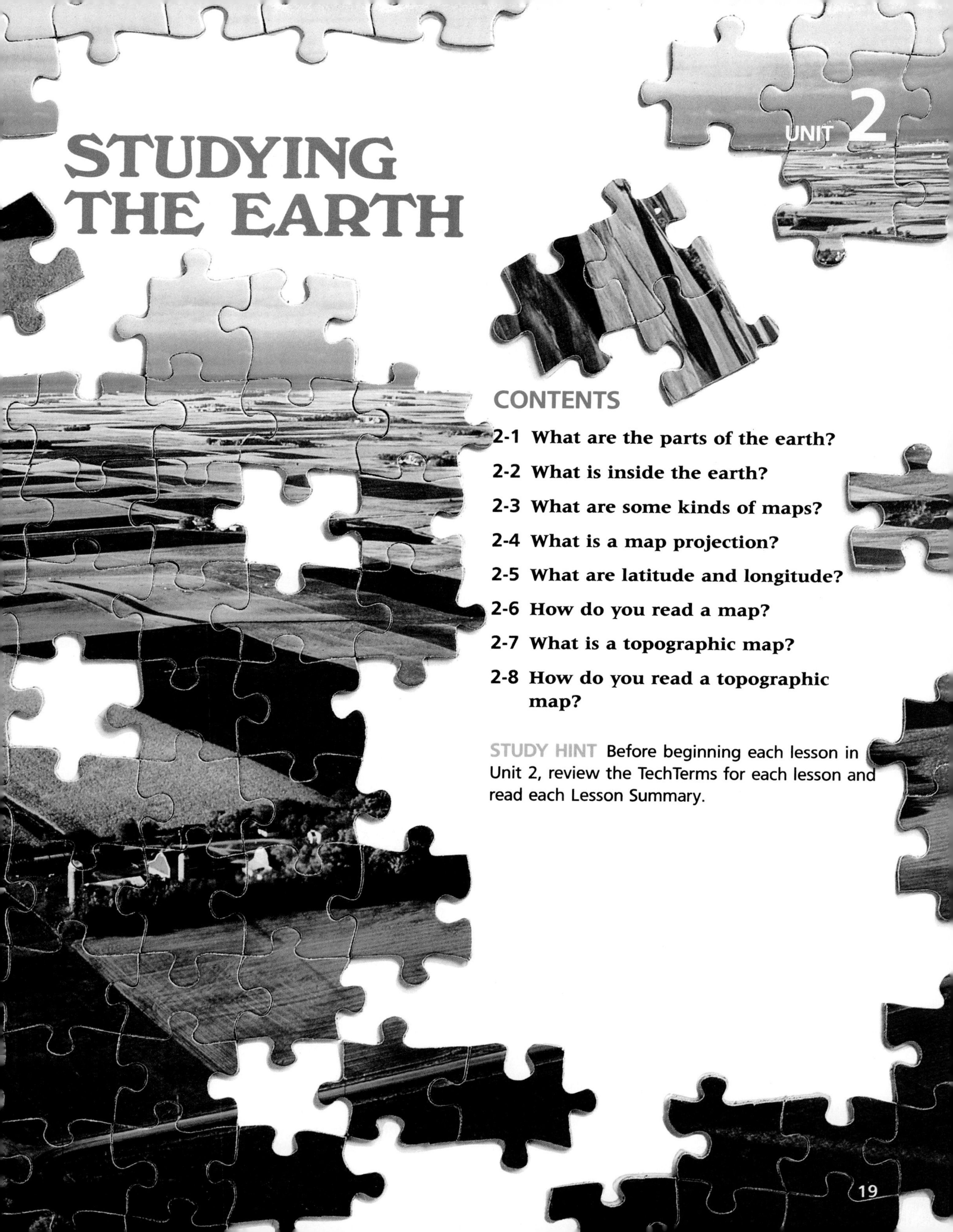

UNIT 2

STUDYING THE EARTH

CONTENTS

STUDY HINT Before beginning each lesson in Unit 2, review the TechTerms for each lesson and read each Lesson Summary.

2-1 What are the parts of the earth?

Objective ▶ Name and describe the three parts of the earth.

TechTerms

- ▶ **atmosphere** (AT-muhs-feer): envelope of gases surrounding the earth
- ▶ **hydrosphere** (HY-droh-sfeer): part of the earth that is water
- ▶ **lithosphere** (LITH-oh-sfeer): solid part of the earth

A Flattened Sphere The earth is not a perfect sphere. A sphere has no top, bottom, or sides. Any point on the surface of a sphere is the same distance from the center. The earth is slightly flattened at its North and South poles. The middle of the earth also bulges a little. Figure 1 compares the shape of the earth to a perfect sphere.

Figure 1

Observe: Using Figure 1, explain why the earth is not a perfect sphere.

The Lithosphere The solid part of the earth is the **lithosphere** (LITH-oh-sfeer). The ground you walk on is part of the lithosphere. Mountains are raised parts of the lithosphere. Valleys are low areas between mountains. The lithosphere extends under the oceans and makes up the continents (KAHNT-un-unts). Continents are the large landmasses on the earth. The continents are shown in Figure 2.

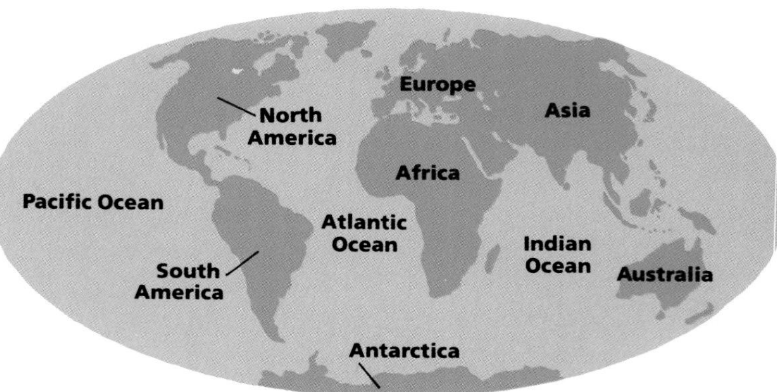

Figure 2

Name: Name the solid part of the earth.

The Hydrosphere The part of the earth that is water is the **hydrosphere** (HY-droh-sfeer). The hydrosphere includes all of the salt water and fresh water on the earth. Salt water makes up about 97% of all the water on the earth. Most of the salt water is in the oceans. Fresh water is found in rivers, lakes, and streams. However, most of the fresh water on the earth is frozen in glaciers, such as ice caps and other areas.

Analyze: Name the bodies of salt water that are shown in Figure 2.

The Atmosphere The **atmosphere** (AT-muhs-feer) is the envelope of gases surrounding the earth. The air you breathe is part of the atmosphere. Nitrogen and oxygen make up most of the atmosphere. Living things need these and other gases. The atmosphere also protects living things from harmful rays given off by the sun. These rays, called ultraviolet (ul-truh-VY-uh-lit) rays, cause sunburn.

Identify: What are the two main gases in the earth's atmosphere?

LESSON SUMMARY

- The earth is shaped like a slightly flattened sphere.
- The lithosphere is the solid part of the earth.
- The hydrosphere is the part of the earth that is water.
- The atmosphere is the envelope of gases that surrounds the earth.

CHECK *Complete the following.*

1. The ground you walk on is part of the ______ .
2. The air you breathe is part of the ______ .
3. The ______ includes rivers, lakes, and oceans.
4. Describe the shape of the earth.
5. What is the lithosphere?
6. What percentage of the hydrosphere is salt water?
7. What is the atmosphere?

APPLY *Use the map on page 20 to answer the following.*

8. **Observe:** How many continents are shown on the map?
9. **Observe:** Which is the smallest continent?
10. Which is the largest continent?
11. How many oceans are shown on the map?

Complete the following.

12. Draw a pie graph that shows the percentages of salt water and fresh water on the earth.

Skill Builder

Using Prefixes Prefixes are word parts that are placed at the beginnings of words. Prefixes have definite meanings. Knowing the definition of a prefix can help you remember the meaning of a word. Two prefixes used in this lesson are "litho-" and "hydro-." Use a dictionary to find the meanings of these prefixes. Then, write the definitions of the following words that use these prefixes: hydroelectric, hydrologist, lithology, lithographer. Circle the part of the definition that relates to each prefix.

SCIENCE CONNECTION

THE BIOSPHERE

The part of the earth that supports all living things is the biosphere (BY-uh-sfeer). Parts of the lithosphere, hydrosphere, and atmosphere make up the biosphere. It has all the materials living things need to live, grow, and reproduce.

Comparing the earth to an apple, the biosphere would be the skin of the apple. The biosphere is a very thin zone. Yet, you may be thinking living things are almost everywhere. You are right. Some kinds of fishes live in the deepest parts of the ocean. Some spiders live high in the air. Worms and ants dig burrows into the ground. Compared to the entire earth and its atmosphere, however, living things can live only on and in a small area of the earth and air.

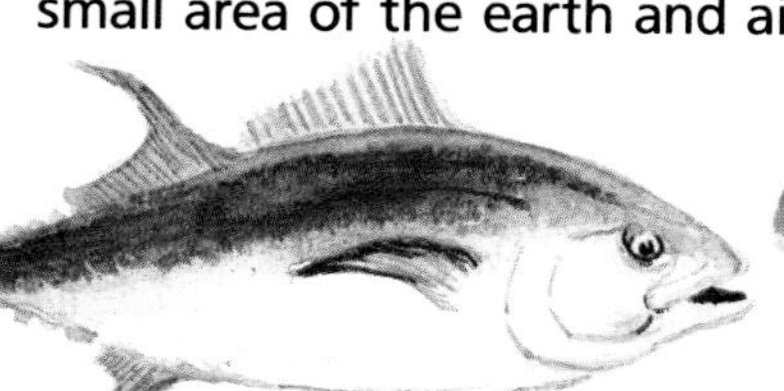

2-2 What is inside the earth?

Objective ▶ Name and describe the layers of the earth.

TechTerms

- ▶ **core:** inner layer of the earth
- ▶ **crust:** thin, solid, outer layer of the earth
- ▶ **mantle** (MAN-tul): thick layer of rock below the crust

Layers of the Earth When you were a child, did you ever plan to dig a hole through the earth to the other side? What do you think the inside of the earth is like? The inside of the earth can be compared to a hard-boiled egg. If you cut a hard-boiled egg with the shell on, you can see that the egg has three different layers. The earth also has three layers. These layers are the crust, the mantle (MAN-tul), and the core.

▶ ***Identify:*** What are the three layers of the earth?

The Crust The **crust** is the solid, outer layer of the earth. The crust forms the upper part of the lithosphere. Beneath the oceans, the crust is between 5 km and 10 km thick. Beneath the continents, the crust is between 32 km and 70 km thick. The thickest crust is beneath mountains. Compared to the whole earth, the crust is very thin. The whole earth is about 12,700 km in

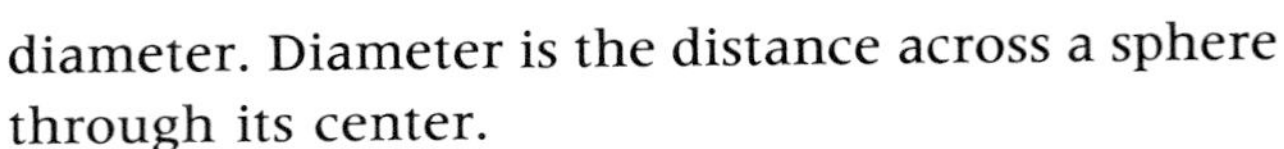

diameter. Diameter is the distance across a sphere through its center.

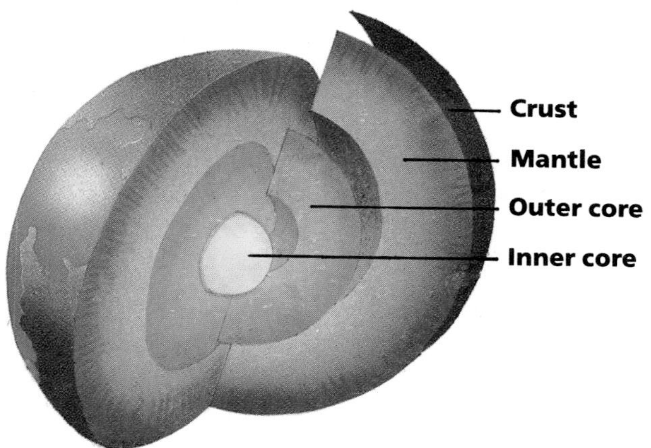

▶ ***Contrast:*** How does the crust beneath the oceans and the continents differ?

The Mantle The layer of the earth beneath the crust is the **mantle.** The mantle is about 2800 km thick. More than two-thirds of the mass of the earth is in the mantle.

The mantle has two parts. The upper part is solid rock. The solid rock of the mantle is part of the lithosphere. Below the solid rock, the mantle rock has the ability to flow like a liquid. Most of the mantle is made up of rock that can flow.

Observe: Where is the mantle located?

The Core The inner layer, or center, of the earth is the **core.** The core is about 3500 km thick. Scientists think that the core is made mostly of iron.

Table 1 Layers of the Earth

LAYER	THICKNESS
Crust	70
Mantle	2800
Outer core	2190
Inner core	1300

The core has two parts. The outer core is a liquid layer. The inner core is a solid layer. These two parts of the core make up almost one-third of the earth's mass.

Analyze: Which part of the core is thicker?

LESSON SUMMARY

- The earth has three layers.
- The crust is the thin, solid, outer layer of the earth.
- The mantle is a thick layer of the earth located beneath the crust.
- The mantle has an upper part made up of solid rock and a lower part that can flow like a liquid.
- The core is the inner layer of the earth.
- The core has an outer liquid layer and an inner solid layer.

CHECK *Complete the following.*

1. The thickest layer of the earth is the ________ .
2. The thickest crust is located beneath ________ .
3. The core is made up mostly of ________ .
4. You can touch the layer of the earth called the ________ .
5. The diameter of the earth is about ________ .

APPLY *Complete the following.*

6. **Sequence:** Place the layers of the earth in order from thickest to thinnest.
7. **Analyze:** A research company wants to drill through the earth's crust to the mantle. The drilling rig can reach down only 6 km. Where would you set up the drilling rig to drill into the mantle? Why?

Skill Builder

Measuring and Calculating Find the diameter of each model planet. Make your measurements in millimeters and centimeters.

If each cm equals 5000 km and each mm equals 500 km, what is the diameter of each planet? What is the distance to the center of each planet?

ACTIVITY

MODELING THE EARTH'S LAYERS

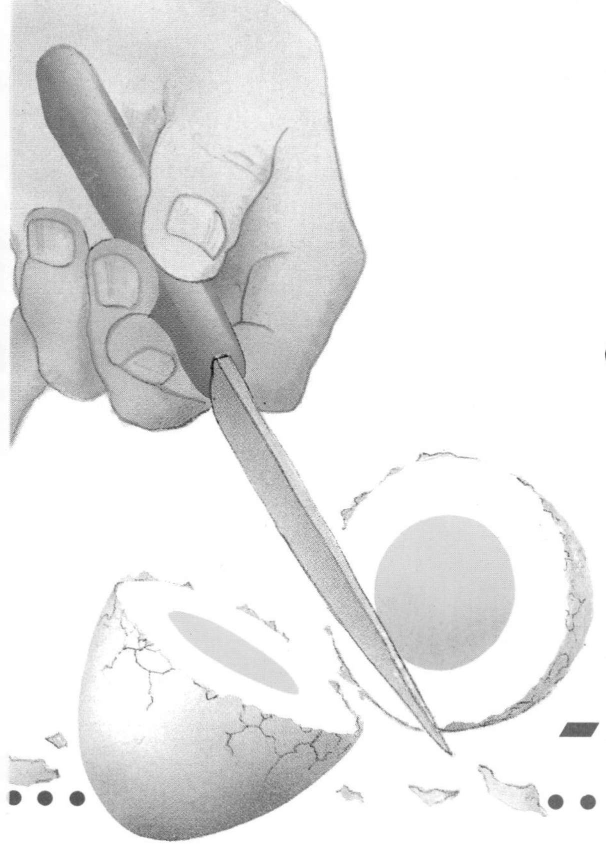

You will need a hard-boiled egg, a knife, and 3 straight pins.

1. Obtain a hard-boiled egg with the shell on.
2. Use a knife to cut the hard-boiled egg in half. **CAUTION: Be very careful when working with sharp objects.**
3. Label each part of the egg with the name of the layer of the earth it represents. Use straight pins to attach your labels to the egg.

Questions

1. **a.** Which part of the egg can be compared to the earth's crust? **b.** How is this part of the egg like the crust of the earth?
2. **a.** Which part of the egg can be compared to the mantle? **b.** How is this part of the egg like the mantle?
3. **a.** Which part of the egg can be compared to the core? **b.** How is this part of the egg like the core?
4. How do the thicknesses of the layers of the egg compare to the thickness of the layers of the earth?
5. **Analyze:** What feature of an egg does not make it a good model of the earth?

2-3 What are some kinds of maps?

Objectives ▶ Explain why a globe is the best model of the earth. ▶ Describe what happens when the round earth is shown on a flat map.

TechTerms

- ▶ **distortion** (dis-TOHR-shun): error in shape, size, or distance
- ▶ **globe:** spherical model of the earth
- ▶ **map:** flat model of the earth

Globes A **globe** is a spherical model of the earth. A model is something that represents a real object, such as a ship or an airplane. A globe correctly shows the shapes and sizes of features on the earth. For this reason, a globe is the best model of the earth. Most globes, however, are too small to show details. Larger globes are too big to handle. Imagine carrying a globe to school every day.

▶ ***Define:*** What is a globe?

Maps A **map** is a flat model, or drawing, of the earth. There are many kinds of maps. Some maps show the whole earth. Other maps show only a part of the earth. Maps that show a small part of the earth can show many details.

Maps can show many different things. Maps can show the locations of and distances between places on the earth. Some maps show city streets. Other maps show the buildings in a town. Some maps even show the weather or types of soil in an area.

▶ ***Identify:*** What are some features that can be shown on maps?

Distortion When a round surface such as the earth is shown on a flat map, changes occur in the flat map. These changes are errors. If the shapes on the map are correct, the distances may be wrong. If the distances are correct, the shapes may be wrong. These errors in shape, size, or distance are called **distortions** (dis-TOHR-shunz). All flat maps of large areas have some distortions. Maps of small areas have almost no distortions.

▶ ***Compare:*** Would a map of the United States or a map of Florida have more distortions? Explain.

LESSON SUMMARY

- A globe is a spherical model of the earth.
- A map is a flat model of the earth that shows surface features.
- Maps are very useful, because they can show many different things.
- All flat maps have some errors, or distortions.

CHECK *Write true if the statement is true. If the statement is false, change the underlined term to make the statement true.*

1. A globe is a <u>flat</u> model of the earth.
2. The best model of the earth is a <u>map</u>.
3. A map of a city shows <u>more</u> details than a map of the whole country.
4. Errors on a map are called <u>distortions</u>.

APPLY *Complete the following.*

5. Why is a globe the best model of the earth?
6. **Hypothesize:** When would a flat map be more useful than a globe?
7. **Hypothesize:** When would a globe be more useful than a flat map?
8. Why does a map of a large area have more distortions than a map of a small area?

State the Problem

Globes and maps can be used to find the distances between different places. Maria wanted to know how far it was from her house to her friend's house in the next town. She tried to use the globe to find out. Why might Maria have a problem using a globe to find the distance between the two towns?

Ideas in Action

IDEA: A globe can be used to locate different places in the world.
ACTION: Describe two situations in which you might use a globe to find out where a place is located.

TECHNOLOGY AND SOCIETY

EARTH OBSERVATION SATELLITES

Some maps are made using satellites high above the earth. One group of satellites is called *Landsat*. *Landsat* satellites orbit the earth from pole to pole. These satellites send back information about the earth's resources and weather.

Landsat satellites have television cameras and special sensors (SEN-surs). The pictures from the cameras and sensors are used in many ways. Countries use the information to plan land use, forest, and water projects. For example, the photographs help scientists predict the amount of water that runs off from melting snow. This information can be used to help predict floods. *Landsat* photographs also help scientists find out how quickly rain forests are being destroyed. Photographs from the French SPOT satellites show more detail than *Landsat* but do not cover as wide an area.

Other earth observation satellites are *SarSat* and *NavStar*. *NavStar* is made up of 18 satellites that orbit the earth over different areas. The system is used to keep track of airplane traffic. It also is used to help during search and rescue missions. *SarSat* is a **S**earch and **R**escue **S**atellite-**A**ided **T**racking system. Many different countries have satellites in the system. *SarSat* is used to find ships and aircraft in distress.

2-4 What is a map projection?

Objectives ▶ Explain what a map projection is. ▶ Describe three kinds of map projections.

TechTerm

- ▶ **map projection** (pruh-JEK-shun): drawing of the earth, or part of the earth, on a flat surface

Map Projection A **map projection** (pruh-JEK-shun) is a flat map that represents all or part of the earth's curved surface. Imagine a clear plastic globe with a light in the middle. If a piece of paper is wrapped around the lighted globe, the outlines of the continents are projected onto the paper. A mapmaker can trace these outlines to make a flat map. The result is called a map projection because the outlines from the globe are projected onto the paper.

Define: What is a map projection?

Different Map Projections A Mercator (mur-KAYT-ur) projection is made by wrapping a piece of paper into a tube around a globe. A Mercator projection is shown in Figure 1. In a Mercator projection, the distances between land areas are distorted. The sizes of areas near the poles also are distorted.

Figure 1 A Mercator projection

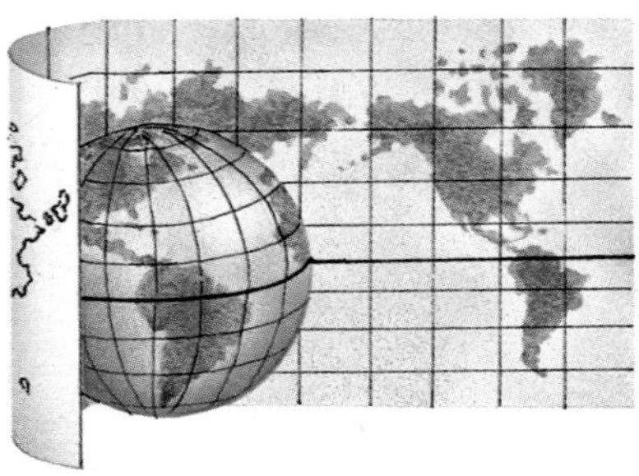

A polar projection is made by holding a flat piece of paper to one pole of a globe. A polar projection is shown in Figure 2. A polar projection has little distortion near the pole. Farther from the pole, however, both direction and distance are distorted.

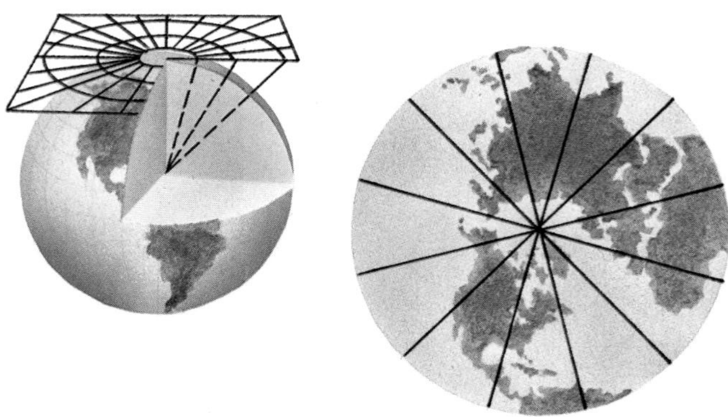

Figure 2 A polar projection

A conic (KAHN-ik) projection is made by wrapping a piece of paper into a cone and placing it over a globe. A conic projection is shown in Figure 3. When several conic map projections are put together, the relative shapes and sizes of land areas are almost the same as on a globe.

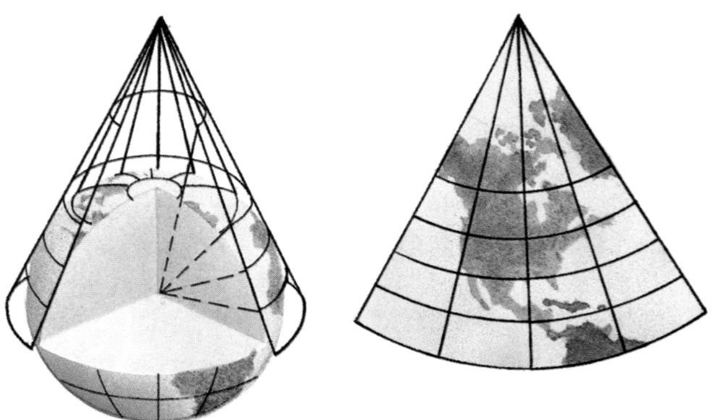

Figure 3 A conic projection

Infer: Which kind of map projection has the least amount of distortion?

LESSON SUMMARY

- A map projection is a drawing of the earth, or part of the earth, on a flat surface.
- A map projection is made by projecting the outlines of features on a globe onto paper.
- A Mercator projection is made by wrapping a piece of paper into a tube around a globe.
- A polar projection is made by placing a flat piece of paper on one pole of a globe.
- A conic projection is made by wrapping a paper cone around a globe.

CHECK *Complete the following.*

1. A flat map of a curved surface is called a ______ .
2. A Mercator projection is made by wrapping a paper ______ around a globe.
3. A conic projection is made by wrapping a paper ______ around a globe.
4. How are mapmakers able to show the earth's surface on a flat map?
5. How is a polar projection made?

APPLY *Complete the following.*

6. Describe how a map projection is made.
7. **Compare:** Compare the amount of distortion in the different kinds of map projections.
8. **Infer:** Why do you think a conic projection and a polar projection were given these names?

InfoSearch

Read the passage. Ask two questions about the topic that you cannot answer from the information in the passage.

Map Projections Although no map projection is completely accurate, each kind of map projection is useful in a different way. For example, a Mercator projection shows the correct shapes of coastlines. For this reason, Mercator projections are helpful to navigators at sea. Another kind of map projection is useful in plotting routes for air travel. It is important to know which kind of map projection to use in a specific situation.

SEARCH: Use library references to find answers to your questions.

LOOKING BACK IN SCIENCE

MAPMAKING

When do you think the first maps were made? The earliest known maps are more than 4000 years old. These early maps were carved on clay tablets. Maps during this time showed rivers, mountains, and settlements. Early people may have used these maps to help build roads, canals, and towns.

The first people to draw the earth as a sphere were Greek geographers. Ptolemy (TOWL-uh-mee), a Greek philosopher, wrote a book called *A Guide to Geography.* In his book, Ptolemy described how to make maps and globes. Columbus used Ptolemy's maps when he set out on his voyage.

During the fifteenth and sixteenth centuries, the explorations of Columbus, da Gama, and Magellan led to more accurate maps of the earth. The most famous mapmaker during this time was Gerardus Mercator. He developed the Mercator projections.

During the eighteenth century, new tools and methods were used to make maps. As a result, more information and detail could be included on maps and globes. Today, aerial photographs, space satellites, and computers all are used to make accurate maps of the earth.

2-5 What are latitude and longitude?

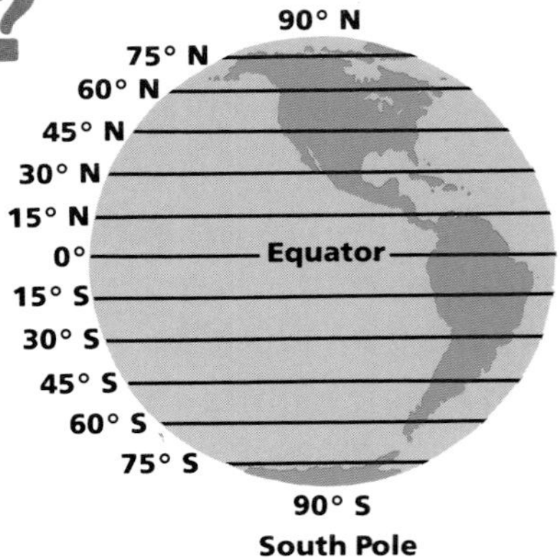

Objective ▶ Explain the relationships among hemispheres, latitude, longitude, meridians, and parallels.

TechTerms

- **hemisphere** (HEM-uh-sfeer): one-half of a sphere
- **latitude** (LAT-uh-tood): number of degrees by which a place is north or south of the equator
- **longitude** (LON-jih-tood): number of degrees by which a place is east or west of the prime meridian
- **meridian** (muh-RID-ee-un): imaginary line running from the North Pole to the South Pole
- **parallel** (PAR-uh-lel): imaginary line running horizontally around the earth

The Equator Imaginary lines called **parallels** (PAR-uh-lels) run horizontally around the earth. The longest parallel runs around the middle of the earth. It is called the equator (uh-KWAY-tur).

The equator divides the earth into two halves. Each half of the earth is called a **hemisphere** (HEM-uh-sfeer). The top half of the earth is the Northern Hemisphere. The bottom half is the Southern Hemisphere.

▶ *Identify:* What are the names of the two halves into which the equator divides the earth?

Latitude The amount by which a place is north or south of the equator is called its **latitude** (LAT-uh-tood). Latitude is measured in degrees. The equator is at 0° latitude. The North Pole is at 90° north latitude. The South Pole is at 90° south latitude. A point on the earth can be anywhere from 0° to 90° north or south latitude.

Measure: What is the latitude of the South Pole?

Meridians Imaginary lines called **meridians** (muh-RID-ee-uns) run from the North Pole to the South Pole. Meridians can be used to locate places east and west of a special starting meridian. The starting meridian is the prime meridian. It passes through Greenwich, England.

▶ *Name:* What is the name of the starting meridian?

Longitude The amount by which a place is east or west of the prime meridian is called **longitude** (LON-jih-tood). Like latitude, longitude is measured in degrees. There are 180° of east longitude and 180° of west longitude. The prime meridian is at 0° longitude.

Every place on the earth has its own latitude and longitude. Lines of latitude and longitude cross each other. If you know the latitude and longitude of a place on the earth, you can locate that place on a map.

▶ *Relate:* How are latitude and longitude related?

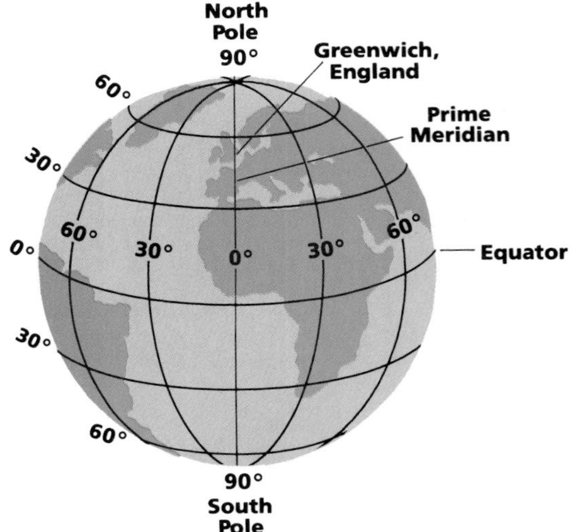

LESSON SUMMARY

- Parallels are imaginary lines that run horizontally around the earth.
- The equator divides the earth into the Northern Hemisphere and the Southern Hemisphere.
- The amount by which a place is north or south of the equator is its latitude.
- Meridians are imaginary lines that run from the North Pole to the South Pole.
- The amount by which a place is east or west of the prime meridian is its longitude.
- Every place on the earth has its own latitude and longitude.

CHECK *Write the letter of the term that best completes each statement.*

1. The imaginary line around the middle of the earth is the _______.
2. Each half of the earth is called a _______.
3. Imaginary lines running horizontally around the earth are called _______.
4. Imaginary lines running from pole to pole are called _______.

APPLY *Complete the following.*

5. Explain how you could locate a particular city on a map of the earth.
6. Where is a place with a latitude of 0° and a longitude of 0° located?
7. **Infer:** What do you think the hemispheres formed by the prime meridian are called?
8. What is the latitude and longitude of the North Pole?

Skill Builder

Modeling When you model, you use a copy or imitation of an object to represent the real object. Globes and maps are models of the earth and its features. Use a globe or a map to identify the cities with the following latitudes and longitudes.

CITY	LATITUDE	LONGITUDE
A	38° N	77° W
B	30° N	90° W
C	35° N	140° E

ACTIVITY

LOCATING PLACES ON A MAP

1. Find the following cities on the map: New Orleans, LA; Pittsburgh, PA; San Antonio, TX; Jacksonville, FL; Springfield, IL.
2. Write the latitude and longitude of each city. Estimate as closely as possible.

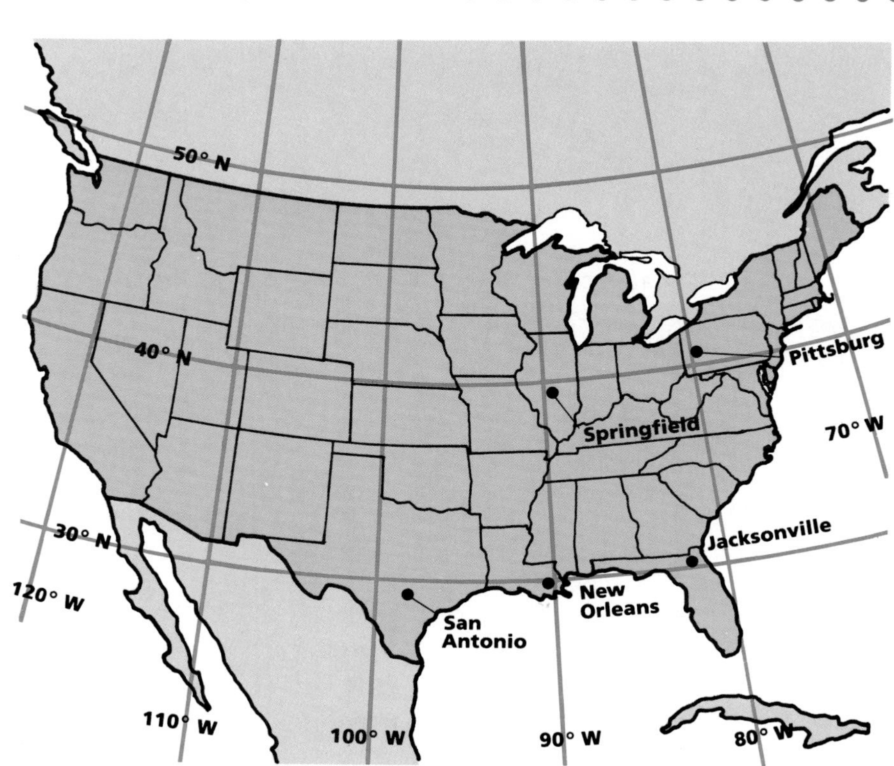

Questions

1. Why do you need to know both latitude and longitude to locate places on a map?
2. What are the latitude and longitude for each of the cities?
3. **Analyze:** What are the latitude and longitude of your city?

2-6 How do you read a map?

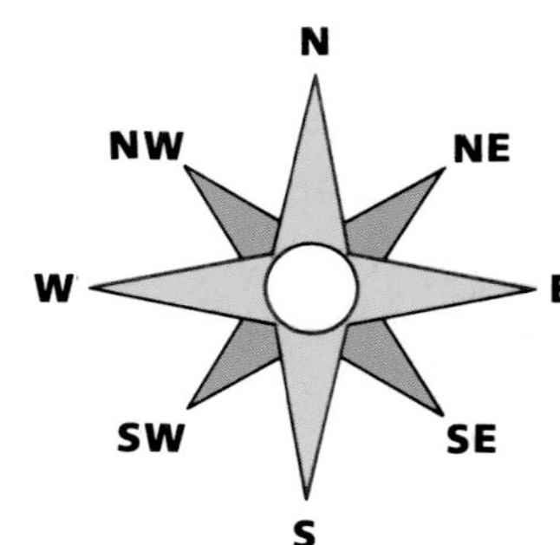

Objective ▶ Interpret the scale and symbols on a map.

TechTerms

- ▶ **legend** (LEJ-und): list of map symbols and their meanings
- ▶ **scale:** feature that relates distances on a map to actual distances on the earth
- ▶ **symbols:** drawings on a map that represent real objects

Direction Most maps show directions. If you look at the map on this page, you will see an arrow marked N. The arrow shows the direction north. On most maps, north (N) is at the top of the map, and south (S) is at the bottom. East (E) is to your right, and west (W) is to your left.

Most places on a map are not exactly north, south, east, or west. On the map, you can see that Snake River flows both south and west. This direction is southwest (SW). The direction between north and east is northeast (NE).

A
Snake River
Main street
B
N
0 1 2
(1 cm = 5km)

LEGEND

Road
Railroad
Bridge
Buildings
School
Church
Park
Water

Observe: On the map, in what direction is point A from point B?

Scale The **scale** on a map shows how the distance on the map compares with the real distance on the earth. Look at the scale for the map shown. This scale shows that 1 cm on the map equals 5 km on the earth. Measure the distance on the map from point A to point B. The distance is 4 cm. To find the actual distance between points A and B, you multiply 4 × 5 km because each centimeter on the map equals 5 km on the earth. On the earth, the actual distance from point A to point B is 20 km.

Calculate: Use the scale 1 cm = 5 km. The main street in a town is 10 km long. How many cm long would the street be on a map?

Map Symbols Simple drawings called **symbols** are used to show real objects on a map. Many different symbols are used on maps. The symbols used on a map are listed in a table called a **legend** (LEJ-und). Each map has a different legend. The legend of each map explains the symbols used on the map.

Analyze: What does the symbol ═╫═ mean?

Color Color often has a meaning on maps. Black usually is used for anything made by people. Symbols for buildings, railroads, and bridges are colored black. Blue is used to show bodies of water. Forests and parks are colored green.

Identify: What color would be used to show your school on a map?

LESSON SUMMARY

- Most maps show directions.
- Most places on a map are not exactly north, south, east, or west.
- The scale on a map compares the distances on the map with the real distances on the earth.
- Simple drawings called symbols are used to show real objects on maps.
- Map symbols and their meanings are explained in a legend.
- Colors are used to show different features on a map.

CHECK *Complete the following.*

1. The direction northwest would be shown on a map by the letters ______ .
2. The ______ on a map shows distance.
3. Simple drawings used to show real objects on a map are called ______ .
4. The symbols used on a map are listed in a ______ .
5. A river would be colored ______ on a map.

APPLY *Use the map on page 30 to answer the following.*

6. **Observe:** How many buildings are shown on the map?
7. **Observe:** What kinds of buildings are shown?
8. What direction is to your left on the map?
9. In which direction does Main Street run?

Complete the following.

10. **Model:** Draw a simple map of your neighborhood. Include a scale and a legend of all the symbols you use.

Ideas in Action

IDEA: Map reading is an important skill.
ACTION: Describe two situations when it would be helpful for you to be able to read a map.

LEISURE ACTIVITY

ORIENTEERING

Orienteering is an exciting sport that uses a compass and a map to find specific areas marked on a given course. As you move through the course, you race against other people, who are looking for the same marked points as you. To win, you must know how to read a map and use a compass. Classes in map and compass reading usually are offered at orienteering meets.

Before an orienteering meet begins, the course is set up. Markers are left at different checkpoints throughout the course. Each orienteering participant is given a map that identifies each checkpoint. The first person to cross the finish line with each checkpoint marker wins.

Orienteering is a sport in which you can participate regardless of where you live. Courses can be set up in cities, as well as wooded areas. You do not need any special equipment except a pair of walking shoes or hiking boots.

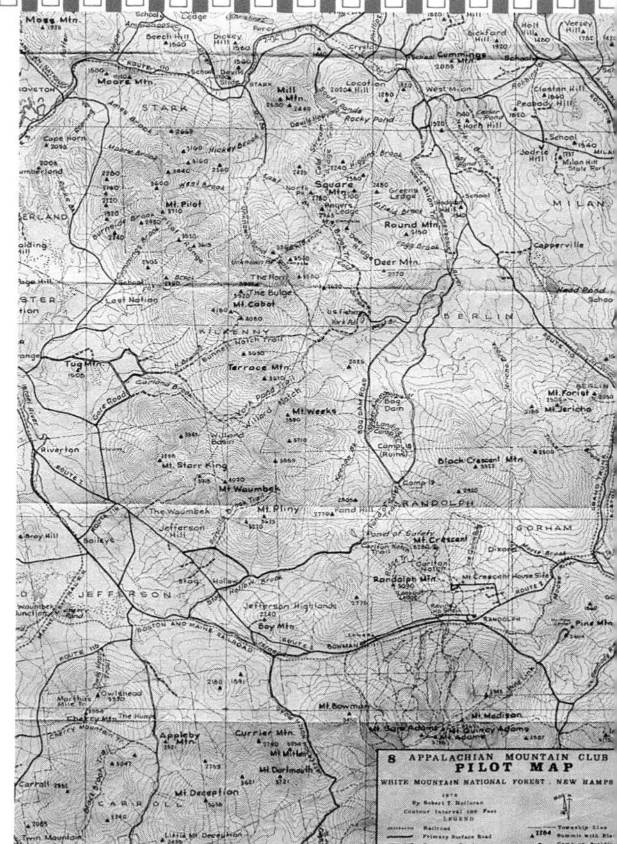

2-7 What is a topographic map?

Objective ▶ Describe what is shown on a topographic map.

TechTerms

- ▶ **contour** (KON-toor) **line:** line on a map that connects all points having the same elevation
- ▶ **elevation** (el-uh-VAY-shun): distance of a point on the earth above or below sea level
- ▶ **topography** (tuh-PAGH-ruh-fee): surface features of the earth

Elevation The level of the water in the oceans is about the same from place to place on the earth. The average level of the water in the oceans is called sea level. The height of a place on land is measured from sea level. For example, the height of Mount McKinley, Alaska, is more than 6 km above sea level. The distance of a point on the earth above or below sea level is called **elevation** (el-uh-VAY-shun).

▶ ***Define:*** What is elevation?

Topography The shape of the earth's surface is called **topography** (tuh-PAGH-ruh-fee). There are three main regions of the earth's topography. These three regions are mountains, plains, and plateaus (pla-TOHS). Mountains have high elevations and steep slopes. Deep valleys often are found between mountains. Plains are flat areas that are not far above sea level. Plateaus are flat areas of land that are at least 600 m above sea level.

▶ ***Identify:*** Name the three main regions of the earth's topography.

Contour Lines The elevations of surface features can be shown on a map using **contour** (KON-toor) **lines.** A contour line is a line that passes through all points on a map that have the same elevation. When you look at the contour lines on a map, you can identify the shape, or contour, of the land.

▶ ***Describe:*** What do contour lines on a map show?

Topographic Maps A map with contour lines shows the surface features, or topography, of the land. For this reason, these maps are called topographic maps. The contour lines on a topographic map connect places on the map with the same elevation.

▶ ***Identify:*** What is a topographic map?

LESSON SUMMARY

- The distance of a place on the earth above or below sea level is called elevation.
- Topography is the shape of the earth's surface features.
- The elevation of different surface features can be shown on a map using contour lines.
- Maps with contour lines are topographic maps.

CHECK *Complete the following.*

1. What is sea level?
2. What is topography?
3. What is a contour line?
4. What is the distance of a point above or below sea level called?

APPLY *Complete the following.*

5. **Contrast:** What is the difference between sea level and elevation?
6. **Infer:** A contour line is marked 50 m. What does this mean?
7. Plateaus are sometimes called "plains in the air." Explain.
8. Why is a map with contour lines called a topographic map?

InfoSearch

Read the passage. Ask two questions about the topic that you cannot answer from the information in the passage.

Contour Plowing Farmers planting on hilly ground are careful to plow their land in a special way. They plow along strips of land that are at the same elevation. In this way, all the furrows follow the slope of the hill. Water collects in the furrows and soaks into the soil. The furrows prevent the water from running down the hill and carrying away valuable topsoil. This kind of plowing is called contour plowing.

SEARCH: Use library references to find answers to your questions.

CAREER IN EARTH SCIENCE

SURVEYOR

Have you ever seen people on the side of a road measuring the land? If you have, you have seen surveyors at work. A surveyor measures the shape and contour of the land. Surveyors usually work in small groups called field parties. One surveyor looks through a telescope-like instrument called a transit. A transit measures land angles. Another surveyor uses an instrument that measures land elevation. Careful notes and measurements are taken. The notes and measurements are used to sketch maps or land surveys.

A land survey is important for determining land and water boundaries. Land surveys also are important for people who plan highways and construction sites.

If you think a career in surveying interests you, you should take courses in mathematics, geology, and mechanical drawing. Most states offer on-the-job training, as well as technical training programs for certification. Some states, however, require a college degree.

2-8 How do you read a topographic map?

Objective ▶ Understand how to read a topographic map.

TechTerm

▶ **contour interval** (IN-tur-vul): difference in elevation between one contour line and the next

Contour Intervals A topographic map shows elevation of features on the earth. Look at the topographic map shown in Figure 1. Every point on a contour line is at the same elevation. Where the contour lines are close together, the land has a steep slope. Where the lines are far apart, the land has a gentle slope.

The difference in elevation between one contour line and the next is called the **contour interval** (IN-tur-vul). If two contour lines are marked 50 m and 70 m, the contour interval between them is 20 m. Mapmakers use different contour intervals for different maps. A large contour interval is used for mountainous areas. A small contour interval is used for flat areas.

Observe: What is the contour interval for the map in Figure 1?

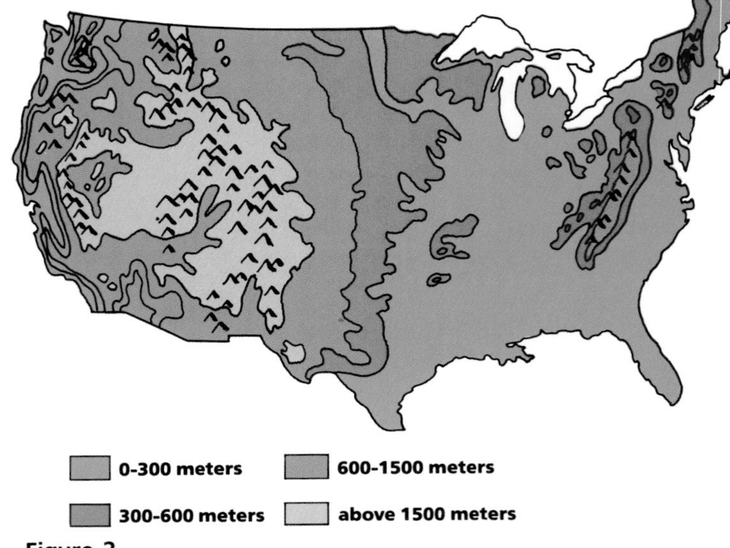

Figure 2

Color A map that uses color to show elevation is called a relief map. On a relief map, one color is used to show high mountains. Another color is used to show areas near sea level. Still other colors are used for elevations in between. A special color may be used for areas that are below sea level.

Explain: How is color used to show elevation on a relief map?

Figure 1

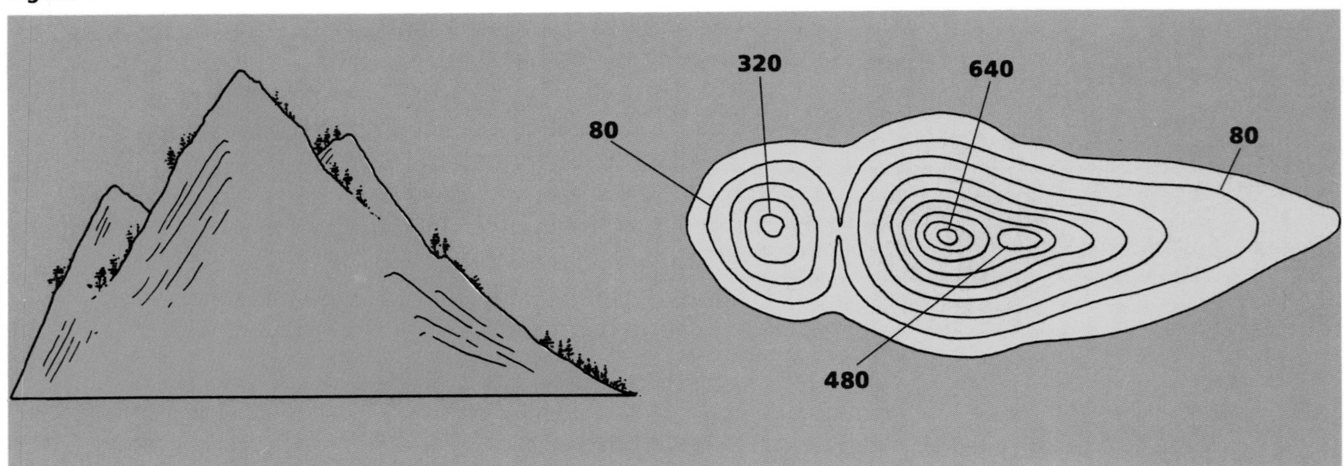

LESSON SUMMARY

- A topographic map shows elevation of features on the earth.
- The difference in elevation between one contour line and the next is the contour interval.
- A relief map uses color to show elevation.

CHECK *Complete the following.*

1. Where contour lines are close together, the land has a _______ slope.
2. The difference in elevation between two neighboring contour lines is called the _______ .
3. A map of a flat area would have a _______ contour interval.
4. Instead of contour lines, some maps use _______ to show elevation.

APPLY *Use the maps on page 34 to answer the following.*

5. **Observe:** What is the highest elevation shown on the map in Figure 1?
6. **Analyze:** Is the land shown on this map flat or hilly? How do you know?
7. **Observe:** What color is used on the map in Figure 2 to show elevations from 200 m to 500 m?
8. **Analyze:** What is the elevation of the land shown in red in Figure 2?

Skill Builder

Reading a Topographic Map The symbol X on a topographic map is called a bench mark. Find out what a bench mark is. A depression is shown on a topographic map by using short, straight lines pointing toward the center of the depression. Look at the following topographic map.

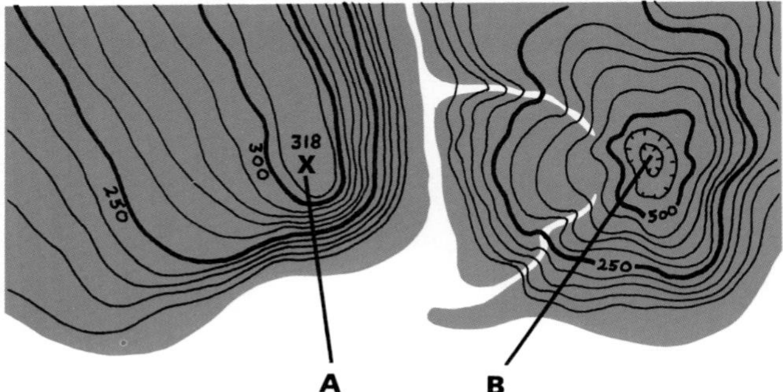

Which point on the map is the bench mark? What is the elevation at the bench mark? Which point shows a depression?

ACTIVITY

INTERPRETING A TOPOGRAPHIC MAP

You will need a pencil, paper, and a metric ruler.

1. Examine the map closely, then answer the questions.

Questions

1. What contour interval is used on this map?
2. What is the elevation of points A, B, and C?
3. How many meters is the highest point on the map?
4. **Observe:** In what direction does the river flow?
5. **Measure:** How many meters is the river from where it begins to where it ends?
6. **a.** The hill shown on the map has three steep sides and one that is gentle. How can you tell which are the steep sides and which is the gentle side? **b.** What is the compass direction of the gentle side of the hill?
7. **a.** Which letter is in a depression? How do you know? **b.** How far below sea level is the bottom of that depression?

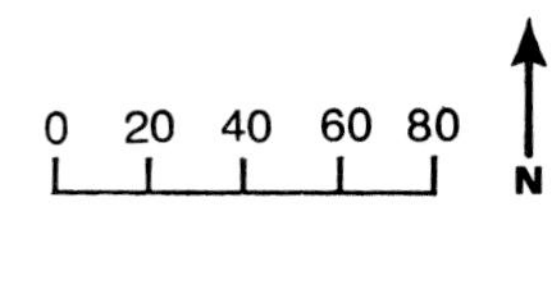

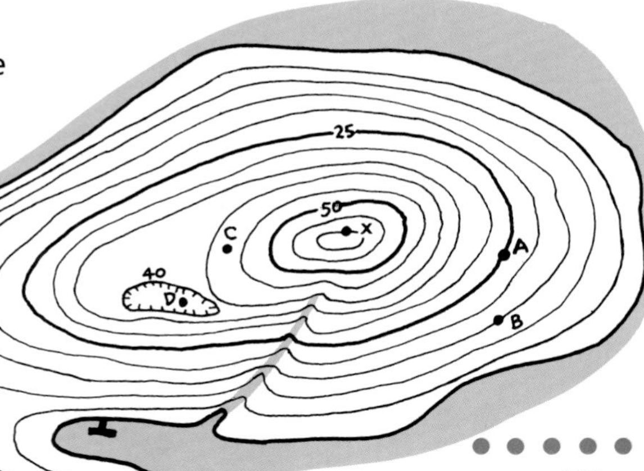

UNIT 2 Challenges

STUDY HINT Before you begin the Unit Challenges, review the TechTerms and Lesson Summary for each lesson in this unit.

TechTerms

atmosphere (20)
contour interval (34)
contour line (32)
core (22)
crust (22)
distortion (24)
elevation (32)
globe (24)
hemisphere (28)
hydrosphere (20)
latitude (28)
legend (30)
lithosphere (20)
longitude (28)
mantle (22)
map (24)
map projection (26)
meridian (28)
parallels (28)
scale (30)
symbols (30)
topography (32)

TechTerm Challenges

Matching *Write the TechTerm that matches each description.*

1. layer of earth below the crust
2. layer of air surrounding the earth
3. one half of the earth
4. shows distance on a map
5. all the water on the earth
6. innermost layer of the earth
7. drawing of part of the earth made on a flat surface
8. error in shape, distance, or size on a map

Identifying Word Relationships *Explain how the words in each pair are related. Write your answers in complete sentences.*

1. contour lines, elevation
2. map, globe
3. crust, lithosphere
4. contour interval, topography
5. latitude, parallels
6. longitude, meridians
7. symbols, legend

Content Challenges

Multiple Choice *Write the letter of the term or phrase that best completes each statement.*

1. The earth's crust forms the upper part of the
   a. atmosphere. **b.** mantle. **c.** hydrosphere. **d.** lithosphere.
2. Rivers, lakes, and streams are part of the earth's
   a. core. **b.** mantle. **c.** hydrosphere. **d.** atmosphere.
3. The two main gases in the atmosphere are
   a. oxygen and nitrogen. **b.** oxygen and hydrogen. **c.** hydrogen and nitrogen. **d.** oxygen and helium.
4. Mountains and valleys are part of the earth's
   a. lithosphere. **b.** core. **c.** mantle. **d.** hydrosphere.
5. Most of the salt water on the earth is found in
   a. the oceans. **b.** lakes and streams. **c.** the core. **d.** the atmosphere

6. The thickest layer of the earth is the
   a. crust. **b.** mantle. **c.** core. **d.** inner core.
7. The best model of the earth is a
   a. topographical map. **b.** relief map. **c.** biosphere. **d.** globe.
8. A map projection made by holding a flat piece of paper to one pole of a globe is a
   a. Mercator projection. **b.** polar projection . **c.** conic projection. **d.** relief projection.
9. Imaginary lines that run from the North Pole to the South Pole are
   a. meridians. **b.** latitudes. **c.** parallels. **d.** contour lines.
10. The North Pole is at
    a. 0° latitude. **b.** 10° longitude. **c.** 90° North latitude. **d.** 90° North longitude.
11. The amount by which a place on the earth is east or west of the prime meridian is called its
    a. longitude. **b.** latitude. **c.** equator. **d.** parallel.
12. The South Pole is located in the
    a. Northern Hemisphere. **b.** Eastern Hemisphere. **c.** Western Hemisphere. **d.** Southern Hemisphere.
13. A relief map shows the elevations of places on the earth by using
    a. symbols. **b.** legends. **c.** color. **d.** contour lines.

Completion *Write the term that best completes each statement.*

1. A relief map uses color to show ______ .
2. Contour lines that are close together show that the land has a ______ slope.
3. If two contour lines are marked 10 m and 20 m, the contour interval between them is ______ .
4. Elevation is the distance of a point above or below ______ .
5. Mountains, plains, and ______ are the three main regions of the earth's topography.
6. The symbols used on a map are listed in a ______ .
7. On a map, SE stands for the direction ______ .
8. Latitude and longitude are measured in ______ .
9. The longest parallel on the earth is the ______ .
10. The prime meridian is located at ______ longitude.
11. A Mercator projection is made by wrapping a piece of paper into a ______ around a globe.
12. Maps of ______ areas have the fewest distortions.
13. The layer of the earth between the core and the crust is the ______ .
14. Scientists think the earth's core is made mostly of ______ .
15. The hydrosphere is the part of the earth that is ______ .

Understanding the Features

Reading Critically *Use the feature reading selections to answer the following. Page numbers for the features are shown in parentheses.*

1. What is the biosphere? (21)
2. What kind of technology is used to make accurate maps of the earth today? (27)
3. How old are the earliest known maps? (27)
4. What is orienteering? (31)
5. What is a transit used to measure? (33)

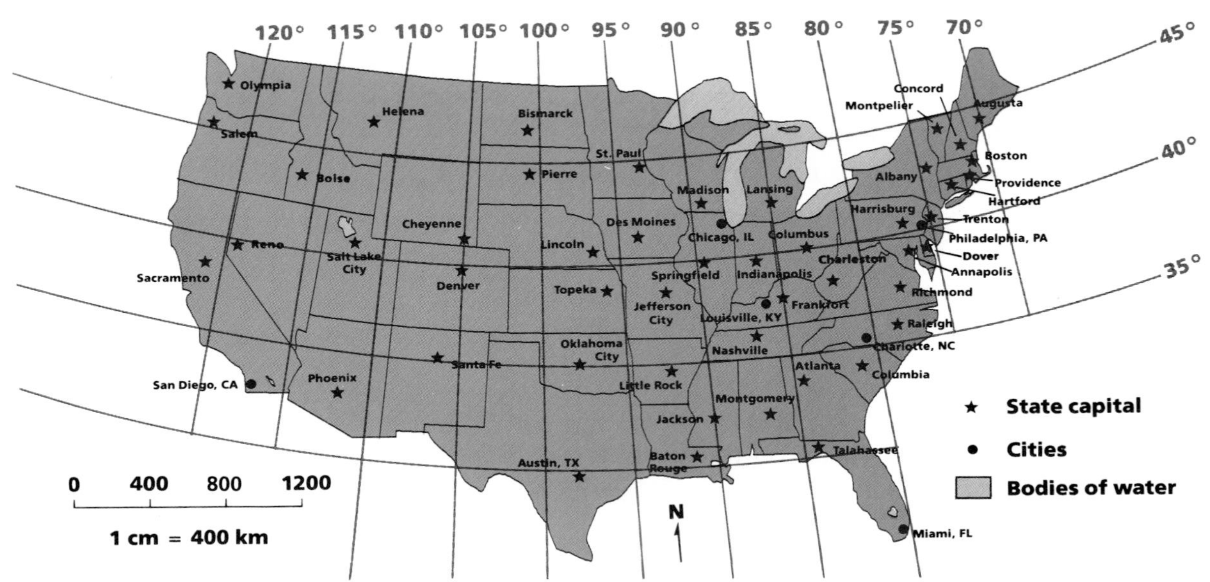

Concept Challenges

Understanding a Map *Use the map to answer the following.*

1. **Observe:** What color on the map is used to show bodies of water?
2. What distance on the map is shown by 1 cm?
3. **Measure:** How many cm is it from Miami, Florida to Austin, Texas?
4. How many kilometers is it from Miami, Florida to Austin, Texas?
5. In what direction is Chicago, Illinois from San Diego, California?
6. In what direction would you travel to go from Philadelphia, Pennsylvania to Charlotte, North Carolina?
7. **Analyze:** What is the latitude and longitude of Louisville, Kentucky?
8. Estimate the latitude and longitude of your home.
9. **Observe:** What symbol on the map is used to show cities?

Critical Thinking *Answer each of the following in complete sentences.*

1. What is the longitude of Greenwich, England?
2. Why must both latitude and longitude be known to find the location of a place on a map?
3. **Analyze:** Why is it not possible for two contour lines to cross each other?
4. Why does a polar projection have less distortion near the poles than it has away from the poles?
5. Is the diameter of the earth larger when measured from pole to pole, or when measured around the equator? Explain.

Finding Out More

1. Write to the United States Geological Survey to request a topographic map of your community. Compare the map with your observations. (United States Geological Survey, Department of the Interior, Washington, DC)
2. Research one of the following careers: architect, cartographer, contractor. Explain how the work of these people relates to one of the topics in this unit.
3. **Model:** A floor plan is a kind of map that shows the sizes and shapes of the rooms in a building. Draw a floor plan of your home. Be sure to include a scale that shows how distances in your floor plan compare to the actual size of the rooms in your house.
4. **Model:** Make a model of the layers of the earth with clay. Label your model.

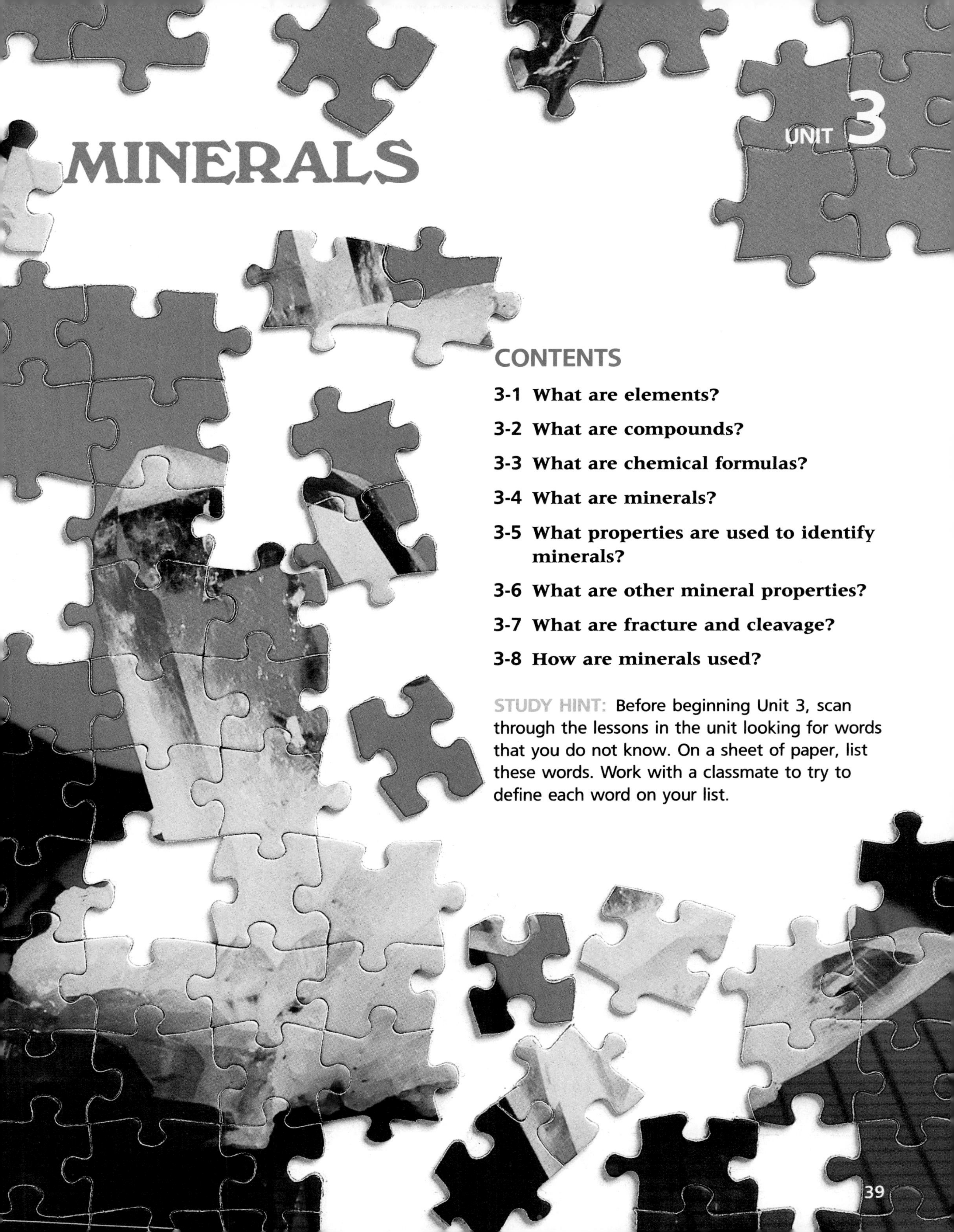

MINERALS

UNIT 3

CONTENTS

STUDY HINT: Before beginning Unit 3, scan through the lessons in the unit looking for words that you do not know. On a sheet of paper, list these words. Work with a classmate to try to define each word on your list.

3-1 What are elements?

Objectives ▶ Define atom and element. ▶ Interpret chemical symbols.

TechTerms

- **atom:** smallest part of an element
- **chemical** (KEM-ih-kul) **symbol:** shorthand way of writing the name of an element
- **element** (EL-uh-munt): substance made up of only one kind of atom

Atoms and Elements All matter is made up of particles that are too small to be seen. These particles are called **atoms.** An atom is the smallest part of a substance.

A substance that is made up of only one kind of atom is an **element** (EL-uh-munt). An element cannot be broken down into a simpler form by ordinary chemical means. Scientists have discovered more than 100 different elements.

Elements can be solids, liquids, or gases at room temperature. Most elements are solids. Oxygen, hydrogen, and nitrogen are gases. Only a few elements are liquids at room temperature. Table 1 shows the states of some elements.

Table 1 States of Common Elements

ELEMENT	STATE	ELEMENT	STATE
Carbon	Solid	Oxygen	Gas
Aluminum	Solid	Helium	Gas
Silver	Solid	Bromine	Liquid
Copper	Solid	Mercury	Liquid

▶ *Relate:* How are atoms and elements related?

Chemical Symbols A **chemical** (KEM-ih-kul) **symbol** is a shorthand way of writing the name of an element. Each element has a chemical symbol. A chemical symbol stands for one atom of an element.

In 1813, a Swedish chemist, Jons Jakob Berzelius (bur-ZEE-lee-us), suggested using the first letter of the name of an element as its chemical symbol. When more than one element has the same first letter, a second letter is added. The chemical symbols for some elements are shown in Table 2. These symbols are used today in all countries.

Table 2 Chemical Symbols

ELEMENT	SYMBOL	ELEMENT	SYMBOL
Oxygen	O	Hydrogen	H
Nitrogen	N	Carbon	C
Aluminum	Al	Helium	He
Iron	Fe	Lead	Pb
Sodium	Na	Mercury	Hg

▶ *Interpret:* What are the chemical symbols for oxygen and hydrogen?

Writing Chemical Symbols The first letter of a chemical symbol is always a capital letter. If a chemical symbol is two letters, the second letter is a lower case letter. Some symbols do not use the first letter of the element's name. How were these symbols developed? The chemical symbols for some elements come from the name of the element in a different language. Look at Table 2 again. The chemical symbol for sodium is Na. Na comes from the first two letters in *natrium* (NAY-tree-um), the Latin name for sodium.

▶ *Identify:* What are the chemical symbols for iron and mercury?

LESSON SUMMARY

- All matter is made up of atoms.
- An element is made up of only one kind of atom.
- Elements can be solids, liquids, or gases.
- Chemical symbols are a shorthand way of writing the names of elements.
- Chemical symbols are made up of one or two letters that come from the names of the elements.
- The first letter in a chemical symbol is a capital letter; the second letter is a lower case letter.

CHECK *Complete the following.*

1. Scientists have discovered more than ______ elements.
2. At room temperature, most elements are ______ .
3. A chemical symbol stands for one ______ of an element.
4. The first letter of a chemical symbol is always a ______ letter.

APPLY *Use the tables on page 40 to answer the following.*

5. **Observe:** The chemical symbol for ______ is He.
6. Oxygen is a ______ at room temperature.
7. What is the chemical symbol for iron?
8. Which elements are liquids at room temperature?

Complete the following.

9. How many atoms of carbon are shown by the chemical symbol C?
10. **Analyze:** Does the chemical symbol for iron come from its English name? Explain.

Skill Builder

Researching Using library resources, find out from which languages the following elements got their symbols: gold (Au), silver (Ag), lead (Pb), and Mercury (Hg).

PEOPLE IN SCIENCE

MARIE CURIE (1867–1934)

Marie Curie worked with her husband Pierre Curie. Together, the Curies studied radioactive (ray-dee-oh-AK-tiv) elements. A radioactive element gives off energy when particles inside its atoms break apart. Most of what is known today about radioactive elements can be traced to the work of Madame Curie.

Marie and Pierre Curie worked with an ore of uranium called pitchblende. The Curies observed that the pitchblende gave off more radiation than expected. The Curies soon discovered that this extra radiation was being produced by two elements contained in the pitchblende. The Curies and another scientist, Henri Becquerel, received a Nobel prize for discovering these new elements. The elements were named polonium and radium. Polonium was named for Poland, the homeland of Marie Curie.

In 1906, Pierre Curie died in a tragic accident. However, Marie Curie continued her work with radium and polonium. In 1911, she received a second Nobel prize in chemistry.

3-2 What are compounds?

Objective ▸ Identify and describe some common compounds.

TechTerms

- ▸ **compound** (KOM-pownd): substance made up of two or more elements that are chemically combined
- ▸ **molecule** (MAHL-uh-kyool): smallest part of a substance that has all the chemical properties of that substance
- ▸ **properties** (PRAHP-ur-teez): features that describe objects

Properties Features that are used to describe objects are called **properties** (PRAHP-ur-teez). Color is a property of an object. Iron is a gray-colored element. Objects made out of iron are attracted to a magnet. Magnetism also is a property of iron. Sulfur is another element. Sulfur has a yellow color. When burned, sulfur gives off a poisonous gas with a bad odor. A yellow color and the formation of a bad-smelling, poisonous gas when burned are properties of sulfur.

▸ ***Identify:*** What are two properties of iron?

Compounds and Molecules Most substances are made up of more than one element. Water is made up of the elements hydrogen and oxygen. Sugar is made up of hydrogen, oxygen, and carbon. Water and sugar are examples of **compounds** (KOM-pownds). A compound is a substance that forms when two or more elements combine chemically.

Compounds are made up of **molecules** (MAHL-uh-kyools). A molecule is the smallest part of a substance that has all the properties of that substance. The atoms that make up a molecule are chemically combined.

▸ ***Explain:*** How are molecules and compounds related?

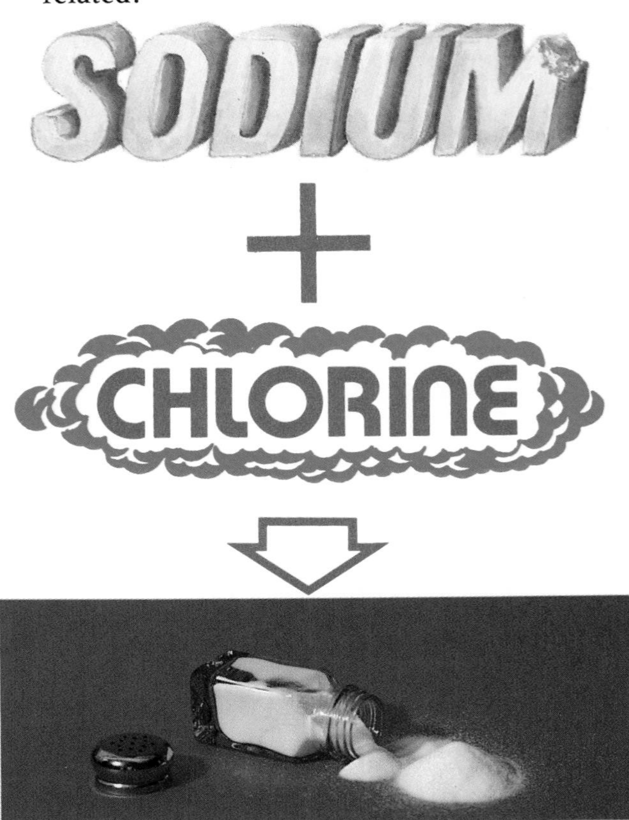

Forming Compounds When elements combine chemically to form a compound, a new substance is formed. The properties of most compounds differ from the properties of the elements from which the compound is formed. Sodium chloride is made up of the elements sodium and chlorine. Sodium is a soft metal that can be cut with a knife. Chlorine is a green-colored gas. Both sodium and chlorine are poisonous substances. Yet, when these elements combine, they form a hard solid that can be eaten. You know this solid compound as table salt.

▸ ***Identify:*** What elements make up table salt?

LESSON SUMMARY

- Properties are features that can be used to describe substances.
- A compound is formed when two or more elements combine chemically.
- A molecule is the smallest part of a compound that still has the properties of that compound.
- The properties of most compounds differ from the properties of the elements making up the compounds.

CHECK *Find the sentence that answers each question. Then, write the sentence.*

1. What is a compound?
2. What is a molecule?
3. What elements make up a molecule of sugar?
4. What happens when elements combine chemically?

APPLY *Complete the following.*

5. **Analyze:** Water is a compound made from the gases oxygen and hydrogen. Use water as an example to explain how the properties of a compound differ from the properties of the elements making up the compound.
6. How are atoms and molecules related?
7. **Compare:** What elements do the compounds sugar and water have in common?
8. How do the properties of sodium chloride differ from the properties of sodium and chlorine?

State the Problem

Objects made of iron are attracted to a magnet. Carlos held a magnet over a variety of metal objects. Not one of the objects was attracted to the magnet.

State two problems that could have caused the objects not to be attracted to the magnet.

ACTIVITY

IDENTIFYING COMPOUNDS AND THEIR ELEMENTS

You will need the labels from three prepared or packaged foods and a reference book that shows the Periodic Table of the Elements.

1. Copy the table on a sheet of paper.
2. Look for the names of compounds in the ingredients list of each food product.
3. In your table, write the name of each compound listed on the label as an ingredient.
4. Write the kind of food in the second column.
5. If the use of the compound is given, write the use in the third column of your table. If no use is given, write "not given."
6. In the last column, write the names of the elements that make up the compound. Use the Periodic Table of the Elements to help you.

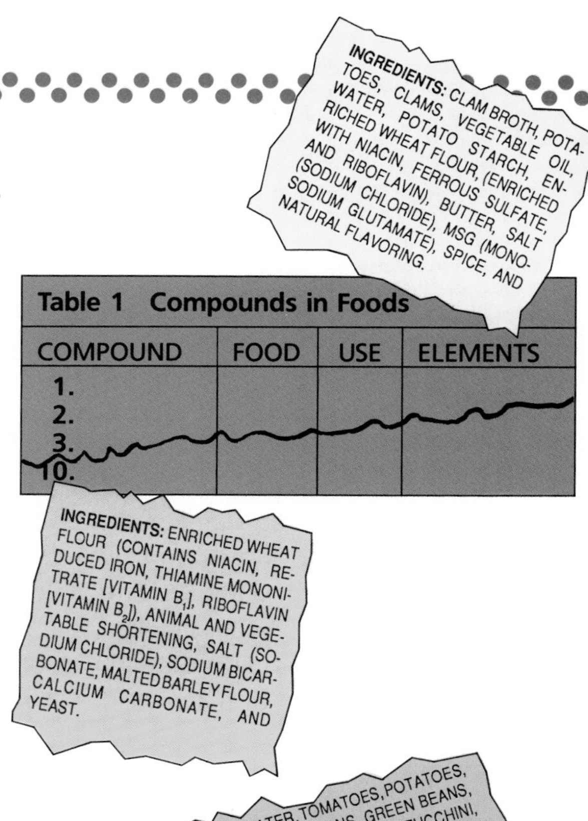

Table 1 Compounds in Foods

COMPOUND	FOOD	USE	ELEMENTS
1.			
2.			
3.			
10.			

Questions

1. Which compound was used most often?
2. For what were most compounds used?
3. **Compare:** Which element was part of the most compounds?
4. **Observe:** Which food had the most added chemical compounds?

3-3 What are chemical formulas?

Objectives ▶ Interpret chemical formulas. ▶ Recognize common chemical formulas.

TechTerms

- **chemical formula** (FOR-myoo-luh): shorthand way of writing the name of a compound
- **subscripts** (SUB-skriptz): numbers in a chemical formula that show the relative amounts of the elements in a compound

Chemical Formulas A **chemical formula** (FOR-myoo-luh) is a shorthand way of writing the name of a compound. Chemical symbols are a shorthand way of writing the names of elements. Chemical symbols also are used to write chemical formulas.

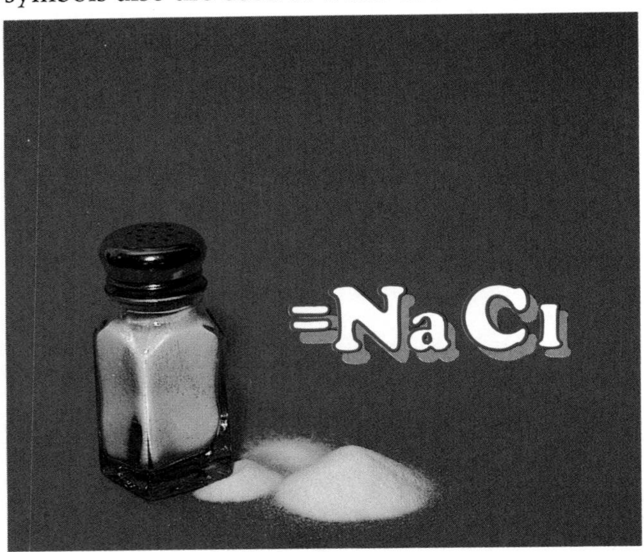

A chemical formula shows the elements that make up a compound. Sodium chloride is the chemical name for table salt. The chemical formula for sodium chloride is NaCl. By looking at the formula, you can see that table salt is made up of sodium and chlorine. The symbol for sodium is Na. The symbol for chlorine is Cl.

Relate: How are chemical symbols and chemical formulas related?

Subscripts Hydrogen peroxide is a compound made from hydrogen (H) and oxygen (O). The chemical formula for hydrogen peroxide is H_2O_2.

Table 1 Chemical Formulas For Common Compounds

COMPOUND	FORMULA
Water	H_2O
Carbon Monoxide	CO
Carbon Dioxide	CO_2
Pyrite	FeS_2
Calcite	$CaCO_3$
Aluminum Oxide	Al_2O_3

The number $_2$ after the H and the O is called a **subscript** (SUB-skript). Subscripts are numbers that show the relative amounts of the elements in a compound. Subscripts are written slightly below the line.

Table 1 shows the chemical formulas for some compounds. The chemical formula for pyrite is FeS_2. This chemical formula shows that a molecule of pyrite contains two atoms of sulfur for each atom of iron. There really are two subscripts in this chemical formula. However, only the subscript for sulfur (S) is written. When a subscript is the number 1, the 1 is not written.

Apply: In the chemical formula for aluminum oxide, what does the subscript 3 mean?

LESSON SUMMARY

- Chemical formulas are a shorthand way of writing the names of compounds.
- A chemical formula shows the elements that make up a compound.
- Subscripts show the number of atoms of each element in a compound.
- Chemical formulas show the relative number of atoms of each element in a compound.

CHECK *Write true if the statement is true. If the statement is false, change the underlined term to make the statement true.*

1. Chemical symbols are a shorthand way of writing the names of elements.
2. Chemical formulas are a shorthand way of writing the names of elements.
3. The chemical symbol for chlorine is Ch.
4. Subscripts are written slightly above the line.
5. When a subscript is the number 1, the 1 is not written.

APPLY *Use Table 1 on page 44 to answer the following.*

6. **Analyze:** Which compound has one atom of oxygen for every two atoms of hydrogen?
7. Which compound has two atoms of aluminum for every three atoms of oxygen?
8. How many elements make up one molecule of carbon dioxide?
9. **Observe:** How many atoms make up one molecule of carbon dioxide?
10. **Analyze:** How does a molecule of carbon monoxide differ from a molecule of carbon dioxide?
11. How many different elements are in calcite?

Ideas in Action

Idea: Chemical formulas are a way of abbreviating the names of compounds.
Action: Identify five other ways you use abbreviations in your daily life.

ACTIVITY

INTERPRETING CHEMICAL FORMULAS

1. Copy Table 1 on a clean sheet of paper.

Table 1 The Meaning of Chemical Formulas

CHEMICAL FORMULA	NAME OF COMPOUND	ELEMENTS IN COMPOUND	RELATIVE NUMBERS OF ATOMS IN COMPOUND
H_2O	Water	hydrogen oxygen	2 atoms of hydrogen for every 1 atom of oxygen
CO_2	carbon dioxide	carbon oxygen	1 atom of carbon for every 2 atoms of oxygen
CO	carbon monoxide		
NaCl	sodium chloride		
Al_2O_3	aluminum oxide		
Al_2S_3	aluminum sulfide		
H_2SO_4	sulfuric acid		

2. Fill in the information that is missing from the chart. Use the tables from the previous two lessons to help identify the elements in each compound.

Questions

1. What information does a chemical formula contain?
2. How does the formula for aluminum oxide differ from the formula for aluminum sulfide?
3. Why do scientists use chemical formulas?

3-4 What are minerals?

Objectives ▶ Define mineral. ▶ Identify and describe some minerals found in the earth's crust.

TechTerm

▶ **mineral** (MIN-uh-rul): natural solid formed from elements and compounds in the earth's crust

Earth's Crust The outer layer of the earth is called the crust. The earth's crust is made up of solid rock, pieces of rock, sand, and soil. Sand and soil are rock that has broken into very small pieces. All materials in the earth's crust are made up of elements and compounds.

▶ ***Define:*** What is the earth's crust?

Elements of the Crust About 75 percent of the earth's crust is made up of the elements oxygen and silicon. When oxygen and silicon combine, the compound silica is formed. Sand is one kind of silica.

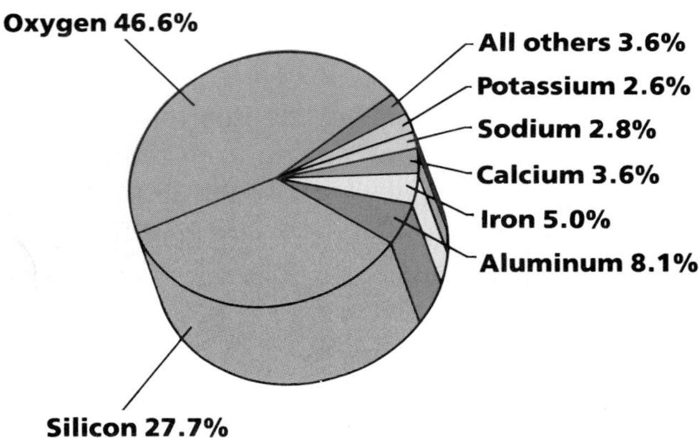

Look at the pie graph. The pie graph shows the elements that make up most of the earth's crust. The pie graph also shows what percentage of the earth's crust is made up of each element. These elements make up many different compounds.

▶ ***Calculate:*** What percentage of the earth's crust is made up of aluminum and iron?

Minerals A **mineral** (MIN-uh-rul) is a natural solid formed from elements and compounds in the earth's crust. All minerals are inorganic. An inorganic substance is not formed from living things or the remains of living things.

A mineral may be either an element or a compound. Thus, a mineral has a definite chemical makeup. Gold and silver are examples of minerals that are elements. Quartz (KWORTZ) is a mineral that is a compound. Quartz is made up of silicon and oxygen. The chemical formulas for some minerals are shown in Table 1.

Table 1 Minerals and Their Chemical Formulas

MINERAL	FORMULA	MINERAL	FORMULA
gold	Au	calcite	$CaCO_3$
silver	Ag	halite	NaCl
copper	Cu	galena	PbS
quartz	SiO_2	pyrite	FeS_2

▶ ***Interpret:*** What elements make up halite?

Rock-forming Minerals The rocks that make up the earth's crust are made up of minerals. Scientists have identified more than 2000 minerals. However, fewer than 20 of these minerals are commonly found in the earth's crust. These common minerals are called the rock-forming minerals. Most of the rock-forming minerals are compounds.

▶ ***Explain:*** Why is calcite classified as a compound?

LESSON SUMMARY

- All materials in the earth's crust are made up of elements and compounds.
- Most of the earth's crust is made up of the elements oxygen and silicon.
- Minerals are natural solids formed from elements and compounds in the earth's crust.
- A mineral may be either an element or a compound.
- Most rock-forming minerals are made up of compounds.

CHECK *Write the letter of the term that best completes each statement.*

1. About three-fourths of the earth's crust is **a.** oxygen. **b.** oxygen and iron. **c.** silicon. **d.** oxygen and silicon
2. Calcite is a compound made up of **a.** calcium and oxygen. **b.** carbon and oxygen. **c.** calcium, carbon, and oxygen. **d.** calcium and carbon
3. Quartz has one atom of silicon for every two atoms of **a.** iron. **b.** hydrogen. **c.** oxygen. **d.** magnesium

APPLY *Use the pie graph on page 46 to answer the following.*

4. **Observe:** Which element makes up almost half of the earth's crust?
5. Which two elements of the earth's crust are found in the smallest amounts?
6. What percentage of the earth's crust is made up of iron?
7. **Sequence:** List the five elements that make up most of the earth's crust from most common to least common.

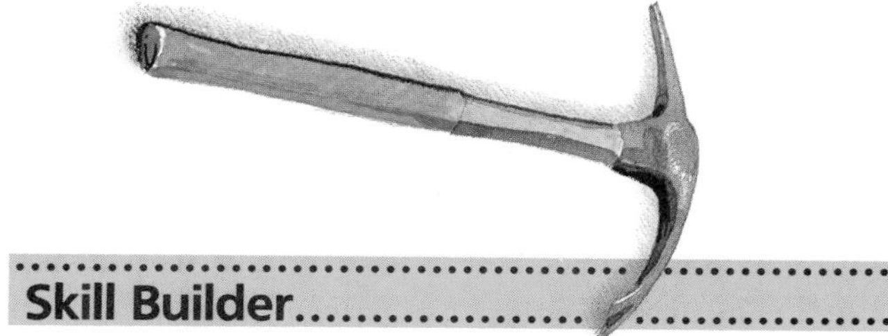

Skill Builder

Recording Data A table is a good way to organize information. Use the information given in the pie graph on page 46, to make a table that identifies the elements that make up the earth's crust. Include a column in your table that identifies what percentage of the crust is made up of each element.

LEISURE ACTIVITY

MINERAL COLLECTING

Collecting minerals can be an exciting and rewarding hobby. There are more than 2000 different minerals. However, only about 100 minerals are common. These 100 minerals are found in different places throughout the world. For this reason, it may take years for a mineral collector to gather samples of the 100 common minerals. Many mineral collectors collect more than one sample of each kind of mineral. For example, samples of white quartz, rose quartz, yellow quartz, or citrine, and purple quartz, or amethyst, all may be included in a mineral collection.

Mineral collecting is a easy hobby to start. All you need is a hammer and chisel, or geologic pick, and a collecting sack. A note pad, a pencil, and a field guide also are useful. This way you can write down the date, place, and name of each mineral you find.

Mountains, rock quarries, deserts, and beaches all are great places for collecting minerals. Mineral collectors also add to their collections at rock and mineral shows. Here, collectors can trade or sell minerals they have collected.

Aquamarine

3-5 What properties are used to identify minerals?

Objective ▶ Describe some properties that can be used to identify minerals.

TechTerms

- ▶ **hardness:** physical property of a mineral to resist being scratched
- ▶ **luster:** the way a mineral reflects light from its surface
- ▶ **streak:** color of the powder left by a mineral

Physical Properties The features of an object that can be observed or measured are its physical (FIZ-ih-kul) properties. Color, size, and shape are some physical properties. Physical properties can be used to help identify minerals. Some physical properties of minerals are color, streak, luster, and hardness.

List: What are four physical properties used to identify minerals?

Color and Streak Most minerals cannot be identified by color alone. Many minerals have the same colors. Gold and pyrite are both brassy yellow. Other minerals have more than one color. Quartz, for example, can be purple, yellow, pink, or colorless. Two minerals that can be identified by their colors are malachite (MAL-uh-kyt) and azurite (AZH-uh-ryt). Malachite is always green. Azurite is always blue.

Calcite

You can find the **streak** of a mineral by rubbing the mineral across a piece of unglazed ceramic tile. **Streak** is the color of the powder left by a mineral. Chalk is made up of the mineral calcite (KAL-syt). When you write with a piece of chalk, the calcite leaves a powder that you can see. A mineral may have different colors, but its streak always is the same color.

Infer: What is the streak of calcite?

Luster The way a mineral reflects light from its surface is called **luster.** The luster of a mineral is either metallic or nonmetallic. Minerals that have metallic luster shine like a new coin. Minerals that have a nonmetallic luster are glassy or dull. Quartz has a glassy luster. Calcite has a dull luster.

Identify: What are two kinds of luster?

Hardness The property of a mineral to resist being scratched is called **hardness.** In 1822, Friedrich Mohs, a German mineralogist, worked out a scale of hardness for minerals. Table 1 shows Mohs' scale of hardness.

Table 1 Mohs Scale of Hardness

MINERAL	HARDNESS	MINERAL	HARDNESS
Talc	1	Feldspar	6
Gypsum	2	Quartz	7
Calcite	3	Topaz	8
Fluorite	4	Corundum	9
Apatite	5	Diamond	10

Mohs' scale ranks ten minerals in hardness from 1 to 10. As the numbers increase, the hardness of the minerals also increases. A mineral with a high number can scratch any mineral with a lower number. However, a mineral with a low number cannot scratch a mineral with a higher number.

Interpret: What is the hardest mineral on Mohs' scale?

LESSON SUMMARY

- Physical properties can be used to identify minerals.
- Color alone cannot be used to identify a mineral.
- The color of the powder left by a mineral is called streak.
- Minerals have either a metallic or a nonmetallic luster.
- The property of a mineral to resist being scratched is called hardness.

CHECK *Find the sentence in the lesson that answers each question. Then, write the sentence.*

1. Why can a mineral with a hardness of eight scratch a mineral with a hardness of six?
2. What is luster?
3. How is the streak of a mineral found?

APPLY *Complete the following.*

4. **Infer:** Why is streak a better way to identify a mineral than color?
5. **Observe:** Use the photograph to describe the color and luster of pyrite.

Designing an Experiment

Design an experiment to solve the following problem.

PROBLEM: Joan found two blue minerals. Upon completing a streak test, she found that one mineral left a blue streak, while the other left a white streak. What other ways could Joan use to identify the minerals?

Your experiment should:

1. List the materials you need.
2. Identify safety precautions that should be followed.
3. List a step-by-step procedure.
4. Describe how you would record your data.

ACTIVITY

HARDNESS TEST

You will need a penny, a butter knife, a piece of glass, and an iron nail.

1. A field hardness scale can help you identify the hardness of a mineral. If a mineral scratches a piece of glass, it is harder than glass. If the glass scratches the mineral, the mineral is softer than glass. Study the field hardness scale.
2. Find out the hardness of each material listed.
3. Try to scratch the glass with your fingernail. **CAUTION: Do not scratch your fingernail with anything. Be careful using the glass.**
4. Find out if the penny is harder than your fingernail.
5. To find out the hardest of the five materials, try scratching each material with the other materials. Look at each place you scratch carefully. Be sure there is a scratch.

Field Hardness Scale

HARDNESS	TESTS
1	Scratched easily with fingernail
2	Scratched by fingernail (2.5)
3	Scratched by a penny
4	Scratched easily by a knife; does not scratch glass
5	Hard to scratch with a knife; barely scratches glass (5.5)
6	Scratched by a steel file (6.5); easily scratches glass
7	Scratches a steel file and glass

Questions

1. List the objects in order from hardest to softest.
2. Which material will scratch all of the others?
3. How could you find the hardness of a mineral using the nail, your fingernail, the glass, a penny, and a butter knife?

What are other mineral properties?

Magnetite

Objective ▶ Explain how density, magnetism, the acid test, and crystal structure can be used to identify minerals.

TechTerms

- ▶ **crystal** (KRIS-tul): a natural solid substance that has a definite shape
- ▶ **density** (DEN-sih-tee): amount of matter in a given volume
- ▶ **magnetism** (MAG-nuh-tiz-um): natural force that occurs when objects made out of iron and steel are attracted by a magnet

Density All matter has mass and volume. Matter also has **density** (DEN-sih-tee). Density is the amount of matter in a given volume. You can calculate the density of an object by using the following formula

$$\text{Density} = \text{mass/volume}$$

Every mineral has its own density. For this reason, density can be used to help identify minerals. Most minerals, however, have a specific density between 2-3 g/cm^3.

▶ ***Explain:*** Why can density be used to identify minerals?

Magnetism Only a few minerals have the property of **magnetism** (MAG-nuh-tiz-um). Magnetism is a natural force that occurs when objects made of iron and steel are attracted by a magnet. Magnetite (MAG-nuh-tyt) is a mineral that contains iron. If you held a small chunk of magnetite near a magnet, the magnetite would be pulled to the magnet. Magnetite also may act as a magnet. Magnetite is the only common mineral that has the property of magnetism.

Hypothesize: How could you use a magnet to determine if an unknown mineral is magnetite.

The Acid Test The acid test is used to test minerals for calcium carbonate ($CaCO_3$). To test for calcium carbonate in a mineral, place a drop of weak hydrochloric acid on a small piece of the mineral. If the surface of the mineral fizzes, the mineral contains calcium carbonate. Calcite, dolomite, and malachite are three minerals that contain calcium carbonate.

▶ ***Explain:*** What is the acid test?

Crystals Almost all minerals are made up of tiny **crystals.** A crystal is a natural solid substance that has a definite shape. The atoms in a crystal are arranged in a certain pattern to form the shape. This pattern is repeated over and over. The crystals that make up a mineral always have the same shape, but may differ in size. Usually the crystals of a mineral are very small. Large, single crystals are rare.

Each kind of mineral has a specific crystal shape. There are six basic shapes of crystals. Scientists use X-rays to study the structure of a crystal. They can use the structure of the crystal to help identify minerals.

▶ ***Identify:*** What is a crystal?

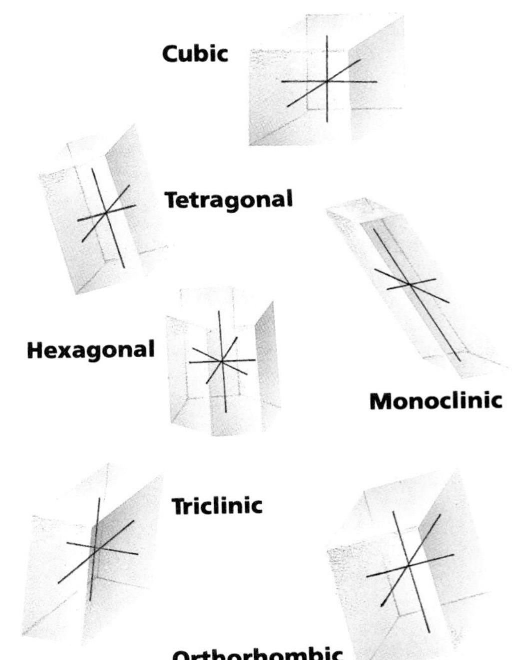

LESSON SUMMARY

- Density is the amount of matter in a given volume.
- Density can be used to identify minerals.
- Magnetism can be used to identify magnetite.
- The acid test is used to identify minerals that contain calcium carbonate.
- Most minerals are made up of crystals.
- Each kind of mineral forms crystals, with one of six basic shapes.

CHECK *Complete the following.*

1. What is density?
2. Which mineral is attracted to a magnet?
3. What kind of minerals can be identified by the acid test?
4. What do scientists use to study crystal structure?

APPLY *Complete the following.*

5. What two properties must be known to calculate the density of a mineral?
6. Halite forms cubic crystals. Draw the crystal form of a piece of halite.
7. Calculate the density of an object with a mass of 49 g and a volume of 7 cm^3.

Designing an Experiment

Design an experiment to solve the problem.

PROBLEM: How can a gold-colored mineral be identified as either gold or pyrite?

Your experiment should:

1. List the materials you need.
2. Identify safety precautions that should be followed.
3. List a step-by-step procedure.
4. Describe how you would record your data.

LOOKING BACK IN SCIENCE

CALCULATING THE PURITY OF GOLD

Pure gold is very soft. It scratches and dents easily. Gold often is mixed with silver or copper to make the gold harder. Jewelers describe the purity of gold in carats, or parts per 24. Twenty-four carat gold is pure gold. Fourteen carat gold is 14/24 pure, or 58% gold. Eighteen carat gold is 18/24 pure, or 75% gold.

Have you ever wondered if a piece of jewelry was real gold? If it was yellow and shiny you may think the gold is real. Color and luster are important properties of minerals. However, other properties must be considered to correctly identify the mineral.

In ancient times, a king asked a goldsmith to make a one-kilogram crown of gold. The goldsmith removed some of the gold and replaced it with copper. The goldsmith then made the king a crown with a mass of 1 kg.

The king thought the goldsmith had stolen some of the gold, but the king was unsure how to prove it. He asked Archimedes (ar-kuh-MEE-deez), a scientist and mathematician, for his help. Archimedes calculated the density of the crown. He compared that density with the density of pure gold. Archimedes discovered that the densities of the crown and the gold were different. The crown could not be pure gold. Archimedes was rewarded for his discovery. The goldsmith was punished for stealing the king's gold.

3-7 What are fracture and cleavage?

Objective ▸ Distinguish between fracture and cleavage.

TechTerms

- ▸ **cleavage** (KLEE-vij): splitting of a mineral into pieces with smooth, flat surfaces
- ▸ **fracture** (FRAK-chur): splitting of a mineral into pieces with uneven surfaces

Figure 1 Mica

Mineral Cleavage Many minerals have **cleavage** (KLEE-vij). Cleavage is the splitting of a mineral into pieces with smooth, flat surfaces. Mica (MY-ka) is a mineral that splits into flat sheets. Mica looks like thin layers of plastic, one on top of another.

▸ ***Define:*** What is cleavage?

Kinds of Cleavage Different minerals have different kinds of cleavage. However, the cleavage of a mineral is always the same for that mineral. Cleavage can be used to identify a mineral. You already know that mica splits into thin, flat sheets. Galena, however, splits into small cubes. Feldspar has steplike cleavage.

Figure 2 Feldspar and galena

▸ ***Identify:*** Which mineral has steplike cleavage?

Fracture Most minerals do not have cleavage. Minerals that do not have cleavage **fracture** (FRAK-chur), or split into pieces with uneven surfaces. The surfaces of minerals that fracture are rough or jagged. Asbestos and copper are minerals that fracture. Asbestos has a fracture that looks like a piece of broken wood. Copper fractures into pieces with sharp edges.

▸ ***Contrast:*** How do the fractures of asbestos and copper differ?

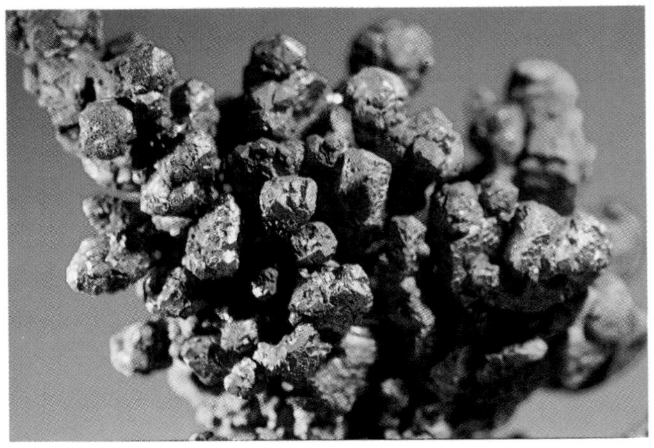

Figure 3 Copper

LESSON SUMMARY

- Cleavage is the splitting of minerals into pieces with smooth, flat surfaces.
- Different minerals have different kinds of cleavage.
- Fracture is the splitting of minerals into pieces with uneven surfaces.

CHECK *Find the sentence in the lesson that answers each question. Then, write the sentence.*

1. What is cleavage?
2. What is fracture?
3. What do the surfaces of a mineral with fracture look like?

APPLY *Complete the following.*

4. Steplike cleavage is a property of ______ .
5. A mineral that splits into pieces with uneven surfaces is ______ .
6. The cleavage of mica can be described as ______ .

Skill Builder

Classifying When you classify, you group things based upon similarities. Look at the minerals in the photographs. Identify whether each mineral shows fracture or cleavage.

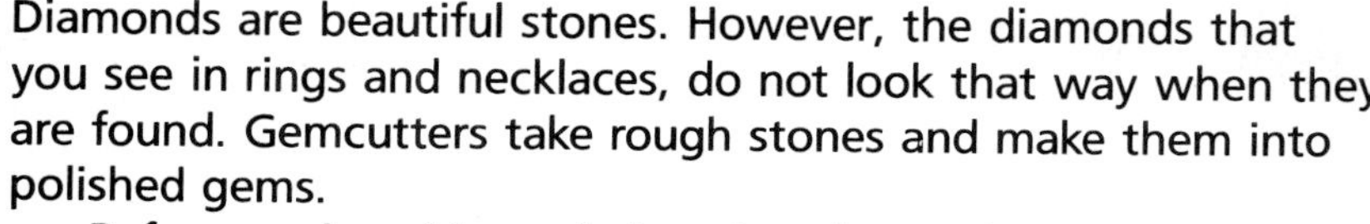

CAREER IN EARTH SCIENCE

GEMCUTTER

Diamonds are beautiful stones. However, the diamonds that you see in rings and necklaces, do not look that way when they are found. Gemcutters take rough stones and make them into polished gems.

Before a mineral is made into jewelry, each rough gemstone is inspected. Some gemstones must be split into two or more parts. After the gem is cut, it is polished. The gemcutter uses a grinding wheel to make many flat surfaces on the gem. These flat surfaces are called facets (FAS-its). Facets give the gem its sparkle.

Gem cutting requires a great deal of skill. It also requires concentration and patience. If a gemcutter makes a mistake, an expensive stone may become worthless. Most gemcutters learn their trade through on-the-job-training. You can begin gem cutting as a hobby by collecting semi-precious gems. The geology department of your local college may be able to help you locate areas near your home to hunt for semi-precious gems in rough form.

3-8 How are minerals used?

Objective ▶ State some common uses of minerals.

TechTerms

- **gem:** gemstone that has been cut and polished
- **ore:** mineral that is mined because it contains useful metals or nonmetals

Mineral Uses Many products are made from minerals. Diamond crystals are used to make jewelry. Because they are so hard, diamonds also are used to make cutting and drilling tools. Gypsum is a mineral that is used to make plaster of Paris. Many walls and ceilings are made of plaster of Paris. Table 1 shows some minerals and their uses.

Table 1 Minerals and Their Uses

MINERAL	USES
quartz	glass, sandpaper, telephone, radio
feldspar	porcelain, china, dishes
mica	insulators, toasters, irons, motors
talc	talcum powder, crayons, soap
calcite	building materials, medicine
graphite	pencil lead

Minerals are needed to keep your body in good health. Have you ever taken a vitamin or mineral supplement? Calcium and phosphorus are two minerals needed by your body. These minerals are needed for strong bones and teeth. Iron is used by the body to make red blood cells.

▶ ***Identify:*** Name two minerals used by the human body?

Ores Many minerals contain useful metals and nonmetals. A mineral that is mined because it contains useful metals or nonmetals is called an **ore.** Hematite is an ore of iron and steel. Bauxite is an ore of aluminum. Serpentine and halite are nonmetal ores. Serpentine is used to make asbestos. Halite is mined for table salt.

▶ ***Define:*** What is an ore?

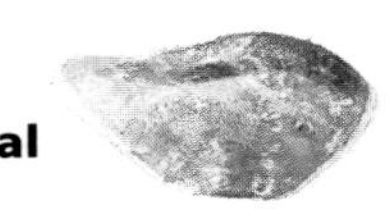
Opal

Jade

Gemstones and Gems Some minerals are valued because they are rare, beautiful, and long-lasting. These minerals are called gemstones. Rare and beautiful gemstones are called precious (PRESH-us) stones. Gemstones that are easier to find are called semi-precious (SEM-ee-PRESH-us) stones. Because they are beautiful and long-lasting many precious and semiprecious gemstones are used to make jewelry.

Gemstones often are cut and polished for use as jewelry. Gemstones that have been cut and polished are called are called **gems.** Table 2 shows some gems that are made from precious and semiprecious gemstones. Diamonds and emeralds are precious gemstones that often are made into gems. Opals and jade are semiprecious gemstones that are made into gems.

Table 2 Precious and Semi-Precious Gems

PRECIOUS GEMS	SEMIPRECIOUS GEMS	
diamond	amethyst	turquoise
emerald	garnet	zircon
ruby	jade	topaz
sapphire	opal	

Classify: Name three gems that are made from semiprecious gemstones.

Diamond

Turquoise

Ruby

LESSON SUMMARY

- Minerals are used to make many products.
- Minerals are needed by the human body.
- A mineral that is mined because it contains a useful metal or nonmetal is called an ore.
- Gemstones are rare, beautiful, and long-lasting minerals.
- Gems are gemstones that are cut, polished, and made into jewelry.

CHECK *Write true if the statement is true. If the statement is false, change the underlined term to make the statement true.*

1. Calcium and iron are needed by the body for strong bones and teeth.
2. Bauxite is an ore of aluminum.
3. Plaster of Paris is made from serpentine.
4. Very rare and beautiful minerals are semiprecious stones.
5. Halite is a nonmetallic ore.

APPLY *Use Table 1 on page 54 to complete the following.*

6. Which minerals are used to make items found in the bathroom?
7. What is the most common use of graphite?
8. Which mineral do objects that require heat insulation usually contain?

APPLY *Use Table 2 on page 54 and Table 3 on page 55 to complete the following.*

9. **Classify:** Classify 5 birthstones as precious or semi-precious gems.

Health & Safety Tip

Minerals are needed as part of your diet to keep your body working properly. Using library resources, find out which minerals your body needs. Then, identify different foods in which these minerals are present. Make an illustrated table of your findings.

SCIENCE CONNECTION

GEMS

A birthstone is a precious or semiprecious stone worn by people who are born in a certain month. If you were born in October, your birthstone is an opal. All birthstones have some kind of meaning or symbol. The September birthstone is the sapphire. It stands for clear thinking. You can find out what your birthstone is by looking at the table.

Precious stones are rare. They are prized for their color, luster, and hardness. Any combination of these properties, makes a precious stone desirable and costly.

Many precious stones are now made in the laboratory. For example, crystals of quartz are heated until they change color. They are then sold as topaz. Such stones are called treated gems. A three-piece sandwich of quartz inside of green glass can be substituted for emerald. This is an example of an assembled gem. Corundum is the second hardest of all minerals. It can be specially treated to form gems resembling rubies and sapphires. These precious stones are synthetic (sin-THET-ik) gems. Manufactured gems are not rare. While many are very beautiful and hard to tell from the real thing, they are not as valuable as natural gemstones.

Table 3 Birthstone Calendar

MONTH	BIRTHSTONE
January	garnet
February	amethyst
March	aquamarine
April	diamond
May	emerald
June	pearl
July	ruby
August	peridot
September	sapphire
October	opal
November	topaz
December	turquoise

UNIT 3 Challenges

STUDY HINT Before you begin the Unit Challenges, review the TechTerms and Lesson Summary for each lesson in this unit.

TechTerms

atom (40)
chemical formula (44)
chemical symbol (40)
cleavage (52)
compound (42)
crystal (50)
density (50)
element (40)
fracture (52)
gem (54)
hardness (48)
luster (48)
magnetism (50)
mineral (46)
molecule (42)
ore (54)
properties (42)
streak (48)
subscripts (44)

TechTerm Challenges

Matching *Write the TechTerm that best matches each description.*

1. features used to describe objects
2. natural solid formed from elements and compounds in the earth's crust
3. way a mineral reflects light
4. property of a mineral to resist being scratched
5. natural solid substance with a definite shape
6. amount of matter in a given volume
7. natural force between iron and a magnet
8. color of a mineral's powder

Identifying Word Relationships *Explain how the words in each pair are related. Write your answers in complete sentences.*

1. gem, gemstone
2. streak, color
3. cleavage, fracture
4. compound, molecule
5. atom, element
6. chemical symbol, element
7. ore, bauxite
8. chemical formula, subscripts

Content Challenges

Multiple Choice *Write the letter of the term that best completes each statement.*

1. The chemical symbol for oxygen is
   a. OG. **b.** OX. **c.** O. **d.** ox.
2. The smallest part of a substance that has all the properties of the substance is
   a. an atom. **b.** a molecule. **c.** an element. **d.** a compound.
3. CO_2 is
   a. an atom. **b.** a chemical symbol. **c.** a chemical formula. **d.** an element.
4. All materials in the earth's crust are made up of elements and
   a. compounds. **b.** minerals. **c.** silicon. **d.** crystals.
5. Two minerals that can be identified by their colors are
   a. pyrite and gold. **b.** calcite and pyrite. **c.** quartz and malachite. **d.** malachite and azurite.
6. The softest mineral on Mohs' hardness scale is
   a. quartz. **b.** diamond. **c.** feldspar. **d.** talc.
7. The luster of pyrite can be described as
   a. metallic. **b.** glassy. **c.** dull. **d.** nonmetallic.

8. The acid test is used to test minerals for
   a. quartz. b. calcium carbonate. c. crystals . d. feldspar.
9. Diamonds and emeralds are examples of
   a. semiprecious gemstones. b. ores. c. precious gemstones. d. metals.
10. Scientists study the crystal structure of minerals using
   a. a microscope. b. X rays. c. the acid test. d. luster.
11. The formula for density is
   a. $D = M/V$. b. $D = V/M$. c. $D = V \times M$. d. $D = M \times M$.
12. A mineral that breaks into thin, flat sheets is
   a. feldspar. b. mica. c. asbestos. d. quartz.

True/False *Write true is the statement is true. If the statement is false, change the underlined term to make the statement true.*

1. Most elements are liquids at room temperatures.
2. A chemical formula stands for one atom of an element.
3. Magnetism is a property of iron.
4. The properties of a compound often differs from the properties of the elements making up the compound.
5. Mohs' scale is used to compare the lusters of minerals.
6. There are six basic crystal shapes.
7. A mineral with cleavage breaks into pieces with uneven edges.
8. A substance that is not formed from living things or the remains of living things is inorganic.
9. The only common mineral with the property of magnetism is calcite.
10. On Mohs' hardness scale, a mineral with a high number cannot scratch a mineral with a lower number.
11. One molecule of CO_2 has one atom of carbon for every two atoms of oxygen.
12. Precious gemstones are less rare than semiprecious gemstones.

Understanding the Features

Reading Critically *Use the feature reading selections to answer the following. Page numbers for the features are shown in parentheses.*

1. What has Marie Curie accomplished that no other person has? (41)
2. What mineral property did Archimedes use to show that the king's crown was not pure gold? (51)
3. Why is gold used in jewelry sometimes mixed with other metals? (51)
4. Why does a gemcutter need good hand-eye coordination? (53)
5. What is a birthstone? (55)
6. How is a field guide helpful to a mineral collector? (47)

Diamond

Turquoise

Opal

Ruby

Jade

Concept Challenges

Interpreting a Table *Use Table 1 to complete the following.*

Table 1 Mineral Properties

MINERAL	CHEMICAL FORMULA	COLOR	STREAK
Pyrite	FeS_2	yellow	greenish, brownish black
Magnetite	Fe_3O_4	black	black
Hematite	Fe_2O_3	reddish brown to black	light to dark red
Gold	Au	gold	yellow
Silver	Ag	silver white	silver to light grey
Diamond	C	colorless, pale yellow, black	colorless
Quartz	SiO_2	colorless white	colorless white
Corundum	Al_2O_3	brown	white
MINERAL	**LUSTER**	**HARDNESS**	**FRACTURE OR CLEAVAGE**
Pyrite	metallic	6–6.5	cleavage
Magnetite	metallic	5–6	cleavage
Hematite	metallic	5.5–6.5	cleavage
Gold	metallic	2.5–3	fracture
Silver	metallic	2.5	fracture
Diamond	nonmetallic	10	cleavage
Quartz	nonmetallic	7.5–8	cleavage
Corundum	nonmetallic	9	cleavage

1. Which minerals listed in the table are elements?
2. What elements do pyrite and magnetite have in common?
3. Which minerals fracture?
4. Which minerals have a metallic luster?
5. What are the two hardest minerals listed?
6. What property would be most useful in distinguishing between black hematite and magnetite?
7. List the minerals in order form softest to hardest.
8. Why might streak not be a useful property for distinguishing between quartz and corundum?

Critical Thinking *Answer each of the following in complete sentences.*

1. Why do you think it is important to test more than one physical property of a mineral, in order to identify it?
2. If you were going to buy a piece of gold jewelry, what carat of gold would you choose? Why?
3. Why would the acid test not be useful when identifying a diamond?
4. Glass has a hardness of about 6. Which minerals on Moh's scale will scratch glass?
5. Explain how you would test an unknown mineral to see if it was magnetite.

Finding Out More

1. Using library references, find out where uranium, sulfur, halite, aluminum, iron, and gold deposits are located. Draw a map of the world. Create a legend that identifies each kind of deposit. Show the locations of each kind of deposit on your map.
2. **Classify:** Using library references, find out what is meant by the following terms: silicates, carbonates, sulfates, sulfides, halides, and oxides. Write a definition for each term. Then find examples of two minerals that can be classified in each group.

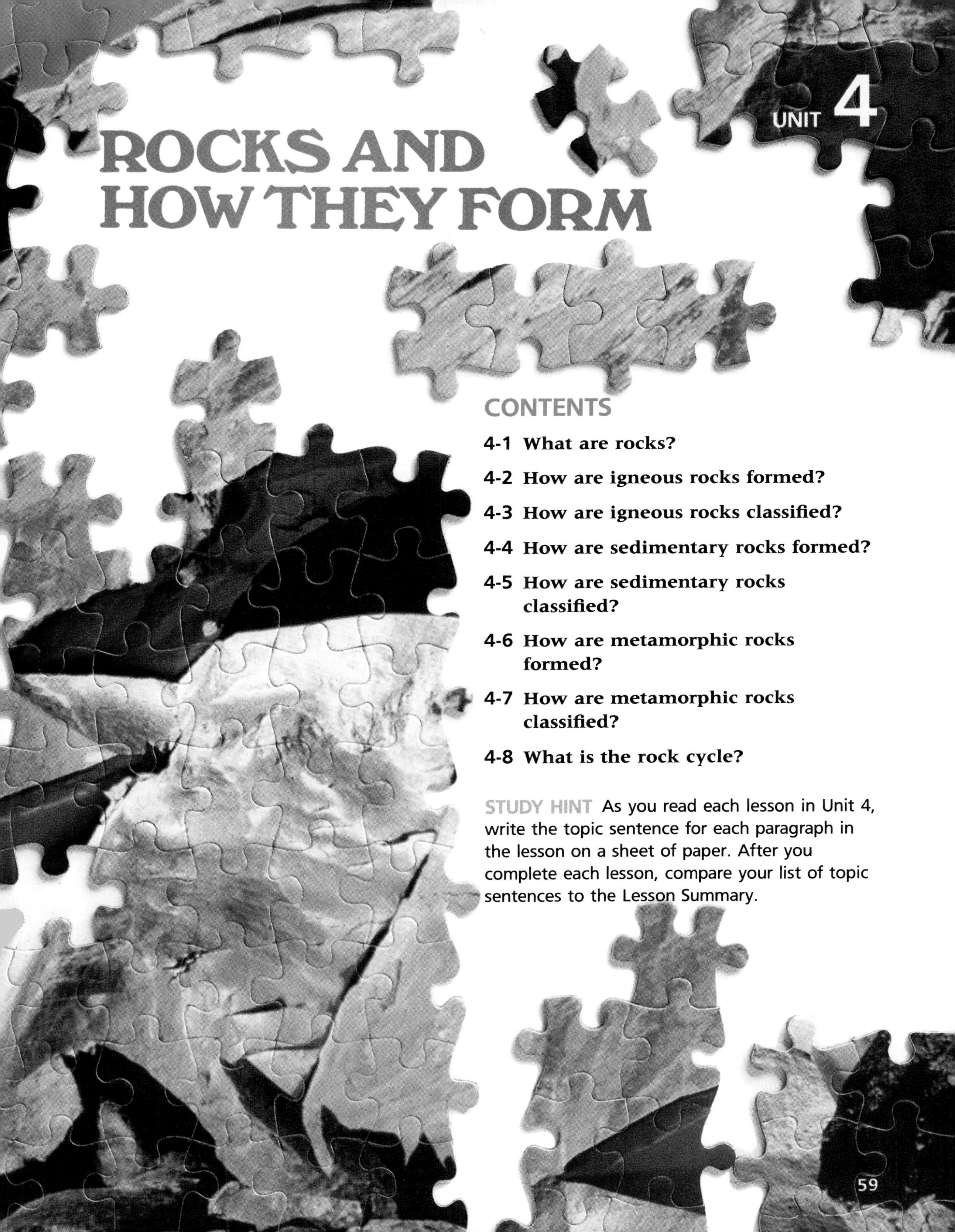

UNIT 4

ROCKS AND HOW THEY FORM

CONTENTS

STUDY HINT As you read each lesson in Unit 4, write the topic sentence for each paragraph in the lesson on a sheet of paper. After you complete each lesson, compare your list of topic sentences to the Lesson Summary.

4-1 What are rocks?

Objective ▶ Identify and describe the three classes of rocks.

TechTerms

- ▶ **igneous** (IG-nee-us) **rock:** rock that forms from melted minerals
- ▶ **metamorphic** (met-uh-MOR-fik) **rock:** rock that forms when existing rocks are changed by heat and pressure
- ▶ **sedimentary** (sed-uh-MEN-tuh-ree) **rock:** rock that forms from pieces of other rocks or the remains of once-living things

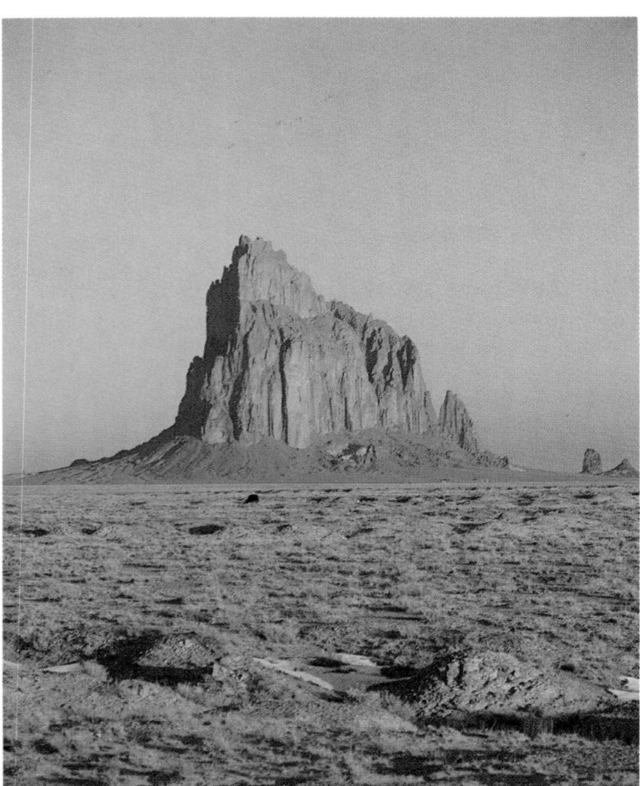

Figure 1

Rocks The earth's crust is made up of many kinds of rocks. All of these different rocks are made up of one or more minerals. There are more than 2000 different minerals in the earth's crust. However, fewer than 20 of these minerals are found in most rocks.

▶ ***Identify:*** What are rocks made up of?

Classification The grouping of things that are alike is called classification (klas-uh-fih-KAY-shun). Scientists often classify things to make them easier to study. Biologists classify things as living or nonliving. Chemists classify elements as metals or nonmetals. A petrologist (puh-TRAHL-uh-jist) is a scientist who studies rocks and minerals. Petrologists classify the rocks of the earth's crust.

▶ ***Define:*** What is classification?

Classes of Rocks Petrologists classify rocks according to the way the rocks form. Some rocks form when melted minerals cool and harden. These rocks are classified as **igneous** (IG-nee-us) **rocks.** Rocks that form when pieces of minerals and rocks become cemented together, or from the remains of living things, are classified as **sedimentary** (sed-uh-MEN-tuh-ree) **rocks.** Other rocks form when existing rocks are slowly changed by heat and pressure. These rocks are classified as **metamorphic** (met-uh-MOR-fik) **rocks.**

▶ ***Identify:*** What are the three classes of rocks?

Figure 2 Petrologists study rocks and minerals.

LESSON SUMMARY

- Rocks are made up of one or more minerals.
- Classification is the grouping of things that are alike in some way.
- The three classes of rocks are igneous, sedimentary, and metamorphic.

CHECK *Complete the following.*

1. Rocks are made up of _______ .
2. There are more than _______ different minerals in the earth's crust.
3. There are _______ classes of rocks.
4. Rocks are classified as igneous, _______, or metamorphic.
5. When melted minerals cool, _______ rocks form.
6. Scientists who study rocks and minerals are _______ .

Find the sentence that answers each question. Then, write the sentence.

7. How do petrologists classify rocks?
8. What are sedimentary rocks?
9. What is classification?

APPLY *Complete the following.*

10. **Classify:** How would you group cars to make shopping for a new car easier?
11. **Contrast:** How do sedimentary rocks differ from metamorphic rocks?

Skill Builder

Applying Definitions A definition is an explanation of what a word means. The term, "metamorphic," means "changed in form." Explain how the word "metamorphic" relates to each of the three classes of rock.

Ideas in Action

IDEA: When you classify, you group things based upon similar characteristics.
ACTION: Give two examples of how you classify things in your daily life.

CAREER IN EARTH SCIENCE

GEOLOGIST

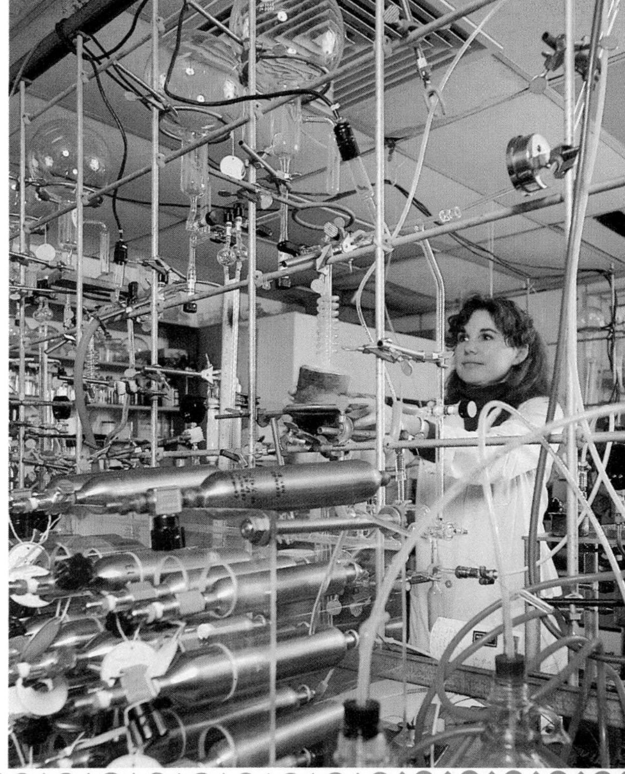

Do you enjoy collecting rocks or fossils? Do you like to explore new places? If you do, you may be interested in a career in geology (jee-AHL-uh-jee). Geology is the study of the features of the earth's crust. Scientists who study geology are geologists.

Geologists do many different kinds of work. Some geologists help build roads, dams, and pipelines. Some geologists find ways to clean polluted rivers or lakes. Many geologists work for oil companies. These geologists locate deposits of oil and natural gas. Other geologists study the earth's history by collecting fossils. Geologists also explore areas for valuable minerals.

To become a geologist, you must complete four years of college. After receiving a college degree, you may find employment in industry or with the government. Some geologists teach in high schools or colleges. A geologist who teaches usually must have a masters degree in science. However, to teach geology in a college, a doctoral degree usually is required.

4-2 How are igneous rocks formed?

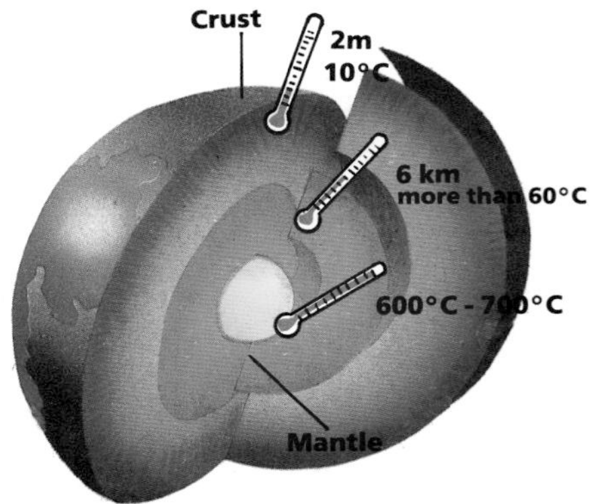

Figure 2

Objective ▶ Identify two ways that igneous rocks are formed.

TechTerms

- ▶ **lava** (LAH-vuh): magma that reaches the earth's surface
- ▶ **magma** (MAG-muh): molten rock inside the earth
- ▶ **molten** (MOHL-tun) **rock:** melted minerals

Heat Inside the Earth The temperature of the earth becomes hotter as you dig deeper into the earth. Two meters beneath the earth's surface, the temperature is about 10 °C. The deepest oil wells have been drilled about 6 km into the earth. Here, the temperature is more than 60 °C. Between the earth's crust and the mantle (MAN-tul), the temperature is between 600 and 700 °C. The mantle is the layer of the earth below the crust.

The temperature between the crust and the mantle is high enough to melt minerals. Melted minerals are called **molten** (MOHL-tun) rock. When molten rock cools, igneous rocks form. Igneous rocks are sometimes called "fire-formed" rocks. Although fire does not form igneous rocks, tremendous heat melts rock.

▶ ***Explain:*** How do igneous rocks form?

Magma and Igneous Rocks Molten rock inside the earth is called **magma** (MAG-muh). There are large pools of magma deep inside the earth. Sometimes, magma rises through cracks between rocks into the upper part of the earth's crust. Here, the temperature is much cooler than deep inside the earth. As magma rises through cracks in the earth's crust, the magma cools and hardens. Igneous rock is formed. Igneous rock can take thousands of years to cool from magma.

▶ ***Define:*** What is magma?

Lava and Igneous Rocks Sometimes magma rises through cracks in rocks and reaches the earth's surface. Magma that reaches the earth's surface is called **lava** (LAH-vuh). Lava cools upon contact with air or water. Cooling makes lava harden into igneous rock. Igneous rocks form from lava in a short period of time.

▶ ***Describe:*** How does lava rise to the earth's surface?

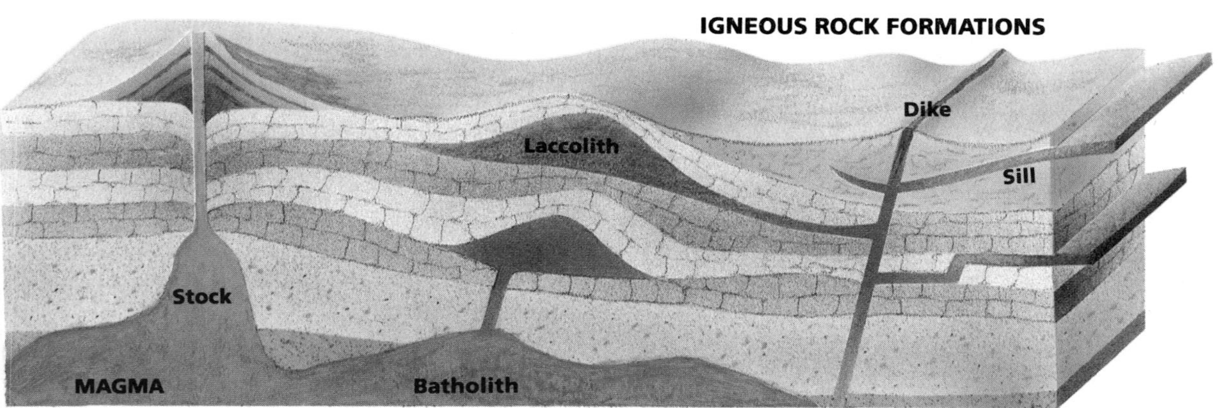

Figure 1 Igneous rock formation

LESSON SUMMARY

- The temperature becomes hotter as you go deeper inside the earth.
- Igneous rocks form from molten rock.
- Magma is molten rock inside the earth.
- Lava is molten rock on the earth's surface.

CHECK *Write true if the statement is true. If the statement is false, change the underlined term to make the statement true.*

1. Igneous rocks formed from magma, form in a short time.
2. Molten rock that reaches the earth's surface is called magma.
3. Large pools of magma are found deep inside the earth's crust.
4. Igneous rock forms from molten minerals.

APPLY *Complete the following.*

5. **Predict:** If you dug a hole two meters deep into the earth's surface, would you find molten rock? Explain.
6. Explain the difference between the formation of igneous rocks from magma and lava.
7. When molten rock pours out of a volcano, what is the rock called?

InfoSearch

Read the passage. Ask two questions about the topic that you cannot answer from the information in the passage.

Plutons Large bodies of igneous rock with different shapes are formed when magma cools inside the earth. These bodies of igneous rocks are called batholiths (BATH-uh-liths), stocks, laccoliths (LAK-uh-liths), dikes, and sills. A general name for all of these bodies of igneous rock is pluton (PLOO-tahn). An example of each kind of pluton is shown in Figure 1 on page 62. Plutons form inside the earth. However, in some areas of the United States, you can see plutons at the earth's surface.

SEARCH: Use library references to find answers to your questions.

PEOPLE IN SCIENCE

JAMES HUTTON (1726–1797)

James Hutton was born in Edinburgh, Scotland. He was trained to be a doctor. However, after Hutton inherited a farm from his father, he became interested in the natural forces at work on the earth's surface. At the time, scientists thought that all rocks were sedimentary rocks. Hutton had a different idea. He said that many rocks, such as granite, were once molten. Hutton also showed that mountains could be formed by the upward push of molten, or igneous, rocks. Hutton published his ideas in a book called *Theory of the Earth* in 1795.

As a result of his studies of the earth, Hutton proposed a theory about the history of the earth. Hutton's theory said that the earth was shaped in the past by the same forces that are still at work today. These forces include erosion. Hutton's theory was the beginning of the modern science of geology. Hutton is sometimes called the father of geology.

4-3 How are igneous rocks classified?

Objective ▶ Identify and describe igneous rocks by their minerals and textures.

TechTerm

▶ **texture** (TEKS-chur): size of the crystals in an igneous rock

A Mixture of Minerals Igneous rocks are made up of different kinds of minerals. There are six minerals that are commonly seen in igneous rocks. These six minerals are listed in Table 1.

Table 1 Minerals in Igneous Rocks	
quartz	olivine
feldspar	amphibole
mica	pyroxene

Igneous rocks can be identified by their minerals. Granite (GRAN-it) is an igneous rock made up of quartz, feldspar, and mica. Look at the photograph of granite. You can see each mineral.

Figure 1 Granite

Observe: Look at the photograph of granite. How do the colors of the quartz and feldspar crystals in granite differ?

Crystal Size Igneous rocks have crystals of different sizes. Crystal size depends upon the amount of time it takes the magma in a rock to cool. Large crystals take a long time to form. Igneous rocks formed from magma have large mineral crystals. Small crystals take a short time to form. Most igneous rocks formed from lava have very small crystals. Sometimes lava cools so quickly that no crystals form. For this reason, a few igneous rocks do not have any crystals. Obsidian is an igneous rock that does not have any crystals.

Figure 2 Obsidian

Relate: How are cooling rate and crystal size related?

Texture The size of the crystals in an igneous rock is called its **texture** (TEKS-chur). Texture can be used to identify different igneous rocks that are made up of the same minerals. Granite and rhyolite (RY-oh-lite) are igneous rocks that are made up of the same minerals. You can tell if a rock is granite or rhyolite by looking at its texture. Granite has large crystals that you can see and feel. Rhyolite has very small crystals that cannot be seen.

Igneous rocks are classified according to their textures. Igneous rocks with large crystals have a coarse texture. Igneous rocks with small crystals have a fine texture. Igneous rocks that do not have crystals have a glassy texture.

Classify: Classify granite, obsidian, and rhyolite according to their textures.

LESSON SUMMARY

- The minerals in an igneous rock can be used to identify the rock.
- Crystal size is determined by the rate at which magma cools.
- The size of the crystals in an igneous rock is its texture.
- Igneous rocks can be classified according to their textures.

CHECK *Complete the following.*

1. Granite is made up of the minerals feldspar, ______, and mica.
2. Igneous rocks formed from magma usually have ______ mineral crystals.
3. An igneous rock with very small mineral crystals most likely formed from ______ .
4. The texture of an igneous rock with no crystals is described as ______ .
5. The texture of rhyolite would be described as ______ .

APPLY *Complete the following.*

Analyze: A rock collector found five igneous rocks. The rocks had mineral crystals with these sizes: Rock A = 2 mm; Rock B = 7 mm; Rock C = 4.5 mm; Rock D = 10 mm; Rock E = .5 mm

6. Which rocks probably cooled from lava?
7. Which rocks probably cooled from magma?
8. Which rock probably took the longest time to cool?

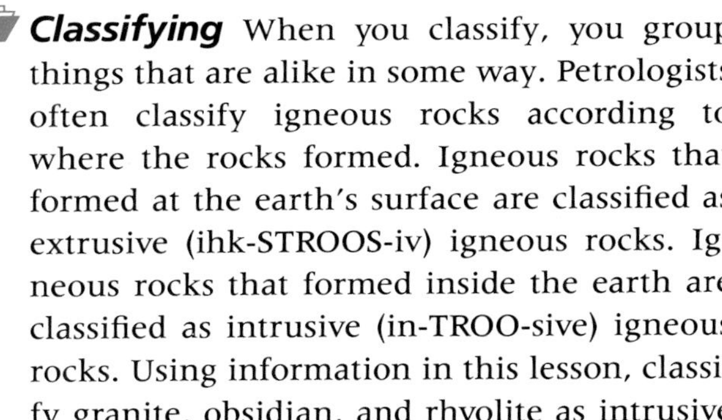

Skill Builder

Classifying When you classify, you group things that are alike in some way. Petrologists often classify igneous rocks according to where the rocks formed. Igneous rocks that formed at the earth's surface are classified as extrusive (ihk-STROOS-iv) igneous rocks. Igneous rocks that formed inside the earth are classified as intrusive (in-TROO-sive) igneous rocks. Using information in this lesson, classify granite, obsidian, and rhyolite as intrusive or extrusive.

ACTIVITY

CLASSIFYING IGNEOUS ROCKS USING CRYSTAL SIZE

You will need a hand lens, samples of diorite, gabbro, and basalt, paper, and a pencil.

1. Copy Table 1 on a clean sheet of paper.
2. **Observe:** Carefully examine each of your rock samples with the hand lens.
3. Record your observations in your table.

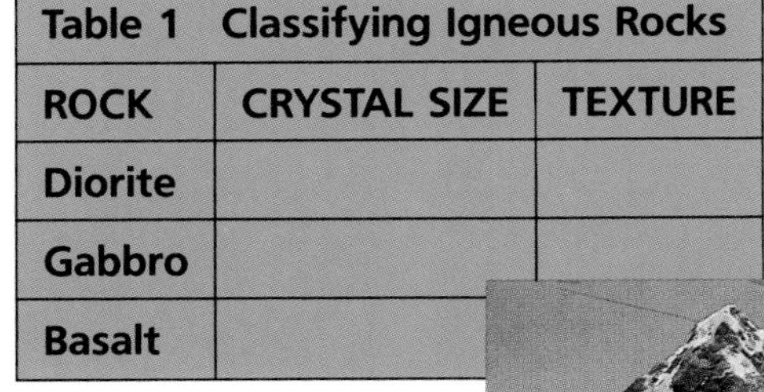

Table 1 Classifying Igneous Rocks

ROCK	CRYSTAL SIZE	TEXTURE
Diorite		
Gabbro		
Basalt		

Questions

1. Which igneous rocks formed deep inside the earth? Explain your answer.
2. Which rocks formed on the earth's surface? Explain your answer.

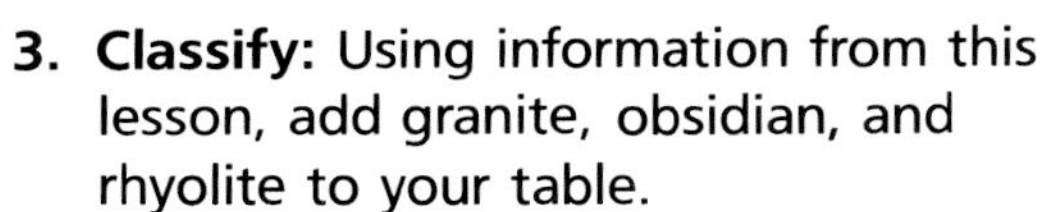

3. **Classify:** Using information from this lesson, add granite, obsidian, and rhyolite to your table.

4-4 How are sedimentary rocks formed?

Objective ▶ Describe two ways that sedimentary rocks are formed.

TechTerm

▶ **sediment** (SED-uh-munt): rock particles that settle in a liquid

Sediments What happens when you mix mud and sand in a jar of water? The particles of mud and sand settle to the bottom of the jar. The mud and sand settle in layers. The sand settles first because it is heavier than the mud. The mud settles on top of the sand. Mud and sand are examples of **sediments** (SED-uh-munts). Sediments are rock and mineral particles that settle in a liquid.

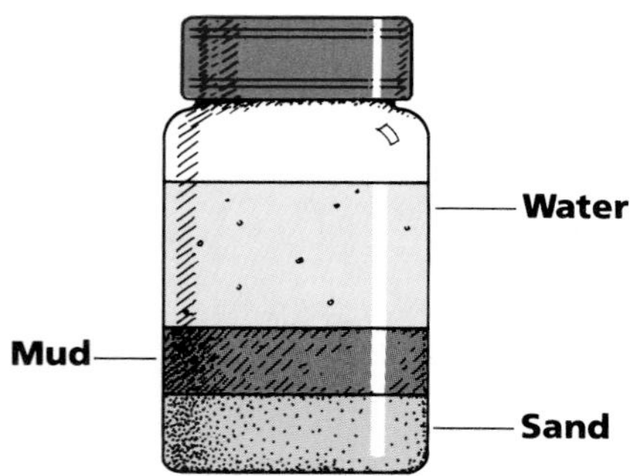

Restate: Define sediment in your own words.

Natural Concrete Many sedimentary rocks form in much the same way as concrete. Concrete is made up of sand and gravel. Have you ever seen the trucks that pour concrete for a building? Inside these trucks, sand, gravel, cement, and water are mixed. After the mixture is poured out, the water evaporates. When the water evaporates, the sand and gravel become cemented together to form solid concrete.

How do sedimentary rocks form? Most sedimentary rocks are formed in water. These rocks form from sediments that settle to the bottoms of lakes, rivers, or oceans. Over millions of years, the sediments pile up in layers. The layers of sediment may be hundreds of meters thick. As more sediment is added to the layers, the lower layers of sediment become tightly packed under the weight of the new layers. The older sediments become solid rock when water and air are squeezed out from between the sediment layers. The sediments also may become rock as dissolved minerals in the water cement the sediments together.

Describe: When does sediment become solid rock?

Sedimentary Rock From Living Things Some sedimentary rocks form from the remains of living things. For example, some sedimentary rocks form from the shells of sea animals. When clams and snails die, their shells are left on the bottom of the ocean. The shells pile up in layers. Minerals in the water cement the shells together. Coquina (koh-KEE-nuh) is a sedimentary rock formed from cemented shells. Shell limestone also forms from shells. However, you cannot see the shells in shell limestone. The shells were smashed into small pieces by ocean waves.

Coquina

Shell limestone

Identify: How do the shells of coquina stick together?

LESSON SUMMARY

- Sediment are small pieces of rocks and minerals.
- Sedimentary rock forms in much the same way as concrete.
- Sedimentary rock is formed when sediments become cemented together by dissolved minerals.
- Some sedimentary rocks form from the remains of living things.

CHECK *Complete the following.*

1. What sedimentary rock is made up of whole shells?
2. What is sediment?
3. Name two examples of sediment.
4. What materials cement the sediments in sedimentary rocks together?

APPLY *Complete the following.*

5. **Infer:** Why does sedimentary rock form in layers?
6. Why must water evaporate for sedimentary rock to form?
7. **Analyze:** How can shell limestone form from coquina?
8. **Compare:** How are shell limestone and coquina alike?
9. How does weight affect the way in which sediments form layers?

Designing an Experiment

Design an experiment to solve the problem.

PROBLEM: How can you find out the order in which mud, sand, gravel, and pebbles settle in water?

Your experiment should:

1. List the materials you need.
2. Identify safety precautions that should be followed.
3. List a step-by-step procedure.
4. Describe how you would record your data.

SCIENCE CONNECTION

WHITE CLIFFS OF DOVER

The city of Dover is located along the southeastern coast of England. Dover is known worldwide for its beautiful white cliffs. The cliffs are composed of deposits of natural chalk. These chalk deposits are more than 100 million years old.

How were the "White Cliffs of Dover" formed? The natural chalk comes from the fossil shells of microscopic animals called forams. Microscopic examination of the chalk deposits reveal the shells of the forams that formed them.

The shells of forams are made up of calcium carbonate ($CaCO_3$). When the forams die, their shells sink to the ocean bottom. In many parts of the oceans, there is a constant rain of these shells. The shells of the forams form fine sediments on the ocean bottom. Gradually, these sediments build up until they are hundreds of meters thick. Because of their great thickness, the sediments are compressed to form solid rock.

4-5 How are sedimentary rocks classified?

Objective ▶ Identify and describe the two main groups of sedimentary rock.

TechTerms

- ▶ **clastics** (KLAS-tiks): sedimentary rocks made up of pieces of rock
- ▶ **nonclastics:** sedimentary rocks made up of dissolved minerals, or the remains of living things

Groups of Sedimentary Rocks There are two groups of sedimentary rocks. One group is made up of sediments that have been cemented and pressed together. These sedimentary rocks are called **clastics** (KLAS-tiks). Another group of sedimentary rock is made up of dissolved minerals, or the remains of plants and animals. These sedimentary rocks are **nonclastics.**

Define: What are clastics?

Figure 1 Clastic Sedimentary rocks

Particle Size Clastics are classified according to the sizes and shapes of their sediments. Conglomerates (kun-GLAHM-uh-rayts) are clastic rocks made up of rounded pebbles and gravel. Sandstones are made up of small grains of sand. Shales are a group of clastic rocks made up of mud and clay. Mud and clay are the smallest kinds of sediment.

Identify: Name three groups of clastic sedimentary rocks.

Dissolved Minerals Most nonclastics form from dissolved minerals. Rocks formed in this way are chemical rocks. When water evaporates from salt lakes and shallow seas, the salts are left behind. These salts form a mineral called halite (HAY-lyt). Rock salt is a sedimentary rock made up of halite. Some kinds of limestone also form from dissolved minerals. The dissolved mineral that forms some kinds of limestone is calcite.

Figure 2 Mono Lake

Name: What mineral makes up rock salt?

Plants and Animals Some nonclastics form from the remains of plants and animals. Rocks formed from the remains of living things are organic (or-GAN-ik) rocks. Coals are nonclastic rocks formed from the remains of plants. Coal forms when the remains of plants are pressed together for a long time. Coquina (koh-KEE-nuh) is a nonclastic made up of the skeletons of sea animals. Chalk is a kind of limestone made up of the shells of very small one-celled organisms.

Describe: How is coal formed?

LESSON SUMMARY

- Clastics and nonclastics are two groups of sedimentary rock.
- Clastics are classified according to the size and shape of their sediments.
- Most nonclastics form from minerals dissolved in water.
- Some nonclastics form from the remains of plants and animals.

CHECK *Complete the following.*

1. Most nonclastics are made up of ______ .
2. Mud and ______ are two kinds of sediment in shale.
3. Coal is a ______ sedimentary rock.

APPLY *Complete the following.*

4. **Hypothesize:** Which group of nonclastic rock is most likely to form from plants buried for a long time?
5. **Classify:** Which group of clastic rock might form from the largest kinds of sediment?

InfoSearch

Read the passage. Ask two questions about the topic that you cannot answer from the information in the passage.

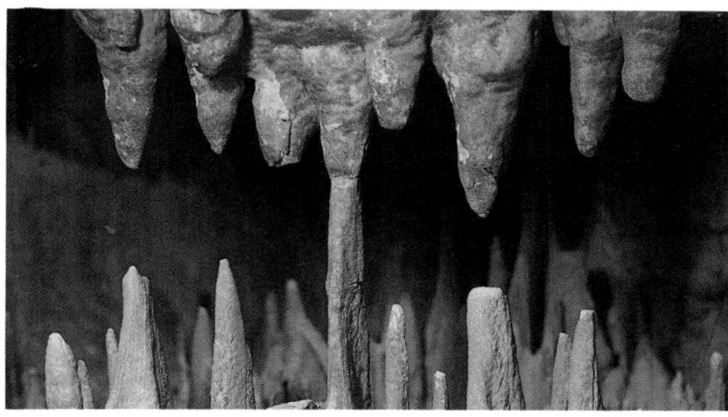

Limestone Caves Some caves have icicle-shaped deposits of limestone hanging from their ceilings. These deposits are called stalactites (stuh-LAK-tyts). These caves also have cone-shaped deposits of limestone rising from their floors. These deposits are called stalagmites (stuh-LAG-myts). Stalactites and stalagmites are formed from dissolved calcite. Sometimes, a stalactite and stalagmite may join to form a structure called a column.

SEARCH: Use library references to find answers to your questions.

ACTIVITY

MODELING STALAGMITE AND STALACTITE FORMATION

You will need 2 plastic cups, plastic wrap, water, Epsom salts, and a 15-cm long piece of unwaxed string.

1. Put some Epsom salts in two glasses of water and stir to dissolve the salts. Keep adding and stirring the salts until no more salts will dissolve in the water.
2. Wet the string. Then, place one end of the string in one glass and the other end of the string in the other glass. Be sure each end of the string is in the water. Let the string hang between the glasses, without touching the table.
3. Place a piece of plastic wrap under the string.
4. Let the glasses and the string stand. Observe the string for two days.

Questions

1. **Compare:** How is your Epsom salts deposit similar to the formation of stalactites and stalagmites?
2. **a. Classify:** Would sedimentary rock formed in this way be classified as a chemical rock or an organic rock? Explain. **b.** Would this rock be classified as a clastic or a nonclastic?

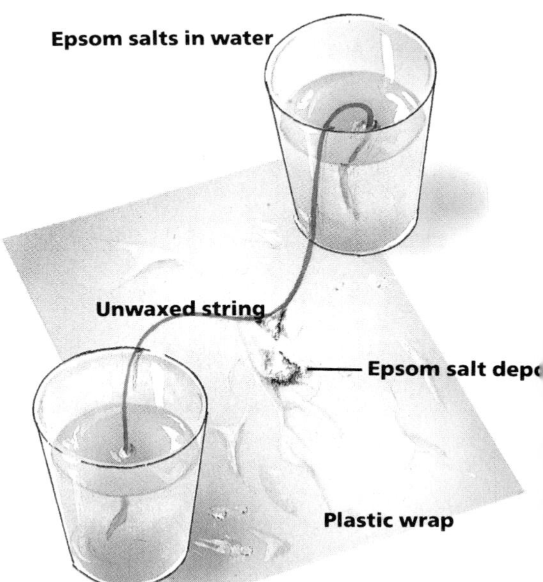

4-6 How are metamorphic rocks formed?

Objective ▶ Describe three ways in which metamorphic rocks form.

TechTerm

▶ **pressure** (PRESH-ur): force that pushes against an object

Changed Rock You can make bread from eggs, milk, flour, and salt. First, you mix the ingredients. Then, you bake the mixture in an oven. After baking the mixture, you cannot recognize any of the ingredients. The heat of the oven changes the eggs, milk, flour, and salt. The inside of the earth is like an oven. Heat inside the earth "bakes" rocks and changes the minerals in them. These changed rocks are metamorphic rocks.

▶ ***Explain:*** Why are metamorphic rocks called changed rocks?

Heat and Pressure Minerals in rocks go through a chemical change when rocks are heated. Minerals change chemically at temperatures between 100 °C and 800 °C. Minerals do not change when the temperature is below 100 °C. Above 800 °C, minerals melt into magma.

Rocks buried deep inside the earth also are affected by **pressure** (PRESH-ur). Pressure is a force that pushes against an object. Pressure deep inside the earth's crust, changes the form of minerals. A lot of pressure makes minerals flatten out into bands.

▶ ***Define:*** What is pressure?

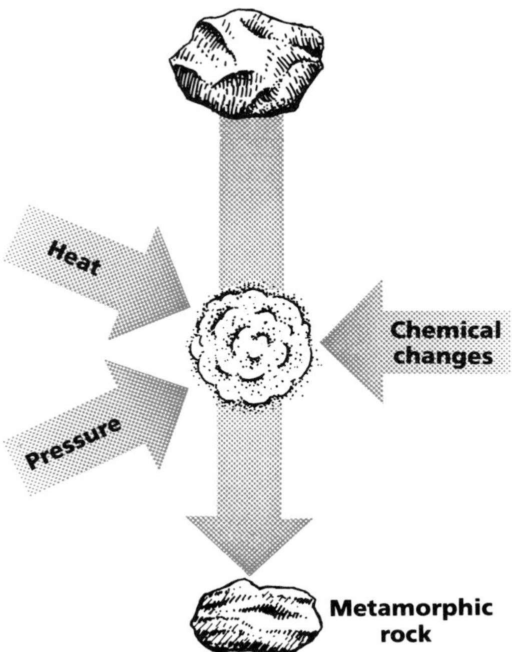

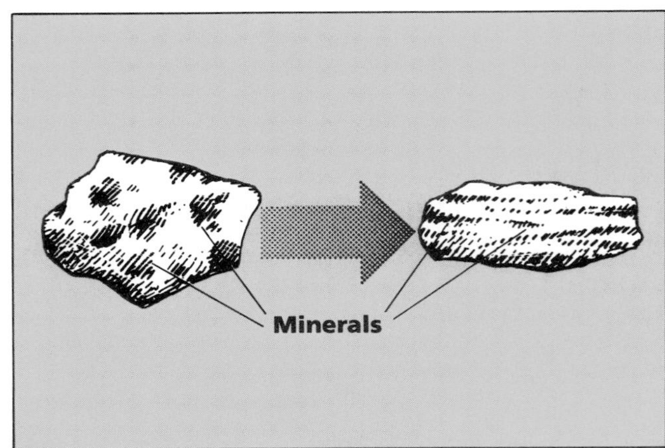

Magma and Metamorphic Rocks Some metamorphic rocks are formed when existing rocks come in contact with magma. Magma can move into cracks in deeply buried sedimentary rocks. Magma may also flow between the layers of sedimentary rocks. The heat and chemical solutions in the magma change the minerals inside the sedimentary rocks. Magma also changes minerals in igneous rocks and other metamorphic rocks.

▶ ***Identify:*** How are rocks changed by magma?

LESSON SUMMARY

- Metamorphic rock is formed when heat inside the earth changes the minerals in rocks.
- Minerals in rocks change chemically when they are heated.
- Great pressure inside the earth changes the form of minerals.
- The heat and chemical solutions in magma can change the minerals in rocks.

CHECK *Complete the following.*

1. Igneous and sedimentary rocks can be changed into metamorphic rocks by ______ .
2. Minerals in deeply buried rocks are flattened by great ______ .
3. The minerals in rocks can be changed by the heat and chemical solutions in ______ .
4. Pressure is a ______ that pushes against an object.
5. When rocks are heated, the minerals in the rocks go through a ______ change.

APPLY *Complete the following.*

6. **Hypothesize:** Can a metamorphic rock be formed at a temperature of 95 °C? Explain.
7. Can a metamorphic rock be formed at a temperature of 950 °C? Explain.
8. **Predict:** Would minerals in a rock buried 2 m beneath the earth's surface be affected by pressure? Explain.

Skill Builder

Calculating Pressure The amount of pressure placed on an object can be calculated using the formula:

$$\text{Pressure} = \text{Force}/\text{Area}$$

or

$$P = F/A$$

In this formula, force is measured in units of mass and area is measured in square units. Calculate the pressure placed on the heel of a shoe if a person's mass is 54 kilograms and the heel of the shoe is 60 cm^2.

CAREER IN EARTH SCIENCE

STONEMASON

One of the oldest professions in the world is that of the stonemason. A stonemason is a person who works with stone. Stonemasons measure, cut, and set stone into place. The great pyramids in Egypt were built by stonemasons.

Today, stone is not the only material used in building. However, the job of a stonemason is still important. Stonemasons may work indoors building fireplaces, putting up walls, or installing marble floors. Stonemasons also may work outdoors, building walls, chimneys, or the outsides of buildings, such as homes or schools.

To become a stonemason, you must first graduate from high school. Courses in mathematics and in reading blueprints are useful to a future stonemason. On-the-job training is provided in the form of an apprenticeship. As an apprentice, you learn while you work. After several years of experience, many stonemasons become building contractors.

4-7 How are metamorphic rocks classified?

Objective ▶ Explain the difference between foliated and unfoliated metamorphic rocks.

TechTerms

- **foliated** (FOH-lee-ay-ted): texture of a metamorphic rock that has mineral crystals arranged in bands
- **unfoliated:** texture of a metamorphic rock that does not have mineral crystals arranged in bands

Classifying Metamorphic Rocks Metamorphic rocks have two kinds of textures. Petrologists classify metamorphic rocks based upon the textures of the rocks. The texture of a metamorphic rock is determined by the arrangement of its mineral crystals.

Identify: How are metamorphic rocks classified?

Banded Metamorphic Rocks The mineral crystals in some metamorphic rocks are arranged in bands. The texture of a metamorphic rock with minerals arranged in bands is called **foliated** (FOH-lee-ay-ted). Foliated rocks tend to break along their mineral crystal bands.

Foliated metamorphic rocks are formed when existing rocks are placed under great heat and pressure. Under great heat and pressure, the minerals in the rocks flatten out into bands. Gneiss (NICE) is a foliated metamorphic rock. Gneiss is formed when shale and granite are heated and pressed together. Schist (SHIST) is another rock that has bands of minerals. Schist is formed from shale, basalt, and mica.

Gneiss

Contrast: How do gneiss and shale differ?

Metamorphic Rocks Without Bands The texture of a metamorphic rock that does not have minerals arranged in bands is **unfoliated.** Unfoliated metamorphic rocks do not break in layers. Marble and quartzite are unfoliated metamorphic rocks. Marble is formed when limestone is heated. Marble contains large mineral crystals of calcite. Quartzite is formed when sandstone is heated. Quartzite has large crystals of quartz.

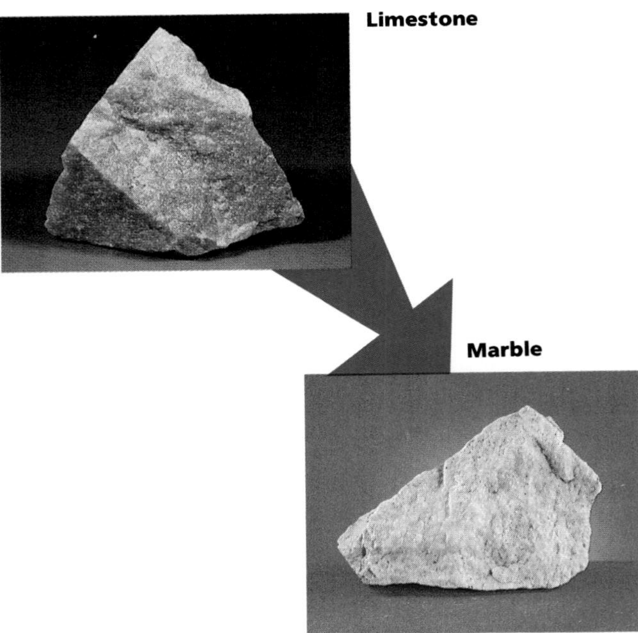

Table 1 Classification of Metamorphic Rocks

METAMORPHIC ROCK	TEXTURE	ORIGINAL ROCKS
Gneiss	foliated	granite, shale
Schist	foliated	granite, shale, mica
Slate	foliated	shale
Quartzite	unfoliated	sandstone
Marble	unfoliated	limestone

Infer: In which metamorphic rock do large crystals of quartz form from sand?

LESSON SUMMARY

- Metamorphic rocks have two kinds of textures.
- The mineral crystals in foliated metamorphic rocks are arranged in bands.
- Foliated metamorphic rocks are formed when existing rocks are placed under great heat and pressure.
- The texture of a metamorphic rock that does not have bands is unfoliated.

CHECK *Complete the following.*

1. Name the two textures of metamorphic rock.
2. What causes rocks to flatten into bands?
3. How do foliated rocks break?
4. What kind of texture does a rock with minerals that do not arrange in bands have?

APPLY *Use Table 1 on page 72 to answer the following.*

5. Which metamorphic rock is formed when shale and basalt are heated?
6. Which metamorphic rock is formed when limestone is heated?
7. Which metamorphic rocks can be formed from shale?
8. From which sedimentary rock is quartzite formed?
9. **Classify:** Is slate a foliated or unfoliated metamorphic rock? Why?

Skill Builder

Researching When you research, you gather information about a topic. Metamorphic rocks, such as marble and slate, are economically important. Use reference books to find out where in the United States deposits of marble and slate are found. Also, list some ways in which marble and slate are economically important.

LEISURE ACTIVITY

ROCK COLLECTING

People who collect rocks are called "rock-hounds." Anyone who has ever picked up a rock and taken it home is a beginning rock collector. Rock collecting is probably one of the oldest hobbies.

Why do people collect rocks? Some people collect rocks because of their attractive colors. Others collect rocks because of their pleasing shapes or textures. Studying rocks can tell you about the history of the land. You can identify land that was once under water, or that was a desert or a lush forest, by the kind of rocks in the ground.

For a rock hound, a field trip to the beach, a river bank, a quarry, or an excavation site is an exciting activity. Who knows what you might find? Will it be a geode filled with colorful crystals, or a piece of coal with the imprint of a fossilized fern?

If you go rock hunting, remember to ask for permission before visiting private lands. Visitors to national parks and monuments may not remove anything when they leave. The motto of most parks is "Take only pictures, leave only footprints."

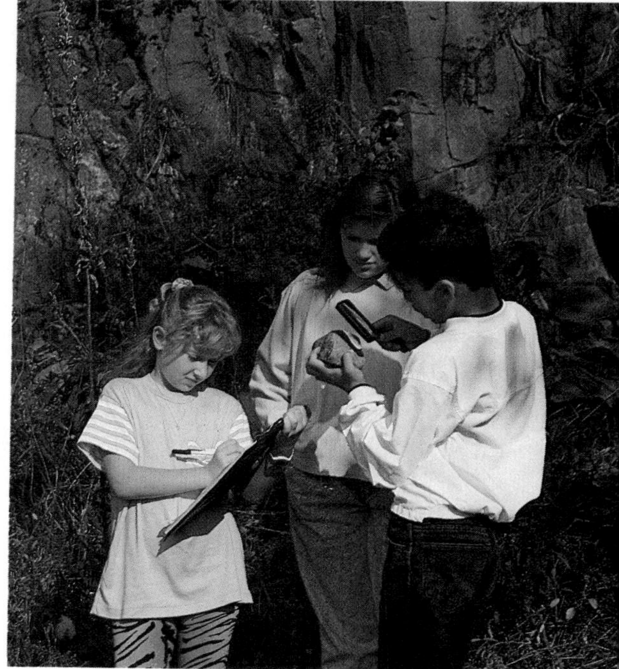

4-8 What is the rock cycle?

Objective ▶ Interpret the rock cycle.

TechTerm

▶ **rock cycle:** series of natural processes by which rocks are slowly changed from one kind of rock to another kind of rock

Cycles A series of events that happen over and over is called a cycle (SY-kul). The rise and fall of the tides is a cycle that occurs twice each day. The movement of the earth around the sun is a cycle that takes place once each year.

Define: What is a cycle?

Rock Cycle Rocks are constantly changing. Some of the changes in rocks take place inside the earth. Here, heat and pressure can change rocks from one kind of rock to another. Other changes in rocks take place at the surface. On the earth's surface, rocks are changed by rain, ice, and wind. The series of natural processes by which rocks are slowly changed from one kind of rock to another kind of rock is called the **rock cycle.** Look at the diagram of the rock cycle. The diagram shows the many ways that rocks are changed.

Infer: How do you think ice, rain, and wind can change rocks?

Examining the Rock Cycle Look at the diagram of the rock cycle. Notice that all three classes of rock may form sedimentary rock. The three classes of rocks also can be changed into metamorphic rocks or back to magma. However, only igneous rocks form directly from magma.

At the earth's surface, rocks are broken apart by rain, ice, and wind. The particles of rock may then settle in lakes or oceans to form sedimentary rock. Deeply buried igneous and sedimentary rocks can change into metamorphic rock or melt back into magma. Heat and pressure can change any rock into a metamorphic rock. A temperature of more than 800 °C can change any rock back to magma.

Observe: How does magma form igneous rocks?

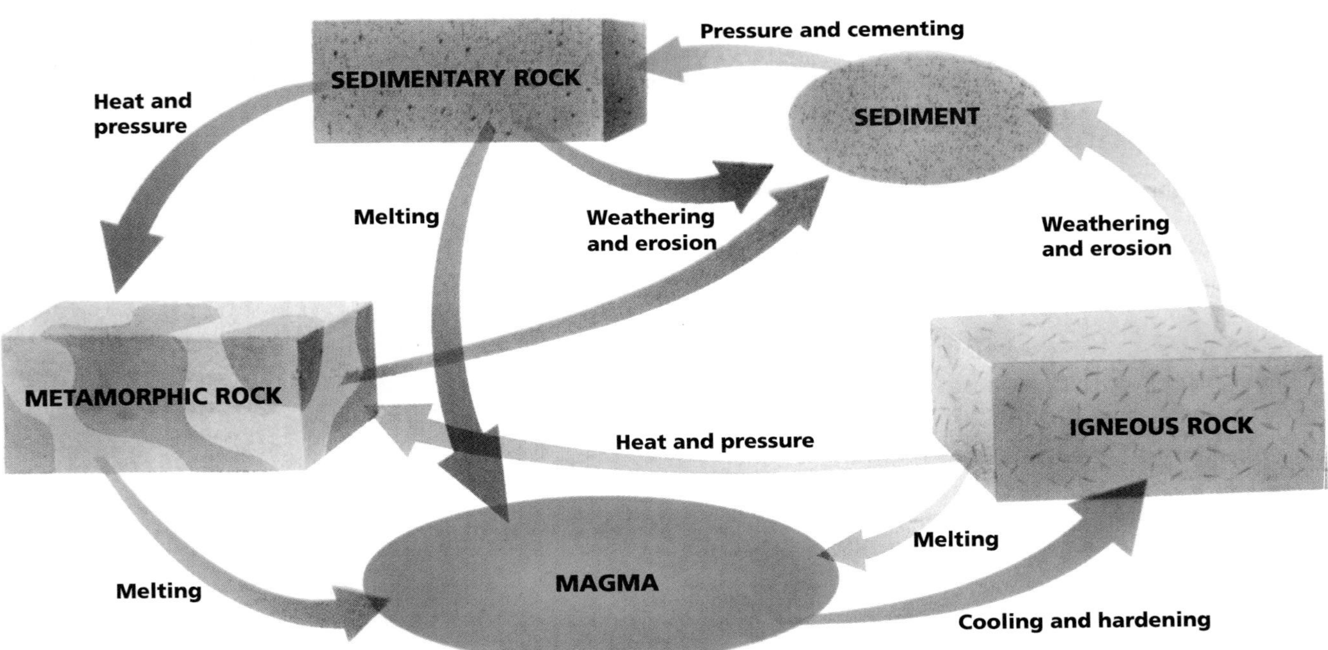

LESSON SUMMARY

- A cycle is a series of events that happen over and over.
- Rocks change slowly both inside the earth and at the earth's surface.
- The rock cycle is a series of natural processes by which rocks are slowly changed from one kind of rock to another kind of rock.
- All rocks can change into another class of rock or back to magma.
- Heat and pressure can change any rock into metamorphic rock.

CHECK *Write true if the statement is true. If the statement is false, change the underlined term to make the statement true.*

1. Inside the earth, rocks are changed by heat and rain.
2. All rocks can be broken down into sediment.
3. Magma cools and hardens into sedimentary rock.
4. Igneous rocks may be broken down and cemented into sedimentary rocks.

APPLY *Use the rock cycle diagram on page 74 to answer the following.*

5. How does an igneous or metamorphic rock become a sedimentary rock?
6. What processes change sedimentary rocks into metamorphic rocks?
7. What process changes a metamorphic rock into an igneous rock?

Ideas in Action

IDEA: Many cycles in nature affect people every day.

ACTION: Identify three natural cycles and explain how they affect you.

ACTIVITY

CLASSIFYING ROCKS

You will need 10 different rocks, a hand lens, paper, pencil, and a field guide to rocks or other reference books (optional).

1. Collect 10 different rocks from around your neighborhood.
2. Place each rock on a piece of paper. Write a number next to each rock.
3. **Observe:** Starting with rock #1, observe each of your rocks. Look at each rock with a hand lens. Record your observations on a sheet of paper.
4. **Classify:** Use your observations to classify each rock as sedimentary, igneous, or metamorphic.
5. Using this book or other reference books, identify as many of your rock samples as you can. Write the name of each rock next to your observations.

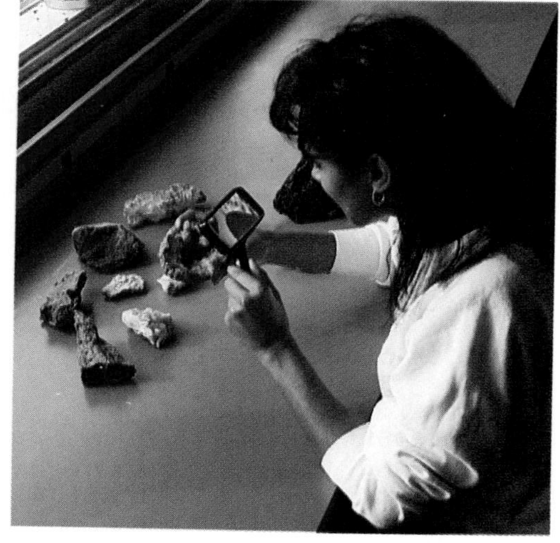

Questions

1. **a.** How many rocks did you classify as sedimentary? **b.** Why did you classify these rocks as sedimentary?
2. **a.** How many rocks did you classify as igneous? **b.** Why did you classify these rocks as igneous?
3. **a.** How many rocks did you classify as metamorphic? **b.** Why did you classify these rocks as metamorphic?
4. How many of your rocks were you able to identify?

UNIT 4 # Challenges

STUDY HINT Before you begin the Unit Challenges, review the TechTerms and Lesson Summary for each lesson in this unit.

TechTerms

clastics (68)
foliated (72)
igneous rock (60)
lava (62)
magma (62)
metamorphic rock (60)
molten rock (62)
nonclastics (68)
pressure (70)
rock cycle (74)
sediment (66)
sedimentary rock (60)
texture (64)
unfoliated (72)

TechTerm Challenges

Matching *Write the TechTerm that matches each description.*

1. rock formed from molten material
2. magma that reaches the earth's surface
3. size of crystals in a rock
4. sedimentary rocks made up of dissolved minerals
5. texture of a metamorphic rock with mineral crystals arranged in bands
6. force that pushes against an object
7. texture of a metamorphic rock that does not have mineral crystals arranged in bands
8. rock formed when another rock is changed by heat and pressure

Fill in *Write the TechTerm that best completes each statement.*

1. A rock that forms when rocks and minerals are cemented together is classified as a ______.
2. Conglomerates belong to a group of sedimentary rocks called ______.
3. Molten rock inside the earth is called ______.
4. Lava and magma are two kinds of ______.
5. The process by which rocks slowly change from one kind of rock to another is the ______.
6. Small pieces of rock material that settle in a liquid are called ______.

Content Challenges

Multiple Choice *Write the letter of the term or phrase that best completes each statement.*

1. All rocks are made up of one or more
   a. sediments. **b.** minerals. **c.** magmas. **d.** metals.
2. A scientist who studies and classifies rocks is a
   a. chemist. **b.** geographer. **c.** biologist. **d.** petrologist.
3. The kind of rock formed when melted minerals cool and harden is
   a. a molten rock. **b.** a sedimentary rock. **c.** an igneous rock. **d.** a metamorphic rock.
4. A rock formed when an existing rock is changed by heat and pressure is
   a. a molten rock. **b.** a sedimentary rock. **c.** an igneous rock. **d.** a metamorphic rock.
5. Molten rock is made up of
   a. melted minerals. **b.** sediments. **c.** the remains of living things. **d.** heat and pressure.
6. Rocks formed from the remains of living things are classified as
   a. molten rocks. **b.** igneous rocks. **c.** sedimentary rocks. **d.** metamorphic rocks.

7. Magma that reaches the earth's surface cools and hardens into
   a. igneous rock. b. sedimentary rock. c. molten rock. d. metamorphic rock.
8. The only kind of rock that can form directly from magma is
   a. sedimentary rock. b. molten rock. c. igneous rock. d. metamorphic rock.
9. The crystal size in an igneous rock is determined by the rate at which the magma in the rock
   a. cools. b. melts. c. reaches the earth's surface. d. freezes.
10. Mud and sand are examples of
   a. molten rock. b. magma. c. lava. d. sediments.

True/False *Write true if the statement is true. If the statement is false, change the underlined term to make the statement true.*

1. Most nonclastic sedimentary rocks are made up of mud.
2. Magma that reaches the earth's surface is called lava.
3. Metamorphic rocks are formed when existing rocks are changed by heat and pressure.
4. The texture of a sedimentary rock that does not have minerals arranged in bands is described as unfoliated.
5. Limestone is formed from dissolved halite.
6. Igneous rocks can be identified by their minerals.
7. Igneous rocks formed from lava usually have large crystals.
8. Marble is an igneous rock formed when limestone is heated.
9. Slate is a foliated metamorphic rock.
10. Some metamorphic rocks form when magma changes the minerals inside igneous or sedimentary rocks.

Understanding the Features

Reading Critically *Use the feature reading selections to answer the following. Page numbers for the features are shown in parentheses.*

1. What is a rock hound? (73)
2. **Infer:** Why are courses in mathematics and reading blueprints helpful to a stonemason? (71)
3. What is the chemical formula for calcium carbonate? (67)
4. What organisms are responsible for the formation of the White Cliffs of Dover? (67)
5. What is geology? (61)

Concept Challenges

Critical Thinking *Answer each of the following in complete sentences.*

1. The Law of Conservation of Matter states that matter cannot be created or destroyed, but matter can be changed from one form to another. Explain how the rock cycle supports the Law of Conservation of Matter.
2. **Classify:** Pumice is a kind of rock often formed from volcanic lava. In what class of rocks should pumice be classified?
3. Explain the difference between magma and lava.
4. How do igneous rocks formed from lava differ from igneous rocks formed from magma.
5. **Classify:** Slate is a metamorphic rock that breaks into sheets along its crystal bands. Is slate classified as a foliated or unfoliated metamorphic rock?

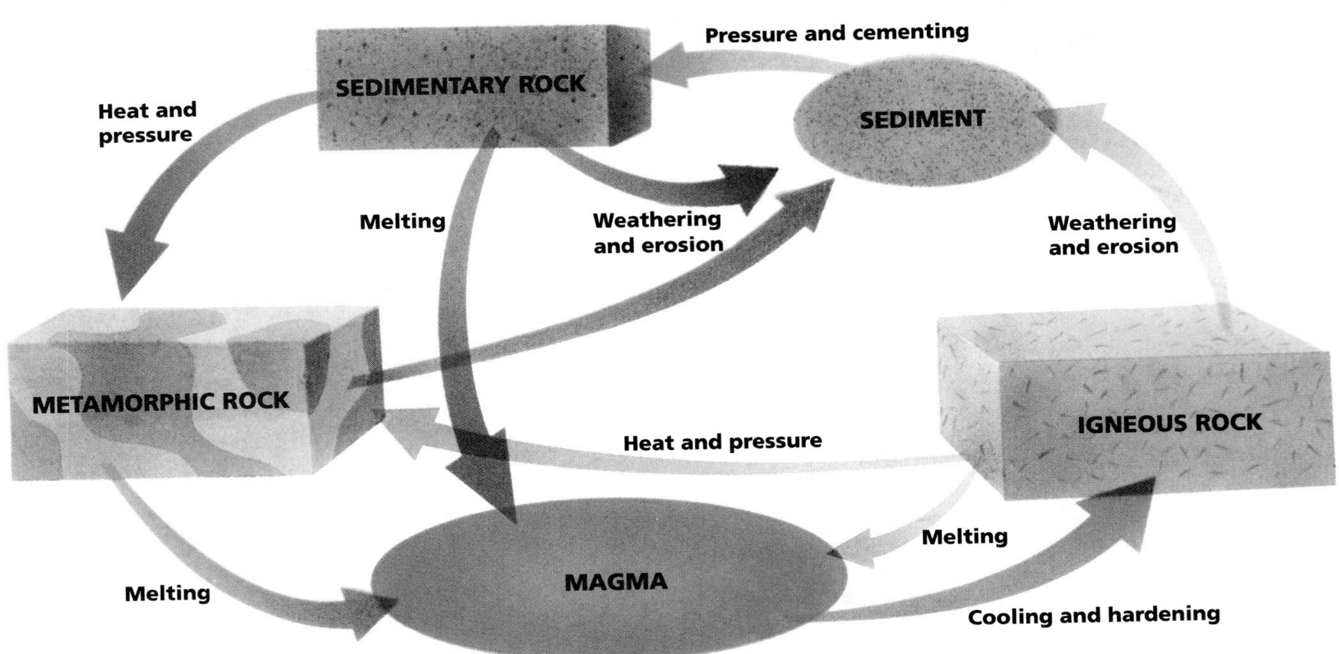

Interpreting a Diagram *Use the diagram of the rock cycle to complete the following.*

1. What are the three classes of rocks?
2. How does magma form igneous rock?
3. What processes break down igneous rocks into sediments?
4. Explain how metamorphic rocks can be changed into sedimentary rocks.
5. What changes sedimentary rock to metamorphic rock?
6. What happens when the minerals in igneous, sedimentary, and metamorphic rocks melt?
7. Explain how igneous rocks can be changed into metamorphic rocks.
8. What are two ways that sediments can form sedimentary rock?
9. What is the only kind of rock that can form directly from magma?
10. What kinds of rocks can be changed to form metamorphic rocks?

Finding Out More

1. Using an encyclopedia or other reference books, write a report on Abraham Gottlob Werner. In your report explain why Werner's theory about the formation of all rocks was wrong.
2. **Classify:** Begin a rock collection by collecting rocks you find in your neighborhood. Use an encyclopedia or a field guide to rocks to classify each rock you find as igneous, sedimentary, or metamorphic. Label each of your rocks with the name of the rock and its class.
3. **Classify:** Collect photographs and postcards of famous monuments and buildings made from stone. Use your photographs and postcards to create a bulletin board display for your classroom. Label each picture with the name of the monument or building, its location, and the kind of stone it is made from.
4. Human history has passed through several ages. Three of these ages are the Stone Age, the Bronze Age, and the Iron Age. Use reference materials to find out how each of these historical ages got its name.
5. **Observe:** Find out what kinds of tools a petrologist uses to study rocks. Make a poster that shows what each tool looks like and how the tool is used.

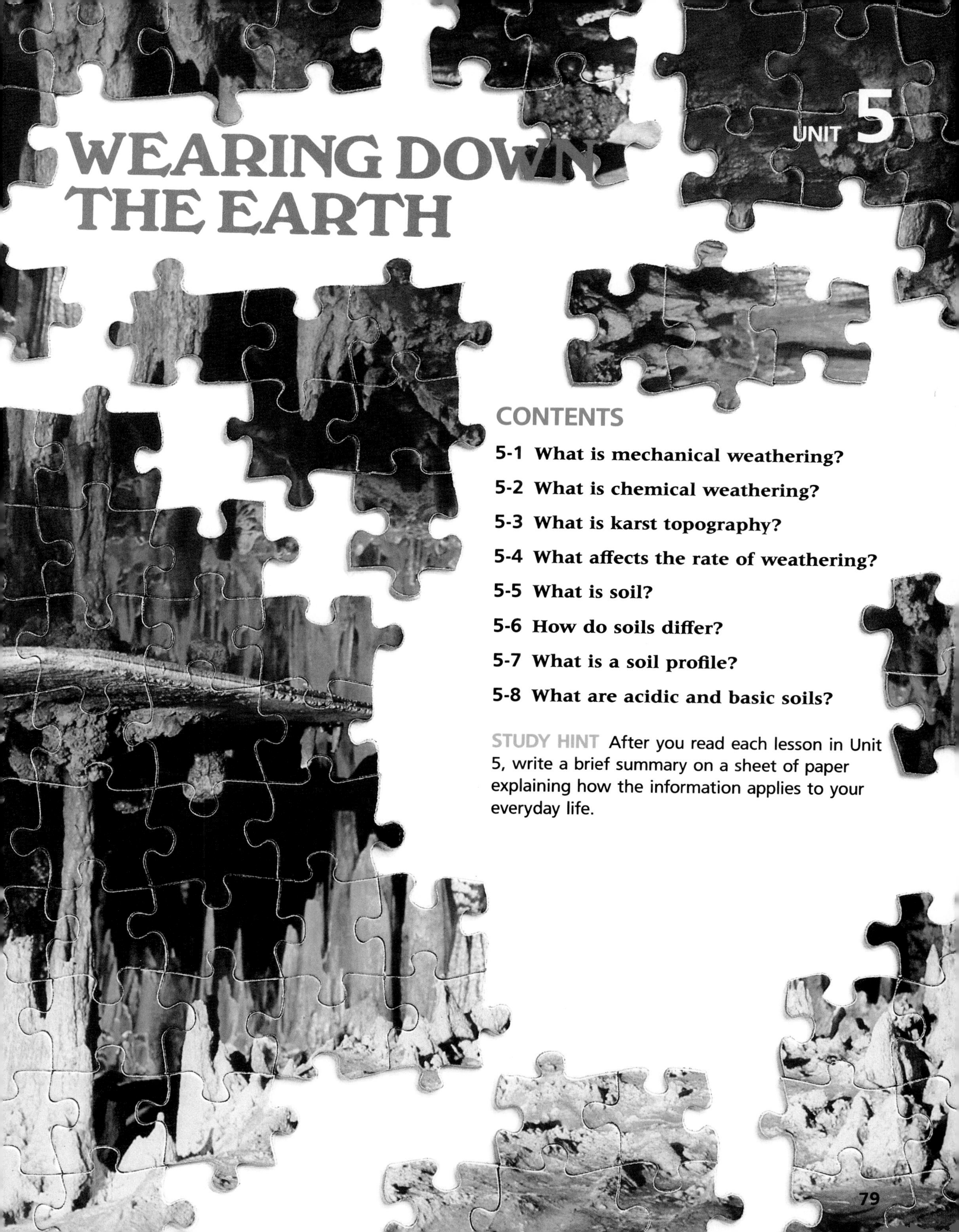

WEARING DOWN THE EARTH

UNIT 5

CONTENTS

STUDY HINT After you read each lesson in Unit 5, write a brief summary on a sheet of paper explaining how the information applies to your everyday life.

5-1 What is mechanical weathering?

Objective ▶ Understand how the earth's surface is worn down by mechanical weathering.

TechTerms

- ▶ **chemical** (KEM-ih-kul) **weathering:** weathering in which the chemical makeup of rocks changes
- ▶ **ice wedging:** mechanical weathering caused by the freezing and melting of water
- ▶ **mechanical** (muh-KAN-ih-kul) **weathering:** weathering in which the chemical makeup of rocks does not change
- ▶ **weathering:** breaking down of rocks and other materials on the earth's surface

Weathering The breaking down of rocks and other materials on the earth's surface is called **weathering.** New bricks are bright red. They have sharp corners and edges. Old bricks are darker red. They have rounded corners and edges. What causes bricks to change color and shape? The answer is weathering.

There are two kinds of weathering. **Mechanical** (muh-KAN-ih-kul) **weathering** occurs when the sizes and shapes of rocks are changed. These are physical changes. The chemical (KEM-ih-kul) makeup of the rocks does not change. **Chemical weathering** occurs when the chemical makeup of the rocks changes. The sizes and shapes of the rocks also may change.

▶ ***Name:*** What are the two kinds of weathering?

Temperature Changes Rocks can be broken apart by changes in temperature. Heat makes things expand, or become larger. Cooling makes things contract, or become smaller. During the day, heat causes the outside of rocks to expand. The inside of the rocks stays cool. At night, the rocks cool and contract. The repeated heating and cooling of rocks each day causes pieces of the rocks' surface to flake or peel off.

Classify: What kind of weathering do changes in temperature cause?

Ice Wedging The repeated freezing and melting of water causes **ice wedging.** Potholes in streets are caused by ice wedging. Water enters cracks in rocks. When the temperature drops below freezing (0 °C), the water in the cracks freezes. Unlike most liquids, water expands when it freezes. The expanding water is like a wedge making the crack wider. After repeated freezing and melting of water, the rock breaks apart.

▶ ***Identify:*** What property of water causes water to act like a wedge when it freezes in cracks?

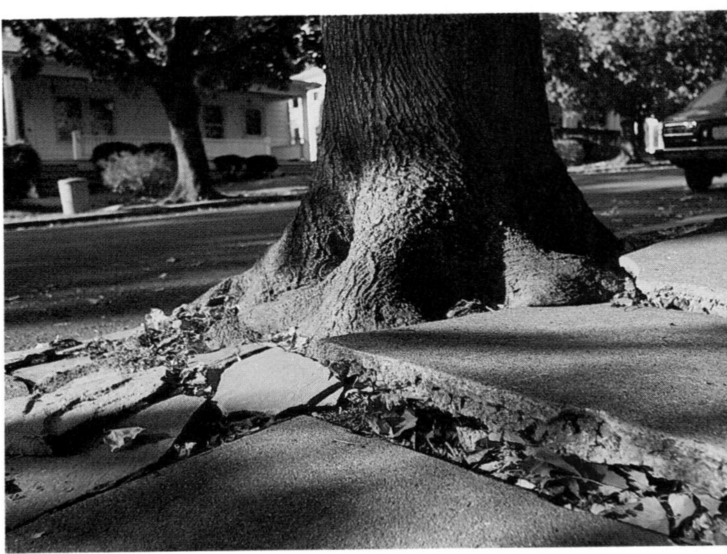

Root Action Plant roots can grow into cracks in rocks. Look at the sidewalk near a tree. Is the sidewalk cracked or raised? The tree roots may have caused the cracks or lifted the sidewalk. The pressure of the growing root can make cracks in rocks larger. As the roots grow, they can break rocks apart.

 ***Classify:*** What kind of weathering is caused by root action?

LESSON SUMMARY

- Weathering is the breaking down of rocks and materials on the earth's surface.
- The two kinds of weathering are mechanical and chemical weathering.
- Changes in temperature can break rocks apart.
- Ice wedging is a kind of mechanical weathering caused by the repeated freezing and melting of water.
- Pressure from the roots of growing plants can cause mechanical weathering.

CHECK *Write true if the statement is true. If the statement is false, change the underlined term to make the statement true.*

1. Breaking a rock into pieces does not change the <u>chemical makeup</u> of each piece.
2. Potholes are caused by <u>chemical</u> weathering.
3. Ice wedging is caused by the repeated <u>freezing</u> and melting of water.
4. When water freezes, it <u>contracts</u>.

APPLY *Complete the following.*

5. **Hypothesize:** Why should trees not be planted near underground water pipes?
6. The breaking apart of rocks by growing roots is sometimes called root-pry. Do you think this is a good name? Explain.
7. **Predict:** Would you find potholes in the roads of regions where temperatures are above freezing all the time? Why?

Skill Builder

Classifying When you classify, you group things based upon similarities. Use a reference book to find the definitions of "chemical change" and "physical change." Use the definitions to classify each of the following as a chemical change or a physical change. **a.** A rock breaks into many pieces. **b.** A match burns. **c.** A can rusts. **d.** A sidewalk becomes cracked by a tree root. **e.** When acid is put on calcite, bubbles form.

ACTIVITY

OBSERVING THE EFFECTS OF MECHANICAL WEATHERING

You will need plaster of Paris, a paper cup, safety goggles, a hammer, a stirring rod, water, a plastic container with a tight-fitting lid, and some small pebbles.

1. Fill a paper cup halfway with plaster of Paris. Add water slowly to the plaster while stirring until the plaster becomes thick and creamy. Let the cup stand overnight.
2. Peel away the paper cup. Use a hammer to break up the plaster into small pieces. **CAUTION: Wear safety goggles.**
3. Place some of the plaster pieces together with an equal amount of pebbles into the container. Fill the container halfway with water and close the lid tightly.
4. Shake the container about 75 times.
5. Pour out the water and remove two pieces of plaster. Compare these pieces with the original pieces of plaster.

Questions

1. **a. Observe:** How did the pieces of plaster look after you shook the container? **b.** What did the water look like?
2. **Predict:** What do you predict would happen to all the pieces of plaster if this process continued?
3. How does this activity show mechanical weathering?

5-2 What is chemical weathering?

Objective ▶ Understand how the earth is worn down by chemical weathering.

TechTerms

- ▶ **carbonation** (kar-buh-NAY-shun): chemical reaction of carbonic acid with minerals
- ▶ **hydrolysis** (hy-DRAHL-uh-sis): chemical reaction between water and another substance
- ▶ **oxidation** (ok-suh-DAY-shun): a chemical change between oxygen and another substance

Chemical Weathering Changes that produce new substances are chemical changes. Chemical changes cause chemical weathering of rocks. Chemical changes take place when the minerals in rocks are broken down into other substances. Chemical changes also take place when minerals are added to or removed from rocks. Most chemical weathering is caused by oxygen, water, and acids.

▶ ***Name:*** What causes most chemical changes during chemical weathering?

Oxidation One kind of chemical weathering is **oxidation** (ok-suh-DAY-shun). Oxidation takes place when oxygen combines with another substance. New substances called oxides are formed. Rust is iron oxide (Fe_2O_3). Many rocks are made up of iron-containing minerals. Pyrite and magnetite are minerals containing iron. When rocks with these minerals are exposed to the air, the iron undergoes oxidation. The rock weakens, and may crumble.

▶ ***Define:*** What is oxidation?

Water Most chemical weathering is caused by water. The chemical reaction of water with other substances is called **hydrolysis** (hy-DRAHL-uh-sis). Many minerals in rocks undergo hydrolysis. For example, a type of feldspar combines chemically with water. Feldspar is changed into clay. Many minerals formed by hydrolysis dissolve in water. Water carries away the minerals holding the rocks together. The rocks then fall apart.

▶ ***Explain:*** How does hydrolysis cause weathering?

Acids Many acids cause chemical weathering of rocks and minerals. Carbon dioxide is a gas in the air. When it rains, carbon dioxide dissolves in the rainwater. Water and carbon dioxide form carbonic (kar-BON-ik) acid. When carbonic acid touches some minerals, a chemical change takes place. The reaction of carbonic acid with minerals is called **carbonation** (kar-buh-NAY-shun). The mineral calcite is changed by carbonation. Limestone and marble are two rocks made of calcite.

Buildings made of limestone or marble often are weathered by carbonation.

Some plants also produce acids. Have you ever seen mosses growing on a rock? Mosses produce weak acids. The weak acids can cause chemical changes in rocks. The surfaces of the rocks are worn away. When acids seep deeper into cracks, the rocks can break apart.

▶ ***Identify:*** What acid is formed when carbon dioxide and water combine?

LESSON SUMMARY

- Chemical weathering takes place when rocks break apart as a result of chemical changes.
- Oxidation is the chemical reaction of oxygen with other substances.
- Most chemical weathering is caused by hydrolysis, the chemical reaction of water with other substances.
- Carbonation occurs when carbonic acid breaks down minerals in rocks.
- Plants produce acids that cause chemical weathering.

CHECK *Complete the following.*

1. List three factors that cause most chemical weathering.
2. What happens to minerals in a rock that undergo oxidation?
3. What is hydrolysis?
4. What happens to minerals in a rock that undergo carbonation?
5. Name two rocks affected by carbonation.
6. How do some plants cause chemical weathering?
7. If a rock has iron in it, what process causes chemical weathering?

APPLY *Complete the following.*

8. **Infer:** Why do you think steel bridges must be painted?
9. Explain how the color of a rock may help you tell if the rock is made up of pyrite and if the rock has undergone chemical weathering.
10. **Classify:** Which kind of chemical weathering is described in each example? **a.** Water dissolves rock salt. **b.** The features on the face of a marble statue can no longer be seen. **c.** A bicycle's fenders rust. **d.** Rock layers in the Valley of Fire, Nevada, have turned dark red-brown.

Skill Builder

Experimenting Place a piece of steel wool outside your house. Be sure the steel wool is in a place where it is exposed to the weather. Place another piece of steel wool in your room. Pick a place where the steel wool will not be disturbed. Examine each piece of steel wool for two weeks. Keep a record of your observations. Write a report explaining your findings. Include changes you observed; the differences in the two pieces of steel wool; and why there are differences.

SCIENCE CONNECTION

PREVENTING CORROSION

Corrosion is the chemical weathering of metals. The most common kind of corrosion is rust. Rust affects iron and steel. It changes the color and also weakens these metals.

Rusting is a problem in buildings, highways, and bridges. If rust cannot be slowed, it can destroy the iron and steel used to build these things. Rust also affects pipes in houses. It also can damage the bottoms of cars.

Rusting is not easy to slow or stop. One of the easiest ways to slow rusting is to paint metals. Paint keeps water and heat from rusting metals. Building steel is often coated with the metal zinc. The zinc coating protects the steel. This kind of steel is called galvanized steel. Have you ever heard someone ask for car undercoating or rust-proofing. This is a coat of tar-like paint used to protect the bottom of a car.

5-3 What is karst topography?

Objective ▶ Name and describe some features of karst topography.

TechTerms

- ▶ **cavern:** series of underground caves formed by groundwater erosion
- ▶ **sinkhole:** large hole in the ground formed when the roof of a cavern collapses

Karst Topography In some places in the world, the topography (tuh-PAGH-ruh-fee), or shape and look of the land, is unusual. The land is bare and rocky with little or no plant growth. There are no lakes or streams on the surface of the land. Instead, there are underground rivers, caves, and large holes in the ground. This kind of topography is called karst topography. Karst topography gets its name from a region in Yugoslavia where these kinds of features are common. In the United States, karst topography can be seen in Florida and Kentucky.

▶ ***Locate:*** Where can karst topography be seen in the United States?

Chemical Weathering of Limestone Karst topography results from the action of groundwater on limestone. In many areas of the world, layers of limestone rock are found under a thin layer of other rocks. These areas of limestone rock are very large. As groundwater seeps through the layers of rock, the groundwater mixes with carbon dioxide in the rocks to form carbonic acid. When carbonic acid reaches the limestone layers, carbonation takes place. The acid dissolves the limestone. The limestone is chemically weathered, or broken down, by the acid.

▶ ***Identify:*** How does carbonic acid affect limestone?

Caverns When carbonic acid dissolves underground limestone deposits, **caverns** are formed. Carbonic acid seeps into small cracks and holes.

Through the years, the holes increase in size and form caves. A series of connected caves form a cavern. Underground streams often flow through caverns.

▶ ***Define:*** What is a cavern?

Sinkholes When water empties out of a cavern, the cavern roof may collapse. **Sinkholes,** or sinks, are formed. Sinkholes may become entrances to the caverns. Tourists enter these sinks to visit places like Carlsbad Caverns, New Mexico and Howe Caverns, New York. If a sinkhole fills with water, a sinkhole lake results.

▶ ***Define:*** What are sinkholes?

Natural Bridges Sometimes only part of the roof of a cavern collapses. The remaining section of the roof becomes a natural bridge. A natural bridge also can form when a surface stream runs through a crack beneath the surface and then flows back onto the surface. The stream wears away the rock, and the crack gets bigger. Scientists think that Natural Bridge in Virginia formed as a result of a stream wearing away rock.

▶ ***Predict:*** What would happen if part of a cavern roof collapsed?

LESSON SUMMARY

- Bare, rocky land with little or no plant growth is called karst topography.
- Karst topography results from the chemical weathering of limestone by carbonic acid.
- Caverns are formed when underground limestone deposits are dissolved by carbonic acid.
- Sinkholes are formed when a cavern roof collapses.
- Natural bridges are formed when part of a cavern roof collapses.

CHECK *Complete the following.*

1. The reaction of carbonic acid on limestone is a form of ______ .
2. Karst topography gets its name from a region in ______ .
3. A ______ is a series of connected caves.
4. A large opening from the surface into a cavern is a ______ .
5. What are three features of karst topography?

APPLY *Complete the following.*

6. Why does karst topography develop in an area where the underground rock is limestone?
7. **Hypothesize:** Why could karst topography not develop in a desert?
8. Why would you find few surface streams in a karst topography region?

Skill Builder

Mapping Trace an outline map of the United States on a piece of paper. Look up the locations of the following caverns: Carlsbad Caverns, New Mexico; Howe Caverns, New York; Mammoth Cave, Kentucky; Luray Caverns, Virginia; Wind Cave, South Dakota. Plot the location of each cavern on your outline map. Are any of these caverns near where you live? Have you ever visited any of these caverns? If so, describe what the caverns looked like.

SCIENCE CONNECTION

SINKHOLES AND THE ENVIRONMENT

You might say that plans to build a basketball court in the parking lot at Flatkinder Park in Lakeland, Georgia "fell through." The land around Lakeland has all of the features of karst topography. The underlying rock of Lakeland is limestone. There is no parking lot in the park any more. In fact, there is no land there. The land fell into a sinkhole. The sinkhole was 24 meters wide and 9 meters deep. The sinkhole has now been connected to a nearby pond and turned into a fish pond.

The people in Winter Park, Florida had a similar problem. However, they suffered greater losses. Damage to the community of Winter Park, Florida was about 2 million dollars. The sinkhole was more than 100 meters, or the size of a football field, across. Several houses, a truck, some cars, and a swimming pool fell into this huge sinkhole. Even a four-lane highway became part of the sinkhole. The formation of eight more sinkholes a few days later did even more damage.

5-4 What affects the rate of weathering?

Objective ▶ Identify three factors that affect the rate of weathering.

TechTerm

▶ **acid rain:** rain containing nitric acid and sulfuric acid

Climate The climate of an area affects the rate of weathering. The amount of water in the air and the temperature of an area are part of climate. Moisture speeds up chemical weathering. The more water there is in the air, the faster is the weathering rate. Weathering is fastest in hot, wet climates. Weathering is very slow in hot, dry climates. Without liquid water, most chemical weathering cannot occur. Without temperature changes, ice wedging cannot occur. In areas that are very cold and wet, there is not much weathering.

▶ ***Identify:*** What two climate factors affect the rate of weathering?

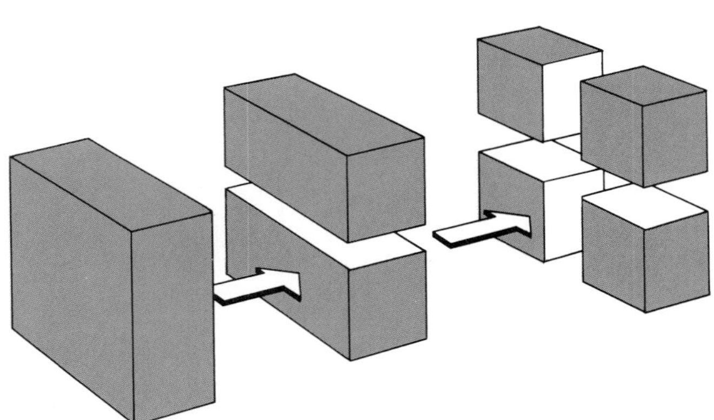

Surface Area The rate of weathering of a rock is affected by the rock's surface area. Picture a block of wood painted red. It has six exposed sides. If you cut the block in half, two more surfaces, or sides, are exposed. Cut each half in half. How many surfaces are exposed on the four pieces? Each cut makes smaller blocks. Cutting the blocks gives the blocks more surface area. If the block were a rock, more surfaces of the rock would be exposed to the weather. The more surfaces exposed, the faster the rock will weather. As a rock is broken into smaller pieces, it weathers faster.

▶ ***Describe:*** How does the amount of surface area exposed to the air affect weathering of a rock?

Rock Composition Different kinds of rock weather at different rates. The minerals that hold some rocks together dissolve faster than other minerals. These differences make one kind of rock weather faster than another. Quartz weathers slowly while feldspar weathers much faster. If a rock has a lot of quartz in it, the rock will weather slowly. Some rocks have a lot of calcite in them. These rocks weather very quickly. They are affected by chemical weathering, especially carbonation. Rocks containing iron weather faster than rocks without iron.

▶ ***Infer:*** Limestone is made up of calcite. Would limestone weather slowly or quickly? Explain.

Acid Rain Weathering is usually a slow process. However, pollution is speeding up the weathering process. Factories and cars release carbon dioxide and other gases into the air. Some of these gases form acids when they mix with rainwater. Two acids are sulfuric acid and nitric acid. Rain containing these acids is called **acid rain.** Acid rain causes rocks and minerals to weather faster. You can see the effects of acid rain on buildings and statues.

▶ ***List:*** What two acids are present in acid rain?

LESSON SUMMARY

- Weathering is affected by moisture and temperature.
- The more surface area of rock exposed, the faster the rock will weather.
- The rate of weathering is affected by the minerals that make up a rock.
- Acid rain speeds up the weathering process.

CHECK *Complete each sentence with the word **"increases"** or **"decreases"**.*

1. As the amount of moisture in a region increases, the rate of weathering ______ .
2. In a rock that has more quartz than feldspar, the rate of weathering ______ .
3. As a rock is broken into smaller pieces, the rate of weathering ______ .
4. In very polluted air, the weathering of a statue probably ______ .

APPLY *Complete the following.*

5. List the factors that affect weathering rate.
6. **Predict:** In which place would you find the most weathered building stones? Explain. **a.** a major city **b.** a farm **c.** the desert
7. **Hypothesize:** Which rock will weather faster? Why?

a.

b.

InfoSearch

Read the passage. Ask two questions about the topic that you cannot answer from the information in the passage.

Cleopatra's Needle In 1880, a large stone monument called Cleopatra's Needle was moved from Egypt to New York City. The climate in Egypt is hot and dry. Cleopatra's Needle stood for more than 3000 years in Egypt. In that time, the writings carved on the surface of the monument changed very little. A short time after the Needle was moved to New York City, Cleopatra's Needle was badly weathered. Most of the writing on the monument had weathered away.

SEARCH: Use library references to find answers to your questions.

ACTIVITY

OBSERVING THE EFFECT OF SURFACE AREA ON WEATHERING

You will need 2 plastic cups, a hammer, a piece of chalk, a paper towel, vinegar, and safety goggles.

1. Break a piece of chalk in half. Place one piece of chalk into a plastic cup.
2. Place the other piece of chalk on a paper towel. Break the chalk into small pieces with a hammer. **CAUTION: Wear your safety goggles.** Place these pieces into another cup.
3. Pour enough vinegar into each cup to cover the chalk.
4. Observe what happens to the chalk in each cup.

Questions

1. **Observe:** What happened to the surface area of the chalk when you broke it into two pieces?
2. **Compare:** Of the two pieces of chalk, which has the greater surface area?
3. What kind of weathering takes place when the pieces of chalk are placed in vinegar?
4. What happens to the rate of weathering as the surface area of the chalk is increased?

5-5 What is soil?

Objective ▶ Explain how soil is a product of weathering and organic processes.

TechTerms

- **bedrock:** solid rock that lies beneath the soil
- **humus** (HYOO-mus): decaying remains of plants and animals

Formation of Soil If you dig a hole through the soil, sooner or later you will hit a layer of solid rock called **bedrock.** In some areas, bedrock is at the earth's surface. Bedrock is the parent material of soil. Soil formation begins when bedrock is broken down by weathering. Weathering breaks the parent material into smaller and smaller pieces. Over time, the weathered rock is broken down into soil particles.

▶ ***Identify:*** From what material does soil form?

Living Things and Soil Many different kinds of organisms live in or on the soil. Living things also help form soil. Some, such as mosses and lichens (LY-kuns), form acids that help break down rocks. Bacteria (bak-TIR-ee-uh) in the soil cause dead plants and animals to decay. Fungi, such as mushrooms, also help break down dead animals and plants. Acids formed by decay speed up soil formation. The decayed remains of plants and animals form **humus** (HYOO-mus). Humus is the organic material in soil.

Animals that live in the soil help to form soil. Living things such as earthworms, ants, and moles burrow through the ground. As these animals burrow, they help break apart large pieces of soil. The burrowing also lets more water into the soil. The water helps speed up the breakdown of rock.

▶ ***Describe:*** What is humus?

Soil Soil is a mixture. Weathered pieces of rocks, minerals, and humus make up most of soil. Rock pieces make up between 50% and 80% of soil. Clay and quartz are the minerals that make up most of soil. Humus has a lot of minerals in it. These minerals are important to plants. Soil that is rich in humus is very dark in color. Air and water are also in soil. They fill the spaces between soil particles.

▶ ***List:*** What things make up soil?

Importance of Soil Soil is important to plants. It supplies water and support for plants. Most plants need the nutrients (NOO-tree-unts), or chemical elements, in soil to grow properly. Important nutrients such as potassium, phosphorus, and nitrogen are part of soil.

Soil also is important to people. Houses, cities, and roads are built on soil. Food crops are grown in soil. Many animals eat plants. Without plants, plant-eating animals would not survive. Other animals hunt and kill plant-eating animals for food. Without soil, few things could live on the earth.

▶ ***Name:*** What are three important nutrients needed by plants?

LESSON SUMMARY

- Bedrock is the parent material of soil.
- Living things help form soil.
- Living things that burrow in the ground help break apart large pieces of soil.
- Soil is a mixture.
- Soil supplies plants with water, support, and nutrients.
- Soil is important to people.

CHECK *Complete the following.*

1. The parent material of soil is _______ .
2. The organic material in soil is _______ .
3. Air and _______ fill the spaces between soil particles.
4. The chemical elements in soil that are needed by plants are called _______ .
5. Soil is made up mostly of weathered _______ .
6. The process that forms soil is _______ .

APPLY *Complete the following.*

7. **Infer:** Why is bedrock called the parent material of soil?
8. How do ants help to speed up the formation of soil?
9. Explain how soil meets the needs of plants for support, water, and nutrients.

Skill Builder

Building Vocabulary In some parts of the world, two kinds of soil form. These two kinds of soil are pedalfer (puh-DAHL-fur) and pedocal (PED-uh-kul). Look up the prefix "pedo-" in the dictionary. Write the meaning of the prefix on a piece of paper. Look up the words "pedalfer" and "pedocal." From the information in the dictionary, what nutrients are in each kind of soil? Write the words "pedalfer" and "pedocal." Circle the part of each word that would help you identify the nutrients in each kind of soil.

SCIENCE CONNECTION

LICHENS

Not many living things can live on a bare rock. The rock surface absorbs very little water. The sun beats down on the rock. The rock surface is not protected from winds. Lichens, however, can live and grow on rocks.

Lichens are made up of two small living things. These living things are an alga and a fungus. Both living things live together as one. The alga makes food, and needs water. The fungus can absorb a lot of water, but cannot make food. The alga and the fungus are helped by the partnership. This is called mutualism (MYOO-choo-wuhl-iz-um).

Lichens help to form soil. Besides helping to form soil, lichens are important in many other ways. Many lichens grow in the Arctic. They keep the frozen soil from melting. They also help to prevent erosion. Lichens also are food for reindeer and caribou. Lichens are used as food in some cultures. In the Middle East, lichens are used in bread and stews. In Japan, lichens are used to make soups. Some lichens are used in perfumes, soaps, and dyes. Lichens also are used to find out the amount of air pollution in an area. Scientists use lichens to find out the amount of sulfur dioxide in the air. Lichens die when there is too much sulfur dioxide in the air. The scientists study how many lichens are growing in polluted areas.

5-6 How do soils differ?

Objective ▶ Describe differences in soils in terms of texture, mineral content, and where the soil was formed.

TechTerms

- ▶ **leaching** (LEECH-ing): removing, or washing away of minerals in soil
- ▶ **residual** (rih-ZIJ-oo-ul) **soil:** soil that remains on top of the bedrock from which the soil was formed
- ▶ **texture** (TEKS-chur): size of soil particles
- ▶ **transported** (trans-POR-tid) **soil:** soil that has been moved from above the bedrock from which the soil was formed

Texture Soils have different **textures** (TEKS-churs). Texture describes the size of soil particles. Sandy soils have a coarse texture. Sand particles are between 0.06 mm and 2 mm in diameter. Some soils contain silt. Silt particles are only 0.002 to 0.06 mm in diameter. Silty soils are not as coarse as sandy soils. The smallest particles in soil are clay. Clayey soils have a fine texture. When clayey soils are wet, they feel sticky and muddy.

▶ *Describe:* What is meant by the texture of soil?

Bedrock and Soil Sometimes soil is carried away from the place where it is formed. Soil can be moved by running water, glaciers, wind, and waves. The soil is then deposited in a new place. Soil that is moved from the place where it was formed is called **transported** (trans-POR-tid) **soil.** To transport something means to carry it to another place. Transported soil may differ from the bedrock, or parent material, that formed the soil.

Many soils are not transported. These soils stay on top of the bedrock from which they were formed. These soils are **residual** (rih-ZIJ-oo-ul) **soils.** Residual soils have a chemical makeup like that of their parent material.

▶ *Contrast:* What is the difference between transported soil and residual soil?

Minerals in Soil The kinds and amounts of minerals in soil vary. The kinds of minerals in soil depend on the parent material. For example, the minerals in granite are different from those in limestone. One kind of soil comes from granite bedrock. Another kind of soil comes from sandstone bedrock. Chemical weathering also affects the minerals in soil.

Minerals are removed from soils by plants and by **leaching** (LEECH-ing). Leaching is the removing, or washing away, of minerals by water. The minerals in the soil are dissolved and washed deeper into the soil. Sometimes the minerals are washed away completely. On farmland, these minerals need to be replaced. Plants use minerals to grow properly. Farmers add fertilizers to the soil to replace minerals used by plants or washed away by leaching.

▶ *List:* How are minerals removed from soil?

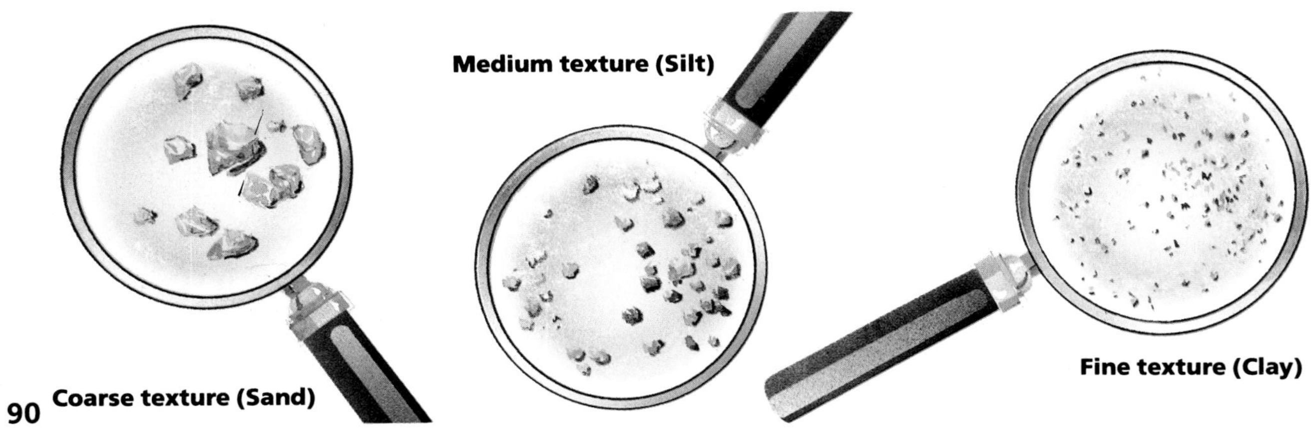

LESSON SUMMARY

- Soils have different textures.
- Transported soils have been moved from the place where they formed.
- Residual soils stay on top of the bedrock from which they formed.
- Different soils contain different kinds and amounts of minerals.
- Minerals are removed from soil by plants and by leaching.

CHECK *Complete the following.*

1. The size of particles in soil describes the _______ of the soil.
2. If a soil is very different from the bedrock beneath it, the soil is probably a _______ soil.
3. A soil with a fine texture probably has a lot of _______ in it.
4. The movement of minerals by water deeper into the soil is called _______ .
5. List four agents that can transport soil from one place to another.
6. Name two ways minerals are removed from soil.

APPLY *Complete the following.*

7. **Sequence:** Put the soils in order from most coarse to least coarse. Write the letter for each soil. **a.** 95% sand, 5% silt **b.** 10% silt, 90% clay **c.** 50% clay, 50% silt **d.** 100% clay
8. **Hypothesize:** Why would chemical weathering affect the kinds of minerals in soil as the soil is formed?

InfoSearch

Read the passage. Ask two questions about the topic that you cannot answer from the information in the passage.

Soil Conservation Service The work of the Soil Conservation Service, or SCS, began during the 1930s. The SCS works with local conservation groups to help protect natural resources such as soil and water. SCS soil conservationists help farmers and ranchers to use their land wisely. The goals of the SCS include reducing soil erosion, protecting wildlife, and keeping water supplies clean.

SEARCH: Use library references to find answers to your questions.

CAREER IN EARTH SCIENCE

SOIL SCIENTIST

Do you like to grow plants? Do you enjoy being outdoors? If so, you might enjoy a career working as a soil scientist. Soil scientists gather information about soils and help to conserve soil. Some soil scientists help farmers care for their land. Others teach and do research in colleges and universities. Fertilizer companies often employ soil scientists.

The Soil Conservation Service is an agency of the United States Department of Agriculture. The Soil Conservation Service was formed in the 1930s. Today, the Soil Conservation Service employs soil conservationists to work with ranchers and farmers to preserve the soil.

A bachelor's degree in soil science is needed to enter this profession. Many colleges have work study programs. In these programs, students work part time in a job related to their studies. The American Society of Agronomy (uh-GRAHN-uh-mee) offers a certification for soil scientists. This certification is not required, but it is important for advancement in the field.

5-7 What is a soil profile?

Objective ▶ Identify and describe the parts of a soil profile.

TechTerms

- **horizon** (hor-Y-zun): soil layer
- **soil profile** (PRO-fyl): all the layers that make up the soil in an area

Soil Layers Soil forms in layers called **horizons** (hor-Y-zuns). Most soils have three horizons. Each horizon is named with a capital letter. The A horizon is the top layer of soil. The B horizon is beneath the A horizon. The C horizon is beneath the B horizon.

All the soil layers together are called a **soil profile** (PRO-fyl). You can see soil profiles in stream banks, where buildings are being built, and in road cuts. A road cut is a place where land has been dug out to build a road.

▶ *List:* Name three places where you can see a soil profile.

Mature and Immature Soils A soil that has three horizons is called a mature (mah-CHOOR) soil. A mature soil takes hundreds of years to form. In some soils, there are only two horizons. A soil with two horizons is called immature (im-uh-CHOOR) soil. After a long time, weathering changes immature soil into mature soil.

▶ *Describe:* What is immature soil?

A Horizon The A horizon is below a thin layer of organic material. This thin layer is called the O horizon. The A horizon is the topsoil. Topsoil is made up of a mixture of humus and tiny rock particles. Humus gives topsoil its dark color. Topsoil is rich in nutrients. Most organisms that live in the soil are found in the A horizon. Plants grow best in topsoil.

▶ *Identify:* What is topsoil made up of?

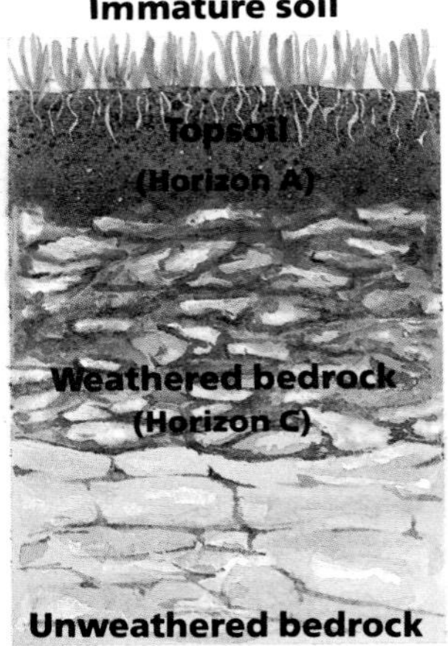

B Horizon The B horizon is beneath the A horizon. The B horizon is the subsoil. Subsoil is made up mostly of clay, small pieces of weathered rock, and minerals. Leaching moves minerals into the B horizon. Because the subsoil has a lot of clay, it is much harder than the A horizon. For this reason, only the roots of large plants grow into the B horizon.

▶ *Compare:* Why is the B horizon harder than the A horizon?

C Horizon The C horizon is the bottom layer of a soil profile. The C horizon is made up of large pieces of rock. Weathering of these large pieces of rock is the first step in forming soil. At the bottom of the C horizon is solid bedrock. The large pieces of rock in the C horizon come from the weathering of bedrock.

▶ *Describe:* Where is the C horizon located in a soil profile?

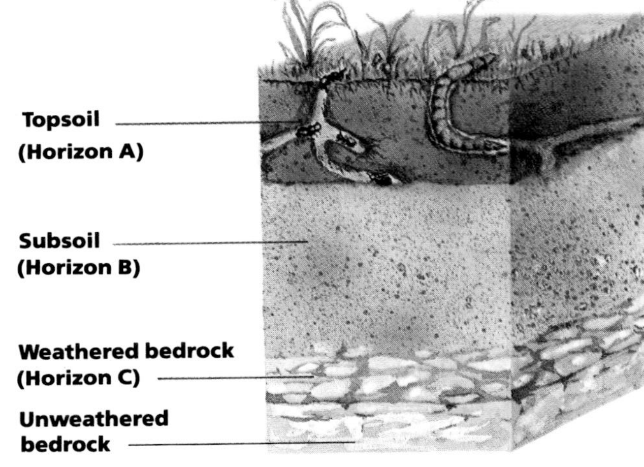

LESSON SUMMARY

- Soil forms in layers called horizons.
- The soil horizons make up a soil profile.
- Mature soil has three horizons. Immature soil has only two horizons.
- The A horizon is the top layer of the soil.
- The B horizon is the subsoil.
- The C horizon is the bottom layer of a soil profile, containing large pieces of bedrock.

CHECK *Complete the following.*

1. Soil forms in layers called _______ .
2. The B horizon is the _______ .
3. The number of horizons in immature soil is _______ .
4. The A horizon is made up of a dark colored soil called _______ .
5. If a soil has 3 horizons, it is a _______ soil.
6. In the C horizon, the large pieces of rock are weathered _______ .

APPLY *Complete the following.*

7. What is the relationship between soil horizons and a soil profile?
8. What is the difference between mature and immature soils?

Skill Builder

Using Prefixes A prefix is a word part that appears at the beginning of another word. A prefix can change the meaning of a word. Look in a dictionary to find the meaning of the prefix "sub-." Then, use the meaning of the prefix "sub-" to help you define the following words:

subsoil	submarine
submerge	subsurface
subheading	subway

Write a definition for each word. Circle the word or words in the definition that relate to the meaning of the prefix "sub-."

ACTIVITY

MODELING A SOIL PROFILE

You will need a clear plastic cup, clay, sand, gravel, dirt, and a marking pen.

1. In a clear plastic cup, arrange layers of clay, sand, gravel, and dirt to make a model of a soil profile. Let the clay represent the bedrock.
2. Use a marking pen to identify each layer of your soil profile. Label the A, B, and C horizons, and the bedrock.
3. **Model:** Draw a diagram of your soil profile. Compare your drawing with the soil profiles on page 92.

Questions

1. Which material did you use to represent the A horizon? the B horizon? the C horizon?
2. **Classify:** Does your soil profile show a mature soil or an immature soil? Explain.
3. **a.** Which horizon of a soil profile is the topsoil? **b.** Which horizon is the subsoil?

5-8 What are acidic and basic soils?

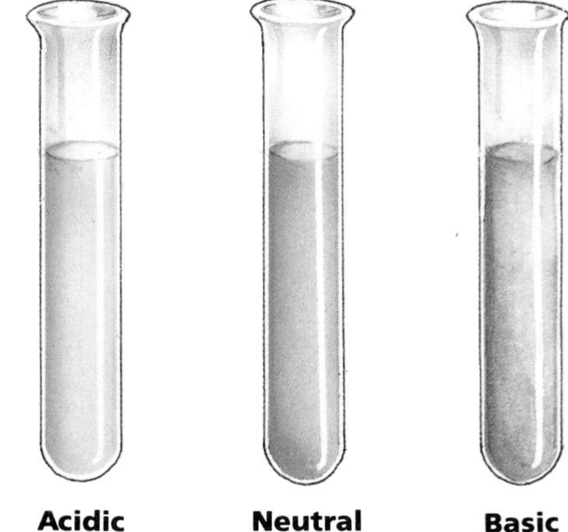

Objective ▶ Identify basic and acidic soils and how to test for them.

TechTerms

- ▶ **indicator** (IN-dih-kay-tur): chemical used to identify the presence of other substances
- ▶ **pH scale:** number scale used to measure acidity

pH Scale Chemists measure the acid content of a solution on a scale. The scale is called the **pH scale.** The pH scale uses numbers between 0.0 and 14.0. A pH of 7 means a solution is neutral. Neutral solutions are neither basic nor acidic. Any number above 7 means a solution is basic. The higher the number is, the more basic the solution. Any number below 7 is acidic. The lower the number is, the more acidic the solution. The acidity of soil can be checked quickly with an instrument called a pH meter.

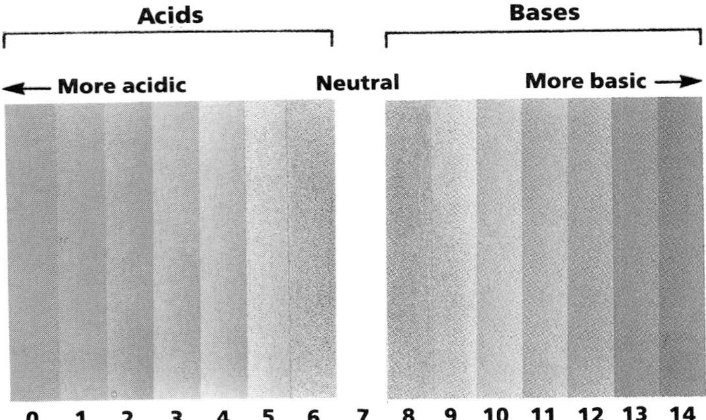

Classify: Pure water has a pH of 7. Is it neutral, acidic, or basic?

Soil Acidity Soil usually measures between a 4.0 and 10.0 on the pH scale. Basic soils contain a lot of calcium, potassium, magnesium, and sodium. These elements form compounds called bases. When these elements are removed from soil by leaching, the soil becomes acidic. Farmers call an acidic soil a sour soil. They call a basic soil a sweet soil.

List: Name four elements that make a soil basic.

Testing Soil Acidity You can test the pH of soil using **indictors** (IN-dih-kay-turs). Indicators change color in acidic and basic solutions. Two indicators are litmus paper and bromthymol (BROM-thy-mol) blue. Red litmus paper turns blue in basic soils. Blue litmus paper turns red in acidic soils. The colors of litmus paper do not change in neutral soils. Bromthymol blue turns different colors. When bromthymol blue passes through a very acidic soil, it turns yellow. In a very basic soil, bromthymol blue turns blue. Neutral soils turn bromthymol blue to a greenish blue color.

Explain: What effect does acidic soil have on bromthymol blue?

Plants and Soil Acidity The kinds of plants that grow in soil depend on the acidity of the soil. Most plants grow best in soils with a pH of 5.0 to a little over 7.0. Some plants grow well in acidic soils. Pine trees and evergreens are examples. Some plants, such as grasses, grow better in basic soils.

You can add lime to acidic soils to make them basic. Farmers often do this when soil becomes too acidic. Lime is calcium carbonate. The calcium in lime makes the soil more basic. Lime is a kind of fertilizer. Farmers must be careful not to add too much lime to soil. In very basic soil, iron does not dissolve. Plants then do not get enough iron to grow.

Identify: In what pH range do most plants grow best?

LESSON SUMMARY

- The pH scale is used to measure the acid content of a solution.
- Soils can be basic or acidic, and usually measure 4.0–10.0 on the pH scale.
- Indicators can be used to test the acidity of soils.
- Some plants grow better in acidic soils while other plants grow better in basic soils.
- Lime can be added to acidic soils to make them more basic.

CHECK *Write true if the statement is true. If the statement is false, change the underlined term to make the statement true.*

1. Bleach has a pH of 12.5. It is acidic.
2. Grasses grow best in sweet soils.
3. Red litmus paper will turn blue in acidic soil.
4. You can check the pH of a solution by using a pH meter.
5. Adding lime to soil turns it sour.

APPLY *Classify: Use the descriptions below to classify each soil as **acidic, basic,** or **neutral.***

6. A soil has a pH of 7.
7. A soil is called a sour soil.
8. A soil has a pH of 5.
9. A soil after lime has been added to it.
10. A soil in which pine trees grow very well.
11. A soil turns bromthymol blue yellow.

Skill Builder

Classifying When you classify, you group things based upon similarities. Use the pH scale on page 94 to classify these common substances as acidic, basic, or neutral. **a.** lye: 14.0 **b.** lemon juice: 2.0 **c.** car battery acid: 0.0 **d.** baking soda: 8.4 **e.** milk: 6.6 **f.** orange juice: 4.1 **g.** blood: 7.4 **h.** ammonia: 11.5 **i.** ocean water: 8.0 **j.** soap: 10.0

1. **a.** Which substance is the most acidic?
   b. The most basic?
2. **a.** Which substance is the least acidic?
   b. The least basic?
3. **Sequence:** List the materials in order from most acidic to most basic.

LEISURE ACTIVITY

GARDENING

Gardening is a hobby that is enjoyed by both homeowners and apartment dwellers. A garden can be as small as a window box or a flower pot, or as large as an outside vegetable garden. In both cases, the gardeners receive great satisfaction for their efforts.

A vegetable garden can supply a variety of fresh fruits and vegetables throughout the growing season. Flower gardens add color and beauty to property. Flowers also attract birds and insects necessary for fruit and seed production. Houseplants can make a room more cheerful. They also clean the air in a home. Plants clean the air by filtering pollutants from the air.

All plants need soil, water, light, and the proper temperature to grow. Plants should be watered regularly, especially when the weather is hot and dry. Plants use minerals from the soil for growth. These minerals can be supplied by adding fertilizers to the soil. To receive sunlight most of the day, plants should be grown on the south side of a house if possible. Indoor plants should be placed away from radiators and open windows.

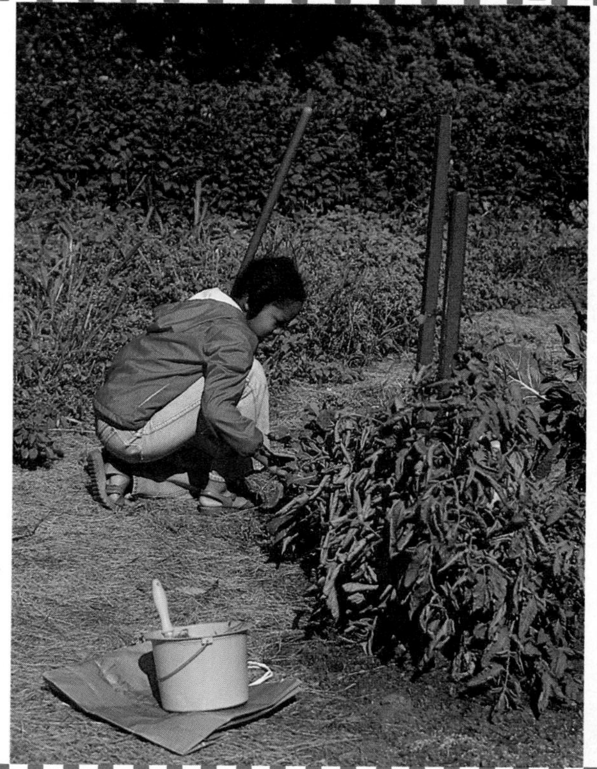

UNIT 5 Challenges

STUDY HINT Before you begin the Unit Challenges, review the TechTerms and Lesson Summary for each lesson in this unit.

TechTerms

acid rain (86)
bedrock (88)
carbonation (82)
cavern (84)
chemical weathering (80)
horizon (92)
humus (88)
hydrolysis (82)
ice wedging (80)
indicator (94)
leaching (90)
mechanical weathering (80)
oxidation (82)
pH scale (94)
residual soil (90)
sinkhole (84)
soil profile (92)
texture (90)
transported soil (90)
weathering (80)

TechTerm Challenges

Matching *Write the TechTerm that best matches each description.*

1. layer of rock beneath soil
2. size of soil particles
3. breaking down of rocks and materials on the earth's surface
4. rain containing sulfuric and nitric acids
5. washing away of minerals in soil
6. large hole in the ground formed by a collapsed cavern
7. soil layer

Identifying Word Relationships *Explain how the words in each pair are related. Write your answers in complete sentences.*

1. cavern, natural bridge
2. residual soil, transported soil
3. chemical weathering, mechanical weathering
4. ice wedging, hydrolysis
5. oxidation, carbonation
6. indicator, pH scale
7. horizon, soil profile
8. humus, soil

Content Challenges

Completion *Write the term that best completes each statement.*

1. Caverns, sinkholes, and natural bridges all are features of _______ .
2. Mechanical weathering does not change the _______ of rocks.
3. Potholes in streets are caused by _______ .
4. Root action and ice wedging are kinds of _______ weathering.
5. Oxidation forms new substances called _______ .
6. Karst topography results from the action of groundwater on _______ .
7. A rock containing quartz weathers _______ than a rock containing calcite.
8. Bedrock is the _______ material of soil.
9. Sandy soils have a _______ texture.
10. Farmers add _______ to the soil to replace minerals washed away by leaching.

Multiple Choice *Write the letter of the term that best completes each statement.*

1. Hydrolysis, carbonation, and oxidation are kinds of
   a. leaching. **b.** mechanical weathering. **c.** chemical weathering. **d.** karst topography.
2. Bromthymol blue and litmus paper are two kinds of
   a. acidic substances. **b.** basic substances. **c.** humus. **d.** indicators.
3. Subsoil is located in the
   a. O horizon. **b.** A horizon. **c.** B horizon. **d.** C horizon.
4. A substance with a pH of 7 is
   a. neutral. **b.** acidic. **c.** an indicator. **d.** basic.
5. A soil that has only two horizons is classified as a
   a. sweet soil. **b.** sour soil. **c.** mature soil. **d.** immature soil.
6. Topsoil is located in the
   a. O horizon. **b.** A horizon. **c.** B horizon. **d.** C horizon.
7. Feldspar is changed into clay by the process of
   a. hydrolysis. **b.** oxidation. **c.** carbonation. **d.** leaching.
8. Most chemical weathering is caused by
   a. acid rain. **b.** carbonation. **c.** oxidation. **d.** hydrolysis.
9. Karst topography results mostly from
   a. acid rain. **b.** carbonation. **c.** oxidation. **d.** hydrolysis.
10. Weathering is fastest in
   a. hot, dry climates. **b.** cold, dry climates. **c.** cold, wet climates. **d.** hot, wet climates.

Understanding the Features

Reading Critically *Use the feature reading selections to answer the following. Page numbers for the features are shown in parentheses.*

1. What kind of rock is Flatlander Park in Georgia built on? (85)
2. What are lichens? (89)
3. What are the responsibilities of a soil scientist? (91)
4. Who provides soil scientists with certification? (91)
5. What are four things plants need to grow? (95)

Concept Challenges

Critical Thinking *Answer each of the following in complete sentences.*

1. Why would weathering be slow in a cold, wet climate?
2. What kind of chemical weathering is most likely to affect a rock containing calcite? Why?
3. How do living things help to form soil?
4. How does leaching affect plantlife?
5. How does the pH of a soil affect the kinds of plants that can grow in the soil?

Interpreting a Diagram *Use the diagram to complete the following.*

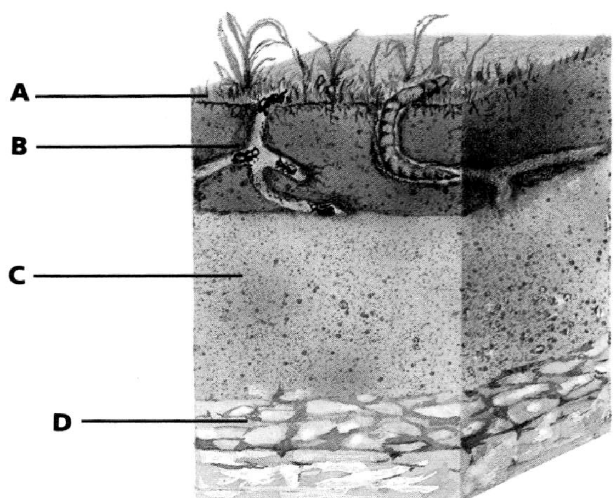

1. What is shown in the diagram?
2. What is each layer of soil called?
3. What is the name of the layer shown in A?
4. What is the name of the layer shown in B?
5. What kind of soil makes up the layer labelled b?
6. What is the soil that makes up layer C called?
7. What material makes up the bottom part of the layer labelled D?
8. Is the soil shown a mature or an immature soil? Explain your answer.

Finding Out More

1. **Observe:** Survey your neighborhood for signs of mechanical and chemical weathering. Draw symbols for each kind of weathering. Draw a map of the area you surveyed. Use the symbols to show where the weathering was observed. Identify the material being weathered.
2. Design an experiment to show how corrosion can be slowed down. Obtain two iron or steel nails. Paint one nail. Place each nail into small jars filled with water. Observe the nails each day for two weeks. Write a laboratory report of your findings.
3. Use library resources to find out about the many kinds of fertilizers added to soil. Find out which fertilizers may have harmful effects as well as being helpful. Prepare a poster that shows the kinds of fertilizers and their uses. Be sure to include any harmful effects.

AGENTS OF EROSION

UNIT 6

CONTENTS

STUDY HINT Before beginning each lesson in Unit 6, review the TechTerms for each lesson and read each Lesson Summary.

6-1 What are erosion and deposition?

Objectives ► Define erosion and list five agents of erosion. ► Define deposition.

TechTerms

- **deposition** (dep-uh-ZISH-un): process by which material carried by erosion is dropped in new places
- **erosion** (eh-ROH-zhun): process by which weathered material is moved from one place to another

Erosion The rocks that make up the earth's crust are broken down by weathering. Weathering, however, is not the only force that acts upon the earth's surface. After rocks are broken down, they may be moved from one place to another. The process by which weathered material is moved from one place to another is called **erosion** (eh-ROH-zhun).

Define: What is erosion?

Agents of Erosion During erosion, parts of the earth's surface are worn away. Have you ever seen the Grand Canyon? The Grand Canyon is a gash in the earth more than 2 km deep. At the bottom of the Grand Canyon is the Colorado River. As the river flows, it carries away small pieces of weathered rock. Over millions of years, enough rocks have been carried away to carve out the Grand Canyon.

Running water, glaciers, wind, waves, and gravity are the five agents of erosion. How do these agents of erosion wear away the earth's surface? Running water and glaciers can carry away large amounts of rocks and soil. Waves can move sand onto and off a beach. Wind can carry sand, dirt, and dust. Gravity can cause soil and rocks to move down a slope.

List: Name five agents of erosion.

Deposition Materials moved by erosion are dropped in new places. The process by which weathered materials carried by agents of erosion are dropped in new places is called **deposition** (dep-uh-ZISH-un). Deposition builds landforms on the earth's surface.

Define: What is deposition?

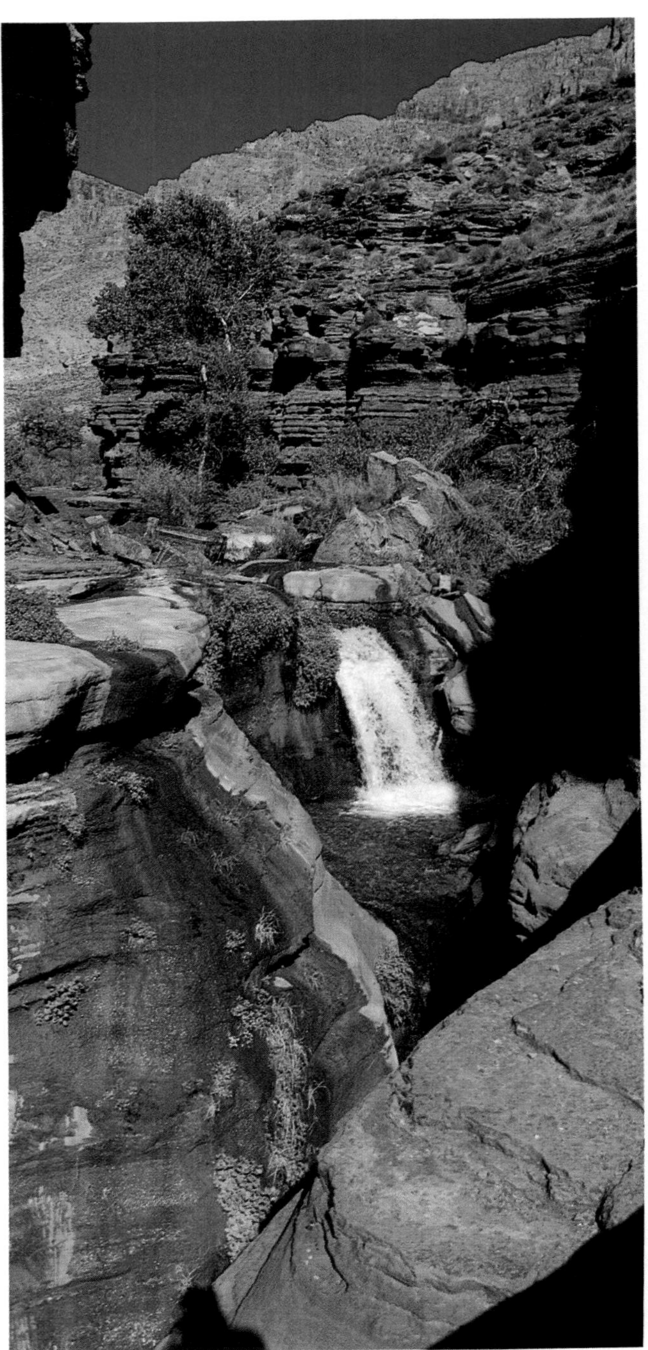

LESSON SUMMARY

- Erosion is the process by which weathered material is carried from one place to another.
- During erosion, parts of the earth's surface are worn away.
- The five agents of erosion are running water, glaciers, wind, waves, and gravity.
- Deposition is the process by which weathered material moved by erosion is dropped in new places.

CHECK *Complete the following.*

1. The Grand Canyon was formed by the process of ______ .
2. There are ______ agents of erosion.
3. Running water, wind, ______, gravity, and glaciers are agents of erosion.
4. The dropping of rocks carried by a glacier is an example of ______ .

APPLY *Complete the following.*

5. **Contrast:** Explain the difference between erosion and deposition.
6. **Infer:** A roadside sign in a mountain area says, "Beware of Falling Rocks." Which agent of erosion is probably at work in the area?

Use the photograph to answer the following.

7. Are the shells on the beach an example of erosion or deposition?
8. **Infer:** How do you think the shells were carried onto the beach?

Ideas in Action

IDEA: The federal government spends millions of dollars each year repairing damage caused by erosion and weathering.

ACTION: Describe the damage done by erosion and weathering in your area. Explain what is being done to correct the damage, and whether you think the effort is worth the money spent.

CAREER IN EARTH SCIENCE

URBAN PLANNER

Urban planners design new cities and help renovate older cities. Many cities in the United States are built on waterways or near the oceans. In the past, cities were built near water so goods and supplies could be transported by water. Urban planners help plan the layout of a city. This includes roads, railroads, and air travel. Because of the work of urban planners, it is no longer necessary for cities to be on the water.

Planners must consider the needs of all the members of the community. As cities get larger, their needs for electric power, sanitation, schools, roads, and other services increase. An urban planner helps bring all of these services to the community.

An urban planner must have a college degree. A bachelors degree in architecture, public administration, or civil engineering usually is helpful.

6-2 How does gravity cause erosion?

Objective ▶ Name and describe examples of erosion caused by gravity.

TechTerms

- ▶ **mass movement:** downhill movement of weathered materials caused by gravity
- ▶ **talus:** pile of rocks and rock particles that collects at the base of a slope

Gravity Gravity is a force. On the earth, the force of gravity pulls all things toward the earth's center. This downward pull of gravity can cause materials to move from areas of higher elevation to areas of lower elevation.

Gravity is the only agent of erosion that is not in motion. However, gravity can cause motion. For example, the force of gravity can cause rocks and glaciers to move down mountain slopes. Gravity also causes rivers to flow toward the oceans.

Infer: Why is gravity an agent of erosion?

Mass Movement The downhill movement of weathered materials caused by gravity is called **mass movement.** Mass movement can occur quickly or slowly. Materials moved by gravity come to rest in piles, called **talus** at the base of the slope. The talus can be carried away by running water and other agents of erosion.

Define: What is mass movement?

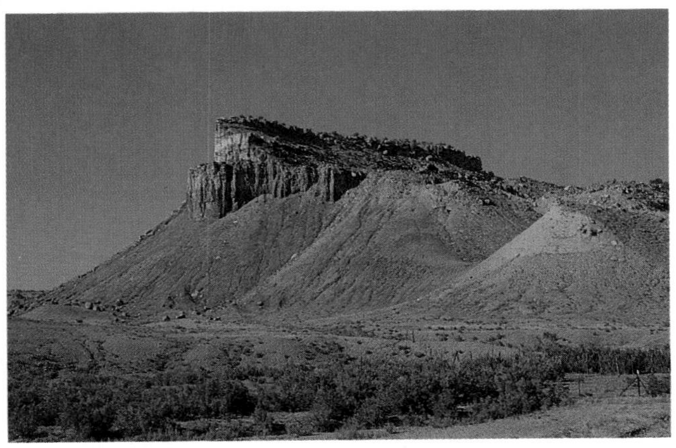

Landslides and Mudflows The sudden movement of rocks down a hill is called a landslide. Rocks on a hill can be loosened by earthquakes, volcanic eruptions, and heavy rains. The force of gravity then pulls the loosened rocks down the slope of the hill. The moving rocks of a landslide cause great damage to anything in their path.

A mudflow is the rapid movement of mud down a hillside. Mudflows usually happen in dry, mountain regions after a heavy rainfall. Like landslides, mudflows can damage property. In the United States, mudflows often happen in the hillside communities of southern California.

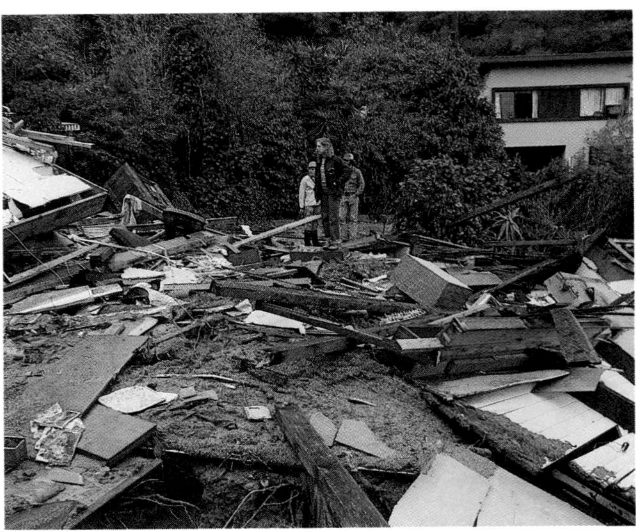

Infer: What kind of damage might be caused by a mudflow?

Earthflow and Creep Earthflow and creep are slow mass movements. An earthflow is the slow movement of soil and plantlife down a hillside. Earthflows usually occur after a heavy rain. Creep takes place when animals, water, or periods of freezing and thawing cause soil and rock particles to move. As the soil and rock begin to move, gravity slowly pulls the materials downhill. Tilted trees and telephone poles usually indicate that creep is happening.

Identify: Name two examples of slow mass movement.

LESSON SUMMARY

- Gravity is a force that pulls all things toward the earth's center.
- Gravity is the only agent of erosion that is not in motion.
- Mass movement is the downhill movement of weathered materials caused by gravity.
- A landslide is the rapid movement of rocks down a hillside.
- A mudflow is the rapid movement of mud down a hillside.
- Earthflow and creep are two kinds of slow mass movement.

CHECK *Complete the following.*

1. The force of gravity can cause rocks and ________ to move down mountain slopes.
2. Gravity causes rivers to flow toward the ________ .
3. The sudden movement of rocks down a hillside is called a ________ .
4. Piles of weathered material that collect at the base of a slope are called ________ .

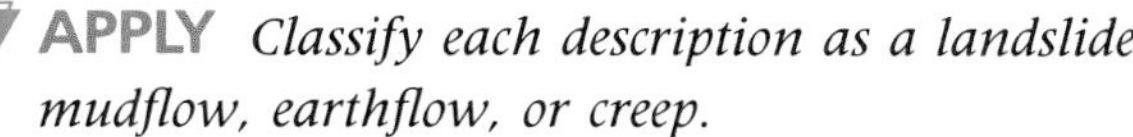

APPLY *Classify each description as a landslide, mudflow, earthflow, or creep.*

5. A tree that was at the top of a hill ten years ago is now at the bottom.
6. A car driving on a mountain road must swerve out of the way of rocks falling down the mountain.
7. After a heavy rain, a large pool of mud blocks a road at the base of a mountain.
8. The fenceposts on a slope are tilted away from the slope.

State the Problem

Study the illustration. Then, state the problem.

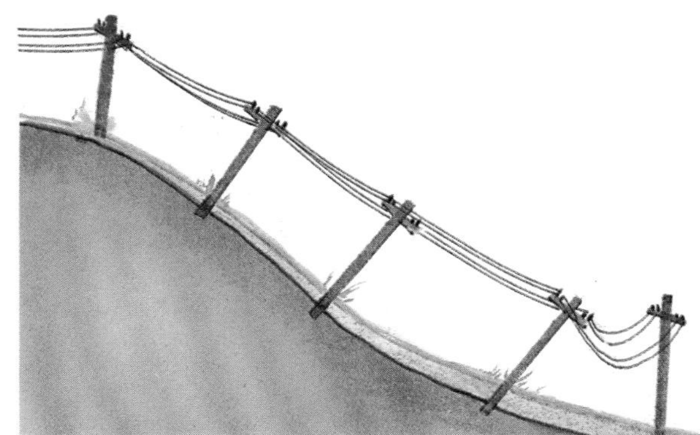

CAREER IN EARTH SCIENCE

ROAD CREW WORKER

Have you ever been in a traffic jam caused by road work? Usually, a large road crew is busy repairing a roadway or a bridge. Road crews maintain and build roads and bridges.

Road crew workers do many different jobs. They remove ice and snow, paint stripes on roads, put up signs, and take care of the sides of roads. Road crew workers also repave roadways and bridges.

Many different people work on a road crew. Some people run the big machinery. Others direct traffic. Usually the civil engineer who plans the project reports to the site. The civil engineer supervises the project.

If you are interested in maintaining or building roads and bridges, you may want to contact your local Department of Transportation or Public Works to find out about road work opportunities.

6-3 How does wind cause erosion?

Objective ▶ Describe the kinds of wind erosion and deposition.

TechTerms

- **abrasion** (uh-BRAY-zhun): wearing away of rock by particles carried by wind and water
- **deflation** (dih-FLAY-shun): removal of loose material from the earth's surface
- **loess** (LESS): deposits of wind-blown dust

Deflation Energy is the ability to do work. Work is done when an object is moved. Wind has energy. Wind can move a sailboat across a lake. Wind also can move loose materials such as sand and dust particles. The removal of loose materials from the earth's surface by the wind is called **deflation** (dih-FLAY-shun). Deflation most often occurs in deserts, plowed fields, and on beaches.

▶ *Describe:* Why is wind an agent of erosion?

Abrasion Sand particles carried by the wind can wear away rocks. Have you ever rubbed sandpaper against a piece of wood? The sand on the sandpaper wears away the surface of the wood. The same thing happens when sand and rock particles are blown over exposed rock or soil. Sand particles carried by the wind are bounced along close to the ground. As the sand particles hit rocks and exposed soil, some of the surface of the rock and soil are worn away. The process by which rock and soil are worn away by particles carried by wind and water is called **abrasion** (uh-BRAY-zhun).

▶ *Define:* What is abrasion?

Sand Dunes Fast-moving wind can carry more sand than slow-moving wind. When a rock or other barrier blocks the wind, the wind slows down. As the wind slows down, it drops the sand it is carrying. The sand is dropped and builds up. A mound called a sand dune is formed. Sand dunes are common in deserts and on beaches.

A sand dune has two sides. The side facing the wind is the windward side. The windward side has a gentle slope. Sand is blown up the windward side and over the top, or crest, to the other side. The side away from the wind is called the slipface. The slipface has a steep slope.

▶ *Infer:* The north side of a sand dune has a gentle slope. From which way is the wind blowing?

Loess Wind carries dust higher and farther than it carries sand. Thick deposits of wind-blown dust may build up many kilometers away from the source of the dust. This wind-blown dust is called **loess** (LESS). The photograph at the top of the page shows a loess deposit. Loess deposits are found in parts of the Mississippi River valley, Washington State, and Oregon.

▶ *Define:* What is loess?

LESSON SUMMARY

- Deflation is the removal of loose materials from the earth's surface by the wind.
- The process by which rock and sand particles carried by wind or water wear away the surface of rocks and soil is called abrasion.
- Sand dunes form when wind is blocked by a barrier in its path.
- A sand dune has two sides: a windward side and a slipface.
- Wind-blown dust forms deposits of loess.

CHECK *Complete the following.*

1. The removal of loose materials from the earth's surface is called ______ .
2. Wind erosion is common in deserts and ______ fields.
3. The ______ of a sand dune has a steep slope.
4. Wind-blown ______ is called loess.

APPLY *Complete the following.*

5. **Infer:** Why are rocks placed around the bottom of telephone poles in the desert?
6. **Classify:** Is abrasion an example of chemical or mechanical weathering? Explain.
7. Label the parts of the sand dune.

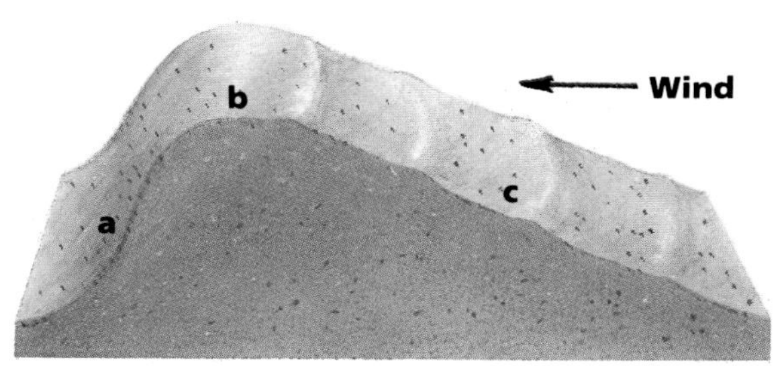

State the Problem

Study the illustrations. Then, state the problem affecting Farm B.

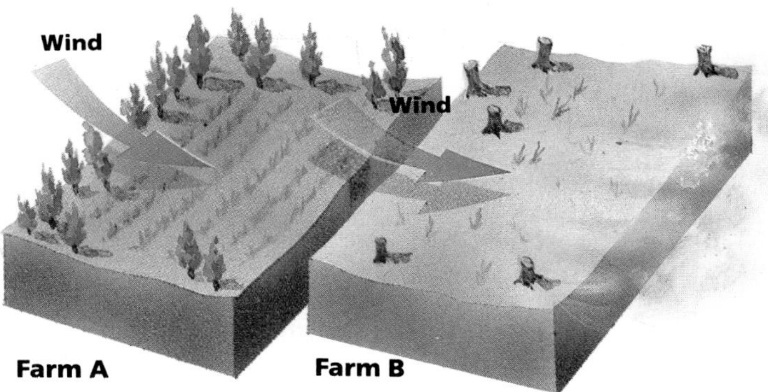

LOOKING BACK IN SCIENCE

THE DUST BOWL

Imagine a huge cloud of black dust almost 10 km high. A cloud this big could block the sun and turn day into night. On April 14, 1935, a huge dust cloud darkened the skies from Oklahoma to New York. The day became known as "Black Sunday."

During the 1930s, huge dust clouds blew across parts of Texas, Oklahoma, Kansas, and Arkansas. This area became known as the Dust Bowl. The Dust Bowl covered more than 20 million hectares.

What caused the Dust Bowl? Ranchers let their cattle overgraze the land. Without much grass, the soil could be carried away by wind and water. Farmers plowed their land to plant wheat. The farming methods they used were poor. Also, there was a long period without rain. Wind blowing across the dry fields carried away millions of tons of topsoil. Topsoil is the layer of soil in which plants grow. Without a layer of good topsoil, the land could not be used for farming. Many people left the Dust Bowl. They moved to other states to find a new way of life.

6-4 How does running water cause erosion?

Objective ▶ Describe how running water causes erosion.

TechTerms

- ▶ **runoff:** rainwater that flows into streams and rivers
- ▶ **tributary** (TRIB-yoo-ter-ee): small stream that flows into the main stream of a river

Running Water Running water changes more of the earth's surface than any other agent of erosion. Rivers, streams, and runoff are forms of running water. Runoff is rainwater that flows over the earth's surface. Runoff empties into streams and rivers.

▶ *List:* What are three forms of running water?

Runoff and Erosion As runoff flows over the earth's surface, the running water carries away soil particles. The faster the water moves, the more soil the water can carry away. Have you ever seen gullies in a hillside? Gullies are formed by erosion caused by runoff.

The amount of rainfall, plant growth, and shape of the land affect the amount of runoff in an area. During heavy rains, there is a lot of runoff. The roots of plants take in some water and hold soil particles in place. For this reason, areas with a lot of plant growth have less runoff than areas with little plant growth. Areas with steep slopes have the most runoff. The greater the amount of runoff, the more erosion there will be.

▶ *Predict:* Would erosion be greater on a hillside or on flat land? Explain.

River System A river system is made up of a main stream and all the streams that flow into the main stream. The streams that flow into the main stream of a river system are called **tributaries** (TRIB-yoo-ter-ees), or branches. The Mississippi River is the main stream of a large river system. The Mississippi River has many tributaries. Two tributaries are almost as large as the Mississippi River. These tributaries are the Ohio and Missouri rivers. Runoff from the surrounding land feeds the many tributaries of a river system.

▶ *Identify:* Name three rivers that are part of the Mississippi river system.

Formation of a River A river system usually begins to form in mountains or in hills. The place where a river starts is its source. When water cannot soak into the ground, runoff flows down the slope of the hill or mountain. The running water erodes the soil and cuts gullies into the slope. A small channel forms. Channels are the paths that streams follow. The small stream may join other small streams to form a larger stream. Larger streams may flow together to form the tributaries of the main stream, or river, of a river system.

▶ *Explain:* How do channels form?

LESSON SUMMARY

- Running water is the major agent of erosion.
- Runoff causes erosion by carrying away soil particles.
- Runoff is affected by the amount of rainfall, plant growth, and shape of the land in an area.
- A river system is made up of a main stream and all the streams that flow into the main stream.
- A river system usually begins to form in mountains or in hills.

CHECK *Complete the following.*

1. How does runoff cause erosion?
2. What causes gullies in a hillside?
3. What is a tributary?
4. What is a river system?

APPLY *Complete the following.*

5. **Predict:** Would planting trees on a hillside help to prevent running water from eroding the land? Explain.
6. **Sequence:** Place the terms in the correct order to show river formation: channel, small stream, river, large stream, tributary
7. **Infer:** How do you think snow helps to form rivers?

Skill Builder

Diagraming A diagram is a drawing that explains something by outlining its parts and their relationships. Draw a labeled diagram comparing a river and its tributaries to a tree and its branches. What part of a tree is like the main stream of a river?

Skill Builder

Researching When you research, you gather information about a topic. Use library references to find the names of two tributaries of each of the following rivers: Nile River, Colorado River, the Thames, and the Tigris. Where is each river located?

SCIENCE CONNECTION

EROSION OF TOPSOIL

Small streams of water come rushing down mountains and hillsides. In the spring, snow melts and more water flows into these streams. The rushing streams empty into small rivers. Some rivers may overflow and cause flooding. Flooding removes topsoil from the land. Topsoil is the layer of soil in which plants can grow.

Farmers need to protect their lands from erosion by running water. If topsoil is eroded, valuable crops will be lost. One way to prevent the erosion of topsoil is terracing. In terracing, farmers plow a slope into level steps, or terraces. The terraces slow the movement of water down the slope.

Another method used to prevent erosion of topsoil is contour farming. In contour farming, land is plowed across a slope. Plowing the land across the slope helps to slow the flow of water down the slope. When the flow of the water is slowed, less topsoil can be carried by the water. As a result, erosion is slowed.

6-5 What are the stages of a river?

Objective ▶ Name and describe the three stages in the life cycle of a river.

TechTerms

- ▶ **meanders** (mee-AN-durs): loops in a mature river
- ▶ **oxbow lake:** lake formed when a meander is cut off from the rest of the river

Life Cycle of a River Rivers go through three stages in their life cycles. The three stages in the life cycle of a river are youth, maturity (muh-CHOOR-ih-tee), and old age. The stage of a river's life cycle is not determined by the age of the river in years. The stage of a river depends upon how fast the water in the river flows and other features of the river.

▶ ***Identify:*** What are the three stages in the life cycle of a river?

Youthful River A youthful river has a steep slope and fast-moving water. The Colorado River and the Niagara River are examples of youthful rivers. The fast-moving water erodes the river bed, or bottom. A narrow, V-shaped valley is formed by a youthful river. The river fills almost the whole valley from side to side.

Many rapids and waterfalls are found along a youthful river. As the moving water rushes over steep slopes, rapids are formed. Sometimes the slope drops straight down. Then a waterfall is formed.

▶ ***Infer:*** What evidence indicates that the Niagara River is a young river?

Mature River The waters of a mature river move slower than the waters of a youthful river. A mature river does not have rapids and waterfalls. As a result of erosion, the river becomes wider. It winds back and forth in loops called **meanders** (mee-AN-durs). The Missouri River and the Ohio River are mature rivers.

▶ ***Define:*** What are meanders?

Old River Water moves very slowly in an old river. The Mississippi River is an old river. An old river has a nearly flat slope. Because of the flat slope, an old river often overflows during periods of heavy rain. The overflowing of river water is called flooding.

As a result of flooding, erosion and deposition take place along the meanders of an old river. Sometimes a meander is cut off from the rest of the river. As a result, a C-shaped lake called an **oxbow lake** is formed.

▶ ***Describe:*** How is an oxbow lake formed?

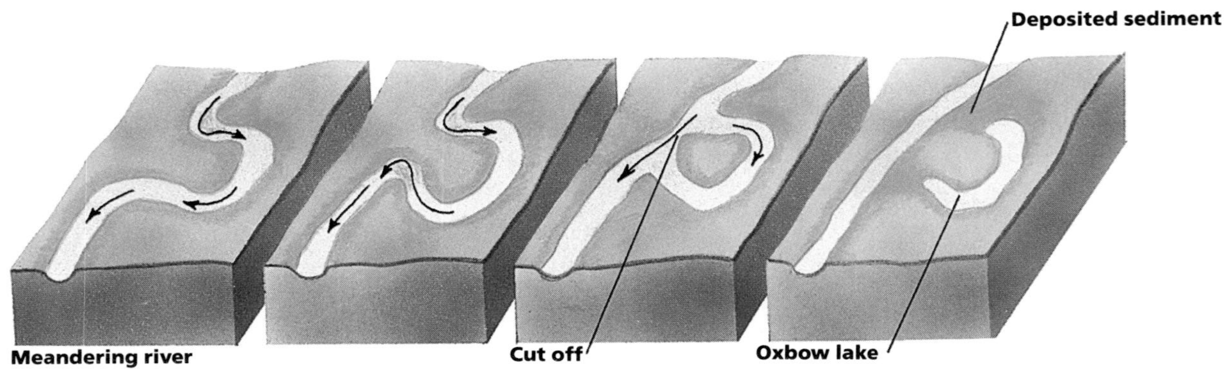

LESSON SUMMARY

- The three stages in the life cycle of a river are youth, maturity, and old age.
- A youthful river has fast-moving water, V-shaped valleys, and many rapids and waterfalls.
- A mature river is slow-moving and forms meanders.
- An old river has slow-moving water, a flat slope, and forms oxbow lakes.

CHECK *Use the terms "youth," "mature," or "old age" to identify the stage of each river described.*

1. has a steep slope
2. has a nearly flat slope
3. forms oxbow lakes
4. has many rapids and waterfalls
5. has meanders

Complete the following.

6. The Colorado River is an example of a _______ river.
7. The Ohio River is an example of a _______ river.

APPLY *Complete the following.*

8. A river with meanders is sometimes said to "snake along." Explain.
9. **Predict:** Can an oxbow lake form from a river that does not meander? Explain.

Skill Builder

Organizing Information When you organize information, you put the information in some kind of order. A table is one way to organize information. Make a table with the following headings: "Name of River," "Tributaries of River," and "Age of River." Use library references to find this information for the following rivers: Amazon, Danube, Nile, Mississippi, Hudson, Colorado, and Delaware.

LEISURE ACTIVITY

RIVER SPORTS

Many rivers across the United States are used for fun sports and activities. Rafting, canoeing, and inner tubing are some river sports. White-water rafting is one of the most thrilling river sports. White-water rafting is done on fast moving rivers with many rapids. Many white-water rafting trips are available throughout the United States. Tour operators use huge rubber rafts for the trips. These tours are supervised by experienced rafters. One of the most thrilling raft trips is down the Colorado River to see the Grand Canyon. This trip lasts several days. You even camp along the river.

Canoeing and inner tubing are done on slow-moving rivers. In many places, you can rent a canoe. Before you go canoeing, you need to learn the basics and safety rules. Usually, you can learn the basics of paddling in one weekend. Paddling a canoe is good exercise and can be a lot of fun.

Inner tubing is a very relaxing sport. It is the least expensive water sport. You seat yourself in an inner tube from a truck tire and float with the river current. Inner tubing is done on slow-moving rivers.

6-6 How does running water create landforms?

Objective ▶ Describe three landforms created by running water.

TechTerms

- ▶ **delta:** triangular-shaped deposit of sediment located at the mouth of a river
- ▶ **flood plain:** flat area on the side of a river where sediments are deposited during floods
- ▶ **sediment** (SED-uh-munt): soil and rock particles that settle to the bottom of a river

Valleys The bed of a river is often solid rock. Small pieces of rock bounce along the bed of a fast-moving river. Abrasion occurs as these pieces of rock scrape the river bed. Over a long period of time, the bed is cut deeper into the rock and a valley is formed. Fast-moving rivers can cut very deep valleys.

▶ ***Identify:*** What is a valley?

Deltas A triangle-shaped deposit of muddy land called a **delta** often forms at the mouth, or end, of a river. The word "delta" is the name of a Greek letter. The Greek delta looks like a small triangle.

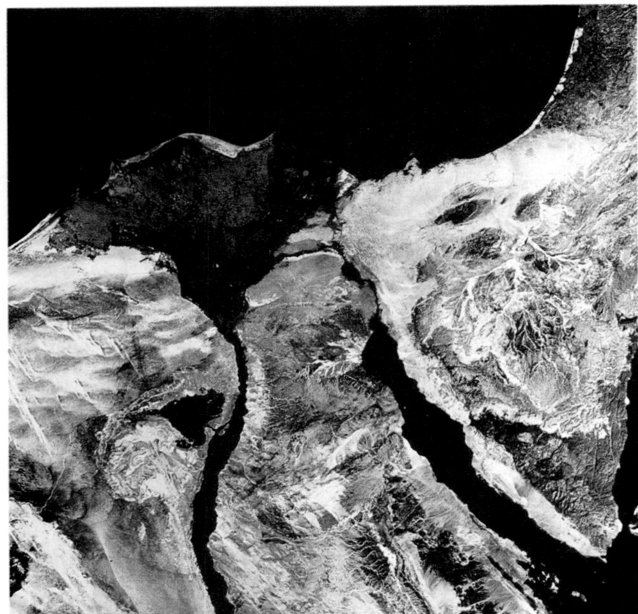

Nile River delta

How does a delta form? The water at the mouth of a river moves very slowly. Pieces of rock and soil carried by slow-moving water are dropped. The particles of soil and rock that settle to the bed of a river are called **sediment** (SED-uh-munt). Sediments in the water are deposited in a delta.

▶ ***Locate:*** Where does a delta form?

Water spills onto the flood plain.

Flood plains During heavy rains, an old river overflows its banks, or sides. When an old river floods its banks, fertile soil carried by the river is deposited at the sides of the river. The fertile soil is deposited in flat areas called **flood plains.** The soil deposited in flood plains was carried to the river by tributaries that feed the river.

▶ ***Define:*** What are flood plains?

LESSON SUMMARY

- A valley is formed when fast-moving water erodes the bed of a river.
- A delta is formed when sediments are deposited by slow-moving water at the mouth of a river.
- Flood plains are formed when a river overflows its banks and deposits fertile soil on both sides of the river.

CHECK *Find the sentence that answers each question. Then, write the sentence.*

1. What is the bed of a river made of?
2. What happens when pieces of rock bounce along the bed of a river?
3. What is sediment?
4. What happens when an old river overflows its banks?

APPLY *Complete the following.*

5. **Infer:** Why is the triangle of sediment deposited at the mouth of a river called a delta?
6. **Hypothesize:** Why does a river flow more slowly at its mouth than at its source?
7. At what stage of its life cycle is a river that is located near flood plains?

State the Problem

Flooding is a natural part of the life cycle of a river. What are some problems that flooding can cause for people who live along the flood plain of a river? Describe ways in which people might try to solve these problems.

Skill Builder

Building Vocabulary Some names for a steep valley are: canyon, gorge, glen, ravine, and chasm. Look up each of these words in a dictionary and write down each definition. Then, use an encyclopedia or other reference book to name an example of each kind of valley.

ACTIVITY

OBSERVING THE SETTLING OF SEDIMENTS

You will need soil, pebbles, sand, water, and a clear plastic container with a lid.

1. Put some pebbles, sand, and soil into a container of water.
2. Cover the container. Gently, shake the container back and forth and observe what happens to the sand, soil, and pebbles.
3. Put the container down. Watch the particles settle out of the water.

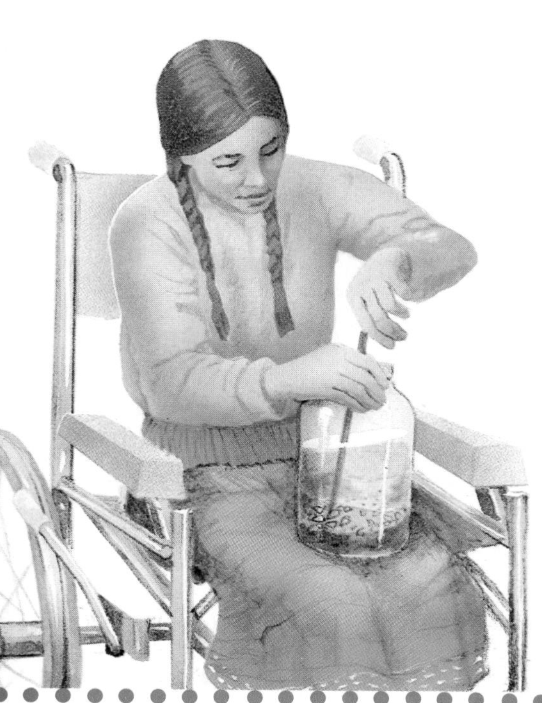

Questions

1. What happened when you shook the container?
2. **Observe:** Did all of the particles settle out of the water at the same time?
3. Which particles settled out first? Why?
4. Which particles settled out last? Why?
5. **Model:** How does this activity relate to the way sediments are deposited by a river?

6-7 What is a glacier?

Objectives ▶ Explain how a glacier is formed. ▶ Name two kinds of glaciers.

TechTerm

▶ **glacier** (GLAY-shur): moving river of ice and snow

Glaciers A **glacier** (GLAY-shur) is a moving river of ice and snow. Glaciers form in places where the temperature is cold for most of the year. In these places, snow does not melt after heavy snowfalls. More snow falls on top of snow that already is on the ground. The snow gets deeper and deeper. Ice forms at the bottom of this deep layer of snow. The pull of gravity and the weight of the snow on top of the ice causes the ice to move. A glacier is formed. Very slowly, the glacier begins to move downhill.

▶ ***Define:*** What is a glacier?

Kinds of Glaciers There are two kinds of glaciers. Glaciers that form in mountains and move slowly downhill through valleys are called valley glaciers. Other glaciers form near the earth's poles. These glaciers form large sheets of ice called icecaps, or continental glaciers.

▶ ***Name:*** What are two kinds of glaciers?

Icebergs When a continental glacier reaches the ocean, a large piece of the glacier may break off and float away. A large piece of floating ice is called an iceberg. Large amounts of sediment may be frozen into an iceberg. As the iceberg melts, these sediments are dropped into the ocean. The sediments sink to the ocean bottom.

Most of an iceberg is below the surface of the water. Only a small part of an iceberg is visible above the surface. Many ships have crashed into icebergs. To protect ships at sea, the U.S. Navy watches for icebergs and keeps track of where they are moving. The Navy also may use icebreakers to break icebergs apart and clear passages for ships.

▶ ***Explain:*** Why are icebergs a problem for ships?

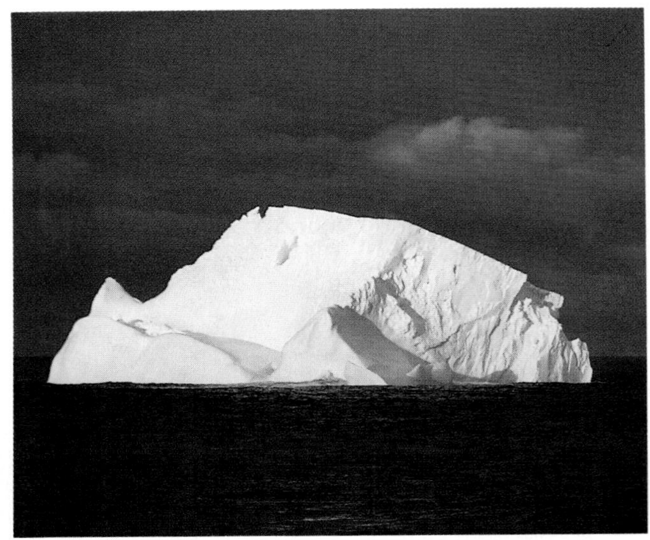

Ice Ages An ice age is a period of very cold temperatures. Glaciers grow and spread during ice ages. There have been many ice ages in the history of the earth. The last ice age ended about 11,000 years ago. During the last ice age, the sheet of ice around the North Pole got larger. The icecap finally covered most of North America.

▶ ***Identify:*** What is an ice age?

LESSON SUMMARY

- A glacier is a slow-moving river of ice and snow.
- Two kinds of glaciers are valley glaciers and continental glaciers.
- An iceberg forms when a large piece of a continental glacier breaks off in the ocean.
- An ice age is a period during which glaciers spread over the earth.

CHECK *Complete the following.*

1. A slow-moving river of ice and snow is called a ________ .
2. A glacier that forms in mountains is a ________ glacier.
3. A glacier that forms near the earth's poles is a ________ glacier.
4. An ________ is a period of very cold temperatures.
5. Antarctica and Greenland are covered by ________ glaciers.
6. The last ice age ended about ________ years ago.

APPLY *Complete the following.*

7. **Infer:** Why are glaciers called "rivers of ice"?
8. **Predict:** Some scientists think that an increase in the average temperature of the earth might cause the icecaps to melt. The melted ice would raise the sea level. How would a rise in sea level effect coastal cities?

InfoSearch

Read the passage. Ask two questions about the topic that you cannot answer from the information in the passage.

The Titanic The British steamer *Titanic* was the largest ship in the world at the time it was built. The great ship was thought to be unsinkable. In April 1912, the *Titanic* set sail on its first voyage. As the ship sailed toward New York, an iceberg was sighted. The captain tried to avoid the iceberg, but it was too late. The *Titanic* struck the iceberg and sank. Of the 2200 people on board, only 705 were rescued.

SEARCH: Use library references to find answers to your questions.

PEOPLE IN SCIENCE

JEAN LOUIS AGASSIZ (1807–1873)

Jean Louis Agassiz (AG-uh-see) was a Swiss naturalist, geologist, and teacher. Agassiz earned degrees in philosophy and medicine. His early research was on fossil fishes.

In 1836, Agassiz began to study glaciers. He built a shack on top of a glacier to study the glacier's movement. Agassiz was the first person to discover that the center of a glacier moves faster than the sides.

Agassiz observed that as glaciers moved, rocks carried by the glacier carved scratches into other rocks the glacier passed over. Using these observations, Agassiz showed that sheets of ice had once covered large areas of land. From his research, Agassiz also concluded that the earth had gone through several ice ages.

In 1846, Agassiz moved to the United States. He taught at Harvard University and founded Harvard's Museum of Natural History. Agassiz also set up an animal laboratory on an island off the coast of Massachusetts. Agassiz died on December 12, 1873. As a memorial, a boulder carried by a glacier was placed at the side of his grave.

6-8 How do glaciers cause erosion?

Objectives ▶ Explain how a glacier causes erosion. ▶ Describe two results of glacial deposition.

TechTerms

- ▶ **erratics** (uh-RAT-iks): rocks left behind by a retreating glacier
- ▶ **hanging valley:** small glacial valley above a main valley
- ▶ **till:** rock material deposited by a glacier

Glacial Erosion Gravel and pieces of rock are frozen into the ice at the bottom of a glacier. As the glacier moves over bedrock, the rocks in the glacier scrape against the bedrock. Small pieces of the bedrock are carved away by the scraping rocks. These pieces of bedrock are pushed along in front of the glacier.

Explain: How does a glacier cause abrasion?

Hanging Valleys As a glacier scrapes away the floor of a valley, the valley becomes U-shaped. Sometimes small side glaciers flow into the main glacier. As the side glaciers melt and disappear, they leave small valleys high above the main valley. These valleys are called **hanging valleys.**

Define: What is a hanging valley?

Glacial Deposition Large rocks and sediments are often frozen into a glacier. As the glacier moves, these rocks and sediments are carried to new places. As a glacier moves into a warmer area, the ice begins to melt around the edges of the glacier. The glacier appears to be shrinking, or retreating. Rocks and sediments that were frozen in the ice are left behind. This loose material deposited by the glacier is called **till.**

Define: What is till?

Erratics Boulders left behind by a retreating glacier are called **erratics** (uh-RAT-iks). Central Park in New York City has many boulders. These boulders are not like the bedrock underneath the park. The boulders are like bedrock located hundreds of kilometers away. The boulders are too large and too heavy to have been moved by running water. How did they get to Central Park? The only way they could have been moved is by a glacier. The boulders were frozen into the ice and left behind when the glacier melted.

Explain: How are erratics moved?

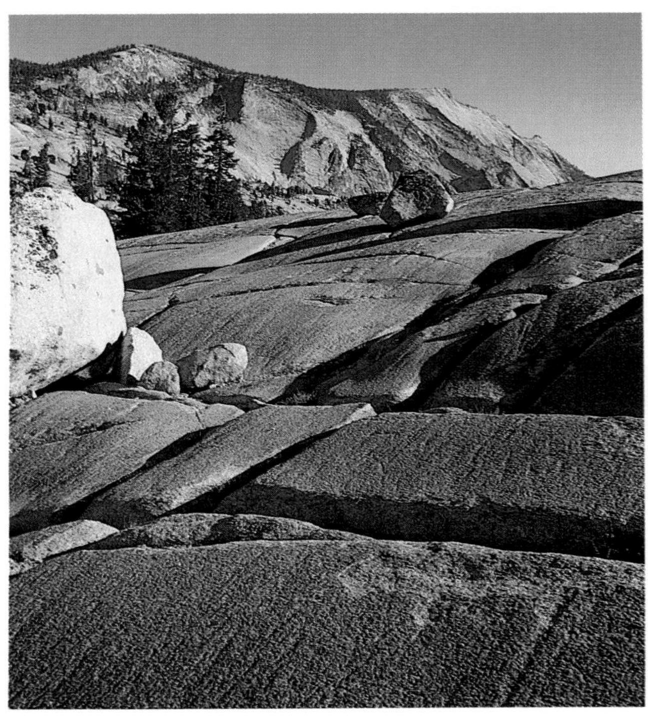

LESSON SUMMARY

- Glaciers cause erosion as a result of abrasion.
- Erosion by glaciers carves out U-shaped valleys.
- A hanging valley is formed when a small side glacier melts and disappears.
- Till is the loose material deposited by a glacier.
- Erratics were carried long distances and deposited by glaciers.

CHECK *Complete the following.*

1. What is frozen into the ice at the bottom of a glacier?
2. By what process is rock broken into smaller pieces by a moving glacier?
3. What happens to the shape of a valley as a result of glacial erosion?
4. What happens when small side glaciers melt and disappear?
5. What happens as a glacier moves into a warmer area?
6. What is the loose material deposited by a glacier called?
7. How were erratics carried to Central Park?

APPLY *Complete the following.*

8. **Hypothesize:** How can you tell if a valley was formed by a glacier?
9. Why is the main valley of a glacier lower than a hanging valley left behind by a side glacier?
10. **Compare:** How is erosion caused by a glacier similar to erosion caused by a river?

State the Problem

Five hundred people live in a village at the edge of a glacier. During the winter, a heavy snow falls on the village and on the glacier. State one problem that a heavy snowfall might cause for the people of this village.

ACTIVITY

OBSERVING ABRASION CAUSED BY GLACIERS

You will need sand, water, a bar of soap, a plastic container, and paper towels.

1. Put some sand into a plastic container.
2. Fill the container with water.
3. Place the container in a freezer until the water turns to ice.
4. Remove the ice from the container.
5. Hold the piece of ice with paper towels. Move the ice, sand side down, over the bar of soap.
6. Press some sand into the soap. Repeat step 5.

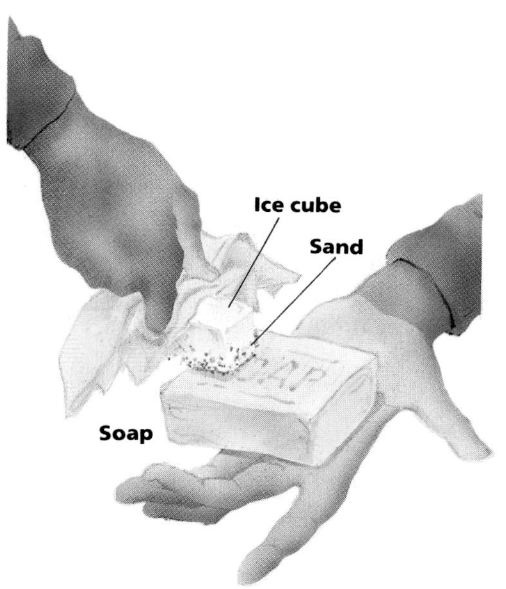

Questions

1. What happened to the soap when you moved the ice and sand over it?
2. Did the sand in the soap become mixed with the sand in the ice?
3. **Observe:** What marks, if any, were left in the soap by the sand?
4. **Model:** How does this activity show how a glacier can erode the land?

6-9 How do glaciers create landforms?

Objective ▶ Describe two landforms created by glaciers.

TechTerms

- ▶ **drumlin:** oval-shaped mound of till
- ▶ **kettle lake:** lake formed by a retreating glacier
- ▶ **moraine** (moor-AYN): ridge of till deposited by a retreating glacier

Moraines When a glacier retreats, it deposits till. The till builds up a long, low ridge. This ridge of till is called a **moraine** (moor-AYN). When till is deposited at the front edge of a glacier, a terminal (TUR-muh-nul) moraine is formed. When till is deposited along the sides of a glacier, a lateral (LAT-uhr-ul) moraine is formed.

▶ ***Name:*** What are two kinds of moraines?

Drumlins Sometimes when a glacier retreats, it leaves behind oval-shaped mounds of till. These mounds of till are called **drumlins.** The tip of a drumlin points in the direction the glacier was moving. Most drumlins form in groups. Drumlins can be seen in the farmlands of Vermont.

▶ ***Define:*** What is a drumlin?

Glacial Lakes During the last ice age, glaciers formed in river valleys. The glaciers eroded the valleys and made them deeper. As the glaciers retreated, till carried by the glaciers was dropped. Then the glaciers melted. The water of a melting glacier is called meltwater. Meltwater filled the valleys with water and formed lakes. Glacial lakes are usually long and deep. The Great Lakes and New York's Finger Lakes are glacial lakes.

Sometimes, a retreating glacier left behind a huge block of ice. The ice blocks were covered with sediments. When the block of ice melted, a large hole was left in the ground. The sediments carried by the glacier were dropped. The hole filled with meltwater and a lake was formed. A lake formed in this way is called a **kettle lake.**

▶ ***Identify:*** What is a kettle lake?

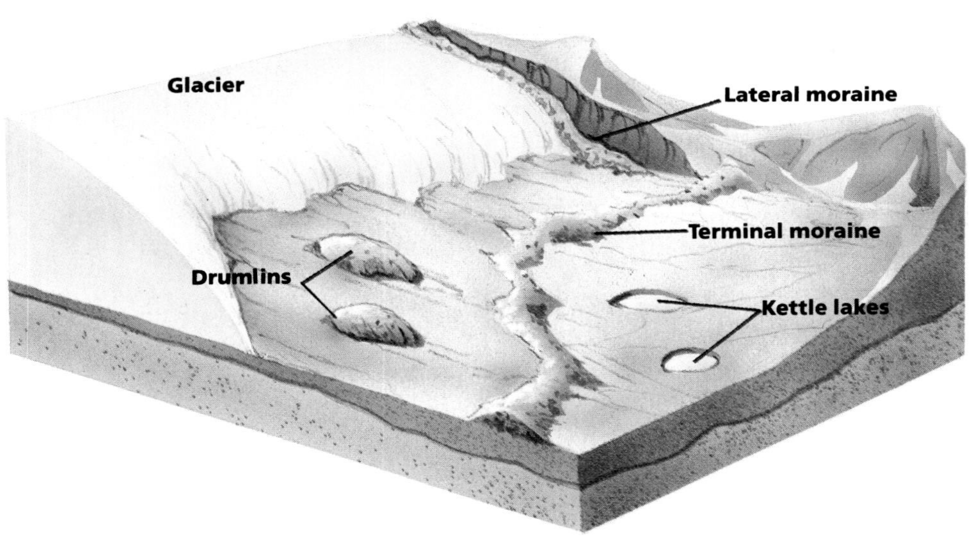

LESSON SUMMARY

- Till deposited by a glacier forms terminal moraines or lateral moraines.
- Oval-shaped mounds of till are called drumlins.
- Glacial lakes are formed when valley glaciers melt.
- Kettle lakes are formed when large blocks of ice are left behind by a retreating glacier.

CHECK *Write true if the statement is true. If the statement is false, change the underlined word or words to make the statement true.*

1. When a glacier retreats, till is left behind.
2. A long, low ridge built up by a glacier is called an erratic.
3. The material deposited at the front edge of a glacier forms a lateral moraine.
4. Glacial lakes are usually long and deep.
5. A lake formed when a block of ice from a glacier melted is called a kettle lake.

APPLY *Complete the following.*

6. What can a scientist learn about a glacier by studying moraines?
7. **Model:** Draw a diagram of a retreating glacier. Label till, terminal moraine, and lateral moraine.
8. **Analyze:** Look up the word "kettle" in a dictionary. Why are some glacial lakes referred to as kettle lakes?
9. **Analyze:** The tip of a drumlin points south. In what direction was the glacier that formed the drumlin moving?

Skill Builder

Using Vocabulary Use a dictionary to find the meanings of the words "lateral" and "terminal." Terms used in other fields of science, such as biology and physics, also include the words "lateral" and "terminal." Use a dictionary or other reference materials to find the definitions for the following terms: lateral line, terminal velocity, terminal bud. Write a definition of each term in your own words. Then circle the part of the definition that relates to the meanings of the words "lateral" and "terminal."

ACTIVITY

MODELING THE FORMATION OF A GLACIAL LAKE

You will need sand, a plastic container, and an ice cube.

1. Fill a shallow plastic container with sand.
2. Push an ice cube deep into the sand.
3. Leave the ice cube in the sand until the ice melts.
4. **Observe:** Examine the sand after the ice melts.

Questions

1. What was left in the sand after the ice melted?
2. **a. Analyze:** What does the ice cube represent in your model? **b.** What does the sand represent?
3. **Analyze:** How is your model like a lake formed by a glacier?
4. **Model:** Draw a diagram showing how the sand appeared after the ice melted.
5. What kind of glacial lake is formed when large blocks of ice melt?

6-10 How do ocean waves cause erosion?

Objectives ▶ Describe how ocean waves cause erosion. ▶ Name five shoreline features that are caused by wave erosion.

TechTerms

- **sea arch:** gap formed when waves cut completely through a section of rock
- **sea stack:** column of rock remaining after the collapse of a sea arch
- **wave:** up-and-down movement of water
- **wave-cut terrace:** flat section of rock formed by the erosion of a sea cliff

Wave Erosion A **wave** is an up-and-down movement of water. Ocean waves are formed when wind blows over the water. Waves also are caused by tides, storms, and earthquakes.

The force of waves striking the shoreline can break up rocks into small pieces. The pieces of rock grind against one another. This grinding causes abrasion. Abrasion wears down the rock and forms particles of sand. The sand is then carried away by the waves.

Waves also cause chemical weathering of the rocks along a shoreline. As waves meet the shoreline, salt water is forced into cracks in rocks. The chemical action of the salt water breaks down the rock and makes the cracks larger. Broken pieces of rock are then carried away by the waves.

Describe: How do waves cause erosion along a shoreline?

Sea Cliffs, Caves, and Terraces Waves pound against the bottom of the rocks on a rocky shoreline. As a result, the rocks are broken down into small pieces. The broken rock is carried away by the waves. A sea cliff is formed. A sea cliff is a steep rock face caused by wave erosion. Soft rock is eroded more quickly than hard rock. When waves erode the soft rock in a sea cliff, a sea cave is formed. A sea cave is a hollowed-out part of a sea cliff.

Over time, the bottom of a sea cliff may be slowly worn away. The sea cliff is worn farther and farther inland. As the sea cliff is worn away, a flat section of rock remains below the surface of the water. This flat platform is called a **wave-cut terrace.**

Define: What is a sea cliff?

Sea Arches and Sea Stacks When waves cut completely through a section of rock, a **sea arch** is formed. A sea arch looks like a natural bridge. In time, the top of a sea arch may fall into the water. The remaining columns of rock are called **sea stacks.** The sea stacks were once the sides of the arch.

Identify: What is left when the top of a sea arch falls into the water?

LESSON SUMMARY

- A wave is an up-and-down movement of water.
- Waves striking the shoreline can break up rocks into small pieces.
- Rocks broken down by salt water are eroded by waves.
- Wave erosion along a rocky shoreline forms sea cliffs and sea caves.
- A wave-cut terrace is formed as a sea cliff is worn inland.
- Sea arches and sea stacks are formed as a result of wave erosion.

CHECK *Complete the following.*

1. What are three possible causes of ocean waves?
2. What are two ways in which rocks are broken down by waves?
3. A steep rock face caused by erosion along a rocky shoreline is a ______ .
4. When part of a sea cliff is hollowed out, a ______ is formed.
5. The shoreline feature that looks like a natural bridge is a
6. A column of rock caused by wave erosion is a ______ .

APPLY *Complete the following.*

7. **Analyze:** In addition to wave erosion, what processes can you name that might change the shape of a shoreline?
8. **Hypothesize:** The rate of wave erosion depends in part on the kind of rock found along the shoreline. The shoreline of Cape Cod, Massachusetts, is made up of loose glacial deposits. Would you expect this shoreline to erode quickly or slowly? Explain.
9. How does the formation of sea caves and sea arches compare with the formation of caves and natural bridges in a desert.

InfoSearch

Read the passage. Ask two questions about the topic that you cannot answer from the information in the passage.

Storms and Erosion Most shoreline erosion takes place during storms. Waves can erode a shoreline at a rate of 1 m to 1.5 m per year. During storms, however, the wave action is stronger. The rate of shoreline erosion is much faster during a storm. Beaches on barrier islands are easily eroded by waves during storms. In fact, the shape of a shoreline can be changed in only one day by a strong storm.

SEARCH: Use library references to find answers to your questions.

SCIENCE CONNECTION

BEACHFRONT PROPERTY

Many people dream of owning a home at the beach. They enjoy the sound of the waves hitting the shore and the fresh ocean breezes. In some cities, large apartment complexes are built right on the beach. However, there are risks to building on beachfront property.

Many owners of beachfront homes learned about these risks during the winter of 1986-1987. In North and South Carolina, tides 2 m above normal destroyed decks and swimming pools. On Long Island, homes and roads were washed away by large waves. Houses that once stood on dry land are now on stilts in the ocean.

Beach erosion is a problem in the United States. Some scientists are in favor of protecting coastal areas and reducing erosion by using jetties, seawalls, and breakwaters. Others say that the shoreline changes naturally and that beachfront development should be limited. What do you think?

6-11 How do waves create landforms?

Objective ▶ Describe three shoreline features created by wave deposition.

TechTerms

- **longshore current:** movement of water parallel to a shoreline
- **sand bar:** long, underwater deposit of sand parallel to a shoreline
- **spit:** long, narrow deposit of sand connected at one end to the shore

Beaches A beach is a nearly flat stretch of shoreline. Waves carry rock particles and other material away from a shoreline. This material may be deposited at another place on the shoreline. A beach is formed when sand and rock particles are deposited on a shoreline by waves.

Materials that form beaches may vary in size and color. Pebble beaches are found along some shorelines. Along the east and west coasts, weathered quartz forms white sand beaches. Weathered volcanic rock forms black sand. Black sand beaches are found in Hawaii. Some beaches in Florida are made up of pieces of broken shells.

Explain: How is a beach formed?

Longshore Currents A **longshore current** is a stream of water moving parallel to a shoreline. Waves do not usually move straight into a shoreline. They come in at an angle. A longshore current is formed as waves approach a beach at an angle. A longshore current can carry sand away from the beach.

Define: What is a longshore current?

Spits A curved or hooked deposit of sand is called a **spit.** One end of a spit is connected to the shore. How is a spit formed? A longshore current carries sand away from a beach in a direction parallel to the beach. The sand keeps moving in a straight line until the beach changes direction. Then the sand is deposited at the spot where the beach curves, forming a spit.

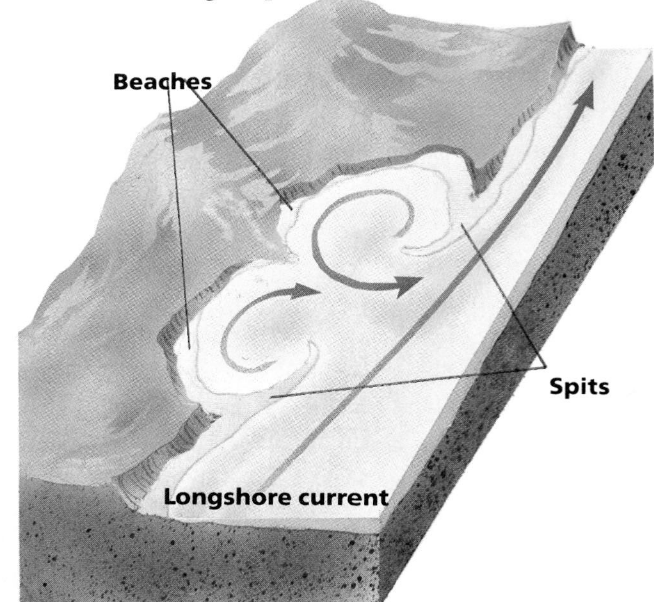

Describe: How is a spit formed?

Sand Bars Waves can carry a lot of sand away from a beach, especially during the winter. Most of the sand is dropped offshore. A sand deposit builds up parallel to the shoreline. A long, underwater deposit of sand is called a **sand bar.** If a sand bar reaches above the water, a barrier beach is formed. Miami Beach, Florida is built on a barrier beach.

Describe: What is a barrier beach?

LESSON SUMMARY

- A beach is formed when sand and rock particles are deposited on a shoreline by waves.
- The material that forms beaches may vary in size and color.
- A longshore current is formed when waves approach a beach at an angle.
- Curved deposits of sand called spits are created by longshore currents.
- Waves deposit sand in underwater sand bars.

CHECK *Complete the following.*

1. A beach is formed when ______ is deposited on a shoreline.
2. The material forming a beach may vary in size and ______ .
3. Weathered ______ forms black sand.
4. A longshore current is formed when waves approach a beach at an ______.
5. Sand bars are ______ deposits of sand.
6. A sand deposit that is created by a longshore current is called a ______ .

APPLY *Complete the following.*

7. Why do some beaches appear different from other beaches?
8. How is a sand bar formed?
9. **Contrast:** What is the difference between a sand bar and a spit?
10. Waves are one way that sand can be removed from a beach. What other agent of erosion removes sand from beaches?
11. **Diagram:** Draw a labelled diagram that shows the position of a longshore current that is approaching a shoreline.
12. **Diagram:** Draw a diagram that shows the relationship of a sand bar to a beach.

State the Problem

Beaches are always changing. State two problems that might result if more sand is carried away from a beach than is deposited by waves.

SCIENCE CONNECTION

COASTAL EROSION

On September 21, 1989, Hurricane Hugo struck the Atlantic coast of the United States. The hurricane hit the shoreline at Charleston, South Carolina. The city of Charleston was heavily damaged. Many nearby coastal communities were almost destroyed. The damage caused by the storm will take many years and billions of dollars to repair.

Large storms such as Hurricane Hugo cause rapid changes along a coastline. A bad storm may wash away beach dunes in one day. However, slow changes are always taking place in coastal areas. Tides, waves, and wind all cause changes in the shape of a coastline. Beaches are moved sand grain by sand grain by wind and waves. When a beach is washed away in one place, a new beach may be built up someplace else. Sand dunes are slowly moved by the wind. Houses that are built on sand dunes, or on hills along the shoreline, may fall into the ocean as the land is washed out from under them.

People have tried to protect shorelines by building breakwaters and jetties. However, they only slow down coastal erosion. They cannot prevent it. Many people think that homes should not be built in some coastal areas.

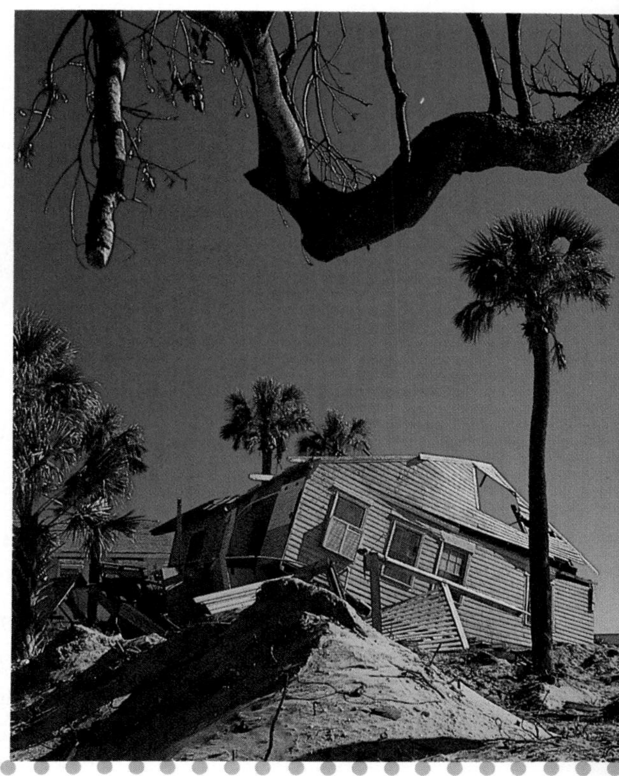

UNIT 6 Challenges

STUDY HINT Before you begin the Unit Challenges, review the TechTerms and Lesson Summary for each lesson in this unit.

TechTerms

abrasion (104)
deflation (104)
delta (110)
deposition (100)
drumlin (116)
erosion (100)
erratics (114)
flood plain (110)
glacier (112)
hanging valley (114)
kettle lake (116)
loess (104)
longshore current (120)
mass movement (102)
meanders (108)
moraine (116)
oxbow lake (108)
runoff (106)
sand bar (120)
sea arch (118)
sea stack (118)
sediment (110)
spit (120)
talus (102)
till (114)
tributary (106)
wave (118)
wave-cut terrace (118)

TechTerm Challenges

Matching *Write the TechTerm that matches each description.*

1. rainwater that flows into streams and rivers
2. up-and-down movement of water
3. small stream that flows into the main stream of a river
4. flat section of rock formed by the erosion of a sea cliff
5. loops in a mature river
6. moving river of ice and snow
7. rocks left behind by a retreating glacier
8. small glacial valley above a main valley
9. underwater deposit of sand
10. downhill movement of weathered materials caused by gravity

Applying Definitions *Explain the difference between the words in each pair. Write your answers in complete sentences.*

1. oxbow lake, kettle lake
2. talus, till
3. sea arch, sea stack
4. deflation, deposition
5. erosion, weathering
6. loess, sediment
7. flood plain, delta
8. abrasion, weathering
9. drumlin, moraine
10. wave, longshore current
11. sand bar, spit
12. wave-cut terrace, sea arch

Content Challenges

Multiple Choice *Write the letter of the term that best completes each statement.*

1. Mudflows, creep, landslides, and earthflow are caused by
   a. wind. **b.** waves. **c.** running water. **d.** gravity.
2. The process by which weathered material is moved from one place to another is
   a. abrasion. **b.** deposition. **c.** erosion. **d.** deflation.
3. The sudden movement of rocks down a hillside is
   a. an earthflow. **b.** a mudflow. **c.** creep. **d.** a landslide.

4. Tilted telephone or fence poles on a hillside is evidence of
   a. creep. b. earthflow. c. runoff. d. meanders.
5. Gullies in a hillside are caused by
   a. creep. b. talus. c. runoff. d. glaciers.
6. The valley of a mature river is
   a. V-shaped. b. U-shaped. c. narrow. d. steep.
7. Sediments carried by a glacier are called
   a. till. b. talus. c. moraines. d. drumlins.
8. The Great Lakes and New York's Finger Lakes are
   a. kettle lakes. b. drumlins. c. oxbow lakes. d. glacial lakes.
9. Sea cliffs, sea stacks, and sea arches are caused by
   a. glacial erosion. b. wind erosion. c. wave erosion. d. gravity.
10. A piece of glacier that breaks off into the ocean is
    a. a continental glacier. b. an iceberg. c. a drumlin. d. a valley glacier.

Completion *Write the term that best completes each statement.*

1. Running water, glaciers, ______, waves, and gravity are the five agents of erosion.
2. The rocks that make up the earth's crust are broken down by ______ .
3. Deposition builds ______ on the earth's surface.
4. Gravity is the only agent of erosion that is not in ______ .
5. Landslides and ______ are rapid mass movements.
6. The side of a sand dune that faces away from the wind is the ______ .
7. A river system usually begins in ______ .
8. The Colorado and Niagara rivers are ______ rivers.
9. A delta usually forms at the ______, or end, of a river.
10. A floating piece of ice is called an ______ .
11. Till deposited at the front of a glacier forms a ______ moraine.
12. A sea stack is formed when the top of a ______ falls into the ocean.
13. In Hawaii, weathered volcanic dust forms ______ beaches.
14. A sand bar that reaches above the surface of the water forms a ______ .
15. The valley of a youthful river is ______ .

Understanding the Features . . . .

Reading Critically *Use the feature reading selections to answer the following. Page numbers for the features are shown in parentheses.*

1. What does an urban planner do? (101)
2. What are some of the jobs done by road crew workers? (103)
3. When was "Black Sunday?" (105)
4. Name two ways that farmers protect their land from erosion of topsoil. (107)
5. What did Agassiz discover about the way a glacier moves? (113)
6. **Synthesize:** How do the ages of the rivers on which white-water rafting and inner tubing are done differ? (109)
7. What are three ways used to reduce coastal erosion? (119)
8. Where did Hurricane Hugo strike the Atlantic coast of the United States? (121)

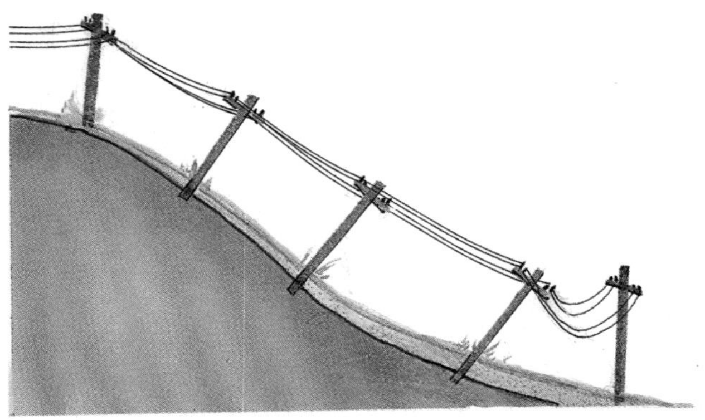

Figure 1

Figure 3

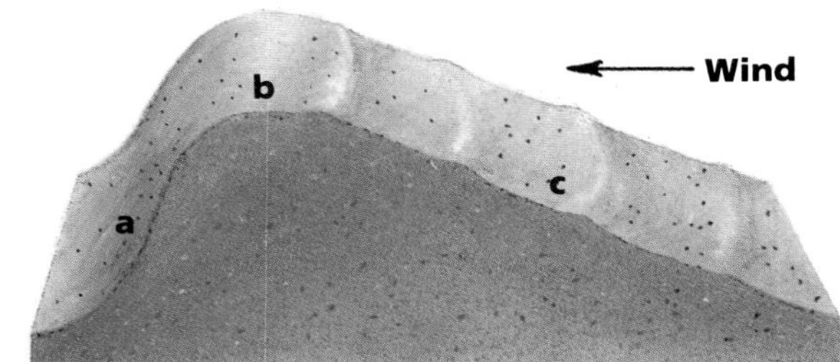

Figure 2

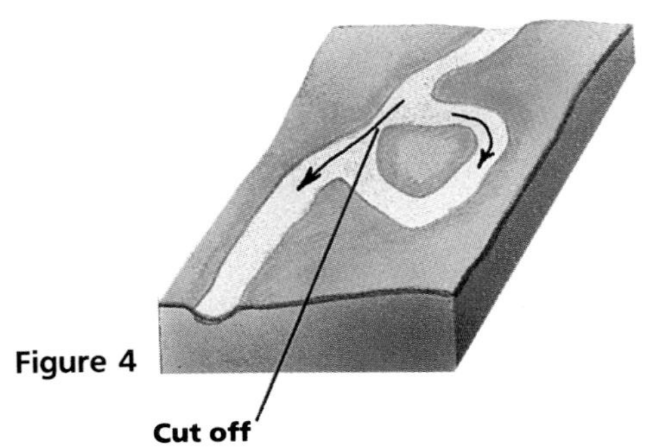

Figure 4

Concept Challenges

Understanding a Diagram *Use the diagrams to complete the following.*

1. What is shown in Figure 1?
2. Which agent of erosion causes what is shown in Figure 1?
3. What is the name of the landform shown in Figure 2?
4. Which agent of erosion formed the landform shown in Figure 2?
5. Is the landform shown in Figure 2 caused by erosion or deposition?
6. What is happening to Farm B in Figure 3?
7. What is preventing erosion of topsoil from Farm A?
8. At what stage of its life cycle is the river in Figure 4?
9. What landform will be formed by the river in Figure 4?
10. Which agent of erosion is at work in Figure 4?

Critical Thinking *Answer each of the following in complete sentences.*

1. How can you tell the age of a river by observing the shape of the river's valley?
2. **Analyze:** If the top of a drumlin points north, in which direction was the glacier that formed the drumlin moving?
3. **Predict:** What would happen to the sea level if the earth's temperature raised and caused glaciers to melt?
4. **Infer:** Why does deflation occur most in deserts, plowed fields, and on beaches?
5. **Infer:** Why can wind carry dust farther than it can carry sand?

Finding Out More

1. Use library references to find out about the ice ages of the earth. Draw a map to show how far down ice reached during the peak of the last glacial period.
2. Imagine that the coastal city of Ocean Side wants you to do a plan to help preserve their coast land. Working with three classmates, prepare a plan with diagrams for the city. Present your plan to the class.
3. Use library references to find out about the different kinds of dunes. Use plaster of Paris and sand to make models of the different shapes that dunes may have. On 3 × 5 cards, write the name of the dune.

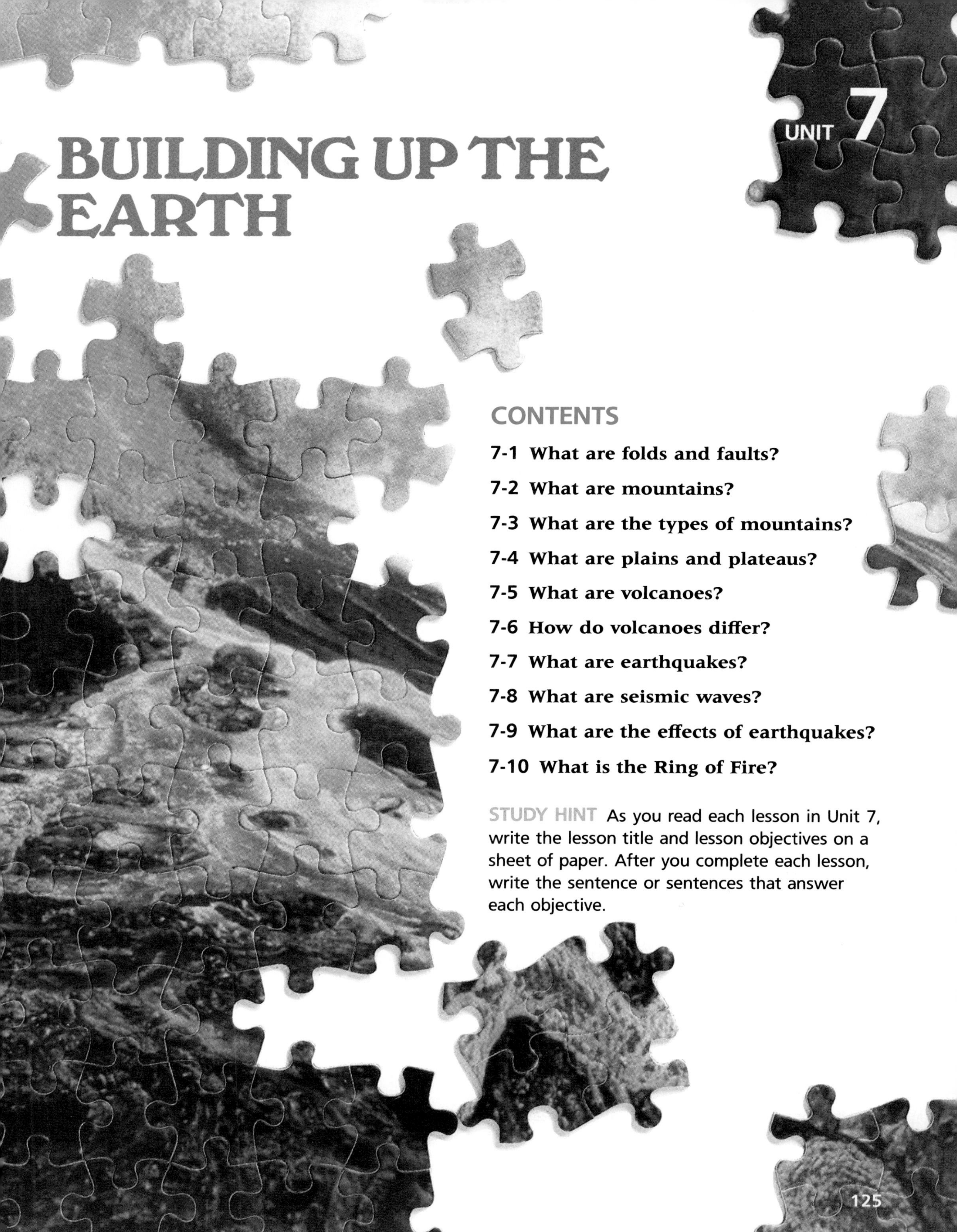

BUILDING UP THE EARTH

UNIT 7

CONTENTS

STUDY HINT As you read each lesson in Unit 7, write the lesson title and lesson objectives on a sheet of paper. After you complete each lesson, write the sentence or sentences that answer each objective.

7-1 What are folds and faults?

Objective Compare folding and faulting in the earth's crust.

TechTerms

- **anticline** (AN-tih-klyn): upward fold
- **fault:** break in the earth's crust along which movement has occurred
- **fracture** (FRAK-chur): break in a rock
- **syncline** (SIN-klyn): downward fold

Folding Over millions of years, pressure in the earth's crust caused sedimentary rock layers to bend, or fold. Flat rock layers were squeezed from the sides. The pressure caused the flat rock layers to move into new positions without breaking. The rocks may have cracked, but the rock layers stayed together.

Folds look like waves in rock layers. The layers curve up in some places. An upward fold is an **anticline** (AN-tih-klyn). A downward fold is a **syncline** (SIN-klyn). Some folds are small enough to be seen in a small rock. Other folds are very large. You often can see anticlines and synclines in road cuts.

Describe: What is a fold?

Figure 1 Folding rock layers

Faulting Pressure deep inside the earth can break rocks. A break in a rock is called a **fracture** (FRAK-chur). If the rocks on either side of a fracture move, the break is called a **fault.**

Four kinds of faults are shown in Figure 2. Faulting causes rocks to move up and down or side to side. The rock layers move only a short distance. Each time movement along a fault occurs, the rock layers move farther apart. The pressure eases. When the pressure builds up again and is released, movement occurs again.

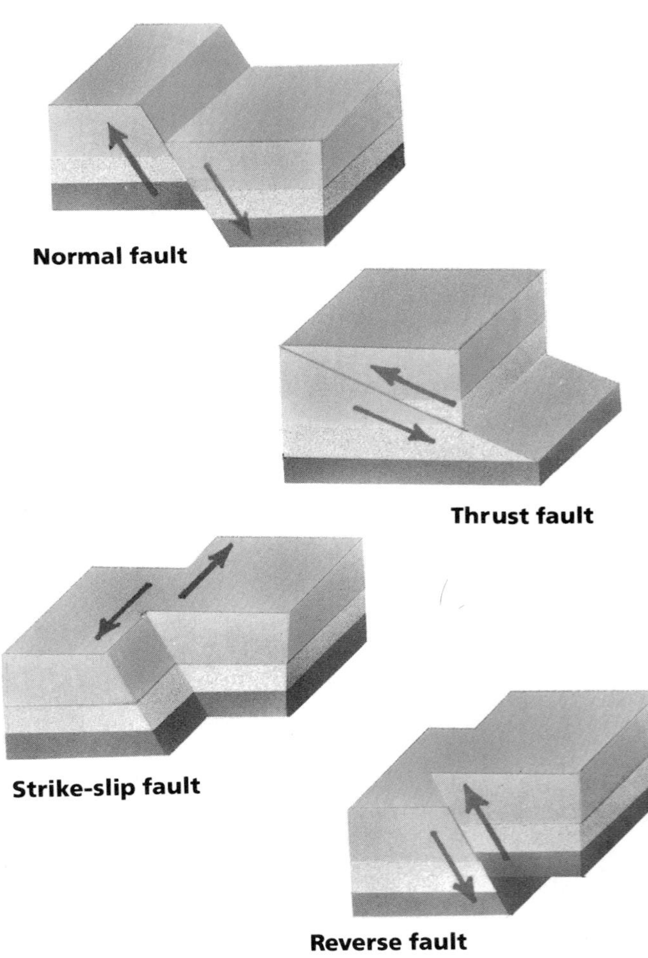

Figure 2 Faults

Observe: How do the rock layers move along a strike-slip fault?

LESSON SUMMARY

- When rock layers bend and move into new positions without breaking, folds form.
- The folds in rock layers may be anticlines or synclines.
- A break in a rock is a fracture.
- Faulting causes rocks to move up and down or side to side.

CHECK *Explain the difference between the words in each pair.*

1. fault, fracture
2. anticline, syncline

Complete the following.

3. When rock layers change shape but do not break, a ______ forms.
4. When rock layers break but do not move, a ______ forms.
5. When rock layers break and the layers move, a ______ forms.

APPLY *Use the illustration of the four kinds of faults on page 126 to answer the following.*

6. Along which faults is movement side to side?
7. Along which faults is movement up and down?
8. **Infer:** Why do you think a strike-slip fault was given its name?
9. **Observe:** List the names of the four kinds of faults.

InfoSearch

Read the passage. Ask two questions about the topic that you cannot answer from the information in the passage.

San Andreas Fault There is a huge fault in the earth's crust that extends through California. This fault is called the San Andreas (an-DRAY-us) fault. The San Andreas fault extends from the Gulf of California through San Francisco Bay. The crack of the fault reaches more than 32 km down into the earth's crust. In 1906, movement along this fault caused the Great San Francisco Earthquake. In 1989, another earthquake hit Santa Cruz and the Bay Area. Areas with networks of faults, such as southern California have many earthquakes.

SEARCH: Use library references to find answers to your questions.

ACTIVITY

MODELING THE FOLDING OF ROCK LAYERS

You will need 3 different colors of modeling clay, a plastic knife, a metric ruler, and a sheet of waxed paper 30-cm long.

1. Flatten each color clay into a strip about 9-cm wide and 24-cm long. Each strip should be about 1-cm thick.
2. Choose one of the colors and make a fourth strip.
3. Using the plastic knife, trim the clay strips so that they form a rectangle 8 cm × 23 cm.
4. Stack the four strips on the sheet of waxed paper.
5. Push both ends of the clay layers toward the center.
6. Sketch the folded layers. Label the layers by color.
7. Label the anticlines and synclines on your drawing.

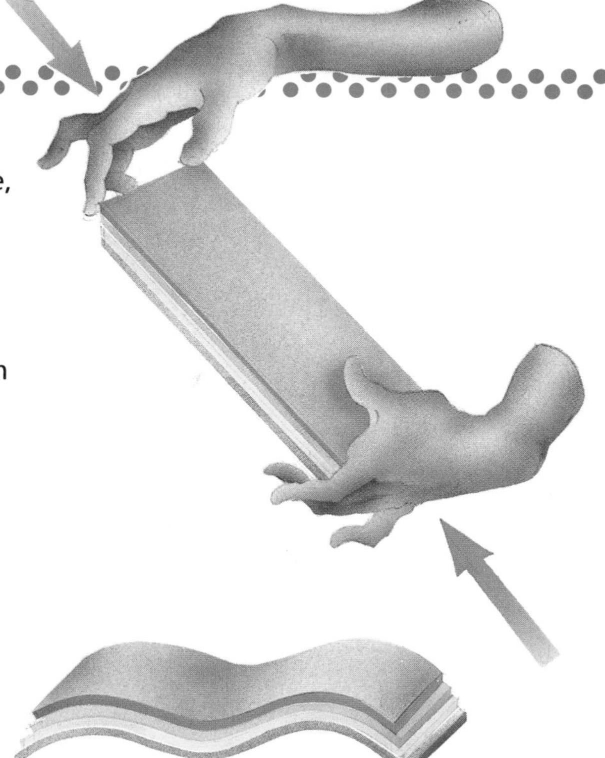

Questions

1. **Model:** What do the clay layers represent?
2. **Analyze:** What caused the clay layers to fold?
3. **Observe:** Did any cracks appear in the clay layers? If so, what are these cracks called?

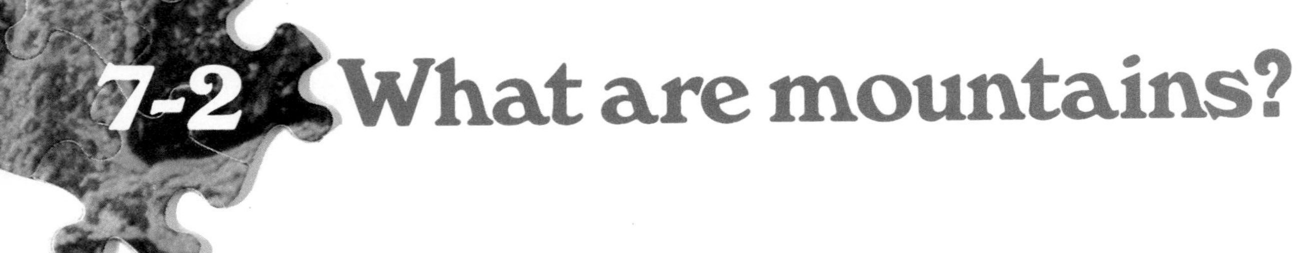

7-2 What are mountains?

Objective ▶ Identify the organization of the world's mountain systems.

TechTerm

- ▶ **elevation** (el-uh-VAY-shun): distance above or below sea level

Mountains A mountain is a landform that reaches a high **elevation** (el-uh-VAY-shun). Elevation is the distance above or below sea level. For a hill or mound of land to be classified as a mountain, its summit, or top, must be at least 600 m higher than that of the surrounding land.

Compare: How does the elevation of a mountain compare with the elevation of the surrounding area?

Young and Old Mountains Mountains, like rivers, can be described in three stages. The three stages are young, mature, and old. A young mountain has a steep slope. Its peaks are sharp and jagged. The valleys in young mountains are narrow. As a mountain becomes mature, the peaks are worn down by weathering. Weathering makes the peaks rounded. The slopes become less steep and more gentle. As the mountain becomes old, its peaks become almost flat. There are no jagged peaks. An old mountain looks like rolling hills. The valleys in old mountains are wide.

Classify: The Appalachians have very rounded peaks. Are these mountains young or old?

Mountain Systems Most mountains do not stand alone. They are part of a group of mountains. A group of mountains with the same general shape and structure is called a mountain range. For example, Mount St. Helens in Washington State is part of the Cascade range. Groups of mountain ranges form mountain systems. The Appalachian mountain system is in the eastern United States. The Blue Ridge and Great Smokey mountain ranges are part of the Appalachian system. Mountain systems make up mountain belts. There are two major mountain belts. Look at the mountain belts on the map.

Observe: What are two major mountain belts?

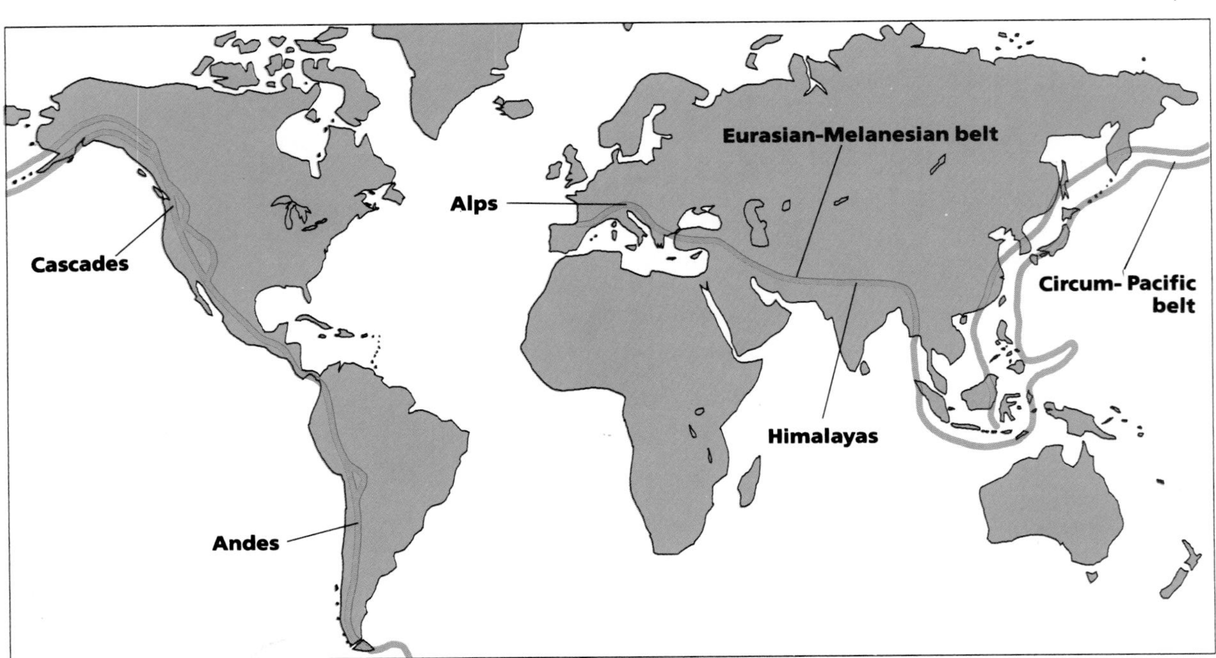

LESSON SUMMARY

- Mountains are landforms that have high elevations.
- The three stages of mountains are young, mature, and old.
- Most mountains are part of larger groups of mountains.

CHECK *Complete the following.*

1. The highest point of a mountain is its ______ .
2. You would find narrow valleys in a ______ mountain.
3. Mountain systems make up mountain ______ .
4. If the peaks of a mountain are like rolling hills, the mountain is ______ .

APPLY *Complete the following.*

5. **Sequence:** Place the mountain groups in order from smallest to largest.

6. **Classify:** Label the stage of each mountain.

a.

b.

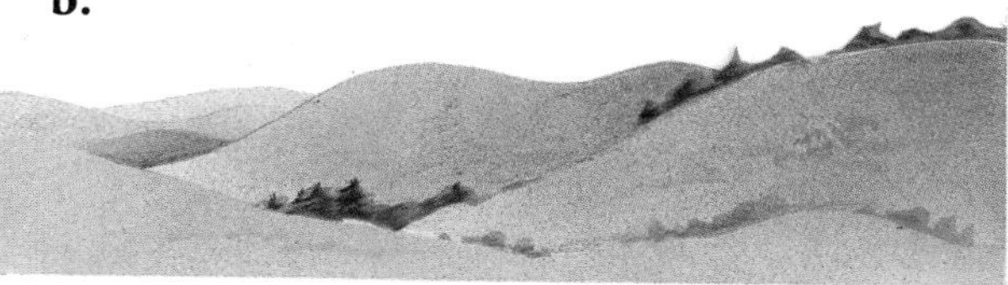

Skill Builder

Organizing Here are the names of six mountains: Mount McKinley, Mount Whitney, Mount Everest, Mont Blanc, Mount Nebo, and Mount Logan. Find out the height in meters or kilometers of each mountain and the country in which it is located. Also, find out the name of the mountain range in which each mountain is located. Organize the information in a table.

PEOPLE IN SCIENCE

EDMUND P. HILLARY (1919–present)

Dateline: May 29, 1953. **Place:** 8848 meters above sea level. **World News:** Two mountain climbers reach the summit of Mount Everest.

Sir Edmund Hillary and Tenzing Norgay were the first mountain climbers to reach the summit of Mt. Everest. Sir Hillary is a New Zealand mountain climber. Norgay was a Sherpa tribesman from Nepal. Many people had tried before them, but no one had succeeded in climbing to the top. Heavy snow, strong winds, and thin air make climbing the cliffs of Mt. Everest very difficult.

Hillary has returned many times to the region near Mt. Everest to aid the Sherpa people living there. He helped build schools, hospitals and airfields. Hillary wrote the book *High Adventures* which describes his experiences of the 1953 climb.

In 1957 Hillary set forth on an expedition to the South Pole. On January 4, 1958 he reached the South Pole by tractor. In 1977 he led the first jet boat expedition up the Ganges River to find its source. After the boat could travel no longer, Hillary climbed the Himalayas to reach the source of the river.

7-3 What are the types of mountains?

Objective ▶ Identify three types of mountains and how they were formed.

Folded Mountains Mountains formed by the folding of rock layers are called folded mountains. Most folded mountains formed when the continents collided. The movements of the continents squeezed rock layers together. Over millions of years, the pressure built up. The rock layers of the crust buckled and folded. Large upfolds, or anticlines, formed folded mountains. The largest mountains in the world are folded mountains. The Himalayas and Urals are folded mountains. In the United States, the Appalachian mountains are folded mountains.

▶ ***Describe:*** How are folded mountains formed?

Fault-block Mountains You may recall that fractures can form in the earth's crust. These fractures may break the crust into large blocks. Sometimes faulting lifts these large blocks. One side of the fault slips up past the crust on the other side. If the blocks are pushed up enough, a mountain is formed. Mountains formed in this way are called fault-block mountains. The Grand Tetons in Wyoming are fault-block mountains. The Sierra Nevadas in California also are fault-block mountains.

▶ ***List:*** Name two fault-block mountains in the United States.

Dome Mountains Some mountains form when hot melted rock called magma (MAG-muh) rises through the crust. Sometimes the magma forms giant pools in the crust. As the pools get bigger, the magma pushes up the rock layers above it. A rounded mountain forms on the earth's surface. The molten rock cools and hardens. The pushed-up rock layers are worn away, leaving separate peaks. These mountains are called dome mountains. The Black Hills of South Dakota are dome mountains.

Observe: What does a dome mountain look like?

LESSON SUMMARY

- Folded mountains are formed by the folding of rock layers.
- Fault-block mountains are formed when large blocks of the earth's crust are lifted and tilted by faulting.
- Dome mountains are formed when molten rock pushes up rock layers of the crust forming rounded domes on the earth's surface.

CHECK *Complete the following.*

1. Which type of mountain is usually formed by colliding continents?
2. Which type of mountain is formed by hot, melted rock?
3. Which type of mountain is formed by upward movements of chunks of the earth's crust?

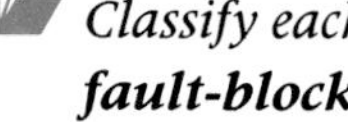 *Classify each mountain range listed as **dome, folded,** or **fault-block.***

4. Appalachian Mountains
5. Grand Tetons
6. Himalaya Mountains

APPLY *Identify the type of mountain shown.*

7.

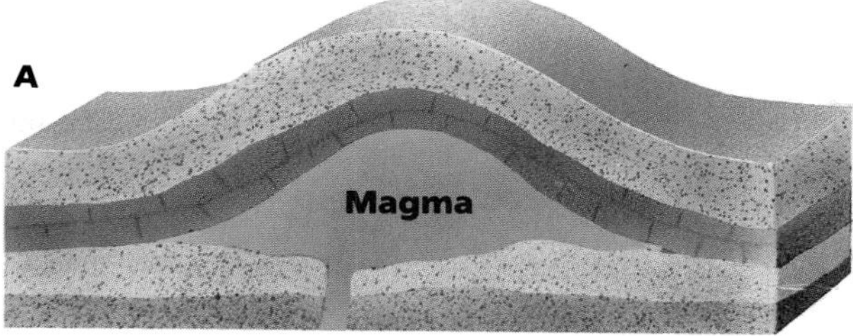

Skill Builder

Modeling When you model, you make a copy of something to help explain it. On a sheet of white, 11″ × 17″ construction paper, make a series of drawings to show the formation of a dome mountain. Use arrows to show the movement of magma and pressure. Color your drawings. Use a key to show what the colors mean.

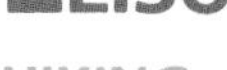

LEISURE ACTIVITY

HIKING

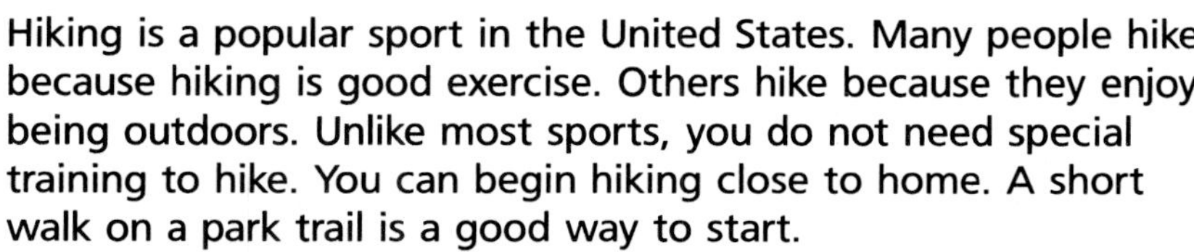

Hiking is a popular sport in the United States. Many people hike because hiking is good exercise. Others hike because they enjoy being outdoors. Unlike most sports, you do not need special training to hike. You can begin hiking close to home. A short walk on a park trail is a good way to start.

Usually people hike for several hours. You do not need any special equipment for a short hike. However, it is a good idea to carry a small knapsack with a spare jacket and a light snack. If you plan a long hike on rough grounds, you should wear hiking boots. Strong boots protect your feet from cold, water, and jagged rocks. Boots also prevent slipping.

Serious hikers often go on hiking trips that take several days. For these trips, you need to take along a backpack. The backpack should contain food, water, and a first aid kit. A sleeping bag and tent also are needed.

You should never hike alone. There are many local and regional hiking clubs in the United States. Many of these clubs plan organized trips for hikers. Check your area to see if you have a hiking club nearby. Happy hiking.

7-4 What are plains and plateaus?

Objective ▶ Compare and contrast plains and plateaus.

TechTerm

- ▶ **landform:** physical feature of the earth's surface

Plains Plains are large, flat areas that are not far above sea level. The two kinds of plains are coastal plains and interior plains. Coastal plains are located along coastlines. Interior plains are located inland. All plains gently slope over great distances.

Plains are formed in several ways. One way is for land of uneven elevation to be worn down by erosion. The Great Plains of the United States were formed this way. Another way is for earth material to be deposited by a body of water. Some plains are formed when sediments are deposited in a body of water. Then the water level drops or the land rises. A flat, dry area of land remains.

Name: What are the two kinds of plains?

Plateaus Plateaus have much higher elevations than do plains. Yet, plateaus are large flat areas just like plains. Most plateaus are located inland. Some are near oceans. These plateaus end with a cliff.

Many plateaus have canyons. A canyon is a steep-sided valley formed by a river. The Colorado Plateau has been cut through by the Colorado River. The river formed the Grand Canyon.

Plateaus are formed by the same forces that build mountains. Large areas of the crust are raised upward. The Colorado Plateau was formed in this way. Some plateaus are formed by lava pouring out of a volcano. The lava cools and hardens, forming a large raised table-like area. The Colombia Plateau in Washington State is a lava plateau.

Describe: What is a plateau?

Landform Regions Mountains, plains, and plateaus (pla-TOHS) are the three main kinds of landforms. A **landform** is a physical feature of the earth's surface. These landforms make up regions in the world. The map shows the locations of the landform regions in the United States.

Observe: In what landform region do you live?

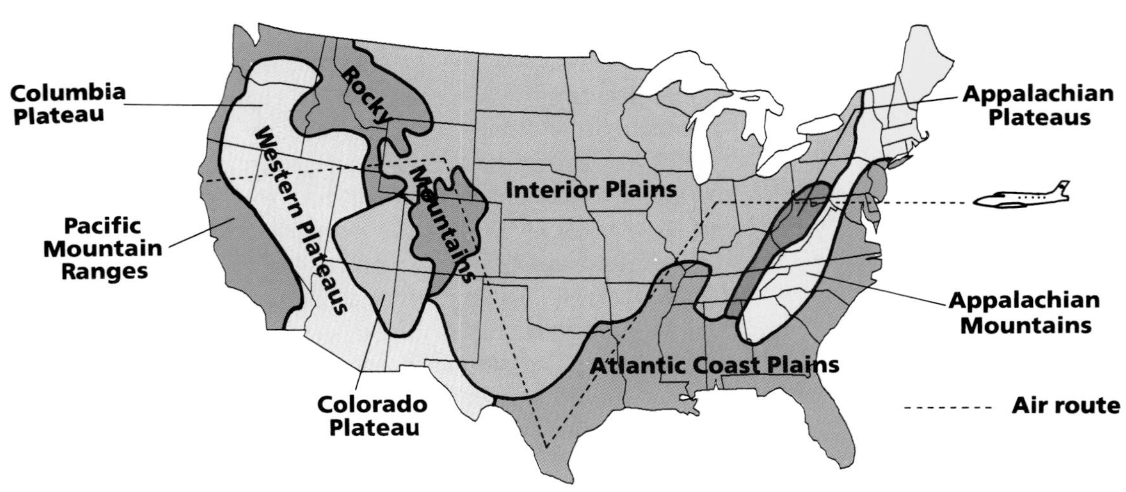

LESSON SUMMARY

- Two kinds of plains are coastal plains and interior plains.
- Plains are formed by erosion, deposition of river sediments, uplifting of land, or dropping water levels.
- Plateaus are large, flat areas that have high elevations.
- Canyons are deep, steep-sided valleys worn into plateaus by rivers.
- The same forces that build mountains also form plateaus.
- The three main landforms are plains, plateaus, and mountains.

CHECK *Complete the following.*

1. What are the three main kinds of landforms?
2. Which landform has the lowest elevation?
3. Name a lava plateau in the United States.
4. What river formed the Grand Canyon?

APPLY *Use the map on page 132 to answer the following.*

5. **Sequence:** Pretend you are taking an airplane across the United States from the east coast to the west coast. You are following the air route shown. List the landform regions of the United States in the order that you will pass over them as you make the trip.
6. **Classify:** Choose 5 states. In which landform region or regions is each state located?

Skill Builder

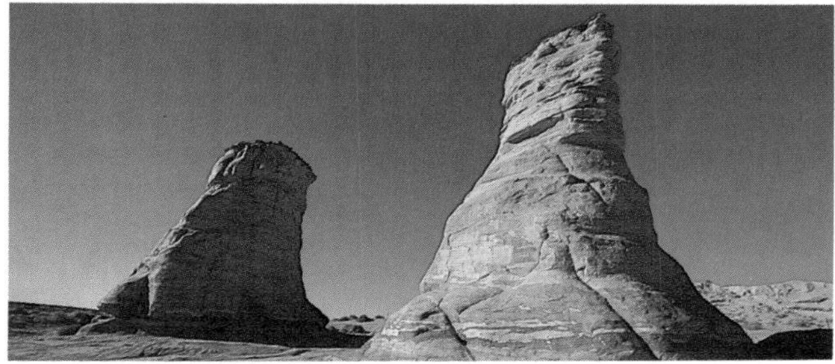

Researching Some landforms have special names. Find out what these landforms are: butte; peneplain; monadnock; mesa. How are they formed?

SCIENCE CONNECTION

BREADBASKET OF THE UNITED STATES

The interior plains of the United States cover a large area. The north central part of this area is called the Great Plains. The states in the Great Plains have rich soil. The soil is very good for growing crops. Besides rich soil, the area has enough rainfall and a good climate for growing food crops.

The twelve states that are in the Great Plains are nicknamed the "breadbasket" of the United States. The nickname is used because most grains and food crops are grown here. Oats, wheat, and rye are some grains grown in the Great Plains. Much of this grain is used to make bread. Other food crops grown in the "breadbasket" are corn, potatoes, soybeans, and alfalfa. The plains also are good grazing areas. Beef cattle and sheep are raised here. Hogs are also raised on hog and corn farms. In the more northern states, dairy farms are common.

7-5 What are volcanoes?

Objective ▶ Describe volcanism and the formation of a volcano.

TechTerms

- **crater** (KRAY-tur): funnel-shaped pit at the top of a volcanic cone
- **lava:** magma on the earth's surface
- **vent:** opening from which lava flows
- **volcanism** (VAHL-kuh-niz-um): movement of magma on or inside the earth
- **volcano** (vahl-KAY-noh): vent and the pile of volcanic material around the vent

Volcanism Any movement of magma on or inside the earth is called **volcanism** (VAHL-kuh-niz-um). Sometimes magma flows between rock layers of the crust and hardens. A sill forms. If magma cuts across rock layers and hardens, a dike forms. You already know that magma forms dome mountains. They form when magma pushes up the crust of the earth. Sometimes magma breaks through the crust. The magma flows onto the surface of the earth. Magma on the earth's surface is called **lava.**

▶ ***Define:*** What is lava?

Volcano Would you like to watch a mountain form? In 1943, a Mexican farmer did just that! First the ground started shaking. A few weeks later, the farmer found large cracks, or fissures (FISH-ers), on his farmland. Hot gases came out of the fissures. The fissures widened. Lava began to come out. The opening from which lava flows is called a **vent.** Dust, ash, and rock particles were thrown out of the vent. A **volcano** (vol-CAY-no) was formed. A volcano is the vent and the volcanic cone. The volcanic cone is the pile of lava, dust, ash, and rock particles around the vent. After several months, a volcanic cone built up that was 450 m high. It had a base 5 km wide. The volcano was called Paricutín (pah-ree-koo-TEEN).

▶ ***List:*** What are four kinds of volcanic material?

Craters and Calderas At the top of a volcanic cone, there may be a funnel-shaped pit. This pit is called a **crater** (KRAY-tur). A crater is formed as material is blown out of the vent of a volcano.

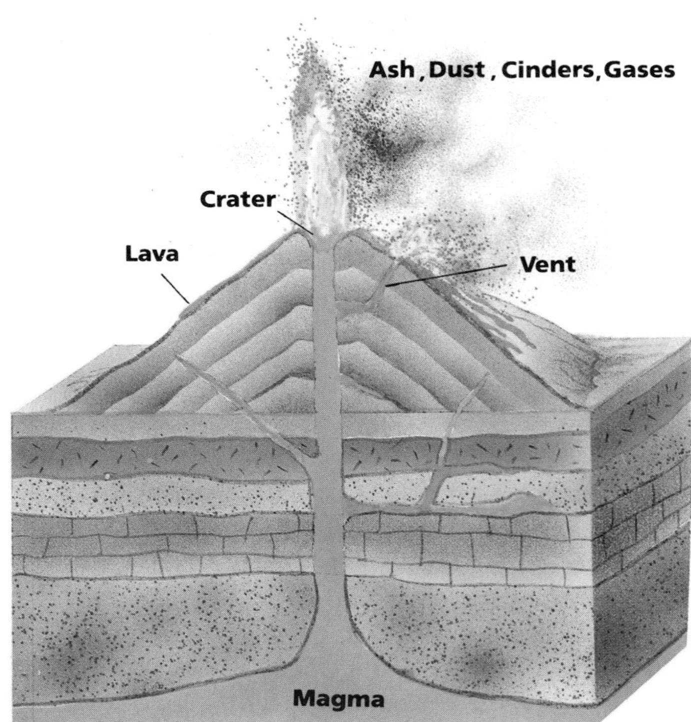

Sometimes the walls of the crater fall back into the vent. The crater gets wider. Sometimes the top of a volcano explodes. A wide opening is left. This wide opening is a caldera (cal-DUR-uh). Some calderas fill with water. They form large lakes such as Crater Lake in Oregon. Crater Lake is 9.6 km long and 8 km wide. It is about 600 m deep.

▶ ***Compare:*** What is the difference between a crater and a caldera?

LESSON SUMMARY

- ► Volcanism is the movement of magma on or inside the earth.
- ► A volcano is the vent and the pile of lava, dust, ash, and rock particles around the vent.
- ► A crater is a funnel-shaped pit at the top of a volcanic cone.
- ► A caldera forms when the walls of a crater fall back into a vent or the top of a volcano explodes.

CHECK *Explain the difference between the words in each pair.*

1. magma, lava
2. caldera, crater
3. dike, sill

Complete the following.

4. What is a volcanic cone?
5. What is a vent?

APPLY *Complete the following.*

6. **Infer:** What do you think is meant by the statement "Volcanoes are windows to the inside of the earth."

InfoSearch

Read the passage. Ask two questions about the topic that you cannot answer from the information in the passage.

Krakatoa Krakatoa (krah-kah-TOH-uh) is a group of volcanic islands in Indonesia. In 1883, many volcanic eruptions occurred. The eruptions began in May and continued into the summer. In August, a huge volcanic explosion destroyed the islands. The explosion was heard in Australia. Australia is 3500 km away.

The volcanic explosion changed the shape of the entire island. A huge caldera was formed. Volcanic ash buried what was left of the island. The area was in total darkness for 2 ½ days because of the ash cloud.

SEARCH: Use library references to find answers to your questions.

SCIENCE CONNECTION

AFTER THE ERUPTION OF MOUNT ST. HELENS

On May 18, 1980, Mount St. Helens in Washington State blew its top. The eruption sent ash high into the air. Nearby towns were covered by several centimeters of the ash. The force of the blast caused great damage to the area around the mountain. Forests were destroyed. Rivers were blocked with mud, ash, and fallen trees. All plant and animal life were killed. The area around the mountain was as lifeless as the moon.

In 1981, life began returning to the area around Mount St. Helens. Ecological succession (suhk-SESH-uhn) had started. Ecological succession is a series of changes in the kinds of plants and animals that live in an area.

Scientists observed lichens growing on bare rocks. Birds flying over the area deposited seeds in their droppings. The seeds soon sprouted. A few years later, larger plants began to grow. The kinds of animals that once lived in the area began returning.

Today, the Mount St. Helens area is an outdoor laboratory for scientists. Biologists and ecologists are studying the area as it changes. Their studies will help put together the pattern of succession.

7-6 How do volcanoes differ?

Objective ▶ Identify and describe the three kinds of volcanic cones.

TechTerms

- ▶ **cinder cone:** volcanic cone made up of rock particles, dust, and ash
- ▶ **composite** (kum-PAHZ-it) **cone:** volcanic cone made up of alternating layers of lava and rock particles
- ▶ **shield cone:** volcanic cone made up of layers of hardened lava

Volcanic Eruptions Volcanic eruptions may be quiet or explosive (eck-SPLO-siv). During a quiet eruption, lava flows freely through a vent or a fissure. Explosive eruptions shoot rocks, lava, gases, ash, and dust high into the air. Different kinds of volcanic eruptions form different volcanic cones.

Name: What are the two kinds of volcanic eruptions?

Shield Cones A **shield cone** is made up of hardened lava. A shield cone forms from quiet eruptions. Lava flows over a large area and hardens. Layers of lava build up to form a cone. The cone has a wide base. The sides of the cone have gentle slopes. Mauna Loa in the Hawaiian Islands is the largest shield cone. It is more than 4 km above sea level.

Describe: What forms a shield cone?

Cinder Cones Volcanoes made up of rock particles thrown out of a vent are called **cinder cones.** They are formed by explosive eruptions. Cinder cones have steep sides and narrow bases. Cinder cones are usually not very high. The rock particles are loose and roll down the slope. Paricutín in Mexico is a cinder cone.

Name: What kind of eruption forms a cinder cone?

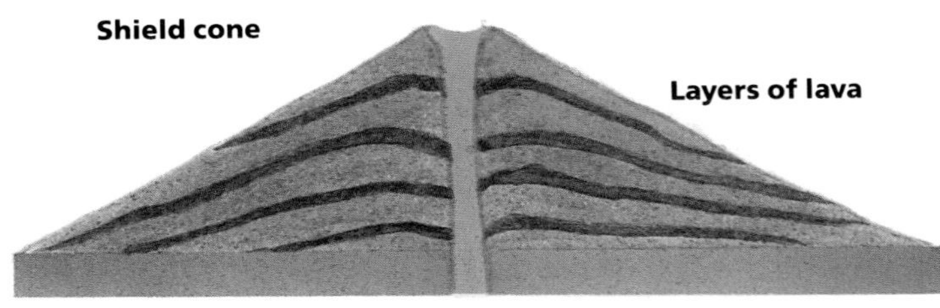

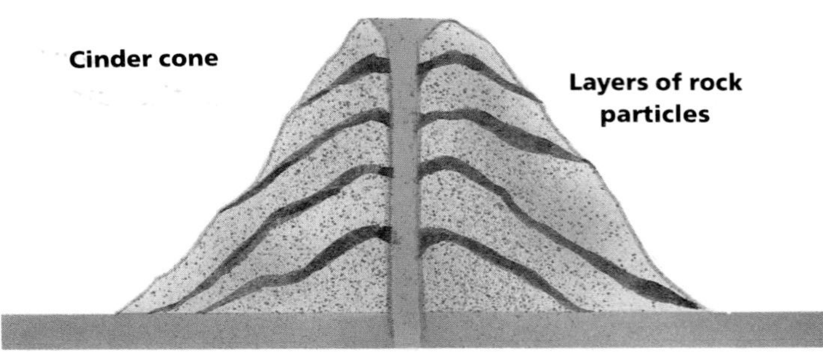

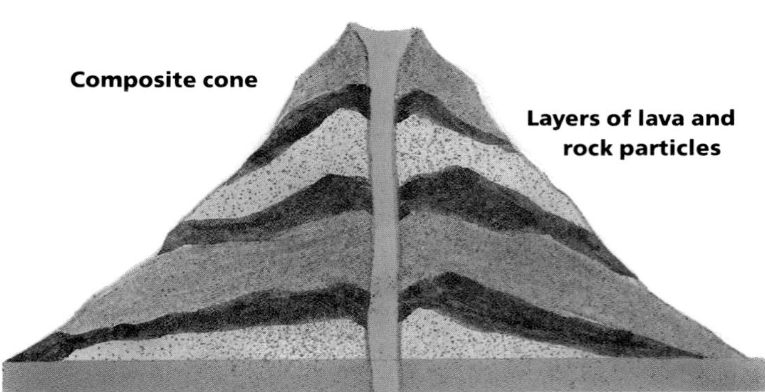

Composite Cones A **composite** (kum-PAHZ-it) cone is formed from layers of lava and rock particles. These cones are formed from both quiet and explosive eruptions. During a quiet eruption, lava forms a wide base. An explosive eruption adds a layer of dust, ash, and rock particles. Then another quiet eruption adds a lava layer. After many quiet and explosive eruptions, a very high volcanic cone is formed. The cone is wide with steep sides. In the United States, Mount St. Helens and Mount Hood are composite volcanoes.

Infer: How could you tell if a layer of a composite cone was formed by a quiet or an explosive eruption?

LESSON SUMMARY

- Volcanic eruptions may be quiet or explosive.
- Different kinds of volcanic eruptions form different volcanic cones.
- Shield cones are lava cones with wide bases and gentle slopes.
- Cinder cones are made up of rock particles and have narrow bases and steep sides.
- Composite volcanoes are very high volcanic cones made up of alternating layers of lava and rock particles.

CHECK *Complete the following.*

1. A volcanic eruption that shoots rocks, dust, ash, lava, and gases high into the air is ______ .
2. Cinder cones are formed by ______ eruptions.
3. There are ______ kinds of volcanic cones.
4. Volcanic cones with gentle slopes and wide bases are ______ cones.
5. Very high volcanic cones are ______ volcanoes.
6. Shield volcanoes are formed by ______ eruptions.

APPLY *Complete the following.*

7. **Sequence:** Place the kinds of volcanic cones in order from highest to lowest.

Classify: *Classify each of these volcanoes as composite cone, shield cone, or cinder cone.*

8. Mauna Loa
9. Mount Hood
10. Paricutin
11. Mount St. Helens

InfoSearch

Read the passage. Ask two questions about the topic that you cannot answer from the information in the passage.

Io Io is one of the moons of Jupiter. Io is a bright yellow and red moon. Scientists think its color is caused by volcanic material. Other than the earth, Io is the first moon or planet on which scientists have seen active volcanism. Mars' has an inactive volcano on it. The earth's moon has hardened lava on it.

The volcanoes on Io seem to be very powerful. They shoot out thousands of metric tons of material every month. The material shoots up hundreds of kilometers into Io's atmosphere.

SEARCH: Use library references to find answers to your questions.

ACTIVITY

MODELING VOLCANIC CONES

You will need cereal flakes, 2 paper plates, a metric ruler, plaster of Paris, a measuring cup, and a spoon.

1. In the measuring cup, mix 3 spoonfuls of plaster of Paris with about 75 mL of water. Be sure the mixture is not too runny.
2. Hold the measuring cup about 15 cm over a paper plate. Pour the plaster of Paris slowly onto one spot of the plate.
3. Let the plaster harden. Clean out the measuring cup.
4. Fill the measuring cup halfway with the cereal flakes.
5. Hold the measuring cup about 15 cm above the second paper plate. Slowly pour the cereal flakes onto one spot of the plate.
6. Measure and record the base of each volcanic cone.

Questions

1. What does the plaster of Paris represent?
2. What do the cereal flakes represent?
3. **Measure:** What is the width of each base?

4. **Model:** Which kind of volcanic cone does the plaster of Paris model represent? Explain.
5. **Model:** Which kind of volcanic cone does the cereal flakes model represent? Explain.

7-7 What are earthquakes?

Objective ▶ Explain what happens during an earthquake.

TechTerms

- **earthquake:** sudden, strong movement of the earth's crust
- **epicenter** (EP-ih-sen-ter): place on the surface of the earth directly above the focus
- **focus** (FOH-kus): place inside the earth where an earthquake starts
- **seismic** (SIZE-mik) **waves:** earthquake waves
- **seismograph** (SIZE-muh-graf): instrument that detects and measures earthquakes

Earthquake! The earth's crust is always moving, but usually very slowly. Small movements of the crust that you may or may not feel are called tremors (TREM-ers). There are more than six million tremors each year. Sudden, strong movements of the earth's crust are called **earthquakes.** They can cause a lot of damage.

▶ ***Define:*** What is an earthquake?

Focus and Epicenter Earthquakes begin deep inside the earth. The place inside the earth where an earthquake starts is the **focus** (FOH-kus). The place on the surface of the earth directly above the focus is called the **epicenter** (EP-ih-sen-ter). The surface of the earth shakes the hardest at the epicenter.

▶ ***Define:*** What is the focus?

Causes of Earthquakes Earthquakes are caused mostly by faulting. Usually, the rocks on both sides of a fault are pushed together very tight. The rocks do not move. Geologists say that the fault is "locked," Pressure in the rocks increases. When the pressure becomes too great, the rocks break at a weak point. Rocks first slip and move at the focus. As the rocks move, they release energy in the form of vibrations. These vibrations are called **seismic** (SYZ-mik) **waves,** or earthquake waves.

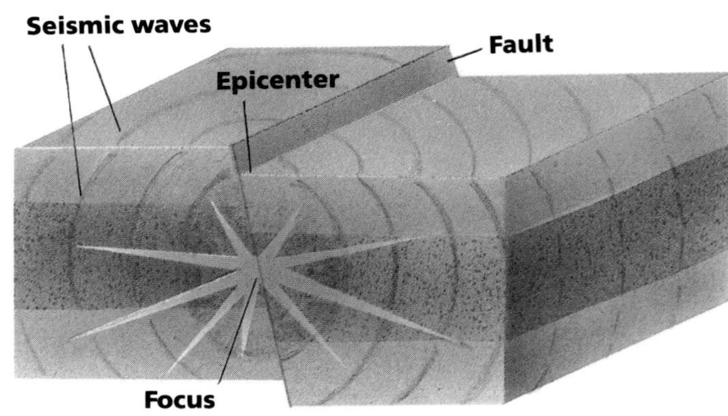

Seismic waves travel out from the focus in all directions. Imagine throwing a pebble into a pond. At the point where the pebble hits the water, you see waves move outward in all directions. Earthquake waves move out from the focus in the same way.

▶ ***Name:*** What is the main cause of earthquakes?

Measuring Earthquakes A **seismograph** (SIZE-muh-graf) is an instrument that detects and measures earthquakes. A seismograph can even measure very small tremors that people cannot feel. It makes a record of the movements in the earth's crust on a piece of paper. The record is called a seismogram (SIZE-muh-gram). It looks like wavy lines. The higher the wavy lines are on the seismogram, the stronger is the earthquake.

▶ ***Describe:*** What is a seismogram?

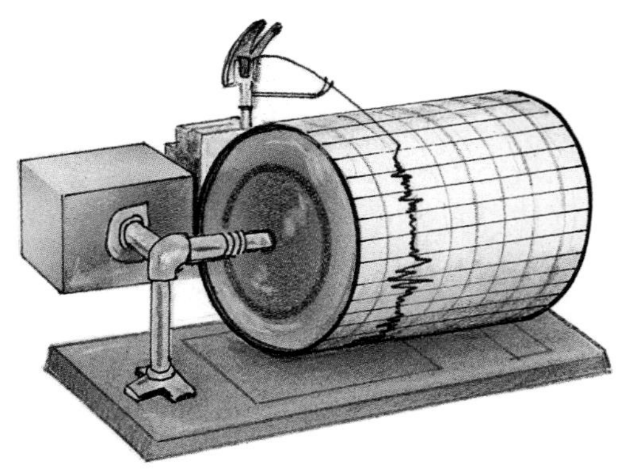

LESSON SUMMARY

- An earthquake is a sudden, strong movement of the earth's crust.
- Earthquakes start deep inside the earth's crust at the focus.
- Most earthquakes are caused by faulting.
- Seismic waves travel out from the focus in all directions.
- A seismograph is used to detect and measure earthquakes.

CHECK *Find the sentence in the lesson that answers each question. Then write the sentence.*

1. What are small movement of the earth's crust called?
2. Where does the earth shake the hardest during an earthquake?
3. How do seismic waves travel?

Explain the difference between the words in each pair.

4. focus, epicenter
5. earthquake, tremor
6. seismogram, seismograph

APPLY *Complete the following.*

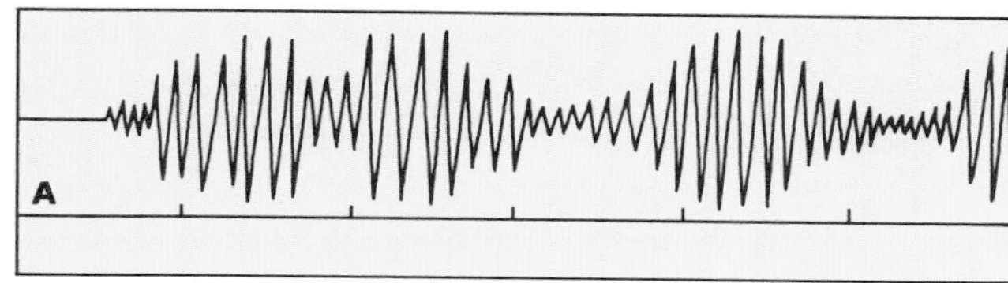

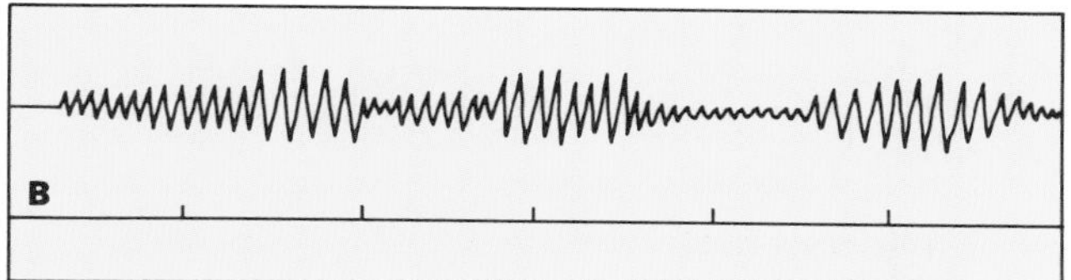

7. What are figures A and B?
8. Which figure shows the stronger earthquake?

Skill Builder

Understanding Word Relationships Use the dictionary to find the meaning of the prefix "seismo-". Write the definintion. Make a list of the words in the lesson and the career that use this prefix. Write definitions for the words on your list in your own words. Circle the words in your definitions that mean "seismo-".

CAREER IN EARTH SCIENCE

SEISMOLOGIST

Today, the study of earthquakes is a special branch of earth science. The science is called seismology (size-MAHL-uh-jee). Earthquake scientists are called seismologists (size-MAHL-uh-jists). Seismologists study areas of the earth where earthquakes happen. After an earthquake occurs, seismologists study the earth along the faults. When the 1989 earthquake occurred near San Francisco, California, seismologists studied the San Andreas Fault. They wanted to see how the earth's crust moved along the fault.

Seismologists collect a lot of data about earthquakes. They take measurements and examine the damage caused by the earthquake. They analyze seismograms, which show the record of the movement of the earth during an earthquake. Using the data, seismologists can try to predict where earthquakes will most likely happen. They also may be able to find ways to prevent earthquakes.

7-8 What are seismic waves?

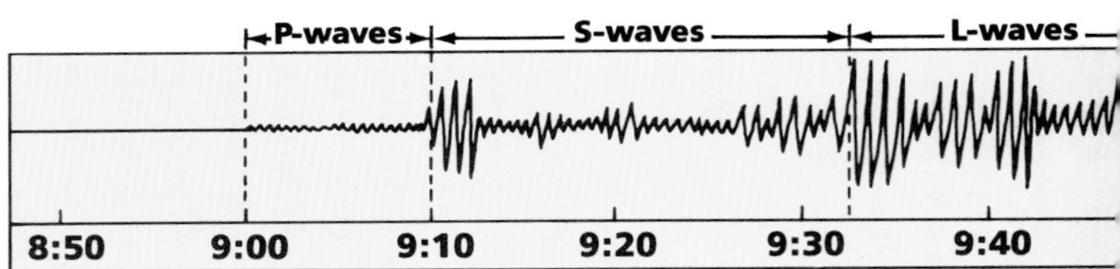

Objective ▶ Describe the three kinds of seismic waves and what they tell scientists about earthquakes.

TechTerms

- ▶ **L-waves:** surface waves
- ▶ **P-waves:** fastest earthquake waves
- ▶ **S-waves:** second earthquake waves to be recorded at a seismograph station

Primary Waves The fastest moving seismic (SYZ-muk) waves are primary waves, or **P-waves.** P-waves are push-pull waves. They cause particles in materials to move back and forth in place. The wave itself moves out from the focus. The particles move together and apart along the direction of the wave. P-waves move through solids, liquids, and gases.

Describe: What kind of waves are primary waves?

Secondary Waves The second waves to be recorded by a seismograph are secondary waves, or **S-waves.** S-waves move slower than P-waves. S-waves travel only through solids. S-waves cause the particles in materials to move from side to side. The waves move at right angles to the direction in which the waves are traveling.

Compare: Are S-waves or P-waves faster moving?

Surface Waves Surface waves are called long waves, or **L-waves.** L-waves are the slowest moving waves. They are the last waves recorded on a seismogram. They cause the surface to rise and fall like ocean waves. L-waves cause the most damage because they bend and twist the surface of the earth.

List: What are three names that can be used for the slowest moving seismic waves?

Studying Earthquake Waves Studying a seismogram can tell scientists much about an earthquake. They can tell where the epicenter is and the force of the earthquake. Look at the seismogram. When did the first P-wave arrive? The time shows 9:00 am. When did the first S-wave arrive? It arrived at 9:10 am. There was a 10 minute difference between the times the P and S waves arrived. Using this time, scientists can tell the distance of the epicenter from the seismograph. Table 1 on page 141 shows the time it takes P-waves and S-waves to travel different distances. This is called travel time.

Describe: What two things does a seismogram tell you?

Finding the Epicenter To find the epicenter, seismograms from three stations are needed. A circle is drawn on a map around each station. Each station is at the center of its circle. There is only one point where all three circles cross. The epicenter is near the point where all three circles cross.

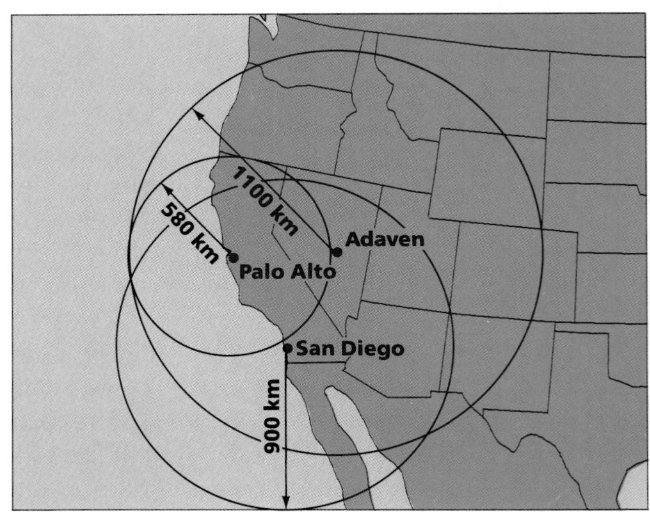

Observe: Where is the epicenter of the earthquake shown on the map?

LESSON SUMMARY

- The fastest moving seismic waves are called P-waves.
- The second waves that are recorded by a seismograph are S-waves.
- L-waves are the slowest moving seismic waves.
- A seismogram can be used to find out the distance of the epicenter from a seismograph and the force of an earthquake.
- The epicenter of an earthquake can be found by using three different seismogram readings.

CHECK *Complete the following.*

1. There are ______ kinds of seismic waves.
2. Seismic waves that travel through solids, liquids, and gases are ______ .
3. The slowest moving waves are ______ .
4. You need seismograms from ______ seismograph stations to find an earthquake's epicenter.

APPLY *Use the table to answer the questions.*

Table 1 Travel Time and Distance

TRAVEL TIME	DISTANCE FROM EPICENTER
1 minute	700 km
2 minutes	1200 km
3 minutes	1800 km
4 minutes	2500 km
5 minutes	3400 km

5. **Infer:** A seismograph station is less than 600 km from an earthquake's focus. What is the travel time?
6. **Analyze:** If travel time is 4 minutes, how far away is the seismograph station that recorded the time?

Health & Safety Tip

People who live in earthquake risk areas should always keep a portable radio, batteries, and a supply of ready-to-eat food and bottled water in their homes. Why do you think it is important to keep each of these things handy?

SCIENCE CONNECTION

EARTHQUAKE SAFETY

The key to earthquake safety is awareness. If you live in, or are visiting, an area that has earthquakes you should follow certain safety rules.

Before: Be prepared

1. Keep a supply of ready-to-eat food and bottled water in the house.
2. Be sure to have a flashlight, batteries, and a portable radio.
3. Learn how to turn off the electricity, gas, and water in your house.

During: Stay calm

1. If you are indoors, stay indoors. Protect yourself from falling materials by standing in a doorway or taking cover under a desk or large table.
2. Stay away from glass, especially windows.
3. If you are outdoors, move away from buildings, and overhead electrical and telephone wires.
4. If you are in a car, stop when you are in a place away from buildings, bridges, tunnels, and so on. Stay in the car until the shaking stops.

After: Be careful

1. Check the gas, water, and electricity. Look for fires or fire hazards.
   a. If you smell gas, open windows and turn off the gas. Leave the building. Contact the gas company or police. Do not go back into the building.
   b. If water pipes are broken, turn off the main water valve.
   c. If there are electrical shorts, turn off the electricity at the main fuse box or circuit breaker.
2. Do not use the telephone except for emergencies.
3. Turn on a radio to get emergency information. Use the television if you can.
4. Do not enter badly damaged buildings.
5. Do not go sightseeing.

7-9 What are the effects of earthquakes?

Objective ▶ Understand the power of earthquakes and the damage that they can cause.

TechTerms

- ▶ **Richter** (RIK-ter) **scale:** scale that measures the energy released by an earthquake
- ▶ **tsunami** (tsooh-NAHM-mee): ocean wave caused by an earthquake

The Richter Scale In 1935, Charles Richter (RIK-ter) developed a scale to measure the energy released by earthquakes. The scale is called the Richter scale. On the Richter scale, an earthquake is given a number between 1 and 9. If a stronger earthquake occurs, a higher number will be used. The higher the number is, the stronger is the earthquake.

An earthquake measuring 7 or more on the Richter scale can cause a great deal of damage. Earthquakes that measure 2.5 or less on the Richter scale are usually not felt by people. The largest earthquake recorded so far measured 8.9 on the scale.

▶ ***Explain:*** What is the Richter scale?

Earthquake Damage Many new buildings are built to be "earthquake-proof." They do not fall during an earthquake. Old buildings, however, may be destroyed completely during an earthquake. Tall buildings may sway. Sometimes tall buildings may move back and forth so much that they tip over. Earthquakes also damage electrical lines, telephone lines, and water pipes. Explosions are caused by broken electric and gas lines. Fires caused by broken gas lines often destroy many buildings.

▶ ***Explain:*** What is meant by "earthquake proof?"

Tsunami A great wave that is sometimes caused by an earthquake is called a **tsunami** (tsooh-NAHM-mee). A tsunami forms when the epicenter of an earthquake is on the ocean floor. Out in the open ocean, a tsunami is not very high. Near the shore, the height of the tsunami increases. A tsunami may be 30 m to 40 m high. When a tsunami hits land, it can cause a lot of damage. In 1964, a tsunami was caused by an earthquake in Alaska. The tsunami almost destroyed an entire fishing fleet. Some of the fishing boats were swept into downtown Kodiak, Alaska.

▶ ***Describe:*** What is a tsunami?

Predicting Earthquakes Scientists use past earthquakes to predict future earthquakes. Their predictions may be off by 25 years or more. Scientists use small movements in the earth's crust as a signal to a future earthquake. They look at the ground in the area to see if it has moved up or down. Laser field stations record the smallest movements along faults. Lasers are thin, strong light beams. The laser beam is shot into a reflector. By measuring the time it takes the beam to hit the reflector and come back, scientists can find out if any movement has happened along a fault. Using earthquake information, scientists have developed a Seismic Risk Map. The map shows where earthquakes may occur and the kind of damage they may cause.

▶ ***Infer:*** Why would predicting an earthquake be helpful?

LESSON SUMMARY

- The Richter scale measures the energy released by an earthquake.
- Major earthquakes on the Richter scale measure 7 or more.
- Most buildings have been built to be "earthquake proof."
- Earthquakes damage electrical lines, and gas and water pipes.
- A tsunami is a giant wave caused by earthquakes on the ocean floor.
- Scientists use many different observations to try to predict earthquakes.

CHECK *Complete the following.*

1. A strong earthquake on the Richter scale measures ______ or more.
2. You probably would not feel an earthquake that is less than ______ on the Richter scale.
3. Many new buildings are built to stand during an earthquake. These buildings can be called "______".
4. A map that shows where an earthquake may happen and the kind of damage it may cause is called a ______ map.

APPLY *Complete the following.*

5. **Sequence:** Place these earthquakes in order from weakest to strongest on the Richter scale. **a.** San Francisco, California, 1906, 8.3 **b.** Santa Cruz, California, 1989, 7.0 **c.** Mexico City, Mexico, 1985, 8.1 **d.** New York, New York, 1984, 5.0 **e.** Tokyo, Japan, 1923, 8.2 **f.** Sumatra, Indonesia, 1994, 7.2
6. **Building Vocabulary:** Find out what the letters in the word "laser" stand for.

Skill Builder

Researching When you do research, you gather information about a topic. The Mercalli scale also is used to measure earthquakes. Use reference materials to find out about the Mercalli scale. Make a poster that shows the Mercalli scale. Illustrate the poster. How does this scale measure earthquakes? How is it different from the Richter scale?

ACTIVITY

MODELING A TSUNAMI

You will need a small plate, masking tape, a shallow baking-pan, a felt-tip marker, scissors, and an unsharpened pencil.

1. Place the plate upside down in one end of the pan.
2. Tape one edge of the plate to the bottom of the pan. The plate should be able to move up and down.
3. Tape the pencil to the opposite edge of the plate.
4. Cut a piece of paper the width and height of the pan. Use the marker to draw a city, beach, or town half way up the paper. Tape the paper on all sides to the inside wall of the pan.
5. Fill the pan with water up to the bottom of the city.
6. Lift and lower the plate with the pencil several times to form a tsunami.

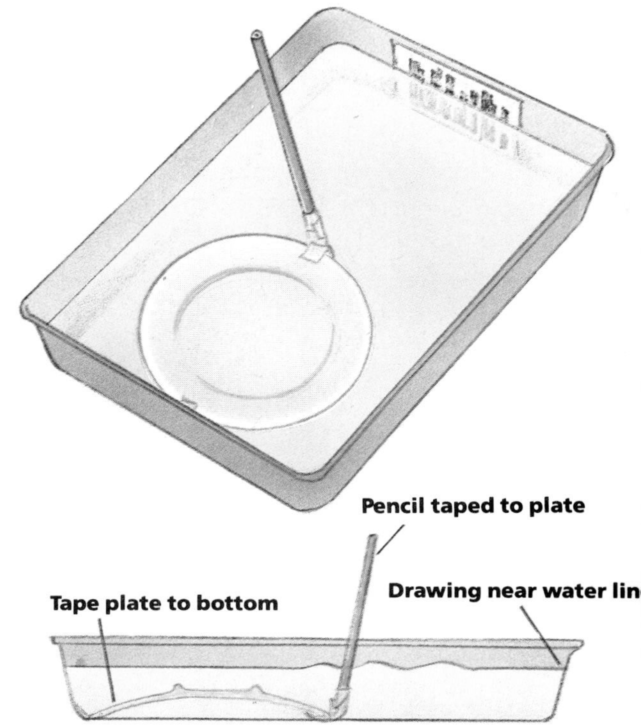

Questions

1. What does the point where you lift the plate represent?
2. **a. Observe:** What happens to the water level in the pan when you lift and lower the plate? **b.** What happens to the city, beach, or town?

7-10 What is the Ring of Fire?

Objective ▶ Identify three volcano and earthquake zones.

TechTerm

▶ **Ring of Fire:** major earthquake and volcano zone that almost forms a circle around the Pacific Ocean

Zones of Activity Most big earthquakes and volcanic eruptions occur in three areas, or zones. In these zones scientists think there is a lot of movement and activity in the earth's crust. There are many active volcanoes. Active volcanoes are volcanoes that have erupted at least once within recorded history. There are 500 to 600 active volcanoes on land. There are many more under the oceans.

▶ ***State:*** How many major volcano and earthquake zones are there?

The Ring of Fire The **Ring of Fire** is the major volcano and earthquake zone that almost forms a circle around the Pacific Ocean. Most of the active volcanoes on landmasses are located in the Ring of Fire. Many earthquakes occur in this area. The western coasts of North and South America are in the Ring of Fire.

▶ ***Identify:*** What is the name of the earthquake and volcano zone around the edge of the Pacific Ocean?

Mid-Atlantic Ridge A second major volcano and earthquake zone is in the Atlantic Ocean. This zone is the Mid-Atlantic Ridge. It is a long underwater chain of volcanic mountains. In this zone, earthquakes and volcanoes are caused by the formation of new parts of the earth's crust. Iceland is part of this zone. Iceland is a volcanic island.

▶ ***Describe:*** What is the Mid-Atlantic Ridge?

A Mountain Belt Zone Many of the countries in Europe have big earthquakes. Many also have active volcanoes. These countries are in the third zone. The third major volcano and earthquake zone is a major mountain belt. Scientists think this zone is so active because the mountains along the belt were formed when parts of the earth's crust crashed into each other.

Observe: Along which mountain belt is the third major volcano and earthquake zone?

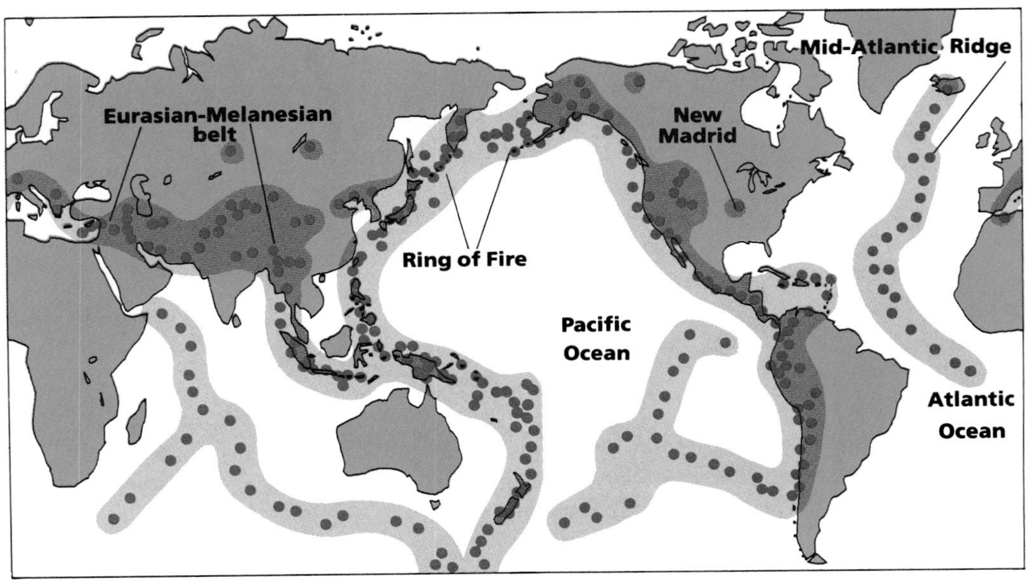

LESSON SUMMARY

- There are three major volcano and earthquake zones.
- The Ring of Fire is the largest zone of earthquake and volcano activity that almost forms a circle around the Pacific Ocean.
- The Mid-Atlantic Ridge is the second major earthquake and volcano zone.
- The third zone is a large zone that is the mountain belt called the Eurasian-Melanesian Belt.

CHECK *Complete the following.*

1. The Ring of Fire nearly surrounds the ______ Ocean.
2. The second major earthquake and volcano zone is located in the middle of the ______ Ocean.
3. The third major volcano and earthquake zone is a major ______ belt.
4. A volcanic island that is part of the Mid-Atlantic Ridge is ______ .

APPLY *Complete the following.*

5. **Observe:** Name two states in the United States that are part of the Ring of Fire. Use the map on page 144 to help you.
6. **Infer:** Which zone do you think has the most earthquakes and volcanic activity? Why?

InfoSearch

Read the passage. Ask two questions about the topic that you cannot answer from the information in the passage.

New Madrid, Missouri Find New Madrid on the map shown on page 144. Between 1811 and 1812, major earthquakes hit New Madrid. They caused flooding. They even changed the course of the Mississippi River. Scientists did not know why earthquakes happened in New Madrid. In the late 1970s, scientists discovered three faults in the area. The faults were buried deep in the earth's crust. Scientists think that movement along these faults caused the earthquakes.

SEARCH: Use library references to find answers to your questions.

LOOKING BACK IN SCIENCE

MOUNT VESUVIUS AND POMPEII

Mount Vesuvius (veh-SOO-vee-us) is the only active explosive volcano in Europe. In 79 AD, Vesuvius had an explosive eruption that spilled hot, wet ashes and cinders on the city of Pompeii (PAHM-pay). The entire city was completely covered with ash and cinders. Most of the people of Pompeii escaped. However, some people died from the hot ash and poisonous fumes in the air.

In the 1500s, people were digging a tunnel when they came across some of the remains of Pompeii. For hundreds of years, people continued to dig to uncover Pompeii. The ash and cinders had preserved the city over time. Today, more than half of Pompeii has been uncovered. Much of the city has been restored to the way it once was.

Mount Vesuvius has not erupted since 1944. However, the longer the volcano is quiet, the more explosive the next eruption may be. Six hundred thousand people live around the slopes of Vesuvius. To help protect people from a violent eruption, scientists constantly study the volcano. They measure escaping gases and slight ground movements. Scientists hope to predict an eruption two or three weeks ahead of time. With an early warning, people would have time to leave the area.

UNIT 7 Challenges

STUDY HINT Before you begin the Unit Challenges, review the TechTerms and Lesson Summary for each lesson in this unit.

TechTerms

anticline (126)
cinder cone (136)
composite cone (136)
crater (134)
earthquake (138)
elevation (128)
epicenter (138)
fault (126)
focus (138)
fracture (126)
L-waves (140)
landform (132)
lava (134)
P-waves (140)
Richter scale (142)
Ring of Fire (144)
S-waves (140)
seismic waves (138)
seismograph (138)
shield cone (136)
syncline (126)
tsunami (142)
vent (134)
volcanism (134)
volcano (134)

Matching *Write the TechTerm that best matches each description.*

1. earthquake waves
2. second earthquake waves to be recorded at a seismograph station
3. distance above or below sea level
4. feature of the earth's surface
5. movement of magma
6. ocean wave caused by an earthquake
7. major earthquake and volcano zone around the Pacific Ocean
8. magma on the earth's surface
9. opening from which lava flows

Applying Definitions *Explain the difference between the words in each pair. Write your answers in complete sentences.*

1. anticline, syncline
2. fault, fold
3. epicenter, focus
4. L-waves, P-waves
5. cinder cone, shield cone
6. crater, caldera
7. seismograph, Richter scale
8. composite cone, shield cone
9. fracture, fault
10. volcano, earthquake

Content Challenges

Multiple Choice *Write the letter of the term or phrase that best completes each statement.*

1. Folding and faulting are caused by
   a. heat. **b.** earthquakes. **c.** volcanoes. **d.** pressure.
2. The peaks of a young mountain are
   a. sharp and jagged. **b.** worn. **c.** rounded. **d.** flat.
3. A group of mountains with the same general shape and structure make up a mountain
   a. range. **b.** system. **c.** cascade. **d.** belt.
4. Mountains formed when magma rises through the crust are classified as
   a. folded mountains. **b.** fault-block mountains. **c.** dome mountains. **d.** volcanoes.
5. The kind of mountains formed by upward movements of chunks of the earth's crust are
   a. folded mountains. **b.** fault-block mountains. **c.** dome mountains. **d.** volcanoes.
6. The kind of plain formed by a volcano is a
   a. coastal plain. **b.** flood plain. **c.** interior plain. **d.** lava plain.
7. Magma that reaches the earth's surface is called
   a. crater. **b.** lava. **c.** magma. **d.** volcanic ash.

8. The opening through which lava flows from a volcano is a
   a. vent. **b.** sill. **c.** dike. **d.** crater.
9. Magma that flows between rock layers and hardens forms a
   a. dike. **b.** composite cone. **c.** sill. **d.** cinder cone.
10. A volcanic cone made up of rock particles, dust, and ash is a
    a. fault-block cone. **b.** composite cone. **c.** shield cone. **d.** cinder cone.
11. A volcanic eruption that shoots rocks, lava, gases, ash, and dust into the air is
    a. a quiet eruption. **b.** an explosive eruption. **c.** an active eruption.
    d. a composite eruption.
12. An instrument that detects and measures earthquakes is a
    a. seismogram. **b.** focus. **c.** seismic map. **d.** seismograph.
13. Earthquake waves that can travel through solids, liquids, and gases are
    a. P-waves. **b.** S-waves. **c.** L-waves. **d.** long waves.
14. The earthquake waves that cause the most damage are
    a. P-waves. **b.** S-waves. **c.** L-waves. **d.** D-waves.

True/False *Write true if the statement is true. If the statement is false, change the underlined term to make the statement true.*

1. Most active volcanoes are located on land.
2. The Ring of Fire is a major earthquake and volcano zone located in the Pacific ocean.
3. On the Seismic scale, an earthquake is given a number between 1 and 9.
4. The second seismic waves to be recorded by a seismograph are P-waves.
5. The fastest moving seismic waves are P-waves.
6. Earthquake waves that move along the surface are called S-waves.
7. Paracutin in Mexico is an example of a cinder cone.
8. The kind of volcanic cone formed from layers of lava and rock particles is a shield cone.
9. A funnel-shaped pit at the top of a volcanic cone is called a crater.
10. Any movement of magma on or inside the earth is called a dike.
11. A large flat landform with a high elevation is a plateau.
12. Mountains, plateaus, and sills are the three landforms of the earth's crust.
13. The Great Plains of the United States are coastal plains.
14. The Appalachian Mountains of the United States are folded mountains.
15. The Grand Tetons are dome mountains.

Understanding the Features

Reading Critically *Use the feature reading selections to answer the following. Page numbers for the features are shown in parentheses.*

1. What were the names of the first two people who climbed to the summit of Mount Everest? (129)
2. **Infer:** Why should you never hike alone? (131)
3. Why are the twelve states that make up the Great Plains sometimes called the 'breadbasket?' (133)
4. **Define:** What is ecological succession? (135)
5. **Infer:** Why should you not got sightseeing in an area that has been damaged by an earthquake? (139)
6. **Define:** What is a seismologist? (139)

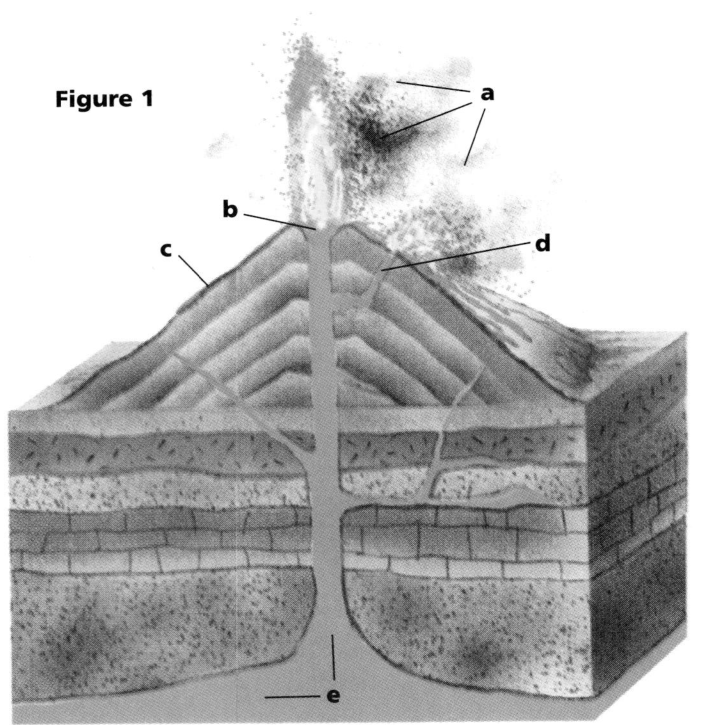

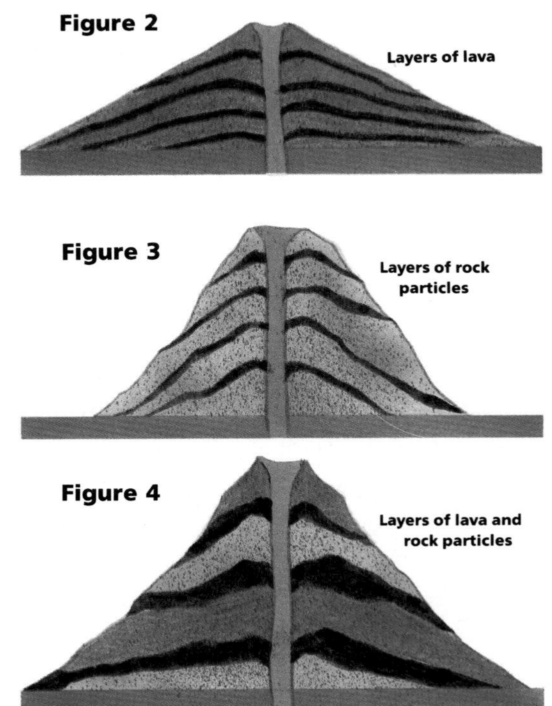

Concept Challenges

Interpreting a Diagram *Use the diagrams to complete the following.*

1. Identify each of the lettered parts in Figure 1.
2. **Observe:** What kind of volcano is shown in Figure 2?
3. **Observe:** What kind of volcanic cone is shown in Figure 3?
4. **Observe:** What kind of volcanic cone is shown in Figure 4?
5. **Contrast:** How does the makeup of the volcanic cone in Figure 2 differ from the makeup of the volcanic cone in Figure 3?
6. **Contrast:** How does the makeup of the volcanic cone in Figure 2 differ from the makeup of the volcanic cone in Figure 4?

Critical Thinking *Answer each of the following in complete sentences.*

1. Explain how you could use observations to distinguish between a cinder cone and a shield cone.
2. **Contrast:** How does a mountain differ from a plateau?
3. How does a dike differ from a sill?
4. Which is likely to do more damage, an earthquake that occurs on land or an earthquake that occurs beneath the ocean? Explain.
5. **Predict:** What kind of damage is likely to be caused by a tsunami?

Finding Out More

1. Use library references to write a short biography on Charles Richter.
2. Observe an area where road cuts have been made. Draw a diagram of the area you observe. Label any synclines or anticlines.
3. Find out about the career of a volcanologist. Describe your findings to the class in an oral report.
4. Research the names of the 10 tallest mountains in the United States. Make a chart listing the mountains, their heights, and where they are located.
5. Using library references, find out about the 1985 eruption of the Nevada del Ruiz volcano in Colombia. Describe the effects of this eruption in a written report.

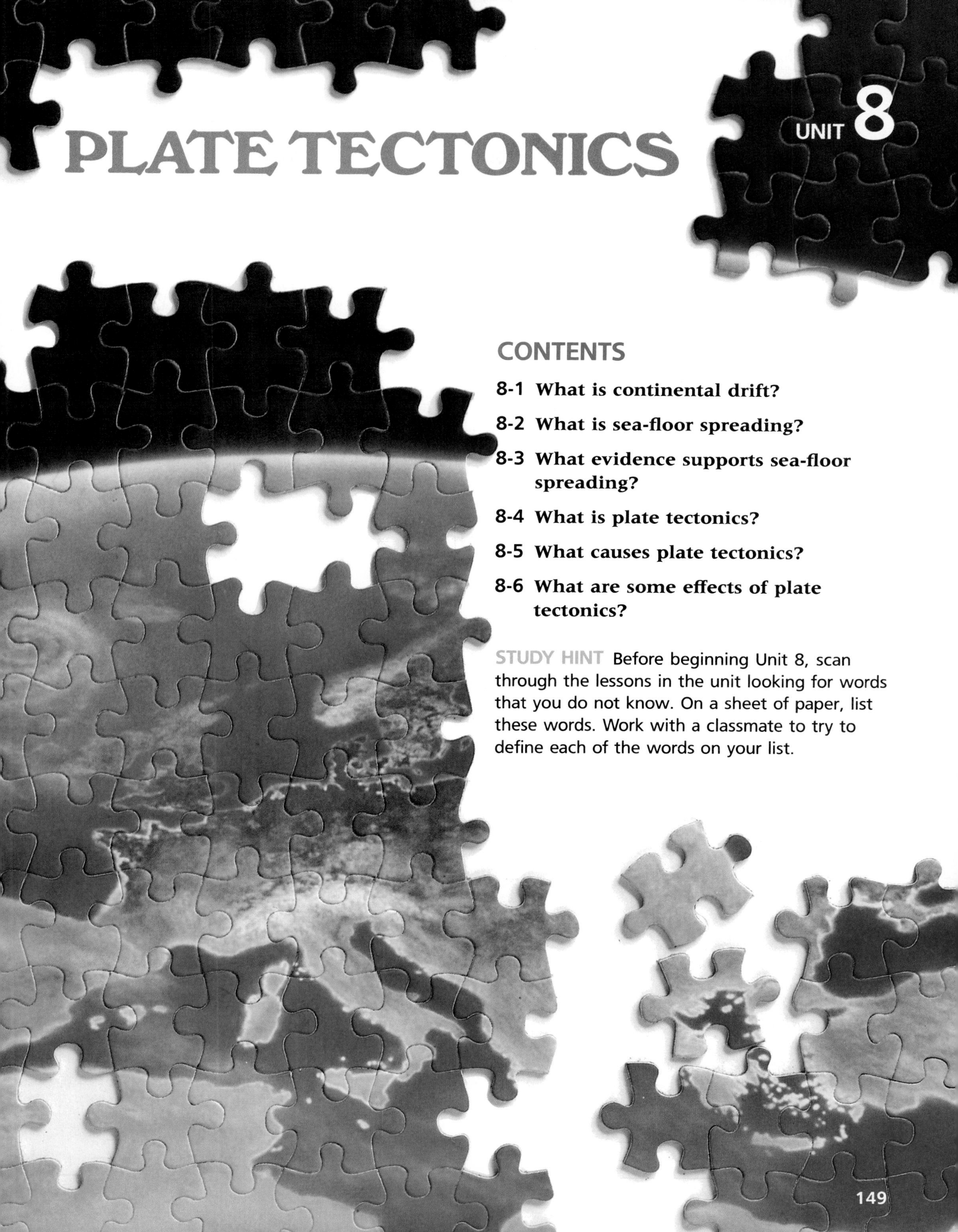

PLATE TECTONICS

UNIT 8

CONTENTS

STUDY HINT Before beginning Unit 8, scan through the lessons in the unit looking for words that you do not know. On a sheet of paper, list these words. Work with a classmate to try to define each of the words on your list.

8-1 What is continental drift?

Mesosaurus

Objective ▶ Explain continental drift and the evidence that supports the theory.

TechTerm

▶ **continental** (KAHNT-un-ent-ul) **drift:** idea that states the continents were once a giant landmass, and broke into pieces that moved to the positions they are in today

Continental Drift Most scientists think that millions of years ago there was one giant continent (KAHNT-un-ent). A continent is a large landmass. This giant continent had water all around it. Millions of years ago, the continent began to break apart. The pieces of the continent slowly drifted apart. They became today's seven continents.

The idea that the continents were once part of a giant landmass that split apart was stated by Alfred Wegener. Wegener was a German scientist. Wegener called the giant landmass Pangaea (pan-JEE-uh). He called his idea **continental** (KAHNT-un-ent-ul) **drift.**

▶ ***Identify:*** Who first stated the idea of continental drift?

A Giant Jigsaw Puzzle In the early 1900s, Wegener noticed that the continents seemed to fit together. Look at the shapes of the coastlines of South America and Africa on the map. The coastlines seem to fit together like jigsaw puzzle pieces. Other places can be found that might once have fitted together. The shapes of coastlines are only one clue that supports continental drift.

▶ ***Describe:*** How are coastlines on both sides of the Atlantic Ocean alike?

Fossil Evidence Fossils of once-living things provide clues that support continental drift. Some of these fossils have been found in places that are far apart. Wegener studied the fossils of Mesosaurus (meh-soh-SAWR-us). Mesosaurus fossils were found in Africa and in South America. Mesosaurus lived in fresh water. How could it swim across the salty Atlantic Ocean? Wegener concluded that the animal must have lived on one landmass. When the landmass broke apart, some of the animals were trapped on each part.

▶ ***Identify:*** What animal fossil is used to support continental drift?

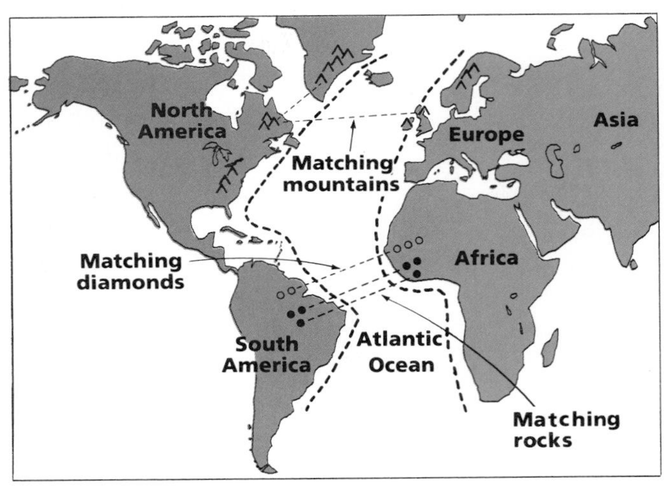

More Evidence Today, most scientists accept the idea of continental drift. Here are some reasons.

▶ Some mountain ranges on different continents seem to match. A mountain range along the eastern United States and Canada is similar to one in Greenland and northern Europe. On a model of Pangaea, the mountains seem to fit together as one long chain.

▶ The age and kind of rocks along the edge of one continent match rocks along the edge of another continent. Even the sizes of the diamonds in Brazil and West Africa are the same.

▶ ***Explain:*** How are mountain ranges used to support continental drift?

LESSON SUMMARY

- Most scientists think that millions of years ago there was one giant continent.
- The theory of continental drift states that Pangaea split apart to form today's continents.
- The coastline on one side of the Atlantic Ocean looks as though it may have once been joined to the land on the other side.
- Studies of fossils provide clues that support continental drift.
- Matching mountains and rocks on different continents support continental drift.

CHECK *Complete the following.*

1. What is a continent?
2. What is the theory of continental drift?
3. How do the shapes of different coastlines support continental drift?
4. List three things that scientists use to support the theory of continental drift?
5. Name two continents that seem to fit together.

APPLY *Complete the following.*

6. **Relate:** How does Pangaea fit into the theory of continental drift?
7. **Infer:** Fossils of a plant called *Glossopteris* have been found on three continents. They are Africa, Asia, and Australia. What might these fossils tell scientists about these continents?
8. Wegener stated the theory of continental drift in the early 1900s. Do you think most scientists accepted his theory? Explain your answer.

Skill Builder

▲ ***Researching and Modeling*** In his model showing continental drift, Wegener named continents, oceans, and seas. He used these names Pangaea, Panthalassa Laurasia, Gondwana, and Tethys. Use library references to find out what each of these names were used for. Then, draw models of what the earth looked like. Label the parts of the earth with these names.

ACTIVITY

MODELING PANGAEA

You will need a sheet of tracing paper, scissors, glue, and 2 sheets of construction paper.

1. Trace the continents shown on the map.
2. Glue the tracing onto a sheet of construction paper.
3. Carefully cut out the continents. You should have seven. **CAUTION: Be careful when using scissors.**
4. Arrange the pieces to form Pangaea. Glue the model of Pangaea on a sheet of construction paper.

Questions

1. Which continents seem to fit together?
2. ▲ **Model:** Label your model of Pangaea.
3. **Compare:** Why is the reconstruction of Pangaea like a jigsaw puzzle?

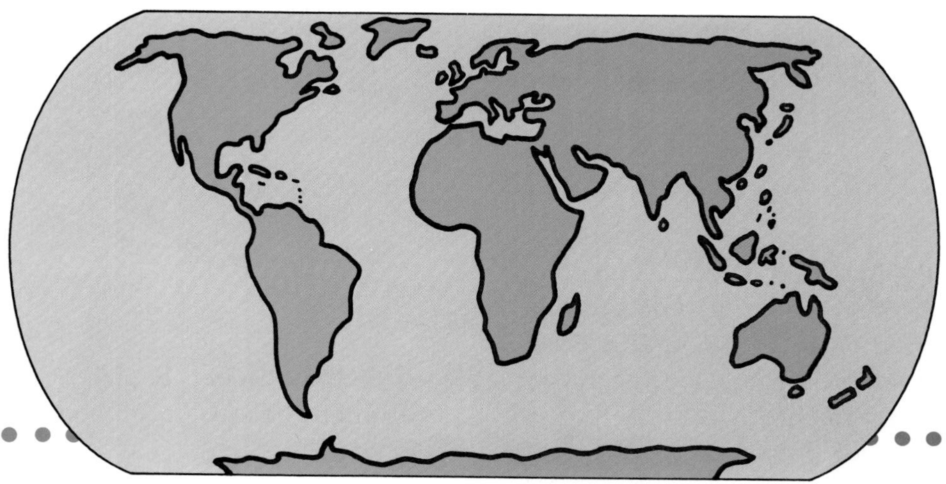

8-2 What is sea-floor spreading?

Objective ▶ Recognize that sea-floor spreading forms new oceanic crust.

TechTerms

- ▶ **mid-ocean ridge:** underwater mountain chain
- ▶ **rift valley:** deep crack running down the center of the mid-Atlantic ridge
- ▶ **sea-floor spreading:** process that forms new sea floor

Kinds of Crust There are two kinds of crust. One kind is oceanic (oh-shee-AN-ik) crust. This crust makes up the ocean floor. The other kind of crust is continental (KAHNT-un-ent-ul) crust. It makes up the earth's continents. Oceanic crust is made of material that is heavier and denser than continental crust.

▶ ***Name:*** What are the two kinds of crust?

Mid-ocean Ridges Some of the longest mountain ranges and the tallest mountains are under the ocean. These mountains form a chain 73,600-km long. The mountain chain is called the **mid-ocean ridge.** Some of its peaks are 3048 m above the ocean floor. In a few places, the peaks rise above the surface of the ocean. These peaks form islands. Iceland is a mountain peak of the Mid-Atlantic Ridge. The Mid-Atlantic Ridge runs down the middle of the Atlantic Ocean.

▶ ***Identify:*** What are the longest mountain ranges on the earth?

The Rift Valley In the late 1940s, scientists began to map the mid-ocean ridges. Along the Mid-Atlantic Ridge, they discovered a deep crack running down the center of the ridge. This deep crack is called a **rift valley.** Magma pouring out of the rift hardened and formed a broad valley with steep sides. Scientists discovered that a lot of earthquakes and volcanic activity take place along mid-ocean ridges.

▶ ***Define:*** What is a rift valley?

Formation of New Sea Floor Deep-sea drills have been used to bring up samples of oceanic crust. Scientists discovered that these samples were younger than samples of continental crust. The crust near a mid-ocean ridge was younger than the crust farther away. The youngest crust was in the center of the ridge.

At the mid-ocean ridges, magma, or molten rock, was rising through the crust. As the magma cooled, it formed new crust on both sides of the ridge. On both sides of the ridge, the sea floor was being pushed away. The sea floor was spreading apart at the ridges. New oceanic crust was being formed at the ridge, and pushing out the older crust next to it. Scientists called this process **sea-floor spreading.** Sea-floor spreading helped to explain continental drift.

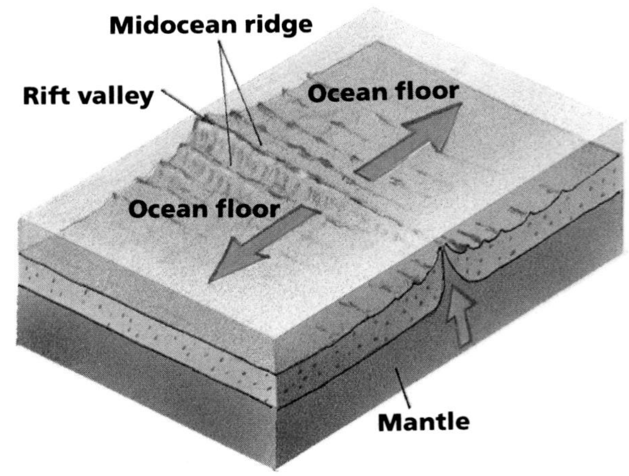

▶ ***Describe:*** What happens as magma rises through the crust at mid-ocean ridges?

LESSON SUMMARY

- The two kinds of crust are oceanic crust and continental crust.
- The longest mountain chain is the mid-ocean ridges.
- A rift valley is a deep crack running down the center of mid-ocean ridges.
- Oceanic crust near the mid-ocean ridge is younger than ocean crust farther away.
- Magma rising through the crust forming new crust on each side of the mid-ocean ridges, and pushing out older crust is the process called sea-floor spreading.

CHECK *Complete the following.*

1. Which kind of crust is made up of heavy, dense material?
2. What is the Mid-Atlantic Ridge?
3. What is the deep crack called that runs down the center of a mid-ocean ridge?
4. Where would scientists find the youngest crust on the ocean floor?

APPLY *Complete the following.*

5. **Model:** Draw a diagram that can be used to explain sea-floor spreading. Label your diagram.
6. **Infer:** Do you think Iceland is a volcanic island? Explain your answer.

Skill Builder

Modeling When you model, you use a copy or imitation of something to help you understand it. Make a model of sea-floor spreading by taping two sheets of red construction paper together along their short ends. Then push two desks together. Fold the sheets of construction paper together along the tape. Push the open ends of the construction paper through the crack between the tops of the desks until some paper falls on each side. Keep pushing up the paper. What does the crack between the two desks represent? What does the construction paper represent? How could you make your model more accurate?

SCIENCE CONNECTION

TUBE WORMS

While exploring the rift valley in the Pacific Ocean, scientists discovered chimneys rising from the ocean floor. What are these unusual structures?

The chimneys shoot out hot water. The water is heated by magma deep in the ocean's crust. Minerals dissolve in this hot water. When the hot water shoots out, it is cooled by the ocean water. The minerals separate from the water and form the chimneys around the openings, or vents.

Around the chimneys, scientists discovered an entire community of life, including giant tube worms. Some of these worms are more than three meters long. They have bright red plumes coming out of their tubes. They have no mouths or digestive systems. Instead, bacteria living inside the worms help them get food. Bacteria use chemicals from the vents to make food.

Other creatures in these communities include giant clams, giant white crabs, huge yellow mussels, white shrimp, and pink fish. This community does not use sunlight for energy.

8-3 What evidence supports sea-floor spreading?

Objective ▶ Describe some effects of sea-floor spreading.

TechTerms

- ▶ **trench:** long, V-shaped valley
- ▶ **subduction** (sub-DUKT-shun) **zone:** place where old crust is pushed down into a trench

Trenches On the ocean floor, there are long, V-shaped valleys called **trenches.** Trenches are the deepest parts of the oceans. They may be more than 10,000 meters deep. Most trenches are found in the Pacific Ocean. They are along the coasts of continents and near strings of islands. Many trenches are along the Ring of Fire.

Define: What is a trench?

Disappearing Crust The oldest rocks found on the ocean floor are only 175 million years old. Yet the earth is about 4.5 billion years old. Very old sea-floor rocks have not be found. As new crust is made in one place, it must be destroyed someplace else. If the crust were not being destroyed, the earth would be getting bigger. Scientists think that old crust on the ocean floor is pushed into ocean trenches. When the crust is pushed deep enough, the rocks of the crust melt. They become magma again.

State: About how old is the earth?

Subduction Zones The areas where the oceanic crust is pushed down into ocean trenches are called **subduction** (sub-DUKT-shun) **zones.** In these zones, the older oceanic crust is pushed down into the mantle. There is a lot of volcanic activity near subduction zones. There also are many earthquakes in these areas. The Ring of Fire around the Pacific Ocean has many subduction zones.

Define: What are subduction zones?

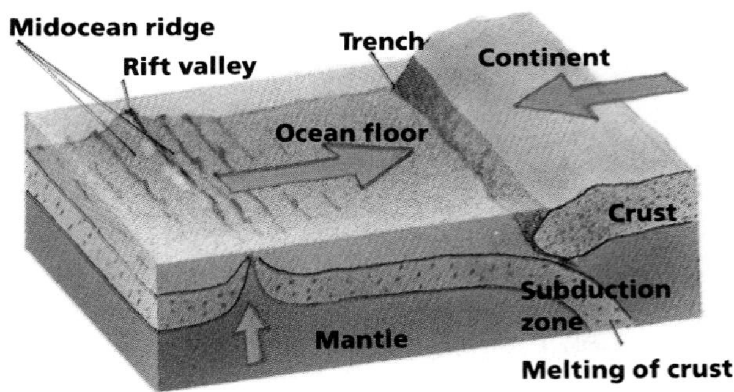

Evidence of Seafloor Spreading The earth is like a giant magnet. It has a magnetic field. If you have ever used a compass, you know that a compass always points north. Some minerals have magnetic properties. When rocks with these minerals form, the magnetic particles are fixed in position. They should point north. Scientists have discovered rocks with magnetic particles that pointed south. The earth's magnetic field changed through its history. North became south; and south became north.

On the sea floor there are stripes of rocks with magnetic particles pointing north and magnetic particles pointing south. Of course, you cannot see the stripes. They are detected by scientific instruments. On either side of the mid-Atlantic ridge, the pattern is the same. This was evidence that the ocean floor was being pushed out from both sides of the mid-Atlantic ridge.

State: What evidence shows the earth's magnetism has changed?

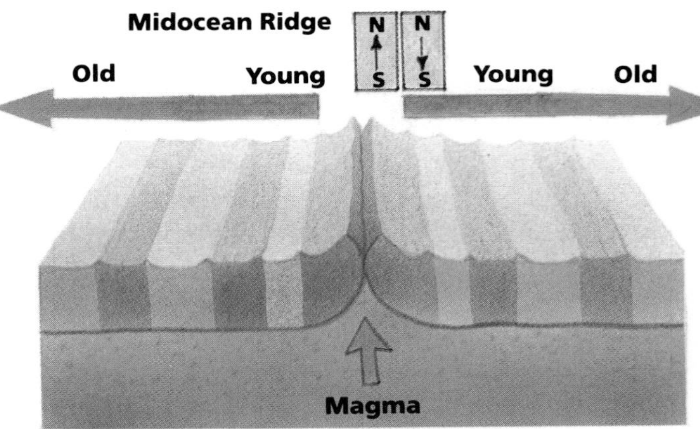

LESSON SUMMARY

- Long, V-shaped valleys on the ocean floor are called trenches.
- Scientists think that old oceanic crust is pushed into ocean trenches where it is changed to magma.
- Subduction zones are areas of the earth where oceanic crust is pushed into ocean trenches.
- The magnetic field of the earth has changed throughout the earth's history.
- The direction in which the magnetic particles in rocks point is evidence that the ocean floor is being pushed out from both sides of the mid-Atlantic ridge.

CHECK *Complete the following.*

1. The deepest parts of the ocean are _______ .
2. The oldest rocks found on the ocean floor are only _______ million years old.
3. A compass always points _______ .
4. Many earthquakes occur near _______ .

APPLY *Complete the following.*

5. **Calculate:** What is the difference in age between the oldest rocks on the ocean floor and the age of the earth?
6. **Model:** Mount Everest is 8848 meters above sea level. The deepest trench is the Challenger Deep. It is 11,033 meters deep. Draw a diagram on graph paper showing Mount Everest in the Challenger Deep. Let each line on the graph paper equal 500 meters.
7. **Infer:** Why is there a lot of volcanic and earthquake activity at subduction zones?
8. **Calculate:** Sea-floor spreading adds about 2.5 cm of new material to Iceland each year. How much wider will Iceland be in 150 years? Give your answer in meters.

InfoSearch

Read the passage. Ask two questions about the topic that you cannot answer from the information in the passage.

Challenger Deep The deepest place on the earth is a trench called Challenger Deep. Challenger Deep is 11,033 meters deep. It is located in the Pacific Ocean. Challenger Deep is part of the Marianas Trench. If you could put Mount Everest into Challenger Deep, it would be covered by 1.6 kilometers of water.

SEARCH: Use library references to find answers to your questions.

LOOKING BACK IN SCIENCE

THE *GLOMAR CHALLENGER*

The *Glomar Challenger* is a research ship. It was built in the late 1960s. The *Glomar Challenger* was built to explore the oceans. It has a giant drill and coring tool built on it. The drill can be used to drill up to 6000 meters into the ocean bottom. It can take cores of the ocean bottom as far down as 750 meters into the crust.

In 1968, the scientists on the *Glomar Challenger* took core and rock samples from both sides of the mid-Atlantic ridge. Deep-sea drills brought up many samples of crust from different places of sea floor. Scientists studied the fossils in the samples. They discovered that the rock samples close to the rift valley of the ridge had the youngest fossils. The fossils farther from the ridge were older. The oldest fossils were the farthest away. This fossil evidence supported the idea that new oceanic crust was forming along the ridge. The old crust was being pushed farther away.

8-4 What is plate tectonics?

Objectives ▶ Name some crustal plates. ▶ Describe the theory of plate tectonics.

TechTerms

- ▶ **crustal plates:** large pieces of the solid part of the earth
- ▶ **theory** (THEE-uh-ree): statement of an idea supported by evidence over a period of time
- ▶ **theory of plate tectonics** (tek-TAHN-iks): theory that states the earth's crust is broken into plates that float on the lower mantle

Crustal Plates Most scientists think that the crust of the earth and solid part of the mantle are broken into **crustal plates.** The mantle is the layer of the earth below the crust. These plates are made up of the solid part of the earth. Most plates are made up of oceanic and continental crust. There are seven main plates and about 13 smaller ones. The largest plate is the Pacific plate. The map shows the crustal plates.

▶ ***Calculate:*** About how many crustal plates have been identified?

Floating Plates Crustal plates float on the lower part of the mantle. This part of the mantle is made up of rock that flows like a thick liquid. The crustal plates float like rafts on a lake. The continents and oceans are carried on the plates like the passengers on a raft.

▶ ***Name:*** On which part of the earth do crustal plates float?

Theory of Plate Tectonics Today, scientists have a **theory** (THEE-uh-ree) to explain how the continents are drifting apart. A theory is a statement of an idea that has been supported by evidence over a period of time. Using information that supports seafloor spreading and continental drift, scientists stated the **theory of plate tectonics** (tek-TAHN-iks). The theory of plate tectonics combines the theories of continental drift and seafloor spreading. The theory of plate tectonics states how and why the continents move. It states that the earth's crust is broken into crustal plates. The continents move because they are carried along on the moving plates.

▶ ***Name:*** What two theories does plate tectonics combine?

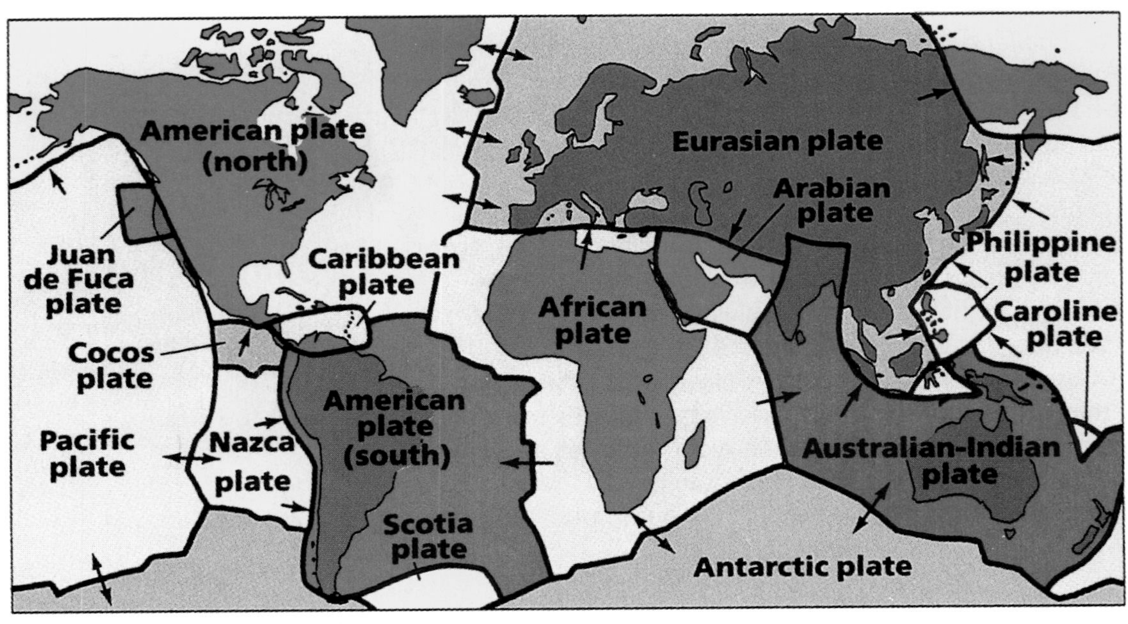

LESSON SUMMARY

- The crust of the earth and the upper solid part of the mantle are broken into crustal plates.
- Crustal plates float on the lower part of the mantle.
- The theory of plate tectonics states how and why the continents drift, or move.

CHECK *Complete the following.*

1. What layer of the earth is below the crust?
2. How many major crustal plates are there?
3. What is the largest crustal plate?
4. Describe the mantle rock on which plates float.
5. What is a theory?
6. What is the theory of plate tectonics?

APPLY *Complete the following.*

7. **Infer:** Since the continents drift, do you think the surface of the earth will look the same 50 million years from today? Explain your answer.
8. **Model:** Draw a picture of a lake with a raft with people on it. Label the parts of your picture with these terms: crustal plate; lower mantle; continents.

Use the map on page 156 to answer the following.

9. **Analyze:** On which plate does Australia float?
10. **Analyze:** On which plate does the United States float?
11. **Analyze:** Name three major plates and two smaller plates.

Skill Builder

Hypothesizing When you hypothesize, you suggest a solution to a problem based on known information. Look at the two maps below. Find the New Ocean. What would you name it? Notice that Europe, Asia, and Africa become one continent. What would you name the continent? Australia has joined with New Zealand and many other islands. What would you name this new continent? Why did you choose these names?

SCIENCE CONNECTION

FUTURE DRIFTING

The earth's crustal plates are still moving. Scientists estimate the plates move between one and five centimeters each year. In 100 million years, they think the earths' continents will look very different. Using computers, scientists can make models of how the earth will look in the future. The models show that the Atlantic Ocean will become bigger. Africa and Europe will collide. New mountain ranges will form. The Mediterranean Sea will disappear. North America will drift farther north and west. Many islands will become parts of larger continents.

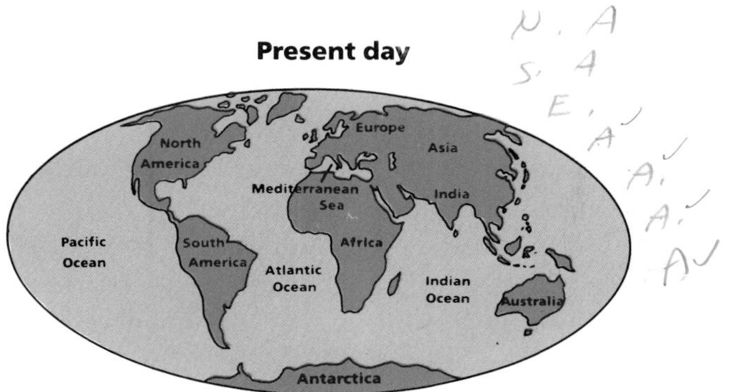

100 million years from now

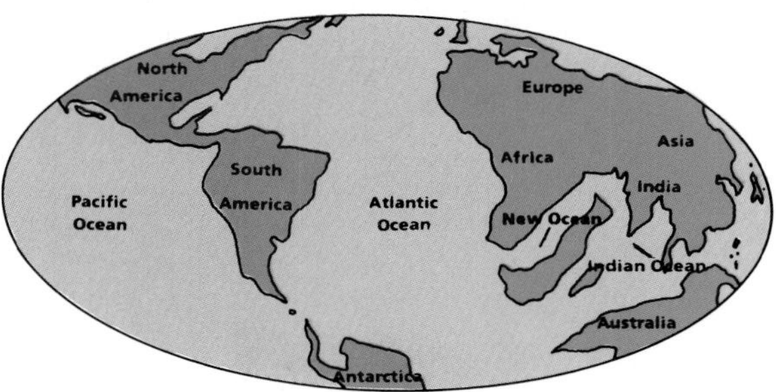

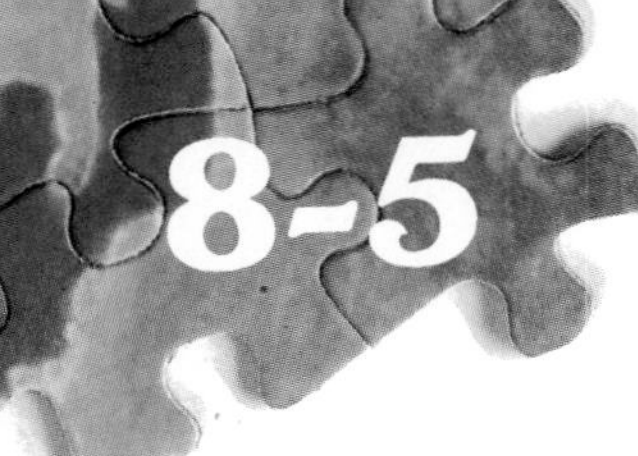

8-5 What causes plate tectonics?

Objective ▶ Describe how convection currents cause plate tectonics.

TechTerm

▶ **convection** (kuhn-VEK-shun) **current:** movement of a gas or liquid caused by changes in temperature

Convection Currents A **convection** (kuhn-VEK-shun) **current** is the movement of a gas or a liquid caused by differences in temperature. For example, warm air rises and cool air sinks to take its place. When you put a pan of water on the stove to boil, the water is heated by convection. The water at the bottom of the pan gets hot first. The hot water rises. Cool water at the top of the pan sinks.

▶ ***Define:*** What is a convection current?

Inside the Mantle Scientists think that giant convection currents in the earth's mantle cause the movement of crustal plates. The mantle rock close to the core, or center of the earth, is hot. The mantle rock farther from the core is cooler. The hot mantle rock rises. The cooler mantle rock sinks deeper into the mantle. As the cooler rock gets closer to the core, it heats up. The hot rock rises. This process repeats in an endless cycle. The crustal plates are carried along like packages on a moving conveyor belt.

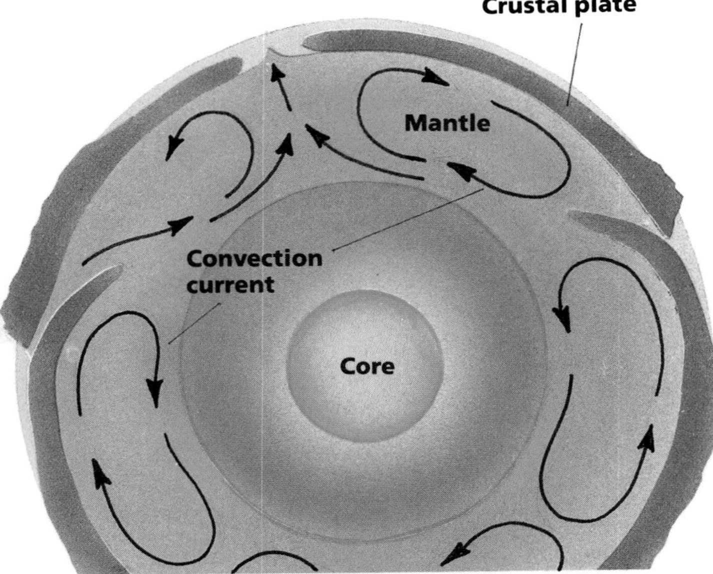

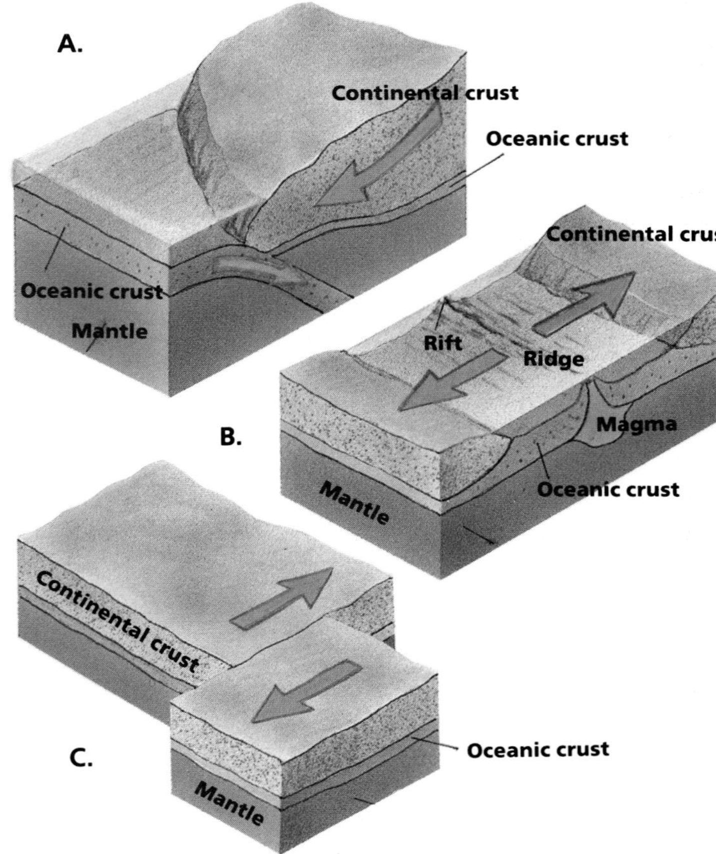

▶ ***State:*** What causes the movement of crustal plates?

The Restless Earth The crustal plates move in different ways. Some plates are moving toward each other. At these places, two plates hit each other. Sometimes the oceanic crust is pushed under continental crust. The oceanic crust is pushed into the mantle. Sometimes the plates crumple up. Other plates are moving apart. These plates are mostly in the oceans along rift valleys. In some places, two plates slide past each other. They do not move smoothly.

▶ ***List:*** What are three ways plates move?

LESSON SUMMARY

- A convection current is the movement of a gas or a liquid caused by differences in temperature.
- Scientists think that giant convection currents in the earth's mantle cause the movement of crustal plates.
- The crustal plates move toward each other, move apart, or slide past each other.

CHECK *Find the sentence in the lesson that answers each question. Then, write the sentence.*

1. Describe the movement of warm and cold air.
2. What do scientists think cause the movement of crustal plates?
3. Where is crustal rock heated inside the earth?
4. Where do most plates move apart?
5. What happens to two plates that move toward each other?

APPLY *Use the diagrams of plate movement to answer the following.*

6. Which diagram shows two plates moving away from each other?
7. **Analyze:** Which diagram shows subduction?
8. **Infer:** If railroad tracks were built over a place where two plates meet, such as diagram C, what would happen to the railroad tracks as the plates moved?

Skill Builder

Building Vocabulary The place where two plates meet is called a plate boundary. Names are used for each boundary. Use library references to find out the meaning of these terms: divergent, convergent, transform, constructive, and destructive. Plate boundaries are named using these terms. Match the name of the boundary to a description of what happens at each boundary.

ACTIVITY

MODELING A CONVECTION CURRENT

You will need a beaker, a clay triangle, 3 large paper clips, 2 small paper clips, pliers, water-color paint, and a heat source.

1. Place the clay triangle over the heat source.
2. Fill the beaker with cold water.
3. Use the pliers to bend the paper clips into the shapes shown.
4. Place a blob of water-color paint into each loop of the paper clips.
5. Carefully lower the 4 loops into the water. Your setup should look like the one shown.
6. Gently heat the beaker. **CAUTION: Be careful when working with a heat source.**
7. Observe what happens.

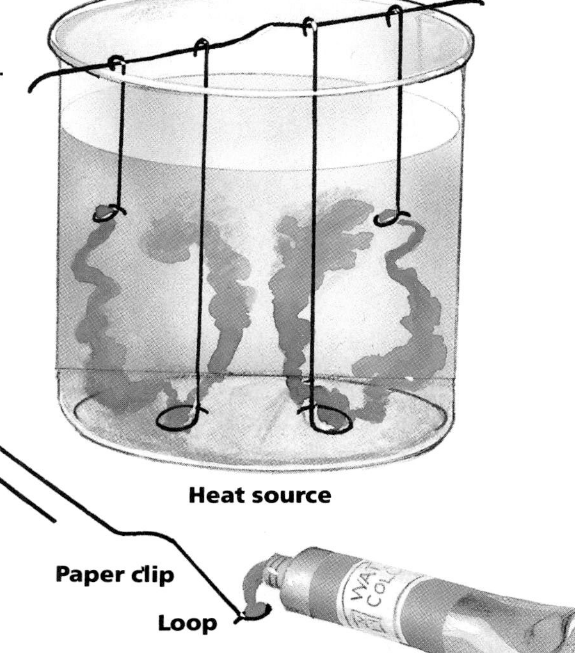

Questions

1. **Observe:** What do you observe?
2. **Model:** Draw a diagram of your setup. Draw arrows to show movement.
3. What does your model show?

8-6 What are some effects of plate tectonics?

Objective ▶ Explain how plate tectonics causes changes on the earth's surface.

TechTerms

- ▶ **hot spot:** place where magma reaches the surface within a crustal plate
- ▶ **magma chamber:** underground pocket of molten rock

Earthquakes In some areas, two crustal plates slide past each other. The San Andreas fault, in California, is one place where two plates are sliding past each other. Many earthquakes are caused by the movement of plates at a fault. The San Francisco earthquakes of 1906 and 1989 were caused by the movement of crustal plates at the San Andreas fault.

▶ ***Name:*** What is caused by two plates sliding past each other at a fault?

Mountain Building When two plates collide, oceanic crust may be pushed down under continental crust. When this happens, the continental crust crumples. It is pushed upward to form new mountains. Mountains along the western coasts of North and South America were formed in this way. They are young mountains and are still rising.

Two crustal plates carrying continents may collide without one plate being pushed down under the other. The Himalaya Mountains were formed in this way. The plate carrying India collided with the Eurasian plate. The edges of the two plates buckled upward, forming the Himalayas.

▶ ***Identify:*** What mountain range was formed by the collision of two continents?

Volcanoes At subduction zones, friction between the oceanic crust and the continental crust produces a great deal of heat. The heat melts the rocks in the crust, forming magma. The magma collects in underground pockets called **magma chambers.** The magma is hotter than the surrounding rock. It works its way to the surface by melting the solid rock around it. Magma also moves through cracks in the rock. When the magma reaches the surface, a volcano forms. Mt. St. Helens and Mt. Hood are volcanoes that formed in this way.

▶ ***Describe:*** How does magma reach the surface?

Islands Some islands are formed by plate tectonics. The Hawaiian Islands are a chain of volcanic islands in the Pacific Ocean. The islands formed one after the other as the Pacific plate moved over a **hot spot.** A hot spot is a place where magma works its way to the surface within a crustal plate. The islands that are farthest west are the oldest. The islands to the east are the youngest. The big island of Hawaii is now over the hot spot. It is still being formed.

▶ ***Describe:*** How were the Hawaiian Islands formed?

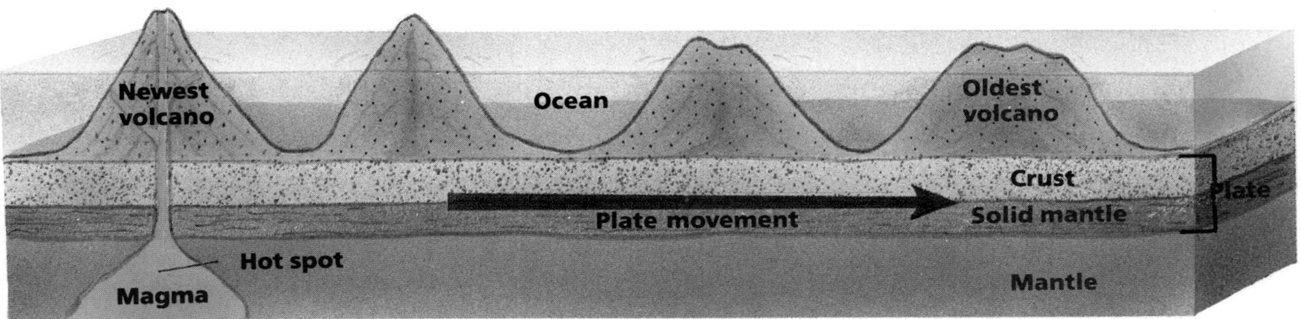

LESSON SUMMARY

- Earthquakes often occur where two crustal plates slide past each other.
- When two plates collide, sometimes the crusts crumple to form mountains.
- Volcanoes often form near subduction zones because the friction between the moving crustal plates produces a great deal of heat.
- Some islands are formed by plate tectonics when crustal plates move over hot spots.

CHECK *Match each event to its cause.*

Cause

1. Plates sliding past each other
2. Collision of two plates
3. Subduction zone
4. Hot spots

Event

a. Mount St. Helens eruption
b. Hawaiian Islands
c. Himalaya Mountains
d. San Francisco Earthquake, 1906

Complete the following.

5. What is a hot spot?
6. What is a magma chamber?
7. Explain how the Himalayas were formed.

APPLY *Use the diagram of hot spots on page 160 to answer the following.*

8. **Infer:** If the plate keeps moving to the right, what will happen to the newest volcano?
9. If the diagram represents the Hawaiian Islands, what island represents the newest volcano?
10. Which volcano could still erupt?

Skill Builder

Inferring When you infer you form a conclusion based upon facts and not direct observation. Volcanoes form over hot spots or near subduction zones. Find out the location of the six volcanoes listed. Decide whether each volcano was formed by a subducting crust or a hot spot. Volcanoes: Mount Hood; Mount Kilimanjaro; Mount Vesuvius; Mount Fuji; Mount Pelee; Mount Erebus.

ACTIVITY

MODELING PLATE MOVEMENTS

You will need clay, a sheet of notebook paper, and 3 sheets of heavy construction paper.

1. Flatten the clay into two long rectangles.
2. Place each rectangle on a different sheet of construction paper. Line the short edge of the clay along the short edge of the paper.
3. Push the pieces of clay together. Observe what happens.
4. Repeat steps 1-3 several times.
5. Lay a sheet of construction paper and a sheet of notebook paper edge to edge on a smooth surface. Be sure the edges touch.
6. Push the papers together. Observe what happens.
7. Repeat steps 5-6 several times.

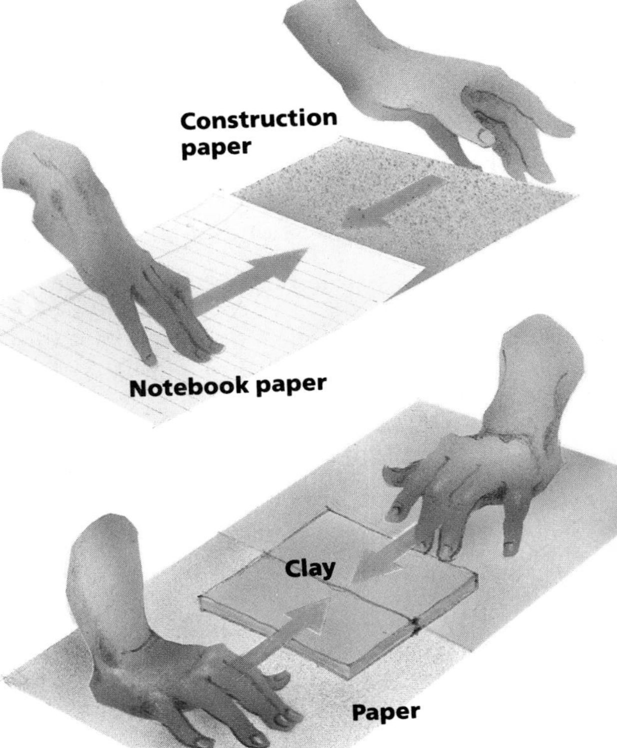

Questions

1. **Relate:** What do the pieces of clay represent?
2. What did you form?
3. What does the construction paper represent in step 5?
4. What does the notebook paper represent?
5. **Model:** Use your model to explain how mountains form and how crust is subducted.

UNIT 8 Challenges

STUDY HINT Before you begin the Unit Challenges, review the TechTerms and Lesson Summary for each lesson in this unit.

TechTerms

convection current (158)
continental drift (150)
crustal plates (156)
hot spot (160)
magma chamber (160)
mid-ocean ridge (152)
rift valley (152)
sea-floor spreading (152)
subduction zone (154)
theory (156)
theory of plate tectonics (156)
trench (154)

TechTerm Challenges

Matching *Write the TechTerm that matches each description.*

1. underwater mountain chain
2. process that forms new sea floor
3. long, V-shaped valley
4. large pieces of the solid part of the earth
5. statement of an idea supported by evidence over a period of time
6. underground pocket of molten rock
7. movement of a gas or liquid caused by changes in temperature
8. deep crack running down the center of the mid-Atlantic ridge

Fill-in *Write the TechTerm that best completes each statement.*

1. The place where magma reaches the surface within a crustal plate is called a ______ .
2. Wegoner's idea that the continents were once part of a giant land mass that broke apart and moved to the positions they are in today is the ______ .
3. The place where old crust is pushed down into a trench is a ______ .
4. The idea that the earth's crust is broken into pieces that float on the lower mantle is the ______ .

Content Challenges

Multiple Choice *Write the letter of the term that best completes each statement.*

1. Wegener called the giant land mass that later formed the seven continents
   a. Mesosaurus. **b.** Pangaea. **c.** Gondwana. **d.** Tethys.
2. The oldest rocks found on the ocean floor are
   a. 175 million years old. **b.** 175 billion years old. **c.** 4.5 million years old. **d.** 4.5 billion years old.
3. Scientists estimate that the age of the earth is
   a. 175 million years. **b.** 175 billion years. **c.** 4.5 million years. **d.** 4.5 billion years.
4. The deepest parts of the ocean floor are
   a. rift valleys. **b.** trenches. **c.** mid-ocean ridges. **d.** subduction zones.
5. The largest crustal plate is the
   a. Atlantic plate. **b.** Pangaea plate. **c.** Pacific plate. **d.** Marianas plate.
6. Crustal plates float on the lower part of the
   a. core. **b.** crust. **c.** mantle. **d.** ocean.

7. Crustal plates sliding past each other are most likely to cause
   a. an earthquake. **b.** a mountain to form. **c.** a volcano. **d.** an island.
8. When continental crust is pushed upward
   a. an earthquake forms. **b.** a mountain forms. **c.** a volcano forms. **d.** an island forms.
9. An animal fossil that is used to support the theory of continental drift is
   a. Tethys. **b.** Gondwana. **c.** Mesosaurus. **d.** Panthalassa Laurasia.
10. In a model of Pangaea, the coastline of South America seems to fit together with the coastline of
   a. Australia. **b.** northern Asia. **c.** North America. **d.** Africa.

True/False *Write true if the statement is true. If the statement is false, change the underlined term to make the statement true.*

1. Peaks of mid-ocean ridges that rise above the surface of the ocean form continents.
2. Earthquakes and volcanic activity often take place along mid-ocean ridges.
3. A deep crack running down the center of a mid-ocean ridge is a trench.
4. The oldest crust on the ocean floor is found in the center of mid-ocean ridges.
5. The deepest parts of the ocean are trenches.
6. The Ring of Fire around the Atlantic Ocean has many subduction zones.
7. A compass always points north.
8. Continental crust is younger than oceanic crust.
9. The theory that states that the earth's crust is broken into plates that float on the lower mantle is the theory of continental drift.
10. Scientists have identified about 20 crustal plates.
11. The theory of plate tectonics was first stated by Alfred Wegener.
12. The movement of crustal plates is caused by convection currents.
13. The Hawaiian Islands formed when the Atlantic plate moved over a hot spot.
14. Magma that works its way to the earth's surface forms an earthquake.
15. The Himalaya mountains were formed by colliding crustal plates.

Understanding the Features

Reading Critically *Use the feature reading selections to answer the following. Page numbers for the features are shown in parentheses.*

1. What organisms help tube worms get their food? (153)
2. From what source do tube worms get their energy? (153)
3. What is the *Glomar Challenger?* (155)
4. How did fossil evidence collected by the *Glomar Challenger* support the idea that new oceanic crust was forming along the mid-Atlantic ridge? (155)
5. **Infer:** What will happen to the size of the Pacific Ocean if the scientists' prediction about future drifting are correct? (157)

Concept Challenges

Critical Thinking *Answer each of the following in complete sentences.*

1. How is the San Andreas fault related to the theory of plate tectonics?
2. How does the activity at subduction zones balance the activity at the mid-ocean ridges?
3. How could mineral deposits formed along the mid-ocean ridge now be on land?
4. How does the theory of plate tectonics combine the idea of continental drift and sea-floor spreading?
5. How did the discovery of rocks with magnetic particles support the idea of sea-floor spreading?

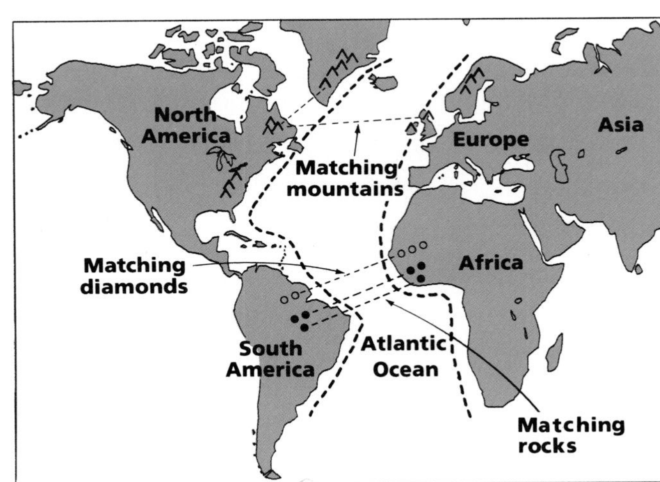

Understanding a Diagram *Use the diagram to answer each of the following.*

1. What are two continents that have mountain ranges that match?
2. What evidence on the continents of South America and Africa supports continental drift?
3. How does the evidence shown in the diagram support the idea of continental drift?
4. How do the coastlines of South America and Africa support the idea of continental drift?

Finding Out More

1. Use library references to write a short biography of Alfred Wegener.
2. Observe an area in your neighborhood where road cuts have been made. Examine the rocks on both sides of the road. In an oral report, describe how the rocks on each side are the same and how they are different. Explain what evidence you could use to support the idea that the rocks had once been connected even if they were very far apart.
3. Research the development of SONAR. Write your findings in a report. Include a description of how earth scientists use sonar to study the ocean floor.
4. Find out the meanings of the term asthenosphere. In a brief report, explain how the asthenosphere fits into the theory of plate tectonics.

THE ROCK RECORD

UNIT 9

CONTENTS

STUDY HINT Before beginning Unit 9, write the title of each lesson on a sheet of paper. Below each title, write a short paragraph explaining what you think each lesson is about.

9-1 What are fossils?

Objective ▶ Describe how different kinds of fossils formed.

TechTerms

- ▶ **cast:** mold that has filled with sediments
- ▶ **fossil** (FOSS-il): remain or trace of a living thing that lived long ago
- ▶ **mold:** cavity, or opening, in a rock that has the shape of an extinct organism

Fossils Have you ever gone to a natural history museum? If you have, you probably saw many **fossils** (FOSS-ilz). Fossils are the remains, or traces, of organisms (OWR-guh-niz-umz) that lived long ago. Organisms are living things. A fossil can be a bone, a footprint, or a shell. A fossil can even be the body of an extinct (ik-STINKT) organism. Extinct organisms are organisms that once lived on the earth, but are no longer found alive. Dinosaurs are extinct organisms. Remains of dinosaurs have been found in many places.

Observe: How many extinct organisms are shown on pages 166-167?

Fossils in Rocks Most fossils are found in sedimentary rocks that once were under water. Fossils take millions of years to form. Only dead organisms that are buried quickly or are protected from decay become fossils. A fossil begins to form when an organism is buried by sediment soon after it dies. The soft parts of the organism decay. Only the hard parts, such as shells and bones, are left. The sediments harden into rock. The organism is now preserved, or kept, as a fossil.

Name: In what kind of rock are most fossils found?

Molds and Casts Two types of fossils are **molds** and **casts.** Molds form when an organism is buried by sediments, and the sediments change into rock. The organism decays, and leaves a cavity, or opening, in the rock. The cavity is a mold. Sometimes, the mold fills with sand or mud. The sand or mud hardens and a cast is formed.

Analyze: Study the fossils in Figure 1. Which is the mold? Which is the cast?

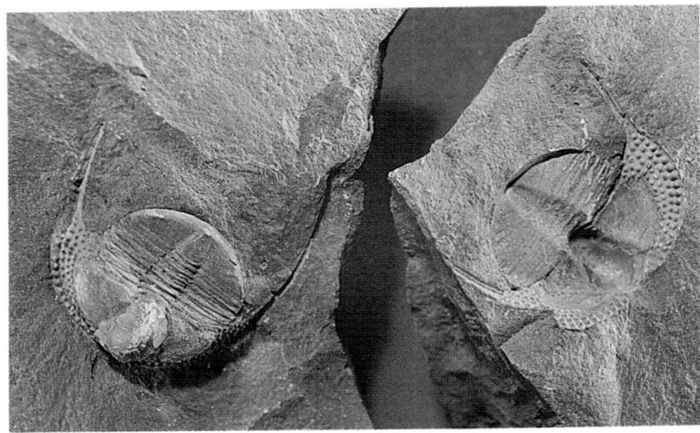

Figure 1

Imprints Some fossils are imprints. Imprints usually are made from the soft parts of organisms. Scientists have found many leaf and fish imprints. Some leaf imprints even show the veins of the leaf. Footprints also are imprints. They were made when an animal stepped into soft mud. The mud hardened, and the footprint was preserved.

Describe: What is an imprint?

Figure 2

LESSON SUMMARY

- Most fossils are the remains, or traces, of organisms that are now extinct.
- Fossils form in sedimentary rock.
- Molds and casts are two kinds of fossils.
- Some fossils are imprints of footprints, fishes, and leaves.

CHECK *Answer the following.*

1. List three kinds of fossils.
2. Which kind of fossil is a dinosaur footprint?
3. What is a fossil?

APPLY *Answer the following.*

4. How do scientists know that dinosaurs once lived on the earth?
5. **Hypothesize:** Igneous rocks are formed when molten rock hardens. Why would fossils probably not be found in igneous rocks?
6. **Predict:** Which of the following organisms would most likely be found as a fossil? Why? **a.** clam shell **b.** ancient dragonfly **c.** ancient worm

InfoSearch

Read the passage. Ask two questions about the topic that you cannot answer from the information in the passage.

Petrified Fossils Sometimes fossils are preserved by petrification (pe-truh-fi-KAY-shun). To petrify means to turn into stone. Many of the hard parts of dead plants and animals have been petrified. Minerals dissolved in groundwater replace the original parts of the plant or animal atom by atom. The minerals then harden, and turn to rock. An exact copy of the plant or animal is left.

SEARCH: Use library references to find answers to your questions.

ACTIVITY

MAKING FOSSILS

You will need 3 large paper cups, clay, a small object such as a shell, a key, or a coin, plaster of Paris, petroleum jelly.

1. Press some clay into each of two paper cups so that the clay is 2-3 cm high in each cup. Do not tear the cups.
2. Push a small object down into the clay of one cup. Then carefully remove the object.
3. Coat the object with petroleum jelly. Very lightly press the object into the clay of the second cup.
4. Prepare the plaster of Paris according to the directions.
5. Pour some of the plaster into each cup. Let the cups stand overnight. After the plaster hardens, tear away the cups. Remove the clay from the plaster.

Questions

1. **Observe:** Describe the two fossils.
2. How are the two fossils alike? How are they different?
3. **Analyze:** Which fossil is the mold? Which is the cast? How do you know?

9-2 How were entire organisms preserved?

Objective ▶ Describe different ways entire organisms were preserved as fossils.

TechTerm

▶ **amber:** hardened tree sap

Fossils in Ice You probably know that freezing helps preserve things by preventing decay. Many food products are frozen to help preserve them. Some extinct animals have been preserved by freezing. The bodies of 50 wooly, elephantlike animals called mammoths (MAM-uths) were found frozen in soil and ice in Siberia and Alaska. These animals had hair and skin on them. Furry rhinoceroses (ry-NAHS-ur-us-es) also have been found.

Identify: What is a mammoth?

Fossils in Tar The remains of animals also have been found in pits of thick, sticky tar. Tar for paving streets is taken from tar pits. Tar pits often were covered with water. Animals that came to the tar pits to drink the water, were trapped in the tar. Other animals came to the tar pits to eat the trapped animals. These animals also became trapped. The animals sank into the tar, and were preserved.

Hundreds of thousands of bones from extinct organisms have been found in tar pits. In the LaBrea Tar Pits in southern California, the bones of animals such as saber-toothed cats have been found. The bones of extinct camels, wolves, vultures, and bison also have been found in these tar pits. In Poland, entire furry rhinoceroses have even been found in tar pits.

Locate: Where are the LaBrea Tar Pits?

Fossils in Amber Flies, bees, wasps, and other insects have been found preserved in hardened tree sap. Hardened tree sap is called **amber.** A clear, sticky sap flows from some kinds of trees. Millions of years ago, insects were trapped in the sticky sap. More sap covered the insects. The sap hardened. The insects, including their wings and legs, were perfectly preserved in the amber.

Define: What is amber?

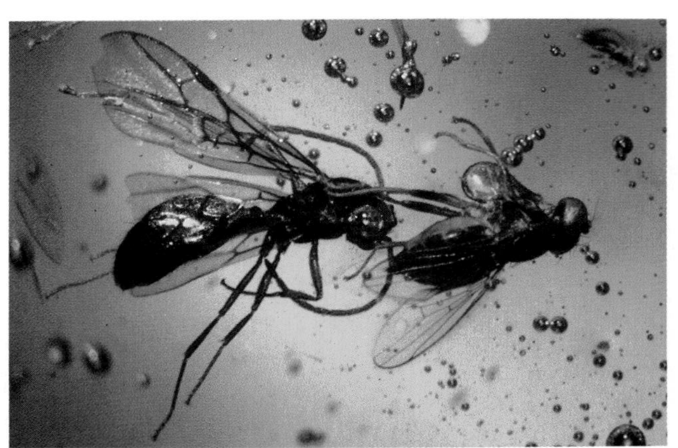

LESSON SUMMARY

- Some extinct organisms have been preserved in frozen soil or ice.
- Animals trapped in tar pits were preserved in them.
- Many different kinds of animal bones have been preserved in tar pits.
- Insects are perfectly preserved in amber.

CHECK *Complete the following.*

1. Name the three substances which help to preserve the remains of organisms.
2. Name two animals found preserved in frozen soil and ice.

For each of the extinct organisms listed, name the most likely way in which it was preserved. Use the terms ***ice, tar,*** *or* ***amber.***

3. wasp
4. vulture
5. camel
6. ant
7. mammoth
8. saber-toothed tiger

APPLY *Write a description of what is happening in the drawing below.*

Skill Builder

Researching When you research, you gather information about a topic. Use reference materials in the library. Find out about an extinct animal that you are interested in. In an oral report, explain to the class when the animal lived, where it lived, and when it became extinct. If possible, show the class a drawing of the animal.

LEISURE ACTIVITY

FOSSIL COLLECTING

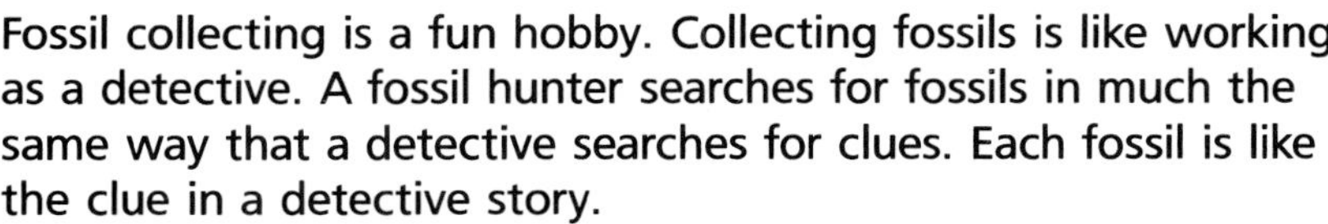

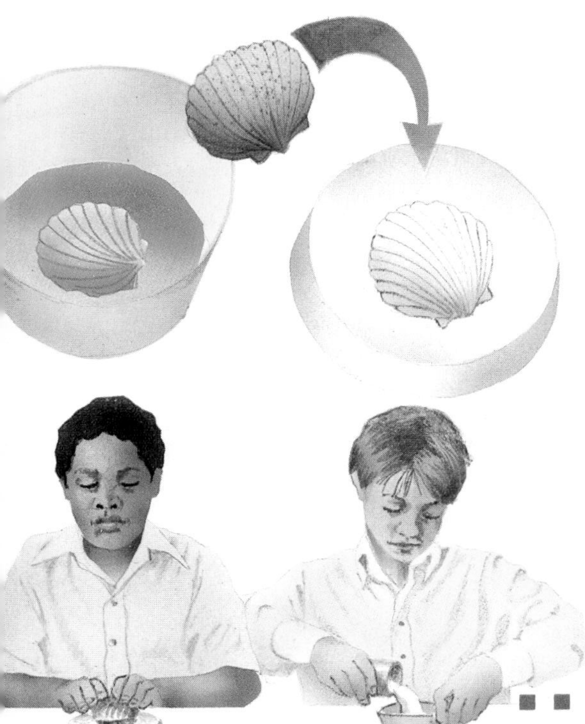

Fossil collecting is a fun hobby. Collecting fossils is like working as a detective. A fossil hunter searches for fossils in much the same way that a detective searches for clues. Each fossil is like the clue in a detective story.

You can go to special places, such as quarries, to hunt for fossils. When you go fossil hunting, bring along a small hammer, a small chisel, and a collecting bag, such as a knapsack, in which to put your fossil discoveries. Take along some newspaper in which to wrap your fossils. You also should have some labels and a pen. Label your fossils with the place where you found the fossils and the date. If you can identify the fossil, write its name on the label.

Some fossil collectors buy fossils from small shops that specialize in fossils and minerals. When they get their fossils home, they may place each fossil in its own small box. Fossil collectors often use a magnifying glass to observe and identify their fossils. Once you know the name of the fossil, you can use books to find out more about the organism from which your fossil formed.

9-3 What are fossil fuels?

Objective ▶ Describe how coal, oil, and natural gas formed.

TechTerm

- ▶ **fossil fuels** (FEWLS): natural fuels that come from the remains of living things

Fossil Fuels Most of the energy that you use comes from **fossil fuels** (FEWLS). Fossil fuels are natural fuels that come from the remains of living things. A fuel is a substance that gives off energy when it is burned. A fuel may be a solid, a liquid, or a gas. Coal and natural gas are fossil fuels. The liquid fuel, petroleum (puh-TRO-lee-um), also is a fossil fuel.

Infer: Which fossil fuel is a solid?

Hydrocarbons Fossil fuels are made up mostly of hydrocarbons (hy-druh-KAR-buns). Hydrocarbons are compounds made up of hydrogen and carbon. Hydrocarbons contain energy. The energy was obtained from sunlight by plants and animals that lived millions of years ago. When hydrocarbons are burned, they give off this energy as light and heat.

Name: What two forms of energy are given off when hydrocarbons are burned?

Forming Coal Coal is formed in swamps. Swamps are areas of shallow water with a lot of plant life. When the plants in the swamps die, they are covered by water and sediments, such as mud. Bacteria, pressure, and heat slowly cause chemical changes to take place in the plants. After many, many years, the decaying plant material changes to peat. Peat is the first stage in coal formation. After millions of years, peat changes into soft coal. Very high heat and pressure change soft coal into hard coal. Soft and hard coal are mostly carbon, so they give off a lot of heat when they burn.

Analyze: What are the three types of coal?

Forming Oil and Gas Geologists think that petroleum, or crude oil, and natural gas formed from decaying sea plants and animals. When these sea plants and animals died, they were covered with sediments. The sediments changed into sedimentary rock. Just like coal, bacteria, heat, and pressure helped to form petroleum and natural gas. Petroleum moved with water through the cracks and holes in rock. When the petroleum reached a rock layer it could not pass through, the petroleum and water began to collect. Petroleum is usually found in oil pools. Oil pools are usually found in rock layers of shale or sandstone. The petroleum floats on water. If natural gas is formed, it is on top of the petroleum. To get to the crude oil and natural gas, it is necessary to drill into the earth's crust.

List: What are three names for liquid fossil fuel?

LESSON SUMMARY

- Petroleum, coal, and natural gas are fossil fuels.
- When hydrocarbons are burned, they give off energy as light and heat.
- Coal was formed from decaying plants by bacteria, heat, and pressure.
- Oil and natural gas are formed from decaying sea plants and animals by bacteria, heat, and pressure.

CHECK *Answer the following.*

1. What compounds are found in fossil fuels?
2. Name three fossil fuels.
3. What three things act on decaying organisms to help form fossil fuels?
4. In what kind of rock layers would you most likely find petroleum and natural gas?

APPLY *Complete the following.*

5. **Infer:** Why are coal, petroleum, and natural gas called fossil fuels?
6. What is the source of the energy stored in hydrocarbons?
7. **Infer:** Why is natural gas found above the petroleum in an oil deposit?

Skill Builder

Reading a Pictograph A pictograph is a graph that uses a picturelike symbol to show an idea. Use the pictograph to answer the questions.

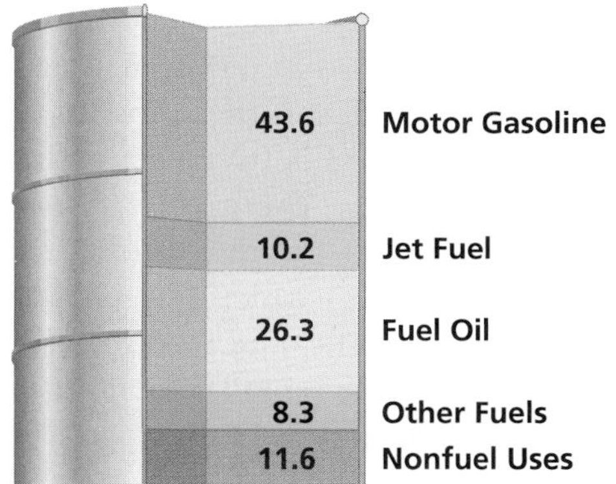

1. List five products that are made from petroleum.
2. Place the uses of petroleum in order from greatest use to least use.
3. What substance is most petroleum used for?
4. What percentage of petroleum is used to make all fuels?

CAREER IN EARTH SCIENCE

MINING INSPECTOR

Imagine putting on a hard hat with a flashlight attached to the front. Then, you go deep into a coal mine to check the structure of the mine. This is one of the jobs of a mining inspector. Mining inspectors work in different kinds of mines. They may work in rock quarries or metal mines.

Mine inspectors check mines for poison or explosive gases. They make sure safety and health rules are being followed. Mine inspectors prepare reports about their findings. They then make sure that any safety or health problems are corrected. Some mine inspectors also teach miners about safety and first aid. To find a job as a mine inspector, you must have a high school diploma. You can enter the field as an apprentice and get on-the-job training. You must have experience working in mines or have four years of related education after high school to get a job as a mine inspector.

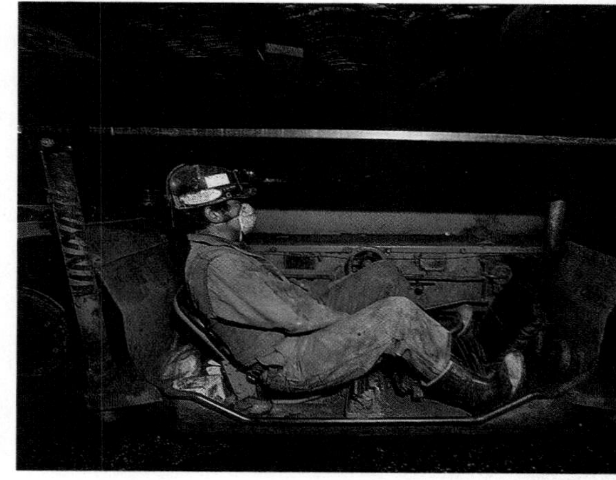

9-4 Why do scientists study fossils?

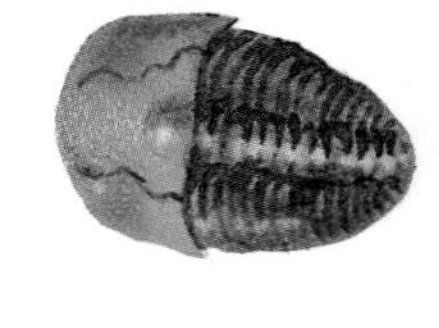

Figure 1 Trilobites

Objective ▶ Understand how fossils are clues to the earth's history.

Clues to Living Things Fossils show that many kinds of organisms lived at different times in the earth's history. Many of these organisms are extinct. Dinosaurs lived between 65 million and 100 million years ago. There were hundreds of kinds of dinosaurs, but not one dinosaur lives on the earth today. Other extinct animals are saber-toothed cats, giant sloths, and trilobites (TRY-loh-bites). Trilobites were small, shelled animals. There were many different kinds of trilobites.

▶ ***Name:*** What are some extinct animals that are preserved as fossils?

Clues to the Past Fossils show that the earth's climate and surface have changed. Fossils of alligatorlike animals have been found in Canada. Today, alligators live in warm climates. The fossils in Canada indicate that at some time in the earth's history, Canada had a warmer climate then it does today. Fossil ferns have been found in Antarctica. The fern fossils indicate that Antarctica was once very warm. Today, Antarctica is covered with ice and snow. Coral fossils have been found in the Arctic. In 1835, fossils of ocean animals were found in the Andes Mountains in South America. The Andes are more than 4000 m above sea level. Scientists infer that this land was once covered by an ocean.

▶ ***Compare:*** Based on fossil records, describe the climate of Canada millions of years ago and today.

Clues to Changes Fossils show that living things have changed over time. For example, many fossils of horses have been found. These fossils show changes in the animals' size and the number of toes. Scientists have found fossils of a four-toed horse that was about the size of a large cat. Fossils of horses also show changes in teeth and in the size and shape of the legs. Today, horses have one large hoof and are quite large. Other fossils show that animals such as elephants, giraffes, and camels also are related to animals that are now extinct.

▶ ***Explain:*** How do scientists infer that the horse has changed during millions of years?

Figure 2 Fossil record of horses

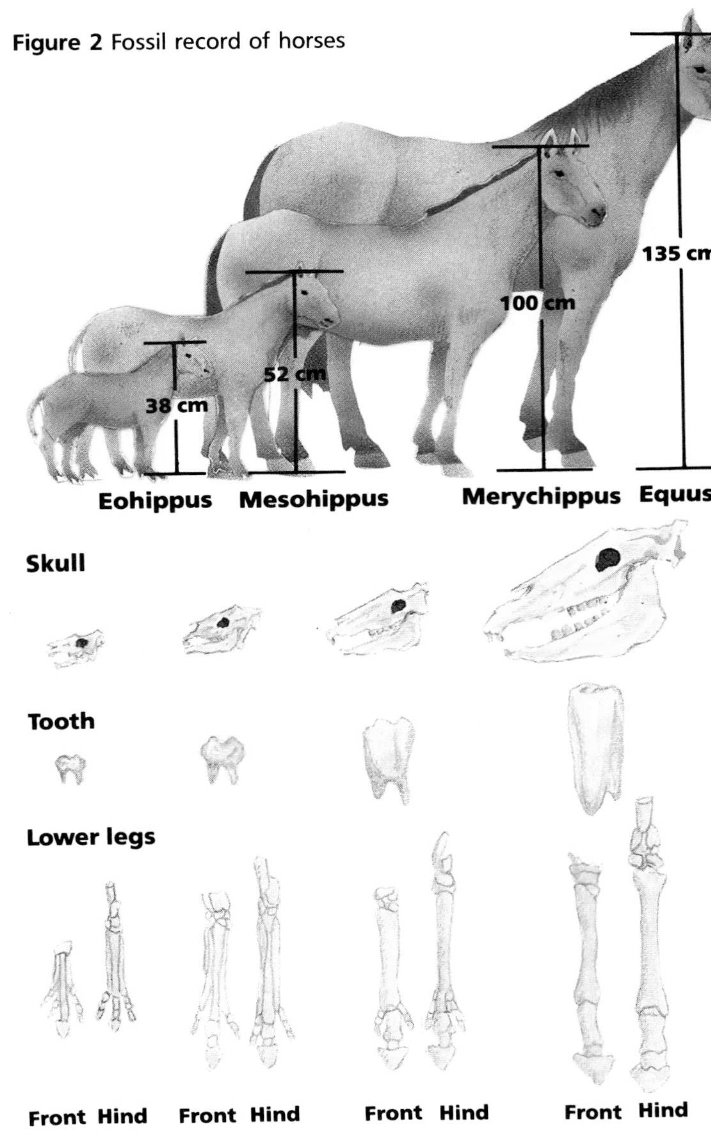

LESSON SUMMARY

- Fossils show that many living things have become extinct.
- Fossils show that the earth's climate and surface have changed over millions of years.
- Fossils show that some living things have changed over millions of years.

CHECK *Write an "E" for each organism that is extinct. Write an "N" for each organism that is living on the earth today.*

1. mastodon
2. saber-toothed cat
3. horse
4. alligator
5. trilobite
6. elephant

Answer the following.

7. What do fossils tell scientists about the earth's surface and climate?

8. What do fossils tell scientists about living things?

APPLY *Use the diagram of the fossil record of the horse on page 172 to answer the questions.*

9. Observe: How many toes did the earliest horse have?

10. Observe: Which horse has the largest skull?

11. Analyze: How has the size of the horse changed over time?

InfoSearch

Read the passage. Ask two questions about the topic that you cannot answer from the information in the passage.

Trilobites Trilobites were tiny ocean animals. There were many kinds of trilobites. They floated on the ocean surface, crawled along the bottom, and swam in between. Trilobites had three body parts—a head, a trunk, and a tail. Trilobites also had a skeleton. The skeletons were made up of chitin (KYT-in). Chitin is a substance like your fingernails.

SEARCH: Use library references to find answers to your questions.

PEOPLE IN SCIENCE

MARY NICOLE LEAKEY (1913–1996)

Imagine finding a humanlike skull that is millions of years old. In the late 1950s, the Leakeys did just that. The Leakeys are a family of anthropologists (an-thruh-PAHL-uh-jists). Anthropologists are scientists who study the history of humans.

Mary Leakey and her husband Louis Leakey studied fossils for more than 50 years. Much of their work involved looking for fossils of early humans. The Leakeys did most of their work in the Olduvai Gorge in East Africa. In 1959, Mary Leakey made an exciting discovery. She found a humanlike skull that was more than 1.75 million years old. About the same time, Mary and her husband discovered other humanlike fossils. These fossils were unlike any others. Because the Leakeys found stone tools near the fossils, the Leakeys called their discovery "Handyman."

Louis Leakey died in 1972. Mary died in 1996. However, their son Richard continues to study fossils. The work of the Leakeys has helped scientists learn about people of the past.

9-5 How can the relative ages of rocks be determined?

Objective ▶ Understand how the relative age of fossils and rock layers can be determined.

TechTerms

- ▶ **index fossil:** remains of an organism that lived only during a short part of the earth's history
- ▶ **relative age:** age of an object compared to the age of another object

Reading Rock Layers Sediments are carried from one place and deposited in another. These sediments pile up layer upon layer. The bottom layer is deposited first. Each layer is deposited on top of other layers. The sediments are pressed together and harden into sedimentary rock layers, or beds. The law of superposition (SOO-pur-puh-zish-un) is used by scientists to read the rock layers. The law of superposition states that each rock layer is older than the one above it. Each rock layer also is younger than the layers below it. Where would you expect to find the oldest layer? Usually, the bottom layer is the oldest layer. The youngest layer is the top layer.

Observe: Which rock layer is the youngest in this rock bed?

Relative Age Using the law of superposition, scientists can tell the **relative age** of a rock layer. Relative age is the age of an object compared to the age of another object. The relative age of a rock tells scientists that one rock layer is older or younger than another rock layer. Relative age does not tell the exact age of a rock.

Figure A

Infer: What is the relative age of rock layer C?

Index Fossils Certain fossils can be used to help find the relative age of rock layers. These fossils are called **index fossils.** To be an index fossil, an organism must have lived only during a short part of the earth's history. Many fossils of the organisms have to be found in rock layers. The fossils must be found over a wide area of the earth. The fossil organisms also must be unique.

Graptolites (GRAP-tuh-lites) and trilobites (TRY-luh-bites) are two large groups of index fossils. The trilobites appeared about 590 million years ago and lived until 250 million years ago. The graptolites appeared about 500 million years ago and lived until 335 million years ago. Individual species lived for short periods of time. Scientists can date rock layers by these short-lived species. Index fossils also can be used to date rock layers from two different parts of the world. Suppose rock layers found in different places contain the same type of trilobite fossils. Scientists can infer that the layers are about the same age.

Explain: What are fossils that scientists call index fossils used for?

LESSON SUMMARY

- Scientists use the law of superposition to tell if a rock layer is older or younger than another rock layer.
- Using the law of superposition, scientists can tell the relative age of a rock layer.
- Index fossils can be used to help find the relative age of rock layers.
- Index fossils can be used to date rock layers in the same area or from two parts of the world.

CHECK *Complete the following.*

1. The youngest layer in a rock bed is usually the ______ layer.
2. Trilobites are examples of ______ fossils.
3. If scientists know that one rock layer is older than another layer, they know the ______ ages of the rock layers.
4. Sedimentary rock layers are called ______ .

APPLY *Complete the following.*

5. List the four requirements a fossil must have to be an index fossil.
6. Draw a rock bed that has four layers. In one rock layer, there are 25 trilobite fossils. In another layer there are 37 graptolite fossils. The oldest layer is about 600 million years old. Label the oldest and youngest layers. Label the layers that have the graptolite and trilobite fossils.

Skill Builder

Building Vocabulary and Modeling Two igneous rock formations can be used to find relative age. These formations are called extrusions and intrusions. They are always younger than the sedimentary rock beds in which they are found. Find out what an extrusion and an intrusion are. Draw a model of a rock bed that has an intrusion and an extrusion. Color the oldest rock layer in your drawing red. Color the youngest rock layer yellow.

ACTIVITY

ANALYZING ROCK LAYERS

You will need a pencil and paper.

1. Study the rock layers and the fossils in both samples.
2. Use the rock layers and the fossils to answer the questions.

Questions

1. **a.** Which are the oldest layers? **b.** The youngest?
2. **a.** Which is the oldest fossil? **b.** The youngest?
3. **Sequence:** List the rock layers in the order that they were laid down.
4. **Infer:** Which fossils are about the same age?

Sample A

Sample B

How is absolute age determined?

Objective ▶ Describe ways used to measure absolute age.

TechTerms

- ▶ **absolute age:** specific age of a rock or a fossil
- ▶ **half-life:** length of time it takes for one-half the amount of a radioactive element to change into another element

Absolute Age How old are you? How do you measure your age? You use the number of years since you were born. This number is your exact age. Scientists need to find out the number of years ago rock layers were formed. They also want to find out the age of fossils. The specific age of a rock layer or a fossil is called its **absolute age.** Absolute age is a more exact age than relative age. Absolute age tells scientists the number of years ago a rock layer formed or an organism lived.

▶ ***Describe:*** What is meant by absolute age?

Natural Clocks The process of a radioactive element changing into another element is called radioactive decay. Radioactive elements were discovered in 1896. They are elements that give off particles and energy. As a radioactive element gives off particles and energy, new elements form. The new elements are not radioactive. The rate at which radioactive decay happens can be measured. Each radioactive element decays at a regular, steady rate. So the radioactive elements are like natural clocks.

▶ ***Explain:*** What is radioactive decay?

Half-life The **half-life** of a radioactive element is the length of time it takes for half the mass of a sample radioactive element to decay. Each element has a different half-life. Uranium is a radioactive element. It slowly decays into lead. It takes 4.5 billion years for one half the uranium in a rock to decay into lead. If you begin with 6 kg of uranium, 3 kg will decay into lead after one half-life. After a second half-life, only 1.5 kg of uranium would be left. By comparing the amount of the radioactive element in a rock to its decay element, scientists can find the absolute age of a rock or fossil.

Measure: If a rock has equal amounts of lead and uranium in it, how old is the rock?

Carbon-14 Carbon-14 is used to date the remains of living things. When living things are alive, they take in carbon-14. Carbon-14 is a radioactive form of carbon. It decays into nitrogen. The half-life of carbon-14 is 5800 years. Carbon-14 is used to find out the absolute ages of wood, bones, skulls, and so on. It also is used to date "young" fossil samples. If a sample is more than 50,000 years old, almost all of the carbon-14 has decayed into nitrogen.

▶ ***Describe:*** What is carbon-14?

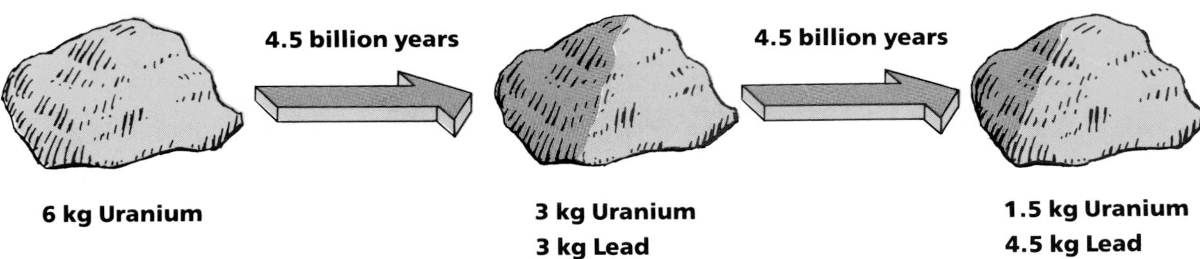

LESSON SUMMARY

- The actual age of a rock or a fossil is its absolute age.
- Radioactive elements and their decay rate make these elements like natural clocks.
- The half-life of radioactive elements can be used to find the absolute age of a rock or fossil.
- Carbon-14 is used to find the absolute age of the remains of living things.

CHECK *Answer the following.*

1. The decay element of uranium is ______ .
2. Radioactive uranium gives off particles and ______ .
3. If you read that a fossil is 350-400 billion years old, you are reading its ______ age.
4. The radioactive element ______ is used to find out the absolute age of once living things.
5. If you tell someone it takes 5800 years for half the amount of carbon-14 in a sample to decay into nitrogen, you are explaining the ______ of carbon-14.

APPLY *Complete the following.*

6. Suppose a radioactive element has a half-life of 10 million years. How much of the original element will be left after 20 million years?
7. Suppose a radioactive element has a half-life of 70 million years. How much of a 10-g sample will be unchanged after 140 million years?

Calculate: *Study each rock sample. Each sample has a radioactive element in it. The radioactive element has a half life of 10,000 years. How old is each rock sample?*

8. 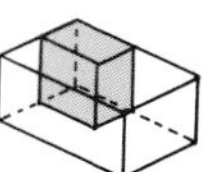

10. 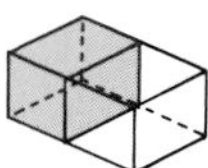

9. 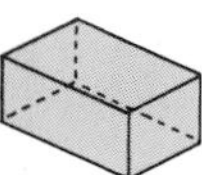

11. 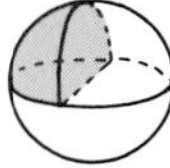

Radioactive element **Decay element**

12. Suppose you found a fossil tooth that you think is about 20,000 years old. Would you use carbon-14 or uranium to find the age of the teeth? Why?

Health & Safety Tip

Large amounts of radioactivity are harmful to living things. Radioactivity harms cells. Find out what the universal symbol for radioactivity danger looks like. Draw the symbol on a sheet of paper. What two colors are used in the symbol?

TECHNOLOGY AND SOCIETY

LASER DATING

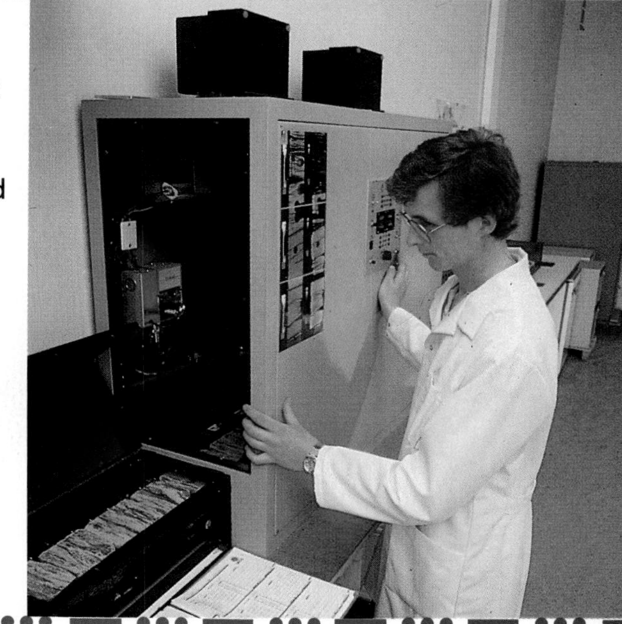

What is a laser? A laser is a very strong beam of light. The light has only one wavelength, or color. You may have several appliances in your house that use laser beams. Compact disc players and videodisc players use laser beams to read the stored sounds and images on the discs. In earth science, lasers are used to estimate the age of sediments.

How can lasers be used to estimate the age of sediments? Scientists bombard sediment layers with lasers. The lasers free electrons from the sediments. Electrons are negative particles trapped in sediments. When the electrons are freed, they give off light. Scientists can measure how much light is given off. Older sediments give off more electrons than younger sediments. Laser dating is used to find out the ages of sediments that are up to 700,000 years old. It can be used to find the age of river sediments and glacier deposits.

9-7 What is the geologic time scale?

Objective ▶ Describe and read the geologic time scale.

TechTerm

▶ **geologic** (jee-uh-LAJ-ik) **time scale:** outline of the major events in the earth's history

Age of the Earth Scientists use radioactive dating to help them find the ages of rocks found on the earth and the moon. The oldest rocks found on the earth are about 4 billion years old. Moon rocks are older. Scientists think the earth and moon were formed at about the same time. Using the age of the moon and earth rocks, scientists estimate that the earth may be more than 4.6 billion years old.

▶ ***Describe:*** About how old is the earth?

Geologic Time Scale By making many observations of rocks and fossils, geologists have developed a **geologic** (jee-uh-LAJ-ik) **time scale.** The geologic time scale is an outline of the major events in the earth's history. The time scale also outlines the kinds of organisms that lived on the earth in the past. The geologic time scale begins when the earth was formed and goes on until the present.

▶ ***Describe:*** What is the geologic time scale?

Divisions of Geologic Time How is a year divided? It is divided into units called months, weeks, and days. Geologic time also is divided into units. The largest unit is an era. Each era lasted for millions of years. There are four eras in geologic time. The eras are divided into periods. The more recent periods are divided into epochs (EP-uks). The divisions of geologic time are based on changes that occurred on the earth.

▶ ***Name:*** What are the divisions of geologic time?

Table 1 Geologic Time Scale

ERA	PERIOD	EPOCH	START DATE (MILLIONS OF YEARS AGO)	ORGANISMS
Cenozoic	Quaternary	Recent	0.025	Modern Humans
		Pleistocene	1.75	Mammoths
	Tertiary	Pliocene	14	Large carnivores
		Miocene	26	Many land mammals
		Oligocene	40	Primitive apes
		Eocene	55	Early horses
		Paleocene	65	Primates
Mesozoic	Cretaceous		130	Flowering plants
	Jurassic		180	Dinosaurs, birds
	Triassic		225	Conifers
Paleozoic	Permian		275	Seed Plants
	Carboniferous		345	Reptiles
	Devonian		405	Insects, amphibians
	Silurian		435	Fishes
	Ordovician		480	Algae, fungi
	Cambrian		600	Invertebrates
Precambrian			4,600	Bacteria, blue-green algae

LESSON SUMMARY

- Scientists estimate that the earth is more than 4.6 billion years old.
- The geologic time scale is a record of the major events and living things in the earth's history.
- The divisions of geologic time are eras, periods, and epochs.

CHECK *Complete the following.*

1. How many geologic eras make up the geologic time scale?
2. What is the age of the oldest earth rocks ever found?
3. List two things that the geologic time scale outlines.
4. What is the largest unit of geologic time?

APPLY *Complete the following.*

5. **Infer:** Why do you think only the most recent period is divided into epochs?
6. **Hypothesize:** If the oldest earth rocks are only 4.1 billion years old, why do scientists think the earth is 4.6 billion years old?

InfoSearch

Read the passage. Ask two questions about the topic that you cannot answer from the information in the passage.

Dinosaurs The dinosaurs lived during the Mesozoic (mes-uh-ZOH-ik) Era. They first appeared during the Triassic (try-AS-ik) Period. You probably think of dinosaurs as giant animals. Actually, some dinosaurs were small. The smallest dinosaur was less than 1 m tall. The largest dinosaur was more than 30 m tall. Some dinosaurs that you may know about are *Apatosaurus* and *Stegosaurus*. *Apatosaurus* was about 25 m long. It weighed about 50 tons. *Stegosaurus* was about 9 m long. Probably the most famous dinosaur was *Tyrannosaurus rex*. It was more than 6 m tall.

SEARCH: Use library references to find answers to your questions.

ACTIVITY

MAKING A MODEL OF GEOLOGIC TIME

You will need 5 meters of adding machine tape, a metric ruler, and a pencil.

1. Use the adding machine tape to make a time line. Each centimeter equals 10 million years.
2. Calculate the length of each era in centimeters for the time line. Draw a line across the tape to show where each era begins.
3. Mark each of these events on your time line.

Questions

1. During which era did the first birds appear?
2. During which era did the first reptile appear?
3. During which era was the last ice age?
4. During which era did the age of dinosaurs begin?
5. During which era did the first humanlike animals appear?

Table 2 Events in Geologic Time

EVENT	YEARS AGO
Precambrian Era	4,600,000,000
First fossils	3,500,000,000
First primitive fish	500,000,000
Paleozoic Era	375,000,000
First reptile	290,000,000
Age of dinosaurs starts	225,000,000
First mammals	200,000,000
Mesozoic Era	160,000,000
First birds appear	160,000,000
Cenozoic Era	65,000,000
First humanlike animal	1,000,000
Last ice age	10,000

UNIT 9 Challenges

STUDY HINT Before you begin the Unit Challenges, review the TechTerms and Lesson Summary for each lesson in this unit.

TechTerms

absolute age (176)
amber (168)
cast (166)
fossil (166)
fossil fuels (170)
geologic time scale (178)
half-life (176)
index fossil (174)
mold (166)
relative age (174)

TechTerm Challenges

Matching *Write the TechTerm that best matches each description.*

1. outline of the major events in the earth's history
2. cavity in a rock that has the shape of an extinct organism
3. length of time it takes for one-half of a radioactive element to change into another element
4. specific age of a rock or fossil
5. age of an object compared to the age of another object

Fill-in *Write the TechTerm that best completes each statement.*

1. Oil, coal, and natural gas are three kinds of ______ .
2. A mold that has filled with sediments forms a ______ .
3. The bodies of entire insects have been found preserved in hardened tree sap called ______ .
4. The traces or remains of living things that lived long ago are called ______ .
5. A trilobite can be used as an ______ .

Content Challenges

Multiple Choice *Write the letter of the term that best completes each statement.*

1. An organism that once lived on the earth, but is no longer found alive is
   a. a fossil. **b.** an imprint. **c.** a cast. **d.** extinct.
2. Most fossils are found in
   a. metamorphic rock. **b.** sedimentary rock. **c.** mud. **d.** igneous rock.
3. Footprints are a kind of fossil called
   a. a mold. **b.** a cast. **c.** an imprint. **d.** an amber.
4. The bodies of wooly mammoths and furry rhinoceroses have been found preserved in
   a. amber. **b.** sedimentary rocks. **c.** ice. **d.** petrified forests.
5. Three ways in which the entire bodies of organisms are preserved are
   a. ice, tar, and amber. **b.** ice, molds, and casts. **c.** tar, molds, and casts. **d.** molds, petrified wood, and amber.
6. Graptolites and trilobites are two kinds of
   a. radioactive elements. **b.** molds. **c.** casts . **d.** index fossils.
7. Fossil fuels are made up mostly of
   a. hydrogen and carbon. **b.** hydrogen and oxygen . **c.** oxygen and carbon. **d.** carbon and nitrogen.

8. Peat is the first stage in the formation of
   a. natural gas. b. tar. c. coal. d. petroleum.
9. The law of superposition states that each rock layer is older than the one
   a. beside it. b. above it. c. below it. d. to its left.
10. The decay element of uranium is
   a. lead. b. nitrogen. c. carbon. d. carbon-14.
11. Uranium has a half-life of
   a. 45 billion years. b. 4.5 billion years. c. 50,000 years. d. 5800 years.

True/False *Write true if the statement is true. If the statement is false, change the underlined term to make the statement true.*

1. Imprints usually are formed from the hard parts of organisms.
2. Elephantlike animals called saber-toothed cats have been discovered preserved in ice.
3. The LaBrea Tar Pits are located in southern California.
4. The bodies of entire insects have been found preserved in amber.
5. When fossil fuels are burned, they give off energy in the forms of heat and electricity.
6. Fossil fuels are formed when bacteria, heat, and pressure act upon decaying plants and animals.
7. Fossils of alligatorlike animals found in Canada indicate that the climate of Canada was always cold.
8. The horses that lived long ago were larger than those that live today.
9. Horses that lived long ago had more toes than horses that live today.
10. Scientists use the law of superposition to tell the absolute age of rocks and fossils.

Understanding the Features

Reading Critically *Use the feature reading selections to answer the following. Page numbers for the features are shown in parentheses.*

1. **Infer:** What tools are helpful to a fossil collector? Why? (169)
2. How could you find out more information about a career as a mine inspector? (171)
3. What kind of scientist was Mary Leakey? (173)
4. Why did the Leakeys name the humanlike fossil they found "Handyman"? (173)
5. How are lasers used in earth science? (177)

Concept Challenges

Critical Thinking *Answer each of the following in complete sentences.*

1. **Infer:** Suppose you find fossils of clams in rock high on a mountain. What can you infer about the mountain?
2. During which period of geologic time are you living?
3. Why is carbon-14 not useful for dating rocks that are more than 50,000 years old?
4. **Analyze:** What method would you use to date a sedimentary rock that you think is about 1 million years old? Why?
5. **Infer:** Suppose you discovered a clam fossil in a layer of rock that also contained trilobite fossils. What inferences could you make from this discovery?

Interpreting a Table *Use the geologic time scale to answer the following questions.*

Table 1 Geologic Time Scale				
ERA	PERIOD	EPOCH	START DATE (MILLIONS OF YEARS AGO)	ORGANISMS
Cenozoic	Quaternary Tertiary	Recent Pleistocene Pliocene Miocene Oligocene Eocene Paleocene	0.025 1.75 14 26 40 55 65	Modern Humans Mammoths Large carnivores Many land mammals Primitive apes Early horses Primates
Mesozoic	Cretaceous Jurassic Triassic		130 180 225	Flowering plants Dinosaurs, birds Conifers
Paleozoic	Permian Carboniferous Devonian Silurian Ordovician Cambrian		275 345 405 435 480 600	Seed Plants Reptiles Insects, amphibians Fishes Algae, fungi Invertebrates
Precambrian			4,600	Bacteria, blue-green algae

Figure 1

Figure 2

1. What are the three divisions of geologic time?
2. **Analyze:** What is the name of the most recent era in geologic time?
3. How long ago did dinosaurs roam the earth?
4. What is the geologic time scale?
5. **Observe:** What organisms are shown in Figure 1?
6. **Synthesize:** During which period did plants such as pine trees first appear?
7. **Observe:** What organisms are shown in Figure 2?
8. **Synthesize:** During which period did snakes first appear?

Finding Out More

1. Visit a natural history museum to observe the fossils. Choose one organism that you would like to learn more about. Use library sources to write a report about the organism you chose.
2. A time capsule is a way to preserve objects and information for people of the future. You can make a time capsule by placing objects in a plastic container and burying the container in the ground. Make a time capsule with five of your classmates. Each classmate should place one object in the time capsule. Explain to the class why you included each object in your time capsule. Explain also why you buried your time capsule where you did.
3. The dodo and moa are extinct birds. Use library references to write a report about one of these birds. Present your findings in an oral report to the class.
4. Many organisms living on the earth today are near extinction. These organisms are called endangered species. Write to your state wildlife agency for a list of the endangered species that live in the United States. Draw a map of the United States. On your map, indicate where each of the species on your list lives. Make a key for your map. Beside the key describe why and how the species became endangered and what is being done to save it.

UNIT 10

THE HYDROSPHERE

CONTENTS

STUDY HINT Before beginning each lesson in Unit 10, write the title of each lesson on a sheet of paper. Below each title, write a short paragraph explaining what you think each lesson is about.

10-1 What is the water cycle?

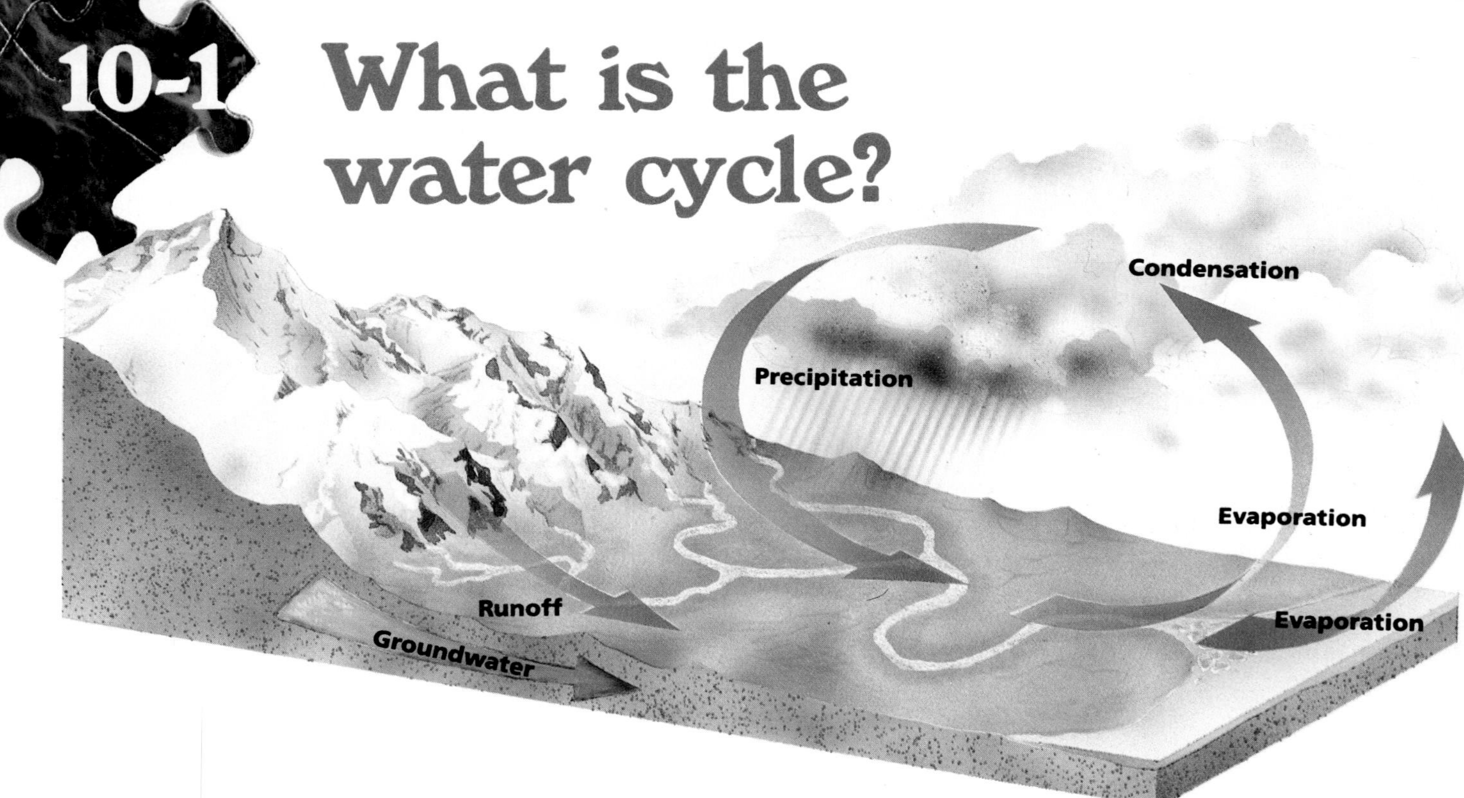

Objective ► Trace the steps in the water cycle.

TechTerms

- ► **condensation** (kahn-dun-SAY-shun): changing of a gas to a liquid
- ► **evaporation** (ih-vap-uh-RAY-shun): changing of a liquid to a gas
- ► **precipitation** (prih-sip-uh-TAY-shun): water that falls to the earth from the atmosphere
- ► **water cycle:** repeated movement of water between the earth's surface and the atmosphere

Evaporation The changing of a liquid to a gas is **evaporation** (ih-vap-uh-RAY-shun). Most of the earth is covered with water. When liquid water takes in heat energy from the sun, it changes to a gas. This gas is called water vapor. The water vapor formed by evaporation goes into the air. Air always contains some water vapor.

► ***Define:*** What is evaporation?

Condensation The changing of a gas to a liquid is called **condensation** (kahn-dun-SAY-shun). When air containing water vapor is cooled, the water vapor loses heat. If the water vapor loses enough heat, it changes back to a liquid. The water vapor condenses into tiny water droplets. These water droplets form clouds. A cloud is a collection of water droplets.

► ***Describe:*** What is a cloud?

Precipitation Water that falls to the earth from the atmosphere is called **precipitation** (prih-sip-uh-TAY-shun). Rain and snow are the two main forms of precipitation. As the water droplets in a cloud get bigger, they become too heavy to stay in the air. Gravity pulls the water droplets toward the earth. The water falls to the earth as rain. If the air is very cold, the water may change to a solid. Then the water falls to the earth as snow, sleet, or hail.

► ***Name:*** What are the two main forms of precipitation?

The Water Cycle Water on the earth is always changing its state, or phase. As water evaporates from the earth's surface, the water changes from a liquid to a gas. In the atmosphere, the water condenses back to a liquid. This water forms clouds. Finally, the water falls to the earth as precipitation. These changes happen over and over. The repeated movement of water between the earth's surface and the atmosphere is called the **water cycle.**

► ***State:*** What is the water cycle?

LESSON SUMMARY

- When liquid water takes in heat energy, it evaporates, or changes to a gas.
- When water vapor loses heat, it condenses, or changes to a liquid.
- Precipitation is any form of water that falls from the atmosphere to the earth.
- The water cycle is the repeated movement of water between the earth's surface and the atmosphere.

CHECK *Complete the following.*

1. When liquid water takes in ______, it evaporates.
2. Condensation is the changing of a gas to a ______ .
3. The main forms of ______ are rain and snow.
4. A cloud is a collection of ______ .
5. Condensation, precipitation, and ______ are parts of the water cycle.

APPLY *Complete the following.*

6. **Hypothesize:** Suppose that dust in the air blocks sunlight from the earth's surface. What effect would this have on the water cycle?
7. **Model:** Draw a diagram showing the three steps in the water cycle.

Skill Builder

Classifying When you classify, you group things based upon similarities. Like all matter, water can exist as a solid, a liquid, or a gas. Write the words "Solid," "Liquid," and "Gas" across the top of a sheet of paper. Classify each form of water listed below in its correct phase by listing it under its correct heading.

rain	river	lake
snow	cloud	fog
water vapor	steam	mist
ocean	ice	puddle

ACTIVITY

OBSERVING THE PHASES OF WATER

You will need a tall drinking glass, plastic wrap, hot water, and ice cubes.

1. Fill a drinking glass halfway with hot water from the faucet. **CAUTION: Be careful not to burn yourself.**
2. Place a piece of plastic wrap tightly over the opening in the glass.
3. Place 5 or 6 ice cubes on the plastic wrap.
4. Allow the jar to stand for about 5 minutes. Observe the mist that forms between the hot water and the cold cover.
5. After 5 minutes, pick up the plastic wrap. Feel the side of the cover that covered the jar.

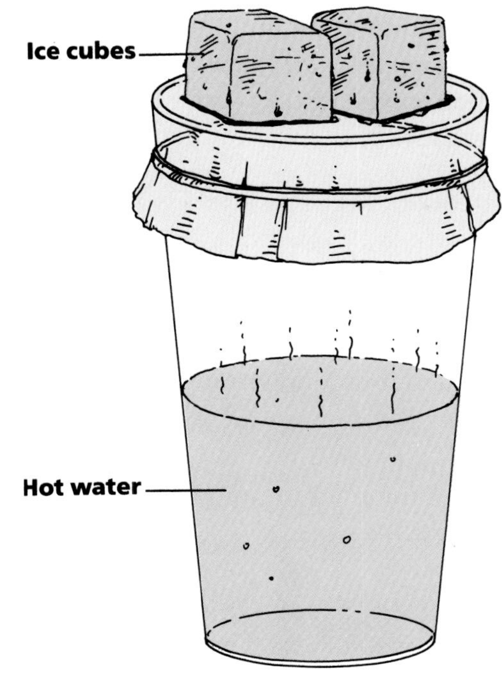

Questions

1. **a.** What phase of water was the hot water? **b.** The ice cube? **c.** Which phase could not be seen?
2. **a. Observe:** What happened to the ice? **b. Analyze:** What caused this to happen?
3. Why did the mist form?
4. **a. Observe:** What did you observe on the bottom of the plastic wrap? **b. Analyze:** How did it get there?

10-2 What is groundwater?

Objective ▶ Explain how groundwater collects in soil.

TechTerms

- ▶ **groundwater:** water that collects in pores in the soil
- ▶ **pores:** tiny holes or air spaces
- ▶ **water table:** upper layer of saturated rock

Groundwater Some of the rainwater that falls to the earth soaks into the soil. The water collects in the air spaces, or pores, between particles of rock and soil. Water that collects in the pores between rock and soil particles is called **groundwater.** About 90% of the earth's freshwater supply is stored as groundwater.

▶ *Identify:* ***What is groundwater?***

Properties Affecting Groundwater Different kinds of rock and soil can hold different amounts of groundwater. Loosely packed soil has many pores. It can hold a lot of groundwater. Tightly packed soil does not have many pores. It cannot hold much groundwater.

Soil in which the particles are all about the same size also can hold a lot of groundwater. Suppose the soil particles are all different sizes. Then, small particles can fill up some of the pores. As a result, the soil cannot hold much groundwater.

▶ *Explain:* Why can loosely packed soil hold a lot of groundwater?

Movement of Groundwater Groundwater moves through the soil by means of the pores between soil particles. Groundwater easily moves through soil with large, interconnected pores. However, if the pores are not connected, the water cannot move through the soil. As a result, the groundwater cannot sink any deeper into the earth.

▶ *Describe:* How does groundwater move through soil?

The Water Table Groundwater eventually reaches a layer of rock through which it cannot pass. Then groundwater begins to fill up the pores in the rock above this layer. When the pores in the rock are completely filled with water, the rock is saturated (SACH-uh-ray-tid). As the rock becomes saturated, the water level underground rises. The upper level of the saturated rock is called the **water table.**

Not all of the water in soil sinks down to the water table. Some water stays near the surface. The roots of most plants cannot reach the water table. These plants get moisture from water in the upper levels of the soil.

▶ *Define:* What is the water table?

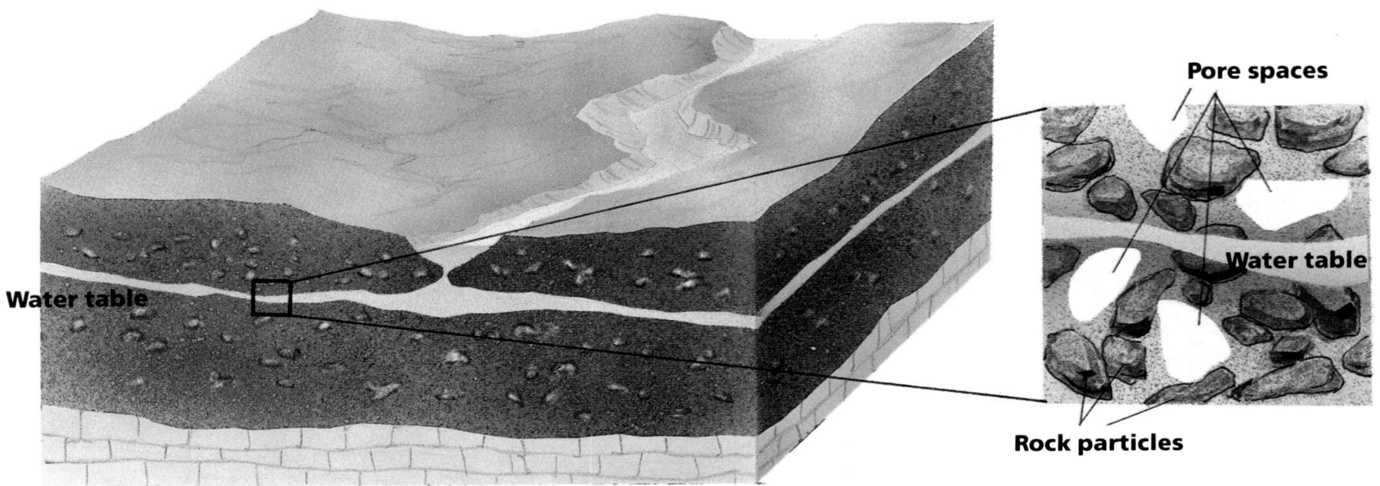

LESSON SUMMARY

- Groundwater collects in air spaces, or pores, between particles of rock and soil.
- Loosely packed soil can hold more groundwater than tightly packed soil.
- Soil with the same size particles can hold more groundwater than soil with different sized particles.
- Groundwater can move easily through soil with large, interconnected pores.
- The upper level of a layer of saturated rock is the water table.
- Some water remains near the surface of the soil instead of sinking down to the water table.

CHECK *Write true if the statement is true. If the statement is false, correct the underlined term to make the statement true.*

1. Rainwater collects in <u>pores</u> between soil particles.
2. About 90% of the earth's <u>salt water</u> is stored as groundwater.
3. <u>Loosely</u> packed soil cannot hold much groundwater.
4. The <u>water table</u> is the upper layer of saturated rock.

APPLY *Complete the following.*

5. **Analyze:** Which of the soils can hold more groundwater? Why?

a.

b.

Ideas in Action

IDEA: Groundwater supplies about 20% of the fresh water used in the United States.

ACTION: Describe two ways in which your life would be affected if the water table in your area dried up.

ACTIVITY

MEASURING GROUNDWATER IN SOIL

You will need three cups, a large plastic container, a marking pencil, water, sand, and soil.

1. Fill one cup half full of sand. Fill the second cup half full of soil. Mix equal amounts of sand and soil. Fill the third cup half full. Label the cups A, B, and C.
2. Pour water into each cup until each of the cups is completely filled.
3. Carefully pour the water in cup A into an empty plastic container. Mark the water level on the outside of the container and label it Level A. Pour the water into the sink.
4. Repeat step 3 with cups B and C.

Questions

1. **Measure:** Which cup held the most water?
2. **Analyze:** Why was the material in one of the cups able to hold more water than the materials in the other two cups?
3. **Compare:** How does this activity relate to the amount of groundwater that can be held in different kinds of soil?

10-3 What are wells, springs, and geysers?

Objective ▶ Describe how groundwater reaches the earth's surface.

TechTerms

- ▶ **geyser** (GY-zur): heated groundwater that erupts onto the earth's surface
- ▶ **spring:** natural flow of groundwater to the earth's surface
- ▶ **well:** hole dug below the water table that fills with groundwater

Wells In many communities, people get their fresh water from **wells.** A well is a hole dug below the water table that fills with water. The water in a well comes from the groundwater in the soil. When a well is dug, a pipe is set into a hole that reaches below the level of the water table. An opening in the pipe allows water to enter the pipe. The water can then be pumped to the surface.

The level of the water table changes from season to season. In dry weather, there is little rainfall. This causes the level of the water table to drop. The pipe for a well must be much deeper than the lowest level of the water table.

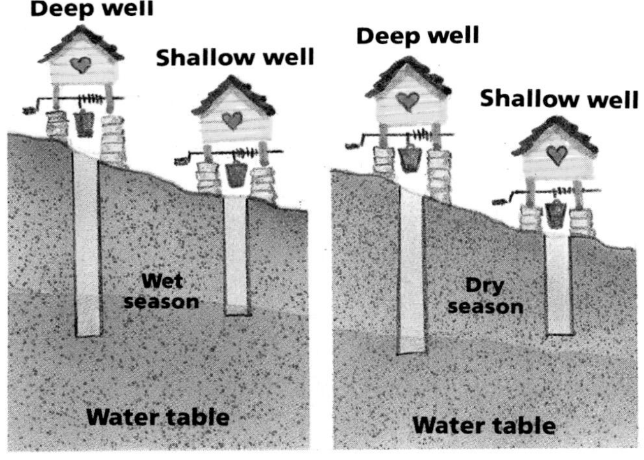

▶ *Infer:* Why should a pipe for a well be deeper than the lowest level of the water table?

Artesian Wells A pump is not necessary to get water out of artesian (ahr-TEE-zhun) wells. Water rises freely from these wells. The water source for an artesian well is trapped between two layers of rock. The water trapped between the rock layers is under pressure. When a pipe is placed into the water, pressure forces the water to rise in the pipe. The water in an artesian well may come from many kilometers away from the well.

▶ *Explain:* Why is it not necessary to pump water out of an artesian well?

Springs A **spring** is a natural flow of groundwater that reaches the earth's surface. The surface of a steep hill may drop below the water table. Water can then flow out of cracks in the rocks. If a pipe is driven into the rock, water will flow from the pipe. For this reason, springs usually are found on hillsides. Spring water usually is cold. However, if the water is near an underground heat source, warm or hot springs are formed.

▶ *Explain:* When are hot springs formed?

Geysers Sometimes, steam and boiling water shoot into the air in a **geyser** (GY-zur). A geyser is heated groundwater that erupts onto the earth's surface. (See photo above.) What causes a geyser to erupt? The water in a deep hot spring may be heated above the normal boiling point of water. This superheated water is trapped by the weight of the water above it. The superheated water turns to steam. The pressure of the steam forces the water above it up and out into the air. Geysers are found only in Wyoming, New Zealand, and Iceland.

▶ *Locate:* Where are geysers found?

LESSON SUMMARY

- Groundwater can reach the earth's surface by means of a well.
- The level of the water table changes from season to season.
- Water rises freely out of an artesian well, so a pump is not needed.
- A spring is a natural flow of groundwater that reaches the earth's surface.
- Superheated groundwater erupts to the surface as a geyser.

CHECK *Complete the following.*

1. To get water from a well, the well must be ______ the water table.
2. Wells that do not require pumps are ______ wells.
3. The temperature of spring water is usually ______ .
4. A ______ is heated groundwater that erupts onto the earth's surface.
5. Hot springs are found near a source of underground ______ .

APPLY *Complete the following.*

6. **Infer:** What kind of springs do you think would be found in Warm Springs, Georgia and Hot Springs, Arkansas?
7. Why does the temperature of spring water stay the same from season to season?

InfoSearch

Read the passage. Ask two questions about the topic that you cannot answer from the information in the passage.

Oases An oasis (oh-AY-sis) is a very fertile piece of land found in the middle of a desert. Oases vary in size from less than one square kilometer to several square kilometers. The land for hundreds of kilometers around an oasis is dry and barren, with little or no rainfall. The oasis, however, has plenty of water and many growing plants. People also live on oases. The number of people living on an oasis varies. Some oases have been called the most crowded places in the world.

SEARCH: Use library references to find answers to your questions.

CAREER IN EARTH SCIENCE

HYDROLOGIST

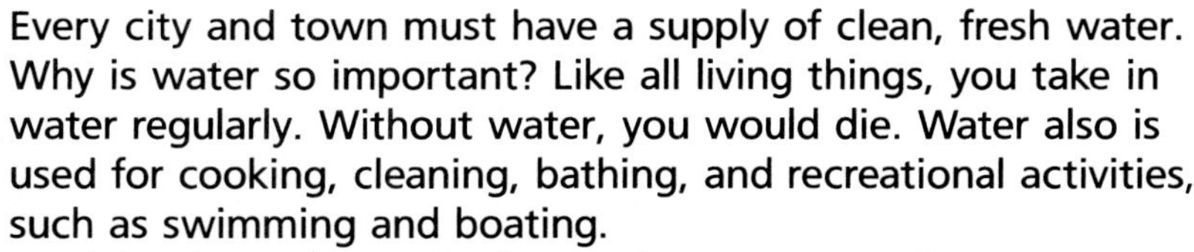

Every city and town must have a supply of clean, fresh water. Why is water so important? Like all living things, you take in water regularly. Without water, you would die. Water also is used for cooking, cleaning, bathing, and recreational activities, such as swimming and boating.

Scientists who study the earth's water supply are hydrologists (hy-DRAHL-uh-jists). Hydrologists work at supplying people with the fresh water they need. For example, hydrologists may choose the best place to dig a well. They also may draw up plans for supplying a city with fresh water from another area. Hydrologists also help farmers irrigate (ir-uh-GAYT) their land. Irrigation is the process of supplying land with water by using artificial canals or sprinkler systems. A hydrologist also may work at keeping water supplies clean.

Hydrologists often work outdoors. A hydrologist must attend four years of college. Courses in mathematics, geology, chemistry, and computer science.

10-4 What is oceanography?

Objectives ▶ Explain what is meant by oceanography. ▶ Describe the world ocean.

TechTerm

▶ **oceanography** (oh-shun-OG-ruh-fee): study of the earth's oceans

The Water Planet About three-quarters, or 75%, of the earth is covered with water. Most of this water is salt water. This large body of salt water is the world ocean. No other planet in the solar system has a covering of liquid water.

Analyze: What percentage of the earth is covered with land?

The World Ocean The world ocean is divided into three major oceans. These oceans are the Atlantic Ocean, the Pacific Ocean, and the Indian Ocean. Geographers (jee-AHG-ruh-furz) are specialists who study the earth's surface. Geographers often name two more oceans. They use the names Arctic Ocean and Antarctic Ocean for areas of the Atlantic and Pacific oceans.

Identify: What are the names of the three major oceans?

Size and Depth The Pacific Ocean covers the largest area of the world ocean. More than half of the earth's ocean water is in the Pacific Ocean. The Pacific Ocean also is the earth's deepest ocean. The average depth of the Pacific Ocean is 3.9 km.

The Atlantic Ocean is the second largest ocean. Several seas and gulfs are part of the Atlantic Ocean. A sea is a small area of the ocean that is partly surrounded by land. The Atlantic Ocean has an average depth of 3.3 km.

The Indian Ocean is the smallest ocean. It is deeper than the Atlantic Ocean, but not as deep as the Pacific Ocean. The average depth of the Indian Ocean is 3.8 km.

Observe: Use the map to name two seas and a gulf that are part of the Atlantic Ocean.

Oceanography The study of the earth's oceans is **oceanography** (oh-shun-OG-ruh-fee). Scientists who study the oceans are oceanographers. There are many kinds of oceanographers. An oceanographer might study the size and depth of the oceans, the living things in the ocean, or the geography of the ocean floor.

Define: What is oceanography?

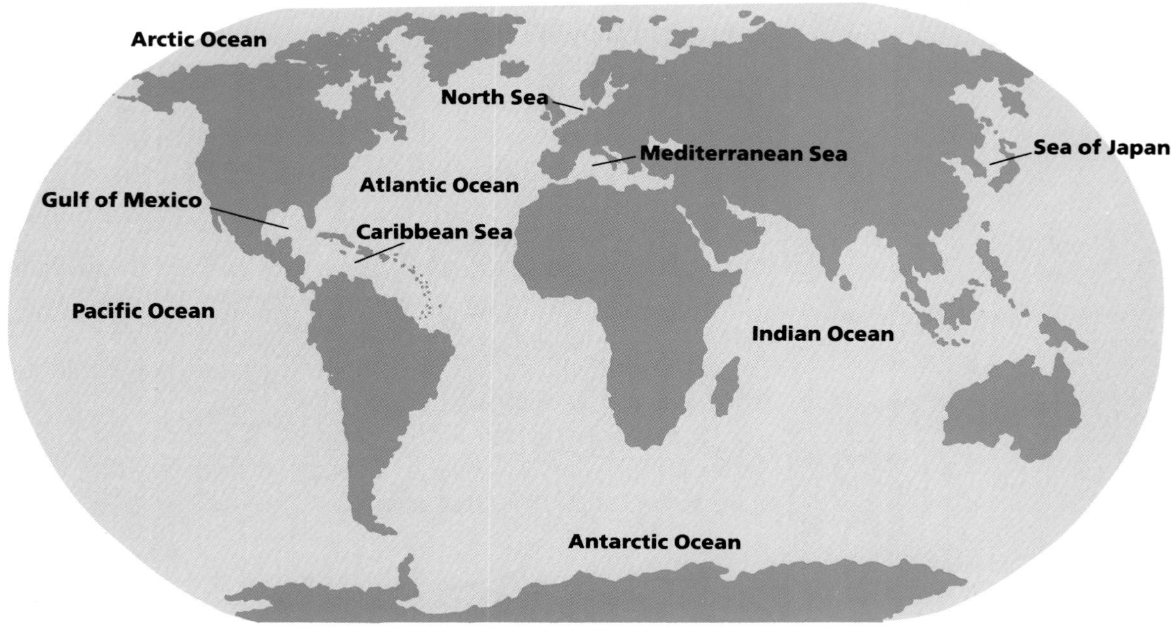

LESSON SUMMARY

- About 75% of the earth is covered with salt water.
- The world ocean is divided into three major oceans.
- The Pacific Ocean is the largest ocean.
- The Atlantic Ocean is the second largest ocean.
- The Indian Ocean is the smallest ocean.
- Oceanography is the study of the earth's oceans.

CHECK *Complete the following.*

1. About how much of the earth's surface is covered with water?
2. How many oceans are named by geographers?
3. Which of the earth's oceans is the deepest?
4. What percentage of the earth's ocean water is in the Pacific Ocean?
5. What is oceanography?

APPLY *Complete the following.*

6. Why is Earth often called the "water planet"?
7. **Hypothesize:** Why do you think most oceanographers study only one area of oceanography?
8. **Sequence:** List the three major oceans in order from the smallest to the largest.

Skill Builder

Graphing A pie graph is a graph in the form of a circle. The circle is divided into sections that represent the parts of a whole. Draw a pie graph that shows the percentage of the earth's surface covered with water and the percentage covered with land. Use different colors for each section of the pie graph. Draw a second pie graph to show the relative sizes of the three major oceans.

CAREER IN EARTH SCIENCE

MARINE TECHNICIAN

Do you enjoy being near the ocean? Are you interested in helping to save the ocean's living things? Does searching for sunken ships or treasure sound exciting? If you answered yes to one of these questions, you may enjoy a career as a marine technician. A marine technician works in many different areas involving the oceans. Some technicians work with marine biologists studying the living things in the oceans. Other marine technicians may help oceanographers map the ocean floor. Still others may take samples of ocean water to test the amount of pollution in it.

Most marine technicians work at sea. They often work aboard research ships or on research platforms built in the oceans. Some marine technicians work in laboratories near shipping areas. To become a marine technician you must complete two years of college. You should take courses in mathematics, biology, and other sciences.

How do scientists explore the oceans?

Objective ▸ Describe three ways in which scientists explore the oceans.

TechTerms

- **sonar:** system that bounces sound waves off the ocean floor
- **submersible** (sub-MUR-suh-bul): underwater research vessel

Deep-Sea Drilling Scientists can study the ocean floor by drilling into the crust beneath the ocean. The Deep Sea Drilling Project is an ocean research program. The Project has helped scientists learn about the ocean floor. The research ship *Glomar Challenger* was specially built for the Deep Sea Drilling Project. Equipment on the *Glomar Challenger* can drill into the ocean floor more than 4 km below the surface. Scientists study samples of rock taken from the ocean floor.

▸ *Identify:* How do scientists get samples of rock from the ocean floor?

Sonar Scientists can map the ocean floor by using **sonar.** The word "sonar" comes from the letters in **so**und **n**avigation **a**nd **r**anging. Sonar is an echo-sounding system.

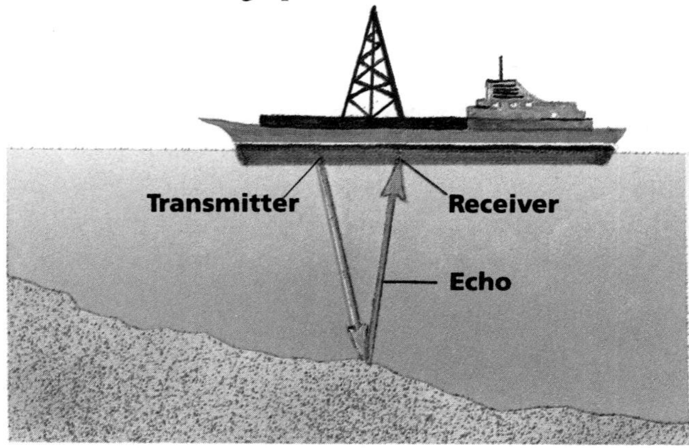

Sonar is used to calculate the depth of the ocean. Sound waves travel through water at a speed of 1500 m/sec. A transmitter bounces a sound wave off the ocean floor. The returning sound wave, or echo, is picked up by a receiver. Scientists can measure the time it takes for the sound wave to return. This time can be used to calculate the depth to the ocean floor. Suppose a sound wave makes a round trip in 10 seconds. The sound wave takes 5 seconds to reach the ocean floor. It takes another 5 seconds to bounce back to the ship. The depth of the ocean floor is 1500 m/sec $\times$ 5 sec = 7500 m.

▸ *Calculate:* A sonar signal is sent out and returns 5 seconds later. How deep is the ocean floor?

Submersibles Scientists also use underwater research vessels to study the oceans. These vessels are called **submersibles** (sub-MUR-suh-bulz). One of the first submersibles was a bathysphere (BATH-uh-sfir). A bathysphere is a round diving vessel. It is lowered into the ocean on a steel cable from a ship.

Another kind of submersible is called a bathyscaphe (BATH-ih-skaf). A bathyscaphe is a small submarine. In 1960, the bathyscaphe Trieste set a record by diving to a depth of almost 11,000 m. Scientists diving in the bathyscaphe *Alvin* have discovered many unusual forms of life deep in the ocean.

▸ *Identify:* What is a bathyscaphe?

LESSON SUMMARY

- Scientists study the ocean floor by drilling into the crust beneath the ocean.
- Scientists use sonar to map the ocean floor.
- Sonar is used to calculate the depth of the oceans.
- A bathysphere is a submersible used to study the oceans.
- A bathyscaphe is a small submarine.

CHECK *Complete the following.*

1. What is the Deep Sea Drilling Project?
2. What does the word "sonar" stand for?
3. What is a submersible?
4. What is the difference between a bathysphere and a bathyscaphe?

APPLY *Complete the following.*

5. **Calculate:** The ocean floor beneath a research ship is 3000 m deep. How long would a sonar signal, moving at 1500 m/sec, take to reach the ocean floor and return to the ship?

InfoSearch

Read the passage. Ask two questions about the topic that you cannot answer from the information in the passage.

Robot Submersibles Scientists use underwater research vessels called submersibles to study the ocean depths. Many submersibles are robots. These robots can take pictures of the ocean floor. Jason Jr. is an example of a robot submersible.

In 1985, Dr. Robert Ballard used the robot submersible *Argo* to find the remains of the sunken *Titanic.* The *Titanic* sank on its maiden voyage in 1912. Dr. Ballard used Jason Jr. to explore the inside of the *Titanic.* Jason Jr. sent back many detailed pictures of the sunken ship.

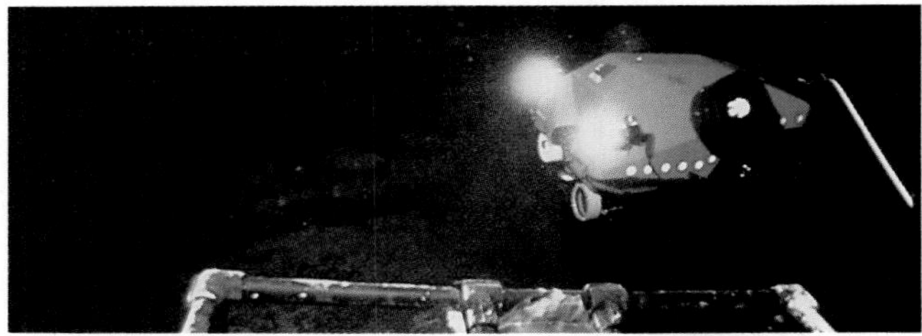

SEARCH: Use library references to find answers to your questions.

LOOKING BACK IN SCIENCE

HISTORY OF OCEANOGRAPHY

People have been studying the oceans for many years. Since the time of the Greeks, people have built ships to explore the oceans. Most of the information was used to make maps.

In the 19th century, modern oceanography began. Matthew Fontaine Maury, an American Naval officer gathered information about ocean currents, temperatures, and climates. Using the information, he developed monthly charts of winds and currents. Maury is known as the "Father of Oceanography."

The first major scientific study of the oceans began in 1872. The study was done from a ship called the *HMS Challenger.* The *Challenger* was a British ship. The *Challenger* expedition lasted for 13 1/2 years. It covered 126,700 kilometers. The expedition gathered information about the ocean from 362 stations. The people took 492 deep soundings. They took 133 samples from the ocean bottom. It took 20 years to write 50 books about the expedition.

Today, ocean studies are still going on. There is still a lot to learn about the oceans. Some people call the oceans the "Last Frontier."

Some Important People
1. Henri Milne-Edwards (1800–1885) French zoologist: First person to use diving gear
2. William Beebe (1877–1962) American naturalist: Developed the bathysphere, a steel ball that people could go into and be lowered into the ocean.
3. August Piccard (1884–1962) Swiss physicist: Built the *Trieste* Jacques Piccard (1922–present) Oceanographic engineer
4. Jacques-Yves Cousteau (1910–present) French explorer and inventor: Developed the aqualung (SCUBA) and built many submersibles.

What are some properties of the ocean?

Objective ▶ Explain why different parts of the ocean have different temperatures and salinity.

TechTerms

- ▶ **salinity** (suh-LIN-uh-tee): amount of dissolved salts in ocean water
- ▶ **thermocline** (THUR-muh-klyn): layer of ocean water in which temperature drops sharply

Salinity The water in the earth's oceans is salt water. Unlike fresh water, salt water contains dissolved salts and other minerals. Figure 1 shows the percentages of salts in ocean water. The amount of dissolved salts in ocean water is called **salinity** (suh-LIN-uh-tee). Salinity is measured as the number of grams of dissolved salt in 1000 g of ocean water. Ocean water contains 33 to 37 grams of salt in every 1000 grams of water.

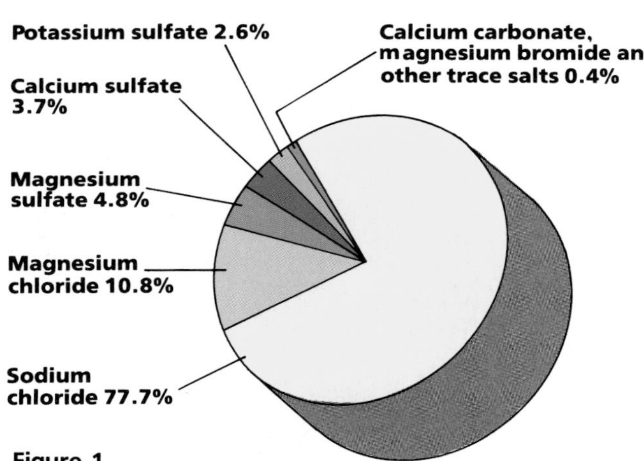

Figure 1

Analyze: Use Figure 1. Which salt is most common in ocean water?

Changing Salinity The salinity of ocean water differs slightly from place to place. The salinity is lowered when fresh water is added to ocean water. Fresh water from rivers, precipitation, and melting glaciers lowers the salinity of the oceans. During the water cycle, water evaporates from the ocean surface. Evaporation leaves behind dissolved salts and raises the salinity. Salinity varies more at the surface than in deeper ocean water.

Infer: Would an area of the ocean that receives a lot of rainfall have a high or low salinity? Explain.

Temperature Heat from the sun warms the water in the oceans. The water is warmest at the surface and coldest at the bottom of the ocean. From top to bottom, there are three different temperature layers in the ocean. The surface layer is about 100 to 300 meters deep. Winds and waves keep the water in the surface layer well mixed. As a result, temperatures are about the same everywhere in the surface layer.

The layer of water below the surface layer is the **thermocline** (THUR-muh-klyn). The thermocline goes down to a depth of about 900 meters. In the thermocline, temperatures drop sharply as the water gets deeper. In the deep layer of the ocean below the thermocline, the water is very cold. The temperature in the deep layer remains constant between 0°C and 4°C.

Identify: What is the thermocline?

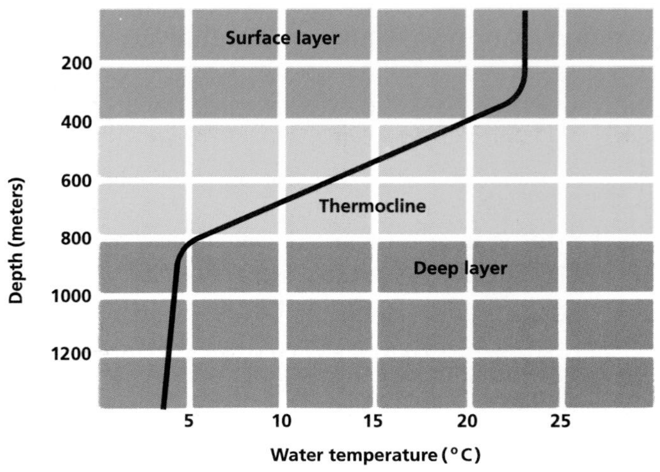

Figure 2

LESSON SUMMARY

- Salt water contains dissolved salts and other minerals.
- The salinity of ocean water differs slightly from place to place.
- There are three different temperature layers in the ocean.
- The thermocline is the layer of ocean water in which the temperature drops sharply.

CHECK *Complete the following.*

1. The amount of salt dissolved in ocean water is ______ .
2. Adding fresh water to salt water ______ the salinity of the water.
3. Ocean water is warmest at the ______ .
4. There are ______ different temperature layers in the ocean.
5. Heat from ______ warms the water in the oceans.

APPLY *Complete the following.*

6. **Sequence:** Use Figure 1 on page 194. List the salts found in ocean water in order, from the largest percentage to the smallest percentage.
7. **Predict:** The area around the Mediterranean Sea is hot and dry, and has a high rate of evaporation. Would the Mediterranean Sea have a high or a low salinity? Explain.

Skill Builder

Using Prefixes Prefixes are word parts that are placed at the beginning of words. Prefixes have definite meanings. Knowing the definition of a prefix can help you remember the meaning of a word. Use a dictionary to find the meaning of the prefix "thermo-." Then, write the definitions of the following words that contain this prefix: thermocline, thermoelectric, thermograph, thermomagnetic, and thermometer. Circle the part of the definition that relates to the prefix "thermo-."

TECHNOLOGY AND SOCIETY

DESALINATION PLANTS

Three-fourths of the earth's surface is covered by water. However, only a small part of this water is potable (POHT-uh-bul), or fit to drink. Fresh water is a valuable natural resource that is in short supply.

As the population of the world increases, more fresh water is needed. Many communities face serious problems as their populations increase and water supplies decrease. Most supplies of fresh water depend on precipitation. During dry periods, those supplies are reduced.

Scientists have discovered a way to use ocean water to meet the increasing need for water. Before people can use the supply of water available in the ocean, minerals or salts in the ocean water must be removed. In many places, desalination (dee-sal-uh-NAY-shun) plants have been built to remove the salts from ocean water. These plants use several different methods to remove salts. The most common method is to heat the water until the water evaporates, leaving the salts behind. The water vapor is then condensed to recover fresh water. Another method is to freeze the ocean water. When ocean water is frozen, the ice that is formed is free of salts. The ice is then cleaned and melted to provide fresh water.

10-7 What are ocean currents?

Objectives ▶ Define current. ▶ Describe how surface currents and density currents are formed.

TechTerms

- ▶ **currents** (KUR-ents): streams of water flowing in the oceans
- ▶ **density currents:** streams of water that move up and down in the oceans

Ocean Currents The water in the earth's oceans is always moving. Have you ever heard of someone throwing a bottle containing a message into the ocean? Some time later, the bottle is found in a distant place. How did the bottle get there? It was carried by ocean **currents** (KUR-ents). Ocean currents are streams of water in the oceans. Currents flow through the ocean water around them. Some currents in the ocean flow along the surface. Some move along the ocean bottom. Currents also can move up and down within the ocean.

▶ *Define:* What is a current?

Surface Currents Winds cause most surface currents. Winds near the equator blow mainly from east to west. In the Northern Hemisphere, winds blow from the northeast. In the Southern Hemisphere, winds blow from the southeast. The earth's rotation causes the winds in the Northern and Southern Hemispheres to curve in different directions. Continents and large islands also make ocean currents change direction. As a result, surface currents move in huge circles. The currents move clockwise in the Northern Hemisphere. They move counterclockwise in the Southern Hemisphere.

▶ *State:* What causes most surface currents?

Warm and Cold Currents Ocean currents can be warm or cold. Currents flowing from areas near the equator are warm currents. They bring warm water into cooler regions. These warm currents tend to warm the air over nearby land areas. Currents coming from areas near the poles are cold currents. They bring cold water into warmer regions. These cold currents cool these areas.

▶ *Name:* Where do warm currents come from?

Density Currents Differences in density can cause currents to move up and down in the ocean. Cold water is denser than warm water. Cold water around the poles sinks to the ocean bottom. Water around the equator is warm. Warm water rises up toward the ocean surface. This up and down movement of water causes **density currents.** Different amounts of salt in ocean water also cause density currents. Water with a lot of salt is more dense than water with a little salt. Dense, salty water sinks. Less salty water rises.

▶ *List:* What causes density currents?

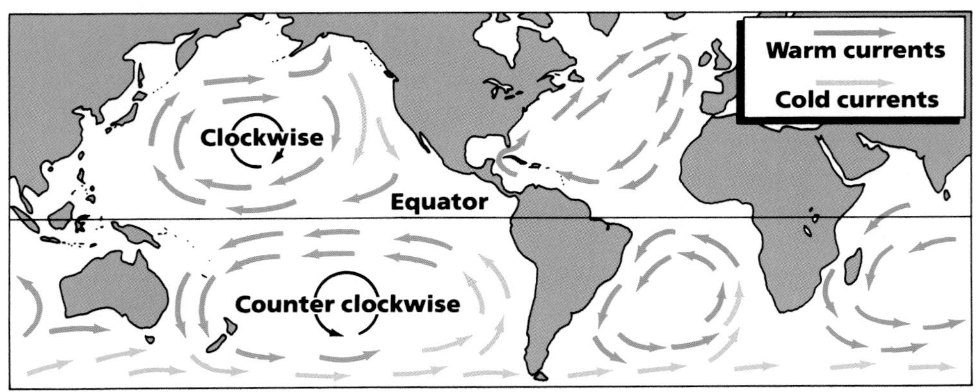

LESSON SUMMARY

- Ocean currents are streams of water that move through the oceans.
- Most surface currents are caused by the winds.
- Surface currents move clockwise in the Northern Hemisphere and counterclockwise in the Southern Hemisphere.
- Ocean currents can be warm or cold.
- Density currents move up and down in the oceans.

CHECK *Write true, if the statement is true. If the statement is false, correct the underlined term to make the statement true.*

1. Ocean currents are streams of water in the oceans.
2. Most bottom currents are caused by winds.
3. Ocean currents flow in straight paths.
4. Surface currents from the poles are cold currents.
5. Surface currents move up and down in the ocean.

APPLY *Complete the following.*

6. What are three kinds of ocean currents?
7. **Infer:** Why do continents and large islands cause surface currents to change direction?
8. **Compare:** Which is probably denser, the water in the Arctic Ocean or the water in the Caribbean Sea? Explain.

Health & Safety Tip

An undertow is a current that moves beneath and in a different direction than a surface current. Undertows can be very strong. For this reason, an undertow can be dangerous to swimmers. This is one reason you should never swim alone. Interview a lifeguard or use reference materials to find out about other safety guidelines for swimming. Make a chart that outlines some of these guidelines.

LEISURE ACTIVITY

SCUBA DIVING

Do you like to swim? Are you fascinated by exotic, brightly colored fishes? If so, you might enjoy scuba diving. Unlike skin divers who use snorkels under water, scuba divers breathe compressed air from a tank. In fact, the word "scuba" comes from the tank used by divers. "Scuba" stands for self-contained underwater breathing apparatus. Scuba divers carry air tanks on their backs.

People of all ages enjoy scuba diving. Why is scuba diving popular? Some people scuba dive because they enjoy swimming and being near the ocean. Many scuba divers take underwater photographs. Others collect interesting and unusual shells.

If you think you would like to try scuba diving, you should begin by taking lessons from a qualified instructor. You might try your local YWCA or YMCA. Community swimming pools and resorts often have certified scuba diving instructors. The National Association of Underwater Instructors is a good source of information. Once you have learned the necessary skills and safety rules, you will be ready to strap on your tank and explore the underwater world.

10-8 What are ocean waves?

Objective ▶ Identify and describe the properties of an ocean wave.

TechTerms

- ▶ **crest:** highest point of a wave
- ▶ **trough** (TROFF): lowest point of a wave
- ▶ **wave:** regular up-and-down movement of water

Ocean Waves When wind blows across water, **waves** are formed. A wave is a regular up-and-down movement of water. On a windy day at the beach, the ocean water gets rough. The waves are high when the wind is strong. On a calm day, the waves are not as high.

▶ ***Define:*** What is a wave?

Shape of a Wave A wave has a high point and a low point. The highest point, or top, of a wave is the **crest.** The lowest point of a wave is the **trough** (TROFF). The height of a wave is the distance measured from the crest to the trough. Waves can sometimes be more than 15 meters high. As you watch waves move across the water, you see one crest following another. The distance from one crest to another crest is the wavelength of the wave.

▶ ***Explain:*** How is wave height measured?

Water Movement in a Wave The water in a wave does not move forward as the wave moves. Only the energy in the wave moves forward. You can see the movement of water by watching a floating cork. As a wave moves by, the cork moves slightly forward. As the wave passes, the cork then falls back about the same distance. The cork appears to be moving up and down in the same place. As a wave moves across the ocean, water particles in the wave move in circles. At the surface, the size of the circles is the same as the height of the wave. The circles get smaller deeper below the surface.

▶ ***Describe:*** What happens to a floating cork as a wave passes by?

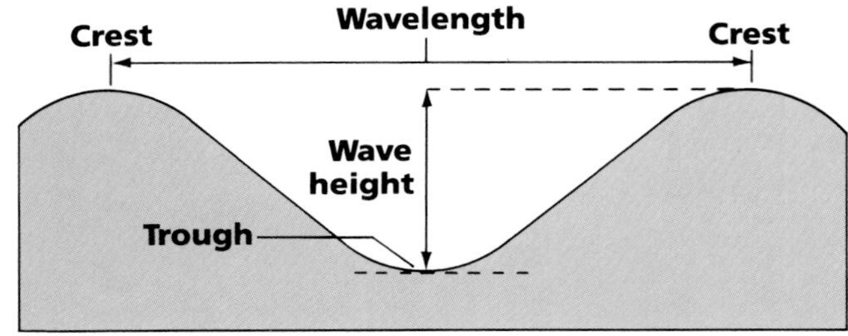

Breaking Waves As waves move toward the shoreline, the trough of each wave touches the ocean bottom. Friction with the ocean bottom slows down the wave. The top, or crest, of the wave keeps moving at the same speed. The crest gets farther and farther ahead of the trough. The wave height increases. Finally, the crest falls over and forms a breaker.

▶ ***Explain:*** What causes a wave to slow down in shallow water?

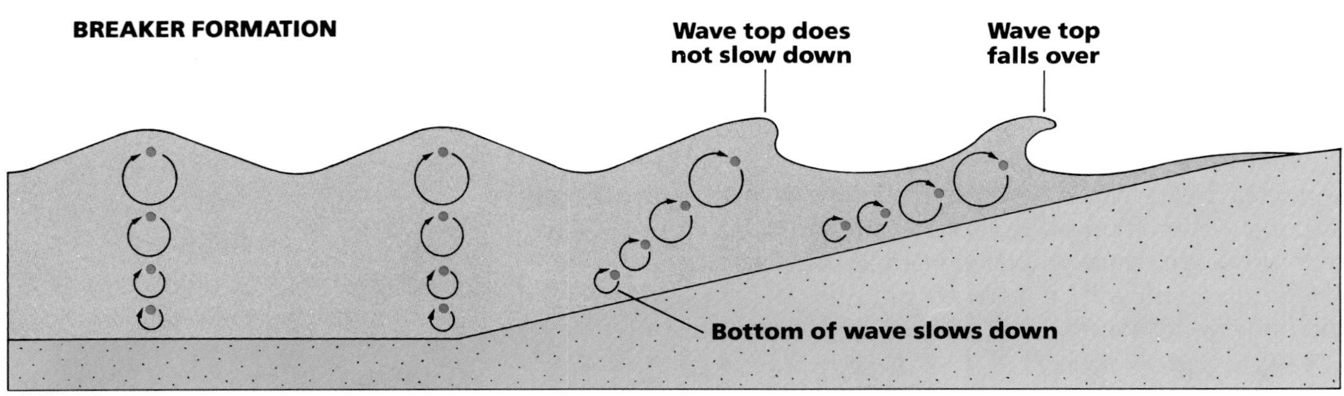

LESSON SUMMARY

- ► Waves are formed when wind blows across water.
- ► Waves have a high point, or crest, and a low point, or trough.
- ► Only the energy of a wave moves forward; the water does not move forward.
- ► Waves slow down and form breakers as they approach a shoreline.

CHECK *Complete the following.*

1. Most waves are caused by _______ .
2. The top of a wave is the _______ .
3. The distance between the crest and _______ of a wave is the wave height.
4. The distance between one crest and the next crest is the _______ of a wave.
5. Only the _______ of a wave moves.

APPLY *Complete the following.*

6. **Model:** Draw a diagram of a wave. Label the crest, trough, wave height, and wavelength.
7. **Infer:** You are at the beach. Early in the day, the water is fairly calm. As the day progresses, the ocean water gets rougher. What do you think causes the water to get rougher?

InfoSearch

Read the passage. Ask two questions about the topic that you cannot answer from the information in the passage.

Tsunamis A tsunami (tsoo-NAH-mee) is a huge ocean wave. Unlike other ocean waves, tsunamis are not caused by wind. A tsunami is not very high, but it carries a great deal of energy. As a tsunami approaches shallow water, the wave height can become much greater that the normal level of the ocean. The height of the wave may reach 30 m. When a tsunami hits shore, it can be very destructive.

SEARCH: Use library references to find answers to your questions.

ACTIVITY

OBSERVING THE PROPERTIES OF A WAVE

You will need a length of rope and a piece of cloth.

1. Tie the cloth to the center of the rope.
2. Tie one end of the rope to a doorknob.
3. Hold the other end of the rope and stand away from the door.
4. Move your end of the rope slowly up and down. Observe the movement of the rope and the piece of cloth.
5. Move the rope faster and observe the movement of the rope and the cloth.

Questions

1. What did the motion of the rope resemble?
2. **Observe:** How did the piece of cloth move?
3. Did you use more energy when you moved the rope slowly or when you moved it fast?
4. How did the height of the rope change as you moved it faster?
5. **Observe:** What features of a wave did you observe in this activity?

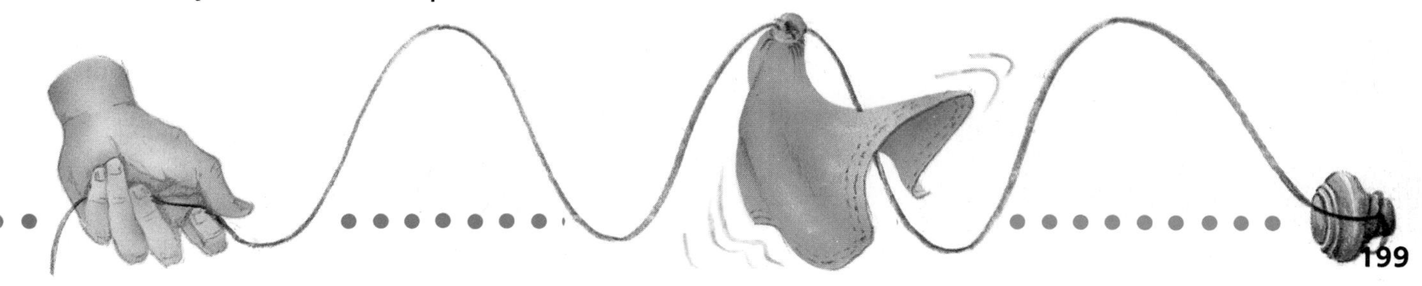

10-9 What are ocean sediments?

Objective ▶ Describe different kinds of ocean sediments.

TechTerms

- ▶ **nodules** (NAHJ-ools): mineral lumps found on the ocean floor
- ▶ **ooze:** ocean sediment formed from volcanic dust and the remains of ocean organisms

Ocean Sediments Ocean sediments are formed by materials that fall and collect on the ocean floor. Some ocean sediments come from rocks eroded from the land. Other sediments are the remains of living things. Dust and ash from volcanoes also sink to the ocean floor.

▶ ***List:*** What materials make up ocean sediments?

Eroded Rock Sediments Most of the sediments found close to shore are eroded rock particles. Rivers carry rocks of all sizes to the ocean. Waves and wind also erode rocks along the ocean shore. These eroded rock particles become part of the ocean sediments. The sediments gradually spread out over the ocean floor. Large particles settle close to shore. Smaller particles settle farther from the shore.

▶ ***Locate:*** Where do eroded rock particles usually form sediments?

Nodules Lumps of minerals called **nodules** (NAHJ-ools) are found on the ocean floor. Nodules are made up mostly of compounds of manganese, nickel, and iron. Small amounts of minerals compounds containing copper, lead, zinc, and silver, also are found in ocean sediments. These minerals can be mined from the ocean floor.

▶ ***Define:*** What are nodules?

Ooze Much of the ocean floor is made up of fine, soft sediments called **ooze.** Ooze is made up of volcanic dust and the remains of ocean organisms. How is ooze formed? When ocean organisms die, their shells and skeletons sink to the ocean floor.

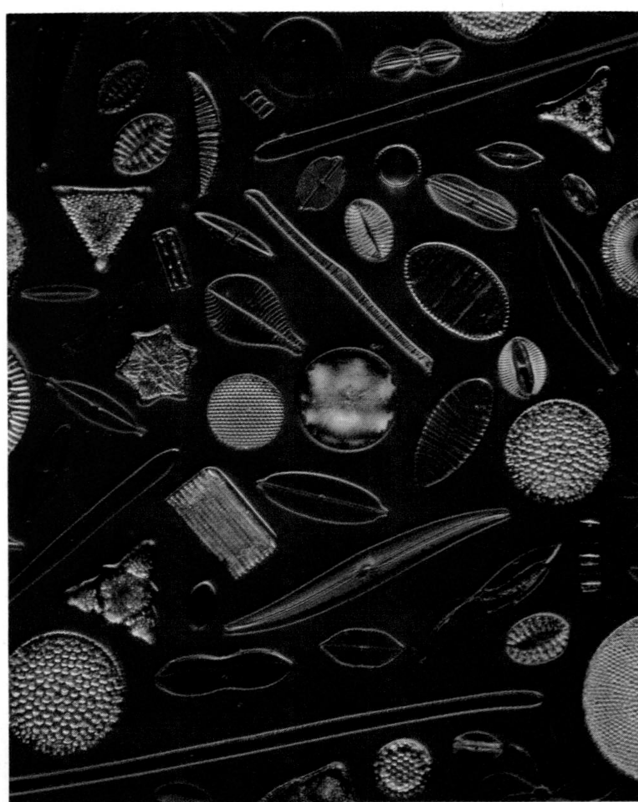

Chemicals in ocean water break apart the shells. The small pieces of shell mix with volcanic dust and water in the ocean to form ooze. Much of the ooze comes from microscopic plants and animals. Larger animals, such as clams and corals, also add to ooze.

▶ ***Define:*** What is ooze?

LESSON SUMMARY

- Ocean sediments are materials that fall and collect on the ocean floor.
- Eroded rock particles form most of the sediments close to shore.
- Minerals form part of ocean sediments.
- Much of the ocean floor is made up of ooze.

CHECK *Complete the following.*

1. Materials that fall to the ocean floor form ______ .
2. The largest rock particles settle ______ to shore.
3. Lumps of ______ called nodules are found on the ocean floor.
4. Nodules are made up mostly of manganese, nickel, and ______ .
5. Ooze is a fine mud formed from ______ and living things.

APPLY *Complete the following.*

6. **Hypothesize:** Why do small rock particles settle farther from shore than larger rock particles?
7. Why is mining nodules from the ocean floor helpful to people?
8. **Infer:** If a volcano erupts on land, how do you think sediments from this volcano get into the ocean?

InfoSearch

Read the passage. Ask two questions about the topic that you cannot answer from the information in the passage.

Underwater Canyons The continental slope is the part of the ocean floor between the continental shelf and the ocean basin. In many places the continental slope has deep canyons. Scientists are not sure how these canyons were formed. Some scientists believe they may have been formed by a landslide under the sea. Scientists infer that ocean sediments collect near the edge of the continental shelf. From time to time, these sediments slide down the continental slope. The sediments cause water to flow down the slope like a river. Gradually, the slope erodes and forms canyons.

SEARCH: Use library references to find answers to your questions.

ACTIVITY

OBSERVING THE SETTLING OF OCEAN SEDIMENTS

You will need a plastic container with a cover, small pebbles, sand, soil, and water.

1. Place a small amount of pebbles, sand, and soil into a plastic container.
2. Fill the container halfway with water. Then place the cover on the container.
3. Do the next three steps outside. Shake the container gently for about 10 seconds.
4. Quickly empty the container onto the ground. Observe where the different particles settle.
5. Leave the particles undisturbed on the ground for several hours. Then observe the pattern that forms.

Questions

1. **a. Observe:** Which particles settled on the ground closest to where you emptied the container? **b.** Which particles settled farther out?
2. **Analyze:** Why did the particles settle out in the way they did?
3. How does this activity relate to the way sediments settle out from the shore?

What are some ocean landforms?

Objective ▶ Describe the ocean floor.

TechTerms

- ▶ **continental shelf:** part of a continent that slopes gently away from the shoreline
- ▶ **continental slope:** part of a continent between the continental shelf and the ocean floor
- ▶ **guyot** (GEE-oh): flat-topped seamount
- ▶ **seamount:** volcanic mountain on the ocean floor
- ▶ **trench:** deep canyon on the ocean floor

Continental Margin The continental margin divides a continent from the ocean floor. The edges of the continents extend into the oceans. At first, a continent slopes gently downward under the ocean. This area is called the **continental shelf.** In some places, the continental shelf is very narrow. In other places, the shelf extends more than 150 km from the edge of the continent. Beyond the continental shelf is the **continental slope.** The continental slope is steeper than the continental shelf.

▶ *Compare:* Which is steeper, the continental shelf or the continental slope?

The Ocean Floor Like the earth's surface, the ocean floor has different landforms. The flat parts of the ocean floor are plains. Plains cover about half of the ocean floor. Ranges of high mountains run through the middle of the oceans. These mountain ranges are called mid-ocean ridges. In some places, mid-ocean ridges rise above the ocean surface. They form islands.

▶ *Identify:* Name two features of the ocean floor.

Trenches Deep **trenches,** or underwater canyons, are found on the ocean floor. The deepest of these is the Marianas Trench in the Pacific Ocean. This trench is more than 11,000 m deep. Mount Everest is the highest mountain on land. It is 8800 m high. Mount Everest would fit into the Marianas Trench and still be more than 2000 m below the ocean surface.

▶ *Compare:* How does the depth of the Marianas Trench compare to the height of Mt. Everest?

Seamounts and Guyots Many mountain peaks are scattered on the ocean floor. These peaks are **seamounts.** Seamounts were once active underwater volcanoes. Seamounts that reach above the ocean surface form volcanic islands. The Hawaiian Islands are the peaks of underwater volcanoes. Some seamounts have flattened tops. These seamounts are called guyots (GEE-ohs).

▶ *Define:* What is a guyot?

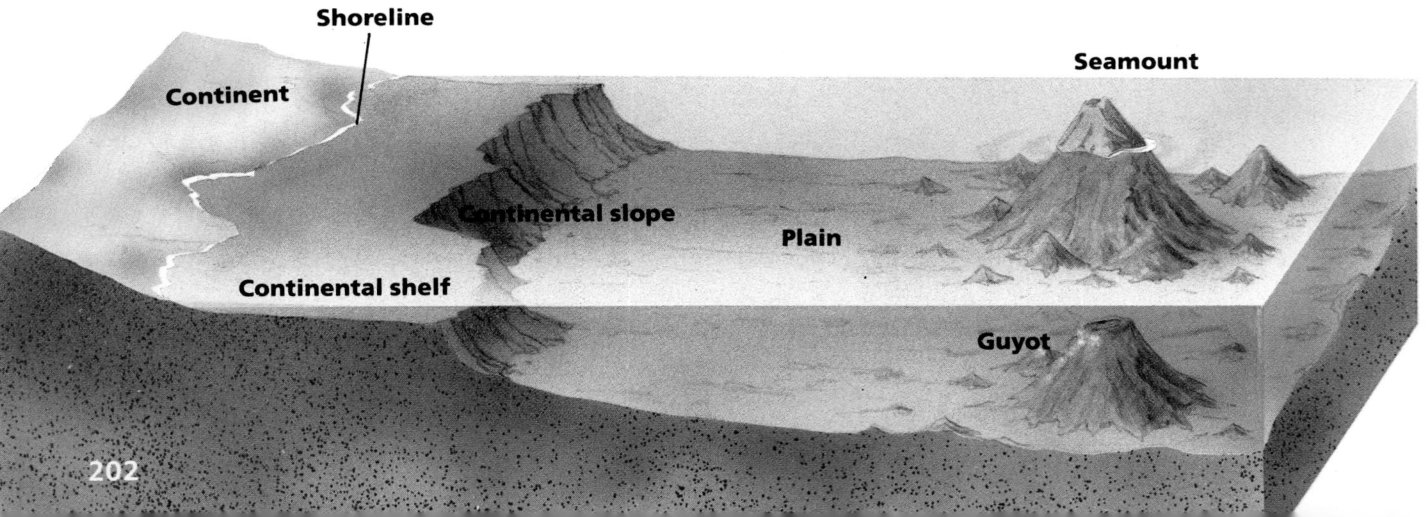

LESSON SUMMARY

- The continental margin divides a continent from the ocean floor.
- The flat parts of the ocean floor are plains.
- Mid-ocean ridges are ranges of high mountains on the ocean floor.
- Deep canyons, or trenches, are found on the ocean floor.
- Seamounts are underwater volcanoes.
- A guyot is a flattened seamount.

CHECK *Complete the following.*

1. The ______ divides a continent from the ocean floor.
2. Two parts of the continental margin are the continental shelf and the continental ______
3. Three landforms on the ocean floor are ______, mountains, and canyons.
4. The deepest ______ on the ocean floor is more than 11,000 m deep.
5. Mountains on the ocean floor are called ______.
6. A ______ is a seamount with a flattened top.

APPLY *Complete the following.*

7. **Predict:** What would happen to the continental shelf if the sea level dropped sharply?
8. On the ocean floor, mountains are higher and plains are flatter than on the earth's surface. Explain.

InfoSearch

Read the passage. Ask two questions about the topic that you cannot answer from the information in the passage.

Fishing on the Grand Banks The most productive fishing grounds in the world are found on continental shelves. One of these fishing grounds is the Grand Banks. The Grand Banks is an area of shallow water off the Atlantic coast of Canada. Because of the available food supply, large numbers of different fishes can be found here. Fishing is an important part of the economy of many countries. Fishing boats from Canada, the United States, Japan, and some European countries catch tons of fish off the Grand Banks every year.

SEARCH: Use library references to find answers to your questions.

PEOPLE IN SCIENCE

JACQUES-YVES COUSTEAU (1910–present)

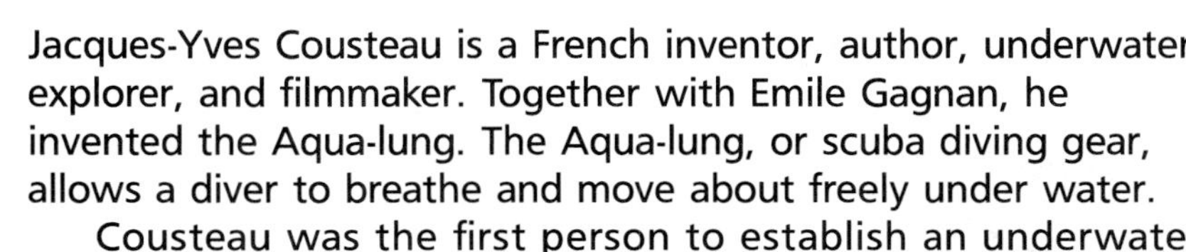

Jacques-Yves Cousteau is a French inventor, author, underwater explorer, and filmmaker. Together with Emile Gagnan, he invented the Aqua-lung. The Aqua-lung, or scuba diving gear, allows a diver to breathe and move about freely under water.

Cousteau was the first person to establish an underwater diving station. He built this station at the edge of the continental shelf. Divers lived and worked at the underwater station for long periods of time. Cousteau also tested other inventions used to explore the oceans.

Cousteau has traveled all over the world exploring the oceans. He has conducted many experiments from his research ship, *Calypso* (kuh-LIP-soh). Cousteau has written many books about his adventures and about ocean life. He also has made over 100 films about nature and the environment. Cousteau's adventures have made people aware of the undersea world and how pollution threatens it. He wants people to help make the oceans clean for future generations.

10-11 What lives in the ocean?

Objectives ▶ Name the two main divisions of the ocean. ▶ Explain how living things in the ocean are classified.

TechTerms

- ▶ **benthos:** organisms that live on the ocean floor
- ▶ **nekton** (NEK-tun): free-swimming ocean animals
- ▶ **plankton** (PLANK-tun): floating organisms

Ocean-Life Zones Many different kinds of organisms live in the ocean. Living things in the ocean are found in two main zones, or divisions. The waters of the ocean are called the pelagic (puh-LAJ-ik) division. The ocean floor is called the benthic (BEN-thik) division.

Classify: What are the two main divisions of the ocean?

Plankton Many organisms float near the surface of the ocean. These living things are called **plankton** (PLANK-tun). Plankton are moved by the motion of the ocean waters. Most plankton are microscopic. There are two kinds of plankton. Phytoplankton (fite-uh-PLANK-tun) are floating plants. These plankton use the energy of sunlight to make food from carbon dioxide and water. Phytoplankton are a source of food for floating animals. Floating animals are zooplankton (zoh-uh-PLANK-tun).

Classify: What are two kinds of plankton?

Nekton Free-swimming ocean animals are classified as **nekton** (NEK-tun). Fishes, whales, dolphins, seals, and squid all are nekton. Nekton can move about freely to find food. Some nekton eat plankton. Others eat animals that have eaten plankton.

List: What are some kinds of nekton?

Benthos Organisms that live on the ocean floor are classified as **benthos.** Benthos are found in shallow waters along a coast. They also are found in the deepest parts of the ocean. Some benthos attach themselves to the ocean floor. They stay in that spot until they die. Mussels, barnacles, and some seaweeds are benthos that remain attached to the ocean floor. Some benthos bury themselves in sand or mud. Others crawl along the ocean bottom. Seastars and crabs are animals that move around on the ocean bottom.

Define: What are benthos?

LESSON SUMMARY

- All life in the oceans is found in two main zones, or divisions.
- Plankton are organisms that float near the surface of the ocean.
- Nekton are free-swimming ocean animals.
- Benthos are organisms that live on the ocean floor.

CHECK *Complete the following.*

1. Living things in the ocean are found in the _______ or the benthic zone.
2. Two kinds of plankton are phytoplankton and _______ .
3. Plankton that make their own food are _______.
4. Whales and dolphins are examples of _______ .
5. Animals and plants that live on the ocean floor are called _______ .

APPLY *Complete the following.*

6. **Classify:** Group the following animals as **plankton, nekton,** or **benthos.**
   - **a.** jellyfish
   - **b.** mussels
   - **c.** squid
   - **d.** seals
   - **e.** barnacles
   - **f.** algae
7. **Hypothesize:** Almost all plants in the ocean grow within 80 meters of the surface. Explain.

Ideas in Action

IDEA: Many plants and animals that live in the ocean are used as food by people.

ACTION: Make a list of plants and animals from the ocean that you and your family have eaten.

Skill Builder

Classifying When you classify, you group things according to similarities. Algae are used to make foods and other products that you use every day. Collect at least 10 different product labels. Use your labels to identify several common products that are made with algae. Classify each kind of product as a food product, a cleaning product, or some other kind of product.

TECHNOLOGY AND SOCIETY

AQUACULTURE

Imagine farms for fishes, lobsters, shrimp and other water animals used for food. The farming of water animals and some plants is called aquaculture (AK-wuh-kul-chur). Water pollution and overfishing have increased interest in aquaculture.

Aquafarms have been springing up where dairy and crop farms used to be. Artificial lakes or even cement tanks are built. The tanks are filled with clean well water. The fish in these tanks are raised under controlled conditions. The fish are fed and protected from disease. There they can be easily harvested.

Other forms of aquaculture are also used. Areas of the ocean are "fenced-in" with nets. In these areas, shrimp and lobsters can be raised. Shellfish also are raised in areas like this.

10-12 What are coral reefs?

Objective ▶ Describe three kinds of coral reefs.

TechTerms

- **atoll** (A-tawl): ring-shaped coral reef
- **coral:** small animals found in shallow ocean waters
- **lagoon:** shallow body of water between a reef and the mainland

Coral Reefs Tiny animals called **coral** are related to jellyfish and sea anemones (uh-NEM-uh-neez). Coral live in warm, shallow ocean waters. These small animals take calcium out of the water. They use the calcium to make hard skeletons of limestone, or calcium carbonate, around their bodies. Coral attach to each other to form large colonies. New coral grow on top of dead ones. In time, a coral reef is formed.

Describe: What is a coral reef made of?

Fringing Reefs and Barrier Reefs Two kinds of coral reefs are fringing reefs and barrier reefs. A fringing reef forms when coral colonies touch the shoreline around a volcanic island. Fringing reefs are located along the coast of Florida.

Locate: Where are fringing reefs located in the United States?

Barrier Reefs Barrier reefs form around sunken volcanic islands. The reef once extended out from the shore. As the island sank, the reef became separated from the mainland by a body of water. This body of water is a **lagoon.** The Great Barrier Reef off the coast of Australia is the world's largest barrier reef. It is more than 2600 km long. In some places, it is almost 200 km wide.

Compare: How does a barrier reef differ from a fringing reef?

Atolls A ring-shaped coral reef is called an **atoll** (A-tawl). An atoll forms around a sunken volcanic island. Only the circular coral reef remains above the ocean's surface. Most atolls are located in the Pacific Ocean. In the center of an atoll is a lagoon. Ships are able to enter the lagoons of some atolls through channels that connect the ocean and the lagoon.

Define: What is an atoll?

LESSON SUMMARY

- A coral reef is made up of the skeletons of living and dead coral.
- Fringing reefs form around the shores of volcanic islands.
- Barrier reefs form around sunken volcanic islands.
- Atolls are ring-shaped coral reefs.

CHECK *Write true if the statement is true. If the statement is false, change the underlined term to make the statement true.*

1. Coral are related to jellyfish.
2. Coral reefs are made up of fish skeletons.
3. Coral reefs are found in deep water.
4. Atolls are found in the open ocean.
5. A pond is the body of water between a reef and the mainland.
6. What are three kinds of coral reefs?

APPLY *Complete the following.*

7. **Infer:** Why is the sand on a coral island white?
8. **Hypothesize:** Fossil coral reefs have been found beneath farmland in New York State. What does this discovery mean?

Designing an Experiment

Design an experiment to solve the problem.

PROBLEM: Do the skeletons of coral contain calcium carbonate?

Your experiment should:

1. List the materials you need.
2. Identify safety precautions that should be followed.
3. List a step by step procedure.
4. Describe how you would record your data.

Skill Builder

Classifying When you classify, you group things based upon similarities. Using reference materials, classify each of the following as a fringing reef, a barrier reef, or an atoll: Great Barrier Reef, Bermuda, Maldive Islands, and Morea Island. After you have classified each of these reefs, plot their locations on a map of the world.

SCIENCE CONNECTION

ARTIFICIAL REEFS

Natural coral reefs are the home to many ocean animals. Some of the best fishing spots are near reefs. To increase the number of fish, especially those used for food, people are building artificial reefs. These reefs also reduce beach erosion by blocking waves before they reach shore.

The Japanese have built artificial reefs for more than 300 years. The first artificial reef in the United States was built in 1830. The reef is made of logs attached to the ocean floor by rocks. This reef is off the coast of South Carolina.

Artificial reefs are built from old oil rigs, sunken ships, concrete blocks, and other large objects. For example, a few dozen battle tanks and armored personnel carriers are part of an artificial reef off the coast of Long Island, New York. Near Miami Beach, Florida, an entire 727 airliner was sunk to serve as a reef. Communities of sea creatures such as sea anemones, mussels, barnacles, and sponges cling to the metal surfaces.

UNIT 10 Challenges

STUDY HINT Before you begin the Unit Challenges, review the TechTerms and Lesson Summary for each lesson in this unit.

TechTerms

atoll (206)
benthos (204)
condensation (184)
continental shelf (202)
continental slope (202)
coral (206)
crest (198)
currents (196)
density currents (196)
evaporation (184)
geyser (188)
groundwater (186)
guyots (202)
lagoon (206)
nekton (204)
nodules (200)
oceanography (190)
ooze (200)
plankton (204)
pores (190)
precipitation (184)
salinity (194)
seamounts (202)
sonar (192)
spring (188)
submersible (192)
thermocline (194)
trench (202)
trough (198)
water cycle (184)
water table (186)
wave (198)
well (188)

TechTerm Challenges

Matching *Write the TechTerm that matches each description.*

1. tiny holes or air spaces
2. upper layer of saturated rock
3. study of the earth's oceans
4. underwater research vessel
5. amount of dissolved salts in ocean water
6. layer of ocean water in which temperature drops sharply
7. streams of water flowing in the oceans
8. regular up-and-down movement of water
9. streams of water that move up-and-down in the oceans
10. mineral layers found on the ocean floor
11. kind of ocean sediment
12. deep canyon on the ocean floor

Applying Definitions *Explain the difference between the words in each pair. Write your answers in complete sentences.*

1. evaporation, condensation
2. crest, trough
3. nekton, benthos
4. continental shelf, continental slope
5. seamount, guyot
6. precipitation, water cycle
7. coral, atoll
8. spring, geyser
9. groundwater, well
10. lagoon, sea
11. plankton, benthos

Content Challenges

Completion *Write the term that best completes each sentence.*

1. Water that evaporates from the earth is changed to a gas called _______ .
2. A cloud is a collection of _______ .
3. The pipe for a well must be _______ than the lowest level of the water table.
4. The temperature of spring water usually is _______ .
5. Most of the water on the earth's surface is _______ water.

6. Geographers are specialists who study the ______.
7. The depth of the ocean is calculated using ______ .
8. There are ______ different temperature layers in the ocean.
9. In the Northern Hemisphere, ocean currents move in a ______ direction.
10. Ocean currents flowing from areas near the equator are ______ than currents flowing from areas near the poles.
11. The distance between the crest of a wave and the trough of a wave is the ______ .
12. The distance between the crest of one wave and the crest of the next wave is the ______ .

Multiple Choice *Write the letter of the term or phrase that best completes each statement.*

1. The process by which a gas changed to a liquid is called
   a. precipitation. **b.** evaporation. **c.** sublimation. **d.** condensation.
2. The main forms of precipitation are
   a. rain and sleet. **b.** sleet and hail. **c.** rain and hail. **d.** rain and snow.
3. About 90% of the earth's fresh water supply is stored
   a. as groundwater. **b.** in wells. **c.** in the oceans. **d.** in geysers.
4. In dry weather, the level of the water table
   a. rises. **b.** drops. **c.** stays the same. **d.** increases, then decreases.
5. Old Faithful is
   a. a warm spring. **b.** an artesian well. **c.** a geyser. **d.** a hot spring.
6. The smallest ocean of the world ocean is the
   a. Indian Ocean. **b.** Pacific Ocean. **c.** Arctic Ocean. **d.** Atlantic Ocean.
7. The study of the world's oceans is
   a. hydrology. **b.** geography. **c.** oceanography. **d.** technology.
8. To find the depth of the ocean, scientists use
   a. hydrology. **b.** sonar. **c.** bathyspheres. **d.** bathyscaphes.
9. Ocean water is warmest
   a. at the surface. **b.** in the thermocline. **c.** in the deep ocean. **d.** at the continental margin.
10. Warm ocean currents come from areas near the
    a. North Pole. **b.** South Pole. **c.** Prime Meridian. **d.** equator.
11. The distance between one crest and the next is the
    a. trough. **b.** wavelength. **c.** wave height. **d.** density.
12. Nodules are made up mostly of nickel, iron, and
    a. manganese. **b.** chlorine. **c.** sodium. **d.** volcanic dust.

Understanding the Features

Reading Critically *Use the feature reading selections to answer the following. Page numbers for the features are shown in parentheses.*

1. **Define:** What is a hydrologist? (189)
2. **Infer:** What do marine biologists study? (191)
3. What is done at desalination plants? (195)
4. **Building vocabulary:** What does the letters in the word "scuba" stand for? (197)
5. What is the name of Jacques Cousteau's research ship?
6. **Define:** What is aquaculture? (205)

Concept Challenges

Interpreting a Diagram *Use the diagram to complete the following.*

1. What letter on the diagram shows evaporation taking place?
2. What is evaporation?
3. Which letter on the diagram shows ground water?
4. Where does groundwater come from?
5. Which letter in the diagram shows precipitation?
6. What form of precipitation is shown is shown?
7. Name three other forms of precipitation.
8. Where does condensation take place?
9. What is condensation?
10. What is runoff?

Critical Thinking *Answer the following in complete sentences.*

1. **Calculate:** If a sonar signal sent from a ship returns 8 seconds later, how deep is the ocean floor?
2. **Contrast:** How does a bathyscaphe differ from a bathysphere?
3. **Synthesize:** If the level of a water table is 10 m below the earth's surface during the wet season and 15 m below the surface during the dry season, at what depth should a pipe for the water table be? Why?
4. How does a hot spring differ from a geyser?
5. **Predict:** How would the salinity of the oceans be affected if increased temperatures caused the polar icecaps to melt into the oceans?

Finding Out More

1. Some tools and instruments used by oceanographers are: corers, dredges, bathythermographs, deep water nets, and floats. Use library references to find out what each of these instruments is used to study. Present your findings in a table. If possible, illustrate your table with drawings.
2. Visit your local water company to find out where the fresh water for your community comes from. Be sure to ask how the water is transported from its source to your area. Present your findings in an oral report to the class.
3. Use clay to make a model of the landforms of the ocean floor. Be sure to include the continental slope, continental shelf, a trench, a seamount, and a guyot. Label each landform on your model.
4. Cut pictures and photographs of 15 ocean animals from newspapers and magazines. Combine your pictures with those of three of your classmates. Use the pictures you collected to make a bulletin board display of benthos and nekton. Use labels to identify each animal in your display.

THE ATMOSPHERE

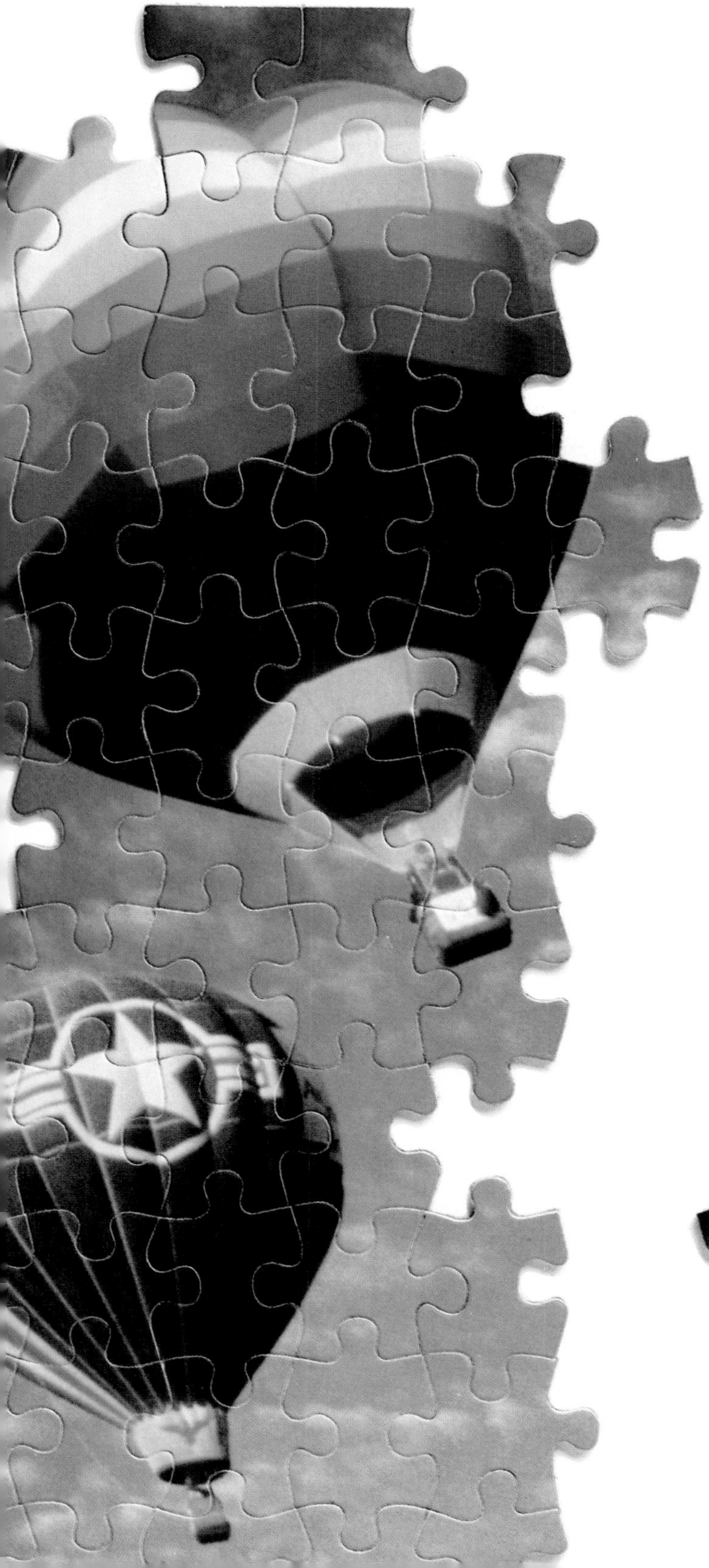

CONTENTS

STUDY HINT As you read each lesson in Unit 11, write the topic sentence of each paragraph in the lesson on a sheet of paper. After you complete each lesson, compare your list of topic sentences to the Lesson Summary.

11-1 What is air?

Objectives ▶ Recognize that air is matter. ▶ Identify and describe the main gases in air.

TechTerms

- **atmosphere** (AT-mus-feer): envelope of gases that surrounds the earth
- **matter:** anything that has mass and volume
- **respiration** (res-puh-RAY-shun): process by which living things combine oxygen with food to get energy

A Mixture of Gases Air is a colorless, tasteless, odorless mixture of gases. Air is **matter.** Matter is anything that has mass and takes up space, or has volume.

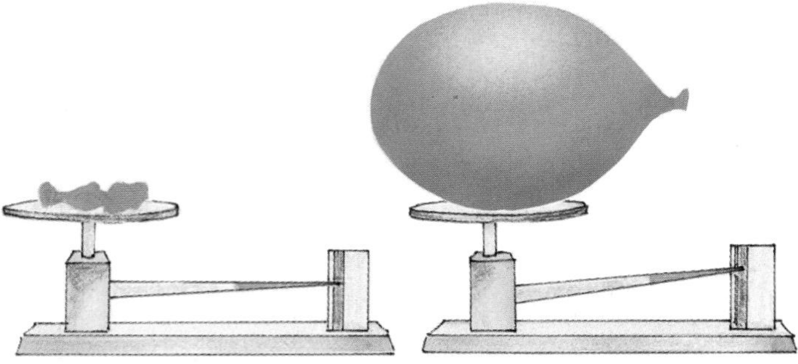

Figure 1 Air has mass and volume.

The **atmosphere** (AT-mus-feer), or air, is the envelope of gases that surrounds the earth. Air is made up mostly of nitrogen and oxygen. Air also is made up of other gases. The pie graph shows the percentages of the gases that make up air.

▶ *Analyze:* What percentage of the air is made up of helium, neon, krypton, and xenon?

Nitrogen About 78% of the atmosphere is nitrogen. Living things, or organisms (AWR-guh-niz-ums), need nitrogen. However, most living things cannot use nitrogen gas from the air. Bacteria (bak-TEER-ee-uh) are microscopic organisms that live in soil, in water, and in the air. Some bacteria can change the nitrogen gas in the air into nitrogen compounds. Plants get the nitrogen they

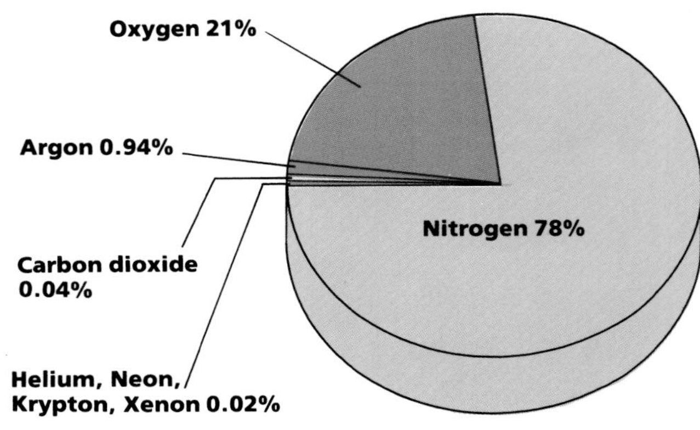

Figure 2 Gases in air

need from the nitrogen compounds made by bacteria. Animals get the nitrogen they need by eating plants.

▶ *Define:* What are bacteria?

Oxygen About 20% of the air is oxygen. Oxygen is needed for things to burn. Living things also need oxygen to carry on **respiration** (res-puh-RAY-shun). Respiration is the process by which living things combine oxygen with food to produce energy. Food is the fuel that provides living things with energy. A fuel is a substance that gives off energy when it is burned. During respiration, oxygen "burns," or breaks down, the food you eat to release energy. Most living things get the oxygen they need from the air.

▶ *Infer:* How do you get the oxygen you need to carry on respiration?

Carbon Dioxide About 0.04% of the air is made up of carbon dioxide. Carbon dioxide is released when things burn. Respiration produces carbon dioxide as a waste product. You get rid of this carbon dioxide when you breathe out. Plants need carbon dioxide to make food.

▶ *State:* How is carbon dioxide added to the air?

LESSON SUMMARY

- Air is matter.
- The atmosphere is an envelope of gases that surrounds the earth.
- About 78% of the air is made up of nitrogen.
- About 20% of the air is made up of oxygen.
- About 0.04% of the air is made up of carbon dioxide.

CHECK *Complete the following.*

1. Name three gases that make up air.
2. What is matter?
3. Why do living things need oxygen?

APPLY *Use the pie graph on page 212 to answer the following.*

4. What gas makes up most of the air?
5. **Calculate:** What percentage of the air is made up of oxygen, nitrogen, and carbon dioxide?
6. What gases make up only 1% of air?

Complete the following.

7. **Hypothesize:** Will a candle burn if no oxygen is present? Explain.
8. Respiration is a chemical process. The formula for respiration is
   glucose + oxygen → carbon dioxide + water + energy
   - **a. Infer:** What is the fuel in this formula?
   - **b. Infer:** What waste products are produced during respiration?

Designing an Experiment

Design an experiment to solve the problem.

PROBLEM: How can you show that air is matter?

Your experiment should:

1. List the materials you need.
2. Identify safety precautions that should be followed.
3. List a step-by-step procedure.
4. Describe how you would record your data.

CAREER IN EARTH SCIENCE

AIR POLLUTION TECHNICIAN

During the year, weather forecasters often tell you whether the air quality is good, fair, or poor. They are telling you about the pollution in the air. Sometimes, a pollution alert will be given. Many people need to know how high the pollution level is. During a pollution alert, older people and people with allergies are advised to stay indoors.

The information about air quality is gathered by air pollution technicians. They collect air samples from different places. Tests are run on the air samples. The tests tell how much of each kind of pollutant is in the air. The results of the tests may be sent to weather information services. The information also is used to find ways to control air pollution.

To be an air pollution technician, you should know mathematics. You will need to take technical courses related to the field.

11-2 What are the layers of the atmosphere?

Objective ▶ Name and describe the layers of the atmosphere.

TechTerms

- **ionosphere** (Y-on-uh-sfeer): upper layer of the atmosphere
- **stratosphere** (STRAT-uh-sfeer): middle layer of the atmosphere
- **tropopause** (TROHP-oh-pawz): place where the troposphere ends
- **troposphere** (TROHP-uh-sfeer): lowest layer of the atmosphere

Layers of the Atmosphere The atmosphere begins at the earth's surface and goes more than 50 km into space. Not all parts of the atmosphere are the same. The atmosphere is made up of three main layers. These layers are the troposphere (TROHP-uh-sfeer), the stratosphere (STRAT-uh-sfeer), and the ionosphere (Y-on-uh-sfeer).

▶ *List:* Name three layers of the atmosphere?

The Troposphere The **troposphere** is the layer of the atmosphere closest to the earth. The air you breathe is part of the troposphere. Winds occur in the troposphere. Most of the water vapor in the atmosphere is in the troposphere. This water vapor forms clouds. Weather takes place in the troposphere.

The higher you go in the troposphere, the colder it gets. Near the top of the troposphere, the temperature stops getting colder. This part of the troposphere is called the **tropopause** (TROHP-oh-pawz).

▶ *Define:* What is the tropopause?

The Stratosphere The stratosphere is the middle layer of the atmosphere. The temperature of the air hardly changes here. There is no weather in the stratosphere. Airplanes travel in this layer. A layer of ozone (OH-zohn) is found in the upper stratosphere. Ozone is a form of oxygen. Ozone stops most of the ultraviolet (ul-truh-VY-uh-lit) light from the sun from reaching the earth. Ultraviolet light causes sunburn. Small amounts of ultraviolet light are needed by living things. Large amounts are harmful.

▶ *Predict:* What might happen if the ozone layer of the stratosphere were destroyed?

The Ionosphere The ionosphere is the top layer of the atmosphere. Charged particles called ions (Y-onz) are found in this layer. Radio waves sent from the earth are reflected, or bounced off, these ions. Because of the ionosphere, radio signals can be transmitted, or sent, from one part of the earth to another.

▶ *Describe:* How is the ionosphere used in communication?

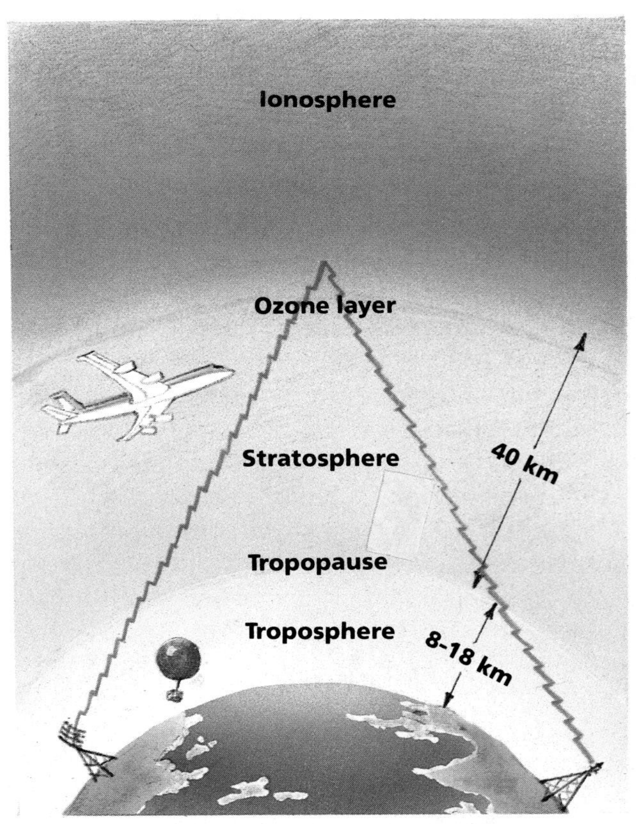

LESSON SUMMARY

- The atmosphere is made up of three layers.
- The troposphere is the lowest layer of the atmosphere.
- The upper layer of the troposphere is the tropopause.
- The stratosphere is the middle layer of the atmosphere.
- The ozone layer protects the earth from the ultraviolet light from the sun.
- The ionosphere is the upper layer of the atmosphere.

CHECK *Complete the following.*

1. The atmosphere is made up of _______ layers.
2. The upper part of the troposphere is the _______ .
3. Ozone is a form of _______ .

Classify: Identify the layer of the atmosphere described by each of the following.

4. stops ultraviolet rays
5. begins at the tropopause
6. has weather
7. reflects radio signals
8. ends at the tropopause
9. has a constant temperature
10. is made up of charged particles

APPLY *Complete the following.*

11. **Infer:** Why do most airplanes travel in the stratosphere?
12. **Compare:** How do air temperatures differ in the troposphere and the stratosphere?

Use the diagram on page 214 to answer the following.

13. **Infer:** Which layer of the atmosphere would be best for flying a kite? Why?
14. How far does the stratosphere go up into space?
15. How far does the troposphere go into space?

Skill Builder

Using Prefixes A prefix is a word part that is placed at the beginning of a word. Use a dictionary to find the meanings of the prefixes "atmo-" and "tropo-." Write the meanings of these prefixes on a sheet of paper. Beside each definition, write a brief statement explaining how the meaning of the prefix relates to the words "atmosphere" and "troposphere."

SCIENCE CONNECTION

A HOLE IN THE OZONE LAYER

In the 1970s, scientists found a hole in the ozone layer. The hole was above Antarctica. Scientists noticed that the hole was getting bigger. In 1988, the hole was about the size of the United States.

Scientists have found that the ozone layer can be destroyed by certain pollutants (puh-LOOT-unts). These pollutants are chemicals called chlorofluorocarbons (KLAWR-oh-FLAWR-oh-KAR-buhns), or CFCs. CFCs are used in spray cans, refrigerators, and air conditioners. Some industrial processes also use CFCs. Scientists think that CFCs are causing the hole in the ozone layer.

In 1978, the use of CFCs in spray cans was banned in the United States. In 1987, other countries joined in this ban. In 1996, the ozone hole was smaller than scientists predicted. The ban seems to be helping. Still, even if all CFCs are banned, the ozone layer will not return to normal for 75 years.

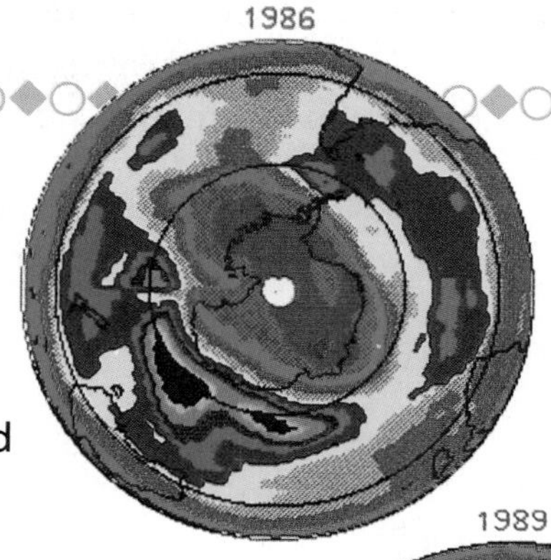

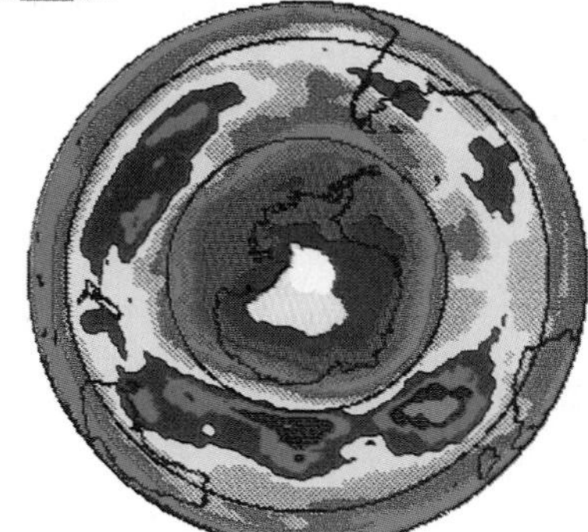

11-3 How does the earth get its heat?

Objective ▶ Describe how energy from the sun reaches the earth's surface.

TechTerms

- ▶ **radiant** (RAY-dee-unt) **energy:** energy that can travel through empty space
- ▶ **radiation** (RAY-dee-AY-shun): movement of energy through empty space

Radiant Energy The sun gives off **radiant** (RAY-dee-unt) **energy.** If you go out into the sunlight, you can feel the radiant energy from the sun warming your skin. Heat and light are forms of radiant energy.

Radiant energy can travel across millions of kilometers of empty space. The movement of energy through empty space is called **radiation** (RAY-dee-AY-shun). Most of the earth's energy comes from radiation from the sun.

▶ ***Name:*** What kind of energy can travel through empty space?

Absorption of Energy When light is absorbed, or taken in, it is changed into heat. Suppose you wrap two ice cubes with cloth. You wrap one ice cube in a dark-colored cloth and the other in light-colored cloth. You place both ice cubes in sunlight. Which one would melt first? The ice cube wrapped in the dark-colored cloth would melt faster than the one wrapped in the light-colored cloth. Dark-colored surfaces absorb light. This light is changed into heat energy. Light-colored surfaces reflect light. Surfaces that reflect light remain cooler than surfaces that absorb light.

▶ ***Describe:*** What happens when light is absorbed?

Energy from the Sun Only a small part of the sun's energy reaches the earth. Some of the sun's energy is absorbed by the ionosphere. Clouds, dust particles, and water droplets in the atmosphere also absorb or reflect some of the sun's energy. The energy that is reflected goes back into space. Energy that passes through the atmosphere is absorbed by the earth's surface. The absorbed energy is changed into heat. As a result, the earth becomes warmer.

▶ ***State:*** What happens when the sun's energy is absorbed by the earth's surface?

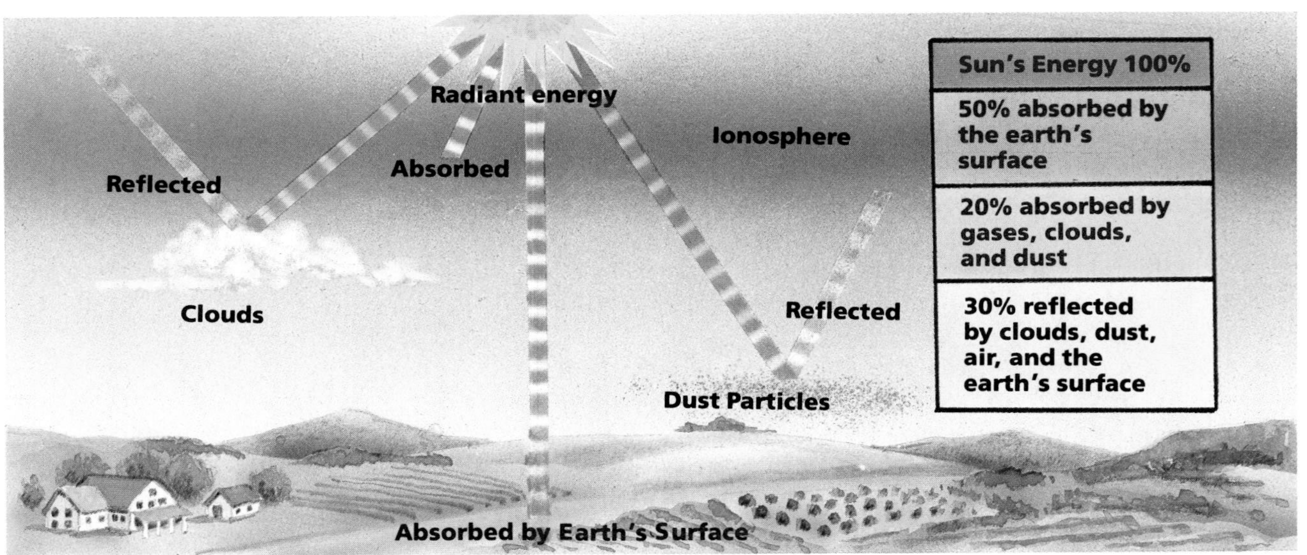

LESSON SUMMARY

- The sun gives off radiant energy.
- Energy is transmitted through empty space by radiation.
- When light energy is absorbed, it is changed into heat energy.
- Light energy that reaches the earth's surface is absorbed and changed into heat energy.

CHECK *Complete the following.*

1. Energy that can travel through empty space is called _______ energy.
2. Heat and _______ are two forms of radiant energy.
3. The sun's energy reaches the earth by _______ .
4. When light is _______, it is changed into heat.
5. Clouds, _______, and water droplets absorb or reflect the sun's energy.

APPLY *Complete the following.*

6. **Infer:** Why do light-colored clothes keep you cooler in the summer than dark-colored clothes?
7. **Predict:** Which would probably be cooler, a cloudy day or a clear day? Explain.

Skill Builder

Inferring When you infer, you form a conclusion based upon facts and not observations. Look at the diagram.

Which of the two houses would be cooler during the hot summer months? Which would be warmer during the cold winter months? Explain your answers.

TECHNOLOGY AND SOCIETY

SOLAR HEATING

The sun's energy, is an unlimited source of energy. It could be used to meet all the world's energy needs. People are working to develop ways to use solar energy.

For example, solar power plants in California's Mojave Desert use solar energy to produce electricity. At one plant, circles of huge mirrors reflect sunlight onto a central tower. A liquid runs through pipes in the tower. The concentrated sunlight makes the liquid hot. The hot liquid is stored in insulated tanks. Later in the day, the hot liquid is used to boil water and produce steam. The steam operates a generator that makes electricity. In this way, solar energy can be stored to produce electricity when people need it—even after sunset.

Different technology uses solar cells to turn solar energy directly into electricity. Panels of solar cells power satellites in space. You might have a calculator or watch that uses a solar cell. These devices can power cars and lightweight airplanes too. However, panels of solar cells are expensive. Scientists and engineers are working on ways to reduce the costs.

11-4 How is the earth's atmosphere heated?

Objective ▶ Explain how the atmosphere is heated.

TechTerms

- **conduction** (kon-DUCK-shun): movement of heat through a solid
- **convection** (kon-VEK-shun): movement of heat through a liquid or a gas

Conduction A metal pan placed over a flame will get hot. The metal molecules directly over the flame begin to move faster. They bump into slower-moving molecules around them and make the slower-moving molecules move faster. In this way, heat moves through the metal pan. The heat moves from an area of higher temperature to an area of lower temperature. This kind of movement of heat is called **conduction** (kon-DUCK-shun). Heat moves through solids by conduction.

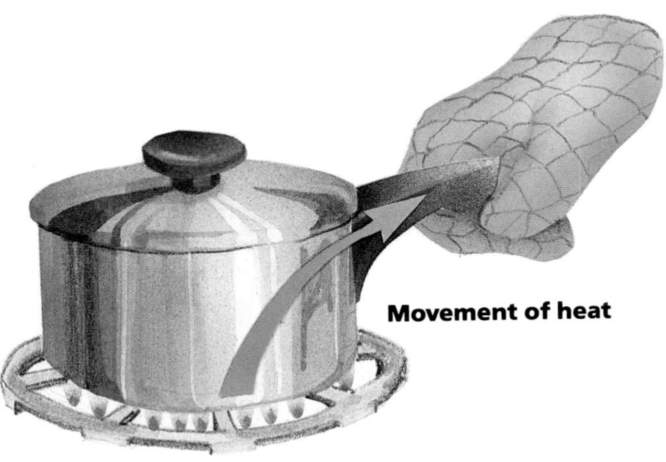

▶ ***Name:*** How does heat move through solids?

Heating the Atmosphere The troposphere, or lower layer of the atmosphere, is heated by conduction. The sunlight that is absorbed by the earth's surface is changed to heat. This heat warms the surface. Air in the troposphere touches the warm surface. It is heated by conduction.

The atmosphere also is heated by radiation. Radiant energy travels through space in waves. Most of the sun's energy is short-wave radiation. Short-wave radiation passes through the atmosphere and is absorbed by the earth. The earth warms up and radiates energy back to the atmosphere. The earth's radiant energy is long-wave radiation. The long-wave radiation is absorbed by the atmosphere and helps to heat the atmosphere.

▶ ***Describe:*** What happens to the energy radiated by the earth?

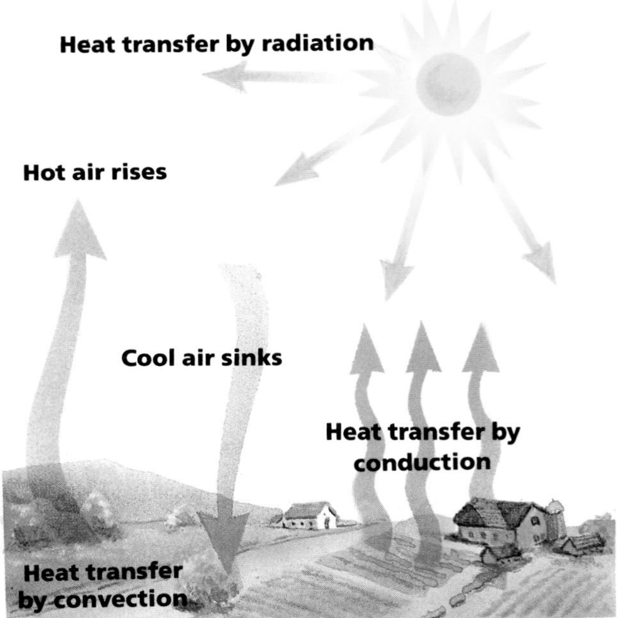

Convection The movement of heat in a gas or liquid is called **convection** (kon-VEK-shun). Heat moves through the atmosphere by convection. When air is heated, it expands. As warm air expands, it becomes lighter. Warm air is lighter than cool air. Warm air rises. Cooler, heavier air sinks.

▶ ***Define:*** What is convection?

LESSON SUMMARY

- Heat moves through solids by conduction.
- The troposphere is heated by conduction.
- Heat from the earth's surface warms the atmosphere by radiation.
- Heat moves through the atmosphere by convection.

CHECK *Write true if the statement is true. If the statement is false, change the underlined term to make the statement true.*

1. When a solid is heated, its molecules move <u>slower</u>.
2. Solids are heated by <u>convection</u>.
3. The troposphere is heated by <u>conduction</u>.
4. The earth radiates <u>short</u>-wave radiation.
5. Heated air <u>rises</u>.
6. Heat moves through air by <u>conduction</u>.

APPLY *Complete the following.*

7. Label each of the following as an example of **radiation**, **conduction**, or **convection**.
 a. The water in a fish tank becomes warmer after the heater is turned on. **b.** The sun warms your skin on a hot, summer day. **c.** A glass bowl is warmed by the food it holds. **d.** A burning log in a fireplace causes the temperature in a room to go up.
8. Look at the diagram. Why does the balloon rise?

Health & Safety Tip

Never grab the handle of a hot pot or pan with your bare hands. Always use a pot holder or oven mitt to remove a pot or pan from the stove. A substance that allows heat to pass through it easily is called a conductor. Do you think metal is a conductor or a nonconductor of heat? Is the material used to make potholders a conductor or a nonconductor of heat?

ACTIVITY

OBSERVING CONDUCTION

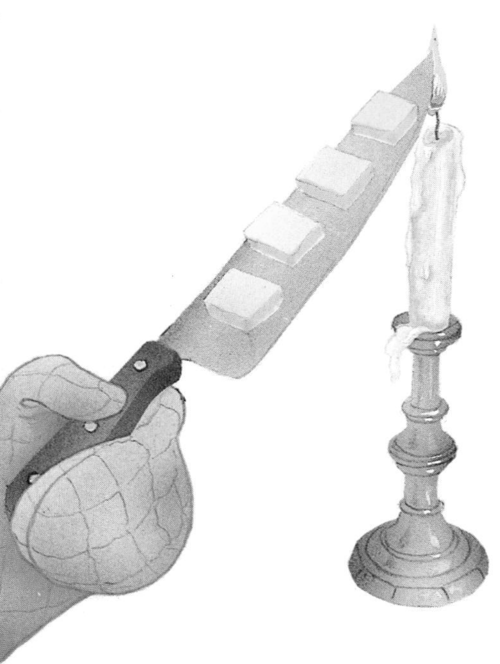

You will need a knife with a wooden handle, a frozen slice of margarine, matches, and a candle.

1. Light the candle with a match. **CAUTION: Be careful when working near an open flame.**
2. Cut the frozen margarine into four equal pieces.
3. Hold the knife sideways. Place the pieces of margarine at four different places on the blade of the knife. Put one piece of margarine near the knife's handle.
4. Hold the tip of the knife in the candle flame. **CAUTION: Use a pot holder or oven mitt. Hold the knife by the handle. Do not touch the blade.** Observe the margarine.

Questions

1. **Describe:** What happened to the margarine when you placed the tip of the knife in the flame?
2. **a. Measure:** How long did it take for the first piece of margarine to melt? **b.** The second? **c.** The third? **d.** The last?
3. Why did the pieces of margarine melt in the order they did?

11-5 What is air pressure?

Objective ▶ Explain how air exerts pressure.

TechTerms

- ▶ **newton:** metric unit of force
- ▶ **pressure:** amount of force on a unit of area

Measuring Weight Weight is a force. If you hold a book on the palm of your hand, you feel the weight of the book pressing down. Weight and other forces are measured in units called **newtons** (N). A 1-kilogram mass has a weight of about 10 newtons, or 10 N.

▶ ***Define:*** What is a newton?

Weight and Pressure The amount of force on a unit of area is called **pressure.** When you hold a book on the palm of your hand, the book's weight is spread over your hand. Suppose the book weighs 10 N and your hand has an area of 100 square centimeters, or 100 cm^2. The force on each square centimeter is then 10 N divided by 100 cm^2, or 0.1 N/cm^2. The pressure of the book on your hand is 0.1 N/cm^2.

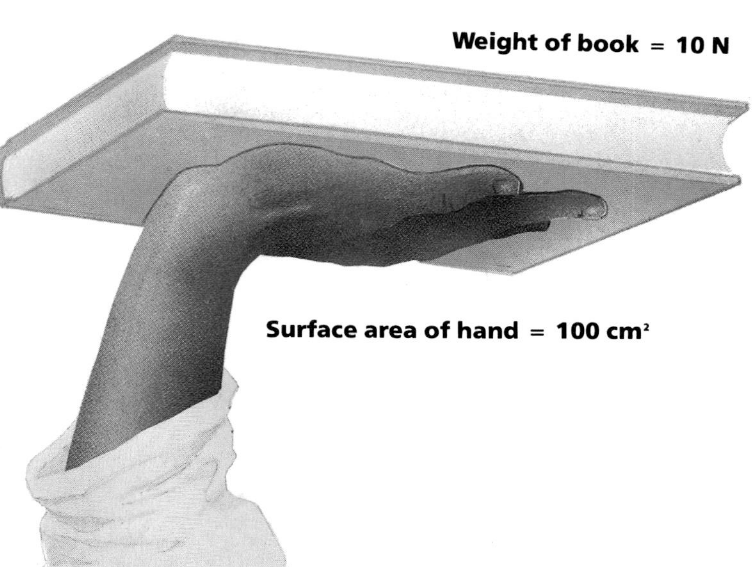

▶ ***Name:*** What is the amount of force on a unit of area called?

pressure = force / area

Air Pressure Air has weight. One liter of air weighs about 0.01 N at sea level. This is about the weight of a paper clip. The surface of the earth is at the bottom of the atmosphere. The weight of the air above the earth's surface pushes down on the surface. As a result, air exerts pressure on the earth's surface. You do not feel the weight of air pressing down on you, because the pressure is equal in all directions. The air inside your body presses outward in all directions.

Air pressure decreases as distance above the earth's surface increases. The air pressure on top of a mountain is less than the air pressure at sea level. Air pressure at sea level is about 10 N/cm^2.

▶ ***Compare:*** Where is air pressure greater, at sea level or on a mountain top?

LESSON SUMMARY

- Weight is a force.
- Pressure is the amount of force on a unit of area.
- The weight of the air in the atmosphere exerts pressure on the earth's surface.
- Air pressure decreases as distance above the earth's surface increases.

CHECK *Complete the following.*

1. Weight is a ______ .
2. Forces are measured in units called ______ .
3. Pressure is the amount of ______ on a unit of area.
4. The ______ of air in the atmosphere exerts pressure on the earth's surface.
5. Air pressure at sea level is ______ than air pressure on top of a mountain.

APPLY *Complete the following.*

6. **Calculate:** A 5-N force pushes down on an area that is 10 cm^2. How much pressure does the force have?

7. **Compare:** Look at the drawings. Which force exerts a greater pressure?

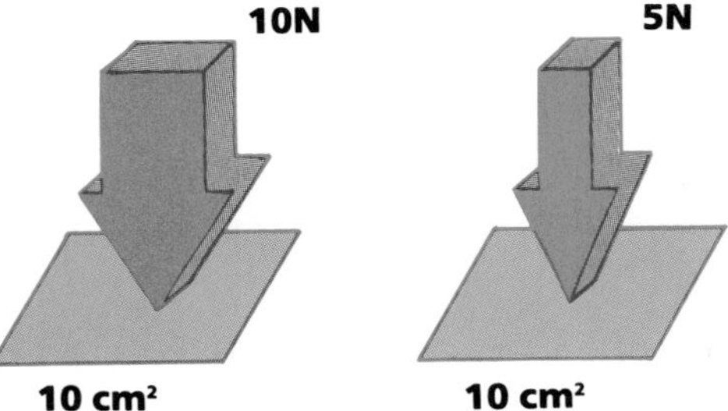

8. **Hypothesize:** Why do you sometimes feel your ears "pop" in an airplane?

Skill Builder

Writing a Laboratory Report Read the experiment. After you read the experiment write a laboratory report explaining why the egg slid into the bottle. Then, write the experiment as a laboratory report. Be sure to include the Problem, Materials, Procedure, Observations, and Conclusions.

Take the shell off a hard-boiled egg. Place a small piece of paper in the top of a juice bottle. Light the paper. Push the paper into the bottle. The burning paper uses up some of the oxygen in the bottle. Place the egg small end down in the top of the bottle. In a few seconds, the egg slides into the bottle.

TECHNOLOGY AND SOCIETY

BALLOONS AND RADIOSONDES

Balloons are used to carry weather instruments into the atmosphere. Some balloons are special. They can reach high into the atmosphere without bursting. These balloons are used to collect small meteorites (MEET-ee-uh-ryts). They also are used to study the stars and planets. Information from these balloons has helped scientists working in space programs.

Some balloons carry a shoebox-sized package of weather instruments called a radiosonde (RAY-dee-oh-sahnd). Radiosondes gather information about conditions in the upper atmosphere. The balloons carry the radiosondes into the air. When the balloon bursts, the radiosondes are carried back to the earth by a parachute. Information sent back by the radiosondes is used by airport personnel, weather forecasters, and weather services.

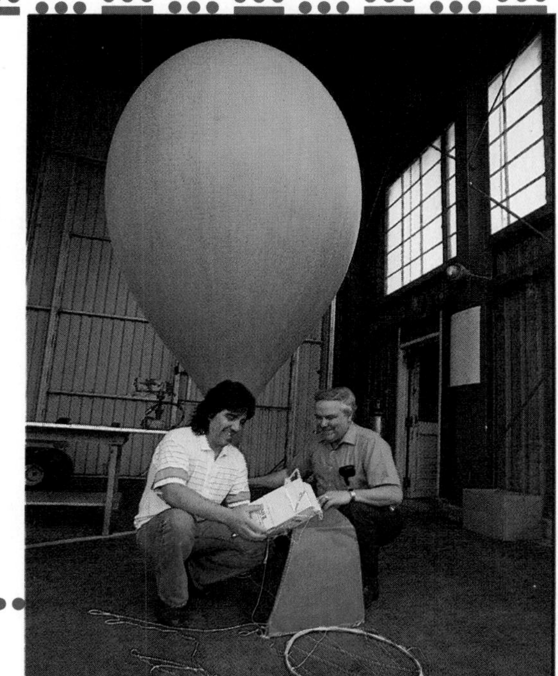

11-6 What factors affect air pressure?

Objective ▶ Identify the three factors that affect air pressure.

Elevation Air pressure changes with elevation, or height above sea level. The atmosphere is hundreds of kilometers thick. The weight of all this air causes a high pressure near the ground. The air molecules are close together. Near the top of the atmosphere, the air molecules are farther apart. There is very little weight of air pressing down. Therefore, the air pressure is low. The higher the elevation is, the lower the air pressure is.

Elevation increases
Air pressure decreases
Mount Everest
8850 meters — 25 cm
5000 meters — 42 cm
1000 meters — 71 cm
Sea level — 76 cm

▶ ***Describe:*** How does elevation affect air pressure?

Temperature The higher the temperature is, the lower the air pressure is. Heat makes air molecules move faster. As the molecules move faster, they get farther apart. Warm air weighs less than cool air. In the summer, the air is warmer than it is in the winter. The warm air has fewer molecules than the cool air. In the summer, the air pressure usually is lower than in the winter. In warm places on the earth, the air pressure is lower than in cold places.

▶ ***Describe:*** How does temperature affect air pressure?

Water Vapor The more water vapor there is in the air, the lower the air pressure is. Water evaporates from lakes, rivers, and oceans. Living things give off water vapor. All of this water vapor goes into the air. The molecules of water vapor take the place of some of the air molecules. Water vapor molecules usually weigh less than air molecules. Air with a lot of water vapor weighs less than dry air. Thus, moist air exerts less pressure than dry air. The pressure of moist air is lower than the pressure of dry air. Air pressure goes down as the amount of water vapor in the air goes up.

▶ ***Describe:*** How does water vapor affect air pressure?

LESSON SUMMARY

- Air pressure goes up with increasing elevation.
- Air pressure goes down as the temperature of the air goes up.
- Air pressure goes down as the amount of water vapor in the air goes up.

CHECK *Complete the following.*

1. Height above sea level is called ______ .
2. Air pressure ______ as elevation increases.
3. Air molecules near the top of the atmosphere are ______ than air molecules near sea level.
4. Warm air weighs ______ than cool air.
5. Molecules of water vapor weigh ______ than air molecules.
6. The pressure of moist air is ______ than the pressure of dry air.

APPLY *Complete the following.*

7. **List:** What three factors affect air pressure?
8. **Infer:** Standard air pressure is always measured at sea level at 0°C. Explain.

InfoSearch

Read the passage. Ask two questions about the topic that you cannot answer from the information in the passage.

The Magdeburg Hemispheres In 1654, Otto von Guericke performed an interesting experiment. Von Guericke was the mayor of a small German town called Magdeburg. He made a hollow metal sphere that had two halves, or hemispheres. The two hemispheres fitted tightly together. The only opening was a valve in one of the hemispheres. Air was pumped out of the sphere through the valve. Few air molecules remained inside. The air pressure inside the sphere was very low. The higher outside air pressure held the hemispheres together. Sixteen horses could not pull the hemispheres apart. Then the valve was opened to let air into the sphere. The two hemispheres came apart easily.

SEARCH: Use library references to find answers to your questions.

ACTIVITY

OBSERVING AIR PRESSURE

You will need a straw, a glass of water, and two glass plates.

1. Place a straw in a glass of water.
2. Put your finger over the top end of the straw.
3. Take the straw out of the water. Carefully observe the water inside the straw.
4. Hold the straw over the glass and remove your finger. Observe what happens.
5. Place two glass plates together. Take them apart. Wet the plates and again place them together. Try to separate the plates by pulling them apart.

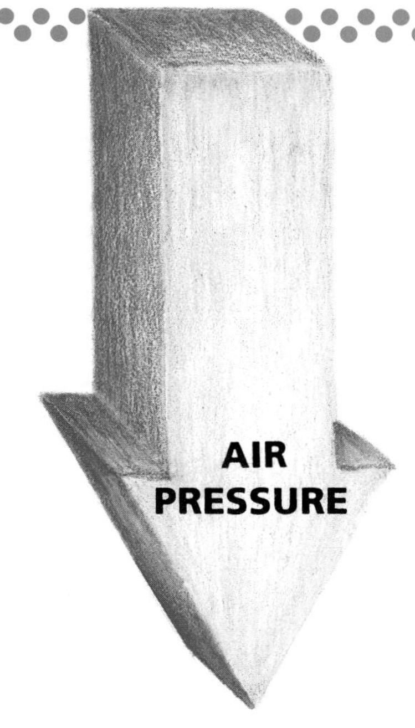

Questions

1. **Observe:** What happened when you removed the straw from the water with your finger on top of it?
2. **Observe:** What happened when you took your finger off the straw?
3. **a.** What holds the water in the straw? **b.** Why does the water fall when you take your finger away?
4. **a.** What happened when you tried to separate the wet glass plates? **b.** Why?

11-7 How is air pressure measured?

Objective ▶ Explain how a barometer is used to measure air pressure.

TechTerm

▶ **barometer** (buh-ROM-uh-ter): instrument used to measure air pressure

Mercury Barometer Air pressure is measured with an instrument called a **barometer** (buh-ROM-uh-ter). One kind of barometer is a mercury barometer. Look at the mercury barometer on page 225. The mercury barometer was invented by an Italian scientist, Evangelista Torricelli (eh-van-jeh-LEE-stuh tor-ih-CHEL-ee). A mercury barometer is made of a glass tube filled with mercury. The tube is open at one end. The open end of the tube is placed in a container of mercury. Air pressure pushes down on the surface of the mercury in the container. The mercury is pushed up the tube. At sea level, air pressure can hold up a column of mercury 760 mm high. As the air pressure changes, the level of mercury in the tube rises or falls.

Define: What is a barometer?

Aneroid Barometer Another kind of barometer is called an aneroid (AN-uh-royd) barometer. The word "aneroid" means "without liquid." An aneroid barometer is made of an airtight metal container. The sides of the container are very thin. They can bend in or out. When the air pressure increases, the sides of the container bend in. When the air pressure decreases, the sides bend out. A pointer is connected to the container. As the container changes shape, the pointer moves along a scale. The scale shows air pressure in millimeters of mercury. Some aneroid barometers keep a continuous record of air pressure.

Define: What does the word "aneroid" mean?

Measuring Air Pressure Standard air pressure is 760 millimeters of mercury. Sometimes, this is called one atmosphere. Air pressure also is measured in millibars (mb). Standard air pressure is equal to 1013.20 millibars.

Analyze: How many millimeters of mercury equal 1013.20 millibars?

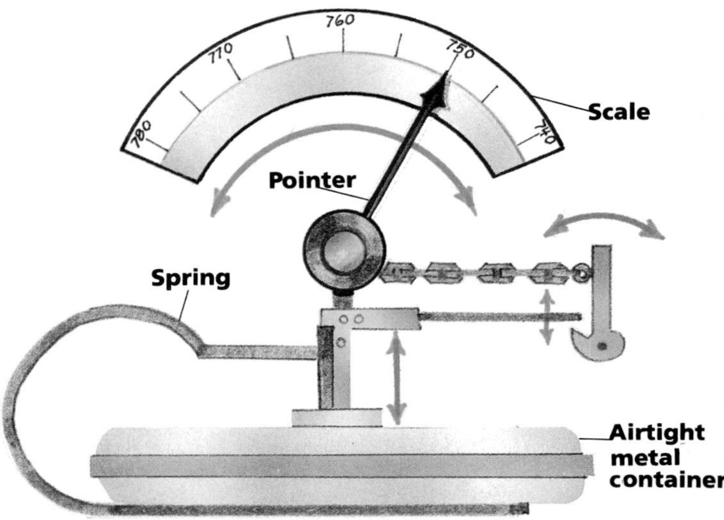

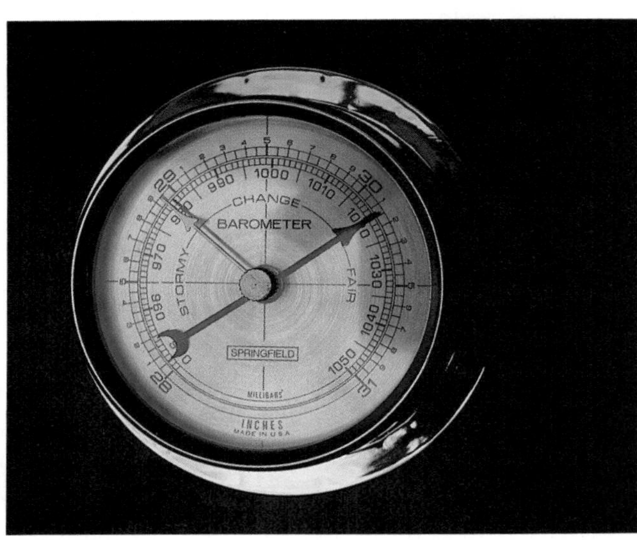

LESSON SUMMARY

- A barometer is used to measure air pressure.
- Two kinds of barometers are mercury barometers and aneroid barometers.
- Air pressure is measured in millibars.
- An altimeter is a barometer used to measure altitude.

CHECK *Complete the following.*

1. Air pressure is measured with a ______ .
2. Two kinds of barometers are mercury barometers and ______ barometers.
3. The mercury column in a mercury barometer is ______ high at sea level.
4. The word "______" means "without liquid."
5. Air pressure is measured in ______ .
6. An ______ is used to measure altitude.

APPLY *Complete the following.*

7. **Calculate:** Mercury is 13.5 times heavier than water. If a container of water can hold 20 g of water, how much more massive would an equal volume of mercury be?
8. **Calculate:** The density of mercury is 13.5 g/cm^3. The density of water is 1.0 g/cm^3. If air pressure at sea level supports a 760-mm column of mercury, how high a column of water can air pressure support at sea level?

InfoSearch

Read the passage. Ask two questions about the topic that you cannot answer from the information in the passage.

Measuring Altitude A barometer called an altimeter (al-TIM-uh-ter) can be used to measure altitude. At sea level, air pressure can hold up a 760-mm column of mercury. As you go higher, air pressure goes down. The mercury column drops. At 1000 meters above sea level, air pressure will support a column of mercury only 710 mm high. At 5000 meters, the mercury column is about 420 mm high. Mount Everest is 8850 meters high. It is the highest point on the earth. Here the mercury column is only about 250 mm high.

SEARCH: Use library references to find answers to your questions.

PEOPLE IN SCIENCE

EVANGELISTA TORRICELLI (1608–1647)

Evangelista Torricelli was an Italian mathematician and scientist. During his time, he improved the microscope and the telescope. His greatest discovery was the first mercury barometer. He made the discovery in 1643.

Torricelli filled a long glass tube that was closed at one end with mercury. He placed his finger over the open end. He turned the tube upside down. Then he placed the tube straight up and down in a container filled with mercury. When the mouth was under the surface of the mercury, he took his finger off the opening. The mercury in the tube dropped. It stopped at a height of about 30 inches. At the top of the tube there was nothing. It was a vacuum (VAK-yoom). Torricelli stated that the mercury was kept in this position because of the air pressure on the mercury in the container. Torricelli's mercury barometer is shown on the right.

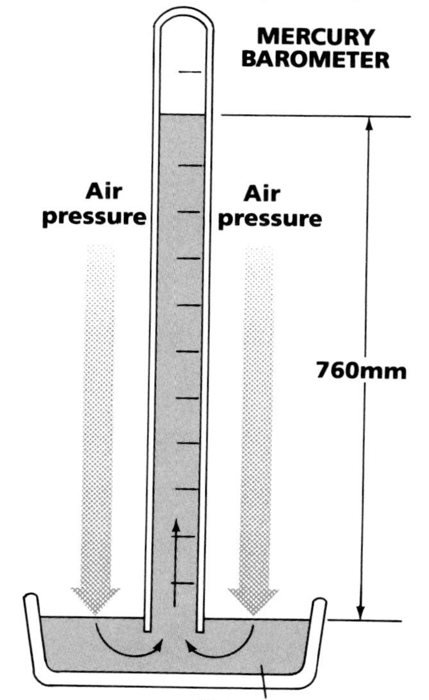

11-8 How do winds form?

Objective ▶ Explain how winds form.

TechTerms

- ▶ **air current** (KUR-unt): up-and-down movement of air
- ▶ **wind:** horizontal movement of air

Air Currents Up-and-down movements of air are called **air currents** (KUR-unts). Air currents are formed because the sun does not heat all parts of the earth equally. Some areas of the earth are warmed more than others. As air over the warmer regions is heated, it expands, or takes up more space. As the warmer air expands, it becomes less dense. As air over cooler regions is cooled, it becomes heavier, or more dense. The cool air moves in under the warm air. It pushes the warm air upward. As the warm air mixes with the cool air, it becomes heavier, and moves downward.

▶ ***Define:*** What is an air current?

Winds The horizontal (howr-uh-ZAHN-tul) movement of air along the earth's surface is called **wind.** Winds form as cool, heavy air moves toward warm, light air. Cool air moves in under warm air. The cool air moves along the surface of the earth toward warmer air.

▶ ***Explain:*** How are winds formed?

Winds and Air Pressure Winds are caused by differences in air pressure. Regions of cold, heavy air have high air pressure. These regions are called "highs." Regions of warm, light air have low air pressure. These regions are called "lows." Air moves from regions of high pressure to regions of low pressure. Winds form when air moves. The speed of the wind depends on the differences in air pressure.

▶ ***Predict:*** Will the speed of a wind be greater if the difference in air pressure is high or low?

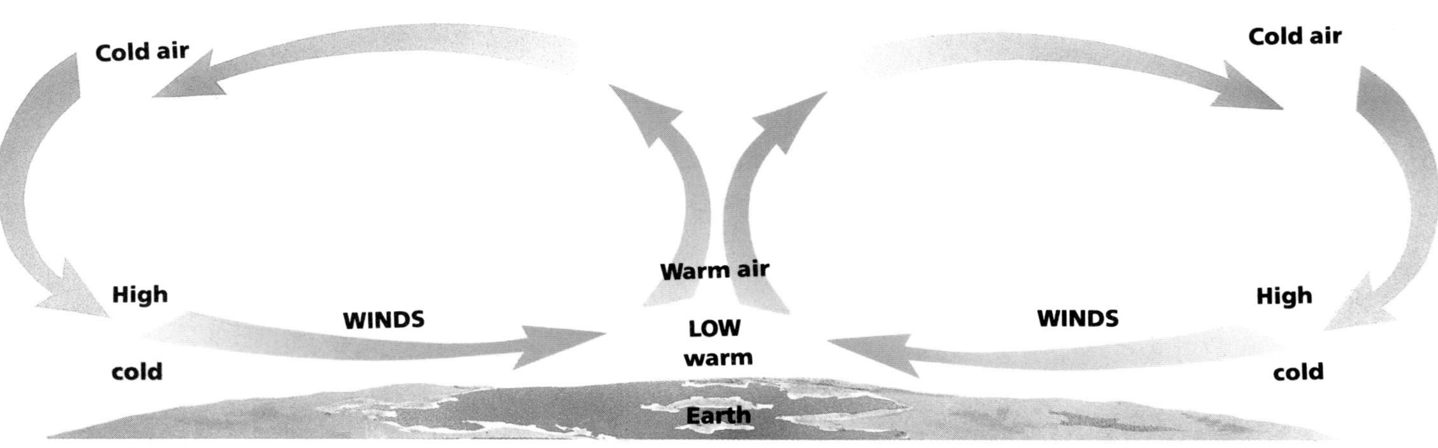

LESSON SUMMARY

- Air currents are caused by the unequal heating of air.
- The horizontal movement of air along the earth's surface is called wind.
- Winds are caused by differences in air pressure.

CHECK *Complete the following.*

1. An air current is an _______ movement of air.
2. Cool air is more _______ than warm air.
3. As cool air moves in under warm air, it pushes the warm air _______ .
4. Wind is the _______ movement of air along the earth's surface.
5. Winds are caused by differences in _______ .
6. Regions of cold, heavy air have _______ pressure.

APPLY *Complete the following.*

7. **Predict:** The map shows the air pressure for four different cities. **a.** Will winds move from Chicago to New York or from New York to Chicago? **b.** Will winds move from New York to Boston or Boston to New York? **c.** Will winds move from Philadelphia to New York or New York to Philadelphia?

Skill Builder

Identifying Winds are named for the direction from which they blow. A wind that blows from the north to the south is called a north wind. The arrows on the map show the movement of several winds. Name each of the winds.

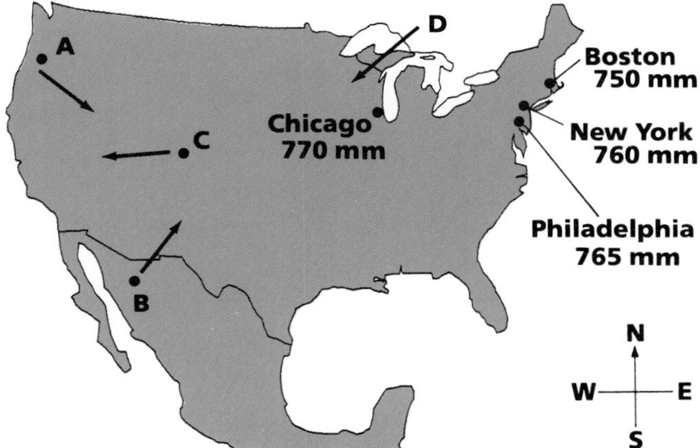

ACTIVITY

OBSERVING THE MOVEMENT OF WARM AIR

You will need a pencil with an eraser, a straight pin, a sheet of paper, scissors, and a lamp.

1. Cut a 10-cm square from the sheet of paper. **CAUTION: Be careful when using scissors.**
2. Make the paper into a pinwheel by following the instructions in the diagram.
3. Attach the pinwheel to the pencil's eraser with a pin.
4. Hold your pinwheel over the lighted bulb of a lamp. Observe what happens.

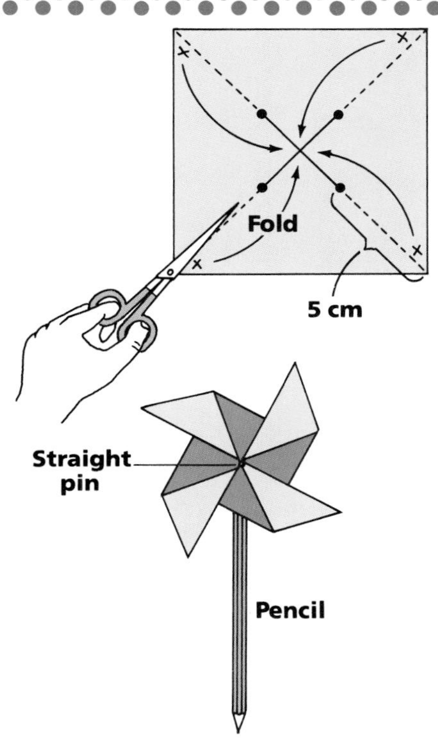

Questions

1. **a. Observe:** What happened when you held the pinwheel over the lighted lamp? **b. Infer:** What caused this to happen?
2. **Infer:** What can you infer about the movement of air from this activity?
3. **Relating Concepts:** Are winds caused by conduction, convection, or radiation? Explain.
4. How does this activity relate to the way winds form?

11-9 What are global winds?

Objective ▶ Describe global wind patterns.

TechTerms

- **global winds:** large wind systems around the earth
- **jet stream:** belt of high-speed wind

Global Winds Winds blow from regions of high pressure to regions of low pressure. Warm air over the equator forms a region of low pressure. Bands of high pressure are found north and south of the equator. Cold air over the poles forms regions of high pressure. These differences in air pressure produce patterns of **global winds.** Global winds are large systems of winds around the earth. At the equator, warm air rises and moves toward the poles. At the poles, cool air sinks and moves toward the equator. The diagram shows global winds.

Explain: What causes patterns of global winds?

Curving Winds Global winds do not move in straight lines. Because the earth rotates, or spins like a top, winds curve as they move from high-pressure to low-pressure regions. Winds moving toward the equator curve to the west. Winds mowing toward the poles curve to the east.

Identify: In what direction do winds near the equator curve?

Jet Streams In the 1940s, global winds called **jet streams** were discovered. They are belts of high-speed air in the upper atmosphere. The jet streams weave back and forth through the atmosphere. Jet streams are located at altitudes between about 6 km and 12 km. Their speeds may be as high as 500 km/hr. The jet streams flow from west to east. Airplanes flying in a jet stream gain speed going from west to east. They lose speed going the other way.

Define: What is a jet stream?

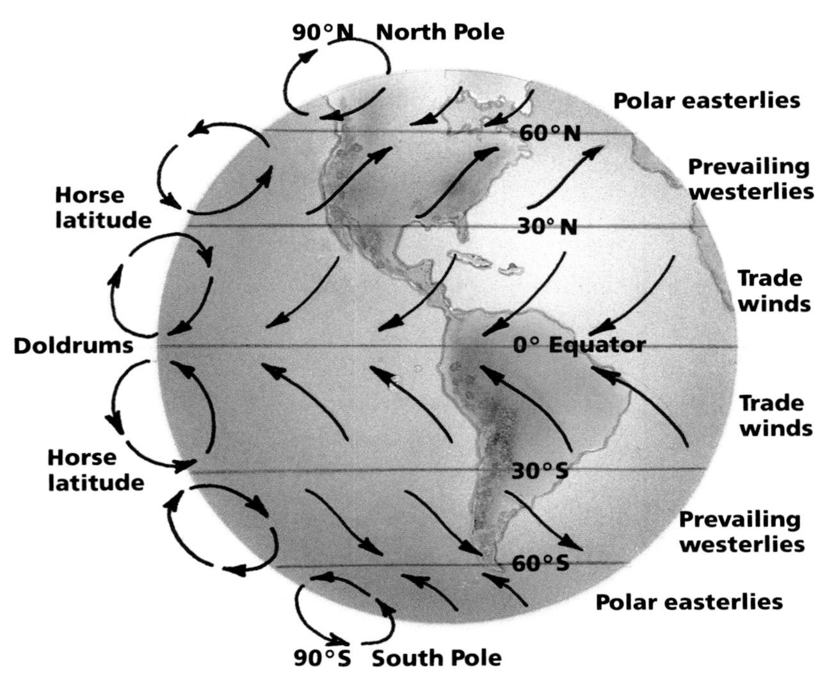

LESSON SUMMARY

- Differences in air pressure create patterns of global winds.
- Global winds curve because of the rotation of the earth on its axis.
- Jet streams are belts of high-speed winds in the upper atmosphere that move from west to east.

CHECK *Complete the following.*

1. Winds blow toward regions of _______ air pressure.
2. Air pressure over the equator is _______ .
3. Air pressure over the poles is _______ .
4. Differences in air pressure form patterns of _______ winds.
5. Because the earth _______, global winds curve.
6. Winds near the poles curve toward the _______ .
7. Belts of high-speed winds in the upper atmosphere are called _______ .
8. Jet streams move toward the _______ .

APPLY *Use the diagram of global winds on page 228 to complete the following.*

9. **Observe:** What are the global winds just north and south of the equator called?
10. What are the global winds between 30° N and 60° N called?
11. What are the global winds between 60° N and 90° N called?

Skill Builder

Researching Use an encyclopedia or other library references to look up the terms "doldrums" and "horse latitudes." Write a brief description of each of these terms in your own words. How do each of these terms relate to global wind patterns?

SCIENCE CONNECTION

WIND ENERGY

The wind is one of the oldest sources of energy. For years, farmers have used windmills to pump water. Today, many communities are using the wind to produce electricity. Modern materials and engineering could combine to make wind energy an important source of power for the future. Wind energy is a promising source of power because it produces no pollution. However, the speed and direction of the winds are unpredictable.

In some places, large windmill farms provide power for electric generators. Windmill farms may include hundreds of windmills. Four hundred wind generators located at Altamont Pass, east of San Francisco, are already in operation and producing electricity. One of the largest windmills is in Medicine Bow, Wyoming. This one windmill can provide enough electricity for 1200 homes.

Modern windmills do not look much like the windmills used to pump water on farms. Some of the newer windmills look more like airplane propellers or eggbeaters. Instead of wood, they are made of new, lightweight materials.

11-10 What causes local winds?

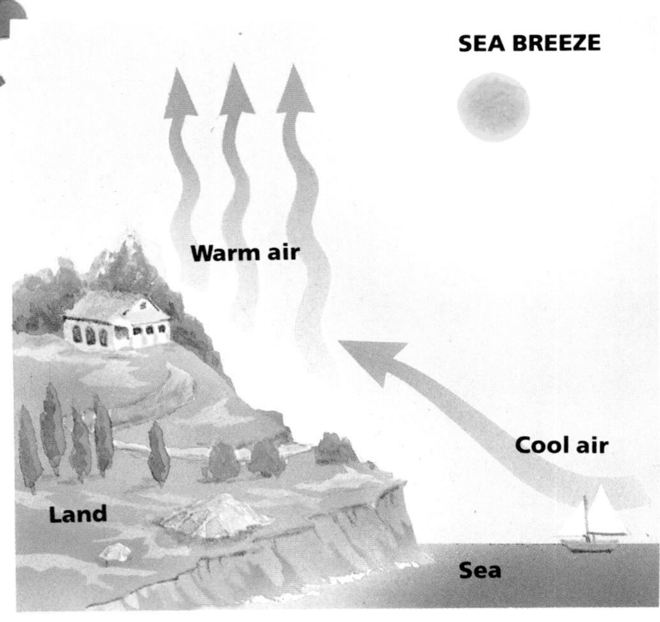

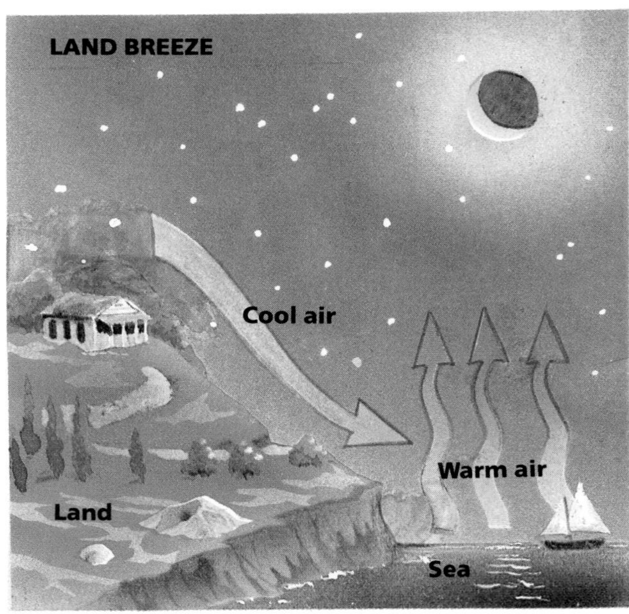

Objective ▶ Describe patterns of local winds.

TechTerm

▶ **monsoon:** wind that changes direction with the seasons

Sea and Land Breezes A breeze coming from the sea toward the land is a sea breeze. A breeze coming from the land toward the sea is a land breeze. Land and sea breezes are local winds.

The sun heats land faster than water. As a result, air over the land is warmer and lighter than air over the water. The cooler, heavier air over the ocean moves in toward the land. The warm light air over the land is pushed upward. The result is a sea breeze.

At night, the land cools faster than the water. The air over the land becomes cooler than the air over the water. The heavier air over the land moves toward the water. The warmer, lighter air over the water is pushed upward. The result is a land breeze.

▶ ***Compare:*** Which cools faster, land or water?

Mountain and Valley Breezes Mountain regions also have local winds. During the day, the air on a mountaintop is warmer than the air in the valleys. Warm air has low pressure. Air in the valley is cooler and has high pressure. Air moves from the high pressure of the valley to the low pressure of the mountaintop. This is a valley breeze. At night, the valleys are warmer than the mountaintops. The heavier mountain air moves downhill toward the valley. This is a mountain breeze.

▶ ***Describe:*** In which direction do valley breezes move?

Monsoons Parts of some continents have winds that change direction with the seasons. These winds are called **monsoons.** In the summer, the continent remains warm both day and night. Winds move from the ocean toward the land all summer. In the winter, the land gets very cold. The air above the oceans is warmer. Winds blow toward the oceans all winter. Monsoons happen near India. The summer monsoon brings warm, moist air with heavy rains. The winter monsoon carries dry air. There is little rain in winter.

▶ ***Define:*** What are monsoons?

LESSON SUMMARY

- Land breezes and sea breezes are local winds.
- A gentle breeze blowing from the sea toward the land is a sea breeze.
- a Land breeze occurs when winds blow from the land toward the sea.
- Mountain regions have local winds called mountain breezes and valley breezes.
- A wind that changes direction with the seasons is called a monsoon.

CHECK *Complete the following.*

1. A _______ breeze blows toward the land from the ocean.
2. Land is heated _______ than water.
3. Movement of air from the land toward the ocean is called a _______ breeze.
4. A _______ breeze moves downhill toward a valley.
5. Winds that change direction with the seasons are _______ .

APPLY *Complete the following.*

6. **Analyze:** During part of the year, monsoons bring heavy rains and warm temperatures to many countries. Do these rainy seasons occur in the summer or winter? Explain.
7. **Interpret:** What type of breeze is shown in the diagram?

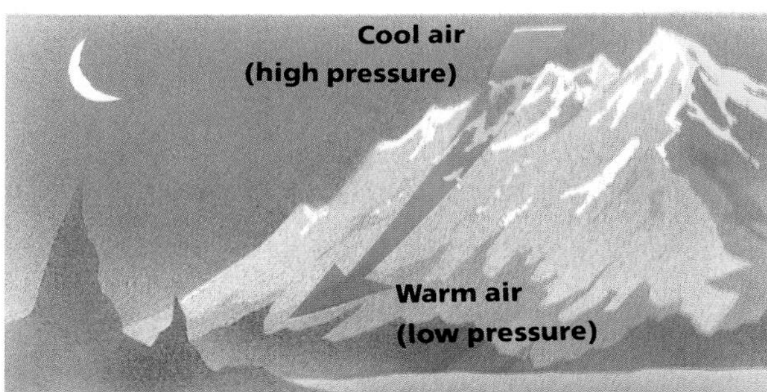

Skill Builder

Building Vocabulary Mistral, foehn (FAYN), and Chinook are the names of three local winds. Use a dictionary or other library references to look up each of these winds. Write a description of each wind on a sheet of paper. Where is each wind located?

LEISURE ACTIVITY

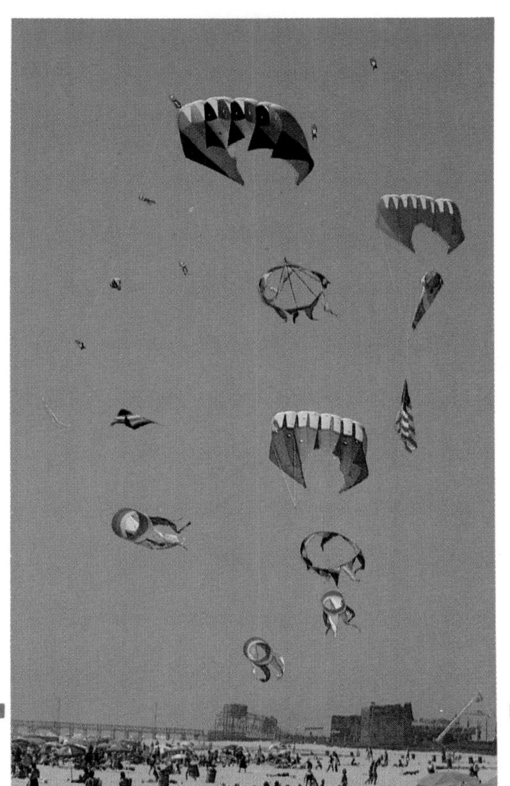

KITE FLYING

Kite flying is over 2000 years old. It probably was invented in China. Kite flying is a hobby that many people still enjoy today. In Japan, kite flying is a national sport. Contests are held and awards are given for design, construction, and flying accuracy.

Would you like to try kite flying as a hobby? All you need is a kite, a roll of string, and a good breeze. A kite does not move on its own. The wind that blows against it carries the kite into the sky. A firm hold on the string keeps the kite from flying away. You will have to exercise some control to keep your kite from becoming entangled in trees or telephone wires. A beach or open field is a good place to begin kite flying.

Some people design and build their own kites. Other people buy kites that are ready-made. Kites come in many shapes and sizes. There are box kites, triangular kites, dragon kites, and bird kites. With a little imagination, you can create your own special kite.

11-11 How is wind measured?

Objective ▶ Explain how weather instruments are used to measure wind.

TechTerms

- ▶ **anemometer** (an-uh-MOM-uh-tur): instrument used to measure wind speed
- ▶ **wind vane:** instrument used to measure wind direction

Measuring Wind Direction A wind is named according to the direction from which the wind comes. If a wind comes from the north, it is a north wind. If it comes from the east, it is an east wind. The direction of a wind is measured with a **wind vane.** A wind vane shows the direction a wind is coming from. Many wind vanes are shaped like arrows. When the wind blows, the arrow turns and points into the wind.

Figure 1 A wind vane

▶ ***Name:*** What is a wind that blows from the northeast named?

Measuring Wind Speed An **anemometer** (an-uh-MOM-uh-tur) is an instrument used to measure wind speed. An anemometer is shown in Figure 2. An anemometer is made of cups turned on their sides and attached to rods. Wind blowing against the cups causes the anemometer to turn. The faster and stronger the wind, the faster the anemometer turns. Some anemometers have a meter attached to them. This meter is like the speedometer in a car. The meter measures how fast the wind is blowing by measuring how fast the cups on the anemometer turn.

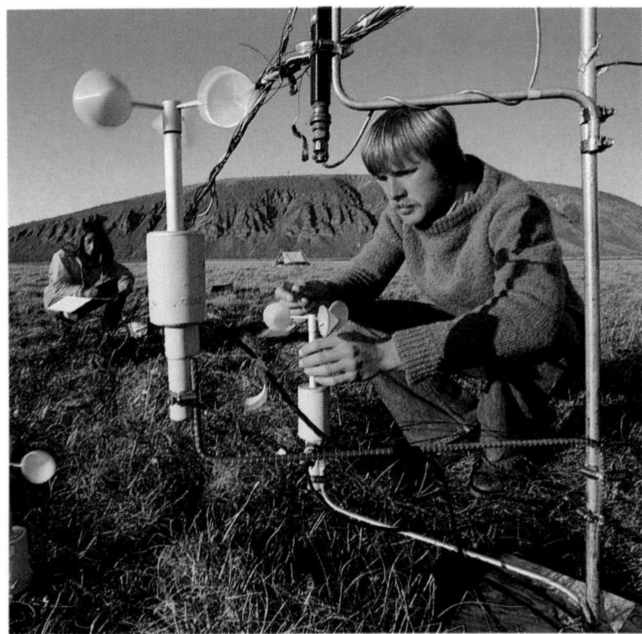

Figure 2 An anemometer

▶ ***Analyze:*** An anemometer turns at a speed of 18 km/hr. At what speed is the wind blowing?

Weather Balloons Scientists sometimes use weather balloons to measure wind speed and direction. A weather balloon is filled with helium gas. Helium gas is lighter than air. As a result, balloons filled with helium gas rise in the air. Winds high in the air move a weather balloon. Scientists can measure the speed of the wind by measuring the speed at which the balloon moves. The direction the balloon moves shows the direction of the wind.

▶ ***Identify:*** What two things are measured by weather balloons?

LESSON SUMMARY

- A weather vane is used to measure wind direction.
- An anemometer is used to measure wind speed.
- Weather balloons are used to measure wind speed and direction.

CHECK *Complete the following.*

1. Winds are named based upon the ______ from which they come.
2. Wind direction is measured with a ______ .
3. Wind speed is measured with an ______ .
4. Weather balloons are filled with ______ .
5. Weather balloons are used to measure wind ______ and direction.

APPLY *Complete the following.*

6. A weather vane points to the north. From which direction is the wind blowing?
7. **Hypothesize:** Carbon dioxide is heavier than air. Would carbon dioxide be useful in a weather balloon? Explain.
8. The cups on an anemometer move at a speed of 12 km/hr. At what speed is the wind blowing?
9. **Analyze:** A weather balloon moves south at a speed of 10 km/hr. Identify the speed and direction of the wind.

Skill Builder

Classifying and Researching Scientists classify winds based upon the wind speed. Wind speed can be measured by observing the way things move. Read the name of each wind and how some things move. Place the names of the winds in order from calmest to strongest.

1. hurricanes: great damage is done to buildings
2. strong breeze: hard to walk against the wind; umbrellas are hard to open
3. calm: smoke goes straight up
4. gale: branches are broken from trees; store windows break; TV antennas break
5. moderate to fresh breeze: small trees sway; papers are blown around
6. strong gale: trees are uprooted

ACTIVITY

MAKING A WIND VANE

You will need cardboard, glue, a ballpoint pen cover, a compass, a pencil, and scissors.

1. Cut out two cardboard arrows. Make them the same size. **CAUTION: Be careful when using scissors.**
2. Clip a ballpoint pen cover in the middle between the two arrows. Then glue the two arrows together.
3. Place the pen cover on the point of a pencil. Move it back and forth until the arrow balances.
4. Go outside and hold your weather vane where the wind will not be blocked by buildings or trees.
5. Use a compass to see which direction the arrow points.

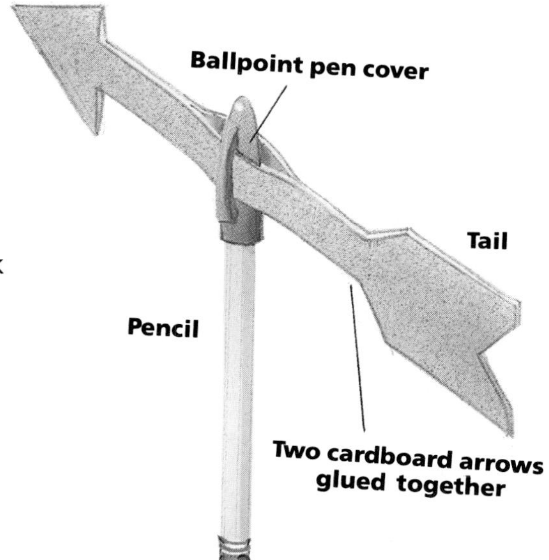

Questions

1. In what direction does a wind vane point?
2. **Analyze:** A strong wind would blow your cardboard vane away. What could you use to make a more sturdy wind vane?

UNIT 11 Challenges

STUDY HINT Before you begin the Unit Challenges, review the TechTerms and Lesson Summary for each lesson in this unit.

TechTerms

air current (226)
anemometer (232)
atmosphere (212)
barometer (224)
breeze (230)
conduction (218)
convection (218)
global winds (228)
ionosphere (214)
jet stream (228)
local wind (230)
matter (212)
monsoon (230)
newton (220)
pressure (220)
radiant energy (216)
radiation (216)
respiration (212)
stratosphere (214)
tropopause (214)
troposphere (214)
wind (226)
wind vane (232)

TechTerm Challenges

Matching *Write the TechTerm that best matches each description.*

1. anything with mass and volume
2. envelope of gases that surrounds the earth
3. process by which living things combine oxygen with food to get energy
4. middle layer of the atmosphere
5. movement of heat through a solid
6. wind that changes direction with the seasons
7. lower layer of the atmosphere
8. horizontal movement of air

Identifying Word Relationships *Explain how the words in each pair are related. Write your answers in complete sentences.*

1. radiant energy, radiation
2. newton, pressure
3. jet stream, global winds
4. wind, anemometer
5. convection, air current
6. troposphere, tropopause
7. breeze, local wind
8. wind, wind vane
9. air pressure, barometer
10. ions, ionosphere

Content Challenges

Completion *Write the term that best completes each sentence.*

1. Heat moves through ______ by conduction.
2. Heat moves through liquids and ______ by convection.
3. During respiration, living things give off ______ and water vapor as waste products.
4. Air is a ______ of gases.
5. Oxygen, carbon dioxide, and ______ are the three main gases in air.
6. The ionosphere is the ______ layer of the atmosphere.
7. The ozone layer of the stratosphere protects the earth from the ______ light from the sun.
8. Ozone is a form of ______.
9. When air is heated, it ______.
10. Cool air is heavier and more ______ than warm air.
11. The newton is the metric unit of ______.

12. As elevation increases, air pressure ______ .
13. A barometer that does not contain a liquid is ______ barometer.
14. A wind vane measures wind ______ .
15. Winds in the Southern Hemisphere curve ______ .

Multiple Choice *Write the letter of the term that best completes each statement.*

1. An altimeter measures
   a. wind speed. **b.** wind direction. **c.** altitude. **d.** rainfall.
2. Seventy-eight percent of the air is made up of
   a. nitrogen. **b.** oxygen. **c.** helium. **d.** carbon dioxide.
3. The amount of space an object takes up is its
   a. matter. **b.** mass. **c.** volume. **d.** density.
4. Burning can only take place in the presence of
   a. nitrogen. **b.** oxygen. **c.** helium. **d.** carbon dioxide.
5. The layer of the atmosphere closest to earth is the
   a. tropopause. **b.** stratosphere. **c.** ionosphere. **d.** troposphere.
6. The layer of the atmosphere that reflects radio signals is the
   a. tropopause. **b.** stratosphere. **c.** ionosphere. **d.** troposphere.
7. Heat from the sun travels through empty space by
   a. convection. **b.** conduction. **c.** ionosphere. **d.** radiation.
8. The troposphere is heated by
   a. convection. **b.** conduction. **c.** ionosphere. **d.** radiation.
9. Air pressure is measured with
   a. a barometer. **b.** an altimeter. **c.** a wind vane. **d.** an anemometer.
10. Regions of cold, heavy air are called
    a. highs. **b.** lows. **c.** convections. **d.** monsoons.
11. A wind that blows from the northeast is a
    a. southwest wind. **b.** monsoon. **c.** local wind. **d.** northeast wind.
12. Belts of high-speed air in the upper atmosphere are
    a. local winds. **b.** monsoons. **c.** jet streams. **d.** sea breezes.
13. Sea breezes and land breezes are two kind of
    a. local winds. **b.** monsoons. **c.** jet streams. **d.** global winds.
14. The movement of air from the land toward the ocean is a
    a. sea breeze. **b.** land breeze. **c.** mountain breeze. **d.** monsoon.

Understanding the Features

Reading Critically *Use the feature reading selections to answer the following. Page numbers for the features are shown in parentheses.*

1. **Infer:** Why do you think people with allergies are advised to stay indoors during a pollution alert? (213)
2. What do air pollution technicians do? (213)
3. Why were CFCs banned? (215)
4. What is the job of solar collectors? (217)
5. What is a radiosonde? (221)
6. Who made the first mercury barometer? (225)
7. Identify one advantage and one disadvantage of using windmills to produce energy. (229)
8. What three things are needed to fly a kite? (231)

Concept Challenges

Understanding a Diagram *Answer the questions about the diagram shown.*

1. What is shown in the diagram?
2. What two gases make up most of the atmosphere?
3. Name the layers of the atmosphere in order from lowest to highest.
4. What is the name of the part of the atmosphere between layers B and C?
5. How far does the troposphere extend into space?
6. Where is the ozone layer located?
7. In which layer of the atmosphere does most weather take place?
8. What kind of particles make up most of layer A?
9. Which layer of the atmosphere is heated by conduction?
10. How does heat move through the atmosphere?

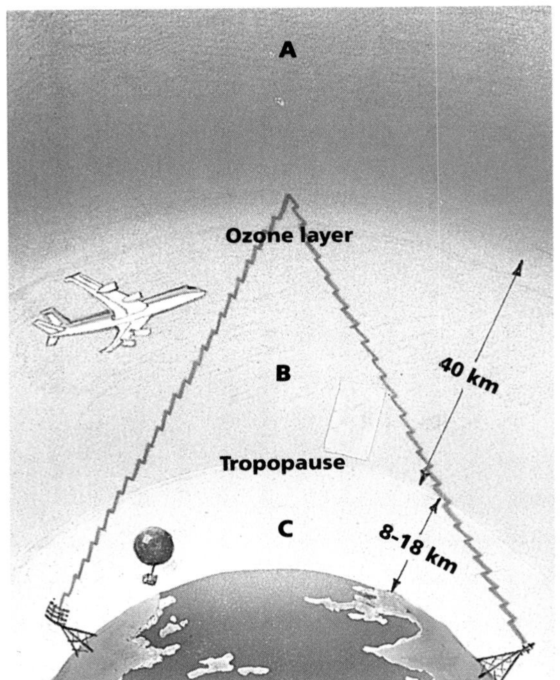

Critical Thinking *Answer the following questions in complete sentences.*

1. **Predict:** Would air pressure on top of a mountain be greater in summer or winter? Explain.
2. Why is mercury used in barometers instead of water?
3. **Infer:** How do mountain and valley breezes get their names?
4. How is a wind vane different from an anemometer?
5. **Hypothesize:** Why would dark-colored clothing be warmer in the winter than light-colored clothing?

Finding Out More

1. Use library references to find the locations and characteristics of the mesosphere and exosphere. Use your information to make a diagram that shows the following: troposphere, tropopause, stratosphere, stratopause, ozone layer, mesosphere, mesopause, ionosphere, exosphere. Compare your diagram to Figure 1 on page 214.
2. At sea level, normal air pressure is 76 cm of mercury. Air pressure decreases about 1 cm for every 123 m increase in elevation. Use this information to calculate normal air pressure for the following locations: Denver, Colorado - 1600 m above sea level; Kansas City, Missouri - 230 m; Mount Whitney, California - 4400 m; Death Valley, California - 85 m below sea level; Mount St. Helens, Washington - 2950 m; Mt. Washington, New Hampshire - 1916 m; Empire State Building, New York City - 380 m. Make a bar graph that shows the air pressure for each location.
3. Use library references to find out what the Coriolis effect is. Explain how wind direction would change if there were no Coriolis effect.
4. Air pressure is sometimes measured in units called kilopascals (kPa). One millimeter of mercury is equal to 0.1333 kilopascals. What is normal air pressure at sea level in kilopascals?

WEATHER

UNIT 12

CONTENTS

STUDY HINT After you read each lesson in Unit 12, write a brief summary on a sheet of paper explaining how the information in each lesson applies to your everyday life.

12-1 How does water get into the atmosphere?

Objective ▶ Explain how water gets into the atmosphere.

TechTerms

- ▶ **evaporation** (ih-vap-uh-RAY-shun): changing of a liquid to a gas
- ▶ **transpiration** (tran-spuh-RAY-shun): process by which plants give off water vapor into the air

Water Vapor On a warm day, droplets of water may form on the outside of a window. The window surface is cooler than the outside air. Where does this water come from? It comes from the air. The water is in the form of a gas. It is water vapor. Water is also in the atmosphere as clouds and fog. They are made up of tiny droplets of water. About 14 million tons of water vapor is in the air.

▶ *Name:* What is water called when it is a gas?

Evaporation Water vapor gets into the air by **evaporation** (ih-vap-uh-RAY-shun). Evaporation is the changing of a liquid to a gas. Most of the water in the air evaporates from the oceans. Every day millions of tons of water evaporates from the surface of the oceans. Water also evaporates from lakes, rivers, puddles, and wet soil. Winds carry the water vapor in the air all over the earth.

▶ *Identify:* Where does most of the water in the air come from?

Heat and Evaporation Molecules in a liquid are always moving. Some are moving faster than others. Some of the fast-moving molecules near the surface escape from the liquid. They go off into the air. They form a gas. That is how evaporation takes place.

When a liquid is heated, its molecules move faster. More of them escape from the surface. Evaporation takes place more rapidly. Water in a pan over a radiator evaporates much faster than water in a pan on a table. Evaporation from the oceans occurs most rapidly around the equator, where the water is heated by the direct rays of the sun.

▶ *Describe:* Does a liquid evaporate faster or slower when heat is added?

Living Things and Water Vapor Living things add water to the air. If you blow on a cold mirror, moisture forms on the mirror. Have you ever heard someone say, "It's so cold out you can see your breath." What you see is water vapor from breathing. The water vapor in your breath condenses in the air. Breathing adds moisture to the air. Plants also give off water. The process by which plants give off water vapor into the air is called **transpiration** (tran-spuh-RAY-shun). The water is given off through tiny openings in the leaves of plants.

▶ *Name:* By what process do plants give off water vapor?

LESSON SUMMARY

- Water is in the air as a gas called water vapor.
- Evaporation is the changing of a liquid to a gas.
- Most of the water in the air evaporates from oceans.
- Living things add water to the air.

CHECK *Find the sentence in the lesson that answers each question. Then, write the sentence.*

1. About how much water vapor is in the air?
2. Where does most of the water vapor in the air come from?
3. How do animals add water to the air?

Complete the following.

4. The changing of a _______ to a gas is evaporation.
5. Water vapor is given off through openings in the _______ of plants.
6. When water is a gas, it is called _______ .

APPLY *Complete the following.*

7. If you wipe a damp cloth across a table top, the table is wet. What will happen to the water after a few minutes?
8. **Hypothesize:** In which diagram will evaporation occur more rapidly? Explain your choice.

Designing an Experiment

Design an experiment to solve the problem.

PROBLEM: How can you show that water evaporates faster when it is heated?

Your experiment should:

1. List the materials you need.
2. Identify safety precautions that should be followed.
3. List a step-by-step procedure.
4. Describe how you would record your data.

ACTIVITY

OBSERVING TRANSPIRATION

You will need a small house plant, an elastic band, a clear plastic bag, a measuring cup, and a measuring spoon.

1. Carefully cover the plant with the plastic bag.
2. Secure the plastic bag near the bottom of the plant stem with the elastic band.
3. Set the plant in a place where it will get enough sun.
4. Observe the inside of the plastic bag for three days. Record your observations each day.
5. On the third day, try to measure how much water was in the plastic bag.

Questions

1. **Observe:** On which day did you first see water in the bag?
2. **Compare:** What happened to the amount of water in the plastic bag each day?
3. How much water did you collect? Where did the water come from?

12-2 What is humidity?

Objective ▶ Explain how water vapor exists in the air as humidity.

TechTerms

- ▶ **capacity** (kuh-PAS-ih-tee): amount of material something can hold
- ▶ **humidity:** amount of water vapor in the air
- ▶ **saturated** (sach-uh-RAYT-ed): filled to capacity
- ▶ **specific humidity** (hyoo-MID-uh-tee): actual amount of water in the air

Humidity The weather reporter says, "The **humidity** (hyoo-MID-uh-tee) was high today." Humidity is the amount of water vapor in the air. High humidity means there is a lot of water vapor in the air. Low humidity means there is a little water vapor in the air.

Define: What is humidity?

Capacity How much water can a 100-mL glass hold? If the glass is filled to the top, its **capacity** (kuh-PAS-ih-tee) is 100 mL. Capacity is the amount of material something can hold. The capacity of a 100-mL glass is always the same. The air has a capacity for holding water. The capacity of the air can change. Warm air can hold more water vapor than cold air. The capacity of the air for holding water vapor changes with temperature. As temperature goes down, the capacity of air for holding water goes down.

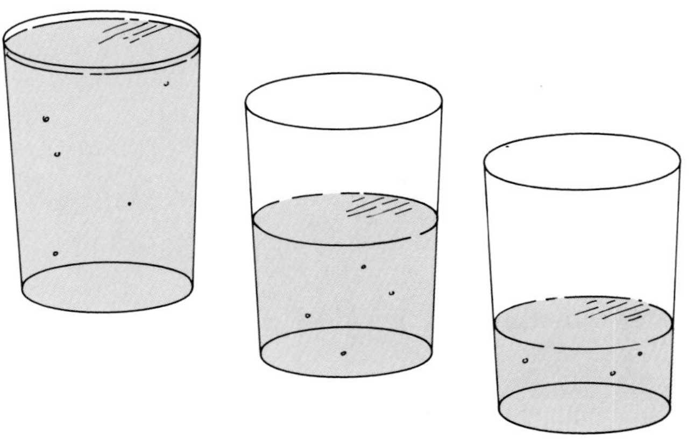

State: What affects the capacity of the air to hold water?

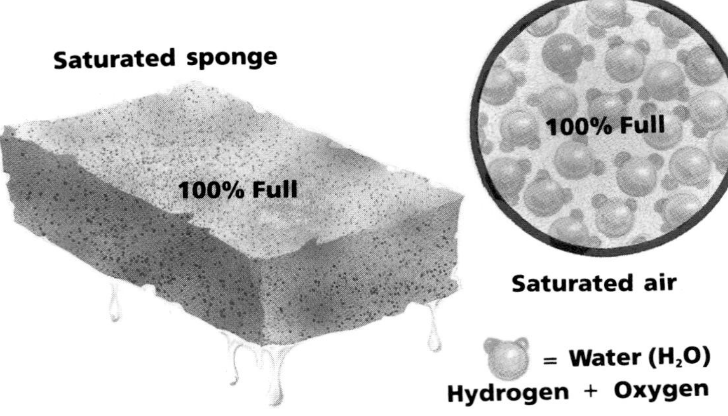

Saturated Air If you place a sponge in a pan of water, the sponge soaks up the water. Soon the sponge is filled with water. It cannot hold any more. It is **saturated** (sach-uh-RAYT-ed). Air can be saturated too. When air is saturated, it holds all the water vapor it can at a certain temperature. Saturated warm air has more water vapor in it than saturated cooler air. As temperature goes up, the capacity of air for holding water goes up.

Infer: At which temperature will air hold more water vapor, 4 °C or 25 °C?

Specific Humidity The actual amount of water vapor in the air is called specific humidity. Meteorologists (meet-ee-uh-RAHL-uh-jists) express specific humidity as the number of grams of water vapor in 1 kilogram of air. Because specific humidity is measured by units of mass, it does not change with temperature or pressure. Only adding more water vapor to the air can change the specific humidity.

Name: How do meteorologists express specific humidity?

LESSON SUMMARY

- Humidity is the amount of water in the air.
- Capacity is the amount of material something can hold.
- Air is saturated, or filled to capacity, when it holds all the water vapor it can at a certain temperature.
- Specific humidity is the actual amount of water vapor in the air expressed in units of mass.

CHECK *Complete the following.*

1. The amount of _______ in the air is its humidity.
2. The amount of water vapor the air can hold is its _______ .
3. The actual amount of water vapor in the air is called _______ .
4. When air is _______, it holds all the water vapor it can at a given temperature.
5. The amount of water vapor that air can hold changes with _______ .
6. Warmer air can hold _______ water vapor than cooler air.

APPLY *Complete the following.*

7. **Infer:** The air temperature in Boise, Idaho is 25 °C. The air temperature in Austin, Texas is 35 °C. In which city could the air hold more water vapor?
8. **Observe:** Which container has the greatest capacity?

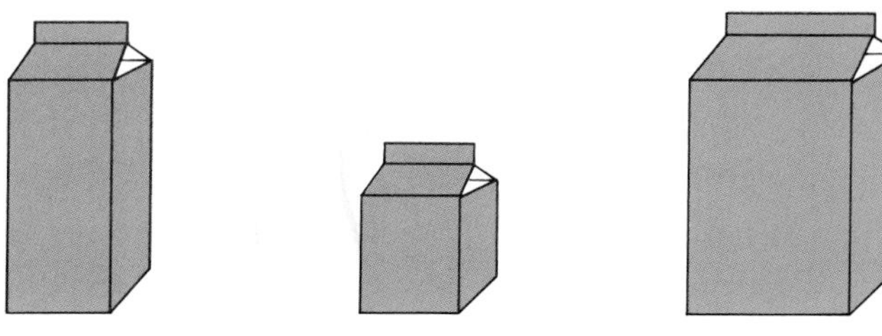

Skill Builder

Experimenting Obtain 1 sheet of paper toweling from 3 different brands. Saturate each of the paper towels with water. Measure the amount of water each paper towel holds at capacity. Use a measuring cup, a graduated cylinder, or a beaker. Which brand has a greater capacity for holding water? Is it the most expensive brand? Compare quality to price for each towel.

CAREER IN EARTH SCIENCE

METEOROLOGIST

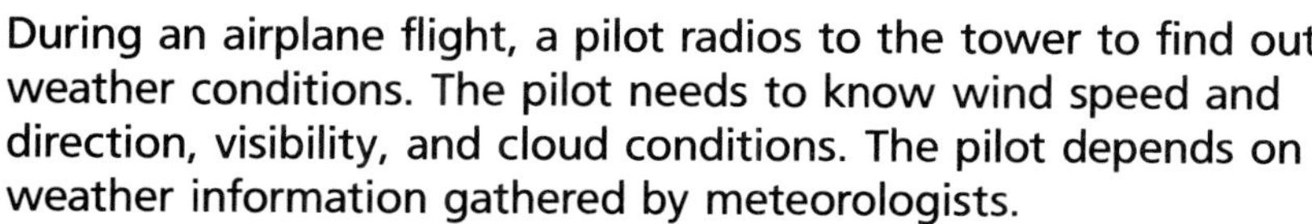

During an airplane flight, a pilot radios to the tower to find out weather conditions. The pilot needs to know wind speed and direction, visibility, and cloud conditions. The pilot depends on weather information gathered by meteorologists.

Meteorologists are scientists who study the atmosphere and how it behaves. They try to understand and predict the weather. Meteorologists gather information about the atmosphere at hundreds of different places and at many altitudes. Tools such as weather satellites and computers are used by meteorologists to gather information.

Meteorologists are employed by the government's National Weather Service, airlines and airports, news bureaus, and groups of farmers. To be a meteorologist, you need a college education. You should enjoy mathematics and science courses. A good way to get started in this field is through the armed services. They offer special training programs in meteorology.

12-3 How is relative humidity measured?

Objective ▶ Explain relative humidity and how it is measured.

TechTerms

- ▶ **psychrometer** (sy-KRAHM-uh-tur): instrument used to find relative humidity
- ▶ **relative** (REL-uh-tiv) **humidity:** amount of water vapor in the air compared to the amount of water vapor the air can hold at capacity

Relative humidity The amount of water vapor in the air compared to its capacity is **relative** (REL-uh-tiv) **humidity.** The relative humidity of air filled to capacity is 100%. Air usually is not filled to its capacity. It may be filled to half its capacity. The relative humidity is then 50%.

The relative humidity of air changes as water vapor leaves the air. It also changes when water vapor goes into the air. If the amount of water vapor stays the same and the temperature drops, the relative humidity changes. Relative humidity goes up if the temperature drops. It goes down if the temperature goes up.

▶ ***Calculate:*** If the air is filled to one-third its capacity, what is the relative humidity?

Humidity and Comfort People living in a hotter city may feel more comfortable than those in a cooler city. High relative humidity makes people uncomfortable. A temperature of 35°C with very low humidity may be quite comfortable. However, a temperature of 25°C with high relative humidity can be uncomfortable.

▶ ***Infer:*** What do you think an air conditioner does to the air temperature and humidity in a room?

Measuring Relative Humidity A **psychrometer** (sy-KRAHM-uh-tur) is used to find relative humidity. A psychrometer is made up of two thermometers. The bulb of one thermometer is covered with a damp piece of cloth. The other is dry. The psychrometer is then spun around. The dry thermometer measures the air temperature. Evaporation of water from the cloth cools the wet thermometer. The wet thermometer is cooled more when the relative humidity is low than when it is high.

Difference Between Dry and Wet Thermometers (°C)	Temperature of Air from Dry Thermometer(°C)								
	−5	0	5	10	15	20	25	30	35
1	75	81	86	88	90	91	92	93	94
2	52	64	72	77	80	83	85	86	87
3	29	46	58	66	70	74	77	79	81
4	6	29	46	55	62	66	70	73	75
5		13	32	44	53	59	63	67	70
6			20	34	44	51	57	61	64
7			0	24	36	44	50	55	59
8				15	28	37	45	50	54
	Relative Humidity (%)								

Relative humidity can be found by using the difference in temperature between the dry and wet thermometers, the temperature of the dry thermometer, and a chart. Suppose the dry thermometer reads 25°C and the wet one reads 18°C. The difference is 7°C. Find 25°C along the top of the chart. Find 7°C down the left side. Where the two rows meet, you see the number 50. This means the relative humidity is 50%.

▶ ***Define:*** What is a psychrometer?

A SIMPLE PSYCHROMETER

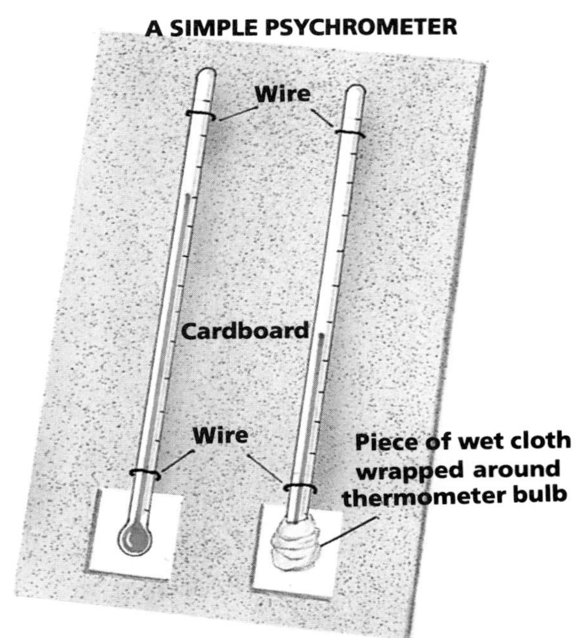

LESSON SUMMARY

- Relative humidity is the amount of water vapor in the air compared to the amount of water vapor the air can hold at capacity.
- Changes in temperature or the amount of water vapor in the air cause the relative humidity to change.
- The amount of humidity in the air and the air temperature affect comfort.
- A psychrometer is an instrument used to find relative humidity.
- To find relative humidity, you need to know the difference in temperature of the dry and wet thermometers, the temperature of the dry thermometer, and a humidity chart.

CHECK *Complete the following.*

1. The relative humidity of air filled to its capacity at a given temperature is _______ %.
2. The relative humidity goes up if the air temperature _______ .
3. A _______ has two thermometers and can be used to find relative humidity.
4. The relative humidity of air changes as _______ leaves the air.

APPLY *Use the chart on page 242 to find the relative humidity when the temperature readings from the psychrometer are:*

5. wet bulb: 12°C dry bulb: 20°C
6. wet bulb: 33°C dry bulb: 35°C
7. wet bulb: 22°C dry bulb: 30°C

Study the information about each city.

8. **Infer:** In which city would people be the most comfortable? The least comfortable?

	TEMPERATURE	HUMIDITY
City A	35°C	44%
City B	35°C	62%
City C	25°C	17%

Ideas in Action

IDEA: Humidity and temperature are important to comfort each day.

ACTION: Keep a record of the temperature and relative humidity where you live for one week. Rate each day according to the comfort factor: 1 = very comfortable; 2 = comfortable; 3 = uncomfortable; 4 = very uncomfortable. Compare your ratings to the ratings of 4 of your classmates. Did everyone agree?

ACTIVITY

EVAPORATION AND COOLING

You will need some isopropyl alcohol, water, an index card, watch with a second hand, and 2 cotton balls.

1. Fan your arm with an index card. Describe how it feels.
2. Dip a small cotton ball into some water and rub it onto your arm. Fan the spot for 25 seconds. Describe how it feels.
3. Dip another cotton ball into some alcohol and rub this on your other arm. Fan this spot for 25 seconds. Describe how it feels.

Questions

1. What happens to the water when you fan your arm? To the alcohol?
2. Why do evaporating liquids make your arm feel cooler?
3. **Infer:** Why do you feel cooler after you come out of the water on a hot day?
4. Which evaporates faster, water or alcohol?
5. **Infer:** How does the speed at which a substance evaporates affect its rate of cooling?
6. How does the amount of moisture in the air affect the rate at which the substance evaporates?
7. **Hypothesize:** Why do you feel warmer on a humid day than on a dry day?

12-4 What is the dew point?

Objective ▶ Explain what happens when air temperature goes above or below the dew point.

TechTerms

- ▶ **condensation** (kahn-dun-SAY-shun): changing of a gas to a liquid
- ▶ **dew point:** temperature to which air must be cooled to reach saturation
- ▶ **frost:** ice formed from condensation below the freezing point of water

Condensation Air always contains some water vapor. As the temperature of the air drops, water vapor changes from a gas to a liquid. The changing of a gas to a liquid is called **condensation** (kahn-dun-SAY-shun). Have you ever seen water form on the outside of a cold can or bottle? The water forms as water vapor in the air condenses into liquid water on the cold metal or glass.

▶ ***Define:*** What is condensation?

Dew Point The temperature at which condensation takes place is called the **dew point.** Condensation takes place when saturated air is cooled. Warm air can hold more water vapor than cold air. As the air cools, it can hold less and less water vapor. If the temperature of the air drops enough, the air becomes saturated. Its relative humidity reaches 100 percent. If saturated air is cooled, some of the water vapor in the air condenses. The water vapor changes to water.

At night, the ground cools fast. Air near the ground is cooled by the ground. The temperature of the air may drop to the dew point. When this happens, condensation takes place. Drops of water called dew begin to form on grass and bushes. Dew also may form on the windows of cars.

▶ ***Define:*** What is dew?

Frost The freezing point of water is 0 °C. At this temperature, water changes from a liquid to a solid. When the humidity is low, the dew point is lower than the freezing point of water. If the air temperature drops below the dew point, water vapor will come out of the air. However, the water vapor will change directly to ice instead of water. Ice that forms in this way is called frost.

Hypothesize: Why will frost not form at temperatures above 0 °C?

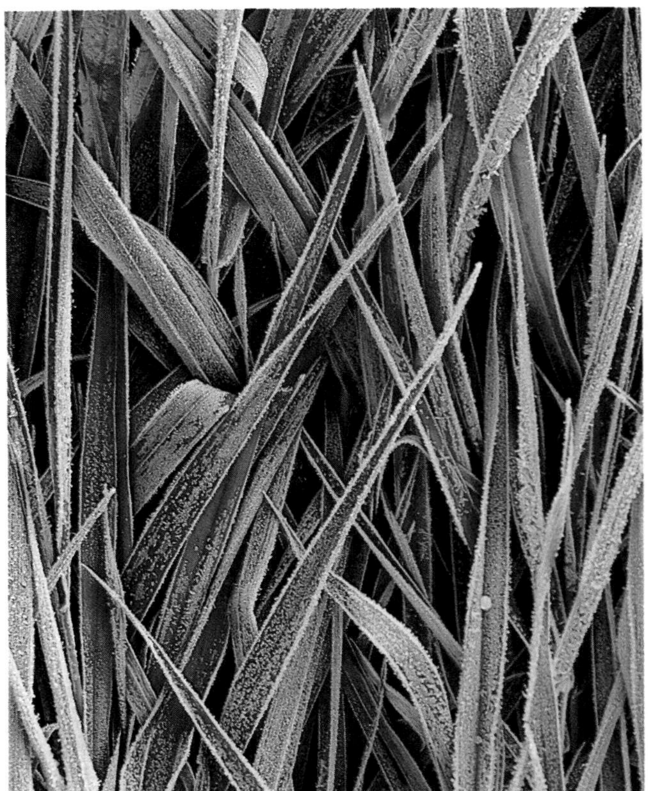

LESSON SUMMARY

- Condensation is the changing of a gas to a liquid.
- When saturated air is cooled, condensation takes place.
- The temperature at which water vapor condenses is called the dew point.
- When saturated air is cooled close to the ground, dew forms.
- Frost forms when the dew point is below the freezing point of water.

CHECK *Find the sentence in the lesson that answers each question. Then, write the sentence.*

1. What is condensation?
2. When does condensation take place?
3. What is dew point?
4. What happens to the relative humidity when the air becomes saturated?
5. What is the freezing point of water?

APPLY *Complete the following.*

6. **Apply:** When the temperature outside reaches 8 °C, condensation begins to form on the window of a car. What is the dew point?
7. Why is the relative humidity of saturated air 100%?
8. **Contrast:** Explain the difference between evaporation and condensation.

InfoSearch

Read the passage. Ask two questions about the topic that you cannot answer from the information in the passage.

Aircraft Icing One of the most dangerous things that can happen to an airplane is aircraft icing. Icing is caused by the freezing of very cold water droplets called supercooled water droplets. Icing sometimes occurs on the wings and body of an airplane. It can reduce the ability of the airplane to fly. Sometimes the air intake openings in the engine ice over, reducing the power of the engines. Icing can also affect the brakes and landing gear. Airports usually de-ice airplanes during weather conditions that can cause icing. Sometimes airports are closed down.

SEARCH: Use library references to answer your questions.

ACTIVITY

MEASURING DEW POINT

You will need an empty can, water, ice cubes, and a thermometer.

1. Fill a can about two-thirds full with ice and water.
2. Place a thermometer into the water. **CAUTION: Do not bang the bulb of the thermometer on the bottom or sides of the can.**
3. Read the temperature on the thermometer as soon as condensation appears on the outside of the can.

Questions

1. **Measure:** At what temperature did condensation appear on the can?
2. **Identify:** What are the water droplets that formed on the outside of the can called?
3. What is the name for the temperature at which condensation took place?
4. What is the dew point of the room?

12-5 How do clouds form?

Objectives ▶ Describe how clouds form.
▶ Identify some kinds of clouds.

TechTerms

- ▶ **cirrus** (SIR-us): light, feathery clouds
- ▶ **cumulus** (KYOOM-yuh-lus): big, puffy clouds
- ▶ **stratus** (STRAT-us): clouds that form layers across the sky

Cloud Formation From space, the earth sometimes seems covered by clouds. Clouds form from condensation in the atmosphere. Water droplets and ice form around dust and other particles in the air. Billions and billions of tiny water droplets and ice crystals form clouds. The smallest air currents keep these droplets and ice crystals from falling to the earth. The way a cloud forms gives it its shape.

▶ ***Name:*** What process forms clouds?

Kinds of Clouds There are three basic kinds of clouds. Light, feathery clouds are called **cirrus** (SIR-us) clouds. They are made up of ice crystals. They form at heights above 10,000 meters. Big, puffy clouds are called **cumulus** (KYOOM-yuh-lus) clouds. They form from rising currents of warm air. As they form, they build up to great heights. The base of a cumulus cloud usually is flat. Sometimes the sky is covered by a layer of sheetlike clouds. These clouds are **stratus** (STRAT-us) clouds. They spread out layer upon layer. Stratus clouds usually form at low heights.

▶ ***List:*** What are the three kinds of clouds?

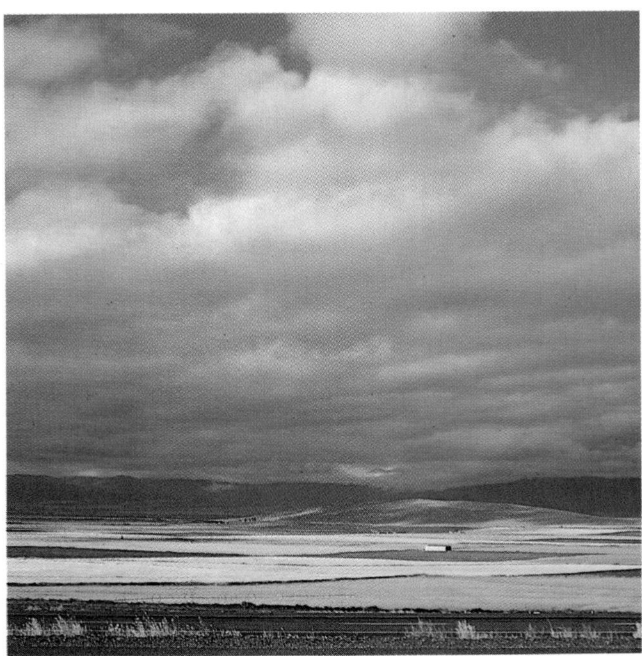

Fog A cloud that forms near the ground is fog. Fog forms when condensation occurs near the ground. At night, the ground cools quickly. It cools the layer of air that lies above it. The air may be cooled to the dew point. If it is, the water vapor condenses and forms fog. Fog usually forms on clear nights. Thick blankets of fog usually covers valleys or other low areas. Sometimes fog forms over rivers and lakes. This kind of fog forms when cool air moves in over warm water.

▶ ***Describe:*** What is fog?

LESSON SUMMARY

- Clouds form from condensation in the atmosphere.
- The three basic kinds of clouds are cirrus, cumulus, and stratus.
- Fog is a cloud that forms near the ground.

CHECK *Complete the following.*

1. What are clouds made of?
2. What are light, feathery clouds called?
3. What are sheetlike, layered clouds called?
4. Name three places you might see fog.
5. What kind of clouds are large and puffy?

APPLY *Complete the following.*

6. **Sequence:** Place the three kinds of clouds in order based on where they form from closest to the ground to farthest from the ground.
7. Look outside at the clouds in the sky. Describe the clouds. What kind of clouds do you think are in the sky?

▲ 8. **Model:** Use cotton balls or cotton to make models of the three kinds of clouds. Mount the clouds on a sheet of blue construction paper. Label the clouds.

Skill Builder

Researching Many clouds are combinations of cirrus, cumulus, and stratus clouds. Prefixes and suffixes are added to name some of these clouds. Use a dictionary to find out what these prefixes and suffixes mean: "alto-" and "-nimbus." Use library references to find the names of five other kinds of clouds. Write a brief description of each kind of cloud. Explain why the word part "alto-" or "-nimbus" is used for some kinds of clouds.

SCIENCE CONNECTION

CLOUD SEEDING

Have you ever wished that you could control the weather? Imagine being able to make it rain on very hot days. How about making snow so that you could go sledding or skiing? There are scientists who can do this. Scientists use cloud seeding to make it rain or snow.

In cloud seeding, crystals of carbon dioxide or silver iodide are dropped on clouds from high-flying airplanes. Water droplets form around these crystals. The droplets grow until they become so heavy that they fall from the clouds. Whether it rains or snows depends on the air temperature.

Scientists are still doing research in cloud seeding because it is only successful about 25% of the time. Cloud seeding can help stop severe storms if scientists can cause rain to fall before a storm becomes too large. It also can help farming areas during droughts.

Some people think of cloud seeding as water rustling. When farmers in one area hire cloud seeders, they may be taking water that is needed by farmers in another area.

12-6 What is precipitation?

Objective ▶ Identify and describe forms of precipitation.

TechTerms

- ▶ **precipitation** (prih-sip-uh-TAY-shun): water that falls to the earth from the atmosphere
- ▶ **rain gauge** (GAYJ): instrument used to measure precipitation

Precipitation Water that falls to the earth from the atmosphere is called **precipitation** (prih-sip-uh-TAY-shun). Precipitation may be liquid or solid. There are four kinds of precipitation. They are rain, snow, sleet, and hail. All precipitation begins when the air cools and water condenses in the air.

▶ *List:* What are the four kinds of precipitation?

Rain and Snow Droplets of water and crystals of ice that make up clouds are very small. They are kept up in the air by air currents. The droplets of water are always moving. They hit into each other. When they hit, they join together. If the droplets become too heavy, they fall as rain. Snow falls when crystals of ice grow larger. When the crystals of ice are too heavy to stay in the clouds, the crystals of ice fall as snow.

Growing ice crystals or water droplets
Warm air
Cold air
Cold air
Warm air
Warm air
Cold air
RAIN
SNOW
HAIL
SLEET

▶ *Compare:* What is the difference between rain and snow?

Sleet and Hail Sometimes rain falls through cold layers of air. The raindrops freeze. Rain that freezes as it falls is called sleet. Sometimes rain does not freeze until it hits the ground. A layer of ice covers everything. This is called freezing rain. The storms that bring freezing rain often are called ice storms.

Hail also forms when raindrops freeze. Hail forms when frozen drops rise and fall many times through warm and cold layers of air. Each time the hailstones move up and down through the warm and cold layers, they get bigger. Hailstones

as large as golf balls may form before they finally fall to the ground. They are made up of layers of ice.

Observe: What does a hailstone look like?

Measuring Precipitation A **rain gauge** (GAYJ) is an instrument used to measure rainfall. Rain gauges collect water in one spot. The amount of rain that falls can be measured in centimeters. Snow also can be measured in a rain gauge. The snow is collected and melted. The amount of water is then measured. The depth of snow is measured with a meter stick.

▶ *Define:* What is a rain gauge?

LESSON SUMMARY

- Precipitation is water that falls to the earth from the atmosphere.
- Rain and snow are two kinds of precipitation.
- Sleet is rain that freezes as it falls.
- Hail forms when frozen raindrops rise and fall many times through warm and cold layers of air.
- Precipitation is measured with a rain gauge.

CHECK *Write true if the statement is true. If the statement is false, change the underlined term to make the statement true.*

1. Precipitation may be a liquid or a gas.
2. There are four kinds of precipitation.
3. A liquid form of precipitation is rain.
4. Rain that freezes as it falls is snow.
5. The depth of rain can be measured with a meter stick.
6. Rainfall is measured using a rain gauge.

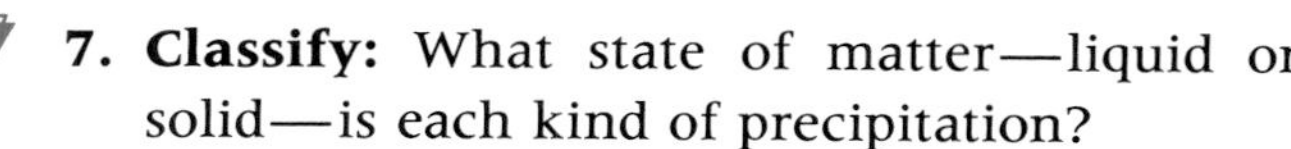

APPLY *Complete the following.*

7. **Classify:** What state of matter—liquid or solid—is each kind of precipitation?
8. What is the difference between sleet and freezing rain?
9. **Infer:** Which type of precipitation do you think can cause damage as it falls? Explain your choice.
10. **Infer:** What effect do you think an ice storm may have on tree branches?

Skill Builder

Building Vocabulary Use a dictionary to find the definition of an avalanche. Write the definition in your own words. From what language does the word come? Explain the statement: "The company received an avalanche of mail after their free offer appeared in the newspaper." Why can avalanche be used in this sentence?

ACTIVITY

MAKING A RAIN GAUGE

You will need a wide-mouth jar, tape, and a ruler with both metric and inch scales.

1. Stand a ruler inside a wide mouthed jar. Tape the ruler to the side of the jar.
2. Place the jar in an open area outdoors.
3. After it rains or snows, measure the rainwater in the jar. If the precipitation is in the form of snow, allow the snow to melt. Read both the inch and millimeter scales on the ruler. Write these measurements on a sheet of paper.
4. Compare your results with those listed in your local newspaper.

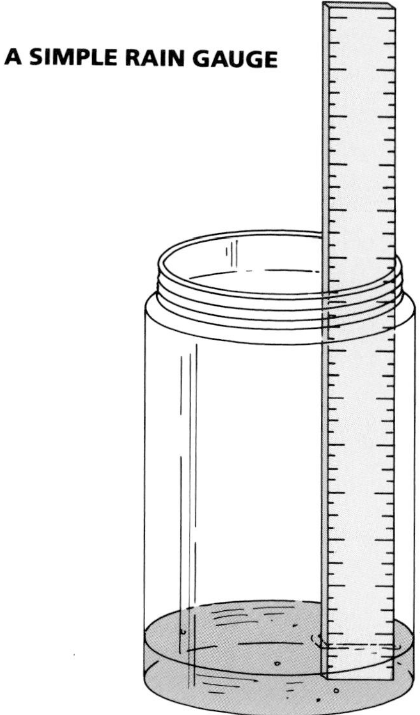
A SIMPLE RAIN GAUGE

Questions

1. **Infer:** Why should a rain gauge be placed in an open area?
2. **a.** How did your readings compare to those listed in the newspaper? **b.** Explain why your readings and the readings of the weather could be different.
3. **Infer:** Why should you allow snow to melt before measuring it?
4. **a.** Would the level of snow be higher or lower than the level of rain? **b.** How many inches of snow would equal one inch of rain?

12-7 What are air masses?

Objective ▶ Describe different kinds of air masses that affect the United States.

TechTerms

- **air mass:** large area of air that has the same temperature and amount of moisture
- **polar air mass:** air mass that forms over cold regions
- **tropical** (TRAHP-ih-kul) **air mass:** air mass that forms over warm regions

Air Masses Why does the weather change? How does weather form? One day it may be rainy. The next it may be cloudy. Then it may be sunny. To learn the answer, you need to know about **air masses.** An air mass is a large area of air that has the same temperature and amount of moisture throughout. Air masses form when air stays over an area for a while or moves slowly over an area. An air mass may cover an area more than 1000 kilometers across.

An air mass is affected by the region it covers. Air masses that form over land are dry. Air masses that form over water are moist. Air masses that form over warm regions are warm. Those that form over cold regions are cold.

Infer: Describe an air mass formed over the ocean in a cold region.

Polar Air Masses Cold air masses that form over cold regions are called **polar air masses.** There are two kinds of polar air masses. The United States is affected by continental (KAHNT-un-ent-ul) polar air masses that form over Canada. They are called continental air masses because the air mass forms over land. Continental air masses that form over Canada in the winter are very cold and dry.

Air masses that form over oceans are moist. They are called maritime air masses. If they are moist and cold, they are called maritime polar air masses. The United States is affected by maritime polar air masses that form over the northern Pacific Ocean.

Name: What is a cold, dry air mass called?

Tropical Air Masses Warm air masses form near the equator. They are called **tropical** (TRAHP-ih-kul) **air masses.** There are two kinds of tropical air masses. If they form over water, they are moist and warm. They are called maritime (MAR-ih-tym) tropical air masses.

The United States is affected by maritime tropical air masses that form over the Caribbean Sea and the Gulf of Mexico. Continental tropical air masses are warm and dry. They form over land areas close to the equator.

Name: What is a warm, moist air mass called?

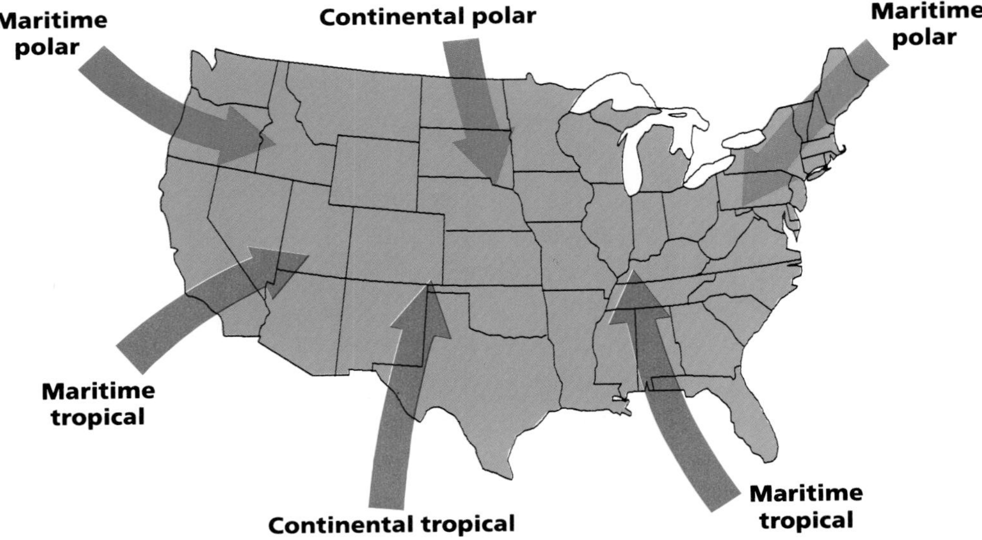

LESSON SUMMARY

- An air mass is a large area of air that has the same temperature and amount of moisture throughout it.
- An air mass is affected by the region it covers.
- Polar air masses form over cold regions, and may be continental or maritime polar air masses.
- Tropical air masses form near the equator, and may be continental or maritime air masses.

CHECK *Complete the following.*

1. What is an air mass?
2. What is a warm, dry air mass called?
3. Does a continental polar air mass form over land or water?
4. List the four main kinds of air masses.
5. What is a cold, moist air mass called?

APPLY *Letters are used to show the four kinds of air masses.*

6. Which air mass is represented by mT?
7. Which air mass is represented by cP?
8. What do you think the letters for a maritime polar air mass are?
9. What kind of air mass do you think the polar Canadian is?

Skill Builder

Inferring Seven air masses affect the weather of North America. Four are tropical air masses and three are polar air masses. A list of the air masses is given. Match the correct air mass to the letters on the map.

Air masses: Polar Pacific; Polar Atlantic; Tropical Pacific; Tropical Gulf; Tropical Atlantic; Polar Canadian; Tropical Continental

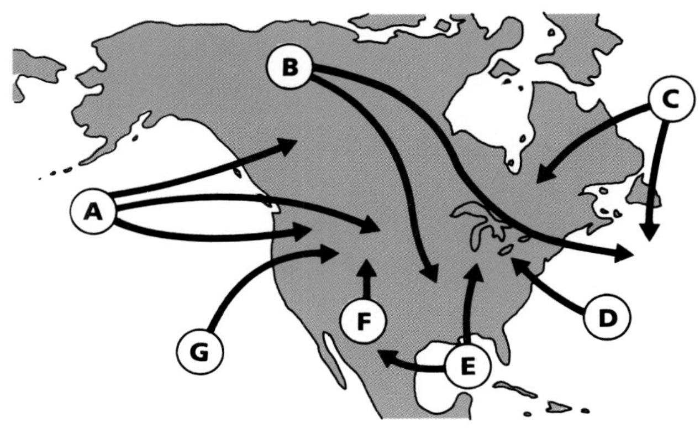

LOOKING BACK IN SCIENCE

DISCOVERING THE JET STREAM

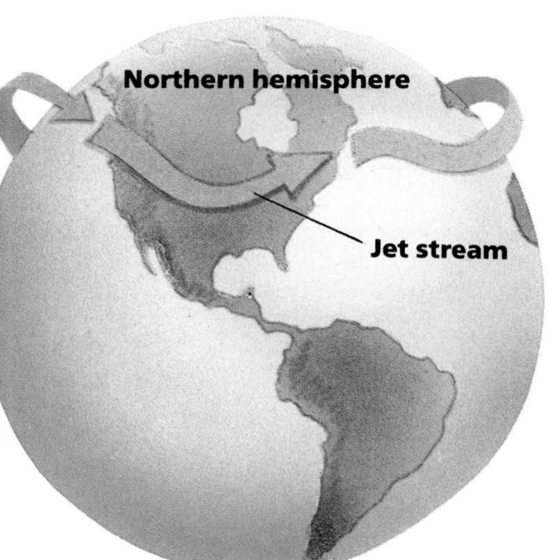

The jet stream is a river of fast-moving air. It is located in the stratosphere. The jet stream was not discovered until the 1940s. Up until the beginning of World War II, planes could not reach to altitudes as high as 16 to 24 km. The jet stream occurs at altitudes of 16 to 24 km. Airplanes used by the United States and Germany during World War II could. American pilots discovered a rapid moving stream of air over Japan. The winds in this stream were measured at up to 500 km per hour. German pilots discovered a jet stream over the Mediterranean Sea. The strong winds in these jet streams affected the speed of the planes flying within them or near them.

Since the discovery of jet streams, meteorologists have studied them with weather balloons. The jet streams seem to affect weather and climate in some places. In Southeast Asia, the jet stream is linked to the heavy rains of the monsoon season. In other areas, jet streams affect the formation of storms, including hurricanes.

12-8 What is a front?

Objective ▶ Describe the different kinds of fronts and the weather they cause.

TechTerms

- ▶ **cold front:** forward edge of a cold air mass, formed when a cold air mass pushes under a warm air mass
- ▶ **front:** surface between different air masses
- ▶ **warm front:** forward edge of a warm air mass, formed when a warm air mass pushes over a cold air mass

Fronts A **front** is the surface between different air masses. Air masses move west to east across the United States. As air masses move across the United States, different air masses meet. Air masses do not usually mix. Instead a front forms between them. A front can cover hundreds of kilometers. Fronts bring changes in the weather.

Explain: What do fronts bring?

Cold Fronts A **cold front** is the forward edge of a cold air mass. A cold front forms when a cold air mass pushes under a warm air mass. Cold air is denser than warm air. As a cold front moves through an area, the warm air over a region is pushed upward. Gusty winds are formed. Cold fronts usually bring rain and cloudy skies. Once the cold front passes, a cold air mass moves in.

Describe: What kind of weather does a cold front bring?

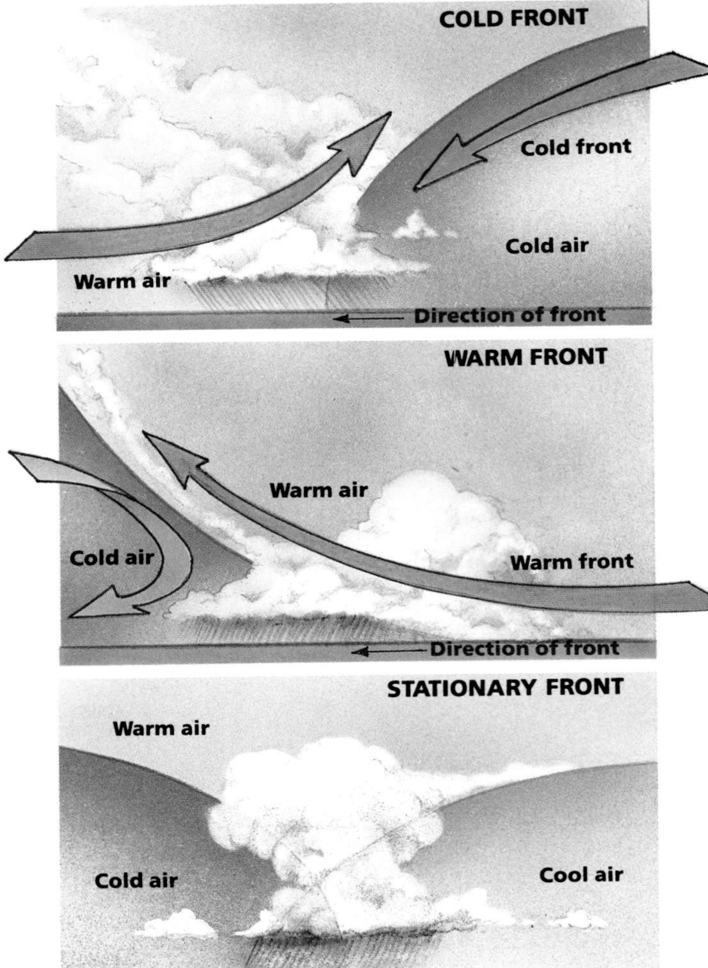

Warm Fronts What happens when a **warm front** moves in? A warm front is the forward edge of a warm air mass. A warm front forms when a warm air mass pushes over a cooler air mass. Warm air moves more slowly than cold air. Warm air rises above cold air. The rising warm air forms a gentle slope. The warm air slowly moves up and over the cold air. As the warm air rises, it cools. Very high cirrus clouds form. They pile up layer upon layer. Each layer is closer to the ground. Long, steady precipitation follows. Slow clearing and warmer temperatures show that a warm front has passed. A warm air mass has moved in.

Define: What is a warm front?

Stationary Fronts Sometimes cold and warm air masses stay in one place for a while. They do not move. They remain stationary. A stationary (STAY-shuh-ner-ee) front forms. A stationary front brings very little change in the weather.

Define: What is a stationary front?

LESSON SUMMARY

- A front is the surface between different air masses.
- A cold front is the forward edge of a cold air mass.
- A warm front is the forward edge of a warm air mass.
- A stationary front forms when two air masses meet and stay in one place for a while.
- The movement of cold and warm fronts causes changes in weather.

CHECK *Complete the following*

1. Name three kinds of fronts.
2. How does a cold front form?
3. What kind of clouds form as a warm front first nears?
4. Which kind of front causes very little change in weather?
5. After a warm front passes, what happens to the air temperature?
6. How many air masses meet to cause each kind of front?

APPLY *Complete the following*

7. If a city is getting an entire day of rain and the next day, it begins to clear, which kind of front passed?
8. If a city has clear skies and warm temperatures for three days, which kind of front is keeping the weather the same?

Skill Builder

Predicting Listen to the weather report for three days. Keep a record of the fronts that are coming toward the place in which you live. Write the weather conditions that are predicted. Using the information, predict the weather for the next two days. Check your predictions with newspaper weather reports.

Skill Builder

Researching A fourth kind of front is called an occluded front. Use library references to find out about an occluded front. Make a labeled drawing of an occluded front.

LEISURE ACTIVITY

WEATHER FORECASTING

Being able to determine future weather conditions is very important to farmers, pilots, airline companies, resort operators, and many others. Television, radio and newspaper forecasters do the public a service by supplying us with up to date weather forecasts. These forecasts are not 100 percent correct because weather varies from one location to the next. Have you ever seen it rain on one side of the road and not on the other? For a person on one side, a prediction of rain would be correct; for a person on the other side, the prediction would be wrong.

By setting up your own weather station with a barometer, thermometer, and hygrometer; you are on the way to doing you own forecasts. You can make your predictions more accurate by adding a wind vane and anemometer, by learning about cloud types and by preparing detailed weather maps. Studying the topography of your immediate area will help you to predict the weather for your local area. Topography is the surface features of the earth.

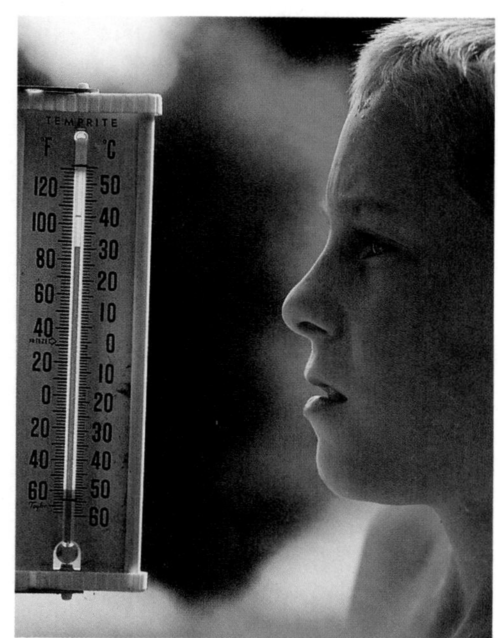

12-9 What are severe storms?

Objective ▶ Identify and describe three kinds of severe storms.

TechTerms

- ▶ **hurricane** (hur-uh-KAYN): tropical storm with very strong winds
- ▶ **thunderstorm:** storm with thunder, lightning, heavy rain, and strong winds
- ▶ **tornado** (tohr-NAY-doh): small, very violent funnel-shaped storm

Thunderstorms A **thunderstorm** is a storm with thunder, lightning, heavy rain, and strong winds. Thunderstorms usually happen when a cold front and warm front meet.

Thunderstorms start when huge cumulus clouds start to form. The cumulus clouds get bigger. They form giant storm clouds. From these clouds, heavy rain falls. Sometimes, hail also falls.

Lightning is caused when giant storm clouds give off electricity. The electricity causes the air to warm and expand quickly. The thunder you hear is caused by the expanding and contracting of the air. You see a flash of lightning first. Then, you hear the thunder. This happens because light moves faster than sound.

▶ *Describe:* List the weather conditions during a thunderstorm.

Hurricanes A **hurricane** (hur-uh-KAYN) is a tropical storm with strong winds. The winds of a hurricane may be as strong as 240 kilometers per hour. The winds of the hurricane spiral toward the center of the storm.

Hurricane hunters often take pictures of hurricanes. Flying over the hurricane, they take photographs of the storm. Some hurricane hunters even fly into the hurricane. Here, they gather information about the hurricane. Hurricane hunters work for the National Weather Service.

From an airplane, a hurricane looks like bands of spinning clouds. Rain is heavy. The wind speeds are greater the closer you get to the eye of the storm. The eye is the center of the storm. You may be surprised to find out that the eye is calm and clear. There is no wind or rain in the eye.

▶ *Describe:* What is the eye of a hurricane like?

Tornadoes A **tornado** (tohr-NAY-doh) is a funnel-shaped cloud that spins. They are very small, but very violent storms. Usually tornadoes form during late spring or early summer. Scientists are not sure how tornadoes form. They do know that part of storm clouds may develop a small, funnel-shaped cloud that reaches the ground. The spinning funnel has very low air pressure. When it touches the ground, it acts like a giant vacuum cleaner. The funnel raises and lowers all the time. Every time it touches the ground, it destroys everything in its path.

▶ *Describe:* What is a tornado?

LESSON SUMMARY

- A severe storm with lightening, thunder, heavy rain, and strong wind is a thunderstorm.
- Thunderstorms begin when huge cumulus clouds develop into giant storm clouds.
- Lightening is caused when storm clouds given off electricity.
- A hurricane is a tropical storm with strong winds that spiral toward the center of the storm.
- Hurricane hunters take photographs of hurricanes and fly into them to gather information.
- A hurricane looks like a band of spinning clouds around an eye.
- A tornado is a small funnel-shaped cloud that spins.

CHECK *Find the sentence in the lesson that answers each question. Then, write the sentence.*

1. When do thunderstorms usually happen?
2. What causes thunder?
3. What is the air pressure in a tornado?
4. During what time of the year do tornadoes usually form?

APPLY *Complete the following.*

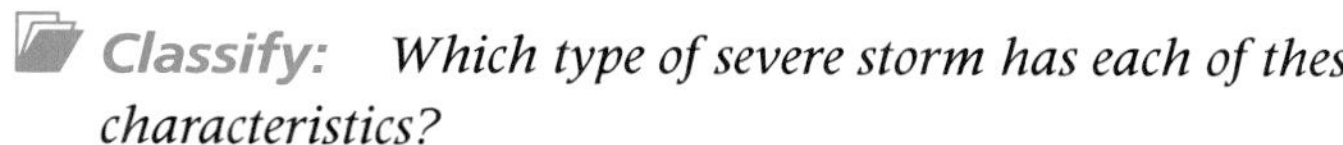

5. **Infer:** After a tornado the houses on one side of a street may be destroyed. On the other side of the street, the houses are not damaged. Explain why this could happen.

Classify: *Which type of severe storm has each of these characteristics?*

6. thunder and lightning
7. funnel-shaped cloud
8. giant cumulus clouds
9. calm eye
10. low air pressure
11. 240-km winds

Health & Safety Tip

The National Weather Service warns communities when hurricanes or tornadoes are approaching. During a hurricane with very strong winds, people are advised to tape their windows with large Xs that reach from corner to corner. During a tornado, the best place to take shelter is a basement. In the basement, you should crouch under a table or other piece of furniture on the side of the basement from which the tornado is coming. Why do you think these safety tips for a hurricane and a tornado are wise?

SCIENCE CONNECTION

TORNADO ALLEY

Tornadoes occur in many parts of the world. They even form over water. Tornadoes that form over water are called water spouts. However, more tornadoes occur in the United States than anywhere else. During some years more than 800 tornadoes are counted in the United States. Oklahoma and Kansas have more tornadoes than any other states. Most of these tornadoes form in the Great Plains and the southwestern United States. This area is called the "Tornado Belt", or "Tornado Alley."

In "Tornado Alley," most tornadoes occur during April, May, and June. Tornadoes rarely form in January or December. Usually tornadoes strike during the middle or late afternoons. Tornadoes occur at these times because these times of day and months are when conditions are best for thunderstorms to develop.

12-10 What is a station model?

Objective ▶ Understand how to read a station model.

TechTerms

- ▶ **millibar:** unit of measurement for air pressure
- ▶ **station model:** record of weather information at a weather station

Station Models A **station model** uses symbols instead of words to describe the weather. Each weather factor has a different symbol. Meteorologists, or weather scientists, use these symbols to make a station model. A station model shows the weather conditions at a particular weather station.

Define: What is a station model?

Reading Station Models Each station model is marked by a circle. The amount of shading in the circle tells how much cloudiness there is. It is given in percentages. Symbols also are used for rain, snow, and other conditions.

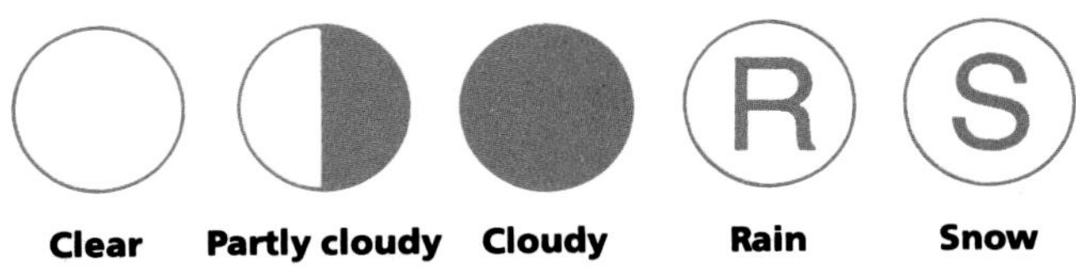

Wind direction is shown by an arrow pointing into the station circle. Wind speed is shown by little lines, or feathers on the arrow. The number and length of the feathers show wind speed. The arrow points into the direction from which the wind is blowing.

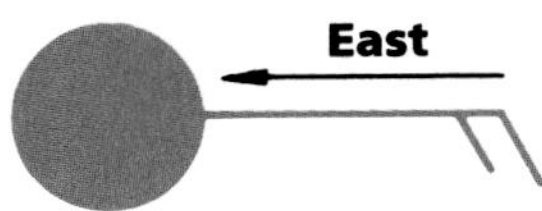

Observe: What is the wind speed for this wind arrow?

WIND SPEED SYMBOLS
(in miles per hour)

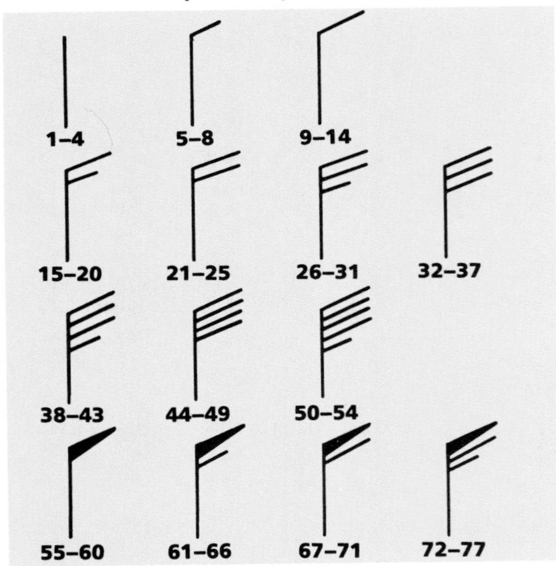

Air Pressure In the United States, air pressure is measured in **millibars** (MIL-uh-bars). Air pressure at the ground is about 1000 millibars (mb). A station model shows air pressure to the tenths of a millibar. The number in the upper right-hand corner of a station model is the last three figures in the air pressure reading. To find the complete reading, put a 9 or a 10 in front of the three figures. Put a decimal point in front of the last figure.

Analyze: What air pressure is shown on the station model?

STATION MODEL

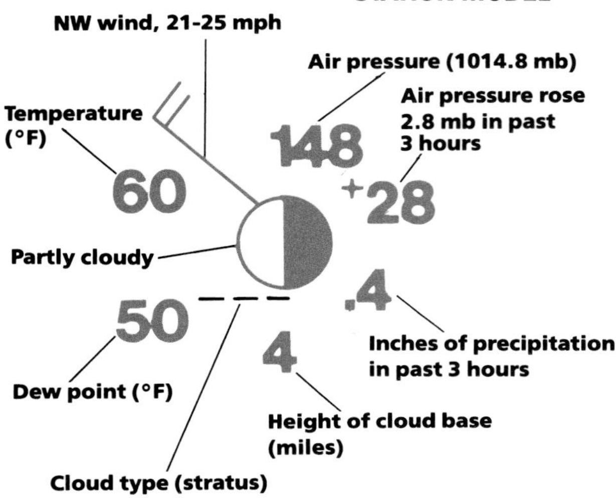

LESSON SUMMARY

- Meteorologists use station models to record and describe weather conditions.
- Each station model is marked by a circle and symbols.
- Wind direction and speed are shown on a station model by an arrow pointing into the station circle.
- In the United States, air pressure is measured in millibars.

CHECK *Answer the following.*

1. What is a meteorologist?
2. What does a station model show?
3. How can you tell how cloudy it is by looking at a station model?
4. How is wind direction shown on a station model?
5. How is air pressure measured?

APPLY *Use the station model on page 256 to answer the following.*

6. From which direction is the wind blowing?
7. What is the dew point?
8. Describe the cloud cover.
9. What is the wind speed?
10. Is the air pressure rising or falling?

Skill Builder

▲ ***Modeling*** When you model, you make a copy of something. Cut a weather map from your local newspaper. Gather other weather information about your local area. Using the weather map and information, draw a station model of your local area.

ACTIVITY

READING A STATION MODEL

Examine the station model shown. Then answer the questions.

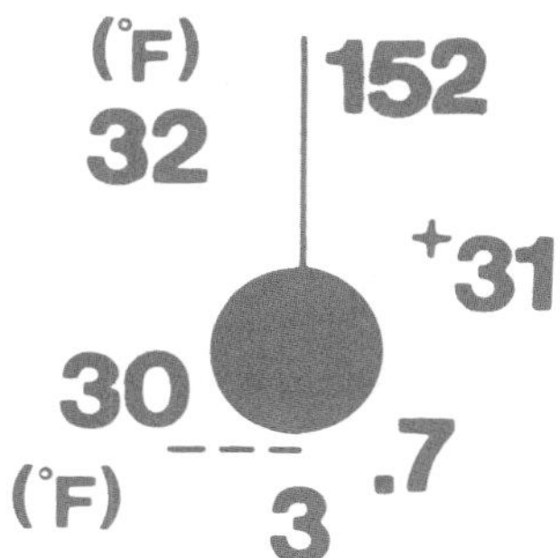

Questions

1. What is the sky condition?
2. **a.** What is the air pressure? **b.** How much has the air pressure risen in the last 3 hours?
3. How much precipitation has there been in the last three hours?
4. What is the height of the cloud base?
5. **a.** What is the temperature? **b.** What is the dew point?
6. **a.** How fast is the wind blowing? **b.** In which direction is the wind blowing?
7. **Infer:** What kind of precipitation do you think is falling?
8. Draw a station model that shows the conditions listed. **a.** air pressure: 1018.8 mb **b.** air pressure change: down 1.7 mb in past 3 hours **c.** amount of precipitation: 0.6 inches in past 3 hours **d.** height of cloud base: 3 miles **e.** dew point: 64 °F **f.** sky condition: cloudy **g.** temperature: 64 °F **h.** wind direction: from the southeast **i.** wind speed: 35 mph.

12-11 How do you read a weather map?

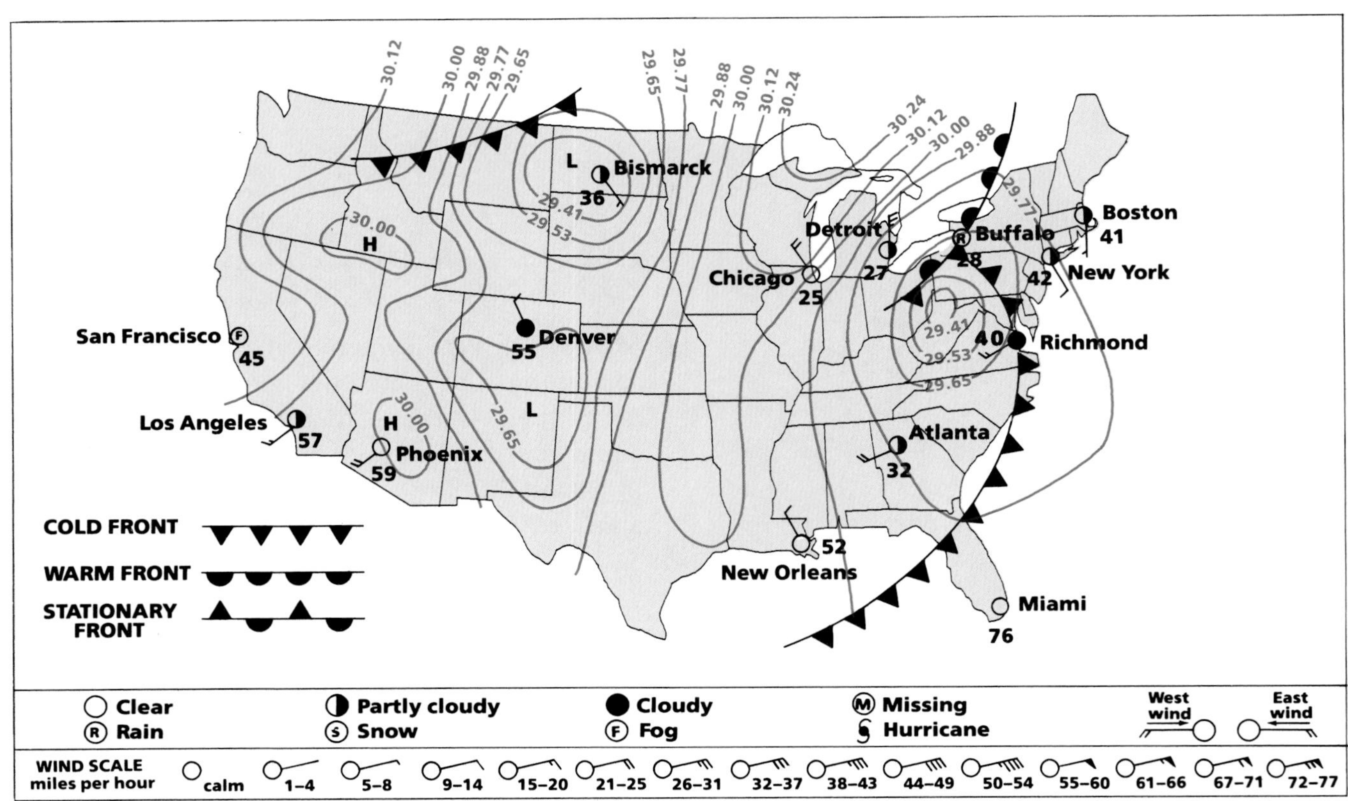

Objective ▶ Understand how to read a weather map.

TechTerm

▶ **isobar** (Y-suh-bar): line on a weather map that connects points of equal air pressure

Weather Maps Look at the weather map. A weather map shows weather conditions for many places at one time. You can find the temperature, cloud cover, wind speed, and so on for many places.

Describe: What do weather maps show?

Reading a Weather Map A key on a weather map helps you to read the station models. The lines that you see on the map are called **isobars** (Y-suh-bars). They connect points of equal air pressure. Places on the same line have the same air pressure. Areas of high pressure are usually called highs. They are shown with an "H." Areas of low pressure are called lows. They are shown with an "L." Symbols are used to show fronts. Precipitation is shown as shading or with symbols.

Observe: What was the temperature in Atlanta on the day this map was made?

Highs and Lows The weather in high-pressure and low-pressure regions is different. Highs usually bring clear skies and cool temperatures. Lows usually bring cloudy skies, some precipitation, and warm temperatures. Highs and lows move from west to east across the United States. As they pass through a region, they bring changes in the weather.

Describe: What type of weather does a low bring?

LESSON SUMMARY

- A weather map shows weather conditions for many places at one time.
- A key with symbols helps you to read the station models on a weather map.
- The weather in high-pressure and low-pressure regions is different.

CHECK *Complete the following.*

1. List three weather conditions that you can find on a weather map.
2. What do isobars show?
3. What are two ways to show precipitation on a weather map?
4. What are areas of low pressure called?
5. What is the symbol for high pressure?

APPLY *Use the weather map on page 258 to find a city that has each of the following weather conditions.*

6. clear skies
7. cloudy
8. partly cloudy
9. highest temperature
10. lowest temperature
11. air pressure 30.00
12. inside a high

Skill Builder

Researching Many different symbols are used on weather maps. Use library references to find out some other weather symbols or different symbols for the same weather conditions. Draw and label the symbols on 3 x 5 index cards. How many different symbols did you find?

Skill Builder

Observing When you observe, you use your senses. Cut out weather maps from a newspaper for four days. Paste them in your notebook. Study the weather maps to see if the highs and lows move in a particular direction. In which direction do the highs and lows move? Predict the fifth day weather for a city. Check the newspaper to see if your prediction was accurate.

CAREER IN EARTH SCIENCE

WEATHER BROADCASTER

If you turn on the television news tonight, you will see a weather broadcaster at work. Weather broadcasters report weather conditions for television and radio stations. They may be employed by local or national news bureaus. During a newscast, weather broadcasters forecast, or predict, the weather. They also report information such as temperature, humidity, wind speed, and air pressure. On television, they may use satellite pictures and maps during their broadcasts.

Some weather broadcasters are meteorologists. Before an actual news telecast begins, meteorologists are busy behind-the-scenes. They spend time gathering information, studying satellite reports, organizing information in charts, and making weather predictions. Other weather broadcasters simply report the information gathered by meteorologists. These weather broadcasters have backgrounds in television and radio broadcasting.

If you are interested in becoming a weather broadcaster, you need a college degree. You also should enjoy communication courses and public speaking.

UNIT 12 Challenges

STUDY HINT Before you begin the Unit Challenges, review the TechTerms and Lesson Summary for each lesson in this unit.

TechTerms

air mass (250)
capacity (240)
cirrus (246)
cold front (252)
condensation (244)
cumulus (246)
dew point (244)
evaporation (238)
front (252)
frost (244)
humidity (240)
hurricane (254)
isobar (258)
millibar (256)
polar air mass (250)
precipitation (248)
psychrometer (242)
rain gauge (248)
relative humidity (242)
saturated (240)
specific humidity (240)
station model (256)
stratus (246)
thunderstorm (254)
tornado (254)
transpiration (238)
tropical air mass (250)
warm front (252)

TechTerm Challenges

Matching *Write the TechTerm that matches each description.*

1. process by which plants give off water into the air
2. filled to capacity
3. line on a weather map that connects points of equal air pressure
4. small, violent, funnel-shaped storm
5. temperature to which air must be cooled to reach saturation
6. amount of material something can hold
7. unit of measurement for air pressure
8. record of weather information at a weather station

Applying Definitions *Explain the difference between the words in each pair.*

1. evaporation, condensation
2. cirrus cloud, stratus cloud
3. air mass, front
4. thunderstorm, hurricane
5. humidity, specific humidity
6. cold front, warm front
7. tropical air mass, polar air mass
8. psychrometer, rain gauge
9. frost, precipitation
10. relative humidity, specific humidity
11. cumulus, cirrus

Content Challenges

Multiple Choice *Write the letter of the term that best completes each statement.*

1. Light, feathery clouds are called
   a. cirrus clouds. **b.** cumulus clouds. **c.** stratus clouds. **d.** nimbus clouds.
2. The changing of a liquid to a gas is
   a. transpiration. **b.** saturation. **c.** condensation. **d.** evaporation.
3. Each station model is marked by a
   a. word. **b.** circle. **c.** square. **d.** triangle.
4. In the United States, air pressure is measured in
   a. millibars. **b.** meters. **c.** milliliters. **d.** kilograms.

5. If air is filled to half its capacity, the relative humidity is
   a. 100%. **b.** 75%. **c.** 50%. **d.** 25%.
6. Fog forms over rivers and lakes when cool air moves in over
   a. cold water. **b.** warm water. **c.** warm air. **d.** cirrus clouds.
7. Air masses do not usually
   a. form fronts. **b.** move. **c.** mix. **d.** meet.
8. Specific humidity is measured by units of
   a. mass. **b.** volume. **c.** length. **d.** temperature.
9. The four kinds of precipitation are rain, snow, sleet, and
   a. fog. **b.** dew. **c.** ice. **d.** hail.
10. Tornadoes usually form during
    a. early winter. **b.** late fall. **c.** early summer. **d.** late winter.
11. Water that forms on grass and bushes when condensation takes place is called
    a. fog. **b.** dew. **c.** rain. **d.** hail.
12. Most of the water in the air evaporates from
    a. the oceans. **b.** the soil. **c.** puddles. **d.** lakes and rivers.
13. Air masses that form over land are always
    a. cold. **b.** warm. **c.** dry. **d.** moist.
14. High-pressure regions usually have clear skies and
    a. precipitation. **b.** warm temperatures. **c.** cloudy skies. **d.** cool temperatures.

Completion *Write the term that best completes each statement.*

1. As the temperature goes down, the capacity of air for holding water goes ______ .
2. Molecules in a liquid are always ______ .
3. Air masses that form over oceans are ______ .
4. Air pressure at the ground is about ______ millibars.
5. As the temperature of the air drops, water vapor changes from a gas to a ______ .
6. Lightening is caused when giant storm clouds give off ______ .
7. The way a cloud forms gives it its ______ .
8. A front brings changes in the ______ .
9. Relative humidity goes ______ if the temperature drops.
10. There is no wind or rain in the ______ of a hurricane.

Understanding the Features

Reading Critically *Use the feature reading selections to answer the following. Page numbers for the features are shown in parentheses.*

1. What are two tools that meteorologists use to gather information? (241)
2. What are two ways scientists can use cloud seeding? (247)
3. What do meteorologists use to study jet streams? (251)
4. What does a weather forecaster do? (253)
5. When do most tornadoes in "Tornado Alley" occur? (255)
6. What are three things weather broadcasters report? (259)

Concept Challenges

	Temperature of Air from Dry Thermometer(°C)								
	−5	0	5	10	15	20	25	30	35
1	75	81	86	88	90	91	92	93	94
2	52	64	72	77	80	83	85	86	87
3	29	46	58	66	70	74	77	79	81
4	6	29	46	55	62	66	70	73	75
5		13	32	44	53	59	63	67	70
6			20	34	44	51	57	61	64
7			0	24	36	44	50	55	59
8				15	28	37	45	50	54
9				6	21	31	39	44	49
10					13	24	33	39	44
	Relative Humidity (%)								

Interpreting a Table *Use Table 1 to answer each of the following.*

1. What is the relative humidity when the dry thermometer reads 5 °C and the wet thermometer reads 0 °C?
2. What is the relative humidity when the dry thermometer reads 20 °C and the wet thermometer reads 13 °C?
3. If the relative humidity is 50%, and the dry thermometer reads 30 °C, what does the wet thermometer read?

Critical Thinking *Answer each of the following in complete sentences.*

1. How are humidity, relative humidity and dew point related?
2. What is the difference between sleet and hail?
3. Why does a cold air mass push under a warm air mass?
4. Why is the wet thermometer of a psychrometer cooled more when the relative humidity is low than when it is high?
5. What air masses affect the United States?

Finding Out More

1. Using library references, find out what a barometer is used to measure, and how an aneroid barometer works. Write your findings in a report.
2. Observe the clouds in your area for one week. Each day, record the date, and a description of the clouds. After 7 days, make a chart listing the dates and the type of clouds you think were in the sky. Compare your chart with your classmates' charts.
3. Draw a diagram showing the structure of a leaf. Label your diagram and describe the function of each part. Circle the structures through which transpiration occurs. Use biology textbooks as guides.
4. Using library references, find out about the last ten hurricanes that occurred in the United States. In an oral report, describe the name of each hurricane, the area it affected, and the damage it caused.

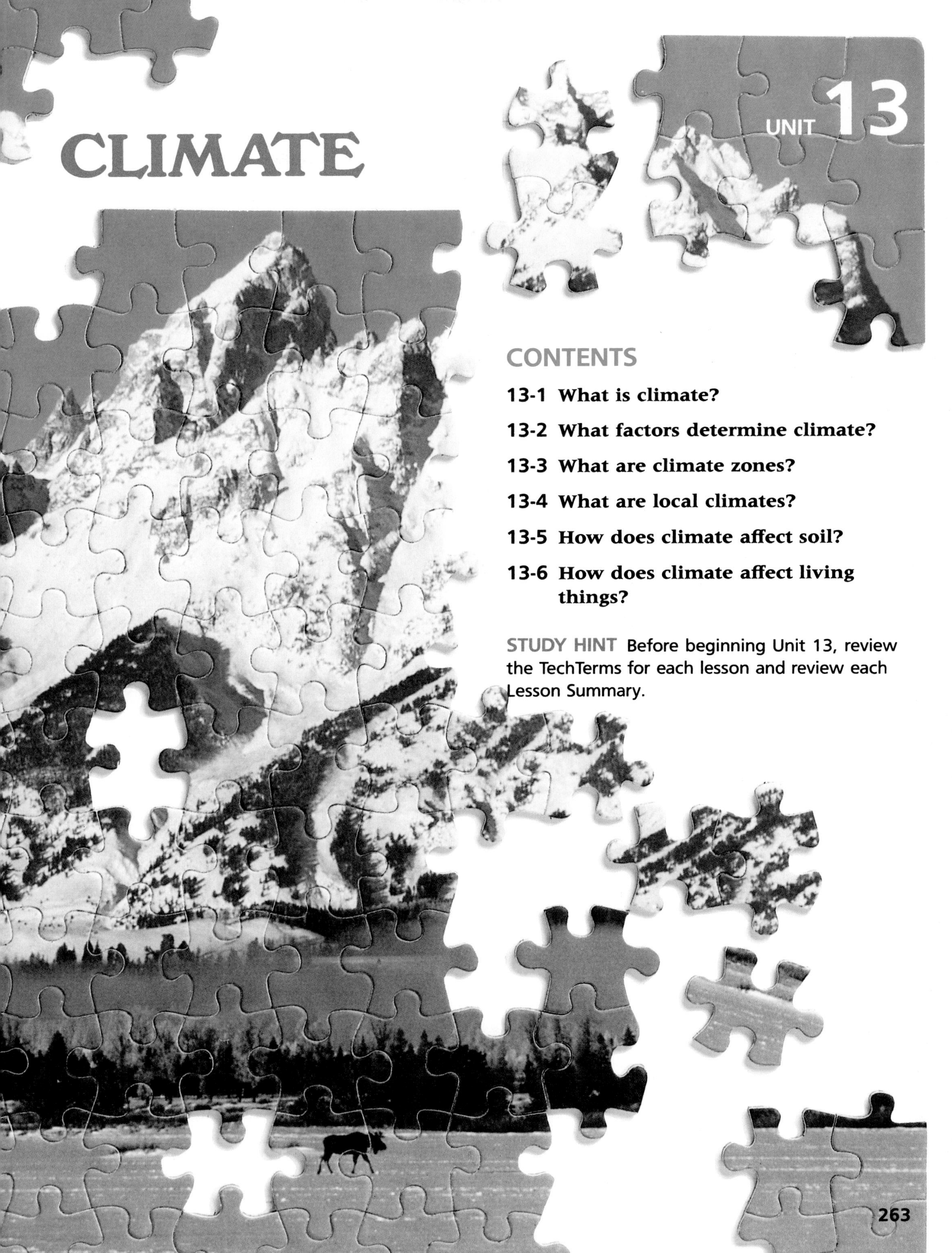

CLIMATE

UNIT 13

CONTENTS

STUDY HINT Before beginning Unit 13, review the TechTerms for each lesson and review each Lesson Summary.

13-1 What is climate?

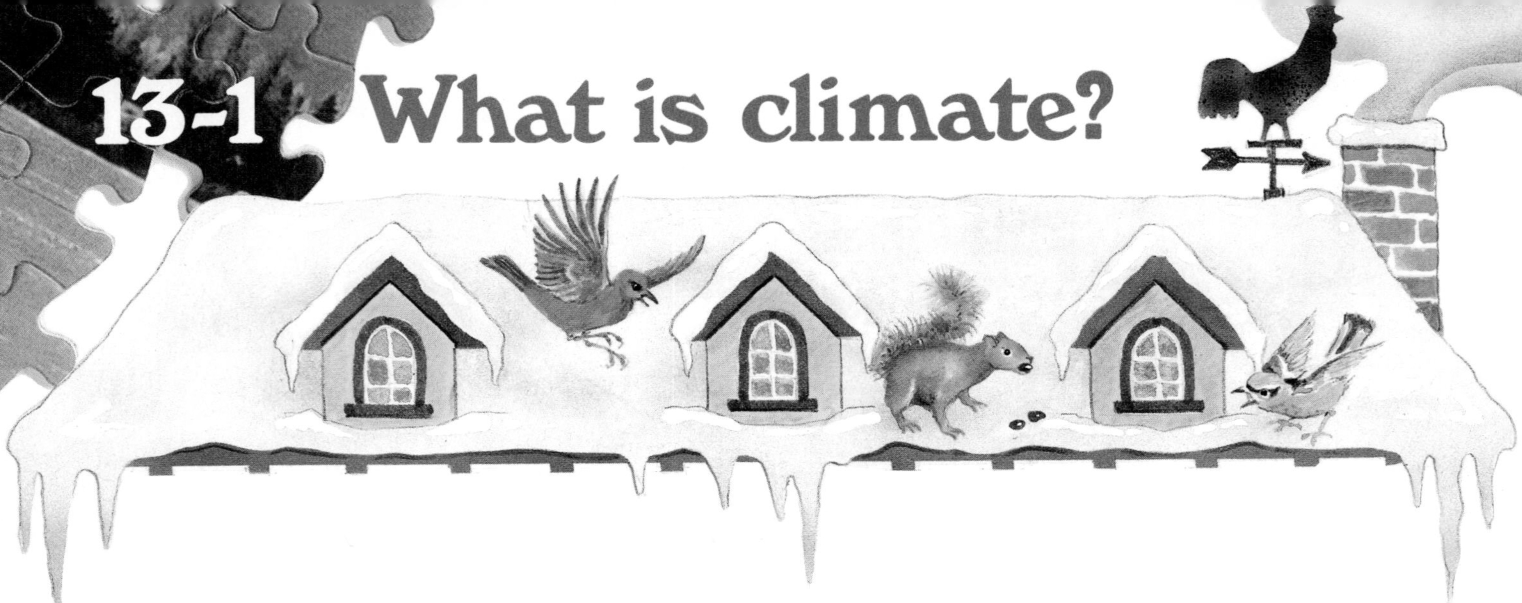

Objectives ▶ Explain the relationship between weather and climate. ▶ Explain how climate is described.

TechTerms

- ▶ **climate** (KLY-mut): average weather conditions of an area over many years
- ▶ **weather:** day-to-day conditions of the atmosphere

Weather and Climate Air temperature, the appearance of the sky, winds, and the amount of moisture in the air all are part of **weather.** Weather is the day-to-day conditions of the atmosphere. The average weather conditions of an area from year to year is the **climate** (KLY-mut). Climate describes the weather patterns of an area.

▶ ***Define:*** What is climate?

Average Temperature Average monthly and yearly temperatures are used to describe climate. To find average temperature, you add two or more temperature readings and divide the sum by the number of readings. For example, to find the average daily temperature, you add the high and low temperatures of the day. Then you divide by 2 because you used 2 readings.

▶ ***Calculate:*** If the high temperature one day is 32°C, and the low temperature is 28°C, what is the average temperature for the day?

Temperature Range The amount of temperature change during the year also is important in describing climate. This is the temperature range. To find the temperature range, subtract the lowest temperature from the highest temperature. Eureka, California and Omaha, Nebraska have the same average yearly temperature—10°C. In Eureka, the average monthly temperature for July is 13°C. The average monthly temperature in January is 8°C. In Omaha, the average monthly temperature goes from 25°C in July to about −6°C in January. Omaha has a greater temperature range than Eureka. The temperature range for Eureka is 5°C. Omaha has a temperature range of 31°C. Eureka and Omaha have different climates partly because they have different temperature ranges.

▶ ***Infer:*** Does Omaha or Eureka have a colder climate?

Average Precipitation Average yearly precipitation (pruh-sip-uh-TAY-shun) also is used to describe climate. Precipitation is rain, snow, sleet, or hail. Average yearly precipitation is the average amount of rain, snow, sleet, or hail that falls in an area in a year. However, average precipitation is not enough to describe climate. Miami, Florida and New York City get about the same amount of precipitation. In New York City, precipitation falls throughout the year. New York City gets rain, snow, sleet, and hail. In Miami, rain falls during a rainy season. The rainy season is May through October. Miami usually does not get snow or hail. New York City and Miami have different climates.

▶ ***Infer:*** Does Miami or New York City have a colder climate? Explain.

LESSON SUMMARY

- Climate is the average weather conditions in an area from year to year.
- Average monthly and yearly temperature is used to describe climate.
- Temperature range is important in describing climate.
- Average precipitation also is used to describe climate.

CHECK *Complete the following.*

1. The condition of the atmosphere today is the ______ .
2. The ______ of an area describes the average weather conditions from year to year.
3. Adding high and low temperature readings and dividing the sum by two gives you the ______ temperature.
4. The temperature ______ describes the change in temperature during the year.
5. Rain and snow are kinds of ______ .

APPLY *Complete the following.*

6. **Calculate:** The high temperature in Chicago, Illinois today was 12°C. The low temperature was 8°C. What was the temperature range?
7. **Calculate:** The high temperature in Houston, Texas was 25°C. The low was 21°C. What was the average temperature in Houston?
8. **Infer:** What two factors have the greatest effect on climate?
9. **Contrast:** Explain the difference between weather and climate.

Skill Builder

Organizing When you organize, you put information in some kind of order. Cut out national weather maps and tables from a newspaper for one week. Choose five cities from the map. Calculate the average daily temperature and daily temperature range for each city. Record the kind of precipitation, if any, for each city. Record this information in a table. Also keep a record of the weather conditions where you live for the same week. Add this information to your table. After one week, write a summary of the weekly weather conditions for each city. Compare the weather conditions of each city with those in your town.

SCIENCE CONNECTION

CLOTHING AND CLIMATE

What did you wear to school today? How did you decide what to wear? You probably dressed according to the weather. You would probably not wear a heavy wool sweater on a hot summer day. In fact, the clothes that you wear during the year are suited to the climate in which you live.

In warm, dry climates, people usually wear loose-fitting clothing. Loose-fitting clothing allows air to move freely through the clothes. This keeps you cool. The fabrics used are light in weight. The colors of the fabrics may be light and bright. Light-colored fabrics reflect sunlight and keep you cool.

In cool climates, people wear snug-fitting clothing. This helps keep in body heat. Snug-fitting clothes help keep you warm. The fabrics used may be wool or synthetics (sin-THET-iks), such as nylon. Synthetic fabrics are warm, but light in weight and less bulky than wool. Dark colors also are used. Dark colors absorb sunlight and help keep you warm.

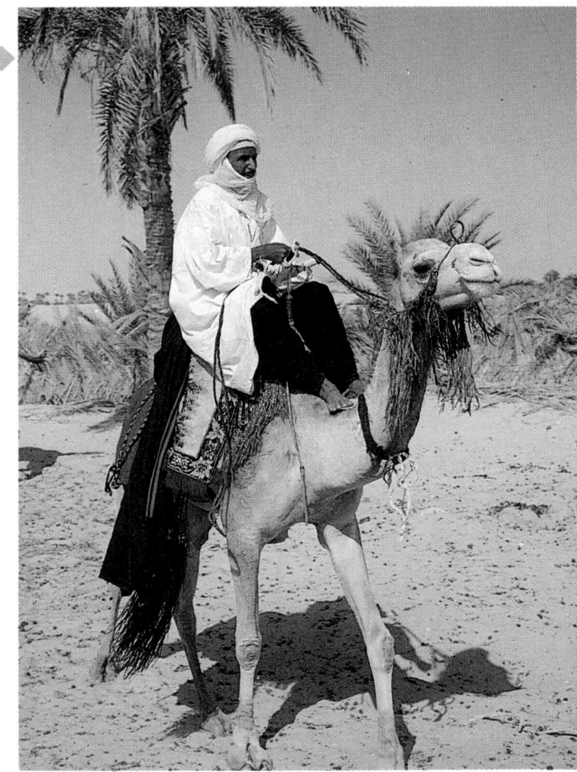

13-2 What factors determine climate?

Objective ► Identify and describe the conditions that determine climate.

TechTerms

- ► **altitude** (AL-tuh-tood): height above sea level
- ► **latitude** (LAT-uh-tood): distance north or south of the equator in degrees

Latitude The climate of an area is affected by its **latitude** (LAT-uh-tood). Latitude is distance north or south of the equator in degrees. Latitude determines how much heat energy an area gets from the sun. At the equator, the sun's rays fall directly on the earth. The closer an area is to the equator, the warmer is its climate. At higher latitudes, the sun's rays strike the earth at an angle. The heat energy from the sun is spread out more. The farther away from the equator an area is, the colder is its climate.

The wind patterns at different latitudes also affect climate. Remember there are global wind belts on the earth. These wind belts affect the direction of the wind. They affect the weather in an area. Thus, the climate of an area is affected. These wind patterns also affect the number and kinds of storms in an area.

► ***Relate:*** How does latitude affect climate?

Altitude The **altitude** (AL-tuh-tood) of an area affects the area's climate. Altitude is distance above sea level. Air is warmer at sea level than at higher altitudes. In fact, the average temperature drops about 2°C for every 300-meter rise in altitude. Even near the equator, mountain tops are covered with snow all year.

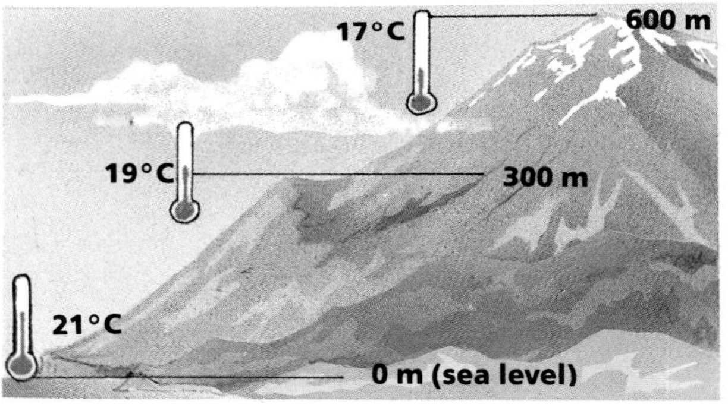

► ***Define:*** What is altitude?

Ocean Currents Ocean currents affect the temperatures of areas along the coast. An ocean current is like a river of water within the ocean. Some currents are warm-water currents. Others are cold-water currents. Winds passing over ocean currents are either warmed or cooled. When these winds pass over nearby land areas, they heat or cool the land. Land areas near cold-water currents have cooler temperatures. Land areas near warm-water currents have warmer temperatures.

► ***Describe:*** How do ocean currents affect land temperatures?

Mountains and Climate Mountains may affect the climate of an area. When air passes over a mountain range, it rises and cools. Moisture condenses from the cooled air, and it rains. As the air moves down the other side of the mountain, it is warmed. Air moving down a mountain usually is warm and dry. It hardly ever rains on the leeward side of a mountain. The leeward side is the side or direction away from the wind. Many deserts are located on the leeward sides of mountains.

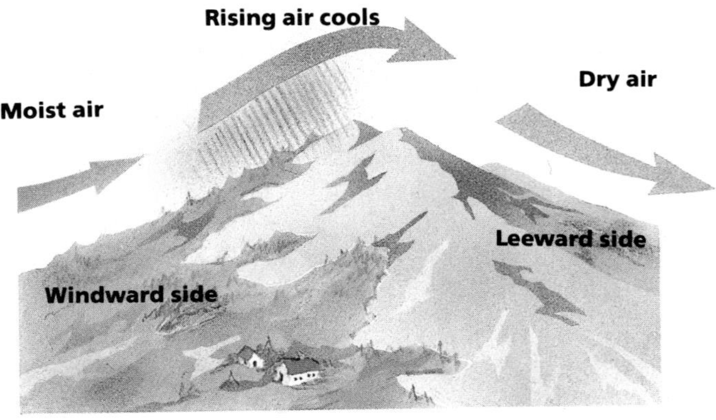

Observe: What is the side of a mountain that faces the wind called?

LESSON SUMMARY

- The climate of an area is affected by its latitude.
- The wind patterns at different latitudes also affect climate.
- The climate of an area is affected by its altitude.
- Ocean currents affect the temperatures of areas along the coast.
- Areas on the leeward sides of mountains have warmer, drier climates than areas on the windward sides of mountains.

CHECK *Explain how the words in each pair are related.*

1. latitude, equator
2. altitude, elevation
3. leeward, windward

Complete the following.

4. The closer an area is to the equator, the _______ its climate.
5. At _______ latitudes, the sun's rays strike the earth at an angle.
6. Air at sea level is _______ than air at higher altitudes.
7. Land areas near cold-water currents usually have _______ temperatures.

APPLY *Complete the following.*

8. **Calculate:** How much lower will the temperature be on top of a 1500-m mountain than at sea level?
9. **Infer:** Miami, Florida is at a lower latitude than San Francisco, California. Which city probably has a warmer climate? Explain.
10. **Infer:** Town A is located on the windward side of a mountain. Town B is located on the leeward side of the same mountain. Which town probably gets more rainfall? Explain your answer.

Ideas in Action

IDEA: Many factors affect climate.
ACTION: Find out the latitude and altitude where you live. Are you near a body of water or a mountain? How does each factor affect the climate where you live?

ACTIVITY

OBSERVING THE EFFECT OF LATITUDE ON CLIMATE

Table 1 World Climates

CITY	LOCATION LATITUDE	TYPE OF CLIMATE	AVERAGE TEMPERATURES JANUARY	JULY
Singapore	1° N			
Pt. Barrow	71° N			
Boston	42° N			

COLDEST MONTH	WARMEST MONTH
Jan Av. 78°F	July Av. 79°F
Jan Av. 30°F	July Av. 73°F
Jan Av. −11°F	July Av. 44°F

You will need a pencil, paper, and a world map.

1. Copy the table on a sheet of paper.
2. Examine the list of cities and their locations. Use the terms "warm," "moderate," and "cold" to fill in the column titled Type of Climate.
3. Study the list of temperatures. Match each city with its temperature. Write the temperatures in the correct column of the table.

Questions

1. Why are regions close to the equator (0° latitude) warmer than those far from the equator?
2. **Infer:** Why is it possible to see snow on the peaks of mountains located near the equator?
3. **Calculate:** What is the yearly temperature range for each city listed in your table?

13-3 What are climate zones?

Objective ▶ Identify and describe the three main climate zones and their climates.

TechTerms

- ▶ **middle-latitude zone:** region between 30° and 60° N and S latitude
- ▶ **polar zone:** cold region above 60° N and 60° S latitude
- ▶ **tropical** (TROP-ih-kul) **zone:** warm region near the equator

Climate Zones A climate zone is an area of the earth with a given temperature range. Each zone also has certain weather conditions. The map shows the three main climate zones. The warm zone near the equator is the **tropical** (TROP-ih-kul) **zone.** It is between 30° N and 30° S latitude. The average monthly temperature is 18°C or more. The coldest climate zones are the **polar zones.** They are above 60° N and 60° S latitude. Temperatures do not go above 10°C. Between 30 °and 60° N and S latitude are the **middle-latitude zones.** The average temperature in the coldest months usually is less then 18°C. The warmest month has an average temperature no colder than 10°C.

Define: What is a climate zone?

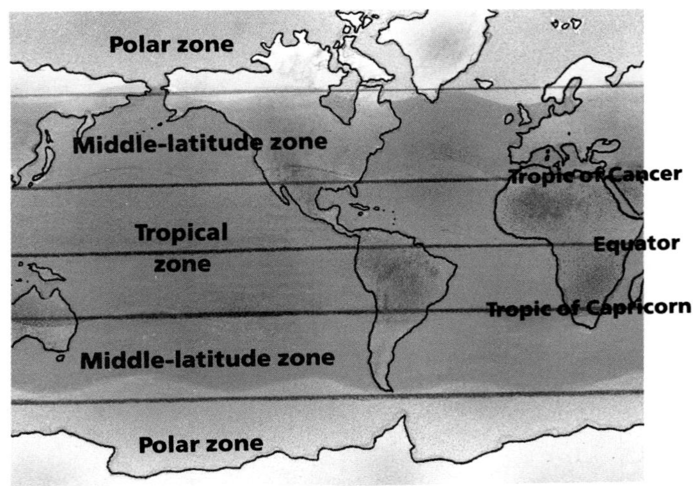

Kinds of Climates The climates in each climate zone can be described by its average temperature and rainfall. Table 1 lists the kinds of climates in each climate zone. In the tropical zone, climates may be very arid, or dry. They also may be very humid, or wet. In the polar zones, the climate is always cold. They are never humid. The middle latitude zones have many different climates.

Analyze: What state in the United States has a taiga climate?

Table 1 Climates

CLIMATE	KINDS OF CLIMATE	DESCRIPTION	EXAMPLES OF PLACES
Tropical	Tropical rain forest Savanna (grasslands) Steppe (grassy plains) Tropical desert	Hot and humid all the time Hot rainy summer, warm dry winter Hot, semiarid Hot and arid	Amazon, Congo Bolivia and Venezuela Parts of central Mexico Sahara Desert, Africa
Middle-latitudes	Mediterranean Humid subtropical Humid continental Marine Steppe (prairies) Deserts	Mild moist winters, dry summers Summers long and rainy, winters short and mild Humid hot summers, wet cold winters Mild rainy summers, cold winters Hot summers, cold winters, light rainfall Hot and dry	Southern California Southeastern U.S. Northern U.S. Pacific Northwest Great Plains Southwest U.S.
Polar	Tundra Taiga	Winters very cold, short summers Long cold winters, short warm summers	Northern Canada Alaska

LESSON SUMMARY

- A climate zone is an area with a given yearly temperature range and regular weather patterns.
- The three climate zones are the tropical zone, the polar zone, and the middle-latitude zone.
- The climates in each climate zone can be described by temperature and amount of rainfall.

CHECK *Complete the following.*

1. The earth is divided into ______ climate zones.
2. Places with the coldest temperatures are located in the ______ zone.
3. Places with the warmest temperatures are located in the ______ zone.
4. Places in the middle-latitude zone have many different combinations of ______ and amount of rainfall.
5. The middle-latitude zone is located between ______ and S latitude.

APPLY *Use the map and table on page 268 to answer the following.*

6. **Observe:** In which climate zone is most of the United States?
7. What are the names of the two boundaries that separate the tropical zone from the middle-latitude zones?
8. **Contrast:** How does the climate of the tropical rain forest differ from the climate of the tropical desert?

Ideas in Action

IDEA: The kinds of clothing people wear usually are suited to the climate in which they live.

ACTION: Imagine that you are going to move from a middle-latitude climate to the polar zone. Describe the kinds of clothing you would need to live in that climate. How does this clothing differ from the clothing you would wear if you moved to the tropical zone?

PEOPLE IN SCIENCE

ALEXANDER VON HUMBOLDT (1769–1859)

Alexander von Humboldt was born in Berlin, Germany. He was a naturalist, geographer, and explorer. Humboldt spent his early career in Germany. Later, he traveled to Mexico, South America, and Central America. On these explorations, Humboldt observed how the physical conditions and climate of the area affected the plants growing there. Much of what is known about world climates and geography is based upon the work of Humboldt. The Humboldt current, a cold-water current in the Pacific Ocean, is named after him.

Humboldt compared the climate conditions of different countries. He was the first person to find out how much the temperatures dropped as you climbed a mountain. Humboldt also studied tropical storms. His studies helped to show weather patterns in certain parts of the world. Using his weather information, Humboldt was the first person to draw temperature lines on a map. These lines, called isotherms (Y-suh-thurms), connect points with the same temperature. Isotherms are still used on today's weather maps.

In 1829, Humboldt was invited to visit Russia and Siberia. Here, he made many weather observations that were important to climatology (kly-muh-TAHL-uh-jee). Climatology is the study of climate.

13-4 What are local climates?

Objective ▶ Describe some factors that affect local climates.

TechTerm

▶ **microclimate** (MY-kroh-kly-mit): smallest climate zone

Local Climates The climate of any place may be affected by local conditions. These conditions make small climate zones called local climates. Altitude, or distance above sea level, affects local climates the most. Large lakes and forests also affect local climates. Like oceans, large lakes can warm or cool the air temperature. Forests slow down winds. Forests also add water vapor to the air. This increases humidity.

▶ *Identify:* Name three factors that can affect local climates.

Microclimates Local climates can be broken down into even smaller climate zones. These very small climate zones are called **microclimates** (MY-kroh-kly-mits). A microclimate can be as small as a schoolyard.

Cities are microclimates. The average temperature in a city is higher than in surrounding areas. You may have heard these differences in temperatures on a weather forecast. The weather forecaster might say that New York City had a high of 32°C. Surrounding areas had high temperatures of 30°C. Heavy traffic in cities warms the air and raises average temperatures. The energy used to heat and light buildings also raises the air temperature in cities. At night, the heat absorbed by streets and buildings radiates back into the air.

The tall buildings in cities also affect the amount of rainfall in the area. Skyscrapers act as mountains and can change patterns of rainfall. Pollution from automobile exhaust and industrial smokestacks adds particles to the air. These extra particles in the air cause more rain over large cities.

▶ *Compare:* Is the average temperature in cities higher or lower than in surrounding areas?

Global Warming Climate has changed many times during the earth's history. Until recently, all of these changes were due to natural causes. Today, human activities can change the earth's climate. Some scientists think that increased air pollution will cause temperatures around the world to increase. This pattern of increased temperature is called global warming. Summers would be hotter. Rainfall patterns might be changed. A temperature increase also might cause the polar icecaps to melt. This would cause a rise in sea level. In fact, if the ice caps of Antarctica and the Arctic melted, the sea level would rise 61 km. New York City would be almost covered with water. Only the tops of very tall buildings would be above the water.

▶ *Predict:* What would happen to coastal cities if the icecaps melted?

LESSON SUMMARY

- Climates are affected by local conditions, forming local climates.
- Very small climate zones are called microclimates.
- Cities are microclimates.
- Human activities and skyscrapers can affect the climate in an area.

CHECK *Write true if the statement is true. If the statement is false, change the underlined term to make the statement true.*

1. The factor that affects local climates most is altitude.
2. Air pollution causes the temperatures in an area to drop.
3. The average temperature in a city is lower than in surrounding areas.
4. Skyscrapers can change the amount of rainfall in a city.
5. Air pollution can affect the amount of rainfall in an area.
6. The pattern of increased temperatures all over the earth is called ______ warming.

APPLY *Complete the following.*

7. Chicago is located in the north central United States. It is on one of the Great Lakes. How does this affect the local climate?
8. **Infer:** Would you expect a city or the suburbs outside the city to get more snow? Explain.
9. What are some weather conditions in your area that are part of the local climate?

Skill Builder

Building Vocabulary The prefix "micro-" means very small. Look at the words listed below. Try to define each word in your own words. Then look up the definition of each word in a dictionary. Compare your definitions with the dictionary definitions. What do all of the words have in common?

WORD LIST

microbiology	micrometer
microchip	microcomputer
microscopy	

CAREER IN EARTH SCIENCE

WEATHER OBSERVER

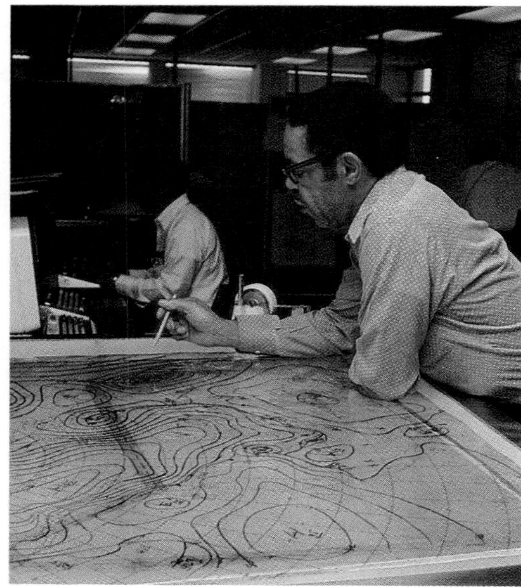

Where does all the information about weather and climate come from? Weather stations are located all over the world. There are even stations on ships and oil rigs at sea. Local areas also have weather bureaus. Weather observers usually work in weather stations. They collect information about weather conditions. Weather observers also analyze weather information, and check to see if the information is accurate. The information is given to meteorologists, or other people studying weather and climate.

To be a weather observer, you must be able to read different kinds of weather instruments. You do not need to go to college to be a weather observer. You do need a high school diploma. You should take some science and mathematics courses. Special training programs also are available.

13-5 How does climate affect soil?

Objective ▶ Relate climate to the six types of soil found in the United States.

TechTerm

- **leaching** (LEECH-ing): downward movement of minerals in soil
- **weathering** (WETH-ur-ing): breaking down of rocks and other materials on the earth's surface

Climate and Soil Climate affects the soil in an area. Rainfall and temperature affect the rate of **weathering** (WETH-ur-ing). Weathering is the breaking down of rocks and other materials on the earth's surface. Weathering forms soil. In hot, wet climates, weathering is fast. Soils are thinner. In warm, moist climates with changing seasons, soils are thicker. In cold, dry climates, weathering is slow. Soils are thinner. In areas with a lot of rain, minerals are moved down into lower soil layers. This process is called **leaching** (LEECH-ing). In areas with little rain, minerals stay in the top soil layers.

Name: What two climate factors affect the kinds of soil in an area?

Types of Soil The major types of soil in the United States are shown on the map. There are six soil types.

- Tropical soil is usually thin. Most of the **humus** is washed away by heavy rainfall. Humus is decayed plants, and animals. However, because decay is fast in hot, wet climates, the humus in the topsoil is replaced quickly. Minerals are leached deep into the soil.
- Grassland and prairie soils have very thick layers of topsoil. The soil is rich in humus. These soils are good for growing corn, wheat, and soybeans.
- Forest soil usually has very thin topsoil. The topsoil usually does not have very much humus in it. Most minerals have been leached away by heavy rainfall.
- Mountain soil is not well-developed. It is made up of rock pieces and small amounts of clay and sand. Water running down the mountains washes topsoil away.
- Desert soil is rich in minerals. There is not much rainfall, so minerals are not leached away. There is not much topsoil in desert soil.
- Tundra soil has very thin layers. Much of the soil is barren rock. The ground is frozen for most of the year.

Observe: What is the only state in the United States with tundra soil?

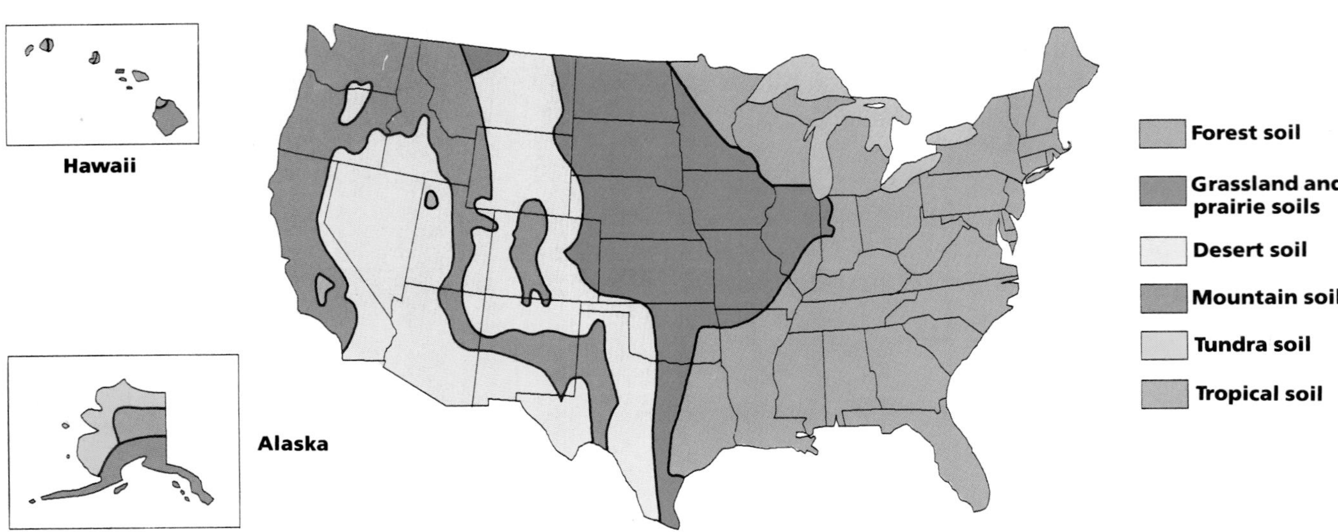

LESSON SUMMARY

- Climate affects the soil in an area, making one soil different from another.
- There are six major types of soil in the United States.
- Six soil types are tropical soil, grassland and prairie soil, forest soil, mountain soil, desert soil, and tundra soil.

CHECK *Complete the following.*

1. What two climate factors make one soil different from another?
2. What affects the minerals in a soil?
3. How many soil types are there in the United States?
4. Which soil type has thick topsoil that is rich in humus?
5. Which soil is rich in minerals?

APPLY *Complete the following.*

6. **Observe:** What type of soil is found in your state?
7. Desert soil is rich in minerals. What else is needed to be able to grow crops in a desert?
8. Why do plants not grow well in tundra soil?
9. **Infer:** Does Hawaii have thick soil or thin soil? Explain.
10. **Observe:** What kind of soil is found along the eastern United States?
11. In what area of the United States would you grow wheat. Explain.

Skill Builder

Researching When you research, you gather information about a topic. The following kinds of farms are found in different parts of the United States: dairy farm, vegetable farm, corn/cattle farm, wheat farm, potato farm. Use library references to find out where each kind of farm is located in the United States. Using the map of the six soil types on page 272 and other reference materials, explain why each kind of farm is suited to its location.

SCIENCE CONNECTION

IRRIGATION OF THE DESERTS

Plants need sunlight, minerals, nutrients, and water to grow properly. Desert soil is rich in minerals and some nutrients. There is more than enough sunlight. The only thing needed to grow crops is water. However, many desert areas are being used as farmland. These desert areas use irrigation (IR-uh-gay-shun). Irrigation is the watering of land by artificial ways.

There are four ways to irrigate land. Water can be run over an entire field or into narrow ditches called furrows. Huge sprinkler systems are built. Plastic tubes can be used that are put next to plants. Water trickles out of the tubes. Underground pipes also can be used.

In desert regions of the western and southwestern United States, much farming is done in irrigated deserts. Large irrigation canals have been built through the desert. They supply water to farmland in the desert. In south-central California, the Imperial Valley is irrigated. It is one of the richest farming areas in the United States.

13-6 How does climate affect living things?

Objective ► Identify ways in which plants and animals are affected by climate.

TechTerms

- **adaptations** (ad-ap-TAY-shuns): features that let living things live and reproduce in their environments
- **biome** (BY-ohm): large area of the earth that has certain kinds of living things
- **vegetation** (vej-ih-TAY-shun): plants

Biomes A large area of the earth that has certain kinds of living things is called a **biome** (BY-ohm). Scientists identify a biome by the main kinds of plants growing in the area. Because many animals eat plants, each biome also has certain kinds of animals.

► *Identify:* How do scientists identify a biome?

Climate and Vegetation Climate affects the **vegetation** (vej-ih-TAY-shun) in an area. Vegetation is the plants in an area. Rainfall and temperature are the climate factors that affect vegetation the most. Some kinds of plants need a lot of water. They grow well where there is a lot of rain. For example, many trees grow only in tropical rainy climates. Some plants grow where there is very little water. Cacti (KAK-tie) are plants that do not need much water. They grow in some desert climates. Many plants cannot survive very cold temperatures. Oak trees, for example, may be killed by frost. Orange trees need both rainfall and warm temperatures to grow well.

► *Define:* What is vegetation?

Climate and Animals The animals in an area are affected by climate. Animals that eat certain plants can live only in areas where those plants grow. For example, eucalyptus leaves are the main food of koalas. Koalas live only in areas where eucalyptus trees grow. Other animals are directly

affected by temperature. The body temperature of these animals is about the same as the air temperature. The animals would die if the air temperature got too low. Most snakes, for example, live in warm climates. They would not be able to survive in a cold climate.

► *Explain:* Why do koalas live in areas where eucalyptus trees grow?

Adaptations Most living things have **adaptations** (ad-ap-TAY-shuns) that help them survive. Adaptations are features of a living thing that let it live and reproduce in its environment. A polar bear is adapted to a cold climate. It has a heavy fur coat and lots of body fat. A polar bear would not be able to survive in a desert. Plants also have adaptations. Cacti have adaptations for living in deserts. They have stems that store water. The stems and leaves of cacti prevent water from escaping from the plant.

► *Name:* What are features that let a living thing live and reproduce in its environment called?

LESSON SUMMARY

- A biome is a large area of the earth that has certain kinds of living things.
- Climate affects the vegetation in an area.
- The animals in an area are affected by climate.
- Living things have adaptations that let them live and reproduce in their environments.

CHECK *Complete the following.*

1. A large area of the earth with certain kinds of plants and animals is a ______ .
2. Scientists identify a biome by the kinds of ______ living there.
3. The kinds of plants in an area are its ______ .
4. Rainfall and ______ are two climate factors that affect vegetation.
5. Most snakes live only in ______climates.
6. Animals and plants have ______ that help them survive.
7. Polar bears are adapted to live in ______ climates.
8. The ______ and leaves of cacti are adaptations for living in deserts.

APPLY *Complete the following.*

9. **Infer:** Giant pandas are racoonlike animals. They eat only bamboo shoots. Bamboo grows only in China and Tibet. Where do you think giant pandas live? Explain.
10. **Hypothesize:** Part of the forest biome in the northern United States is called the "spruce-moose" belt. How do you think it got this name?

Skill Builder

Classifying There are six major land biomes. They are classified by the type of vegetation that grows in the area. The type of vegetation depends on the climate of the area. Use library references to find the names of the six land biomes. Write the name of each biome on a 3″ × 5″ index card. Give the average yearly rainfall and temperature range for each biome. Cut out pictures of the kinds of plants and animals that live in each biome. Use old magazines to find the pictures. Glue the pictures on the index card for the correct biome.

SCIENCE CONNECTION

THE TROPICAL RAINFOREST

Tropical rainforests are very dense areas of vegetation. They have hot, humid climates. Many different kinds of animals and plants live in the rainforests. Scientists estimate that in 10 square kilometers, there may be more than 750 different kinds of trees and more than 1000 different kinds of animals.

Many plants in the rainforests are used to make medicines and other products. Many of the plants and animals here live nowhere else. Scientists are concerned because the rainforests are being destroyed. In many areas, the forests have been cut down and burned. The land is being used for farming and development. The problem is that once the minerals in the soil are used up, the farmers leave the land. They move to a new area, and cut down and burn more forests.

Scientists are working closely with many countries to help stop the destruction of the rainforests. Scientists also are working to save some of the animals in the rainforest from extinction.

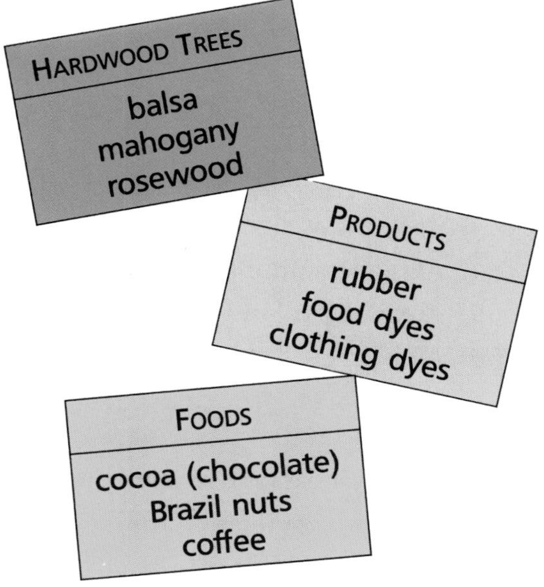

UNIT 13 Challenges

STUDY HINT Before beginning the Unit Challenges, review the TechTerms and Lesson Summary for each lesson in this unit.

TechTerms

adaptations (274)
altitude (266)
biome (274)
climate (264)
latitude (266)
leaching (272)
microclimate (270)
middle-latitude zone (268)
polar zone (268)
tropical zone (268)
vegetation (274)
weather (264)
weathering (272)

TechTerm Challenges

Matching *Write the TechTerm that best matches each description.*

1. warm region near the equator
2. features that let living things live and reproduce in their environments
3. breaking down of rocks and other materials on the earth's surface
4. cold region near the poles
5. downward movement of materials in soil

Identifying Relationships *Explain how the words in each pair are related. Write your answers in complete sentences.*

1. altitude, elevation
2. latitude, longitude
3. biome, vegetation
4. climate, weather
5. microclimate, local climate
6. tropical zone, middle-latitude zone

Content Challenges

Completion *Write the term or phrase that best completes each statement.*

1. To find average temperature, you add two or more temperatures and divide the sum by the number of _______ .
2. The amount of temperature change in an area is its temperature _______ .
3. Rain, snow, sleet, and hail are forms of _______ .
4. At higher latitudes, the sun's rays strike the earth _______ .
5. Areas at low latitudes have a _______ climate than areas at higher latitudes.
6. Air is _______ at sea level than it is at higher altitudes.
7. Land areas near cold-water currents have _______ temperatures than areas near warm-water currents.
8. When air passes over a mountain range, it rises and _______ .
9. It hardly ever rains on the _______ side of a mountain.
10. The leeward side of a mountain is the side of the mountain that faces _______ the wind.
11. The tropical zone is located between _______ north and south latitude.
12. Some scientists think that _______ will lead to global warming.

True/False *Write true if the statement is true. If the statement is false, change the underlined term to make the statement true.*

1. The day-to-day conditions of the atmosphere is <u>climate</u>.
2. The leeward side of a mountain gets <u>more</u> rain than the windward side.
3. Dry climates are described as <u>arid</u>.
4. Antarctica is located in the <u>tropical</u> zone.
5. A city is an example of a <u>microclimate</u>.
6. In hot, wet climates, weathering is very <u>slow</u>.
7. Soils in cool, dry climates are <u>thinner</u> than soils in hot, wet climates.
8. Leaching occurs most in areas with <u>a lot</u> of rain.
9. Tropical soil is rich in <u>humus</u>.
10. Because it gets little rainfall, desert soil is rich in <u>humus</u>.
11. Much of the soil in the <u>forest</u> is barren rock.
12. Tundra soil is <u>frozen</u> for most of the year.
13. Each biome has certain kinds of <u>plants and animals</u>.
14. Most snakes live in <u>cool</u> climates.
15. Cacti grow best in <u>tundra</u> climates.

Understanding the Features

Reading Critically *Use the feature reading selections to answer the following. Page numbers for the features are shown in parentheses.*

1. Why do dark-colored clothes help keep you warm? (265)
2. **Define:** What is climatology? (269)
3. What do weather observers do? (271)
4. **Define:** What is irrigation? (273)
5. What kind of climates do tropical rain forests have? (275)
6. Explain two ways that tropical rain forests are important. (275)

Concept Challenges

Critical Thinking *Answer the following in complete sentences.*

1. **Infer:** Why is tundra soil frozen for most of the year?
2. How is the mineral content of soil affected by the amount of rainfall?
3. Why is having a stem that stores water an important adaptation for a cactus?
4. **Predict:** What kind of temperature would a coastal town located near a cold-water current have?
5. **Infer:** Why are many deserts located on the leeward sides of mountains?

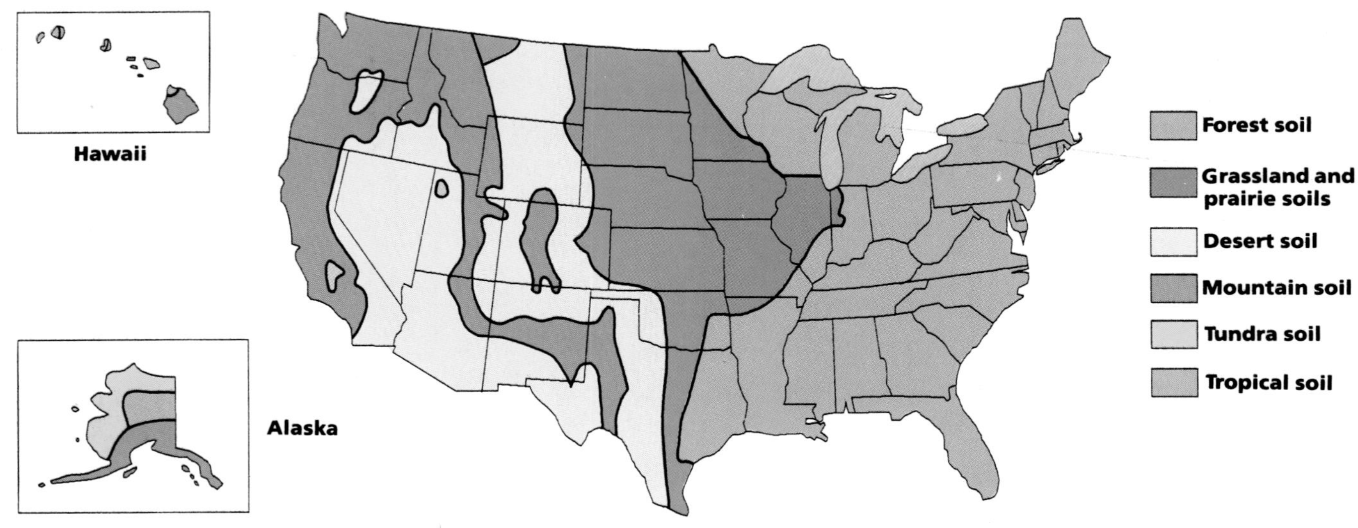

Understanding a Map *Use the map to complete the following.*

1. **Observe:** What states have tropical soil?
2. In which type of soil would cacti grow?
3. How many soil types are shown in the map?
4. Which state has frozen soil for most of the year? Explain.
5. What kind of soil is found along most of the west coast of the United States?
6. Name three states in which grain crops such as wheat and corn are grown.
7. Cattle feed upon grass and grains. Why do you think most cattle ranches are located in states that have grassland and prairie soil?
8. Which state probably gets more rainfall, Florida or Utah? Explain.

Finding Out More

1. Draw a map of the United States. Use an encyclopedia, or other reference book, to find out the locations of each biome in the United States. Use different colored pencils or markers to show the location of each biome on your map. Be sure to include a legend that identifies the biome shown by each color.
2. Use an almanac to find out what kind of weather and climate was predicted for the area in which you live. Compare the predictions to actual weather and climate conditions reported in your local newspaper. Present your findings in a table.
3. Choose a foreign country that you would like to visit. Use library references to find out what the climate is like in the country you chose during each of the four seasons. Write a report explaining why you chose the country you did and the kinds of clothing you would need to visit the country in each season.
4. Choose a wild animal that you would like to know more about. Use library references to find out how the animal you chose is adapted to the climate and area in which it lives.

UNIT 14

NATURAL RESOURCES

CONTENTS

STUDY HINT After you read each lesson in Unit 14, write a brief summary on a sheet of paper explaining how the information in each lesson applies to your everyday life.

14-1 What is the environment?

Objective ▶ Describe cycles in nature and define pollution.

TechTerms

- ▶ **environment** (in-VY-run-munt): everything that surrounds a living thing
- ▶ **pollutants** (puh-LOOT-ents): harmful substances in the environment
- ▶ **pollution** (puh-LOO-shun): anything that harms the environment

Environment Living things get everything they need from the **environment** (in-VY-run-munt). The environment is everything that surrounds a living thing. The atmosphere, hydrosphere, and lithosphere are parts of the environment. The atmosphere, or air, supplies living things with important gases. The hydrosphere is the part of the earth that is water. Living things get water from the hydrosphere. The lithosphere, or solid part of the earth, supplies living things with important materials such as minerals and soil.

▶ *Describe:* What is the environment?

Cycles in Nature Some materials in the environment pass through cycles. You may recall that the water cycle allows the earth's water to be used again. Carbon dioxide, oxygen, and nitrogen also cycle through the environment.

The repeated movement of oxygen and carbon dioxide through the environment is called the oxygen-carbon dioxide cycle. Animals take in oxygen from the air when they breathe in. Animals give off carbon dioxide when they breathe out. The oxygen in the air is not used up by animals because plants release oxygen into the air. Plants use the carbon dioxide that is given off by animals.

Figure 1 The oxygen-carbon dioxide cycle

The nitrogen cycle is shown in Figure 2. In the nitrogen cycle, bacteria in the soil use nitrogen gas from the air to form compounds. The nitrogen compounds are used by plants and animals. When the plants and animals die, the nitrogen compounds are broken down. Nitrogen gas is released back in the air.

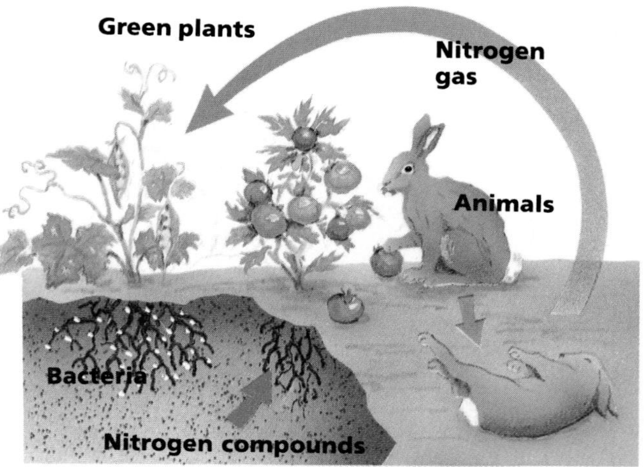

Figure 2 The nitrogen cycle

▶ *Identify:* What gas do animals release when they breathe out?

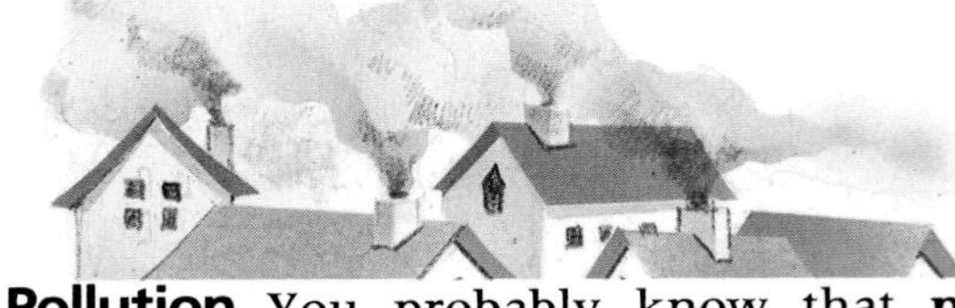

Pollution You probably know that **pollution** (puh-LOO-shun) is a major problem. Pollution is anything that harms the environment. Pollution occurs when harmful substances, or **pollutants** (puh-LOOT-ents), are released into the environment. Pollutants are harming the earth's air, water, and land. This upsets the balance of nature's cycles.

▶ *Define:* What is pollution?

LESSON SUMMARY

- The environment is everything that surrounds a living thing.
- Some materials in the environment pass through cycles.
- Oxygen and carbon dioxide cycle through the environment.
- Nitrogen cycles through the environment.
- Pollution is anything that harms the environment.

CHECK *Find the sentence in the lesson that answers the question. Then, write the sentence.*

1. From what part of the environment do living things get water?
2. What gas do animals take in from the air when they breathe in?
3. What is the environment?
4. What happens to the nitrogen compounds used by plants and animals when the plants and animals die?
5. When does pollution occur?

APPLY *Use Figure 2 on page 280 to answer the following.*

6. **Analyze:** How do animals get nitrogen compounds?
7. **Observe:** What living things make nitrogen compounds?

Complete the following.

8. **Model:** Draw a diagram of the oxygen-carbon dioxide cycle.

InfoSearch

Read the passage. Ask two questions about the topic that you cannot answer from the information in the passage.

Nitrogen-Fixing Bacteria Bacteria that use nitrogen gas from the air are called nitrogen-fixing bacteria. These bacteria live in the soil. They also live in the roots of plants, such as legumes. Farmers often plant legumes in their fields. The bacteria in the legumes add nitrogen compounds to the soil. The compounds are used by crops.

SEARCH: Use library references to find answers to your questions.

PEOPLE IN SCIENCE

RACHEL CARSON (1907–1964)

Rachel Louise Carson was born in Springdale, Pennsylvania. She graduated from Pennsylvania College for Women. From 1936 to 1952, Rachel Carson worked for the United States Fish and Wildlife Service. She was both a marine biologist and a science writer.

Rachel Carson wrote about the ocean and the problems of pollution. Her first book, *Under the Sea Wind,* was published in 1941. Rachel Carson also wrote *The Sea Around Us* and *The Edge of the Sea.* These books have been used as guides in studying ocean life.

Rachel Carson's most famous book is *Silent Spring.* This book was published in 1962. In *Silent Spring,* Carson discusses how pesticides are harmful to the environment. She warns people that pesticides can kill birds and fishes, as well as insects. Carson also points out that pesticides can poison the foods people eat.

Silent Spring has affected how people use pesticides. Some pesticides have been banned as a result of Carson's warnings. Rachel Carson died in Silver Springs, Maryland in 1964.

14-2 What causes air pollution?

Objective ▶ Identify causes of air pollution and explain how pollution harms the environment.

TechTerms

- ▶ **acid rain:** rain containing nitric acid and sulfuric acid
- ▶ **smog:** mixture of smoke, fog, and chemicals

Air Pollution The burning of fossil fuels is the major cause of air pollution. When fuels are burned, harmful substances are released into the air. Air pollution occurs when these harmful substances enter the atmosphere.

Have you ever seen thick, black smoke coming from a chimney? Smoke contains dust and soot. Dust and soot are air pollutants. They can remain in the air for a long time. Heavier pieces of dust and soot may settle on almost everything around you. Dust and soot may irritate your eyes, lungs, and air passages.

Many cities have a **smog** problem. Smog is a mixture of smoke, fog, and chemicals. Smog is harmful to people who have breathing problems because it harms the lungs.

▶ ***Identify:*** What is the major cause of air pollution?

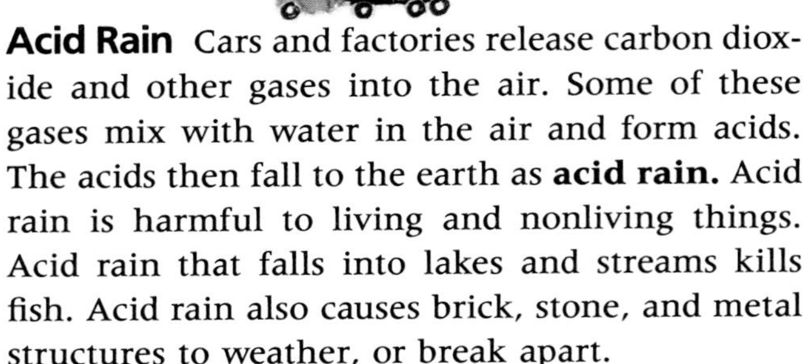

Acid Rain Cars and factories release carbon dioxide and other gases into the air. Some of these gases mix with water in the air and form acids. The acids then fall to the earth as **acid rain.** Acid rain is harmful to living and nonliving things. Acid rain that falls into lakes and streams kills fish. Acid rain also causes brick, stone, and metal structures to weather, or break apart.

▶ ***Explain:*** How does acid rain form?

Carbon Dioxide Levels Fuels need oxygen to burn. When fuels burn, they give off carbon dioxide. Carbon dioxide traps the heat energy from the sun. Scientists think that the increase of carbon dioxide in the air is causing the temperature of the atmosphere to rise. This rise in temperature may cause climate changes.

▶ ***Relate:*** Why might an increase of carbon dioxide in the air cause air temperature to rise?

Protecting the Air Many countries have laws to help control pollution. In the United States, cars must have anti-pollution devices (duh-VISES). These devices prevent some pollutants that are given off by burning fuels from entering the air. Factories use filters on their smokestacks. One of the easiest ways to reduce air pollution is to use less fossil fuel.

Hypothesize: Why will using less fossil fuel reduce air pollution?

LESSON SUMMARY

- The burning of fossil fuels is the major cause of air pollution.
- Dust and soot are two air pollutants.
- Smog is a mixture of smoke, fog, and chemicals.
- Acid rain harms both living and nonliving things.
- The burning of fossil fuels has increased the amount of carbon dioxide in the atmosphere.
- Some countries have laws to help control air pollution.

CHECK *Complete the following.*

1. Smoke contains tiny pieces of dust and _______ .
2. Smog is a mixture of smoke, fog, and _______ .
3. Carbon dioxide traps the _______ energy from the sun.
4. Some pollutant gases combine with _______ in the air to form acid rain.
5. The rise in the temperature of the atmosphere could cause changes in the earth's _______ .

APPLY *Complete the following.*

6. **Predict:** The rising temperature of the earth's atmosphere could cause glaciers to melt. How would this affect sea level, and low-lying coastal cities?
7. **Infer:** Why is smog a serious problem in big cities?
8. **Model:** Draw a model showing the relationship between the burning of fossil fuels, the amount of carbon dioxide in the air, and the temperature of the atmosphere.
9. **Hypothesize:** Do you think acid rain is more of a problem in areas with wet climates or dry climates? Explain.
10. **Infer:** What two words are used to make up the word "smog"?

Health & Safety Tip

Cities with air pollution problems often give warnings when smog is very bad. A smog alert usually is given as part of the weather report. Use library references to find out why people in these cities should not exercise outdoors on days the warnings are given.

ACTIVITY

OBSERVING AIR POLLUTANTS

You will need a hand lens, a microscope slide, a toothpick, and petroleum jelly.

1. Use the toothpick to coat one side of a glass slide with a thin layer of petroleum jelly.
2. Place the slide on a window ledge overnight.
3. Examine the slide with a hand lens the next day.

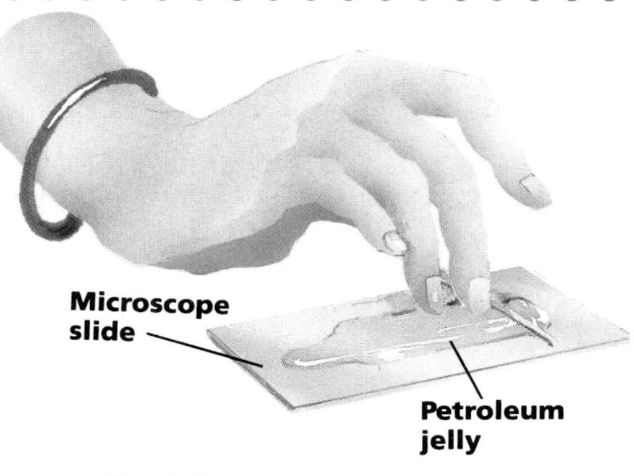

Questions

1. **Observe:** What are some of the things you observed on your slide?
2. **Infer:** What do you think these particles are?
3. Where do you think these particles came from?
4. **a.** Hypothesize: Where in your neighborhood do you think you could place your slide to observe fewer pollutants?
   b. Where in your neighborhood do you think you could place your slide to observe more pollutants?
   c. How could you prove your hypotheses?

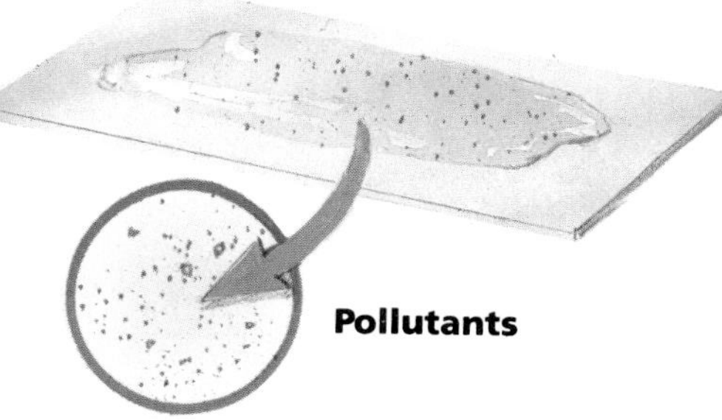

14-3 What causes water pollution?

Objective ▶ Describe the major sources of water pollution.

TechTerm

- ▶ **sewage:** waste that usually is flushed away in water

Water Pollution Water pollution occurs when harmful substances enter the water. Some pollutants dissolve in the water. Other pollutants float in the water. Many lakes and rivers were once used as sources of fresh water. Today, some lakes and rivers are polluted. They cannot be used for drinking or swimming. Some lakes and rivers are so polluted that fish cannot live in their waters.

Explain: Why are many lakes and rivers not used for drinking water today?

Sewage Sewage is made up of wastes that usually are flushed away in water. Sewage is a source of water pollution. Bacteria and other disease-causing organisms live in sewage. Many fish and shellfish cannot be eaten because they contain bacteria that live in sewage. Sewage also contains soaps and chemicals.

Describe: What harmful things are in sewage?

Chemical Pollutants Many chemicals pollute the water. Fertilizers (FUR-tul-y-zuhrs) are chemicals that help plants grow. Pesticides (PES-tuh-sides) are used to kill insect pests. Farmers use fertilizers and pesticides on their crops. Many fertilizers and pesticides seep into the groundwater. This water is then carried to lakes and rivers. The chemicals in the water may harm living things that live in the water.

Chemical pollutants also come from industry. Some industries bury their wastes in barrels, or drums, in the ground. If the drums rust and break apart, the wastes can leak into the groundwater. Industries also dump chemical wastes directly into water. These wastes are harmful to fish living in the water. They also are harmful to people who eat the fish. Mercury is a poisonous element that is sometimes found in polluted water. Many fish cannot be eaten because they contain mercury.

Name: What are two sources of chemical water pollutants?

Protecting the Water Sewage-treatment plants have been built in many cities and towns. Sewage-treatment plants change sewage into less harmful material. Laws also help to fight water pollution. These laws require industries to clean their wastes before dumping them into lakes and rivers. Many pesticides have been banned.

Explain: What happens to sewage at sewage-treatment plants?

LESSON SUMMARY

- Water pollution occurs when harmful substances enter the water.
- Sewage is a source of water pollution.
- Many chemicals pollute water.
- Industries are a source of chemical water pollutants.
- Laws have helped stop water pollution.

CHECK *Find the sentence in the lesson that answers each question. Then, write the sentence.*

1. What are pesticides used for?
2. What causes water pollution?
3. What happens when drums storing industrial wastes become corroded?
4. Where do fertilizers and pesticides that seep into groundwater end up?
5. What are fertilizers?

APPLY *Complete the following.*

6. **Diagram:** Draw a flow chart that shows how a pesticide could end up in a person's body.
7. How could you help stop water pollution?
8. **Predict:** What might happen if drums containing harmful chemicals were buried on a beach? Explain your answer.

Skill Builder

Hypothesizing Sewage increases the amount of algae in water. Algae are plantlike living things. When algae die, their decay uses up the oxygen in the water. Explain what will happen to fish living in the water as the amount of oxygen in the water decreases.

State the Problem

Study the illustration. Then state the problem.

ACTIVITY

SEPARATING SOLUTES FROM WATER

You will need 3 medium-sized glass jars, paper towels (or a paper coffee filter), soil, a paper cup, and a stirrer.

1. Pour 1 cup of water into each of 2 jars. Add 1/2 cup of soil to each jar.
2. Stir the contents of each jar to make a muddy mixture. Put one jar aside. Observe the jar after 30 minutes.
3. Place a paper towel over the empty jar. Pour your other muddy mixture over the towel. Observe what happens.

Questions

1. **Observe:** What happened to the mixture of water and soil in the jar you set aside?
2. **Predict:** What would happen if you added twigs to the mixture you set aside?
3. **a. Observe:** What materials went through the paper towel? **b.** What material was trapped by the paper towel?

14-4 How is water purified?

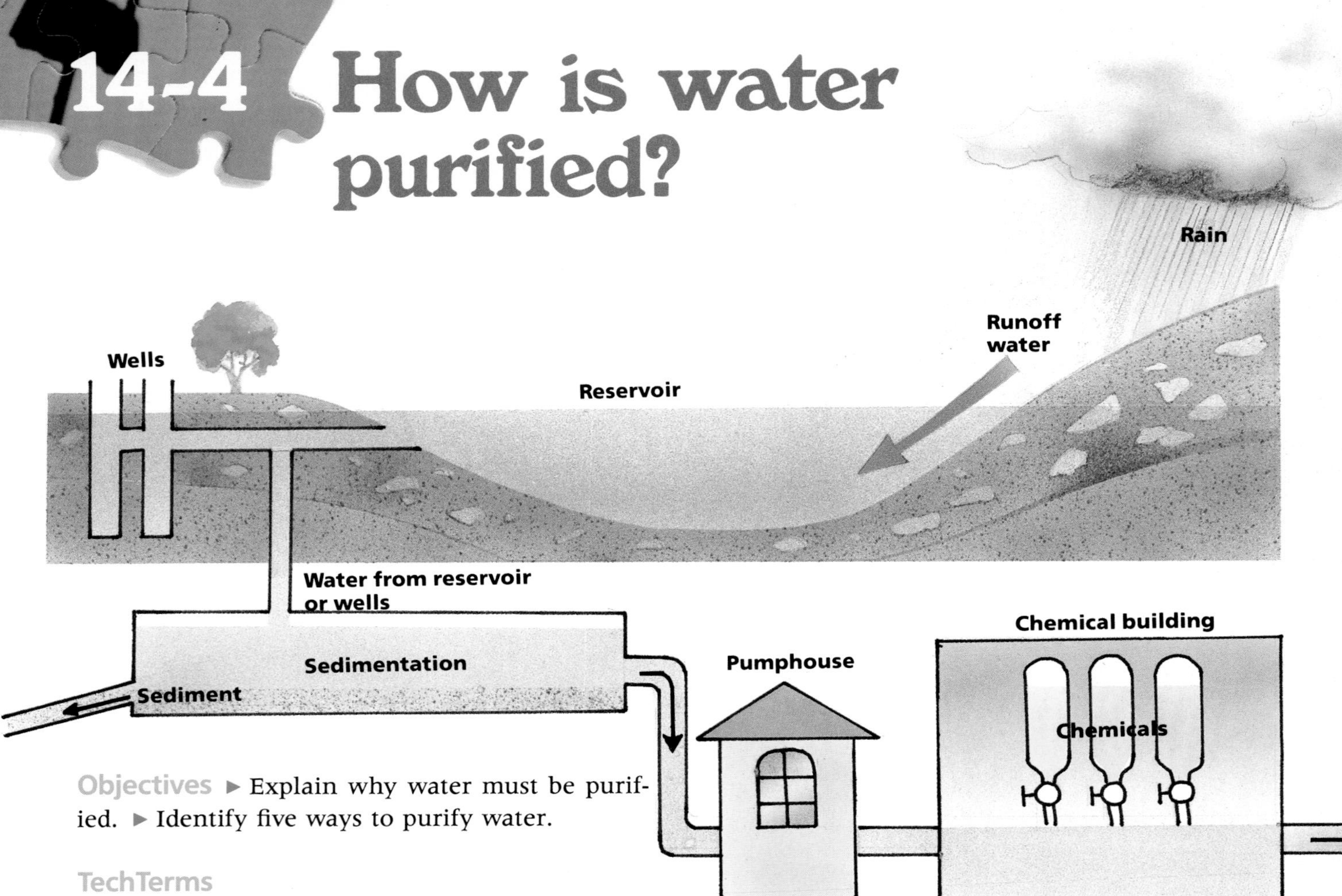

Objectives ▶ Explain why water must be purified. ▶ Identify five ways to purify water.

TechTerms

- **hard water:** water containing a lot of calcium and magnesium minerals
- **soft water:** water containing few or no minerals

Drinking Water Your drinking water comes from reservoirs (REZ-er-vwahrs), springs, or wells. A reservoir is a lake made by people. Reservoirs store large amounts of fresh water. Pipelines carry the water to homes and businesses.

Some water contains dissolved minerals. Calcium and magnesium are minerals often found in some water. Water that has a lot of calcium and magnesium is called **hard water.** It is hard for soap to form suds in hard water. Water with few or no minerals in it is called **soft water.**

▶ *Identify:* What two minerals does hard water contain?

Purifying water Water for drinking and bathing must be purified (PYOOR-ih-fyd), or cleaned. Water is purified in water-treatment plants. Water can be purified in the following ways.

- Sedimentation (sed-uh-mun-TAY-shun): The water is allowed to stand for long periods of time. Heavy particles, such as sand and dirt, settle to the bottom and are removed.
- Coagulation (koh-ag-yoo-LAY-shun): Chemicals that cause particles to clump together are added to the water. The clumps of particles settle to the bottom. The particles are then removed from the water.
- Filtration (fil-TRAY-shun): Water is passed through a filter to remove small particles.
- Aeration (ayr-AY-shun): Water is sprayed into the air. Oxygen from the air dissolves in the water. The oxygen kills some harmful microorganisms.
- Chlorination (klor-uh-NAY-shun): Chlorine is added to the water. Chlorine kills harmful microorganisms in the water.

▶ *Name:* What are five ways to purify drinking water?

Coagulation

Filtration

Sand

Gravel

LESSON SUMMARY

- Drinking water comes from reservoirs, wells, or springs.
- Some water contains a lot of dissolved minerals.
- Five ways to purify water are sedimentation, coagulation, filtration, aeration, and chlorination.

CHECK *Identify the water-purification method described in each statement.*

1. Chemicals that cause particles to clump together is added to water.
2. Water is sprayed into the air.
3. Water is allowed to stand for long periods of time.

Complete the following.

4. Hard water contains a lot of calcium and _______ .
5. A human-made lake that stores fresh water is a _______ .

APPLY *Use the diagram of water purification methods to complete the following.*

6. What materials are used for filtration?
7. **Analyze:** Where does the water in reservoirs come from?
8. What substance is added to water to kill microorganisms?

Ideas in Action

IDEA: Water is needed by all living things.
ACTION: Identify ways that you use water everyday.

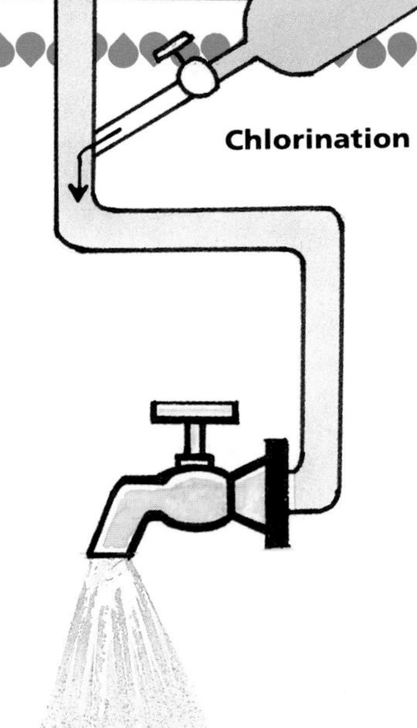

CAREER IN EARTH SCIENCE

WATER PURIFICATION TECHNICIAN

A water purification technician works at a water treatment plant. A water purification technician controls and maintains the equipment at the plant. The technician also takes water samples at different times during the purification process. The water samples are tested for impurities. The technician also checks the amount of chemicals in the water. It is part of the technician's job to make sure that the proper amount of chlorine and other chemicals are being used.

To become a water purification technician, you must have a high school diploma. Water purification technicians may learn through on-the-job training. Some water purification technicians take two year programs in water purification technology.

14-5 What causes land pollution?

Objective ► Describe the causes of land pollution.

TechTerm

- ► **litter:** materials that are thrown away on the ground

Litter and Garbage Have you ever seen cans, bottles, papers, and plastic materials that were thrown on the ground? These thrown-away materials are called **litter.** Litter is one of the causes of land pollution. Litter harms the land and destroys the beauty of many areas.

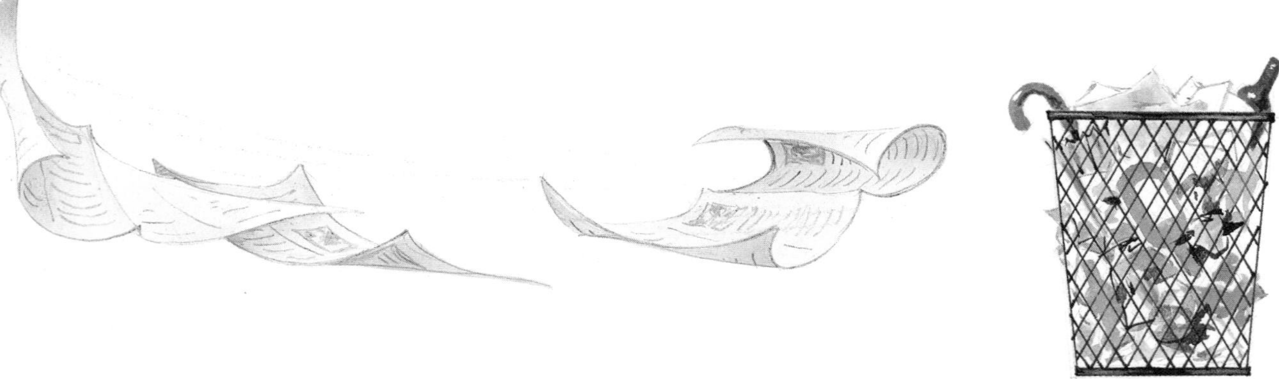

Garbage also causes land pollution. Each year people make billions of tons of garbage. The garbage builds up at dumps or is used as landfill. The garbage is put between two layers of the land in a landfill. Some materials in garbage take many years to be broken down. Materials, such as some kinds of plastic, do not break down at all. Other materials contain harmful substances that seep into the soil.

► *Identify:* Name two causes of land pollution.

Industrial Wastes You may recall that chemical wastes from industry pollute the water. These chemicals also pollute the land. Some industrial wastes are buried in drums in the ground. Many of these wastes contain harmful metals such as mercury and lead. In many places, these wastes are leaking from the drums into the ground. The wastes pollute the land and harm living things.

► *Describe:* How are some industrial wastes disposed?

Protecting the Land Getting rid of garbage and chemical wastes is a growing problem. Cities have taken some steps to reduce land pollution. Garbage is collected regularly. Streets are cleaned of litter. However, much more needs to be done.

One solution to the problem of land pollution is to make use of certain wastes. Some wastes can be used as fertilizers. Others can be burned to produce energy. Still other wastes such as bottles and cans, can be treated and used again.

The clean-up of chemical wastes is a more difficult problem. People are working to clean up wastes leaking into the soil. Cleaning up these wastes is expensive and takes a lot of time.

► *Identify:* What are some solutions to the problem of land pollution?

LESSON SUMMARY

- Litter pollutes the land and destroys the beauty of many areas.
- Garbage is a cause of land pollution.
- Chemical pollutants from farms and industries pollute the land.
- Some harmful wastes buried in the ground are leaking into the soil.
- Collecting garbage and cleaning the streets regularly have reduced land pollution.
- One way to prevent land pollution is make use of certain wastes.
- Cleaning up chemical wastes in the land is a difficult problem.

CHECK *Write true if the statement is true. If the statement is false, change the underlined term to make the statement true.*

1. Materials that are thrown away on the ground are called litter.
2. Some wastes can be burned to produce fertilizers.
3. Garbage put between layers of land creates a landfill.
4. Cleaning up chemical wastes from the soil is inexpensive.

APPLY *Complete the following.*

6. What are some steps you can take to reduce the amount of litter in your neighborhood?
7. **Apply:** Explain how industrial wastes can pollute both land and water.
8. **Infer:** How do you think placing deposits on beverage containers helps to reduce land pollution?

Skill Builder

Observing Take a walk around your school grounds. Observe all the litter on the ground. Make a list of all the different discarded materials you see. How many cans did you find? How many plastic objects did you find? How many pieces of paper did you find? What material is most of the litter made up of?

Ideas in Action

IDEA: Litter is a problem in all areas of the country.

ACTION: List five things you could do to reduce the amount of litter in your community.

SCIENCE CONNECTION

LANDFILLS

One of the biggest problems in large cities is how to get rid of the city's daily garbage. One way cities do this is to use landfills. Solid wastes are placed between layers of soil to form a landfill. The wastes are squeezed together first. Then the wastes are covered with soil. Large machinery such as bulldozers are used to squeeze the wastes together and cover the wastes with soil. The landfill is then covered with different kinds of plants.

Landfills often are used to reclaim land that cannot be used. Sometimes a landfill is used to claim land under water. In San Francisco, a landfill was used to fill in parts of San Francisco Bay. The size of the Bay has been reduced from about 348 square kilometers to about 216 square kilometers. In 1965, the Bay Conservation and Development Commission was formed. The commission now controls the landfill.

14-6 What are natural resources?

Objective ▶ Distinguish between renewable and nonrenewable resources.

TechTerms

- ▶ **conservation** (kahn-sur-VAY-shun): wise use of natural resources
- ▶ **natural resource:** material from the earth that is used by living things
- ▶ **nonrenewable resource:** natural resource that is not replaced by nature
- ▶ **renewable resource:** natural resource that can be replaced or reused

Natural Resources Everything you use, eat, drink, and wear comes from the earth. When a spaceship travels into space, it carries everything its crew needs to live. A spaceship must have a supply of food, air, water, and fuel. The earth can be compared to a spaceship. The earth has everything living things need to survive. Materials from the earth that are used by living things are called **natural resources.**

▶ ***Define:*** What is a natural resource?

Renewable Resources Natural resources that can be reused or replaced are **renewable resources.** Air, water, soil, and living things are renewable resources. The water cycle allows the earth's water to be used over and over. New soil is formed to replace soil that has been carried away by wind and water. Trees and other new plants grow to replace those that have been cut down or died. Animals are born to replace animals that have died.

▶ ***List:*** What are four renewable resources?

Nonrenewable Resources Oil, coal, and natural gas are fossil fuels. They were formed from the remains of plants and animals that lived long ago. Fossil fuels and minerals are **nonrenewable resources.** Nonrenewable resources are natural resources that are not replaced by nature. Nonrenewable resources take millions of years to form. Once nonrenewable resources are used up, their supplies are gone.

▶ ***Define:*** What is a nonrenewable resource?

Conservation The wise use of a natural resource is **conservation** (kahn-sur-VAY-shun). As the number of people on earth gets larger, the need for natural resources increases. People must use natural resources wisely to help them last longer.

▶ ***Relate:*** What happens to the need for natural resources as the number of people on the earth grows?

LESSON SUMMARY

- Natural resources come from the earth and are used by living things.
- Renewable resources can be reused or replaced.
- Nonrenewable resources are not reused or replaced.
- Conservation is the wise use of natural resources.

CHECK *Complete the following.*

1. Water, soil, and air are ______ natural resources.
2. Oil is a ______ natural resource.
3. Natural resources come from the ______ .
4. Resources that can be reused or replaced are ______ .
5. The wise use of natural resources is ______ .
6. Living things are ______ natural resources.

APPLY *Complete the following.*

7. **Classify:** Classify each of the following as a renewable or a nonrenewable resource: trees, coal, nitrogen, people, diamonds, water, natural gas, soil, oil, iron.
8. Why do you think it is important to conserve renewable resources?

Skill Builder

Organizing When you organize, you put information in some kind of order. Use library references to find out the metal that is taken from each of these minerals: hematite, sphelerite, bauxite, and chalcopyrite. Give a use for each metal. Organize the information in a table.

Ideas in Action

IDEA: People use natural resources every day.
ACTION: Make a list of all the natural resources you use in one day. Explain how you used each natural resource.

LOOKING BACK IN SCIENCE

METALLURGY

What do jewelry, radios, cars, skyscrapers, coins, and wires have in common? They all are made up of metal. Metals have many uses. Almost everything around you is made up of metal or requires a metal to be made.

Metallurgy (MET-ul-ur-jee) is the science of removing metals from their ores, and preparing the metals for use. Some of the basic ideas of metallurgy have been used for many centuries. For example, in 500 BC the ancient Assyrians knew how to make steel from iron. Today, steel production is a very important industry. The ancient Egyptians and Chinese used gold, silver, and copper to make jewelry, tools, and weapons. Five thousand years ago, the Egyptians knew how to take iron from its ores.

During the Middle Ages, great advances were made in metallurgy. Alchemists were people who tried to turn less costly metals, such as copper, into gold. Of course, they never could do it. Alchemists, however, learned a great deal about metals and their uses. Their work was important to modern metallurgy. Modern metallurgy has methods and equipment that were developed only within the last fifty years.

14-7 How can resources be conserved?

Objective ▶ Describe ways to conserve natural resources.

TechTerm

- **recycling:** using natural resources over and over again

Recycling Natural resources can be conserved by **recycling.** When a resource is recycled, it is used again. Aluminum cans, glass bottles, newspapers, and some of the metals used to make cars can all be recycled. Recycling conserves minerals. It also conserves living things. For example, when paper is recycled, fewer trees need to be cut down. Recycling uses less energy than finding and using new resources. This conserves fossil fuels.

▶ ***Describe:*** How does recycling conserve natural resources?

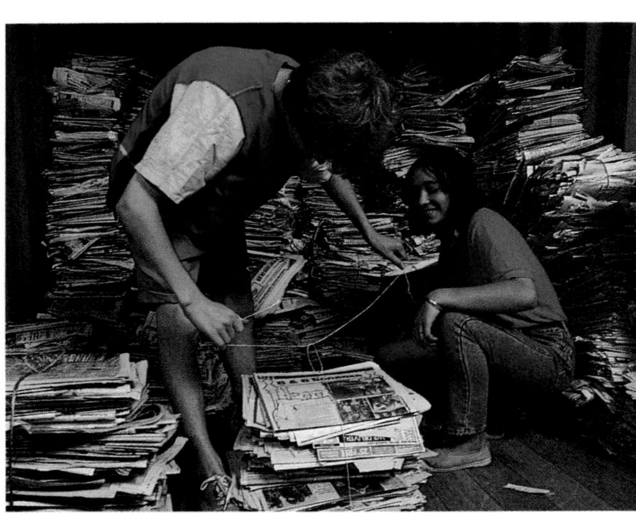

Replacement Materials One way of conserving minerals is to use other materials in their place. For example, some iron and aluminum engines have been replaced with plastic. Lightweight steel cables are being replaced by nylon.

▶ ***List:*** List two materials that are being used to replace minerals.

Water Conservation The supply of clean, fresh water on the earth is limited. One way to conserve water is to not waste water. You can conserve water by turning off the water when you brush your teeth or by taking a shower instead of a bath. Fixing leaking faucets also conserves water.

▶ ***State:*** What are two ways you can conserve water?

Soil Conservation Different farming methods can be used to conserve soil. Soil can be conserved by the following farming practices.

- Contour farming is plowing across the slope of the land. Terracing is the building of flat areas, or terraces up the side of a hill. Both contour plowing and terracing keep water from washing away the soil.
- Strip-cropping is the planting of crops in rows. Grasses are planted between the rows of crops. The grasses hold water and help stop erosion.
- Windbreaks are used to keep wind from blowing soil away. Farmers plant rows of trees along the edges of fields to slow the wind.
- Fertilizers are used to replace the nutrients used up by plants. Fertilizers add nutrients to the soil.

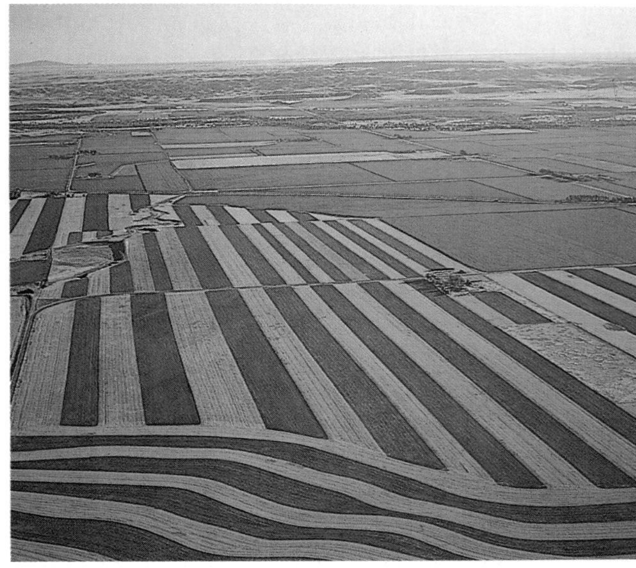

▶ ***Name:*** What are three farming methods that help conserve soil?

LESSON SUMMARY

- Recycling allows resources to be used over and over again.
- One way to conserve minerals is to find other materials that can take the place of minerals.
- One way to conserve water is not to waste water.
- Different farming methods such as contour plowing can be used to conserve soil.

CHECK *Write true if the statement is true. If the statement is false, change the underlined term to make the statement true.*

1. Replacement allows a mineral to be used again.
2. Some iron and aluminum engines have been replaced with plastic.
3. Windbreaks add nutrients to the soil.
4. Contour plowing involves plowing down the slope of a hill.
5. Strip-cropping helps prevent erosion by wind.

APPLY *Complete the following.*

6. How does recycling reduce waste?
7. **Calculate:** About 90 new aluminum cans can be made from 100 recycled cans. If you recycled 1 can each day for a year, about how many new cans would you help to make? If each person in your class recycled 1 can a day, how many new cans would your class make?
8. **Model:** Make or draw a model of a field on which strip-cropping is used. Label each row on your model.

InfoSearch

Read the passage. Ask two questions about the topic that you cannot answer from the information in the passage.

New Mineral Sources The mineral resources on land are running out. The oceans may be a new source of minerals. There are many minerals dissolved in ocean water. Some of the minerals found in ocean water are sodium, sulfur, potassium, magnesium, and bromine. Scientists are studying ways to take minerals from ocean water. At the present time, taking minerals from ocean water is very expensive.

SEARCH: Use library references to find answers to your questions.

TECHNOLOGY AND SOCIETY

SYNTHETIC SUBSTITUTES

Have you ever heard the terms "acrylic," "nylon," and "polyester?" You may associate these terms with clothing. Perhaps you have an acrylic sweater, or a nylon shirt. What do acrylic, nylon, and polyester have in common? They are all synthetic (sin-THET-ik) materials. Synthetics are substances that are made by people.

Synthetics are used in place of natural materials. In clothing, acrylic, nylon, and polyester can be used in place of natural fibers such as cotton, silk, and wool. Look around and you probably will see plastics. All plastics are synthetics. Drinking straws, raincoats, food wrap, containers, buttons, toys, toothbrushes, and jewelry are just some of the many things made of plastic. Plastics are even used in furniture, machines, and cars.

Some synthetics are developed because there is a shortage of a natural resource. Chemists developed synthetic rubber when natural rubber became scarce. At other times, synthetics are developed to meet certain needs, such as the need for a rust-proof, or heat-resistant material.

14-8 What is wildlife conservation?

Objectives ▶ Identify the main threat to wildlife today. ▶ Describe two ways to conserve wildlife.

TechTerm

▶ **wildlife:** all the plant and animals that live in an area

Endangered Wildlife Do you enjoy hiking, camping, or nature photography? Each of these activities depends on **wildlife.** Wildlife is the plants and animals that live in an area.

During the past two hundred years, hundreds of kinds of plants and animals, have died out, or become extinct (EX-tinkt). Once a kind of living thing becomes extinct, it will never return. Today other kinds of plants and animals are in danger of becoming extinct. Plants and animals in danger of becoming extinct are considered endangered. The African elephant is an endangered animal. There are very few African elephants left. Other kinds of living things are threatened. Their numbers are going down.

▶ ***Define:*** What is wildlife?

Loss of Living Space Many places where wildlife live are being destroyed. Loss of living space is the main threat to wildlife. As the number of people on the earth increases, people use up more and more space. Land that was once covered with forest is now used for cities, farms, roads, and industries. One place living space is being rapidly destroyed is in tropical rain forests. About one-third of the kinds of plants and animals that live on the earth live in tropical rain forests.

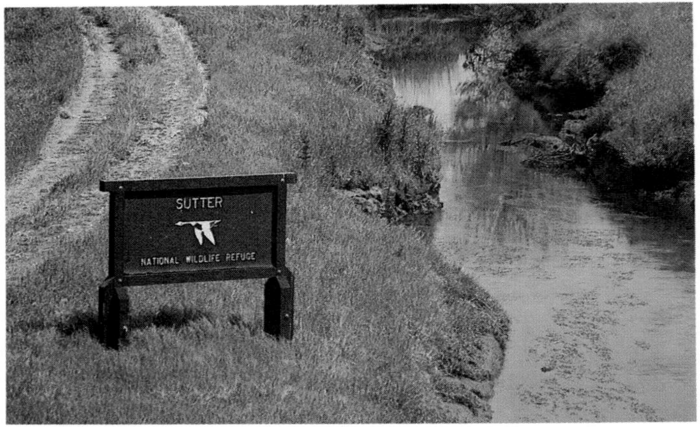

▶ ***Identify:*** What is the major threat to wildlife today?

Laws and Wildlife One way to conserve wildlife is to pass laws that protect wildlife. Laws have been passed setting up rules for hunting and fishing. In recent years, some countries have passed laws stopping the use of certain pollutants. Laws also have been passed to stop the places where wildlife live from being destroyed.

▶ ***Describe:*** How have laws helped to protect wildlife?

Wildlife Parks and Refuges Have you ever visited an animal refuge (REF-yooj), a National Park, or a zoo? An animal refuge is an area where wildlife is protected. Wildlife also is protected in National Parks. Setting up animal refuges and National Parks conserves wildlife. Zoos also help conserve wildlife. Breeding programs at zoos have helped save some kinds of animals from extinction. Endangered animals are bred at many zoos. They are then returned to their natural environment.

▶ ***State:*** List two ways to conserve wildlife.

LESSON SUMMARY

- Wildlife is all the plants an animals that live in an area.
- Many kinds of wildlife are in danger of becoming extinct.
- The main threat to wildlife is loss of living space.
- One way to conserve wildlife is to pass laws that protect wildlife.
- National Parks, animals refuges, and zoos help conserve wildlife.

CHECK *Complete the following.*

1. The main threat to wildlife is loss of living ______ .
2. Wildlife in danger of becoming extinct are called ______ .
3. To conserve wildlife, laws have been passed ruling fishing and ______ .
4. Once a kind of plant or animal becomes ______ it will never return.
5. An animal ______ is an area where wildlife is protected.

APPLY *Complete the following.*

6. Explain the statement "Extinct is forever."
7. Do you think it is important to save the rain forest? Explain your answer.

Skill Builder

Researching Some animals and plants are extinct. Others are endangered or threatened. Use library references to find the names of 6 animals and plants that are extinct, endangered, and threatened. In which country do or did these animals and plants live? The extinct dodo bird is shown below.

CAREER IN EARTH SCIENCE

ANIMAL BREEDER

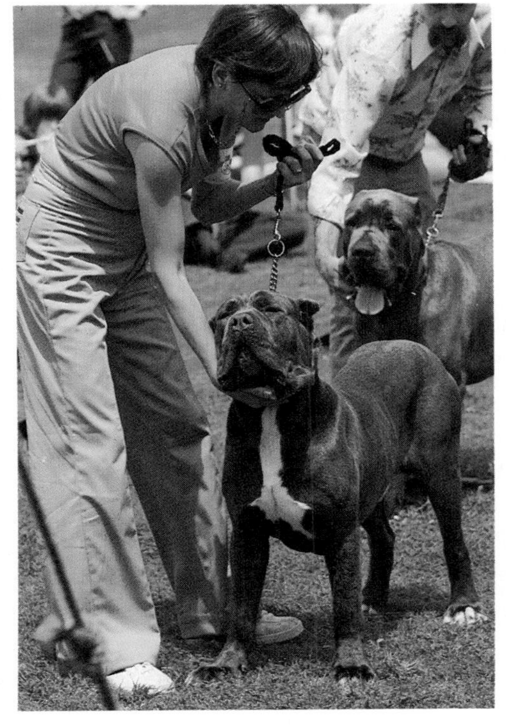

Do you enjoy working with animals? If so, you may want to consider a career as an animal breeder. Animal breeders are people who breed animals to improve their value. Thoroughbred horses, purebred dogs, and prize cattle all are the result of careful breeding.

An animal breeder may work with animals in the field, or may be involved in laboratory research. Some are self-employed. Other animal breeders work for veterinarians, farms, horse ranches, and kennels. Animal breeders involved in research often work for universities, or the government. Keeping records on animals is one of the main jobs of an animal breeder. An animal breeder keeps records of animals' traits, such as size, weight, and coat color.

Much of an animal breeder's training is learned on the job. However, to be an animal breeder, you should have a high school diploma, and take some biology courses. You also should enjoy working with animals.

For more information: write to your local department of agriculture.

14-9 What are energy resources?

Objective ▶ Name and describe the main sources of energy.

TechTerms

- ▶ **hydroelectric** (HY-droh-ih-LEK-trik) **power:** electrical energy produced from moving water
- ▶ **kinetic** (ki-NET-ik) **energy:** energy of motion
- ▶ **potential** (puh-TEN-shul) **energy:** stored energy

Fossil Fuels Fossil fuels are the main sources of energy. Oil, coal, and natural gas are fossil fuels. Fossil fuels are used to produce electricity and

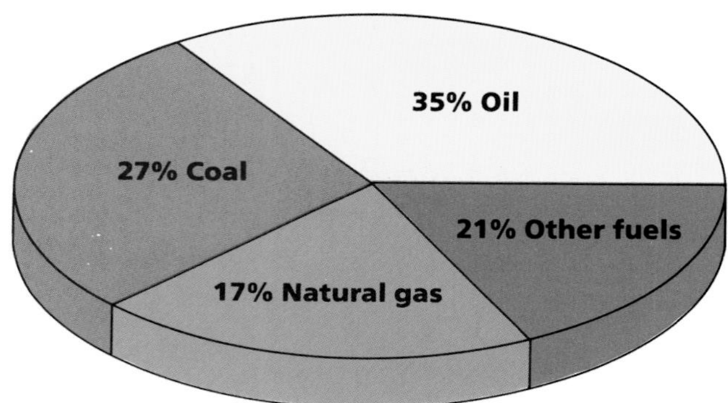

heat. They also are needed to run cars, trucks, and machines.

Large amounts of fossil fuels are being used up rapidly. It is important for everyone to conserve energy to avoid running out of fossil fuels. There are ways people can conserve energy. Driving to school or work in carpools helps save oil. Lowering the heat saves gas or oil. Turning off unneeded lights saves coal and oil burned to produce electricity.

▶ ***Name:*** What are the three main sources of energy in the world?

Hydroelectric Power Water running downhill has **kinetic** (ki-NET-ik) **energy.** Kinetic energy is the energy of motion. Water stored behind a dam has **potential** (puh-TEN-shul) **energy.** Potential

energy is stored energy. When this water falls to a lower level, its potential energy changes to kinetic energy.

The kinetic energy of moving water can be used to produce electricity, or electrical energy. Electrical energy produced by moving water is called **hydroelectric** (HY-droh-ih-LEK-trik) **power.** The moving water turns the blades of a turbine (TUR-byne). The turbine drives an electric generator (JEN-uh-ray-ter). Today falling water is used to produce about one-fourth of the world's electricity.

A place where moving water produces electricity is called a hydroelectric plant. Hydroelectric plants do not pollute the air. Their energy source, moving water, is renewable.

▶ ***Recognize:*** What are two advantages of hydroelectric plants?

Wind Energy The energy from moving air, or wind energy, is a renewable resource. Windmills have been used for years. Farmers use windmills to pump water. Windmills also are used to produce electricity. In California, thousands of windmills are used to make electricity. Windmills do not pollute the air, but there is one big problem. What happens on a windless day? There are not many places where there is a steady wind blowing.

▶ ***Explain:*** What are windmills being used for today?

LESSON SUMMARY

- The main sources of energy are oil, coal, and natural gas.
- It is important for everyone to conserve fossil fuels.
- When water falls to a lower level, its potential energy changes to kinetic energy.
- Energy from moving water can be used to produce electricity.
- A place where moving water produces electricity is called a hydroelectric plant.
- Wind energy is used to produce electricity.

CHECK *Write true if the statement is true. If the statement is false, change the underlined term to make the statement true.*

1. Kinetic energy is stored energy.
2. The main sources of energy are oil, coal, and water.
3. To produce electricity, moving water turns the blades of a turbine.
4. Oil accounts for 35% of the fossil fuels used by people.
5. Water stored behind a dam has potential energy.
6. Wind is a nonrenewable resource.

APPLY *Complete the following.*

7. **Hypothesize:** How could building a dam affect the living things in an area?
8. **Classify:** Classify each of the following things as having potential or kinetic energy:
   a. a book on a shelf
   b. milk in a bottle
   c. a book falling to the floor
   d. a parked car
   e. milk being poured
   f. a moving car
9. Explain how you could use a pinwheel or a kite to show that wind has energy.

Skill Builder

Developing a Flowchart A flowchart is a diagram that shows the order in which events take place. Using drawings and arrows, develop a flowchart showing how water stored behind a dam is used to produce electricity.

LEISURE ACTIVITY

CYCLING

Would you like to improve your physical fitness, have fun, and conserve energy resources all at the same time? If so, you should take up cycling. Cycling is a non-polluting form of transportation that does not use up fossil fuels. Because of today's high energy costs, cycling has become a cost-wise and conservation-wise way of traveling.

People of all ages enjoy cycling. Some people cycle to get to and from work, and other places. Others cycle strictly for fun. Still others cycle to sightsee. No matter what their reason for cycling, all cyclists make their body stronger. Cycling improves your muscle tone and increases the strength of your heart.

If you would like to take up cycling, make sure you have a bicycle in good condition. You should wear a helmet when you cycle, and observe all traffic regulations. Today many areas have bicycle paths and lanes for cyclists. Many areas also have bicycle clubs. If you would like to cycle with a group of people, join a bicycle club in your area.

14-10 What are future energy sources?

Objective ▶ Describe five energy resources.

TechTerm

- ▶ **geothermal** (jee-oh-THER-mul) **energy:** energy produced from heat inside the earth
- ▶ **nuclear** (NOO-klee-ar) **energy:** energy produced by breaking apart atoms
- ▶ **solar cells:** structures that change sunlight into electricity

Solar Energy Energy from sunlight, or solar energy, is an energy resource. Solar energy is used to heat some homes. These houses have solar collectors on their roofs. Solar collectors collect the sun's energy. Solar energy also can be used to produce electricity. Special structures called **solar cells** change sunlight into electricity. Solar energy is a renewable resource. It does not pollute the earth. However, solar energy is a good source of energy only in places with lots of sunlight.

▶ ***Define:*** What are solar cells?

Nuclear Energy Energy that is produced by breaking apart atoms is called **nuclear** (NOO-klee-ar) **energy.** When atoms are split, energy is given off as heat. This heat can be used to produce electricity. Uranium often is used as the nuclear fuel.

Today, nuclear power plants have been built in many places. However, there are drawbacks to using nuclear energy. Radiation is produced in nuclear reactors. An accident could release deadly radiation. Dangerous radioactive wastes also are produced. Storing and getting rid of these wastes is a problem.

▶ ***Identify:*** What are some problems using nuclear energy?

Geothermal and Tidal Energy Heat produced inside the earth is **geothermal** (jee-oh-THER-mul) **energy.** Geothermal energy causes groundwater to boil and change to steam. In some places in the world, the steam is used to produce electricity for homes. In Iceland, about 80% of the homes get their hot water and heat from geothermal energy.

Tidal energy is the energy of rising and falling tides. Tidal energy can be used to produce electricity. However, it can be used only near a shoreline where tides are very high and very low.

▶ ***Describe:*** How is geothermal energy used to produce electricity?

LESSON SUMMARY

- Solar energy is used to heat homes and produce electricity.
- Nuclear energy is the energy given off when atoms are split.
- There are drawbacks to using nuclear energy.
- Heat produced inside the earth is geothermal energy.
- Tidal energy is the energy of rising and falling tides.

CHECK *Find the sentence in the lesson that answers each question. Then, write the sentence.*

1. What is often used as a nuclear fuel?
2. What is geothermal energy?
3. What can tidal energy be used for?
4. What structures change sunlight into electricity?
5. What is nuclear energy?

APPLY *Complete the following.*

6. Which future energy source do you think is best? Give reasons to support your answer.
7. **Infer:** If you were building a house with solar collectors, in which direction would you face the solar collectors? Explain your answer.

InfoSearch

Read the passage. Ask two questions about the topic that you cannot answer from the information in the passage.

Biomass Fuels Energy from the products of living things are called biomass fuels. Wood is a biomass fuel. It is used for energy all around the world. Methane gas and alcohol are two other biomass fuels. Methane comes from sewage and animal wastes. Alcohol is made from plant materials.

SEARCH: Use library references to find answers to your questions.

Health & Safety Tip

The symbol for radiation danger is ☢. Find out why radiation is dangerous to living things.

ACTIVITY

MEASURING SOLAR ENERGY ABSORPTION

You will need a piece of black construction paper, a piece of white construction paper, and two thermometers.

1. Place two thermometers in a sunny place. **CAUTION: Be careful when using thermometers.**
2. Cover one thermometer with a piece of black construction paper and the other with a piece of white construction paper.
3. After fifteen minutes, check the temperature readings of the two thermometers.

Questions

1. **Observe:** What were the temperature readings of the two thermometers?
2. **Compare:** Which thermometer had the higher reading?
3. **Relate:** Which color takes in more heat energy from the sun, black or white?
4. What color do you think is used in solar collectors? Explain your answer.

UNIT 14 Challenges

STUDY HINT Before you begin the Unit Challenges, review the TechTerms and Lesson Summary for each lesson in this unit.

TechTerms

acid rain (282)
conservation (290)
environment (280)
geothermal energy (298)
hard water (286)
hydroelectric power (296)
kinetic energy (296)
litter (288)
natural resources (290)
nonrenewable resource (290)
nuclear energy (298)
pollutants (280)
pollution (280)
potential energy (296)
recycling (292)
renewable resource (290)
sewage (284)
smog (282)
soft water (286)
solar cells (298)
wildlife (294)

TechTerm Challenges

Matching *Write the TechTerm that matches each description.*

1. everything that surrounds a living thing
2. mixture of smoke, fog, and chemicals
3. waste that usually is flushed away in water
4. water that contains a lot of minerals
5. heat energy from inside the earth
6. the natural plants and animals that live in an area
7. stored energy
8. electricity produced from moving water
9. natural resource that can be reused or replaced
10. energy produced by splitting atoms
11. anything that harms the environment
12. wise use of natural resources
13. harmful substances that are released into the environment

Fill-in *Write the TechTerm that best completes each statement.*

1. Gases in the air mix with water and fall to the earth as ______ .
2. Materials, such as paper and cups, that are thrown away on the ground are called ______ .
3. Materials that come from the earth and are used by living things are ______ .
4. Minerals and fossil fuels are examples of ______ .
5. The energy of motion is called ______ .
6. Structures that are used to change sunlight into electricity are called ______ .
7. The use of natural resources over and over again is called ______ .
8. Water that contains few or no minerals is called ______ .

Content Challenges

Multiple Choice *Write the letter of the term that best completes each statement.*

1. Oil, coal, and natural gas are three kinds of
   a. fossil fuels. **b.** water pollutants. **c.** acid rain. **d.** nuclear fuels.
2. Soap, chemicals, and bacteria are commonly part of
   a. acid rain. **b.** litter. **c.** garbage. **d.** sewage.
3. Water that contains a lot of calcium and magnesium is
   a. soft water. **b.** hard water. **c.** polluted. **d.** acid rain.

4. Sedimentation and coagulation are two kinds of
   a. water-purification methods. b. farming methods. c. energy resources. d. air pollutants.
5. The major cause of air pollution is
   a. dust. b. fossil fuels. c. soot. d. smog.
6. Pesticides and fertilizers are two kinds of
   a. sewage. b. natural resources. c. chemical pollutants. d. farming methods.
7. The major threat to wildlife is
   a. air pollution. b. water pollution. c. loss of living space. d. overhunting.
8. The African elephant is an example of an animal that is
   a. extinct. b. threatened. c. preserved. d. endangered.
9. Oxygen and carbon dioxide are examples of
   a. air pollutants. b. nonrenewable resources. c. renewable resources. d. energy resources.
10. Minerals and fossil fuels are examples of
    a. air pollutants. b. nonrenewable resources. c. renewable resources. d. land pollutants.
11. A kind of plant that is no longer found alive is
    a. threatened. b. extinct. c. endangered. d. polluted.
12. Electricity produced from heat inside the earth is
    a. geothermal energy. b. solar energy. c. nuclear energy. d. tidal energy.

True/False *Write true if the statement is true. If the statement is false, change the underlined term to make the statement true.*

1. Living things get water from the atmosphere.
2. The burning of wood is the major cause of air pollution.
3. Acid rain can cause brick, stone, and metal structures to weather.
4. An increase of carbon dioxide in the atmosphere is causing temperatures to go down.
5. Pesticides are an example of chemical pollutants.
6. Water that contains a lot of oxygen and magnesium is called hard water.
7. Soap does not form suds easily in hard water.
8. Industrial wastes cause both water and land pollution.
9. Aluminum cans, glass bottles, and newspapers are examples of replacement materials.
10. Contour farming and terracing prevent water from removing soil from farmland.
11. Farmers plant rows of trees along the edges of their land to prevent water from carrying away soil.
12. Energy from sunlight is called geothermal energy.
13. Uranium is a common fuel for nuclear energy.
14. Tidal energy can be used to produce heat.
15. Fertilizers and pesticides are renewable resources.

Understanding the Features

Reading Critically *Use the feature reading selections to answer the following. Page numbers for the features are shown in parentheses.*

1. Who was Rachel Carson? (281)
2. Where do water purification technicians work? (287)
3. What kind of wastes are placed in a landfill? (289)
4. **Define:** What is metallurgy? (291)
5. **Infer:** What does "synthetic" mean? (293)
6. **Infer:** Why is it important for an animal breeder to keep records of an animal's traits? (295)
7. How is cycling important to good health? (297)
8. How does cycling help to reduce air pollution? (297)

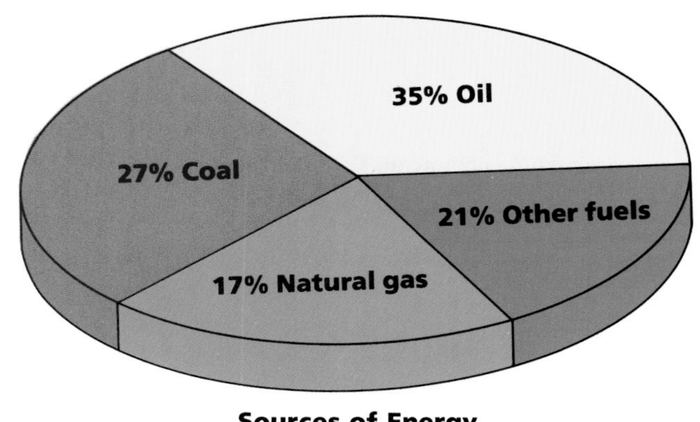

Sources of Energy

Concept Challenges

Interpreting a Graph *Use the graph to answer each of the following.*

1. What energy resource accounts for the most energy use?
2. What percentage of the world's energy use do fossil fuels make up?
3. What percentage of the world's energy use do other fuels make up?
4. What fossil fuel accounts for the least percentage of the total energy use?
5. What percentage of the total energy use does coal account for?

Critical Thinking *Answer each of the following in complete sentences.*

1. How can burning wastes both reduce land pollution and conserve fossil fuels?
2. How does the growth of cities affect wildlife?
3. How does water pollution affect the fishing industry?
4. Why is flat land in less danger of erosion by water than hilly land?
5. Would solar energy be a good energy resource in your area? Explain.

Finding Out More

1. Read *Silent Spring* by Rachel Carson and write a book report.
2. Using library references, find out about the development of the national park system. Describe your findings in an oral report.
3. Animals use oxygen to carry out the process of respiration. Plants use carbon dioxide to carry out the process of photosynthesis. In a brief report, write the equations for these two processes, and describe how they relate to the oxygen-carbon dioxide cycle. Use biology textbooks as references.
4. Research the farming method of crop rotation. On a posterboard, draw a model of crop rotation, and explain its relationship to the nitrogen cycle.
5. For the next two weeks, clip any articles about pollution from the newspaper and save them. At the end of two weeks, read and discuss the articles in class.
6. If possible, read the electric meter in your house when you first get up in the morning, and at sunset. Keep a record of the readings for one week. Using the readings, explain whether your family uses more electric energy during the day or night. Describe ways your family can conserve energy.

EXPLORING SPACE

UNIT 15

CONTENTS

STUDY HINT Before beginning Unit 15, write the title of each lesson on a sheet of paper. Below each title, write a short paragraph explaining what you think each lesson is about.

15-1 What is astronomy?

Objective ▶ Explain what is meant by astronomy and how astronomy was used by ancient peoples.

TechTerms

- ▶ **astronomy** (uh-STRON-uh-mee): study of stars, planets, and other objects in space
- ▶ **solar system:** the sun and all the bodies that circle the sun

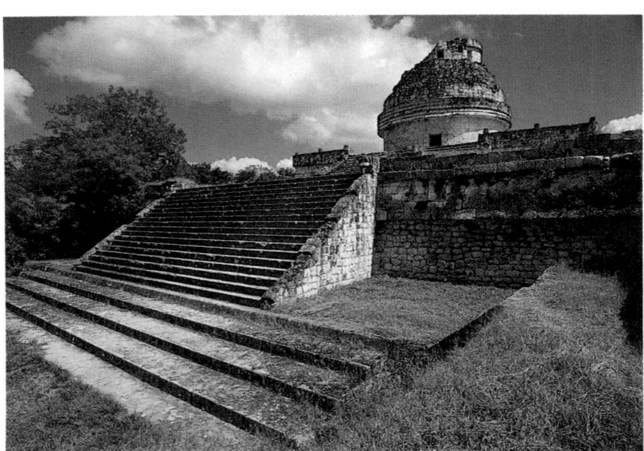

Ancient Astronomy People have studied and wondered about the skies for thousands of years. **Astronomy** (uh-STRON-uh-mee) is one of the oldest sciences. Astronomy is the study of the stars, planets, and other objects in space. Ancient clay tablets predicting eclipses of the sun date back to 131 BC. The planets Mercury, Venus, Mars, Jupiter, and Saturn were known more than 5000 years ago. No new planets were found until 1781 when Uranus was discovered.

▶ *List:* Which of the planets were known in ancient times?

Uses of Astronomy Astronomy helped ancient peoples solve many problems. Most ancient societies were built around the changing seasons. Farmers had to know when was the right time to plant their crops. Astronomers were able to predict the coming of spring so that crops could be planted on time. Sailors were able to use the positions of the stars as a guide to help them find their way at sea.

▶ *Explain:* Give two examples of how ancient peoples used astronomy.

Modern Astronomy Ancient astronomers made observations using only their eyes. Over time, new tools helped astronomers see farther into space. The Italian scientist Galileo (gal-ih-LAY-oh) first used a telescope to get a close-up look at the moon in 1609. In 1957, the first human-made satellite was launched into space by the Soviet Union.

Today, astronomers use telescopes, satellites, and space probes to make their observations. Astronomers are able to take close-up photographs of the planets and study stars billions of kilometers from the earth. What do astronomers study? Modern astronomers study the universe. The universe is everything that exists. Some astronomers, called cosmologists (coz-MOL-uh-jists), study how the universe began. Planetologists study the planets in the **solar system.** The solar system includes the sun and all of the bodies in space that circle the sun.

▶ *Describe:* What do astronomers study?

LESSON SUMMARY

- Astronomy is one of the oldest sciences.
- Astronomy helped ancient societies solve practical problems.
- Ancient astronomers used only their eyes to make observations.
- Modern astronomers use telescopes, satellites, and space probes to study the universe.

CHECK *Write true if the statement is true. If the statement is false, change the underlined term to make the statement true.*

1. Five thousand years ago, there were <u>seven</u> known planets in addition to Earth.
2. Sailors were able to find their way using the positions of the <u>planets</u>.
3. Ancient astronomers made observations using <u>their eyes</u>.
4. The first <u>space probe</u> was launched in 1957.
5. Modern astronomers study the whole <u>universe</u>.

APPLY *Complete the following.*

7. **Infer:** Early astronomers observed that the planets changed their positions in the sky. However, the stars kept the same positions from night to night. Why did sailors use the stars and not the planets to find their way at sea?

Skill Builder

Building Vocabulary Many ancient civilizations studied the stars. The ancient Chinese, Egyptians, Arabs, Greeks, and Romans all had different names for many familiar stars. On a sheet of paper, list the names of the following stars: *Vega, Sirius* (sir-EE-us), *Aldebaran* (al-DEB-uh-run), *Polaris, Algol, Capella, Betelgeuse* (BET-ul-jooz), *Proxima Centauri* (PRAHK-suh-muh sen-TOHR-ee). Use a dictionary or other library references to find out what each name means in its original language. Write the meaning and identify the original language next to each name.

LOOKING BACK IN SCIENCE

THE HISTORY OF ASTRONOMY

Astronomy is one of the oldest sciences. Records dating back to 2000 BC show that ancient people had a calendar based upon the movements of the sun and the moon. Most ancient people believed that the earth was flat, with the stars forming a tentlike cover over the earth.

As early as the sixth century BC, the Greeks made many important observations of the skies. Pythagoras (pi-THAG-ur-us), a Greek mathematician, saw that the masts of ships disappeared over the horizon. He also saw that the earth's shadow on the moon during a lunar eclipse was round. From these observations, he reasoned that the earth must be round.

The Greek philosopher Aristotle (AR-is-taht-ul) claimed that the earth was at the center of the universe. This claim was supported by the philosopher Ptolemy (TAHL-uh-mee). The claim was unchallenged for almost 2000 years. Then, late in the fifteenth century, the Polish mathematician Nicolaus Copernicus (koh-PUR-nih-kus) developed a new theory. Copernicus said that the sun was at the center of the solar system. According to this theory, the earth and the other planets moved around the sun. Later observations by Tycho Brahe, Johannes Kepler, Galileo, and Newton supported Copernicus's theory. This was the beginning of modern astronomy.

15-2 Why do scientists explore space?

Objective ▶ Explain how space exploration helps scientists learn about Earth and about the universe.

TechTerm

▶ **galaxy** (GAL-ack-see): large system of stars

Space Exploration The exploration of space began in 1957. In that year, the first artificial earth satellite was launched. This scientific instrument was launched as part of the International Geophysical Year, or IGY. The IGY lasted from 1957 to 1958. It was planned as a year of astronomical observations by scientists from many countries.

Today, scientists hope that space exploration will answer many questions about the universe. How was the solar system formed? Does intelligent life exist elsewhere in the universe? These are some of the questions that might be answered by space exploration.

▶ *Infer:* Why do scientists explore space?

Studying the Universe Space exploration may provide clues to how the universe was formed. Scientists think that the universe began about 15 billion years ago. A huge explosion, called the "Big Bang," sent matter flying out in all directions. **Galaxies** were formed. A galaxy is a large collection of stars.

The most distant galaxies probably were formed at the time of the Big Bang. These distant galaxies are not visible from Earth. Pollution in Earth's atmosphere makes any kind of space observations difficult. Lights from nearby cities also make nighttime viewing difficult. City lights block out the faint light from distant stars, as sunlight does during the day.

▶ *Define:* What are galaxies?

Hubble Space Telescope Astronomers are learning more about the universe using a telescope in Earth orbit. The Hubble Space Telescope was launched from the shuttle *Discovery* in 1990. The telescope is named after the American astronomer Edwin Hubble. Above the pollution, the atmosphere, and city lights, this telescope has observed and photographed distant galaxies that cannot even be seen on Earth. It can view planets as clearly as *Voyager* did.

▶ *Identify:* What is the goal of the Hubble Space Telescope?

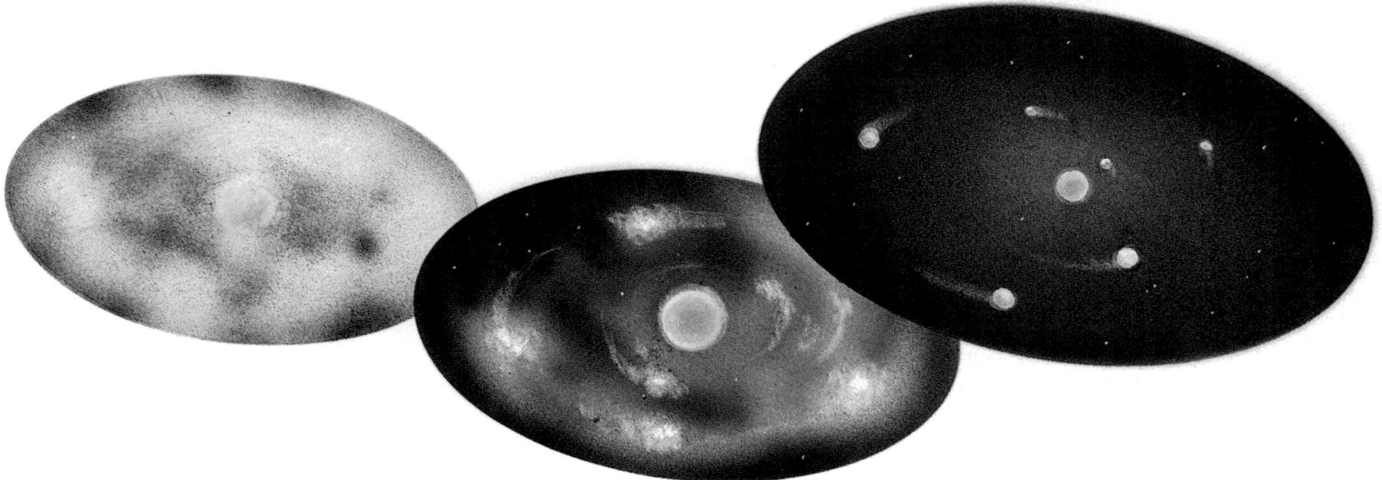

LESSON SUMMARY

- Space exploration began as part of the International Geophysical Year in 1957.
- Space exploration answers many questions about the universe.
- Space exploration provides clues about the formation of the universe.
- Air pollution and city lights make it difficult to view distant galaxies from Earth.
- The Hubble Space Telescope orbits Earth and can photograph distant galaxies.

CHECK *Complete the following.*

1. Space exploration began during the ______ .
2. Scientists think the universe began about ______ years ago.
3. The explosion that started the universe is called the ______ .
4. A galaxy is a large collection of ______ .
5. Nearby city ______ makes it difficult to view distant galaxies from Earth.
6. The ______ is able to see very distant galaxies.

APPLY *Complete the following.*

7. What are some questions that scientists hope to answer through space exploration?
8. What advantages does the Hubble Space Telescope have over other telescopes?

InfoSearch

Read the passage. Ask two questions about the topic that you cannot answer from the information in the passage.

Making Repairs in Space When the Hubble Space Telescope began operating in space, its main mirror was not working properly. Images from deep space were not clear. NASA repaired the telescope during a mission of the space shuttle *Endeavour*. During five space walks, astronauts installed a corrective lens for the mirror. They replaced solar panels and other equipment. They also installed a new camera. The Hubble Space Telescope now works better than was ever expected.

SEARCH: Use library references to answer your questions.

TECHNOLOGY AND SOCIETY

SPINOFFS FROM SPACE EXPLORATION

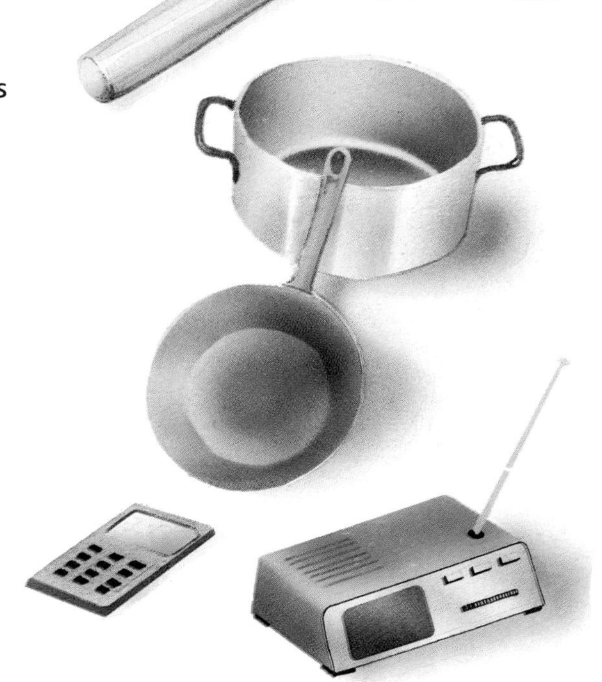

How can space exploration help people on Earth? The answer is spinoffs. A spinoff is a benefit or product that results from an unrelated activity or process. Sending spacecraft into space is very costly. One way to save costs is by developing smaller, lighter equipment. Small radios, computers, televisions, and other products have been made for use in space travel. These products are spinoffs of space exploration. Today, these products are used on Earth.

Other products also have resulted from space travel. For example, many foods sent into space with the astronauts are freeze-dried to make them lighter and longer-lasting. Many freeze-dried foods now are available in supermarkets. Light-weight durable clothing and non-stick cookware also are spinoffs of space exploration.

Scientists need to check the vital signs of astronauts in space. However, a doctor cannot always be sent into space with the astronauts. To meet this need, scientists have developed tiny monitoring, recording, and transmitting devices.

15-3 How does a refracting telescope work?

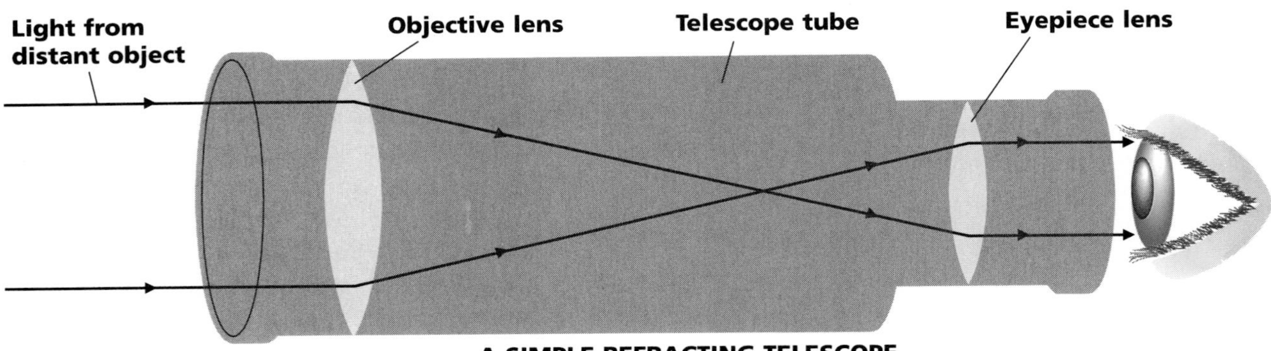

A SIMPLE REFRACTING TELESCOPE

Objective ▶ Explain how a refracting telescope works.

TechTerms

- ▶ **convex** (kon-VEKS) **lens:** lens that is thicker in the middle than at the edges
- ▶ **refracting** (rih-FRAKT-ing) **telescope:** telescope that uses convex lenses to produce an enlarged image

Galileo's Telescope Galileo was the first person to look at the moon through a telescope. Have you ever looked through a telescope? If you have, you know that a telescope makes objects appear much nearer than they are. If you look at the moon through a telescope, you can see many features on the moon's surface that you cannot see with your eyes alone. Galileo looked at the moon soon after the telescope was invented. He was the first to see that the moon's surface is not smooth. Galileo saw craters, plains, and hills on the moon.

▶ *Name:* What features did Galileo see on the surface of the moon?

Refracting Telescopes Galileo used a **refracting** (rih-FRAKT-ing) **telescope** to look at the moon. Galileo's refracting telescope was made of a tube with two lenses inside. A lens is a piece of glass that refracts, or bends, light. The telescope in the illustration is a simple refracting telescope. The lenses in a refracting telescope are **convex** (kon-VEKS) **lenses.** Convex lenses bulge outward. They are thicker in the middle than at the edges. When light passes through a convex lens, the light is bent inward, as shown in the illustration. The bent light produces an image that is larger than the image you would see with your eyes alone.

▶ *Describe:* What kind of lenses are used in a refracting telescope?

Function of Lenses Each of the convex lenses in a refracting telescope has a special job. The lens at the far end of the tube is the objective (ob-JECK-tiv) lens. The objective lens collects light and brings the image into focus. The lens at the other end of the tube is the eyepiece lens. The eyepiece lens acts like a magnifying glass. It enlarges, or magnifies, the image formed by the objective lens. The objective lens and the eyepiece lens work together to produce a sharp, clear image of a distant object.

▶ *Name:* What are the two lenses in a refracting telescope called?

LESSON SUMMARY

- Galileo was the first person to look at the moon through a telescope.
- Galileo's telescope was a refracting telescope.
- A refracting telescope uses two convex lenses to produce an enlarged image.
- The two lenses in a refracting telescope are the objective lens and the eyepiece lens.

CHECK *Complete the following.*

1. A telescope makes the moon appear ______ .
2. Galileo saw ______, hills, and plains on the moon.
3. A refracting telescope uses ______ lenses.
4. A lens bends, or ______, light.
5. The lenses in a refracting telescope are ______ lenses.
6. The two lenses in a refracting telescope are the objective lens and the ______ lens.

APPLY *Complete the following.*

7. **Compare:** Which surface features of the moon also are found on the earth? Which feature is not found on the earth?
8. **Hypothesize:** Why does the image formed by a telescope appear nearer than the object?

Skill Builder

Modeling When you model, you use a copy or an imitation of an object to help explain or understand something. A diagram is one kind of model. Draw a diagram of a simple refracting telescope. Label the objective lens and the eyepiece lens. Beside each label, write a brief summary of the function of each lens.

Ideas in Action

IDEA: Many objects that you use every day contain convex lenses.

ACTION: Make a list of as many common objects that contain convex lenses as you can. Briefly describe how the lenses are used in these objects. Hint: What part of your body has a convex lens?

ACTIVITY

MAKING A SIMPLE TELESCOPE

You will need two convex lenses, or magnifying glasses.

1. Look at a distant object through a convex lens.
2. Move the lens back and forth slowly. Stop when you see the object clearly through the lens.
3. Without moving the first lens, hold a second convex lens close to your eye.
4. Move the second lens back and forth slowly. Stop when you can see the distant object clearly through both lenses.

Questions

1. What part of a telescope does the first lens represent?
2. **Observe:** How does the image appear through the first lens?
3. What part of a telescope does the second lens represent?
4. **Observe:** How does the image appear when you look through both lenses?
5. **Analyze:** Would a telescope with a large objective lens be better than one with a small objective lens? Explain.

15-4 How does a reflecting telescope work?

Objectives ▶ Explain how a reflecting telescope works. ▶ Contrast a reflecting telescope with a refracting telescope.

TechTerms

- **concave mirror:** mirror that curves inward
- **reflecting** (rih-FLEKT-ing) **telescope:** telescope that uses a concave mirror to collect light

Reflecting Telescopes Recall that a refracting telescope uses a convex lens to collect light. Another kind of telescope uses a mirror instead of a lens to collect light. This kind of telescope is called a **reflecting** (rih-FLECKT-ing) **telescope.** A simple reflecting telescope is shown in the illustration.

The mirror used in a reflecting telescope is a **concave mirror.** A concave mirror curves inward. In a reflecting telescope, a concave mirror collects light from distant stars and brings the light to a focus.

▶ *Define:* What is a reflecting telescope?

Newton's Telescope Isaac Newton, an English scientist, made the first reflecting telescope in 1671. Newton used a concave mirror to collect light and form an image. The concave mirror was only 2.5 cm across. Newton used a convex lens as an eyepiece to magnify the image. He could not look at the image formed inside the telescope tube. His head would have blocked the incoming light. Instead, Newton used a flat mirror to reflect the light to one side.

The illustration shows how the mirrors and lenses in Newton's telescope were arranged. Reflecting telescopes usually have the eyepiece at one side of the telescope tube. A camera can be attached to the eyepiece to take pictures of the images. The pictures can be stored and studied by astronomers at a later time.

▶ *Explain:* Why is the eyepiece of a reflecting telescope at one side of the tube?

Modern Reflecting Telescopes Modern reflecting telescopes have very large mirrors. One of the largest reflecting telescopes is the Hale Telescope on Mt. Palomar in California. Its mirror is 5 m across. The mirror is so big that the astronomer using the telescope can sit inside the telescope. The astronomer sits high up near where the image is formed. The amount of light blocked by the astronomer is too small to affect the image.

▶ *Explain:* Why does an astronomer using the Hale Telescope not have to sit at the side of the telescope?

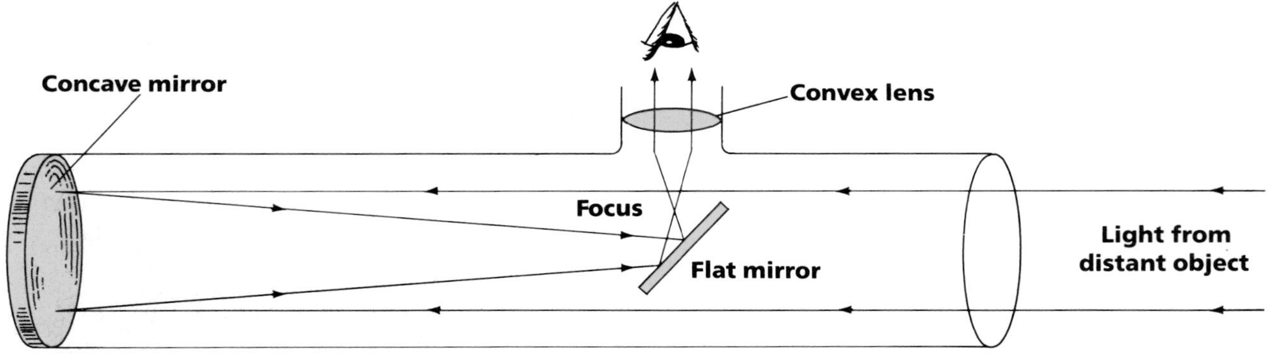

A SIMPLE REFLECTING TELESCOPE

LESSON SUMMARY

- A reflecting telescope uses a mirror instead of a lens to collect light.
- The mirror that collects light in a reflecting telescope is a concave mirror.
- Isaac Newton made the first reflecting telescope.
- Modern reflecting telescopes have very large mirrors.

CHECK *Complete the following.*

1. What kind of telescope uses a mirror to collect and focus light?
2. What kind of mirror collects light in a reflecting telescope?
3. Who made the first reflecting telescope?
4. What kind of lens is used as an eyepiece in a reflecting telescope?
5. Where is the eyepiece usually found in a reflecting telescope?

APPLY *Complete the following.*

6. **Contrast:** What is the difference between a refracting telescope and a reflecting telescope?
7. **Model:** Draw a diagram of a simple reflecting telescope. Label the concave mirror, the flat mirror, and the convex lens.
8. **Analyze:** Why is a reflecting telescope with a large concave mirror better than a telescope with a smaller mirror?

Skill Builder

Researching When you research, you gather information about a topic. An observatory is a building or group of buildings where astronomers use telescopes to study the universe. Use library references to find out what kinds of telescopes are used in each observatory listed. Write a report of your findings.

Kitt Peak National Observatory
Mauna Kea Observatory
Mount Palomar Observatory
Yerkes Observatory
Mount Wilson Observatory

SCIENCE CONNECTION

BUYING A TELESCOPE

Does skywatching interest you? Have you ever dreamed of visiting distant planets? You may never travel through space, but you can bring the planets closer to you. A telescope can be your spaceship.

With so many telescopes to choose from, how do you know which one is right for you? Generally, your best buy is a telescope that is simple, well made, and easy to use. One of the most important features of a telescope is the size, or aperture (AP-ur-chur), and quality of its objective lens or mirror. The larger the lens or mirror, the more light the telescope gathers and the sharper the image it forms. The steadiness of the telescope also is important. The best way to determine a telescope's steadiness is to try the telescope before you buy it. Try to avoid telescopes with too many "gadgets," or small, easy-to-lose parts. Lost parts may be difficult to replace.

Is there a "best" telescope? Probably not. Either a reflector or a refractor will allow you to enjoy the night sky. The best rule is to compare quality and price before buying.

15-5 What is a radio telescope?

Objectives ▶ Describe how a radio telescope works. ▶ Recognize the advantages of a radio telescope.

TechTerm

▶ **radio telescope:** telescope that can receive radio waves from sources in space

Studying Stars Stars are usually not visible during the day. Are there stars in the sky during the day? Yes, but you cannot see them. You cannot see the stars during the day because of the sun. The sun is also a star. It is the closest star to Earth. The bright light of the sun hides the dimmer light from the distant stars. On rainy nights, clouds hide the stars. The light from the stars cannot get through the clouds. For this reason, you cannot see the stars on a cloudy night. An ordinary telescope, such as a refracting telescope or a reflecting telescope, cannot help you see the stars on a cloudy night.

▶ ***Explain:*** Why can you not see the stars during the day?

▶ ***Compare:*** How is a radio telescope like a reflecting telescope?

Radio Telescopes A **radio telescope** can pick up radio waves from sources in space. This telescope can find stars during the day or when the sky is covered with clouds. An American engineer, Karl Jansky, first heard radio signals from space in 1932. He found that the radio waves were coming from the center of our galaxy, the Milky Way. In 1944, Grote Reber built a radio telescope with a 9-m receiver, or antenna (an-TEN-uh). Using his telescope, Reber was able to make the first radio map of the Milky Way galaxy.

The antenna of a radio telescope works like a mirror in a reflecting telescope. The antenna collects and focuses radio waves given off by stars and other objects in space. The antenna transmits the radio waves to a receiver. An astronomer can "listen" to the stars using a radio telescope.

Advantages of Radio Telescopes There are three main advantages to using radio telescopes. First, a radio telescope can detect very distant stars and galaxies. Refracting or reflecting telescopes cannot pick up the faint light from these distant objects. Second, a radio telescope can be used in any kind of weather. Radio waves can travel through clouds in the earth's atmosphere. Reflecting or refracting telescopes can be used only on clear nights. Third, a radio telescope can be used during the day, when the stars are not visible. Reflecting or refracting telescopes can be used only at night, when the sun's light does not block the light from the stars.

▶ ***Explain:*** Why can a radio telescope be used on cloudy nights?

LESSON SUMMARY

- Refracting or reflecting telescopes cannot be used during the day or on cloudy nights.
- A radio telescope picks up radio waves from objects in space.
- Astronomers can "listen" to stars using a radio telescope.
- Radio telescopes have three main advantages over refracting or reflecting telescopes.

CHECK *Complete the following.*

1. The closest star to Earth is _______ .
2. You cannot see stars on a _______ night.
3. A _______ telescope can be used during the day.
4. The first radio map of the Milky Way was made by _______ .
5. The _______ of a radio telescope works like the mirror of a reflecting telescope.

APPLY *Complete the following.*

6. **Contrast:** How does a radio telescope differ from a reflecting telescope and a refracting telescope?
7. What are three advantages of a radio telescope over a refracting telescope or a reflecting telescope?
8. **Infer:** How do you think astronomers can tell if a sound picked up by a radio telescope is from a star or another body in space?

Ideas in Action

IDEA: Radio waves, like light waves, are part of the electromagnetic spectrum.

ACTION: Find out what other kinds of waves are part of the electromagnetic spectrum. Make a list of the appliances and other instruments in your house that use these waves.

Health & Safety Tip

Sound is measured in decibels. Nerve deafness can be caused by repeated exposure to loud sounds such as those at a rock concert. Brief exposure to loud noises can cause ringing in the ears. Long-term exposure can cause permanent damage. Use an encyclopedia or other reference book to find out at what decibel sounds become harmful to the ear. Prepare a poster that shows some ways to protect your ears from damage by loud noises.

TECHNOLOGY AND SOCIETY

SETI: SEARCH FOR EXTRATERRESTRIAL INTELLIGENCE

Many astronomers around the world are part of SETI, or the Search for ExtraTerrestrial Intelligence. SETI rhymes with the word "jetty." National Aeronautics and Space Administration (NASA) scientists are using radio telescopes and computers to listen for radio signals from space. They are hoping that some of these signals may have been sent by intelligent life forms.

The search for extraterrestrial intelligence began in 1960. Dr. Frank Drake was the first astronomer to search for intelligent life elsewhere in the universe. He used a radio telescope in West Virginia to listen for signals.

Although Dr. Drake did not hear any messages from space, scientists did not stop searching. NASA launched a ten-year SETI project. Meanwhile, a private SETI program also was begun.

Jill Tarter, a NASA astronomer, is sure that intelligent beings exist somewhere in the universe. She also thinks that someday these beings will contact Earth. What do you think? How would such an event affect your life?

15-6 How do astronomers measure distance?

Objective ▶ Identify two units of measurement that astronomers use to measure distance.

TechTerms

- ▶ **astronomical** (as-truh-NOM-ih-kul) **unit:** unit of measurement equal to about 150 million kilometers
- ▶ **light year:** unit of measurement equal to about 10 trillion kilometers

Measuring Distances Most distances on the earth can be measured in meters or kilometers. How would you measure the distance from the earth to the stars? You might use kilometers as a unit of measurement. However, astronomers have found that the distance to even the nearest star is too great to measure in kilometers. The distances are so great that the numbers are too large to work with easily. For example, the star Proxima Centauri (PROX-ih-muh sen-TOR-ee) is the closest star, other than the sun, to the earth. Proxima Centauri is 40,000,000,000,000 km from the earth. As you can see, this is a very large number. Astronomers had to invent special units to measure distances in space.

▶ ***Explain:*** Why did scientists invent special units to measure distances in space?

Light Years Astronomers often measure the distance to an object in space in **light years.** A light year is equal to the distance light travels in one year. Light travels through space at a speed of about 300,000 km/sec. A light year is equal to almost 10 trillion km. Light from the sun reaches the earth in a little more than 8 minutes. Light from the North Star, Polaris (poh-LAR-us), takes about 300 years to reach the earth.

▶ ***Interpret:*** How far, in light years, is Polaris from Earth?

Astronomical Units One of the units used by astronomers is equal to the distance from the earth to the sun. Do you know how far away the sun is from the earth? The sun is about 150 million km from the earth. Astronomers call this distance an **astronomical** (as-truh-NOM-ih-kul) **unit.** One astronomical unit, or 1 AU, is equal to 150 million kilometers. Table 1 shows the distances of the planets from the sun in astronomical units.

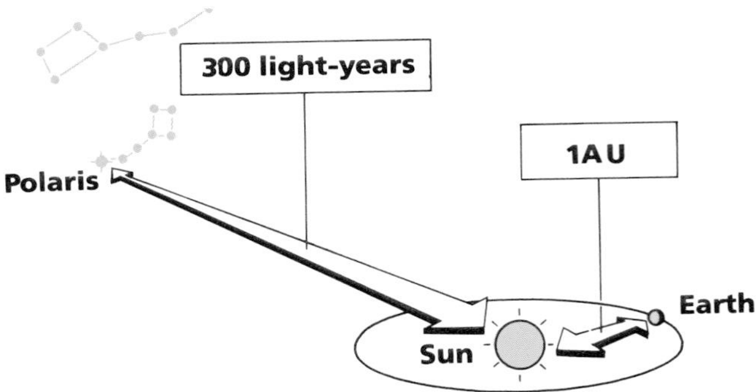

Table 1 Distance of Planets from the Sun in Astronomical Units (AU)

PLANET	DISTANCE
Mercury	0.4
Venus	0.7
Earth	1.0
Mars	1.5
Jupiter	5.2
Saturn	9.5
Uranus	19.2
Neptune	30.1
Pluto	39.4

Observe: What is the distance of Venus from the sun in astronomical units?

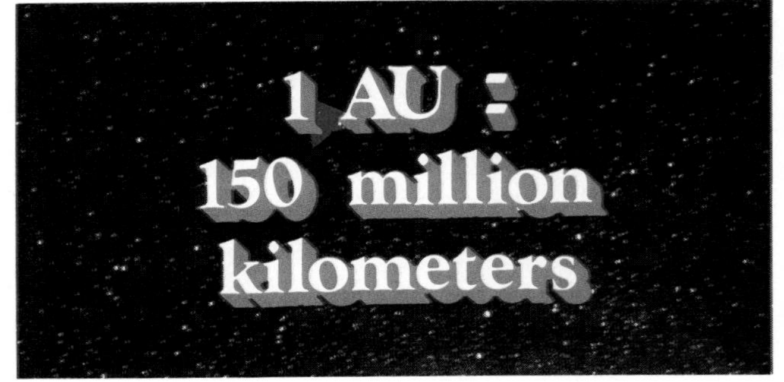

LESSON SUMMARY

- Astronomers use special units to measure distances in space.
- One light year, the distance light travels in one year, is equal to 10 trillion km.
- One astronomical unit, the distance from the earth to the sun, is equal to 150 million km.

CHECK *Complete the following.*

1. Why do astronomers not measure the distances to the stars in kilometers?
2. What is the name of the closest star, other than the sun?
3. What is the distance from the earth to the sun in kilometers?
4. What is an astronomical unit?
5. What is the speed of light in space?
6. What is a light year?

APPLY *Complete the following.*

7. **Calculate:** Use Table 1 on page 314. Convert each of the distances into kilometers.

InfoSearch

Read the passage. Ask two questions about the topic that you cannot answer from the information in the passage.

Parallax Astronomers can use parallax (PAR-uh-lax) to find the distances to the closer stars. Parallax is the change in the position of a distant object when seen from two different places. A nearby star seems to move against a background of distant stars. By measuring how much the star appears to move, astronomers can calculate how far away the star is. Nearby stars have a large parallax. Distant stars have a smaller parallax.

SEARCH: Use library references to find answers to your questions.

ACTIVITY

OBSERVING PARALLAX

You will need three sheets of continuous-feed computer paper, a metric ruler, a drinking straw, and tape.

1. Remove the edges with holes from the computer paper. Tape this strip of paper with holes to a wall.
2. Tape a straw upright on a metric ruler at the 15-cm mark.
3. Stand about 2 to 3 m from the wall.
4. Hold the ruler level with the floor. Close your left eye and line up the straw with the left end of the strip of computer paper.
5. Open your left eye and close your right eye. Count the number of holes the straw appears to move along the strip.
6. Move the straw to the 30-cm mark on the ruler, and repeat steps 3-5.

Questions

1. What does the strip of paper with holes represent in this activity?
2. a. **Observe:** At the 15-cm mark, how many holes did the straw appear to move?
   b. at the 30-cm mark?
3. **Analyze:** Why does the straw appear to change position?
4. **Compare:** Which has a greater parallax, a nearby star or a more distant star?

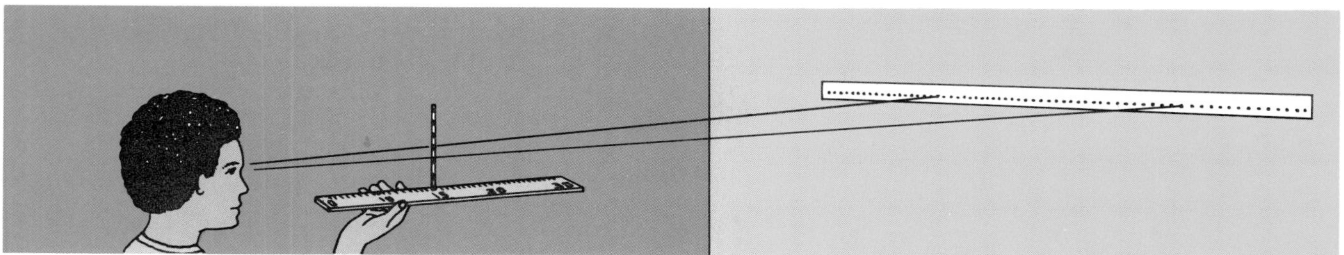

15-7 How does a rocket work?

Objective ▶ Describe how a rocket works.

TechTerm

▶ **thrust:** force produced in a rocket engine

Rockets Rockets were invented by the Chinese more than 800 years ago. The ancient Chinese used rockets for fireworks and weapons. How does a rocket work? To understand how a rocket works, you must know about Newton's Third Law of Motion. Newton's Third Law of Motion says that for every action, there is an equal and opposite reaction. For example, suppose you are sitting in a rowboat on a lake. You throw a rock into the lake. This is the action. At the same time, the rowboat moves backward slightly. This is the reaction.

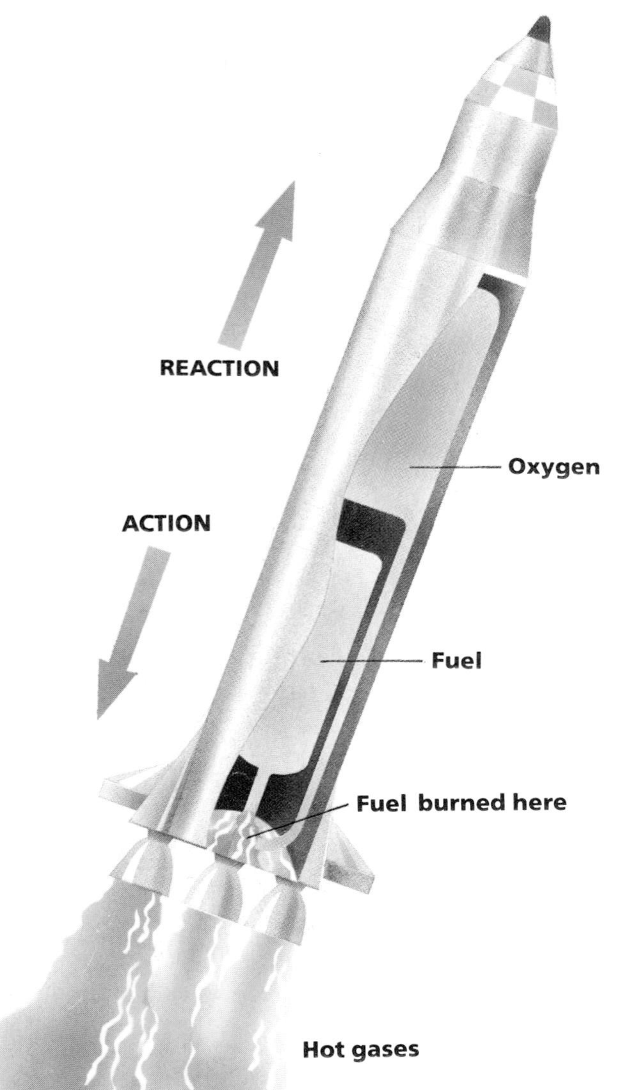

▶ ***State:*** What is the Third Law of Motion?

Rocket Engines The force that pushes a rocket forward is called **thrust.** The greater the thrust, the higher and faster the rocket will travel. What causes thrust? Fuel is burned inside a rocket engine. The fuel can be a solid or a liquid. As the fuel burns, hot gases inside the engine begin to expand. The expanding gases create pressure inside the engine. The pressure forces the hot gases out of the rear of the rocket. This is the action force. The rocket moves in the opposite direction. This is the thrust, or reaction force.

▶ ***Define:*** What is thrust?

Rockets in Space A lot of thrust is needed for a rocket to escape the earth's gravity. To get into space, a rocket must reach a speed of more than 40,000 km/hr. Large amounts of fuel are needed to produce enough thrust to reach this speed. Rocket engines need oxygen to burn fuel. In space, there is no air to supply the oxygen needed to burn fuel. Rockets carry their own oxygen.

As a rocket moves farther away from the earth, the pull of the earth's gravity becomes weaker. Once the rocket is in space, there is nothing to slow down the rocket. The rocket does not need to burn fuel to keep moving. The rocket keeps moving in the same direction at a constant speed. Fuel is needed in space only to change the rocket's speed or direction.

▶ ***Explain:*** Why must rockets carry oxygen?

LESSON SUMMARY

- Newton's Third Law of Motion explains what causes a rocket to move.
- Thrust is the force that pushes a rocket forward.
- Rocket engines must carry their own oxygen to burn fuel in space.
- In space, fuel is needed only to change the speed or direction of a rocket.

CHECK *Complete the following.*

1. Rockets were invented by the ______ .
2. Newton's Third Law of Motion says that for every action, there is an ______ reaction.
3. The force that pushes a rocket forward is called ______ .
4. Rocket fuel needs ______ to burn.
5. In space, fuel is needed to change ______ or direction.

APPLY *Complete the following.*

6. **Predict:** Could a rocket traveling at a speed of 10,000 km/hr get into space? Explain.

Look at the following pictures. Write the letters of the picture that show action forces. Then, identify the reaction forces.

7.

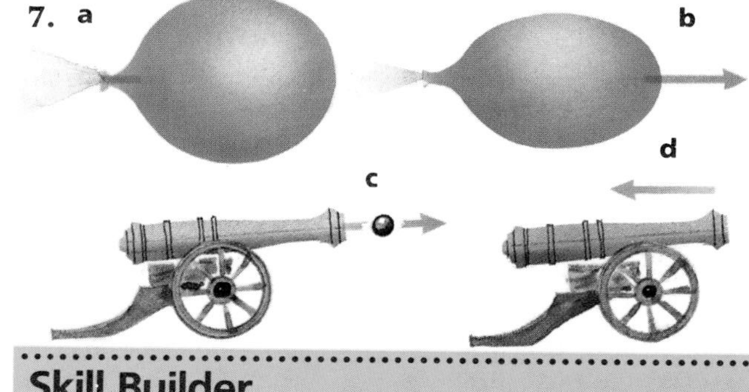

Skill Builder

Calculating Thrust is a force. The unit of force in the metric system is the newton (N). One newton (1 N) is equal to 4.5 lbs. Below is a list of rockets and their thrusts at launch. The thrust is given in pounds. Convert each thrust into newtons. Then list the rockets in order, from least thrust to greatest thrust.

Delta	205,000 lbs.
Saturn V	7,570,000 lbs.
Mercury-Atlas	367,000 lbs.
Space Shuttle	6,925,000 lbs.
Vanguard	28,000 lbs.

ACTIVITY

DEMONSTRATING ACTION AND REACTION FORCES

You will need about 3 m of string, a drinking straw, tape, a balloon, and a twist tie.

1. Inflate a balloon. Use a twist tie to close the opening.
2. Tape a straw lengthwise to the top of the balloon.
3. Thread a piece of string through the straw. Tie one end of the string to a doorknob.
4. Move as far away from the door as you can. Hold the string as tight as possible.
5. Remove the twist tie from the balloon and observe what happens.

Questions

1. What happened to the air in the balloon when you removed the twist tie?
2. **Observe:** In which direction did the balloon move?
3. **Infer:** In which direction did the air move?
4. **a.** What was the action force? **b.** What was the reaction force?

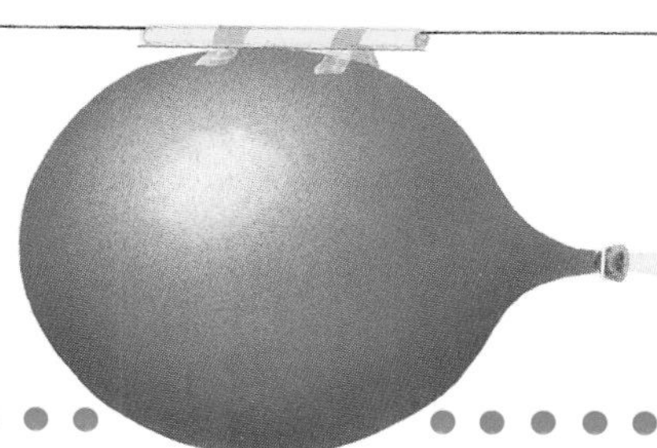

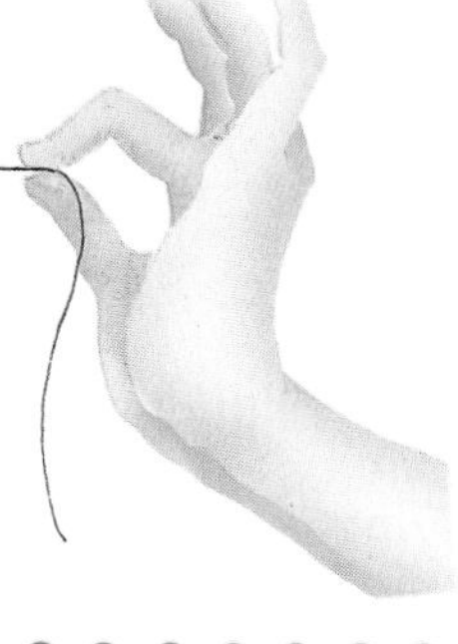

15-8 What are satellites and probes?

Objective ▶ Explain how artificial satellites and space probes are used to explore space.

TechTerms

- ▶ **orbit:** path of a satellite around a planet or other body in space
- ▶ **satellite** (SAT-uh-lite): natural or artificial object orbiting a body in space

Artificial Satellites For thousands of years, astronomers were able to study the skies only from the surface of the earth. Then, on October 4, 1957, the Space Age began. On that day, the Soviet Union launched the first artificial **satellite** (SAT-uh-lite). This satellite was called *Sputnik.* A satellite is an object that follows a curved path around another body in space. The curved path of a satellite is its **orbit.** *Sputnik* orbited the earth every 90 minutes.

Since the launch of *Sputnik,* hundreds of artificial satellites have been placed in orbit around the earth. These satellites collect information about the sun, stars, planets, comets, and other bodies in the solar system. All of this information is sent back to Earth for scientists to study.

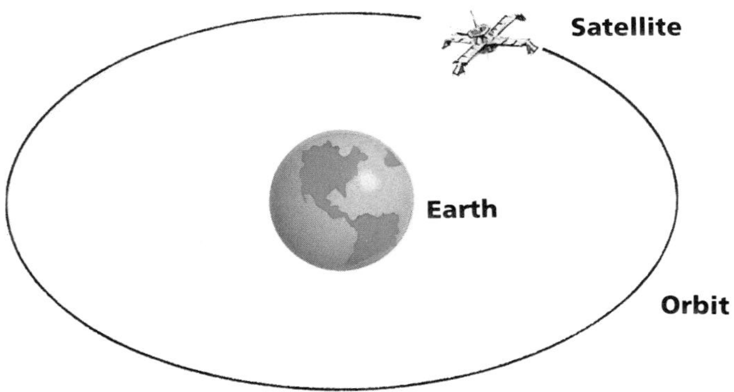

▶ ***Name:*** What is the curved path of a satellite called?

Space Probes Space can be explored by people in spaceships. For example, six *Apollo* spacecraft landed astronauts on the moon and returned them safely to Earth. Space also can be explored by robot space probes. Many kinds of space exploration are best done with space probes. Space probes can go to places that would be too dangerous for astronauts. For example, part of the *Galileo* space probe sent to Jupiter entered the atmosphere of Jupiter in 1995. It radioed important information to Earth before being destroyed by the high temperature and pressure in the atmosphere.

Space probes can be sent on one-way missions. They do not have to return to the earth. Some space probes, such as *Voyager 1* and *Voyager 2,* have even been sent out of the solar system. The *Voyager* space probes were launched in 1977. In 1989, *Voyager 2* became the first human-made object to reach Neptune. At that time, Neptune was the farthest planet from the sun. Both space probes sent back exciting photographs of the outer planets. Scientists estimate that *Voyager 2* will continue traveling for thousands of years. They hope to continue receiving signals from both space probes at least until 2015, and perhaps until 2030.

▶ ***Identify:*** What are *Voyager 1* and *Voyager 2*?

LESSON SUMMARY

- The Space Age began in 1957 when the first artificial satellite was launched.
- Hundreds of artificial satellites are in orbit around the earth.
- Space probes can go to places that are too dangerous for astronauts.
- Space probes can be sent on one-way missions.

CHECK *Complete the following.*

1. What was *Sputnik*?
2. What is the curved path of a satellite called?
3. What is the purpose of the satellites in orbit around the earth?
4. Why was a robot space probe sent to Jupiter instead of a spaceship with astronauts?
5. What was the first space probe to reach Neptune?

APPLY *Complete the following.*

6. What are two advantages that robot space probes have over spaceships with human crews?
7. **Infer:** *Telstar,* one of the first artificial satellites, was launched in 1962. *Telstar* was a communications satellite. What do you think was the function of *Telstar* and of other communications satellites?
8. **Infer:** What is the difference between a natural satellite and an artificial satellite?

Skill Builder

Classifying When you classify, you group things based on similarities. Below is a list of some important satellites. Use library references to find out the function of each satellite. Then classify each satellite according to its function. On a piece of paper, write the words "Communications Satellites," "Weather Satellites," "Navigation Satellites," and "Scientific Satellites." Place each satellite under its correct heading.

Early Bird	*Transit*
Explorer I	*Echo*
Landsat	*Nimbus*
Tiros	*Intelsat*

LEISURE ACTIVITY

BUILDING SCALE MODELS

Do you like airplanes, rockets, and space probes? If so, you may enjoy building scale models of these flying machines. Many people have collections of scale models of different kinds of aircraft rockets, and space probes. A scale model is a miniature copy of the actual object. The model is made so that all parts and its size are in proportion to the real thing. For example, the scale may be 1/14. In this example, the model is 1/14 the actual size of the object.

Model kits may be purchased from hobby shops. Some kits can be ordered from mail-order advertisements and catalogs. Some places have more than 25,000 different models to choose from.

Putting together a model takes time and patience. Some models have a lot of detail. You can even get models that you paint yourself.

15-9 What is a space shuttle?

Objective ▶ Describe how a space shuttle works.

A Reusable Spaceship In the 1960s and 1970s, all space flights were made with spacecraft that could be used only once. This was very expensive and wasteful. In the late 1970s, the National Aeronautics and Space Administration, or NASA, had a better idea. NASA decided to build a spacecraft that could go into space and return many times. This new kind of spacecraft was called a Space Transportation System, or space shuttle.

Infer: Why was the space shuttle an improvement over earlier spacecraft?

The Space Shuttle The space shuttle has three main parts. Two of the parts are needed to get the shuttle into space. They are the solid-fuel booster rockets and the liquid-fuel tank. The third part is the shuttle orbiter. The orbiter is the only part that goes into space.

How does the space shuttle get into orbit? At launch, both the booster rockets and the orbiter's rocket engines are fired. A few minutes after launch, the booster rockets separate from the orbiter. The booster rockets fall back into the ocean. They can be picked up and used again. The large liquid-fuel tank provides fuel for the orbiter's engines. The tank drops away before the orbiter reaches earth orbit.

Once the orbiter is in space, the engines are turned off. They are fired again to change the orbiter's speed and direction when the orbiter is ready to land. When its mission is over, the orbiter returns to Earth. The orbiter glides to a landing on a runway.

List: What are the three parts of a space shuttle?

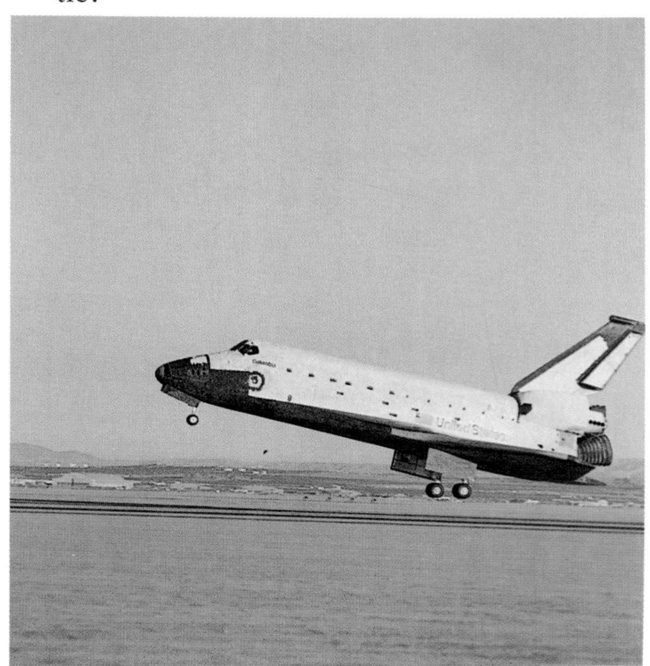

Uses of the Shuttle The shuttle's cargo bay is designed to carry almost 30,000 kg of equipment into orbit. Satellites and space probes can be launched from the shuttle. Shuttle astronauts can repair satellites in orbit, or the satellites can be returned to Earth. The shuttle also can carry a laboratory called Spacelab in its cargo bay. In the future, the shuttle may be used to ferry people and supplies to a space station.

Name: What is the laboratory carried by the shuttle called?

LESSON SUMMARY

- The space shuttle is a spacecraft that can be reused many times.
- The orbiter is the only part of the shuttle that goes into space.
- Both the booster rockets and the liquid-fuel tank drop off before the orbiter reaches space.
- The orbiter returns to Earth and lands on a runway.
- The shuttle has many uses, including launching and repairing satellites.

CHECK *Complete the following.*

1. Another name for the space shuttle is ______ .
2. The space shuttle has ______ main parts.
3. The ______ is the only part of the shuttle that goes into space.
4. The ______ can be picked up in the ocean and used again.
5. The shuttle orbiter lands like an airplane on a ______ .
6. Satellites are carried in the shuttle's- ______ .

APPLY *Complete the following.*

7. What are some uses for the space shuttle?
8. **Infer:** Why can the space shuttle be used as a ferry for an orbiting space station?
9. If you could take a trip on the space shuttle, where would you go? Why?

InfoSearch

Read the passage. Ask two questions about the topic that cannot answer from the information in the passage.

Buran In 1988, the Soviet Union tested its first space shuttle. The shuttle was called Buran. This is a Russian word that means "snowstorm." Buran was launched from a cosmodrome in the Soviet Union. The shuttle was boosted into orbit by a huge Energia rocket. After circling the earth twice, Buran made a remote-controlled landing. Many people who have seen photographs of Buran think that it looks very much like American space shuttles.

SEARCH: Use library references to find answers to your questions.

PEOPLE IN SCIENCE

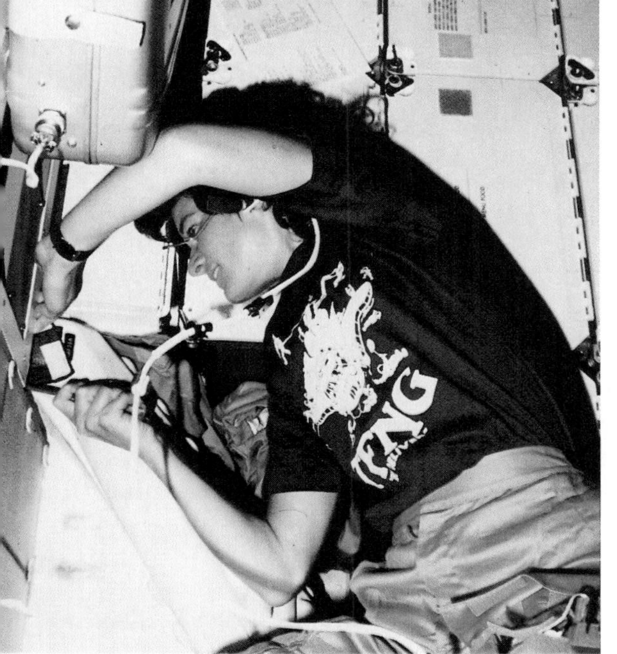

SALLY KRISTON RIDE (1951–present)

In June 1983, the space shuttle *Challenger* took off for a six-day flight. On board was the first American woman to travel in space. She was Sally Kriston Ride.

Dr. Ride was born in Los Angeles, California. She received a Ph.D. in physics from Stanford University in California. Dr. Ride married fellow astronaut Steven A. Hawley in 1982. On her first space flight, Dr. Ride and another astronaut, John M. Fabian, launched two communications satellites. They did some medical experiments and tested the shuttle's remote manipulator arm.

Sally Ride's second space flight took place in October 1984. On this flight, Dr. Ride used the remote manipulator arm to measure the effect of the sun on the earth's weather. On January 28, 1986, the space shuttle *Challenger* exploded, killing all seven crew members on board. The next month, Dr. Ride was appointed to a presidential committee to investigate the cause of the accident. In 1987, Sally Ride resigned from the astronaut program. She accepted a fellowship for International Security and Arms Control at Stanford University.

15-10 What is a space station?

Objective ▶ Explain how space stations are used for space exploration.

Space Stations Artificial satellites and robot space probes are very useful in space exploration. They can gather information and send the information back to scientists on Earth. The scientists do not have to leave the earth. Sometimes, however, scientists find it necessary to make their observations directly. In a space station, scientists can live and work in space for long periods of time.

▶ ***Explain:*** What is the purpose of a space station?

Skylab The first space station was called *Skylab. Skylab* was put into orbit around the earth in May 1973. It was about the size of a small house. *Skylab* stayed in orbit while different teams of astronauts visited it. Astronauts in *Skylab* were able to stay in space for long periods of time. In November 1973, a team of three astronauts lived and worked in *Skylab* for 83 days. The *Skylab* missions showed that people could safely live and work in space.

▶ ***Name:*** What was the first space station called?

Space Station *Freedom* The United States and other countries are planning to build a space station called *Freedom*. The station will be put together piece by piece with parts carried into orbit by space shuttles. Men and women will work and live in space station *Freedom*. They will use the space shuttle as a ferry to travel to and from earth. The *Freedom* space station will consist of laboratories, living quarters, docking bays for space shuttles, and solar panels for energy. *Freedom* will be a full-time research laboratory and satellite repair shop. Scientists expect *Freedom* to function for 20 to 30 years.

▶ ***Describe:*** How will space station *Freedom* be built?

LESSON SUMMARY

- A space station allows scientists to live and work in space for long periods of time.
- *Skylab* was the first space station.
- The space station *Freedom* will be built in orbit from parts carried by space shuttles.
- *Freedom* will be used as a full-time research laboratory and to repair satellites.

CHECK *Complete the following.*

1. In a ______, scientists can live and work in space.
2. ______ was the first space station.
3. In 1973, three astronauts lived on board *Skylab* for ______ days.
4. Parts for space station *Freedom* will be carried into orbit by the ______ .
5. *Freedom* will be used to repair ______ .
6. Scientists expect *Freedom* to function for ______ years.

APPLY *Complete the following.*

7. **Hypothesize:** An engineer has said: "The space shuttle is a lot like camp. The space station will be more like home." What do you think the engineer meant?

Ideas in Action

IDEA: Astronauts living on a space station have to adjust to the weightlessness of space. This makes many ordinary chores much more complicated than they are on Earth. For example, how do you take a shower in space?

ACTION: Identify three things that you do every day that might be difficult or impossible to do on a space station.

InfoSearch

Read the passage. Ask two questions about the topic that you cannot answer from the information in the passage.

Living in Space Astronauts on a space station must live and work in conditions that are very different from those on Earth. Life-support systems are needed on a space station to supply air, water, and food. A special water-management system produces pure, fresh drinking water. Exercise also is important for astronauts living in space.

SEARCH: Use library references to find answers to your questions.

CAREER IN EARTH SCIENCE

AEROSPACE WORKER

Space probes, satellites, and space stations are manufactured by the aerospace industry. This industry employs nearly one million workers. About half of the people in the aerospace industry actually work on putting the spacecraft together. Many inspectors are employed to check the quality of each job as it is completed. Managers and administrators supervise the operation of the plants where the spacecraft are built.

Because the aerospace industry uses the latest technologies, many aerospace workers have a background in science and engineering. In addition to the workers who design and build the spacecraft, the aerospace industry also employs lawyers, accountants, and clerical workers. If you are a high school graduate, and a graduate of a technical school or a college, you probably can find a job in some part of the aerospace industry.

UNIT 15 Challenges

STUDY HINT Before you begin the Unit Challenges, review the TechTerms and Lesson Summary for each lesson in this unit.

TechTerms

astronomical unit (314)
astronomy (304)
concave mirror (310)
convex lens (308)
galaxy (306)
light year (314)
orbit (318)
radio telescope (312)
reflecting telescope (310)
refracting telescope (308)
satellite (318)
solar system (304)
thrust (316)

Matching *Write the TechTerm that best matches each description.*

1. path of a satellite around a planet
2. force that pushes a rocket forward
3. distance of 150 million kilometers
4. mirror that curves inward
5. lens that is thicker in the middle than at its edges
6. large system of stars
7. the sun and all the bodies that circle the sun
8. natural or artificial object that orbits a body in space

Fill-in *Write the TechTerm that best completes each statement.*

1. The study of the stars, planets, and other bodies in space is _______ .
2. A telescope that uses convex lenses to produce an enlarged image of an object is a _______ .
3. A telescope that is used to study sounds coming from space is a _______ .
4. A unit of distance equal to 10 trillion kilometers is the _______ .
5. A telescope that uses mirrors to form an image is a _______ .

Content Challenges

Multiple Choice *Write the letter of the term or phrase that best completes each statement.*

1. The first artificial satellite launched into space was
   a. *Apollo.* **b.** *Voyager 2.* **c.** *Telstar.* **d.** *Sputnik.*
2. Scientists who study how the universe began are
   a. planetologists. **b.** cosmologists. **c.** philosophers. **d.** geophysicists.
3. The Space Telescope is named after
   a. Jansky. **b.** Reber. **c.** Newton. **d.** Hubble.
4. A concave mirror
   a. curves inward. **b.** curves outward. **c.** is flat. **d.** curves inward and outward.
5. The telescope used by Newton was a
   a. refracting telescope. **b.** reflecting telescope. **c.** radio telescope. **d.** scanning telescope.
6. The closest star, other than the sun, to Earth is
   a. Io. **b.** Proxima Centauri. **c.** Polaris. **d.** Voyager.
7. Light travels through space at a speed of about
   a. 3000 km/sec. **b.** 30,000 km/sec. **c.** 300,000 km/sec. **d.** 300,000 km/min.

8. A light year is equal to the distance light travels in one
   a. minute. **b.** day. **c.** month. **d.** year.
9. An astronomical unit is equal to the distance from the
   a. earth to the moon. **b.** sun to the moon. **c.** earth to the sun. **d.** earth to Pluto.
10. To get into space, a rocket must reach a speed of more than
   a. 3000 km/hr. **b.** 4000 km/hr. **c.** 30,000 km/hr. **d.** 40,000 km/hr.
11. The only spaceship that can be reused is the
   a. space shuttle. **b.** space station. **c.** space probe. **d.** *Skylab.*
12. The first space station that was put into orbit was
   a. *Sputnik.* **b.** *Voyager.* **c.** *Freedom.* **d.** *Skylab.*

True/False *Write true if the statement is true. If the statement is false, change the underlined term to make the statement true.*

1. The first artificial satellite was launched in 1957 as part of the International <u>Space</u> Year.
2. Scientists think that the universe began when a huge explosion called the <u>Big Bang</u> occurred.
3. The telescope used by Galileo was a <u>radio</u> telescope.
4. The first person to study the surface of the moon with a telescope was <u>Newton</u>.
5. The lens in a refracting telescope that collects light and focuses the image is the <u>objective</u> lens.
6. A telescope that uses mirrors instead of lenses is a <u>refracting</u> telescope.
7. Stars can be studied on a cloudy night with a <u>radio</u> telescope.
8. Polaris is <u>300</u> light years from Earth.
9. The *Galileo* space probe is studying the atmosphere of <u>Earth</u>.
10. The only part of a space shuttle that goes into space is the <u>liquid fuel tank</u>.
11. The first space station was called <u>*Challenger*</u>.
12. Newton's Third Law of Motion states that for every action, there is an equal and <u>opposite</u> reaction.

Understanding the Selections

Reading Critically *Use the feature reading selections to answer the following. Page numbers for the features are shown in parentheses.*

1. Who first developed the theory that the sun was at the center of the solar system? (305)
2. Name three products that have resulted from space exploration. (307)
3. What are three features to look for when buying a telescope? (311)
4. **Building vocabulary:** What do the letters in the term 'SETI' stand for?
5. **Building Vocabulary:** What do the letters in the term "NASA" stand for?
6. Why is Sally Ride famous? (321)

Concept Challenges

Interpreting a Table *Use Table 1 to answer each of the following.*

Table 1 Distance of Planets from the Sun in Astronomical Units (AU)

PLANET	DISTANCE
Mercury	0.4
Venus	0.7
Earth	1.0
Mars	1.5
Jupiter	5.2
Saturn	9.5
Uranus	19.2
Neptune	30.1
Pluto	39.4

1. What is the distance in AU of Earth from the sun?
2. What is the closest planet to the sun?
3. What is the fourth planet from the sun?
4. How far in AU is Neptune from the sun?
5. How much farther from the sun is Pluto than Uranus?

Critical Thinking *Answer each of the following in complete sentences.*

1. What is the relationship between advances made in technology and astronomy?
2. Why is space exploration important?
3. What is the difference between a refracting telescope and a reflecting telescope?
4. Why does a rocket in space need fuel to change speed or direction?
5. What are the advantages of space probes?

Finding Out More

1. Research the development of the space shuttle. Make a time line of its development and launchings.
2. Using library references, find out about the Hubble Space Telescope. In an oral report, describe how the telescope works, and what astronomers hope to learn from using the telescope.
3. If possible, read newspaper articles from 1957 and 1958 written about the beginning of the Space Age. Your library may have the articles on microfilm.
4. Using library references, find out how convex and concave lenses are used in eyeglasses to correct vision problems. Write your findings in a report.

THE SOLAR SYSTEM

UNIT 16

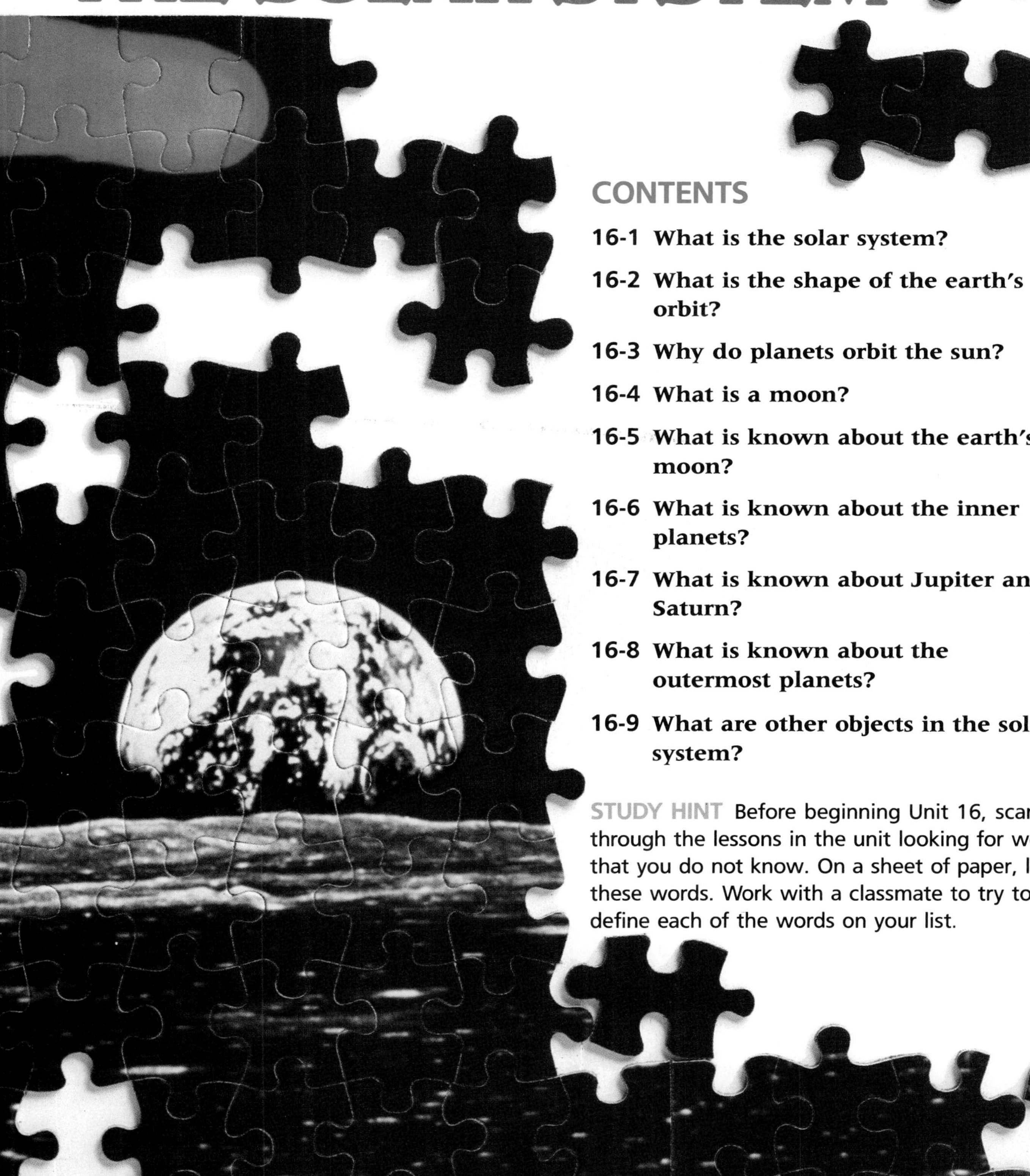

CONTENTS

STUDY HINT Before beginning Unit 16, scan through the lessons in the unit looking for words that you do not know. On a sheet of paper, list these words. Work with a classmate to try to define each of the words on your list.

16-1 What is the solar system?

Objective ▶ Name the planets that make up the solar system.

TechTerms

- ▶ **nebula** (NEB-yuh-luh): spinning cloud of hot gases
- ▶ **orbit:** curved path of one object around another object in space
- ▶ **solar system:** sun and all the objects that orbit the sun

Formation of the Solar System The solar system is the sun and all the objects that orbit the sun. Scientists are not sure how the solar system formed. However, several theories have been developed to explain the formation of the solar system. One theory states that the solar system formed from a spinning cloud of hot gases called a **nebula** (NEB-yuh-luh). Scientists think that the nebula shrank, or contracted, to form the sun, planets, and other objects in the solar system. According to this theory, the solar system formed slowly, over a long period of time.

▶ *Define:* What is a nebula?

The Sun's Family The sun has a "family" of nine planets. Ancient people observed that the planets changed their positions among the stars. The planets seemed to wander in the sky. The word "planet" comes from a Greek word meaning "wanderer." Earth is one of the nine planets in the solar system. Like all of these planets, Earth moves in a path around the sun. The path of a planet around the sun is the planet's **orbit.** All the planets orbit the sun in the same direction.

▶ *Explain:* Why were the planets called wanderers?

Inner and Outer Planets The nine planets often are classified into two groups. These groups are the inner planets and the outer planets. Mercury, Venus, Earth, and Mars are the inner planets. The outer planets are Jupiter, Saturn, Uranus, Neptune, and Pluto.

Classify: Which planets are the inner planets?

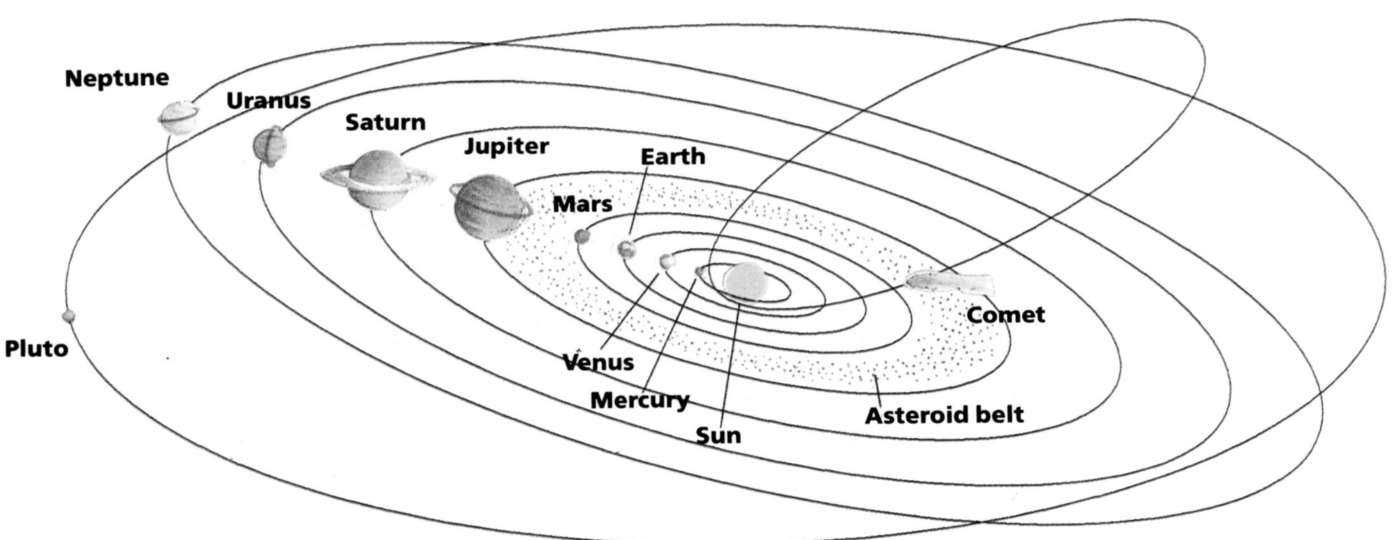

LESSON SUMMARY

- The solar system may have formed from a spinning cloud of hot gases called a nebula.
- There are nine planets in the solar system.
- The planets can be classified into two groups: the inner planets and the outer planets.

CHECK *Write true if the statement is true. If the statement is false, change the underlined term to make the statement true.*

1. The solar system may have formed quickly from a nebula.
2. The solar system contains nine planets.
3. The word "nebula" means wanderer.
4. The path of a planet around the sun is the planet's orbit.
5. The planets can be classified into three groups.
6. Jupiter, Saturn, Uranus, Neptune, and Pluto are the inner planets.

APPLY *Complete the following.*

7. List the planets in order from nearest to the sun to farthest from the sun.
8. **Hypothesize:** Why is the solar system often referred to as the sun's "family"?

Skill Builder

Researching When you research, you gather information about a topic. Astronomers think that many stars other than the sun may have planets in orbit around them. Use library references to find out what evidence astronomers have that stars other than the sun may have planets.

LOOKING BACK IN SCIENCE

THE BIG BANG THEORY

A theory (THEE-uh-ree) is an idea that explains events in nature. According to nebular theories, the solar system came from a spinning cloud of hot gases, called a nebula. Where did the nebula come from? The question of how the universe was formed has always been a scientific puzzle.

In the 1920s, an American astronomer, Edwin Hubble observed some fuzzy patches of light in the sky. He discovered that these patches of light were galaxies, made up of millions of stars. Hubble and other astronomers later found that the galaxies were all moving away from one another. In other words, the universe is expanding, or getting bigger. Astronomers needed a theory to explain this observation. Today, scientists have a theory. The theory explains the origin of the universe. It is called the Big Bang Theory. The Big Bang Theory states that the universe began in a giant explosion about 15 billion years ago. All the matter and energy in the universe exploded outward from a single point. As time passed, the matter formed into stars and galaxies. These galaxies are still flying away from the point of the Big Bang. So the universe is still expanding.

16-2 What is the shape of the earth's orbit?

Objective ▶ Describe the shape of the earth's orbit.

TechTerms

- ▶ **aphelion** (af-FEEL-yun): point in a planet's orbit at which it is farthest from the sun
- ▶ **ellipse** (uh-LIPS): flattened circle, or oval
- ▶ **perihelion** (per-uh-HEEL-yun): point in a planet's orbit at which it is closest to the sun

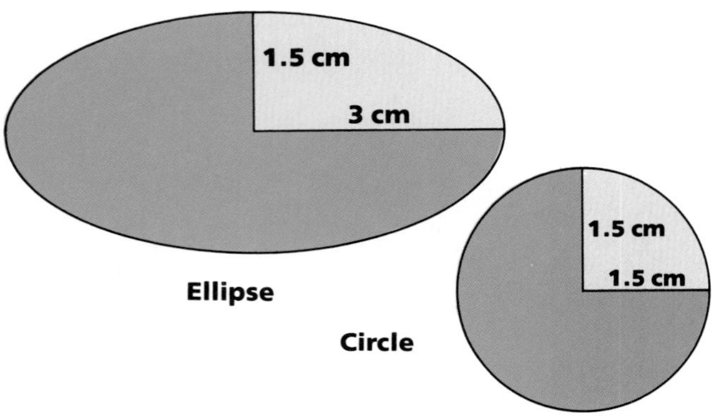

Circles and Ellipses A circle is perfectly round. All lines drawn from the center of a circle to its rim are the same length. An **ellipse** (uh-LIPS) looks like a flattened circle. An ellipse has an oval shape. Lines drawn from the center of an ellipse to different points on its rim are different lengths.

▶ ***Define:*** What is an ellipse?

Earth's Orbit The earth travels around the sun in an elliptical (uh-LIP-tuh-kul) orbit. The earth's orbit looks like an ellipse. The earth is not the same distance from the sun at all times of the year. In January, the earth is at **perihelion** (per-uh-HEEL-yun). Perihelion is the point at which the earth is closest to the sun. The earth is about 147 million kilometers from the sun at perihelion. In July, the earth is at **aphelion** (af-FEEL-yun). Aphelion is the point at which the earth is farthest from the sun. The earth is 152 million kilometers from the sun at aphelion.

▶ ***Describe:*** What is the shape of the earth's orbit?

Orbital Velocity The speed at which the earth travels in its orbit is called its orbital velocity (OR-buh-tul vuh-LOS-uh-tee). The earth travels at different speeds at different parts of its orbit. The closer the earth is to the sun, the greater is its orbital velocity. The earth moves fastest at perihelion. It moves slowest at aphelion.

▶ ***State:*** When does the earth move fastest in its orbit?

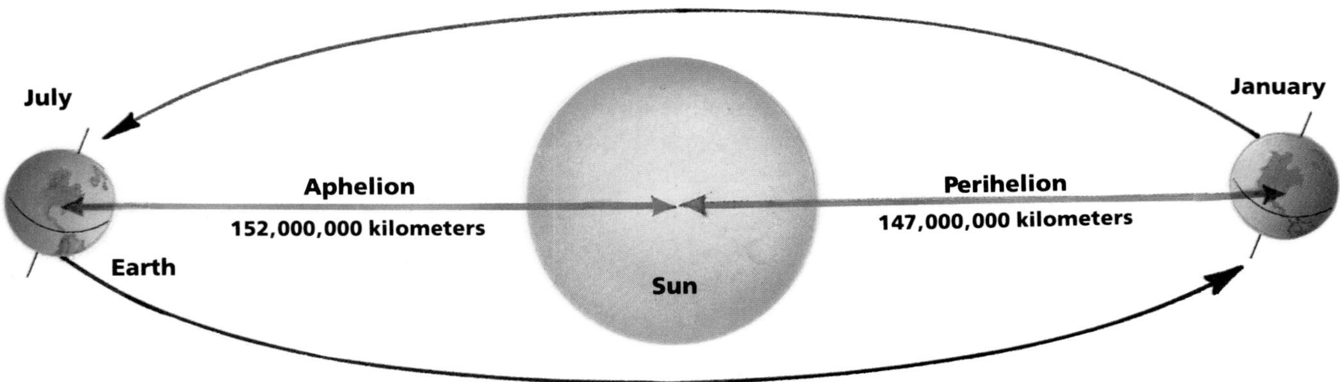

LESSON SUMMARY

- An ellipse has an oval shape.
- The earth travels around the sun in an elliptical orbit.
- Orbital velocity is the speed at which a planet travels in its orbit.
- The earth's orbital velocity is greatest at perihelion and least at aphelion.

CHECK *Complete the following.*

1. An ellipse has an _______ shape.
2. Earth's path around the sun is its _______ .
3. The earth moves in an _______ orbit.
4. The point at which the earth is closest to the sun is _______ .
5. In July, the earth is at _______ .
6. A planet's speed in its orbit is its _______ .

APPLY *Complete the following.*

7. **Hypothesize:** The planets are different distances from the sun. Mercury is closest to the sun. Pluto usually is farthest from the sun. Which of the two planets has the greatest orbital velocity? Explain.
8. **Calculate:** How much farther from the sun is the earth at aphelion than at perihelion?

Skill Builder

Building Vocabulary A root is the main part of a word. Look up the words "perihelion" and "aphelion" in a dictionary. What root do these words have in common? What does the root word mean? A satellite in orbit around the earth has a perigee and an apogee. What do you think the words "perigee" and "apogee" mean? What is the root for these words?

ACTIVITY

DRAWING THE SHAPE OF THE EARTH'S ORBIT

You will need a piece of paper, a piece of cardboard, two push pins, string, a pencil, and a metric ruler.

1. Place a piece of paper on top of a piece of cardboard. Draw a horizontal line 4 cm long in the center of the paper.
2. Stick a push pin through the paper and cardboard at each end of the line.
3. Draw a circle around one of the push pins. Label the circle "Sun."
4. Tie the ends of a piece of string together to make a loop about 12 cm long.
5. Place the loop of string around both push pins on the paper.
6. Hold a pencil against the inside of the loop of string. Move the pencil around the loop. Keep the string tight against the pencil as you move the pencil.

Questions

1. **a. Observe:** What shape did you draw with the pencil? **b.** What does this shape represent?
2. Label the perihelion and aphelion on your drawing?
3. **Measure:** What are the distances from the "sun" at perihelion and aphelion? Label the distances on your drawing.
4. During what two months does the earth reach perihelion and aphelion? Label the months on your drawing.

16-3 Why do planets orbit the sun?

Objective ▶ Explain how the force of gravity keeps planets moving around the sun.

TechTerm

▶ **gravity** (GRAV-uh-tee): force of attraction that exists between all objects in the universe

Gravity When you throw a ball into the air, you know that the ball will fall back to the ground. **Gravity** (GRAV-uh-tee) is the force that pulls the ball to the ground. On the earth, gravity pulls all objects toward the center of the earth.

▶ ***Name:*** What force pulls a ball to the ground?

Curved Motion When you throw a ball, you give the ball a forward motion. At the same time, gravity pulls the ball toward the center of the earth. As a result, the ball has two motions. The ball has a forward motion and a downward motion. These two motions cause the ball to follow a curved path, as shown in Figure 1.

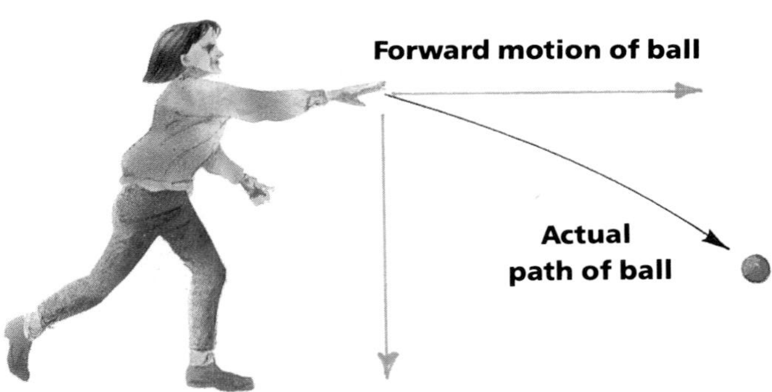

Figure 1

Suppose you tied a ball to the end of a string and swung the ball around your head. You would feel an outward pull on the string. The ball tends to fly off in a straight line. At the same time, your inward pull on the string would keep the ball from flying away. The inward pull on the string keeps the ball moving in a curved path around your head.

▶ ***Explain:*** What keeps a ball on a string moving in a curved path?

Gravitational Attraction Every object in the universe pulls on every other object. This pull is the force of gravity, or gravitational attraction (grav-uh-TAY-shun-ul uh-TRAK-shun). There is a gravitational attraction between all objects in the universe. For example, there is a gravitational attraction between the sun and the planets. This gravitational attraction pulls the planets toward the sun as they move through space. Instead of flying off into space, the planets move in curved, elliptical orbits around the sun.

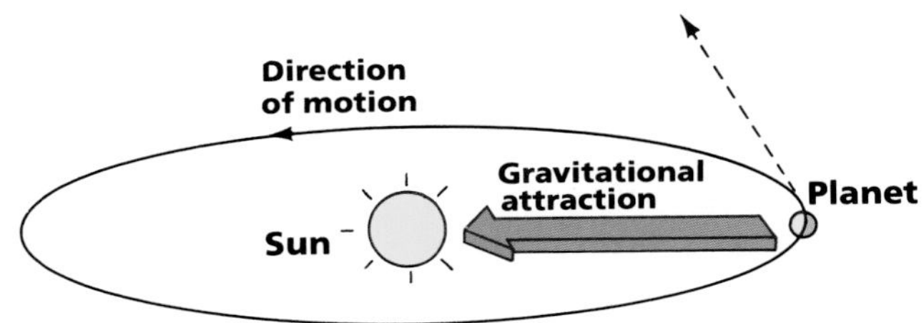

Figure 2

▶ ***Explain:*** What keeps the planets in their orbits around the sun?

Effects of Gravitational Attraction The closer two objects are to each other, the greater is the gravitational attraction between them. As a planet gets closer to the sun, the gravitational attraction between the planet and the sun increases. As a result, the planet moves faster. When a planet is farther from the sun, the gravitational attraction between them decreases. The planet moves slower. This is why a planet moves fastest at perihelion and slowest at aphelion. The difference in gravitational attraction also explains why planets near the sun move faster than planets farther from the sun.

▶ ***Describe:*** What happens as a planet gets closer to the sun?

LESSON SUMMARY

- Gravity pulls all objects toward the center of the earth.
- The downward pull of gravity causes a thrown ball to follow a curved path.
- There is a gravitational attraction between every object in the universe.
- The sun's gravitational attraction keeps the planets moving in elliptical orbits and determines their orbital velocities.

CHECK *Complete the following.*

1. The force that causes a ball to fall to the ground is ______ .
2. When you throw a ball, you give it a ______ motion.
3. Because of gravity, a thrown ball follows a ______ path.
4. The gravitational attraction of the ______ keeps the planets moving in their orbits.

APPLY *Complete the following.*

5. Which planet moves faster in its orbit, Mercury or Pluto?

▲ 6. **Model:** Copy the diagram. Label the sun, the planet, and the planet's orbit.

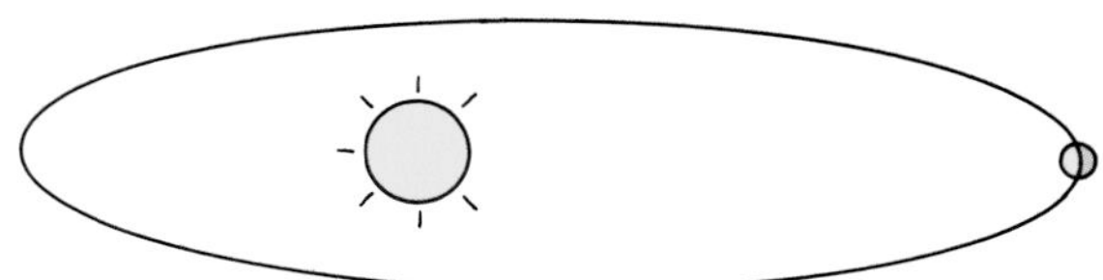

InfoSearch

Read the passage. Ask two questions about the topic that you cannot answer from the information in the passage.

Kepler Johannes Kepler was a German astronomer and mathematician. Kepler was the first astronomer to openly support Copernicus, who said that the sun is at the center of the solar system. Kepler discovered three important laws that describe how planets move in their orbits. Kepler discovered these laws while trying to explain the observations of Tycho Brahe. Kepler found that the orbits of the planets are ellipses, not circles.

SEARCH: Use library references to find answers to your questions.

ACTIVITY

MODELING A PLANET'S ORBIT

You will need a long piece of string and a key.

1. Tie a key securely to the end of a piece of string.
2. **CAUTION: Be sure that you have a clear space around you.** Hold one end of the string tightly. Then swing the key on the other end of the string around your head.

Questions

1. What is the shape of the key's path around your head?
2. What keeps the key from flying off in a straight line?
3. What keeps the key moving in its path?
4. **a. Observe:** In what direction is the pull of the key on your hand? **b.** In what direction is the pull of your hand on the string?
5. How does the movement of the key on the string compare to the movement of the planets in their orbits?

16-4 What is a moon?

Objective ▶ Compare the moons of the different planets in the solar system.

TechTerm

▶ **satellite** (SAT-uh-lite): natural or artificial object orbiting a body in space

Moons and Rings Most of the planets in the solar system have one or more moons. A moon is a natural **satellite** (SAT-uh-lite) of a planet. A satellite is a natural or artificial object that orbits another object in space.

Astronomers have known about some moons for hundreds of years. For example, Galileo discovered the four largest moons of Jupiter in 1610. Other moons of Jupiter have been discovered recently by the space probe *Voyager 2.*

Some planets also have rings. Rings are made up of small particles of rock or ice. Each particle is a tiny satellite. Table 1 lists the planets and the number of their known moons. Table 1 also identifies the planets that have rings.

Table 1 Planets, Moons, and Rings

PLANET	NUMBER OF MOONS	RINGS
Mercury	0	No
Venus	0	No
Earth	1	No
Mars	2	No
Jupiter	16	Yes
Saturn	17	Yes
Uranus	15	Yes
Neptune	8	Yes
Pluto	1	No

▶ ***Describe:*** What is a moon?

Planetary Moons As you can see in Table 1, Mercury and Venus are the only planets in the solar system without at least one moon. Earth has only one moon. Mars has two moons named Deimos and Phobos.

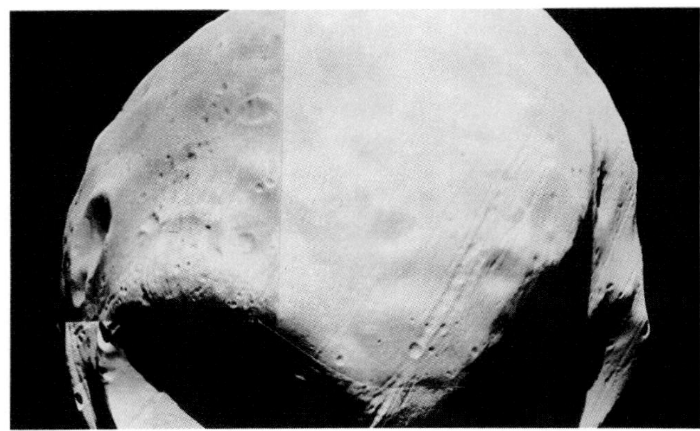

Most of the outer planets have rings as well as many moons. The moons of Jupiter that were seen by Galileo are Io, Europe, Ganymede, and Callisto. Saturn's rings are its most obvious feature, but Saturn also has five large moons. Saturn's largest moon is Titan. Uranus has at least 15 moons. The five largest are Oberon, Titania, Umbriel, Ariel, and Miranda. The two moons of Neptune that are visible from Earth are Triton and Nereid. Pluto, like Earth, has only one moon. Pluto's moon is called Charon.

▶ ***Name:*** Which two planets have only one moon?

LESSON SUMMARY

- Most planets in the solar system have one or more moons.
- Some planets have rings, which are natural satellites made up of rocks and ice.
- Mercury and Venus are the only planets without at least one moon.
- Most of the outer planets have both moons and rings.

CHECK *Match each planet with its correct moon.*

1. Jupiter	a. Charon
2. Mars	b. Triton
3. Uranus	c. Io
4. Pluto	d. Titania
5. Neptune	e. Titan
6. Saturn	f. Phobos

APPLY *Complete the following.*

7. **Sequence:** List the planets in order from the one with the most moons to the ones with the fewest.
8. **Infer:** Why do you think the four largest moons of Jupiter are called the "Galilean moons?"

Skill Builder

Researching When you research, you gather information about a topic. The names given to newly discovered moons are chosen by the International Astronomical Union. The names chosen come from many different sources. For example, recently discovered moons of Uranus were named after characters in the plays of Shakespeare. Choose the moons of one planet. Use library references to find the source of each moon's name. Write a report of your findings.

LOOKING BACK IN SCIENCE

DISCOVERY OF NEW MOONS

People have observed Earth's moon since ancient times. For thousands of years, Earth was the only planet in the solar system known to have a moon, or natural satellite. In the 17th century, Galileo discovered four moons of Jupiter. Today, astronomers know that seven planets—Earth, Mars, Jupiter, Saturn, Uranus, Neptune, and Pluto—have moons.

Until the late 1970s, all of the known moons had been discovered using earth-based telescopes. Then, two space probes called *Voyager 1* and *Voyager 2* were launched in 1977. From 1979 through 1989, these spacecraft sent back to earth the first detailed, close-up photographs of many new moons. Together, *Voyagers 1* and *2* discovered at least 35 new moons. The *Voyager* spacecraft discovered 12 new moons of Jupiter, 7 of Saturn, 10 of Uranus, and 6 of Neptune.

The *Voyager* spacecraft also discovered rings around Jupiter, two new rings around Uranus, and at least four complete rings around Neptune. They also found new details in Saturn's ring system. In fact, much of what astronomers know about the outer planets was discovered by the *Voyager* spacecraft.

16-5 What is known about the earth's moon?

Objective ▶ Describe some features of the moon.

TechTerms

- ▶ **craters** (KRAY-turz): round holes on the moon's surface
- ▶ **maria** (MAHR-ee-uh): broad, flat plains on the moon

Moon Landing On July 20, 1969, American astronauts set foot on the surface of the moon. These astronauts were the first humans to reach the moon. They had traveled 380,000 kilometers from the earth to the moon in five days. Since 1969, 12 astronauts have landed on the moon and returned to Earth. The last moon landing was made by *Apollo 17* astronauts in 1972.

▶ ***State:*** When did humans first land on the moon?

The Moon The moon is the earth's only natural satellite. The moon is much smaller than the earth. It is about 3200 kilometers in diameter. Because the moon has less mass than the earth, the moon's gravity is less than the earth's gravity. Gravity on the moon is only one-sixth as strong as gravity on the earth. As a result, your weight on the moon would be one-sixth of your weight on the earth. The moon's smaller gravity also means that you could jump six times higher on the moon than on the earth.

The moon has no water and no atmosphere. Temperatures on the moon can be as high as 120°C or as low as −153°C. Astronauts need space suits to survive on the moon.

▶ ***Calculate:*** If you could jump 60 cm high on the earth, how high could you jump on the moon?

The Moon's Surface There are three main features on the moon's surface. Galileo called the smooth, dark areas that he saw on the moon **maria** (MAHR-ee-uh). The word "maria" means "seas" in Latin. The first astronauts to land on the moon landed in the Sea of Tranquility. Today, scientists know that the moon's maria are broad, flat plains. Galileo also saw light areas on the moon. These light areas are mountains, or highlands. Some mountains on the moon are as high as the highest mountains on Earth. The most obvious features on the moon's surface are its many **craters** (KRAY-turz). Most craters were caused by large objects striking the moon's surface. Others may have been caused by erupting volcanoes.

▶ ***List:*** What are three features on the moon's surface?

LESSON SUMMARY

- The first humans landed on the moon on July 20, 1969.
- The moon is the earth's only natural satellite.
- There is no air or water on the moon.
- The three main features on the moon's surface are maria, highlands, and craters.

CHECK *Complete the following.*

1. The distance from the earth to the moon is _______ kilometers.
2. The moon is a natural _______ of the earth.
3. The moon is _______ than the earth.
4. The moon's gravity is _______ as strong as the earth's gravity.
5. The word "maria" means _______ .
6. Three features on the moon's surface are maria, _______, and highlands.

APPLY *Complete the following.*

7. **Calculate:** How much would a 60-kilogram person weigh on the moon?
8. **Infer:** Astronauts left their footprints on the moon's surface. These footprints may remain unchanged for millions of years. Why?
9. **Calculate:** How much would you weigh on the moon?

Skill Builder

Observing When you observe, you use one or more of your senses to gather information about your surroundings. Many features on the moon are visible to the unaided eye. Others can be seen clearly through binoculars. Observe a full moon, first using only your eyes and then with binoculars. Compare how well you were able to see certain features with your unaided eyes and with binoculars. Make a labeled drawing of the features you were able to identify.

ACTIVITY

MODELING CRATER FORMATIONS

You will need a shoebox, plaster of Paris, a metric ruler, and 2 rocks of different sizes.

1. Mix the plaster of Paris according to the directions. Make enough plaster of Paris to fill the shoebox one-third of the way up.
2. Pour the plaster of Paris into the shoebox.
3. Just before the plaster of Paris hardens, drop one of the rocks into it from a height of 25 cm. Then drop the other rock from the same height.
4. Remove the rocks and drop them from a height of 10 cm.
5. Remove the rocks and let the plaster of Paris harden.
6. Take as many measurements of the rocks and craters as you can.

Questions

1. What do the rocks represent?
2. **Compare:** Which rock made the deepest crater?
3. **Compare:** Which rock made the widest crater?
4. How do you think craters were formed on the moon?

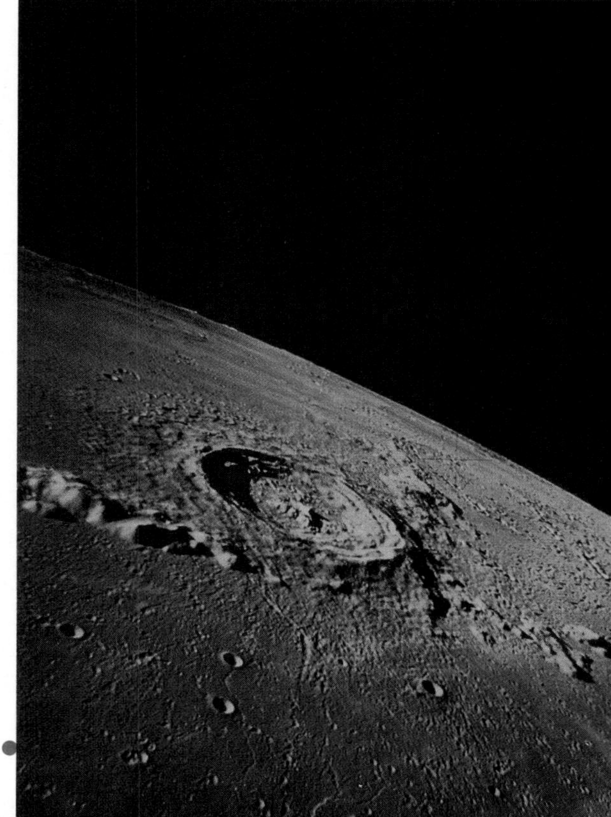

16-6 What is known about the inner planets?

Objective ▶ Identify the basic features of the four inner planets.

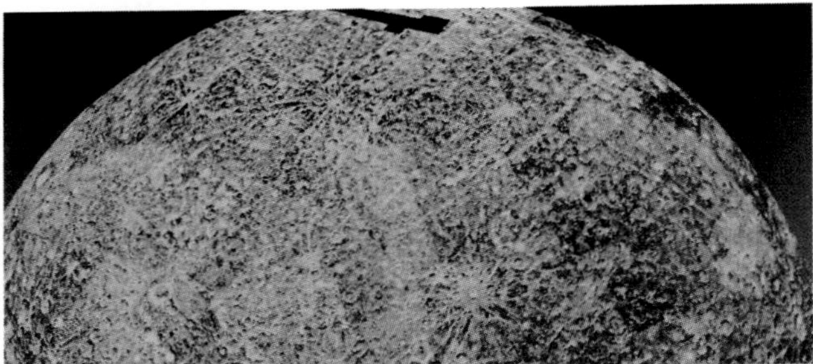

Mercury Mercury is the closest planet to the sun. For this reason, Mercury moves faster in its orbit than any of the other planets. Astronomers cannot take clear photographs of Mercury from Earth because Mercury is so close to the sun. However, the space probe *Mariner 10* has visited Mercury. Photographs taken by the space probe show that the surface of Mercury is covered with craters. Mercury has a thin atmosphere. Temperatures on Mercury range from 500°C during the day to −200°C at night.

▶ ***Explain:*** Why can astronomers not take clear photographs of Mercury from Earth?

Venus Venus has been called Earth's twin. The two planets are about the same size, mass, and density. However, temperatures and pressures on Venus are much higher than on Earth. Astronomers think that the high surface temperature of Venus is related to its thick atmosphere. There is a lot of carbon dioxide in the atmosphere of Venus. Carbon dioxide traps heat close to the planet's surface. Soviet space probes have landed on the surface of Venus. Photographs taken by the probes show smooth plains, mountains, and valleys. Some scientists think that Venus may have had oceans at one time.

▶ ***Infer:*** Why is Venus sometimes called Earth's twin?

Earth The third planet from the sun is Earth. Earth is the fifth largest planet in the solar system. It is the only planet known to have oceans of liquid water. Earth also is the only planet known to support living things. Life is possible on Earth because of its combination of proper temperature, oxygen in the atmosphere, and liquid water.

▶ ***List:*** What three features make life on Earth possible?

Mars Mars is the fourth planet from the sun. Many space probes, including two Viking landers, have studied Mars. Photographs show that the surface of Mars has many craters. It is covered with loose rocks. Mars also has huge volcanoes that are now dead. The atmosphere of Mars is thin and made mostly of carbon dioxide. Winds up to 500 km per hour raise giant dust storms that cover the whole planet. Scientists think that Mars probably once had running water. There is no liquid water on Mars now because temperatures are too low.

▶ ***Explain:*** Why is there no liquid water on Mars now?

LESSON SUMMARY

- Mercury is the closest planet to the sun.
- Venus is often called Earth's twin.
- Earth is the only planet that is known to have life.
- Mars probably had running water in the past.

CHECK *Complete the following.*

1. What are the four inner planets?
2. What does the surface of Mercury look like?
3. What gas in the atmosphere makes the surface of Venus so hot?
4. Which planet is the only one known to have liquid water?
5. What causes the huge dust storms on Mars?

APPLY *Complete the following.*

6. **Compare:** How are the surfaces of Mercury and Mars similar to the surface of Earth's moon?
7. **Hypothesize:** Space probes have identified basalt and granite on Venus. On Earth, these two kinds of rock are usually found near volcanoes. What does the presence of these rocks on Venus suggest?

InfoSearch

Read the passage. Ask two questions about the topic that you cannot answer from the information in the passage.

Martian Canals Is there life on Mars? People have asked this question for hundreds of years. In 1877, an Italian astronomer, Giovanni Schiaperelli (skyah-puh-REL-lee), said that he had seen "channels" on Mars. When Schiaperelli's report was translated into English, the word became "canals." Some people assumed that the canals must have been built by Martians. Today, astronomers know that there are no artificial canals on Mars.

SEARCH: Use library references to find answers to your questions.

SCIENCE CONNECTION

THE GREENHOUSE EFFECT ON VENUS

Both the United States and Russia have sent space probes to Venus. Information from instruments on these space probes and from the Hubble Space Telescope shows that Venus has a very dense atmosphere. The atmospheric pressure on the surface of Venus is 90 times the pressure at sea level on Earth. The atmosphere of Venus is made up mostly of carbon dioxide. Hazy clouds extend up to 40 km into the atmosphere. Clouds of sulfuric acid float through the upper atmosphere.

The temperature on the surface of Venus is nearly 500°C. This is much higher than the temperature of boiling water. The high temperature is the result of the greenhouse effect. Energy from the sun can reach the surface of Venus through the clouds. However, the thick atmosphere of carbon dioxide does not allow the heat energy to escape back into space. The heat is trapped near the surface and causes the temperature to build up to its present levels.

Scientists are interested in studying the greenhouse effect on Venus to help them understand what is happening on Earth. Many scientists think that the build-up of carbon dioxide in Earth's atmosphere will result in a greenhouse effect and higher temperatures on Earth.

16-7 What is known about Jupiter and Saturn?

Objective ▶ Identify some features of Jupiter and Saturn.

Jupiter Jupiter is the largest planet in the solar system. Because it is so large, Jupiter can easily be seen without a telescope. Its mass is twice the mass of all the other planets combined. Jupiter has a diameter of 143,000 km. The earth's diameter is less than 13,000 km. Jupiter has 125 times the surface area of the earth.

Jupiter is a gas giant. It is made up mostly of hydrogen and helium. Because these gases are very light, Jupiter's density is only one-fourth the density of Earth. Astronomers cannot see the surface of Jupiter. The planet is completely covered with clouds. The clouds are arranged in colorful bands around the planet.

▶ ***Name:*** What two gases make up most of Jupiter?

The Great Red Spot The largest and best known feature of Jupiter is the Great Red Spot. Astronomers have been observing this huge storm system since it was discovered in 1664. Astronomers think that the Great Red Spot is caused by heated gases rising through the atmosphere of Jupiter.

▶ ***Describe:*** What is the Great Red Spot?

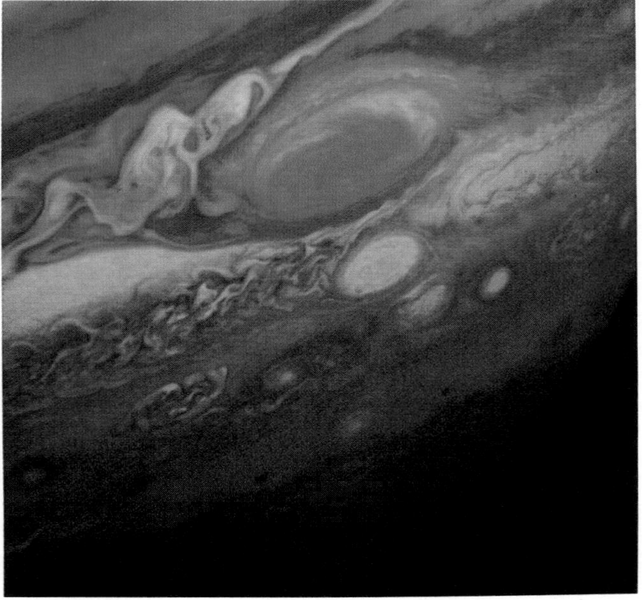

Saturn Saturn is the second largest planet in the solar system. Its diameter is 121,000 km. Like Jupiter, Saturn is a gas giant made up mostly of hydrogen and helium. Saturn has colorful bands of clouds like Jupiter. However, Saturn is much less dense than Jupiter. Saturn's density is less than the density of any other planet. It is even less than the density of water. If you could put Saturn in a bucket of water, it would float.

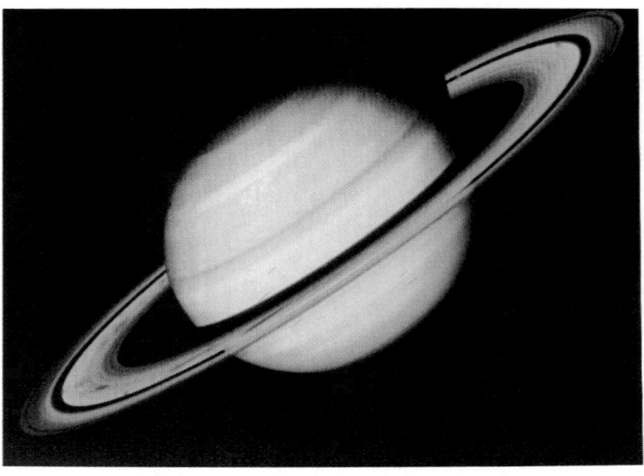

▶ ***Contrast:*** How is Saturn different from Jupiter?

LESSON SUMMARY

- Jupiter is the largest and most massive planet in the solar system.
- Jupiter is made up mostly of the gases hydrogen and helium.
- The Great Red Spot is the best-known feature of Jupiter.
- Saturn is the second largest and least dense planet in the solar system.

CHECK *Complete the following.*

1. The largest planet is ______ .
2. The second largest planet is ______ .
3. Jupiter's mass is more than ______ the mass of the other planets put together.
4. Jupiter and Saturn are made up mostly of ______ and helium.
5. Saturn is ______ dense than water.
6. The Great Red Spot is caused by heated ______ .

APPLY *Complete the following.*

7. **Compare:** What are two ways in which Jupiter and Saturn are alike?
8. **Infer:** Why are Jupiter and Saturn called gas giants?

Skill Builder

Researching When you research, you gather information about a topic. Jupiter and its 16 moons form a miniature "solar system." The space probes *Voyager 1* and *Voyager 2* took close-up photographs of the four largest moons of Jupiter: Io, Callisto, Europa, and Ganymede. Use library references to find out what astronomers have learned about these moons. Write a report of your findings.

TECHNOLOGY AND SOCIETY

GALILEO PROBE TO JUPITER

The *Voyager* space probes gave us the first close-up views of Jupiter and its moons. But until recently, much information about the planet, such as the gases that make it up, was uncertain. Then in December 1995, the space probe *Galileo* entered into orbit around Jupiter. This started a two-year exploration of Jupiter and its moons.

The first task was to collect data on Jupiter's atmosphere. To do this, a smaller probe separated from *Galileo* and fell through the atmosphere, slowed by a parachute. Instruments on the small probe measured the amounts of gases. Scientists found much less helium gas and water vapor than they expected. Scientists were also surprised that winds got stronger instead of weaker as the probe descended.

Galileo also provided new information about Jupiter's largest moons, including the most detailed photographs ever taken. For example, new photographs of the ice-covered moon Europa showed that sections of the ice have moved away from each other. Such movement might be caused by water beneath the ice. The presence of water means life may also be present. One of the most puzzling discoveries was a magnetic field around the moon Ganymede. Usually only planets have magnetic fields. Scientists do not know why Ganymede is different.

16-8 What is known about the outermost planets?

Objective ▶ Identify some features of Uranus, Neptune, and Pluto.

Uranus The seventh planet from the sun is Uranus. It is the third largest planet in the solar system. The diameter of Uranus is about 51,000 km.

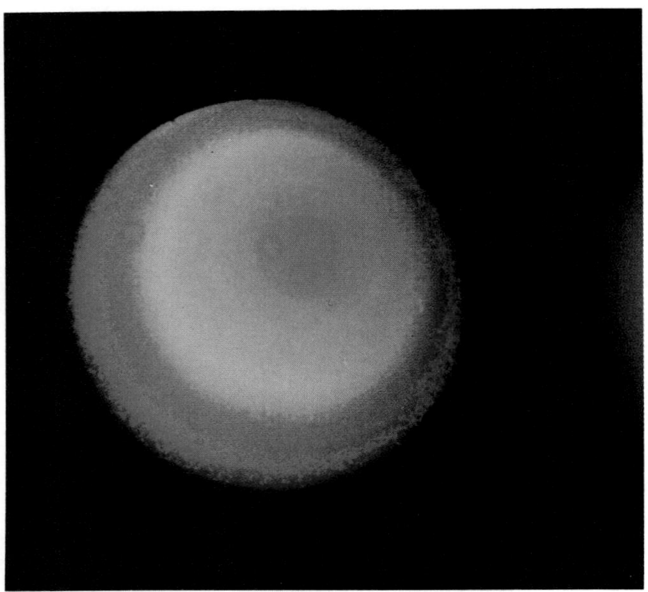

Uranus was the first planet to be discovered since ancient times. Because Uranus is so far from the sun, very little was known about Uranus until very recently. In 1986, the *Voyager 2* space probe flew past Uranus. *Voyager 2* took many photographs of the blue-green clouds of Uranus. The color of the clouds shows that the atmosphere contains methane, as well as hydrogen and helium. The most unusual feature of Uranus is that the planet is tipped on its side.

▶ ***List:*** What three gases are found in the atmosphere of Uranus?

Neptune Neptune is the eighth planet from the sun. It is similar to Uranus in size and mass. Neptune's diameter is about 49,000 km. Neptune is so far from the sun that it takes 165 years to make one orbit around the sun. Neptune has not made a complete orbit since it was discovered in

1845. It was the last planet to be visited by *Voyager 2.* Photographs taken by *Voyager 2* show that Neptune has a Great Dark Spot, similar to Jupiter's Great Red Spot. Neptune also is a gas giant. Neptune's atmosphere is made up mostly of clouds of frozen methane.

▶ ***Identify:*** When was Neptune discovered?

Pluto Pluto is the smallest planet in the solar system. Its diameter is only about 2200 km. Pluto usually is the farthest planet from the sun. However, Pluto's unusual orbit sometimes takes it inside the orbit of Neptune. This means that Neptune will be the most distant planet until about 1999. Scientists think that Pluto probably is made up mostly of frozen methane, with a thin methane atmosphere. Because of its distance from Earth, Pluto is the only planet that has not yet been visited by a space probe.

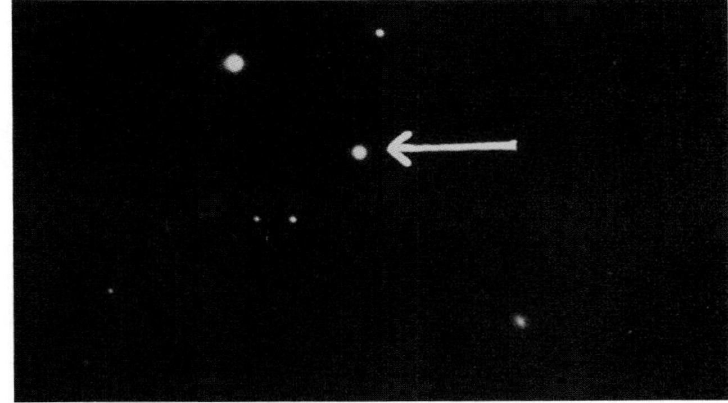

▶ ***Explain:*** Why is Pluto not always the farthest planet from the sun?

LESSON SUMMARY

- Uranus is the seventh planet from the sun, and the third largest planet in the solar system.
- Neptune is the eighth planet from the sun; it is similar to Uranus in size and mass.
- Pluto is the ninth planet from the sun; it is unlike any of the other outer planets.

CHECK *Complete the following.*

1. What is the diameter of Uranus?
2. What is the most unusual feature of Uranus?
3. How is Neptune similar to Uranus?
4. How long does Neptune take to complete one orbit around the sun?
5. Which planet was the last one visited by *Voyager 2*?

APPLY *Complete the following.*

6. **Hypothesize:** Some astronomers think that Pluto may once have been a moon of Neptune. What might have happened to pull Pluto away from Neptune and into its own orbit?

InfoSearch

Read the passage. Ask two questions about the topic that you cannot answer from the information in the passage.

Planet X After the discovery of Uranus and Neptune, astronomers observed a strange wobbling in their orbits. They thought that a ninth planet, called Planet X, beyond the orbit of Neptune could explain the wobbling. Clyde Tombaugh was an American astronomer at the Lowell Observatory in Flagstaff, Arizona. He began searching for Planet X. In 1915, Percival Lowell had predicted the general location of Planet X. Fifteen years later, in 1930, Tombaugh discovered Pluto. The planet was just where Lowell had predicted. But Pluto is too small to cause the wobbling in the orbits of Uranus and Neptune. Is there a tenth planet?

SEARCH: Use library references to find answers to your questions.

TECHNOLOGY AND SOCIETY

VOYAGER

Carl Sagan called the two *Voyager* spacecraft "a triumph of American technology." When they were launched in 1977, the *Voyagers* were programmed to explore only Jupiter and Saturn. However, controllers at the Jet Propulsion Laboratory were able to reprogram the spacecraft. The spacecraft then used the gravitational energy of each planet they passed to push them on to the next planet. In this way, *Voyager 2* reached Uranus in 1986 and Neptune in 1989. Scientists once expected the *Voyager* mission to last for only five years. Now, they expect to receive signals from the spacecraft until about 2020, when *Voyager 2* leaves the solar system and passes into interstellar space.

The technology that made the *Voyagers* possible grew out of the *Apollo* moon-landing missions of the 1960s. Engineers designed a new electrical power system and a new high-frequency communications system for the spacecraft. Today, however, the *Voyager* spacecraft are "technological antiques." Many common laptop computers are more powerful than the computers on the *Voyager* spacecraft.

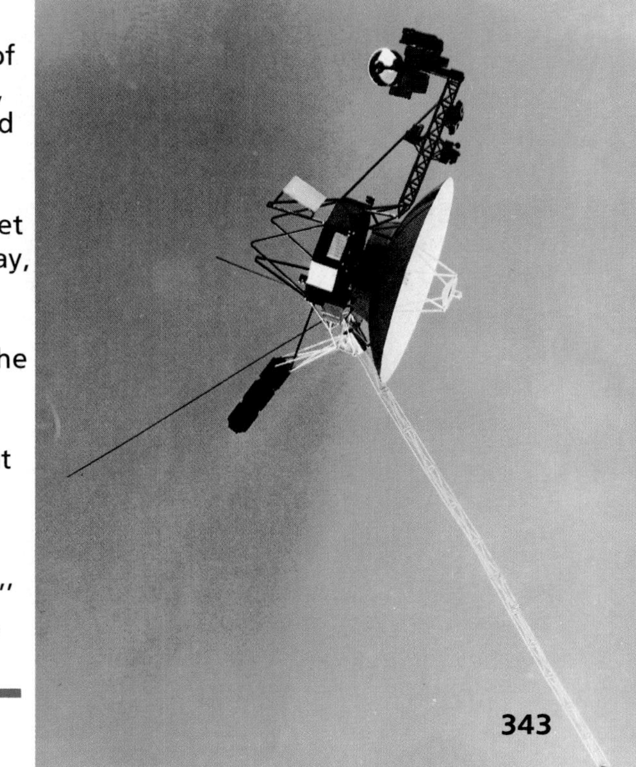

16-9 What are other objects in the solar system?

Objectives ▶ Identify the features of asteroids and comets. ▶ Compare meteoroids, meteors, and meteorites.

TechTerms

- **asteroid** (AST-uh-royd): large chunk of rock that orbits the sun
- **comet:** body made up of rock, dust, gases, and ice that orbits the sun
- **meteor** (MEE-tee-or): piece of rock or metal that enters the earth's atmosphere
- **meteorite** (MEE-tee-or-ite): piece of rock or metal that hits the earth's surface
- **meteoroid** (MEE-tee-or-oyd): piece of rock or metal that orbits the sun

Asteroids Between Mars and Jupiter, a large group of rocks orbit the sun. These rocks are called **asteroids** (AST-uh-royds). The region between Mars and Jupiter is called the asteroid belt. Asteroids are sometimes called minor planets, but they are not round like planets. They look more like chunks of broken rock. There are three kinds of asteroids. One kind is made up mostly of carbon. A second kind consists of iron and nickel. A third kind of asteroid contains silicon. The largest asteroid, Ceres, is about 1000 km in diameter. Most asteroids, however, are smaller than 10 km in diameter.

▶ ***Locate:*** Where are asteroids found?

Comets Like planets and asteroids, **comets** also are members of the solar system. Comets orbit the sun in long ellipses. Comets are made up of rock, ice, and frozen gases. A comet has three parts. The core, or nucleus, of a comet is made up of rock and ice. The core is surrounded by a cloud of gas and dust. This cloud is the coma. The nucleus and coma form the head of the comet.

The most spectacular part of a comet is its tail. The tail forms as the comet comes near the sun. The tail is made up of glowing gas and dust streaming out from the head. A comet's tail always points away from the sun.

▶ ***Name:*** What are the nucleus and coma of a comet called?

Meteoroids Smaller pieces of rock and metal called **meteoroids** (MEE-tee-or-oyds) orbit the sun. Most meteoroids are smaller than a grain of sand. Larger meteoroids may have been formed by collisions between asteroids.

Have you ever seen a shooting star streaking through the sky? These shooting stars are **meteors** (MEE-tee-ors). Meteors are meteoroids that enter the earth's atmosphere. As meteors fall through the atmosphere, friction heats them. They glow brightly and burn up.

Some meteors are large enough to reach the earth's surface. Meteors that strike the earth's surface are called **meteorites** (MEE-tee-or-ites). A meteorite may leave a large crater when it strikes the earth. Barringer Crater, in Arizona, was created when a large meteorite struck the earth 20,000 years ago.

▶ ***Name:*** What is a meteoroid that enters the earth's atmosphere called?

LESSON SUMMARY

- Asteroids orbit the sun between Mars and Jupiter.
- Comets have long, elliptical orbits.
- Meteoroids may enter the earth's atmosphere and become meteors.
- A meteor that strikes the earth's surface is a meteorite.

CHECK *Complete the following.*

1. Chunks of rock that orbit the sun between Mars and Jupiter are ______ .
2. The largest asteroid is ______ .
3. The parts of a comet are the nucleus, coma, and ______ .
4. Comets orbit the sun in long ______ orbits.
5. A meteor is a ______ that enters the earth's atmosphere.
6. Barringer Crater was created by a ______ .

APPLY *Complete the following.*

7. **Infer:** Why is the region of the solar system between Mars and Jupiter called the asteroid belt?
8. Look at the diagram of the comet. Identify the nucleus, coma, head, and tail.

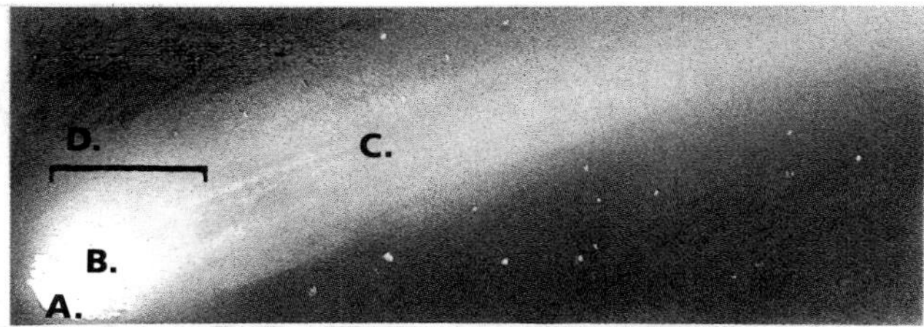

InfoSearch

Read the passage. Ask two questions about the topic that you cannot answer from the information in the passage.

Oort Cloud Astronomers think that comets may come from the Oort Cloud. The Oort Cloud is a cloud of dust and ice surrounding the solar system. It is named after a Dutch astronomer, Jan Oort. As many as 100 billion comets may be in the Oort Cloud. The Cloud is so far from the sun that comets in the Cloud take millions of years to complete one orbit. Sometimes, a comet may fall into a long orbit toward the sun and back to the Cloud.

SEARCH: Use library references to find answers to your questions.

LEISURE ACTIVITY

AMATEUR ASTRONOMY

Using only your eyes, you can see and identify many stars in the summer and winter sky. You do not need binoculars or a telescope to locate some planets in the morning and evening sky. The phases of the moon are easily observed. However, a telescope or good binoculars will allow you to further explore all of these objects.

With a telescope, you can probe the depths of space, and locate stars and galaxies. You can observe the craters and maria of the moon up close. A telescope shows the planets as small disks, not just points of light. Some of a planet's satellites also may be visible through a telescope. An amateur astronomer can track the path of Jupiter's Great Red Spot, count the rings of Saturn, and watch the advance and retreat of the polar icecaps on Mars.

A lifetime of adventure and discovery awaits the amateur astronomer. Amateur astronomers can even contribute to scientific research. Many new asteroids and comets have been discovered by amateur astronomers. The night sky presents a new and ever-changing face each night of the year.

UNIT 16 Challenges

STUDY HINT Before you begin the Unit Challenges, review the TechTerms and Lesson Summary for each lesson in this unit.

TechTerms

aphelion (330)
asteroid (344)
comet (344)
craters (336)
ellipse (330)
gravity (332)
maria (336)
meteor (344)
meteorite (344)
meteoroid (344)
nebula (328)
orbit (328)
perihelion (330)
satellite (334)
solar system (328)

TechTerm Challenges

Matching *Write the TechTerm that best matches each description.*

1. curved path of one object around another object in space
2. flattened circle, or oval
3. body made up of rock, dust, gases, and ice that orbits the sun
4. force of attraction between all objects in the universe
5. object orbiting a body in space

Applying Definitions *Explain the difference between the words in each pair. Write your answers in complete sentences.*

1. asteroid, meteoroid
2. meteor, meteorite
3. aphelion, perihelion
4. craters, maria
5. nebula, solar system
6. satellite, rings

Content Challenges

Multiple Choice *Write the letter of the term that best completes each statement.*

1. The speed at which the earth travels in its orbit is called its orbital
   a. ellipse. **b.** velocity. **c.** perihelion. **d.** aphelion.
2. The planet that has been called earth's twin is
   a. Venus. **b.** Mercury. **c.** Pluto. **d.** Jupiter.
3. The Great Red Spot is the best known feature of
   a. Pluto. **b.** Neptune. **c.** Uranus. **d.** Jupiter.
4. The inner planets are Mercury, Venus, Earth, and
   a. Jupiter. **b.** Mars. **c.** Saturn. **d.** Pluto.
5. As a planet gets closer to the sun, the gravitational attraction between the planet and the sun
   a. decreases. **b.** increases. **c.** goes down. **d.** stays the same.
6. Asteroids are made up of carbon, iron and nickel, or
   a. dust. **b.** helium. **c.** silicon. **d.** hydrogen.
7. The planet that usually is the farthest from the sun is
   a. Pluto. **b.** Neptune. **c.** Uranus. **d.** Jupiter.

8. The only planets in the solar system without at least one moon are
   a. Jupiter and Pluto. b. Earth and Venus. c. Jupiter and Mercury. d. Mercury and Venus.
9. American astronauts first set foot on the moon in
   a. 1957. b. 1969. c. 1972. d. 1975.
10. The second largest planet in the solar system is
   a. Pluto. b. Earth. c. Saturn. d. Jupiter.
11. The earth is closest to the sun in
   a. July. b. September. c. March. d. January.
12. Pluto's orbit sometimes takes it inside the orbit of
   a. Uranus. b. Saturn. c. Neptune. d. Mars.
13. The light areas on the moon are
   a. mountains. b. craters. c. plains. d. oceans.
14. The first planet to be discovered since ancient times is
   a. Pluto. b. Uranus. c. Mars. d. Mercury.
15. The four largest moons of Jupiter were discovered by
   a. Copernicus. b. Galileo. c. Kepler. d. *Voyager 2.*

True/False *Write true if the statement is true. If the statement is false, change the underlined term to make the statement true.*

1. Some scientists think that a nebula expanded to form the solar system.
2. The moon's gravity is greater than the earth's gravity.
3. The core of a comet is made up of rock and ice.
4. The earth moves fastest at perihelion.
5. The largest planet in the solar system is Neptune.
6. Planets near the sun move faster than planets farther from the sun.
7. The closest planet to the sun is Mercury.
8. Barringer Crater in Arizona was created when a large meteor hit the earth.
9. The earth has one ring.
10. Uranus is tipped on its side.
11. Earth is classified as an outer planet.
12. The moon's surface has three main features.
13. The region between Mars and Jupiter is called the meteoroid belt.
14. The earth travels around the sun in a circular orbit.
15. Saturn's density is less than the density of any other planet.

Understanding the Features

Reading Critically *Use the feature reading selections to answer the following. Page numbers for the features are shown in parentheses.*

1. What does the Big Bang Theory state? (329)
2. How had all the known moons been discovered before the late 1970s? (335)
3. Why are scientists interested in studying the greenhouse effect on Venus? (339)
4. What did the small probe from *Galileo* measure as it fell through Jupiter's atmosphere? (341)
5. When will *Voyager 2* leave the solar system? (343)
6. What are three things an amateur astronomer can see through a telescope? (345)

Concept Challenges

Interpreting a Table *Use Table 1 to answer each of the following.*

Table 1 Planets, Moons, and Rings		
PLANET	NUMBER OF MOONS	RINGS
Mercury	0	No
Venus	0	No
Earth	1	No
Mars	2	No
Jupiter	16	Yes
Saturn	17	Yes
Uranus	15	Yes
Neptune	8	Yes
Pluto	1	No

1. How many moons does Neptune have?
2. What is the only outer planet without rings?
3. What planet has the most known moons?
4. Do any of the inner planets have rings?
5. Which planet other than Earth has only one moon?

Critical Thinking *Answer each of the following in complete sentences.*

1. Why is the term "wanderer" inaccurate for describing a planet?
2. Why do rocks on the moon not weather or erode like rocks on the earth?
3. In what way is Pluto more similar to the inner planets than it is to the outer planets?
4. What are some reasons astronauts may go back to the moon?
5. How do you think the rings around some planets formed?

Finding Out More

1. Research the three parts of Isaac Newton's law of gravitation. In an oral report, describe the three parts, and how they apply to planets orbiting the sun.
2. Using library references, find out the distances from the sun (in km) of the nine planets, and their diameters. Make a chart listing the information.
3. Write a report on Halley's comet. Describe the comet, and how often it can be seen from the earth. Use library references as guides.
4. Use library references to write a brief biography about Neil Armstrong, the first person to walk on the moon.

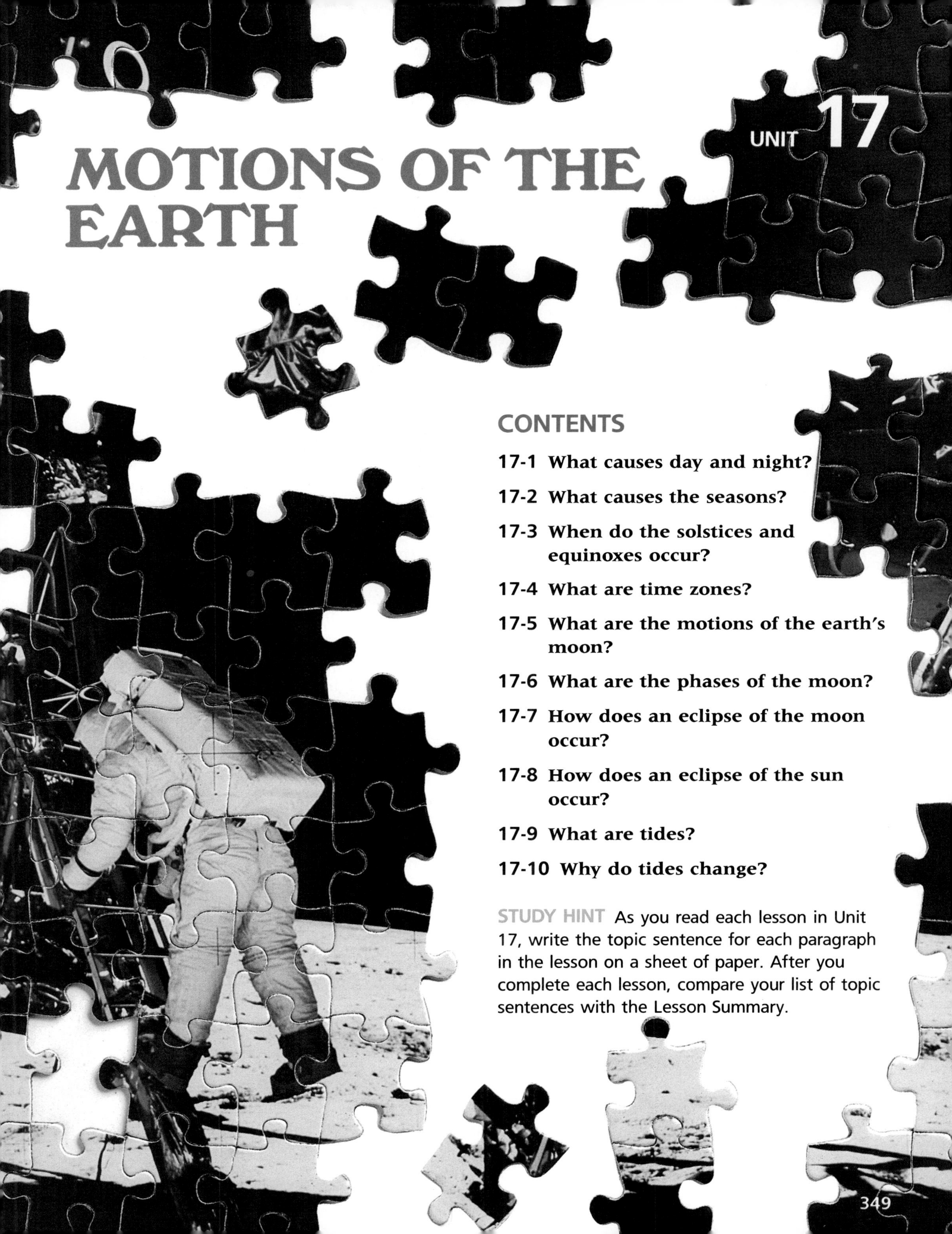

UNIT 17 MOTIONS OF THE EARTH

CONTENTS

STUDY HINT As you read each lesson in Unit 17, write the topic sentence for each paragraph in the lesson on a sheet of paper. After you complete each lesson, compare your list of topic sentences with the Lesson Summary.

17-1 What causes day and night?

Objective ▶ Explain the causes of day and night.

TechTerms

- ▶ **axis** (AK-sis): imaginary line through the center of a planet on which the planet rotates
- ▶ **revolution** (reh-vuh-LOO-shun): movement of a planet in its orbit
- ▶ **rotation** (roh-TAY-shun): spinning of a planet on its axis

Earth's Movements Although you cannot feel it, the earth is always moving. The earth moves in an orbit around the sun. This movement is called **revolution** (reh-vuh-LOO-shun). The earth also spins on its **axis** (AK-sis). An axis is an imaginary line around which something spins. The earth's axis runs from the North Pole to the South Pole. The spinning of the earth on it's axis is called **rotation** (roh-TAY-shun).

▶ ***Identify:*** What are two motions of the earth?

Day and Night The earth's rotation causes day and night. The sun shines on only one side of the earth at a time. The side of the earth that faces the sun has daylight. The side that faces away from the sun has night.

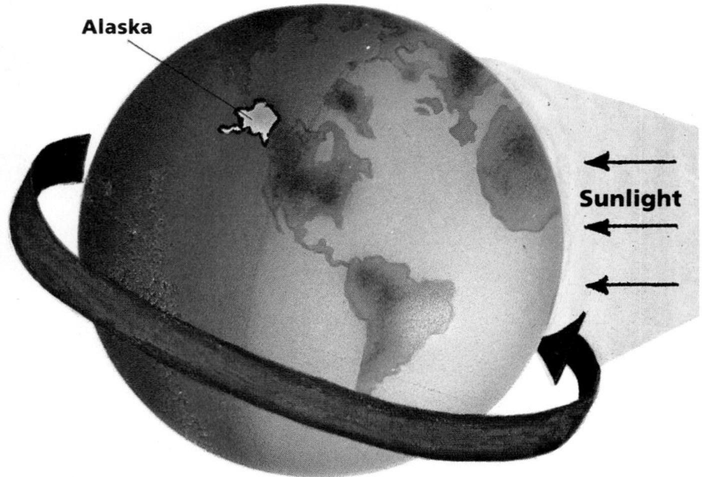

▶ ***Explain:*** What causes day and night?

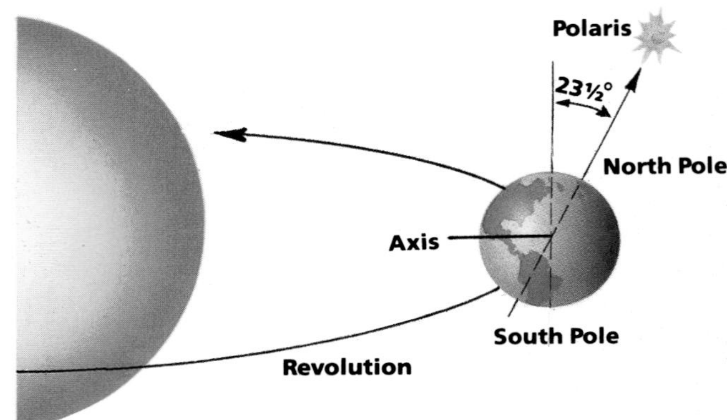

Length of Day and Night You may have noticed that during the year, the number of daylight hours changes. During the summer, there are more hours of daylight than of darkness. During the winter, there are more hours of darkness than of daylight. Why do the number of daylight hours change throughout the year? The number of daylight hours changes because the earth's axis is tilted.

The earth's axis is tilted at an angle of 23 ½°. As a result, the North Pole of the earth points toward Polaris. Polaris also is called the North Star. The axis always points in the same direction as the earth moves in its orbit. If the earth's axis were not tilted, all parts of the earth would always have 12 hours of daylight and 12 hours of night.

▶ ***State:*** Why are the number of hours of daylight and darkness not the same all year?

Sunrise and Sunset When viewed from the North Pole, the earth rotates on its axis from west to east. This rotation makes the sun appear to rise, or come up, in the east and set, or go down, in the west. As the earth rotates, the sun seems to move across the sky from east to west.

▶ ***Relate:*** In which direction does the earth rotate?

LESSON SUMMARY

- Revolution and rotation are the two movements of the earth.
- The earth's rotation causes day and night.
- The number of daylight hours changes throughout the year because the earth's axis is tilted.
- If the earth's axis were not tilted, all parts of the earth would have 12 hours of day and 12 hours of night.
- The sun rises in the east and sets in the west because of the earth's rotation.

CHECK *Write true if the statement is true. If the statement is false, change the underlined term to make the statement true.*

1. The movement of the earth around the sun is called rotation.
2. The change from day to night is caused by the earth's revolution.
3. The sun appears to rise in the east.
4. The earth rotates on its axis from east to west.

APPLY *Complete the following.*

5. **Contrast:** How does the earth's rotation differ from its revolution?
6. **Predict:** What would happen if the earth did not rotate?
7. Like the sun, the moon rises and sets. Explain why the moon appears to rise in the east and set in the west.
8. **Analyze:** During the summer months, northern Alaska has 24 hours of sunlight. During the winter months, northern Alaska has 24 hours of darkness. Use Figure 2 to explain why this happens.

Ideas in Action

IDEA: Daylight savings time extends daylight one hour later in the evening by artificially beginning the day one hour earlier. Many states use daylight savings time during the summer months.
ACTION: Explain why your state uses or does not use daylight savings time.

SCIENCE CONNECTION

EVIDENCE OF EARTH'S ROTATION

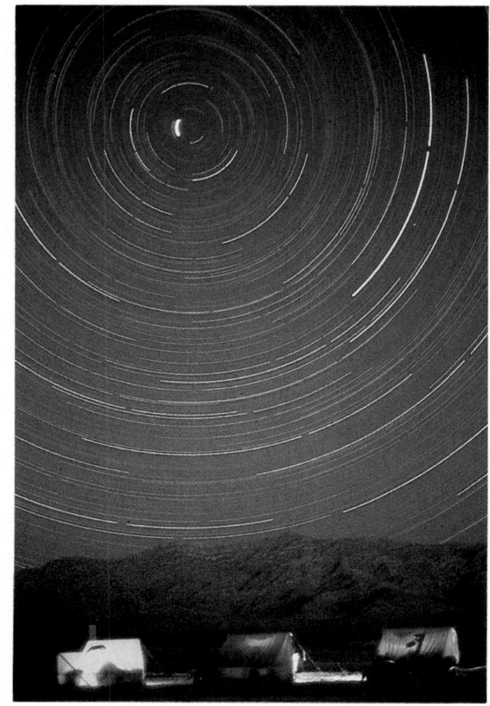

The photograph shows a time exposure of stars. In an ordinary photograph, stars look like tiny dots of light. In this photograph, the stars have made circular paths. When a time exposure is taken, the camera shutter is left open for some time. The earth turned while the shutter was open. This caused the camera to turn, also. The circular paths in the photograph are star trails. The trails are circular because the earth rotated beneath the stars.

A pendulum also can be used to show that earth rotates. A pendulum is a weight attached to a wire or string that swings back and forth. In Washington, DC at the Smithsonian Institute, there is a large pendulum. This pendulum appears to be constantly changing direction. The pendulum is not really changing its direction. The earth is rotating beneath the pendulum. That is what makes the pendulum seem to change direction.

17-2 What causes the seasons?

Objective ▸ Explain how the tilt of the earth's axis causes the change of season.

Near and Far During the year, there are differences in the distance between the earth and the sun. These differences have nothing to do with the change in seasons. The earth is closest to the sun in January. The Northern Hemisphere has winter. In July, the earth is farthest from the sun. Yet, this is when the Northern Hemisphere has summer. The seasons do not depend on the distance of the earth from the sun.

▸ ***Name:*** During which season is the Northern Hemisphere closest to the sun?

Earth's Tilt and Seasons As you know, the earth's axis is tilted. The seasons are caused by the tilt of the earth's axis. The earth's axis is tilted toward the sun for part of the year. Its axis is tilted away from the sun for the other part of the year.

The angle of the sun's rays and the number of daylight hours cause the differences in seasons. When the Northern Hemisphere is tilted toward the sun, it receives direct rays. Direct rays heat best. The Northern Hemisphere also has more hours of daylight during this time. The combination of more daylight hours and direct rays cause the earth to get more heat. The higher temperatures cause summer.

At the same time, the Southern Hemisphere is tilted away from the sun. The sun's rays are slanted. Slanted rays spread out the heat. There also are fewer daylight hours. The combination of fewer daylight hours and slanted rays cause the earth to get less heat. Temperatures drop. Lower temperatures cause winter.

▸ ***Describe:*** What causes the change of season?

Opposite Seasons The Northern and Southern Hemispheres have opposite seasons. Look at the diagram of the earth's seasons. Notice that when the Northern Hemisphere gets slanted rays, it has winter. At the same time, the Southern Hemisphere gets direct rays and has summer. When summer comes to the Northern Hemisphere, it is winter in the Southern Hemisphere.

▸ ***Name:*** If it is summer in the Northern Hemisphere, what season is it in the Southern Hemisphere?

LESSON SUMMARY

- During the year, there are differences in the distance between the earth and the sun.
- The seasons are caused by the earth's tilted axis.
- The combination of direct rays and more daylight hours causes the earth to heat up.
- The combination of slanted rays and less hours of daylight causes the earth to cool off.
- The Northern and Southern hemispheres have opposite seasons.

CHECK *Write true if the statement is true. If the statement is false, change the underlined term to make the statement true.*

1. The North Pole points away from the sun during the summer.
2. During the winter, the sun's rays are slanted.
3. In January, the earth is farthest from the sun.
4. The seasons are caused by the earth's tilted axis.
5. The Northern and Southern hemispheres have the same seasons.

APPLY *Complete the following.*

6. **Analyze:** If the North Pole is having summer, what season is the South Pole having?
7. **Infer:** Why do you think direct sunlight produces more heat than indirect sunlight?

Ideas in Action

IDEA: Places located near the equator always receive direct rays from the sun. As a result, temperatures in these areas are always warm.

ACTION: Explain three ways that your life would change if the area in which you live always had a warm climate.

ACTIVITY

MODELING DIRECT AND SLANTED RAYS

You will need a flashlight, and graph paper.

1. Shine a flashlight straight down on a piece of graph paper. Count how many boxes are lighted by the flashlight. Record the number.
2. Tilt the flashlight, making sure you keep it at the same height. Again, count the number of boxes that are lighted by the flashlight. Record the number.

Questions

1. Which light rays were spread out over a larger area, the direct rays or the slanted rays?
2. **Observe:** Which rays were brighter, the direct rays or the slanted rays.
3. **Hypothesize:** Which rays do you think heat better, direct rays or slanted rays?
4. When do you think areas of the earth get direct rays of the sun, in the summer or in the winter? Explain.
5. When do you think areas of the earth get the sun's rays at a slant, in the summer or in the winter? Explain.

17-3 When do the solstices and equinoxes occur?

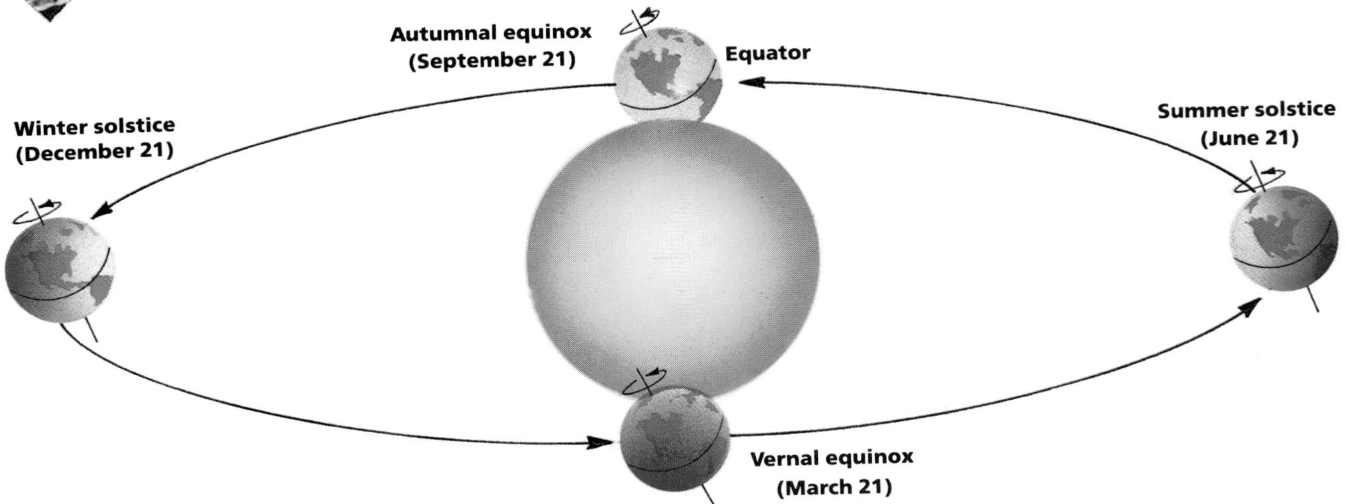

Objective ▶ Define solstice and equinox.

TechTerms

- ▶ **equinox** (EE-kwuh-nahks): "equal night"; day on which the sun shines directly on the equator
- ▶ **solstice** (SAHL-stis): "sun stop"; day on which the North Pole points toward or away from the sun

Solstices and Equinoxes Have you ever heard the words **"solstice"** (SAHL-stis) and **"equinox"** (EE-kwuh-nahks)? If you have, you know that a solstice or an equinox is a day that marks the beginning of a season. "Solstice" means "sun stop." The word "equinox" means "equal night."

▶ ***Define:*** What does the word "equinox" mean?

Summer Solstice In the Northern Hemisphere, the first day of summer is June 21. On this day, the North Pole points directly toward the sun. The sun seems to follow its highest path across the sky. This day is the summer solstice. On this day, the North Pole has 24 hours of daylight. At the same time, the South Pole points away from the sun. The South Pole has 24 hours of darkness. Winter begins on this date in the Southern Hemisphere.

▶ ***Identify:*** What day marks the first day of winter in the Southern Hemisphere?

Winter Solstice The first day of winter in the Northern Hemisphere is December 21. This day is called the winter solstice. On the winter solstice, the North Pole points away from the sun. The sun seems to follow its lowest path across the sky. On this day, the South Pole has 24 hours of daylight.

▶ ***Interpret:*** On which day of the year does the North Pole have 24 hours of darkness?

Equinoxes On two days of the year, the sun shines directly on the equator. These days are the equinoxes. The spring, or vernal, equinox occurs on March 21. This is the first day of spring. The fall, or autumnal (aw-TUM-nul), equinox occurs on September 21. The autumnal equinox marks the first day of autumn. During an equinox, all places on the earth have 12 hours of darkness and 12 hours of daylight.

▶ ***Name:*** On which days of the year does the North Pole have 12 hours of daylight and 12 hours of night?

LESSON SUMMARY

Solstices and equinoxes are days that mark the changes in seasons.

The North Pole points directly toward the sun on the summer solstice.

The North Pole points away from the sun on the winter solstice.

The sun shines directly on the equator on the vernal and autumnal equinoxes.

CHECK *Complete the following.*

1. An ______ occurs on a day with 12 hours of daylight and 12 hours of darkness.
2. December 21 is the ______ solstice in the Southern Hemisphere.
3. The beginning of winter in the Northern Hemisphere is marked by the ______ .

APPLY *Complete the following.*

4. **Relate:** "Equinox" means "equal night." How does this definition relate to the number of hours of daylight and darkness on the spring and autumnal equinoxes?
5. **Infer:** Do the days get longer or shorter in the Northern Hemisphere after the autumnal equinox?
6. What are some characteristics of winter in your area?

Ideas in Action

IDEA: On the winter solstice, the North Pole has 24 hours of darkness.

ACTION: Identify the ways in which 24 hours of darkness would affect your actions during the day.

Skill Builder

Using Prefixes A prefix is a word part that appears at the beginning of a word. The prefix "equi-" means equal. Find five words in the dictionary that contain the prefix "equi-." Write down these words and their definitions on a separate sheet of paper. Circle the part of the definition that relates to the prefix.

SCIENCE CONNECTION

STONEHENGE

An ancient monument called Stonehenge stands on a plain in Wiltshire, England. Stonehenge was built around 1848 BC. The monument is made up of huge blocks of sandstone 4 m high. They form a circle 30 m across. On top of these stones, there are smaller stone blocks. Inside the circle, there are two horseshoe shaped sets of stones. A flat block of sandstone 5 m long sets in the inner horseshoe set of stones. A stone marker is about 73 m away from the flat sandstone block.

Stonehenge acts as a giant calendar. It can be used to predict the seasons. It also can be used to predict the solstices and equinoxes. A shadow is cast by the stone marker onto the flat sandstone block. This happens on the summer solstice.

17-4 What are time zones?

Objectives ▶ Recognize the importance of standard time zones. ▶ Identify four time zones in the United States.

TechTerms

- ▶ **international date line:** the boundary formed where the first and twenty-fourth time zone meet
- ▶ **solar noon:** time when the sun is highest in the sky

Solar Time The sun can be used to tell time. Using the sun to measure time is called solar time. When the sun is highest in the sky, the time is **solar noon.** Because the earth rotates, different places have solar noon at different times. For example, when it is solar noon in Philadelphia, it is 4 minutes later in New York and 17 minutes later in Boston.

Hypothesize: State a problem that is likely to arise using solar time.

Time zones In 1883, the earth was divided into 24 time zones, each 15° of longitude wide. All places within a time zone have the same time. This time is called standard time.

The United States has four time zones. These time zones are Eastern Standard Time, Central Standard Time, Mountain Standard Time, and Pacific Standard Time. All of the states in the United States, except Hawaii and Alaska, are in one of these time zones. As you move west, the time in each zone is one hour earlier than in the previous time zone. As a result, when it is noon in New York, it is 11:00 AM in Chicago.

Look at the map of the time zones shown in Figure 1. Notice that time zones do not have straight boundaries. The boundaries were drawn this way to keep whole states or large neighboring cities in the same time zone.

Calculate: If it is 12:00 noon in California, what time is it in Virginia?

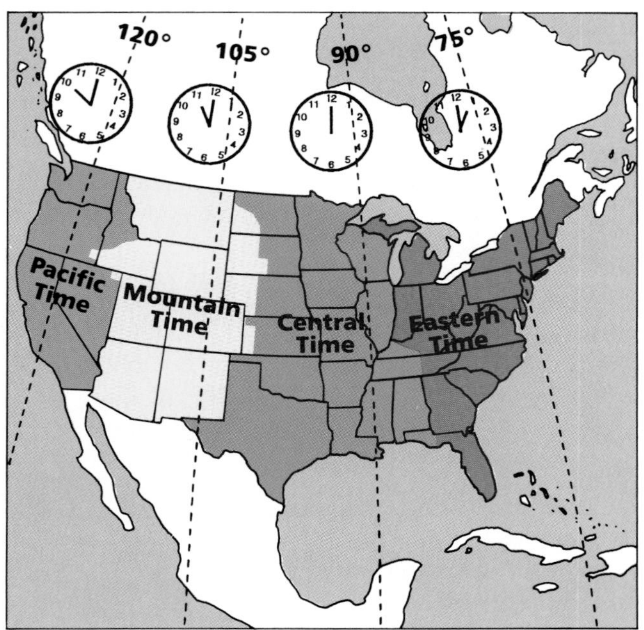

Figure 1

International Date line There are 24 standard time zones and 24 hours in a day. The first time zone is on one side of the **international date line.** The twenty-fourth time zone is on the other side of the international date line. As you cross the international date line, you either gain or lose 24 hours. If you were to travel west, you would have to move your calendar ahead one full day when you crossed the international date line.

Infer: What happens to the date if you cross the international date line going east?

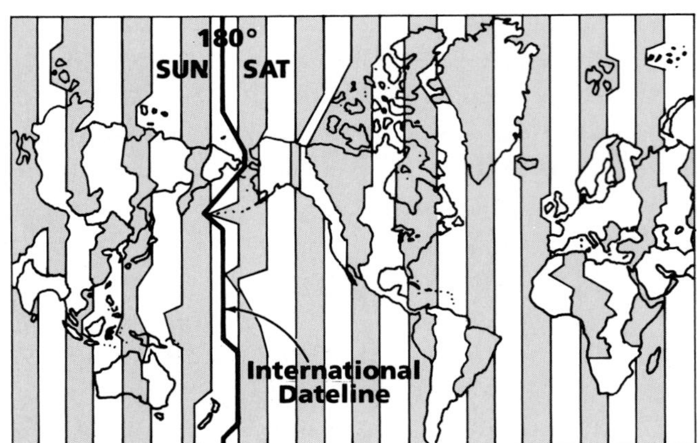

Figure 2

LESSON SUMMARY

When the sun is highest in the sky, the time is solar noon.

The earth is divided into 24 time zones.

The four standard time zones in the United States are Eastern Standard Time, Central Standard Time, Mountain Standard Time, and Pacific Standard Time.

Boundaries between time zones are drawn to keep whole states and neighboring cities in the same time zone.

As you cross the international date line, you either gain or lose one full day.

CHECK *Complete the following.*

1. Using the sun to measure time is _______ .
2. The time in each of the 24 time zones is _______ .
3. If you cross the international date line going east, you would _______ 24 hours.

APPLY *Use Figure 1 on page 372 to answer the following.*

4. In which time zone is most of Texas located?
5. **Analyze:** If it is 3:00 pm in Florida, what time is it in Oregon?
6. **Calculate:** If you left California at 12:00 noon Pacific Time, and took a six hour plane trip to Boston, when would you land in Boston, Eastern Standard Time?
7. In which time zone do you live?

Complete the following.

8. **Analyze:** The earth rotates from west to east. If it is solar noon where you live, would a town to your west have solar noon before you or after you? Explain.

InfoSearch

Read the passage. Ask two questions about the topic that you cannot answer from the information in the passage.

Jet Lag Jet lag is a term given to the general tired feeling people get when they travel across three or more time zones. Jet lag occurs because your body is adjusted to the time where you live, and not to the time zone to which you traveled. It is easier for your body to adjust to a longer day by traveling west, than to a shorter day traveling east. For this reason, jet lag usually affects people who are flying east more than people who are flying west.

SEARCH: Use library references to find answers to your questions.

LEISURE ACTIVITY

TRAVEL

For millions of people, vacation means traveling. People board airplanes, ships, trains, and buses, to travel. They also travel in their own cars. For example, many people in the United States enjoy taking car trips to other states. Traveling by car allows them to see many parts of the country.

Some people travel for rest and relaxation. Others travel to visit historic places, or experience other cultures. Traveling to a foreign country allows you to see the people's customs, sample their food, and so on. Many people also enjoy shopping when they travel. They like to bring home souvenirs of their trip.

Traveling is a way to have fun and learn at the same time. If you need help planning a trip, contact a travel agency in your area. Travel agencies can help you plan your trip, and make travel arrangements. A state or country's Department of Tourism also is a good source of information.

17-5 What are the motions of the earth's moon?

Objective ▶ Describe and identify two motions of the earth's moon.

TechTerms

- ▶ **apogee** (AP-uh-jee): point at which the moon is farthest from the earth
- ▶ **perigee** (PER-uh-jee): point at which the moon is closest to the earth

Rotation and Revolution Like the earth, the moon rotates on an axis. The moon rotates very slowly. In fact, it takes the moon 27 1/3 days to rotate once on its axis.

The moon also revolves around the earth. The moon revolves around the earth at a speed of 3500 km/h. The moon takes 27 1/3 days to make one complete revolution around the earth. This is the same time that it takes the moon to make one rotation on its axis. As a result, the same side of the moon is always facing the earth.

▶ *Calculate:* How many km does the moon travel in one day?

Apogee and Perigee The moon's orbit around the earth is shown in Figure 1. When the moon is farthest from the earth, it is at **apogee** (AP-uh-jee). The distance from the moon to the earth at apogee is 409,000 km. When the moon is closest to the earth, it is at **perigee** (PER-uh-jee). At perigee, the distance from the moon to the earth is 365,000 km.

▶ *Calculate:* How much farther from the earth is the moon at apogee than at perigee?

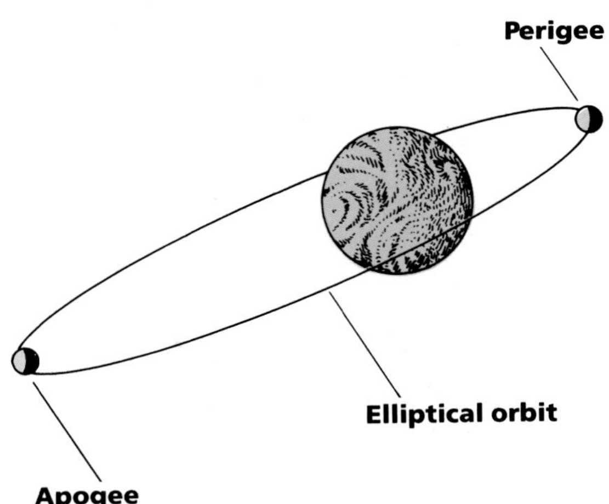

Figure 1

Figure 2

Moon Rise The earth's rotation brings the moon into view every day. Like the sun, the moon appears to rise in the east and set in the west. The moon rises and sets a little later each day. Suppose you saw the moon rise at 9:00 PM on Wednesday. On Thursday, you would see the moon rise at 9:50 PM. As the moon revolves around the earth, the earth must go through more than one rotation to "catch up" with the moon. The earth must rotate 24 hours and 50 minutes to bring the moon back into view. As a result, the moon rises 50 minutes later each day.

▶ *Explain:* Why does the moon rise 50 minutes later each day?

LESSON SUMMARY

- It takes the moon 27 1/3 days to rotate once on its axis.
- The moon revolves around the earth in the same way the earth revolves around the sun.
- The same side of the moon is always facing the earth because the moon rotates at the same speed as it revolves.
- Apogee and perigee are two terms used to describe the moon's position in relation to the earth.
- The moon appears to rise in the east and set in the west.

CHECK *Complete the following.*

1. How long does it take the moon to make one complete revolution around the earth?
2. What are the two motions of the moon?
3. Why do you not see all sides of the moon?
4. The moon does not always rise at the same time. Why?

APPLY *Complete the following.*

5. Why does the moon appear to rise in the east and set in the west?
6. **Analyze:** The moon has completed three-quarters of its revolution around the earth. During the same time, how much has the moon rotated?
7. **Calculate:** If the moon rose at 6:45 on Tuesday, what time will the moon rise on Thursday?

Skill Builder

Researching When you research, you gather information about a topic. The word "month" comes from a variation of the Greek word meaning "'moon." Using library resources, find out how the word "month" got its name.

Skill Builder

Applying Definitions The word "perigee" contains the prefix "peri-". The prefix "peri-" means "around," "surrounding," or "close." Perigee is when the moon is closest to the earth. Using a dictionary, find five words that contain the prefix "peri-". List these words with their definitions. Explain how the prefix "peri-" relates to the meaning of each word on your list.

PEOPLE IN SCIENCE

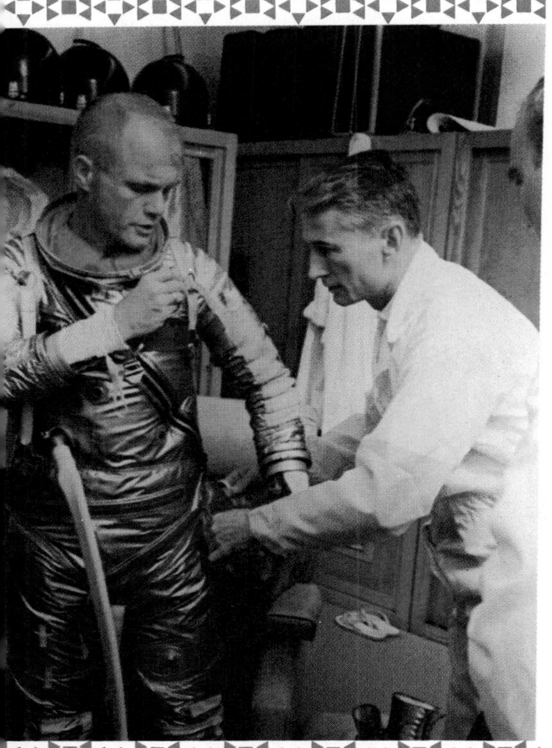

JOHN GLENN (1921–present)

The United States began its space program in 1957. Seven people were chosen to train as astronauts. One of these men was John Glenn. John Glenn made a historic space flight on February 20, 1962. He became the first American to orbit the earth. In his spacecraft, *Friendship 7,* Glenn orbited the earth three times. He was the first person to see the earth rotate. The trip lasted 4 hours and 55 minutes. Glenn flew a distance of 80,996 miles. He returned to earth a national hero.

John Glenn was born in Cambridge, Ohio. He served in World War II as a Marine Corps pilot. After the war, Glenn returned to college and graduated with a degree in chemistry. In 1957, Glenn set a transcontinental speed record by flying from Los Angeles to New York City in 3 hours and 23 minutes. Glenn retired from the space program in 1964. In 1974, Glenn was elected United States senator from Ohio. John Glenn is still a senator today.

17-6 What are the phases of the moon?

Objective ▶ Recognize and identify the different phases of the moon.

TechTerms

- ▶ **crescent** (KRES-ent) **phase:** phase when less than half the moon is visible
- ▶ **gibbous** (GIB-us) **phase:** phase when more than half the moon is visible
- ▶ **phases** (FAYZ-uz): changing shapes of the moon

Phases of the Moon From the earth, the moon sometimes looks round. At other times, the moon looks like a thin sliver. Why does the moon appear to change shape? The moon appears to change shape because of the way it reflects light from the sun. The changing shapes of the moon are called **phases** (FAYZ-uz). The phases of the moon depend upon the positions of the sun, the moon, and the earth.

▶ ***Identify:*** What causes the moon to appear to change shape?

Waxing Phases Look at the picture of the phases of the moon. When the side of the moon facing the earth is dark, it appears as if there is no moon at all. This is called a new moon. As the moon revolves around the earth, a small part of the moon becomes visible. As the part of the moon that is visible increases, the moon is waxing. The first phase is called the waxing **crescent** (KRES-ent) **phase.** During the crescent phase, less than half of the moon is visible. When the moon has moved one-quarter of the way around the earth, it enters the first-quarter phase. At the first-quarter phase, one-half of the side of the moon facing the earth is visible.

As the moon continues in its orbit, more and more of the side facing the earth becomes visible. This is called the waxing **gibbous** (GIB-us) **phase.** During the gibbous phase, more than half of the moon is visible. Finally, the moon completes half of its trip around the earth. The whole surface facing the earth is visible. This is the full moon.

▶ ***Define:*** What is the gibbous phase of the moon?

Waning Phases As the moon continues to move around the earth, less and less of the surface is visible. As the visible part of the moon decreases, the moon is waning (WAYN-ing). After the full moon, the moon enters the waning gibbous phase. At the last-quarter phase, only half of the moon's surface facing the earth is visible. The last phase of the moon is the waning crescent phase. The moon takes 29 1/2 days to go through all of its phases. This is a little longer than the time for one revolution of the moon around the earth.

▶ ***Compare:*** When do the waxing and waning crescent phases of the moon take place?

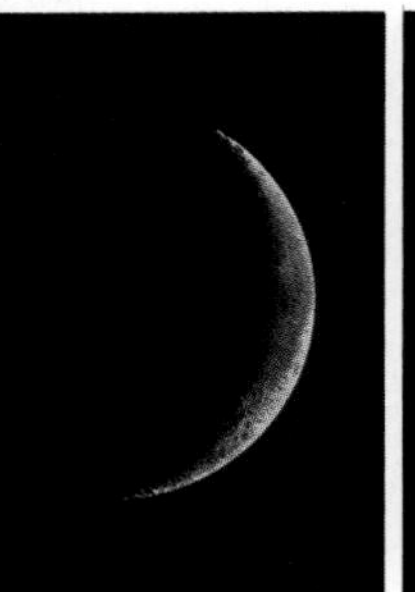
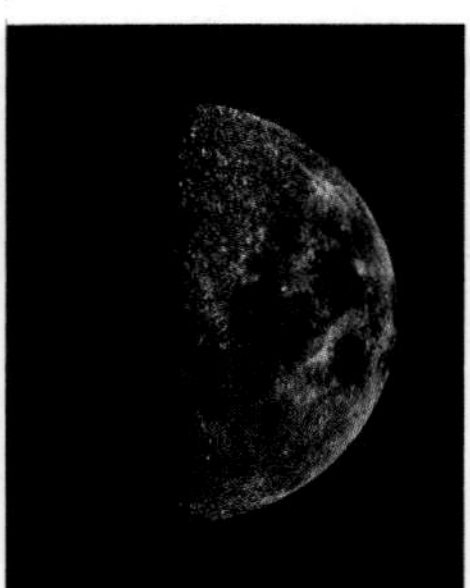

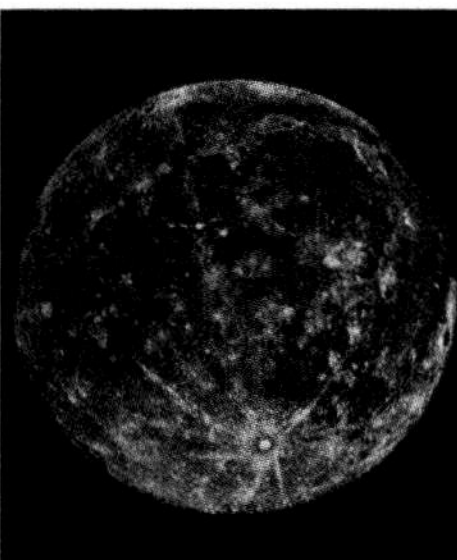

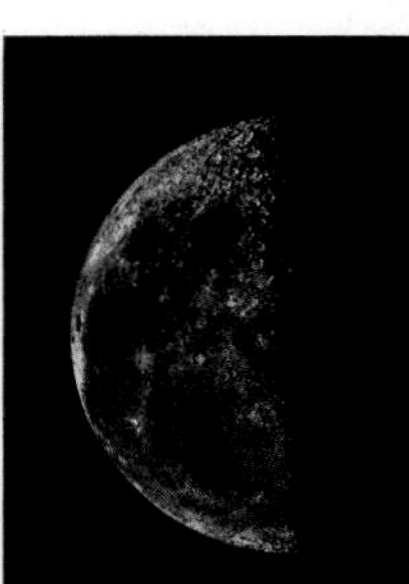
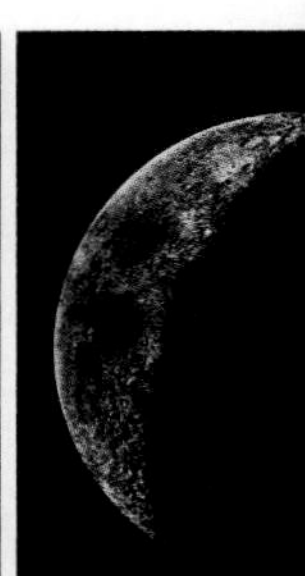

LESSON SUMMARY

- The phases of the moon depend on the positions of the sun, the moon, and the earth.
- After the new moon, the moon goes through waxing phases.
- When the moon has completed half its trip around the earth, it is called a full moon.
- After the full moon, the moon goes through waning phases.

CHECK *Complete the following.*

1. The moon reflects light from the ______ .
2. The phases of the moon depend on the positions of the earth, ______, and sun.
3. During the ______ phase of the moon, half of the side of the moon facing earth is visible.
4. When the moon has finished half of its revolution around the earth, the moon is called a ______ moon.
5. The moon goes through all of its phases in ______ days.

APPLY *Complete the following.*

6. **Contrast:** What is the difference between a crescent phase and a quarter phase of the moon?
7. **Predict:** What would the moon look like if it did not reflect light from the sun?
8. **Sequence:** List the eight phases of the moon in order, beginning with the new moon.
9. **Model:** Draw a sketch of each phase of the moon as it would be seen from the earth. Label each of your sketches.

Skill Builder

Making a Lunar Calendar The time period between one full moon and the next full moon is called a lunar month. On a calendar, identify each of the moon's phases for the next two months. How does the length of the lunar month compare to the length of the actual month?

CAREER IN EARTH SCIENCE

ASTRONAUT

An astronaut is an American pilot or scientist who travels and works in space. Astronauts perform many different duties on their job. Before a space mission, they may help design and test spacecraft, and other space equipment. While in space, astronauts operate their spacecraft and analyze any problems that arise. They also carry out experiments in space. Astronauts gather information that helps people learn more about the earth and the rest of the universe.

Astronauts work for the National Aeronautics and Space Administration, or NASA. Many astronauts also are military officers. NASA puts astronauts through a difficult training program. During their training, astronauts learn how to perform their duties in space. Astronauts get most of their training at the Johnson Space Center in Houston, Texas.

To be an astronaut, you need a good understanding of mathematics and science. Most astronauts have advanced degrees in science or engineering. Pilots also have many hours of flight experience.

17-7 How does an eclipse of the moon occur?

Objectives ▶ Describe a lunar eclipse. ▶ Distinguish between a total and partial lunar eclipse.

TechTerms

- ▶ **lunar eclipse** (uh-CLIPS): passing of the moon through the earth's shadow
- ▶ **penumbra** (peh-NUM-bruh): light part of a shadow
- ▶ **umbra** (UM-bruh): dark part of a shadow

Shadows When you walk outside on a sunny day, you can see your shadow. A shadow is formed when an object blocks a light source. A shadow has two parts. The center of a shadow is very dark. The dark part of a shadow is called the **umbra** (UM-bruh). Around the outside of a shadow, you will see a lighter part. The light part of a shadow is called the **penumbra** (peh-NUM-bruh). People and objects are not the only things that can cast shadows. The earth, the moon, and other bodies in space also cast shadows.

Identify: What are the two parts of a shadow?

Eclipse of the Moon As the moon revolves around the earth, it usually passes above or below the earth's shadow. Sometimes the moon passes directly through the earth's shadow. As a result, sunlight is blocked from reaching the moon. When sunlight is blocked from the moon, a **lunar eclipse** (uh-CLIPS) occurs. A lunar eclipse can occur only during the full-moon phase.

Define: What is a lunar eclipse?

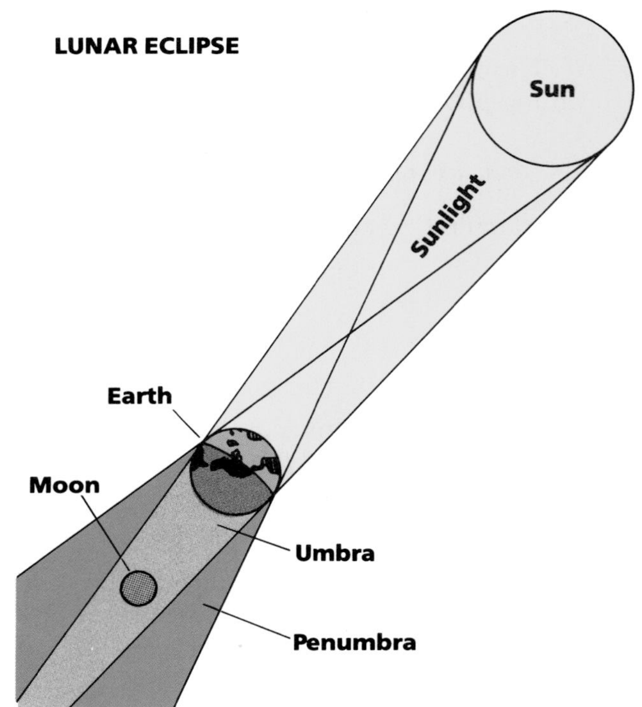

Total or Partial Eclipses Sometimes the moon moves entirely into the earth's umbra. When this happens, all of the sun's light is blocked. The entire face of the moon darkens. This is called a total lunar eclipse. Total lunar eclipses are rare.

Sometimes only part of the moon moves into the earth's umbra. Sunlight can still reach the moon. As a result, only part of the moon darkens. This is called a partial lunar eclipse. A partial lunar eclipse is hard to see.

Describe: What does the moon look like during a total lunar eclipse?

Figure 1

LESSON SUMMARY

- The umbra and the penumbra are the two parts of a shadow.
- A lunar eclipse occurs when the moon passes through the earth's shadow.
- A total lunar eclipse occurs when the moon moves entirely into the earth's umbra.
- A partial lunar eclipse occurs when part of the moon moves into the earth's umbra.

CHECK *Write true if the statement is true. If the statement is false, change the underlined term to make the statement true.*

1. The dark part of a shadow is the umbra.
2. A lunar eclipse occurs when the earth is between the sun and the moon.
3. A partial lunar eclipse occurs when part of the moon is in the earth's penumbra.
4. During a total lunar eclipse part of the moon is dark.

APPLY *Complete the following.*

5. **Hypothesize:** Why would a partial lunar eclipse be difficult to see?
6. Can a lunar eclipse occur during the quarter moon phase? Why or why not?
7. Can a shadow have only an umbra and not a penumbra?
8. **Contrast:** Explain the difference between a total and a partial lunar eclipse.

Skill Builder

Researching When you research, you gather information about a topic. Lunar eclipses can occur only during a full moon. Use reference books or a calendar to find out when the next 12 full moons will occur. Find out if a lunar eclipse is likely to occur during one of these full moons.

ACTIVITY

MODELING LUNAR ECLIPSES

You will need tracing paper, a ruler, and a pencil.

1. The diagram shows the sun, the earth, and three different positions that the moon might be in as it revolves around the earth. Trace the diagram onto a sheet of paper.
2. Use your diagram to show whether each position represents a total eclipse, a partial eclipse, or no eclipse of the moon. Hint: Use Figure 1 on page 362 as a guide.

Questions

1. **Analyze:** Does position 1 represent a total eclipse, a partial eclipse, or no eclipse of the moon? Explain.
2. **Analyze:** Does position 2 represent a total eclipse, a partial eclipse, or no eclipse of the moon? Explain.
3. **Analyze:** Does position 3 represent a total eclipse, a partial eclipse, or no eclipse of the moon? Explain.
4. **Model:** Draw a model of a total eclipse of the moon.

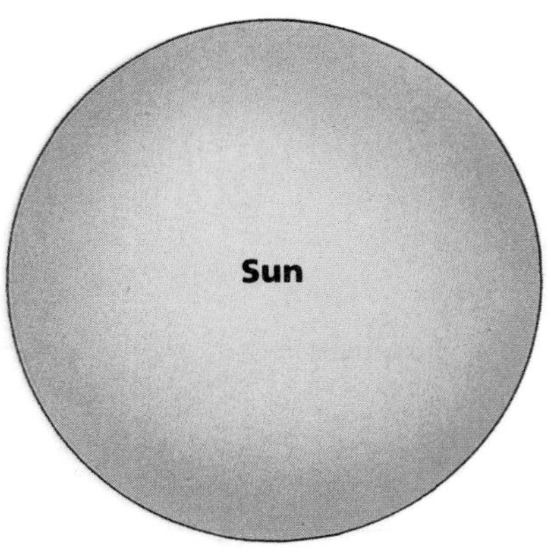

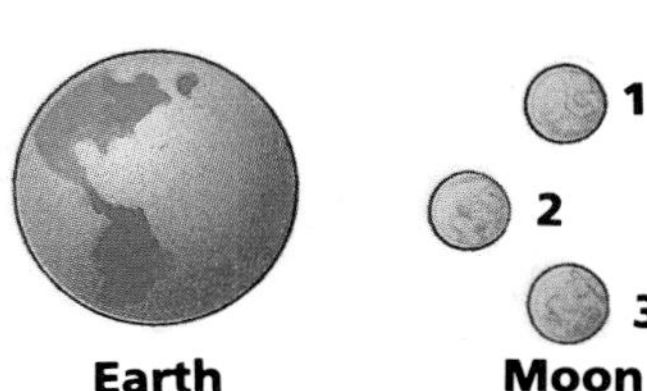

How does an eclipse of the sun occur?

Objective ▶ Explain how a solar eclipse occurs.

TechTerm

▶ **solar** (SOH-ler) **eclipse:** passing of the moon between the earth and the sun

Solar Eclipses An eclipse of the sun is called a **solar** (SOH-ler) **eclipse.** A solar eclipse occurs when the moon passes directly between the earth and the sun. During a solar eclipse, the moon casts a shadow on the earth. Figure 1 shows a solar eclipse. During a solar eclipse the sun looks like it is covered by a black circle. This circle is the moon.

▶ ***Define:*** What is a solar eclipse?

Kinds of Solar Eclipses Like lunar eclipses, solar eclipses can be either total or partial. A total solar eclipse occurs when the entire face of the sun is blocked by the moon. A partial solar eclipse happens when only part of the sun's face is blocked.

▶ ***Describe:*** When does a total solar eclipse happen?

Viewing Solar Eclipses Look at Figure 2. When the moon's umbra touches the earth, people within the umbra see a total solar eclipse. The umbra of the moon is very small. Therefore, a total solar eclipse is visible from only a small area of the earth. People who are in the moon's penumbra see a partial solar eclipse.

The penumbra of the moon's shadow is much larger than the umbra. As a result, a partial eclipse can be seen over a larger area of the earth than a total eclipse. Partial solar eclipses are seen more often than total eclipses.

▶ ***Identify:*** Which kind of solar eclipse is seen more often?

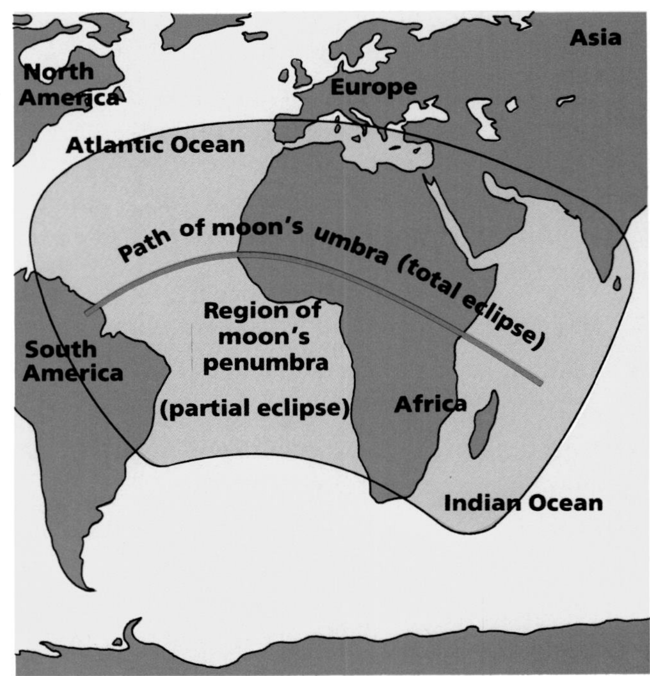

Figure 2

Figure 1

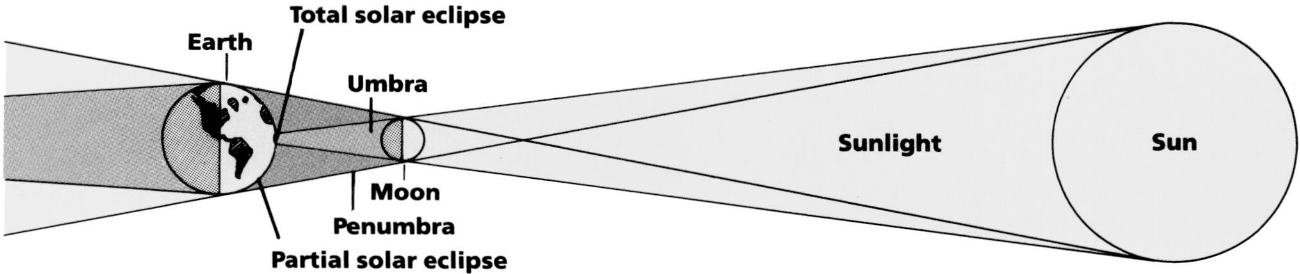

SOLAR ECLIPSE

LESSON SUMMARY

- A solar eclipse occurs when the moon passes between the earth and the sun.
- A solar eclipse can be either a total eclipse or a partial eclipse.
- A total solar eclipse is visible from only a small area of the earth.
- A partial solar eclipse is seen over a larger area of the earth than a total solar eclipse.

CHECK *Find the sentence that answers each question. Then, write the sentence.*

1. When does a solar eclipse occur?
2. What is a partial eclipse of the sun?
3. What happens when the moon's umbra touches the earth?
4. Which part of the moon's shadow is larger?

APPLY *Use Figure 2 on page 364 to answer the following.*

5. **Analyze:** What part of the shadow are you in if you see a total solar eclipse?
6. Can people outside the area of a total solar eclipse see a partial solar eclipse? Explain.

Complete the following.

7. **Compare:** How are total eclipses of the moon and the sun similar?
8. Why is a partial solar eclipse seen more often than a total solar eclipse?

InfoSearch

Read the passage. Ask two questions about the topic that you cannot answer from the information in the passage.

The Corona Like the earth, the sun has an atmosphere. The sun's upper atmosphere is called the corona. The corona is like a halo around the sun. Usually, the corona cannot be seen from Earth, because it is so bright. During a solar eclipse, however, most of the sun's light is blocked out. As a result, the corona can be seen from Earth. Scientists use special instruments to see and study the corona.

SEARCH: Use library references to find answers to your questions.

LOOKING BACK IN SCIENCE

SOLAR ECLIPSES OF THE PAST

People have always been fascinated by solar eclipses. In some cultures, solar eclipses were connected with superstition, mystery, and fear. Some ancient people thought the darkened sky caused by a solar eclipse was a sign of the displeasure of certain spirits. Ancient Chinese thought that solar eclipses happened when a dragon in the sky tried to swallow the sun.

Descriptions of solar eclipses have been found dating back to the 1st century BC. In Babylon, a record of solar eclipses was kept from 747 BC on. In China, 36 solar eclipses were recorded between 720 BC and 495 BC.

Scientists can calculate the exact dates past solar eclipses happened. The records of eclipses in ancient writings have been used to pinpoint the dates of historical events. For example, the description of a solar eclipse during an uprising in the ancient city of Assur has pinpointed the date of that event to June 15, 763 BC. Eclipses also have been used to check Greek history, and the history of the Roman Empire and the Middle Ages.

Today scientists can accurately predict solar eclipses. Solar eclipses are important in the study of the sun and moon. They also can be used for making improved scientific measurements.

17-9 What are tides?

Objectives ▶ Describe how tides change each day. ▶ Identify the cause of tides.

TechTerms

- ▶ **ebb tide:** outgoing, or falling tide
- ▶ **flood tide:** incoming, or rising tide
- ▶ **tide:** daily change in the level of the earth's oceans

Tides Have you ever been at the beach and noticed a change in the ocean level? The water level of the ocean rises and falls throughout the day. During the day, ocean water rises and covers part of the beach. Later, the ocean level falls. The beach is uncovered. The changes in ocean water levels are called **tides.** The time of low water level is low tide. The time of high water level is high tide.

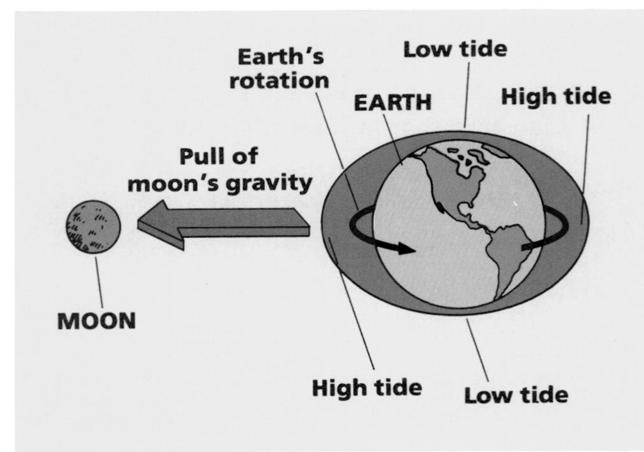

▶ ***Define:*** What are tides?

Cause of Tides Tides are caused mainly by the pull of the moon's gravity. Gravity is a force. The moon's gravitational force pulls water in the oceans toward the moon. The side of the earth facing the moon will have a high tide. The ocean water on that side bulges toward the moon. There is also a high tide on the opposite side of the earth, facing away from the moon. Low tides occur in the areas of the earth between the two high tides.

▶ ***Identify*** What causes tides on the earth?

Changing Tides Newspapers sometimes print tide tables. A tide table tells the times at which high tide and low tide will occur. If you look at a tide table, you will notice that the table shows two high tides and two low tides each day. The tides change about every 6 hours and 15 minutes.

Each quarter rotation of the earth causes a major change in tides. Water floods the beach slowly until high tide is reached. The incoming tide is a **flood tide.** As the earth rotates another quarter turn, the water begins to flow off the beach until low tide is reached. The outgoing tide is an **ebb tide.**

▶ ***Relate:*** How many times a day does a flood tide occur?

LESSON SUMMARY

- Tides are the daily changes in the surface level of the earth's oceans.
- Tides are caused by the pull of the moon's gravity.
- There are two high tides and two low tides each day.
- Each quarter rotation of the earth causes a major change in tides.

CHECK *Complete the following.*

1. What is another name for high water level?
2. What is the outgoing tide called?
3. What causes tides?
4. What is a flood tide?
5. How often do the tides change?
6. Where do low tides occur?

APPLY *Complete the following.*

7. **Infer:** How would a tide table be useful to fishers?
8. **Predict:** If one low tide occurs at 6:30 AM, when will the next low tide occur?
9. Suppose you docked a boat at a marina where the tides rise and fall about 1 m. How would the change in tide affect the use of the boat?

State the Problem

Study the illustrations. Then, state the problem.

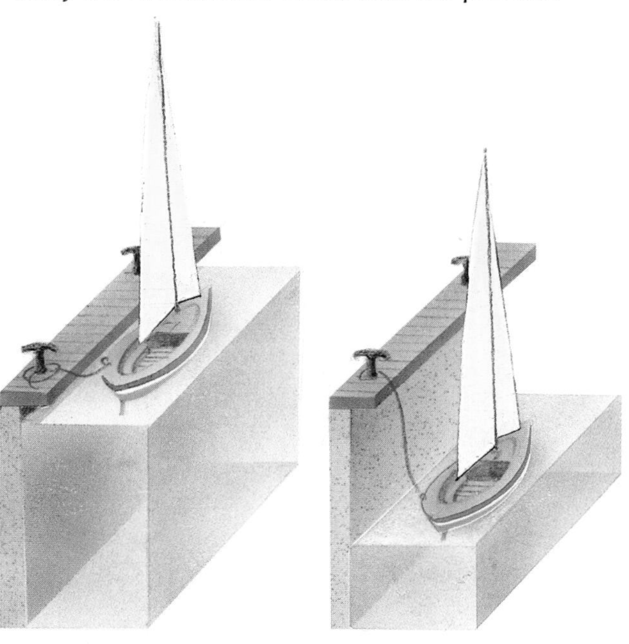

SCIENCE CONNECTION

FISHING AND TIDES

Has a newspaper in your community ever announced a "grunion night?" Grunions are small silver fish that live off the coast of California. Grunions spawn and lay their eggs on sandy beaches from late February to early September, but only on nights of the highest tides. During this time, thousands of grunions cover the beaches. Many people gather on the beaches and catch the fish by hand. Some newspapers announce the nights the fish are expected to be on the beach.

Fishing for grunions is one example of how fishing and tides are related. Much of the fishing industry depends on an understanding of tides. Tides involve the movements of huge volumes of water. The water carries fresh oxygen and microorganisms, which serve as food for fish. Fish carried in with high tides can become trapped in nets as the tide goes out.

The Bay of Fundy, located between Nova Scotia and New Brunswick, is world known for its tides. The difference between high and low tides may be as much as 15 meters. This region has a major fishing industry. The largest sardine cannery in North America is located in New Brunswick.

17-10 Why do tides change?

Objective ▶ Explain the effects of the sun's gravity and the moon's gravity on tides.

TechTerms

- ▶ **neap** (NEEP) **tide:** tide that is not as high or as low as normal tides
- ▶ **spring tide:** tide that is higher and lower than normal tides

The Law of Gravity The British scientist Isaac Newton first stated the law of gravity in the seventeenth century. The law of gravity states that every object in the universe attracts every other object. The attraction between any two objects depends in part on the distance between them. If the objects are close together, the attraction is strong. If the objects are far apart, the attraction is weak.

▶ ***State:*** What is the law of gravity?

Gravity and Tides The sun and the moon both attract the earth. The moon is much closer to the earth than the sun is. Therefore, the moon's gravitational pull on the earth is stronger than the sun's gravitational pull. As a result, the moon's gravitational pull is the main cause of tides on the earth.

▶ ***State:*** Why does the moon have a greater gravitational pull on the earth than the sun?

Spring Tides Twice a month, the earth, the sun, and the moon line up in a straight line. This occurs during the new moon and the full moon phases. During these phases, the gravitational pulls of the sun and the moon on the earth combine. When these forces combine, high tides are higher than normal high tides. Low tides are lower than normal low tides. When tides are higher and lower than normal tides, they are called **spring tides.**

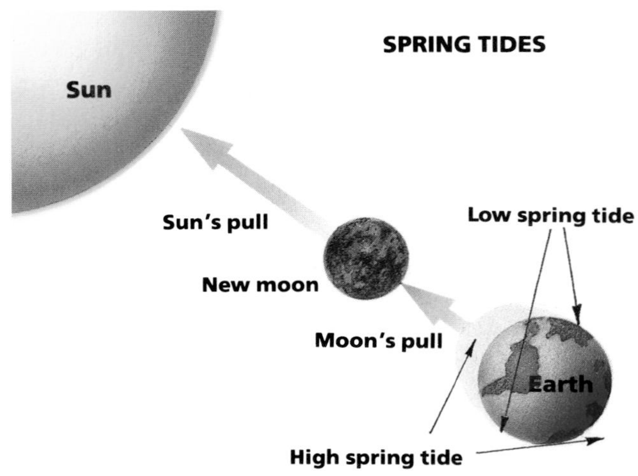

▶ ***Describe:*** When do spring tides occur?

Neap Tides During the moon's first- and last-quarter phases, the sun and the moon are at right angles to the earth. The gravitational pull of the moon works against the gravitational pull of the sun. These opposing pulls on the earth cause high tides that are not as high as usual. Low tides at these times are not as low as usual. Tides that are not as high as usual or as low as usual are called **neap** (NEEP) **tides.**

▶ ***Identify:*** What causes a neap tide?

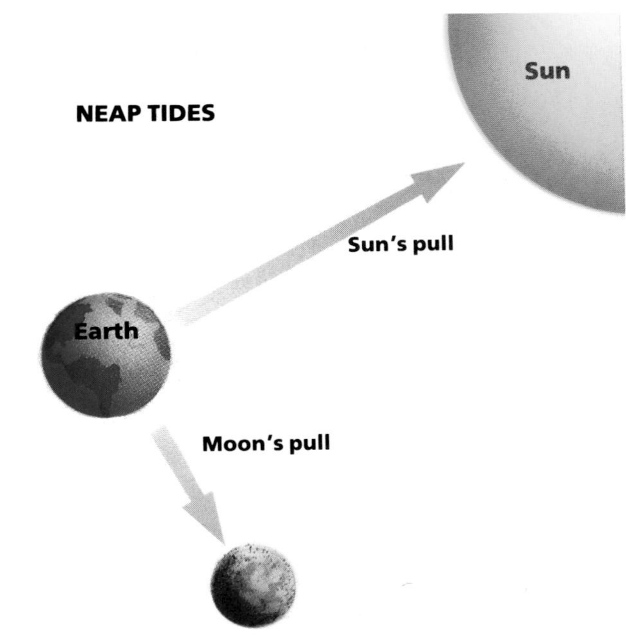

LESSON SUMMARY

- The law of gravity states that every object in the universe attracts every other object.
- Because the moon is closer to the earth than the sun is, the moon has a stronger gravitational pull on the earth.
- During the full moon and new moon phases, spring tides occur.
- During the first- and last-quarter phases of the moon, neap tides occur.

CHECK *Find the sentence in the lesson that answers each question. Then, write the sentence.*

1. What does the law of gravity state?
2. Why is the sun's gravitational pull on the earth weaker than the moon's pull?
3. What happens when the gravitational forces of the sun and the moon combine?
4. What are neap tides?

APPLY *Complete the following.*

5. Why are spring tides higher than normal high tides?
6. **Analyze:** High and low tides occur 50 minutes later each day. Why do you think this happens?
7. Why do spring tides occur?

Designing an Experiment

Design an experiment to solve the problem.

PROBLEM: How can the law of gravity be demonstrated?

Your experiment should:

1. List the materials you need.
2. Identify safety precautions that should be followed.
3. List a step-by-step procedure.
4. Describe how you would record your data.

Ideas in Action

IDEA: On the moon, the force of gravity is one-sixth of the force of gravity on earth.
ACTION: Identify the ways in which your daily life would be affected by less gravity.

CAREER IN EARTH SCIENCE

SHELLFISHER

Do you like to eat clams, oysters, mussels, scallops, lobster, or shrimp? If so, you enjoy eating shellfish. Shellfish are available to you because of the work of shellfishers. Shellfishers make their living catching shellfish.

The shellfish industry is located in towns and cities along the sea coasts. Shellfishers may use nets or traps to catch shellfish. For example, lobsters are caught in traps called lobster pots. A lobster can enter a lobster pot, but cannot get out. Some shellfishers use machines to help them bring shellfish out of the water. Shellfishers also may grow, or farm, some kinds of shellfish. The shellfish are farmed from areas called beds. In an oyster bed, there are large numbers of oysters.

If you would like to spend much of your time at sea and are willing to work long, hard hours, consider a career as a shellfisher. Skills are learned on the job. However, a high school diploma is recommended.

UNIT 17 Challenges

STUDY HINT Before you begin the Unit Challenges, review the TechTerms and Lesson Summary for each lesson in this unit.

TechTerms

apogee (358)
axis (350)
crescent phase (360)
ebb tide (366)
equinox (354)
flood tide (366)
gibbous phase (360)
international date line (356)
lunar eclipse (362)
neap tides (368)
penumbra (362)
perigee (358)
phases (360)
revolution (350)
rotation (350)
solar eclipse (364)
solar noon (356)
solstice (354)
spring tides (368)
tide (366)
umbra (362)

TechTerm Challenges

Matching *Write the TechTerm that best matches each description.*

1. time when the sun is highest in the sky
2. changing shapes of the moon
3. daily change in the level of the earth's oceans
4. imaginary line through the center of a planet on which the planet rotates
5. passing of the moon through the earth's shadow
6. movement of the earth on its axis
7. movement of the earth in its orbit

Identifying Word Relationships *Explain how the words in each pair are related. Write your answers in complete sentences.*

1. rotation, revolution
2. international date line, meridian
3. equinox, solstice
4. apogee, perigee
5. neap tide, spring tide
6. ebb tide, flood tide
7. penumbra, umbra
8. crescent phase, gibbous phase
9. solar eclipse, lunar eclipse

Content Challenges

Completion *Write the term that best completes each statement.*

1. When viewed from the North Pole, the earth rotates on its axis from ______ .
2. The earth's axis is tilted at an angle of ______ .
3. Because of the earth's tilted axis, the North Pole of the earth always points toward ______ .
4. In the Northern Hemisphere, the summer solstice occurs on ______ .
5. During an equinox, the number of daylight hours and nighttime hours are ______ .
6. The continental United States has ______ standard time zones.
7. The moon takes ______ days to make one complete revolution around the earth.
8. The moon takes ______ days to make one complete rotation on its axis.
9. As the visible part of the moon decreases, the moon is ______ .
10. The waxing crescent phase of the moon occurs ______ the full moon.
11. When the moon moves entirely into the earth's umbra, a ______ lunar eclipse occurs.

12. When the moon's umbra touches the earth, people within the umbra see a _______ solar eclipse.
13. Tides are caused mainly by the pull of the _______ gravity.
14. A major change in the tides occurs with each _______ rotation of the earth.
15. When the sun, moon, and the earth form a straight line, _______ tides occur.

True/False *Write true if the statement is true. If the statement is false, change the underlined term to make the statement true.*

1. The change from day to night is caused by the earth's revolution.
2. The number of daylight hours is not equal all year because of the earth's tilted axis.
3. The change in seasons is caused by the earth's rotation.
4. In the Southern Hemisphere, the first day of summer is June 21.
5. The vernal equinox marks the first day of spring.
6. The earth is divided into 24 time zones, each 15° of longitude wide.
7. As you move east, each time zone is one hour earlier than the previous time zone.
8. When the moon is closest to the earth, it is at apogee.
9. The moon rises 50 minutes earlier each day.
10. As the part of the moon that is visible increases, the moon is waxing.
11. The moon appears to change shape because of the way it reflects light from the sun.
12. During a total lunar eclipse, the entire face of the moon is darkened.

Understanding the Features

Reading Critically *Use the feature reading selections to answer the following. Page numbers for the features are shown in parentheses.*

1. Why are star trails circular? (351)
2. Where is Stonehenge located? (355)
3. What are some forms of transportation people use to travel? (357)
4. What are two of the careers that John Glenn has had? (359)
5. **Define:** What is an astronaut? (361)
6. **Infer:** How can a solar eclipse be used to date a historical event? (365)
7. **Identify:** What are grunions? (367)
8. **Identify:** List four kinds of organisms caught by shellfishers. (369)

Concept Challenges

Critical Thinking *Answer each of the following in complete sentences.*

1. **Calculate:** If the moon rises at 6:30 pm on Thursday, what time will the moon rise on Friday?
2. **Calculate:** If high tide occurs at 12:00 noon, what time will low tide occur?
3. How many times a month can neap tides occur? Explain.
4. **Compare:** How does the number of days between one full moon and the next compare to the number of days it takes the moon to make one complete revolution around the earth?
5. **Hypothesize:** Is the moon's gravitational attraction to the earth stronger at apogee or perigee? Explain.
6. **Compare:** How does the number of time zones on the earth compare with the number of hours in a day?

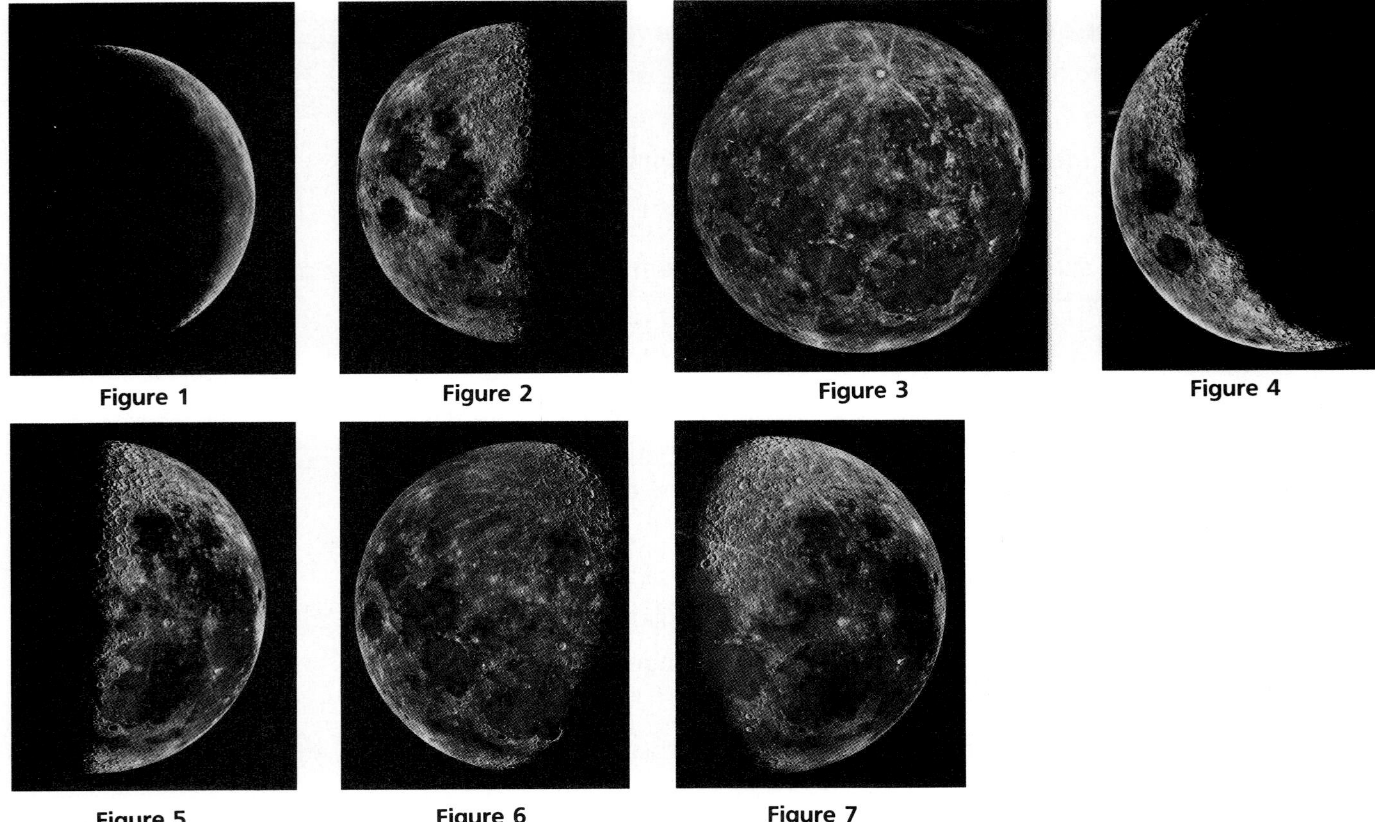

Figure 1 Figure 2 Figure 3 Figure 4

Figure 5 Figure 6 Figure 7

Interpreting Photographs *Use the photographs of the phases of the moon to answer the following questions.*

1. **Observe:** Which phase of the moon is shown in Figure 1?
2. Which phase of the moon is shown in Figure 3?
3. Which phase of the moon is shown in Figure 5?
4. Which phase of the moon is not shown?
5. Why is the phase of the moon shown in Figure 4 called a "waning" phase?
6. Which phase of the moon follows a full moon?
7. How long does it take the moon to go from one new moon phase to the next new moon phase?
8. **Sequence:** Using the Figure numbers, place the phases of the moon in the correct order beginning with Figure 3.

Finding Out More

1. The full moon that appears just after September 23 in the Northern Hemisphere and March 31 in the Southern Hemisphere is often called a harvest moon. Use library resources to find out how the harvest moon got its name. Present your findings to the class in an oral report.
2. Use an almanac to find out when the next five lunar and solar eclipses will occur in your area. Present your findings in a table.
3. Use library references to research historical events that occurred at the same time as solar eclipses of the past. Be sure to include the dates for each event. Use the information you gather to make a time line.

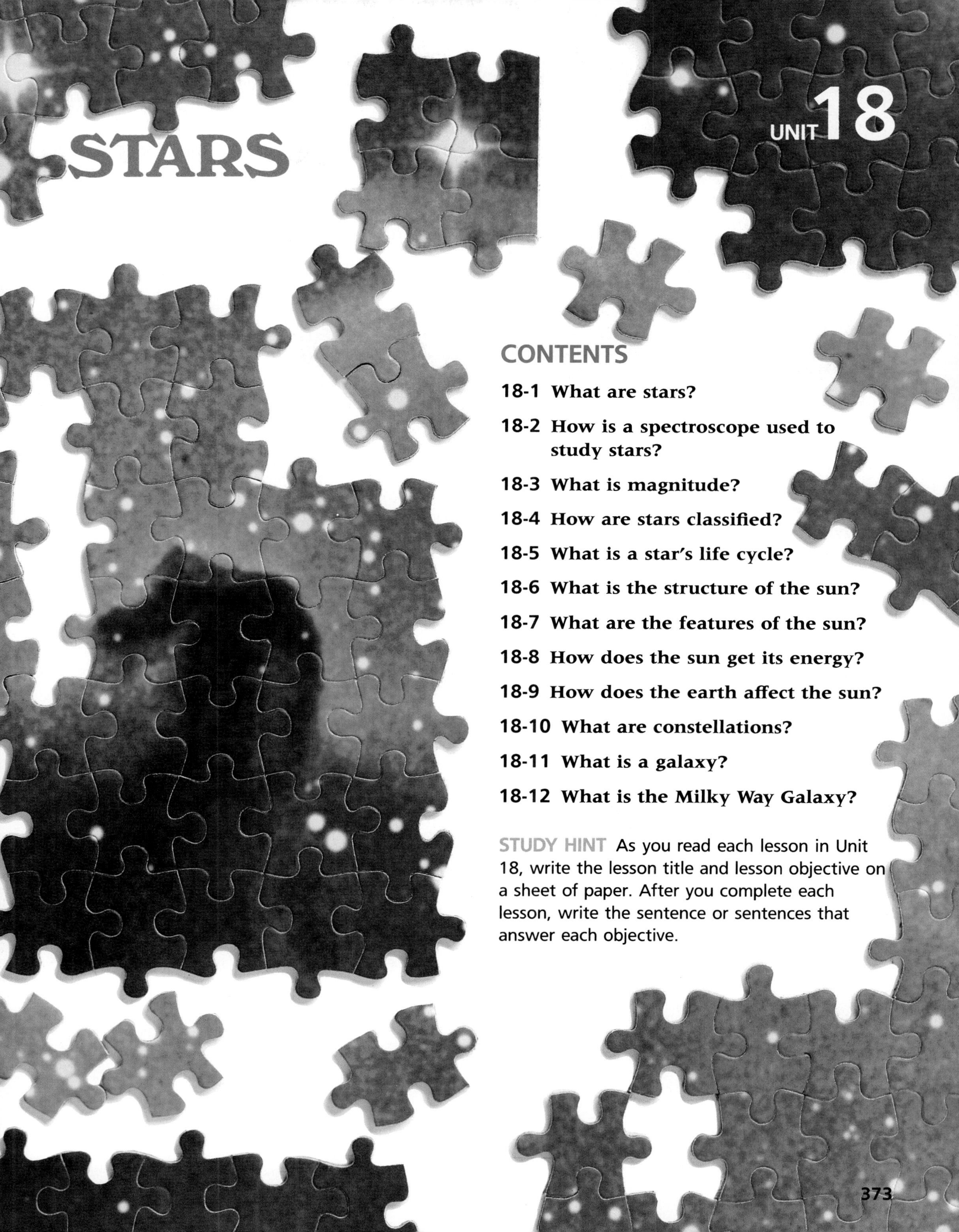

UNIT 18 STARS

CONTENTS

STUDY HINT As you read each lesson in Unit 18, write the lesson title and lesson objective on a sheet of paper. After you complete each lesson, write the sentence or sentences that answer each objective.

18-1 What are stars?

Objective ▶ Describe some characteristics of stars.

TechTerms

- ▶ **nebula** (NEB-yuh-luh): spinning cloud of hot gases
- ▶ **protostar:** material in the center of a nebula that becomes a star
- ▶ **star:** ball of gases that gives off light and heat

Stars The sun is the nearest **star** to Earth. A star is ball of gases that gives off heat and light. The heat and light from the sun makes life on Earth possible. The sun is only one of billions of stars. If you look at the sky on a clear night, you can see thousands of stars. Most of these stars look like tiny points of light. Stars look like points of light because they are so far away.

When you look at the stars at night, most stars appear white. However, if you look closely, you

will see that stars have different colors. For example, Rigel is a blue star. Betelgeuse (BEET-uh-jooz) is red. What color is the sun?

▶ ***Define:*** What is a star?

Composition of Stars Most stars are made up of the gases hydrogen and helium. Other elements in stars are sodium, calcium, and iron. Not every star contains every one of these elements. Different stars may have different amounts of these elements. Hydrogen is the most common element in most stars.

▶ ***Name:*** What is the most common element in most stars?

Formation of Stars A star forms from a spinning cloud of gas and dust called a **nebula** (NEB-yuh-luh). As the nebula spins, gravity causes it to

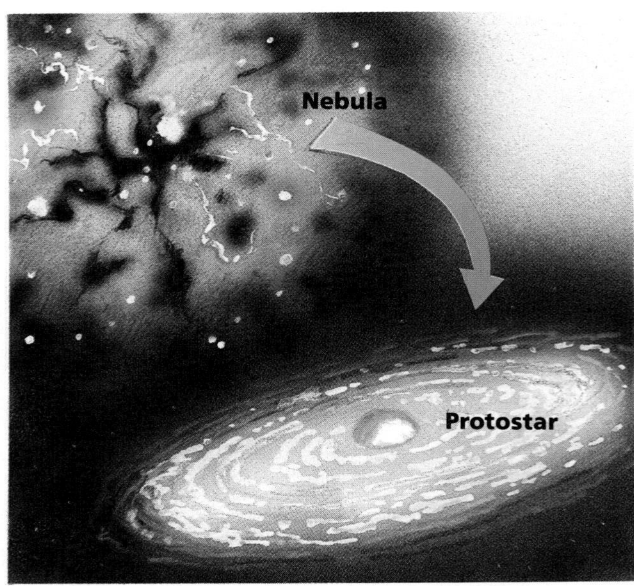

shrink. The spinning nebula flattens into a disk of dust and gas. Material comes together at the center of the disk. A **protostar** begins to form. A protostar is the material in the center of a nebula that becomes a star. The protostar shrinks. As it shrinks, temperature and pressure build up. When the temperature and pressure are high enough, the protostar starts to give off light and heat. It is now a star.

▶ ***Name:*** What is the first stage in the formation of a star?

LESSON SUMMARY

- A star is a ball of gases that gives off light and heat.
- The sun is one of billions of stars.
- Stars are different colors.
- Most stars are made up of hydrogen and helium.
- A star forms from a protostar in a nebula.

CHECK *Complete the following.*

1. What is the closest star to Earth?
2. Why do the stars look like points of light?
3. What color is the star Rigel?
4. What two gases make up most stars?
5. What is a nebula?
6. What causes a spinning nebula to shrink?

APPLY *Complete the following.*

7. **Sequence:** Describe the stages in the formation of a star.
8. **Infer:** Why would life on Earth not be possible without the sun?

Skill Builder

Building Vocabulary A prefix is a word part that is placed at the beginning of a root or base word. Understanding prefixes can help you to remember the meanings of new words.

The word "protostar"is made up of the prefix "proto-" and the root word "star." Look up the prefix "proto-" in a dictionary. Write the definition on a sheet of paper.

Then list the following words: prototype, protozoa, protoplasm, protohistory. What is the prefix for each of these words? What are the root words? Write the prefix and root word next to each word. What do you think each word means? Write a definition for each word in your own words. Look up each definition and write it on a sheet of paper. Compare your definitions with the definitions in a dictionary.

TECHNOLOGY AND SOCIETY

OBSERVATORIES

An observatory is a place from which to make astronomical observations. Most observatories house a reflecting telescope.

Reflecting telescopes have become larger and more powerful as scientists have learned to make large, flawless mirrors. The largest reflecting telescope with a single mirror is the Special Astrophysical Observatory in Russia. Its mirror is 6 meters in diameter. However, problems have made it less useful than other, smaller telescopes. One of the problems with large mirrors is that they sag under their own weight. Then the image becomes unclear.

To solve this problem, scientists have built reflecting telescopes that use many small mirrors acting as one. For example, a very large reflecting telescope is the Keck Telescope at Mauna Kea, Hawaii. Its mirror is made of 36 thin glass hexagonal segments. Together, the segments make a mirror 10 meters in diameter.

18-2 How is a spectroscope used to study stars?

Objective ▶ Describe how astronomers use spectroscopes to study stars.

TechTerms

- ▶ **spectroscope** (SPEK-truh-skohp): instrument that separates light into different colors
- ▶ **spectrum:** bands of the different colors of light

Colors of Starlight A star gives off light. Telescopes collect the light from distant stars. Astronomers can learn about stars by studying their light. A **spectroscope** (SPEK-truh-skohp) is a tool that astronomers use to study the light from stars. A spectroscope separates light into bands of different colors. These bands of color make up the **spectrum** of light. The plural of "spectrum" is "spectra."

Define What is a spectrum?

Color and Composition Astronomers study the spectrum of starlight to find out the chemical makeup of a star. Stars are very hot. When elements are heated to a high temperature, they give off light. Each element gives off its own spectrum of light. Astronomers can study the spectrum of a star to find out what elements are in the spectrum. A spectroscope helps scientists identify the elements in a star.

Explain: What happens when elements are heated?

Color and Temperature Astronomers can find out how hot a star is from its spectrum. You know that stars are different colors. For example, the sun is a yellow star. The surface temperature of a star is related to its color. Blue stars are the hottest stars. Red stars are the coolest. A yellow star is medium-hot. Table 1 shows how stars are classified by color and temperature.

Table 1 Color and Temperature of Stars

COLOR	TEMPERATURE (°C)	EXAMPLE
Red	about 3000	Betelgeuse
Orange	about 4000	Arcturus
Yellow	about 5500	Sun
White-yellow	about 7500	Canopus
White	8000–11,000	Vega
Blue-white	15,000–30,000	Algol
Blue	above 30,000	Rigel

Interpret: What is the temperature of the sun?

LESSON SUMMARY

- Astronomers use a spectroscope to study the light from stars.
- The spectrum of a star helps identify the elements in the star.
- The surface temperature of a star is related to the color of the star.

CHECK *Complete the following.*

1. Astronomers use a _______ to study the light from stars.
2. Bands of different colors of light make up a _______ .
3. When an element is _______, it gives off a spectrum of light.
4. Each _______ in a star gives off its own spectrum.
5. The _______ of a star is related to its color.
6. The hottest stars are _______ .

APPLY *Complete the following.*

7. **Analyze:** A star has a surface temperature of 4000 °C. What color does this star appear?
8. **Sequence:** List the names of the stars in Table 1 in order, from the hottest to the coolest.

InfoSearch

Read the passage. Ask two questions about the topic that you cannot answer from the information in the passage.

Prisms White light is a mixture of different colors of light. A prism (PRIZ-um) separates white light into its colors. When you shine a beam of white light onto a prism, the prism spreads the light out into a band of colors. This band of colors is the spectrum of the light. The colors in the spectrum of white light are red, orange, yellow, blue, green, and violet. These are the colors you see in a rainbow.

SEARCH: Use library references to find answers to your questions.

ACTIVITY

MAKING A SPECTROSCOPE

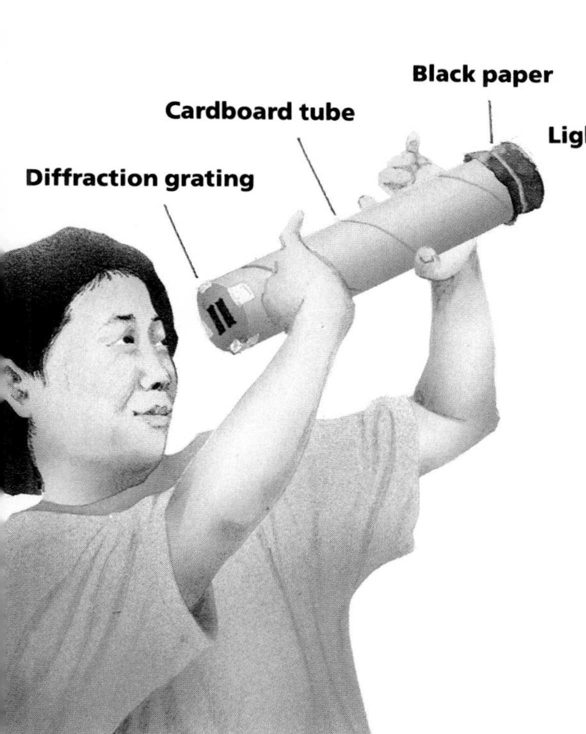

You will need a cardboard tube, a diffraction grating, a piece of black construction paper, scissors, tape, a rubber band, a light source, and different colored crayons.

1. Tape a diffraction grating to one end of a cardboard tube.
2. Cut a thin slit in a piece of black construction paper. **CAUTION: Be careful when using scissors.**
3. Cover the other end of the cardboard tube with the piece of black paper. Use a rubber band to hold the paper in place.
4. Hold the end of the tube with the diffraction grating up to your eye. Look through the tube at a light bulb. Slowly turn the tube until you see a spectrum. Draw the spectrum.
5. Use your spectroscope to look at other light sources, such as a fluorescent light. **CAUTION: Do not look at the sun.** Draw each spectrum that you see.

Questions

1. What does a spectroscope do?
2. **a. Compare:** Were the spectra from different light sources the same or different? **b.** How can you explain the similarity or difference of the spectra?

18-3 What is magnitude?

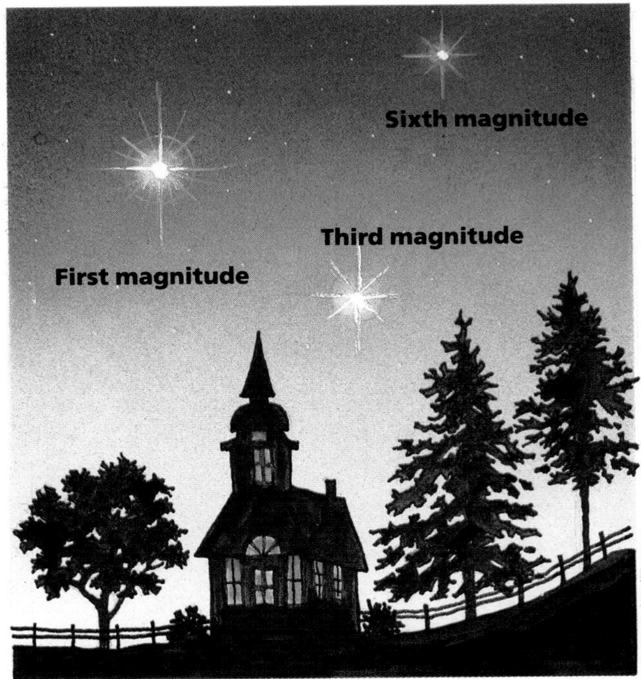

Objective ▶ Compare apparent magnitude and absolute magnitude.

TechTerm

▶ **magnitude** (MAG-nuh-tood): measure of a star's brightness

Brightness of Stars Without a telescope, you can see about 5000 stars in the night sky. Some stars appear brighter than others. The measure of a star's brightness is its **magnitude** (MAG-nuh-tood).

The brightness of a star depends upon its temperature, its size, and its distance from Earth. A hot star is brighter than a cool star. A large star is brighter than a small star. The closer a star is to Earth, the brighter it appears.

Name: What is the measure of a star's brightness called?

Apparent Magnitude The brightness of a star as seen from Earth is the star's apparent (uh-PER-unt) magnitude. Astronomers have developed a scale to identify apparent magnitude. On this scale, a star with a low number appears brighter than a star with a high number. Some of the brightest stars in the sky have an apparent magnitude of 1. These are first-magnitude stars. The dimmest stars you can see using only your eyes are sixth-magnitude stars.

Compare: Which appears brighter, a third-magnitude star or a sixth-magnitude star?

Absolute Magnitude Astronomers also can find the absolute (AB-suh-loot) magnitude of a star. The absolute magnitude of a star is its actual brightness. Absolute magnitude describes how bright a star would be if all the stars were the same distance from Earth. For example, the sun appears very bright because it is so near Earth. If the sun were farther away, it would not appear as bright. A dim star that is close to Earth may appear brighter than a bright star that is far away. All stars have both an apparent magnitude and an absolute magnitude.

Describe: What is absolute magnitude?

LESSON SUMMARY

- The measure of a star's brightness is its magnitude.
- Magnitude depends on temperature, size, and distance from the earth.
- Apparent magnitude is a star's brightness as seen from the earth.
- Absolute magnitude is a star's actual brightness.

CHECK *Complete the following.*

1. Magnitude is a measure of a star's _______ .
2. Magnitude depends upon a star's size, _______, and distance from Earth.
3. A sixth-magnitude star appears _______ than a first-magnitude star.
4. The brightness of a star as seen from Earth is its _______ magnitude.
5. The actual brightness of a star is its- _______ magnitude.

APPLY *Complete the following.*

6. **Hypothesize:** Two stars have the same absolute magnitude, but different apparent magnitudes. Explain.
7. **Compare:** The sun is the closest star to Earth. The sun has an absolute magnitude of 5. The star Altair has an absolute magnitude of 2. Which star is brighter? Which star appears brighter? Explain.

Skill Builder

Classifying When you classify, you group things according to similarities. Astronomers classify stars according to their color. Each group is called a spectral class. The spectral classes are indicated by letters: O, B, A, F, G, K, and M. Blue stars are grouped in spectral class O. Red stars are classified as M stars. Using library references, classify each of the following stars in its correct spectral class:

Canopus	Sun
Arcturus	Betelgeuse
Sirius	Altair
Rigel	Capella

ACTIVITY

OBSERVING MAGNITUDE

You will need one large flashlight and one small flashlight.

1. Work in groups of three. Have one partner hold a large flashlight and another partner hold a small flashlight. Have both partners stand the same distance away from you and turn on their flashlights. Compare the brightness of the two flashlights.
2. Now have the person holding the small flashlight move closer to you. Compare the brightness of the two lights.

Questions

1. **a. Compare:** Which appeared brighter, the large flashlight or the small flashlight? **b.** Which had the greater apparent magnitude? **c.** Which had the greater absolute magnitude?
2. **a. Observe:** What happened when the small flashlight was moved closer? **b.** Which had the greater apparent magnitude? **c.** Which had the greater absolute magnitude?

18-4 How are stars classified?

Objective ► Explain how the Hertzsprung-Russell diagram is used to classify stars.

TechTerms

- **red giants:** large, bright stars that are fairly cool
- **main sequence stars:** stars that fall within a band in the middle of the H-R diagram
- **supergiants:** very large stars
- **white dwarfs:** very small, hot stars

H-R Diagram Two astronomers, Ejnar Hertzsprung and Henry Russell, each made an interesting discovery about stars. They found that there is a relationship between a star's absolute magnitude and its surface temperature, or color. They developed a chart called the Hertzsprung-Russell, or H-R, diagram. The H-R diagram shows that the brightness of most stars increases as the star's surface temperature increases.

Describe: What does the H-R diagram show?

Main Sequence A star's position on the H-R diagram depends upon its absolute magnitude and its surface temperature, or color. Suppose that a star has a blue color and a large absolute magnitude. This star would be placed in the upper left of the diagram. A red star with a small absolute magnitude would appear in the lower right. Most stars fall in a band that runs from the upper left to the lower right of the diagram. Stars that fall in this band are called **main sequence stars.** The sun and most stars that you can see at night are main sequence stars.

Classify: How is the sun classified on an H-R diagram?

Other Stars Some stars do not fall within the main sequence. Some stars are very bright, but not very hot. These stars are red, orange, or yellow in color. Because they are not very hot, they would not be very bright if they were of average size. However, these stars are very large. They give off a great deal of light. They have large absolute magnitudes. These stars are called **red giants.** Red giants are placed in the upper right part of an H-R diagram. Some stars are even larger than red giants. These stars are called **supergiants.**
Other stars that fall outside of the main sequence are hot, but very small. These stars are blue or white. They are called **white dwarfs.** White dwarfs are found in the lower part of an H-R diagram, below the main sequence.

Define: What are white dwarfs?

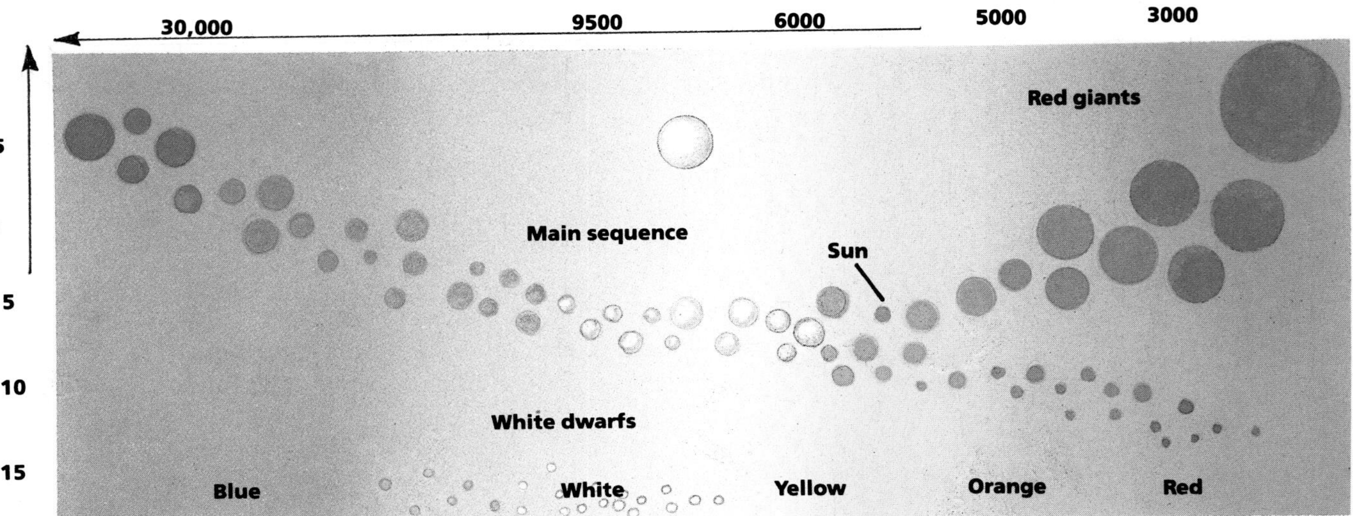

LESSON SUMMARY

- The Hertzsprung-Russell diagram shows the relationship between a star's absolute magnitude and its surface temperature.
- Most stars, including the sun, are main sequence stars.
- Very large, bright stars are red giants or supergiants.
- Very small, hot stars are white dwarfs.

CHECK *Write true if the statement is true. If the statement is false, correct the underlined term to make the statement true.*

1. The H-R diagram shows the relationship between <u>apparent</u> magnitude and temperature.
2. As a star's brightness increases, its surface temperature <u>decreases</u>.
3. The sun is a <u>main sequence</u> star.
4. A very large, bright star is a <u>red giant</u>.
5. Supergiants are found in the <u>lower left</u> of an H-R diagram.
6. White dwarfs are small, <u>cool</u> stars.

APPLY *Use the H-R diagram on page 380 to complete the following.*

7. **Compare:** Which star has a greater absolute magnitude, a red giant or a white dwarf?
8. **Compare:** Which star has a greater surface temperature, a red giant or a white dwarf?
9. **Analyze:** What is the average surface temperature of a white dwarf?
10. What color are supergiants?

Skill Builder

Graphing A graph is a good way to organize information. A line graph is used to plot points along two lines called axes (AKS-eez). Create a line graph that shows where each kind of star appears on the H-R diagram. Plot the absolute magnitude of each kind of star along the vertical, or up-and-down, axis. Plot the temperature of each kind of star along the horizontal, or across, axis. Label each point with the kind of star it represents. Then connect the points to see what pattern is formed. How does this pattern compare to the H-R diagram shown on page 380?

PEOPLE IN SCIENCE

HENRIETTA SWAN LEAVITT (1868–1921)

How do astronomers measure the distances to the stars? The distance of a close star can be found by observing the star's parallax, or how the star seems to change position over time. The distances to stars that are very far away were almost impossible to find. An American astronomer, Henrietta Leavitt, discovered a way to find the distances to stars in other galaxies.

Henrietta Leavitt was born in Lancaster, Massachusetts. She graduated from what is now Radcliffe College. Leavitt worked at Harvard Observatory. She was studying a kind of star called a Cepheid (SEF-ee-id) variable. A Cepheid variable is a star that changes its brightness in a regular period of time.

In 1912, Leavitt identified 25 Cepheid variables in a nearby galaxy. She observed the period of each star, or how long the star took to go from bright to dim and back again to bright. She showed that the longer the period is, the brighter the star is. A star's brightness is related to its distance. Therefore, astronomers could use this relationship to calculate the distance to the star.

18-5 What is a star's life cycle?

Objective ▶ Describe the stages in the life cycle of a star.

TechTerms

- ▶ **nova:** star in which the outer layer has been blown off in an explosion
- ▶ **supernova:** star that has been blown apart in a violent explosion

Life Cycle of Stars Stars are not alive, but they have a life cycle. The life cycle of a star takes billions of years. As time passes, a star changes its mass into energy. The energy is given off as light and heat. A star's mass cannot last forever. In time, most of the mass is used up and the star dies. By studying different stars, astronomers can describe the life cycle of stars.

▶ ***Explain:*** Where does a star's energy come from?

Protostar to Giant Stars are formed from clouds of dust and gas called nebulas. Gravity squeezes the dust and gas together and a protostar is formed. When the protostar is hot enough, nuclear reactions start to take place. In these reactions, hydrogen is changed into helium. Large amounts of energy are produced. At this stage, the protostar has become a star.

The second stage in the life cycle of a star is the main sequence stage. It is the longest stage. A star stays on the main sequence until all its hydrogen fuel is used up. Then the star shrinks and its temperature increases. Helium is changed into carbon in nuclear reactions. These reactions give off energy. The star expands and becomes cooler. The star becomes either a red giant or supergiant.

▶ ***Name:*** What is the longest stage in the life cycle of a star?

Death of a Star The next stage in a star's life cycle depends upon the star's mass. A medium-sized star loses mass and begins to shrink. The star gets cooler and dimmer, and becomes a white dwarf. The white dwarf continues to cool. It becomes fainter and fainter. Finally, it becomes a small, cold, dark object called a black dwarf. Not all white dwarfs change quietly into black dwarfs. Some white dwarfs blow off their outer layers in a huge explosion. A very bright star called a **nova** is formed.

A very massive star may have a much greater explosion. The star blows itself apart and becomes a **supernova.** A supernova may shrink into a very dense ball called a neutron star. A very large supernova may become a black hole. The gravity of a black hole is so great that nothing can escape—not even light.

▶ ***Describe:*** What happens when a medium-sized star loses mass?

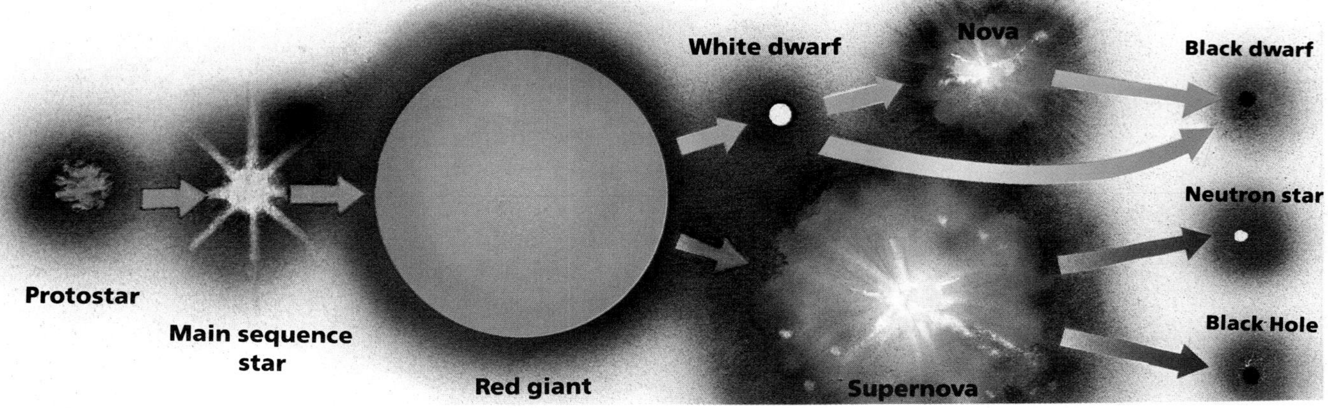

LESSON SUMMARY

- Stars have a life cycle.
- The first stage in a star's life cycle is a protostar.
- The second stage in a star's life cycle is the main sequence stage.
- A medium-sized star becomes first a white dwarf and then a black dwarf.
- A very massive star becomes a supernova, and may then become a neutron star or a black hole.

CHECK *Complete the following.*

1. A star changes ______ into energy.
2. Stars give off energy as light and ______ .
3. A protostar forms in a ______ .
4. The ______ stage is the longest in a star's life cycle.
5. A main sequence star becomes a red giant or ______ .
6. A white dwarf may explode and become a ______ .
7. A supernova may become a ______ .

APPLY *Use the diagram of the life cycle of stars on page 382 to complete the following.*

8. **Sequence:** A flow chart is a diagram that shows a sequence of events. Draw a flow chart showing the stages in the life cycle of a star in order, beginning with a protostar.

InfoSearch

Read the passage. Ask two questions about the topic that you cannot answer from the information in the passage.

Supernova 1987A In 1987, a supernova was seen in the Large Magellanic Cloud, more than 160,000 light years from Earth. The supernova, called supernova 1987A, could easily be seen without a telescope. It was the first supernova to be visible from Earth in almost 400 years.

Astronomers were able to study the light coming from the supernova as it slowly became dimmer. The energy coming from supernova 1987A might be caused by a neutron star or a pulsar. By studying supernova 1987A, astronomers hope to learn more about the evolution of stars.

SEARCH: Use library references to find answers to your questions.

PEOPLE IN SCIENCE

TYCHO BRAHE (1546–1601)

Tycho Brahe was a 16th century Danish astronomer. As a young man, Brahe studied law at the University of Copenhagen. In 1560, he observed a total eclipse of the sun. Brahe was amazed that an eclipse could be predicted. This event turned his interest toward astronomy. While continuing to study law during the day, he began to observe the stars at night.

Brahe found that most of the astronomical information of the time was not accurate. He decided to devote his life to making accurate observations of the stars. In 1572, he observed a nova, or "new star," in the constellation Cassiopei. No star had ever before been seen in that spot. At the time, people thought that the stars were fixed and unchanging. Brahe's observations of the nova of 1572 showed that this is not so. Brahe published his observations in 1573. In 1576, the king of Denmark gave Brahe an island. Here he built an observatory. It had the finest astronomical instruments in the world.

18-6 What is the structure of the sun?

Objective ▶ Describe the parts of the sun.

TechTerms

- ▶ **chromosphere** (KROH-muh-sfeer): layer of the sun's atmosphere above the photosphere
- ▶ **core:** center of the sun
- ▶ **corona** (kuh-ROH-nuh): outer layer of the sun's atmosphere
- ▶ **photosphere** (FOH-tuh-sfeer): inner layer of the sun's atmosphere

Structure of the Sun The sun is an average star in size, mass, and temperature. Its diameter is 1,300,000 km. The sun is a large ball of hot gases. Because the sun is made up of gases, it has no distinct boundaries. However, the sun has two main parts. These parts are the core and the atmosphere.

▶ ***Name:*** What are the two main parts of the sun?

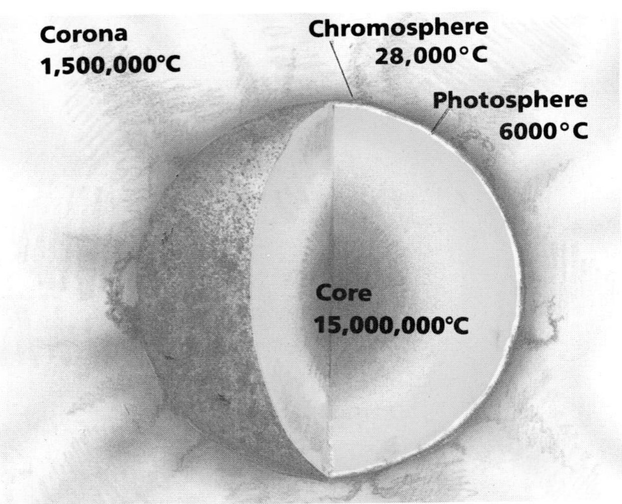

Core The center part of the sun is the **core.** The core makes up about 10% of the sun's diameter. It is the source of the sun's energy. Like the rest of the sun, the core is made up of hot gases. The temperature of the core is about 15,000,000 °C.

▶ ***State:*** What is the temperature of the sun's core?

Atmosphere The sun's atmosphere has three layers. The inner layer is the **photosphere** (FOH-tuh-sfeer), or light sphere. The photosphere is the visible surface of the sun. It is visible because the hot gases in the photosphere glow and give off light.

The **chromosphere** (KROH-muh-sfeer) is the layer of the sun's atmosphere next to the photosphere. The chromosphere is the sun's color

sphere. It gives off a weak red glow that can be seen only under special conditions, such as a solar eclipse. The chromosphere extends for thousands of kilometers beyond the photosphere.

The **corona** (kuh-ROH-nuh) is the outer layer of the sun's atmosphere. The temperature of the corona is about 1,500,000 °C. Like the chromosphere, the corona can be seen only during a solar eclipse.

▶ ***List:*** What are the three layers of the sun's atmosphere?

LESSON SUMMARY

- The two main parts of the sun are the core and the atmosphere.
- The core is the center of the sun.
- The inner layer of the sun's atmosphere is the photosphere.
- The chromosphere is the layer of the sun's atmosphere next to the photosphere.
- The outer layer of the sun's atmosphere is the corona.

CHECK *Complete the following.*

1. What are the two parts of the sun?
2. What is the sun's diameter?
3. What is the temperature of the sun's core?
4. Which part of the sun is the source of the sun's energy?
5. How many layers make up the sun's atmosphere?
6. Which layer of the sun's atmosphere is the light sphere?
7. Which layer of the sun's atmosphere is the color sphere?
8. Which layers of the sun's atmosphere can be seen only during a solar eclipse?

APPLY *Complete the following.*

9. **Infer:** The word "corona" comes from a Latin word meaning crown. Why do you think the outer layer of the sun is called the corona?

Health & Safety Tip

Astronomers use special telescopes to observe the sun during a solar eclipse. **You should never look directly at the sun, even during an eclipse.** The very bright light from the sun can damage your eyes. Use reference materials to find safe ways to observe a solar eclipse.

ACTIVITY

DRAWING A MODEL OF THE SUN

You will need a piece of paper, a pencil, a metric ruler, and a drawing compass.

1. Place a piece of paper on your desk lengthwise. Draw a line across the center of the paper from left to right.
2. Beginning at the left edge of the paper, use a metric ruler to mark points at 10 cm, 17.5 cm, 19.5 cm, and 19.75 cm. Draw a dot at each point.
3. Place the point of a compass on the 10-cm dot. Place the pencil of the compass on the 17.5-cm dot. Draw a circle. Label this circle "Surface of the sun."
4. Keep the point of the compass on the 10-cm dot. Move the pencil to the 19.5-cm dot. Draw a circle.
5. Keep the point of the compass on the 10-cm dot. Move the pencil to the 19.75-cm dot. Draw a circle.

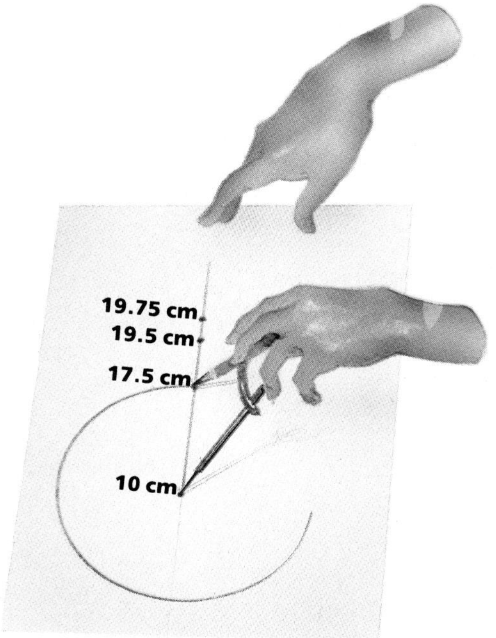

Questions

1. Which layer of the sun is considered the surface of the sun?
2. **Analyze:** The corona extends more than 57,000,000 km beyond the chromosphere out into space. Why can you not draw the corona on your model?

18-7 What are the features of the sun?

Objective ▶ Describe sunspots, solar flares, and prominences.

TechTerms

- ▶ **prominences** (PRAHM-uh-nuns-ez): streams of gases that shoot high above the sun's surface
- ▶ **solar flares:** eruptions of electrically charged particles from the surface of the sun
- ▶ **sunspots:** dark, cool areas on the sun's surface

Sunspots Some areas on the surface of the sun are cooler than the areas around them. The gases in these cooler areas do not shine as brightly as the areas around them. As a result, these areas appear dark. The dark, cooler areas on the sun's surface are called **sunspots.** Sunspots appear in groups that move across the sun in the same direction. The movement of sunspots is caused by the spinning of the sun on its axis. Sunspots may last for days or months. The number of sunspots seen from Earth varies in an 11-year cycle.

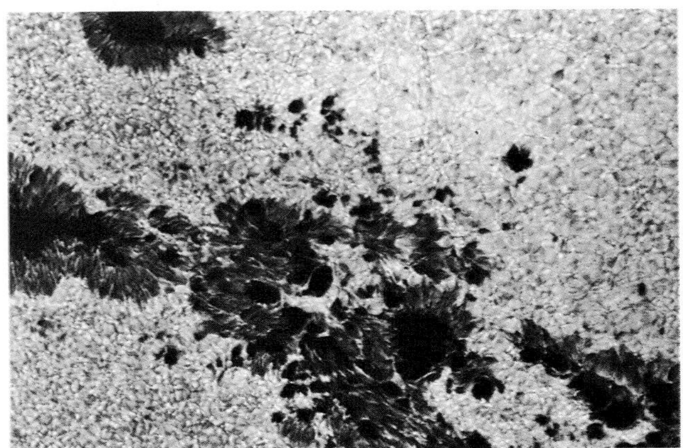

Explain: Why do sunspots all appear to move in the same direction?

Prominences Streams of flaming gas shoot out from the surface of the sun. These streams of gas are called **prominences** (PRAHM-uh-nuns-ez). Prominences usually form high in the chromosphere. They reach thousands of kilometers above the sun's surface. Then they fall back into the sun, forming huge arches. Prominences are best seen during a solar eclipse. They can last for weeks or months.

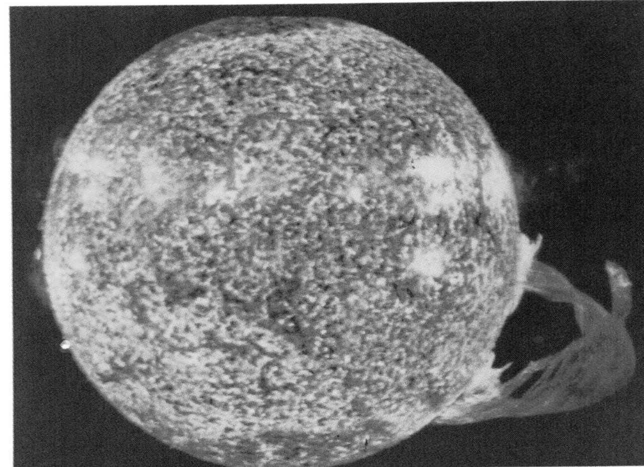

Define: What are prominences?

Solar Flares Energy sometimes builds up in the sun's atmosphere. This usually happens near a group of sunspots. If the energy is given off suddenly, a **solar flare** is formed. Solar flares usually do not last for more than about an hour. Some may last for only a few minutes. Solar flares send streams of electrically charged particles out into space. When these particles reach the earth, they can cause static and disrupt communications.

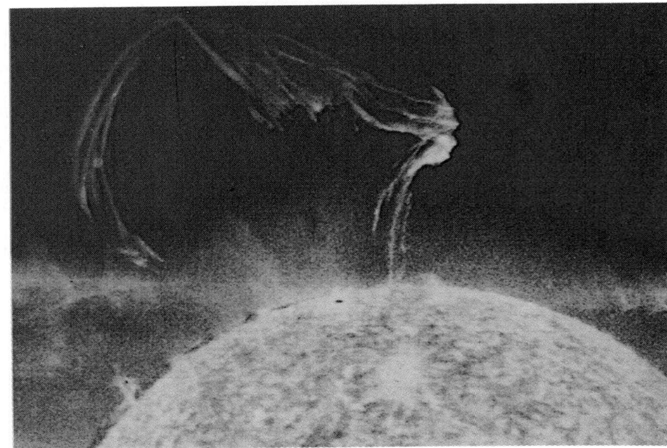

Describe: How do solar flares affect the earth?

LESSON SUMMARY

- Sunspots are dark, cool areas on the sun's surface.
- Prominences are streams of gas that arch high above the sun's surface.
- Solar flares are eruptions of energy and charged particles from the sun out into space.

CHECK *Complete the following.*

1. Sunspots appear dark because they are _______ than surrounding areas.
2. The sunspot cycle lasts for about _______ years.
3. Streams of gas from the surface of the sun are _______ .
4. The best time to observe prominences is during a _______ .
5. Features called _______ usually appear near sunspots.
6. Solar flares release streams of _______ particles.

APPLY *Complete the following.*

7. **Predict:** Suppose the number of sunspots was low in 1988. When do you predict the next period of low sunspot activity will occur?

InfoSearch

Read the passage. Ask two questions about the topic that you cannot answer from the information in the passage.

Auroras Auroras are glowing lights that are seen in the sky at night. They are most often seen in the far north and far south. Most auroras occur in September and October, and in March and April. Auroras are caused when charged particles from the sun enter the earth's atmosphere. High in the atmosphere, the charged particles hit molecules of gas. The gas molecules begin to glow. Different gases in the atmosphere produce different colors. Green is the most common color seen in auroras. Auroras are most often seen during periods of high sunspot activity.

SEARCH: Use library references to find answers to your questions.

SCIENCE CONNECTION

EFFECTS OF SUNSPOTS AND SOLAR FLARES

The sun is too bright to look at directly without damaging your eyes. Astronomers use special telescopes to study the surface of the sun. The McMath Solar Telescope, at Kitt Peak in Arizona, is 800 m long and is built into the ground. With this telescope, astronomers can observe and study sunspots and solar flares.

The sun is constantly bombarding the earth with electrically charged atomic particles. Solar flares release these particles into space. When the charged particles reach the earth, they interact with gases in the upper atmosphere. Spectacular ribbons of colored light called auroras are formed. You may be familiar with auroras as the northern or southern lights.

Astronomers have found that sunspot activity builds up and decreases in an eleven-year cycle. During periods of high sunspot activity, bursts of energy from the sun often interfere with radio and television reception. Meteorologists have related the sunspot cycle to weather and climate changes on the earth. For example, mini-ice ages have been associated with periods of low sunspot activity.

18-8 How does the sun get its energy?

Objective ▶ Describe the process by which energy is released in the sun.

TechTerms

- ▶ **fusion** (FYOO-zhun): reaction in which atomic nuclei combine to form larger nuclei
- ▶ **nucleus** (NEW-klee-us): center, or core, of an atom

Solar Energy The sun gives off energy in the form of heat and light. Where does this energy come from? You know that burning produces heat and light. However, the heat and light of the sun are not produced by burning. The sun produces energy by nuclear (NEW-klee-ur) reactions. The **nucleus** (NEW-klee-us) is the center of an atom. In a nuclear reaction, the nuclei of atoms are changed.

▶ *Describe:* What kind of reaction produces the heat and light of the sun?

Nuclear Fusion The sun is about 80% hydrogen and 18% helium. Other elements make up the remaining 2%. Deep inside the sun, the temperature is more than 15,000,000°C. At these high temperatures, the nuclei of hydrogen atoms combine, or fuse. This kind of reaction is called a **fusion** (FYOO-zhun) reaction. In a fusion reaction, four hydrogen nuclei combine to form one helium nucleus. The mass of a helium nucleus is less than the mass of all four hydrogen nuclei put together. The missing mass is changed into energy.

▶ *Explain:* What happens in a fusion reaction?

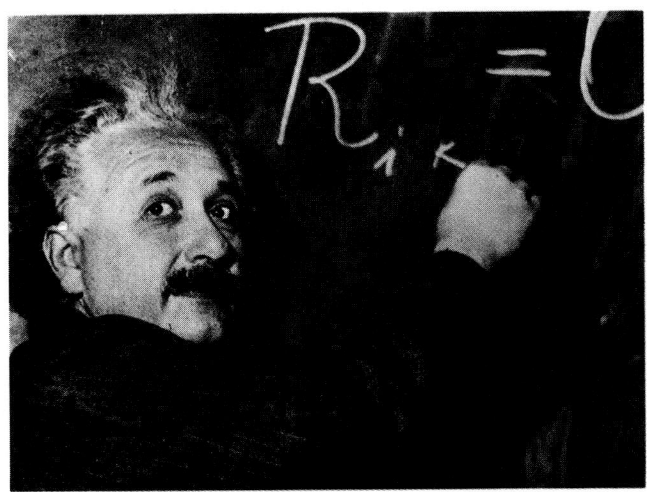

Matter and Energy Albert Einstein helped explain how the sun produces its energy. Einstein said that matter could be changed into energy. His equation, $E = mc^2$, explains how a small amount of matter can be changed into a large amount of energy. In this equation, E is energy. Mass, or the amount of matter, is m and c is the speed of light. The speed of light is 300,000 km per second. Astronomers can use Einstein's equation to calculate how much energy the sun produces.

▶ *State:* What is Einstein's equation?

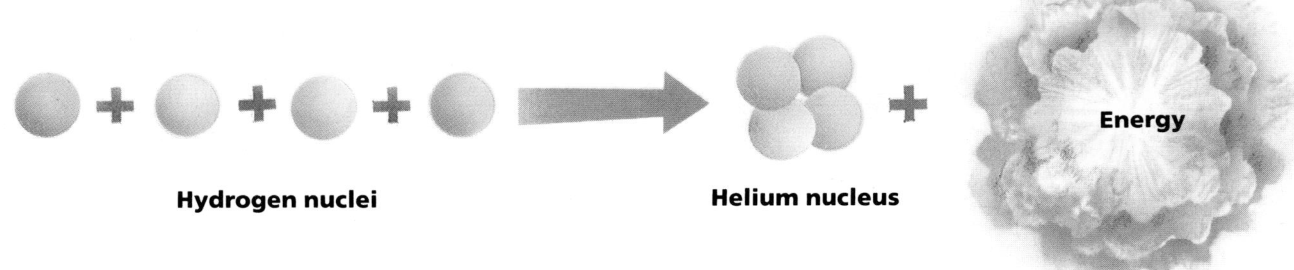

LESSON SUMMARY

- The sun produces energy by means of nuclear reactions.
- In a fusion reaction, four hydrogen nuclei combine to form one helium nucleus.
- Astronomers can use Einstein's equation to calculate how much energy the sun produces.

CHECK *Complete the following.*

1. What two forms of energy does the sun produce?
2. What is the core of an atom called?
3. What happens in a nuclear reaction?
4. What two elements make up 98% of the sun?
5. What happens to the missing mass in a hydrogen fusion reaction?
6. What does E stand for in Einstein's equation?
7. What is the speed of light?

APPLY *Complete the following.*

8. **Infer:** Why are the nuclear reactions that take place in the sun called fusion reactions?
9. **Analyze:** Explain how Einstein's equation, $E = mc^2$, shows that a small amount of matter can be changed into a very large amount of energy.

InfoSearch

Read the passage. Ask two questions about the topic that you cannot answer from the information in the passage.

Albert Einstein Albert Einstein was born in Germany in 1879. He became interested in science as a young child. Einstein studied mathematics and physics in Switzerland. He later moved back to Germany and became a professor of physics in Berlin.

Einstein was one of the greatest scientists of all time. He is best knows for his theory of relativity. His famous equation, $E = mc^2$ led to the development of nuclear energy. In 1921, Einstein received the Nobel Prize in physics. Einstein moved to the United States in 1933. He later became an American citizen. Einstein spent the rest of his life at the Institute for Advanced Study in Princeton, New Jersey. He died in 1955.

SEARCH: Use library references to find answers to your questions.

TECHNOLOGY AND SOCIETY

FUSION ENERGY

Modern society requires a lot of energy. Most of this energy now comes from fossil fuels, such as coal, oil, and natural gas. However, the supply of fossil fuels may run out sometime in the 21st century. Fusion energy is one possible alternative source of energy. In a fusion reaction, hydrogen atoms are smashed together. The reaction produces helium, plus a great deal of energy. Because water contains hydrogen, the oceans could be an almost unlimited source of fusion energy.

Very high temperatures and pressures are needed for fusion reactions to take place. Producing these high temperatures and pressures is not easy. More energy must be put in than is released by the reactions. Scientists are experimenting with different ways to solve this problem. One kind of experimental fusion reactor uses a magnetic trap, or "magnetic bottle," to hold the fusion reaction. Another uses high-powered laser beams to cause a fusion reaction. Fusion reactors may someday provide a clean, safe source of energy for the future.

18-9 How does the sun affect the earth?

Objective ▶ Describe some ways in which the heat and light from the sun affect the earth.

TechTerm

▶ **photosynthesis** (foh-toh-SIN-thuh-sis): process by which plants use light from the sun to make food

The Earth and The Sun The sun is the most important source of Earth's energy. What would happen to Earth if the sun stopped shining? The sun's energy reaches Earth as heat and light. This energy causes water on the earth to evaporate and rise into the air. The water then falls to the earth as rain. Rain helps plants to grow. Plants use sunlight to make food. Without rain and sunlight, plants would die. People and other animals could not survive without plants.

▶ *Explain:* Why do plants need the energy of sunlight?

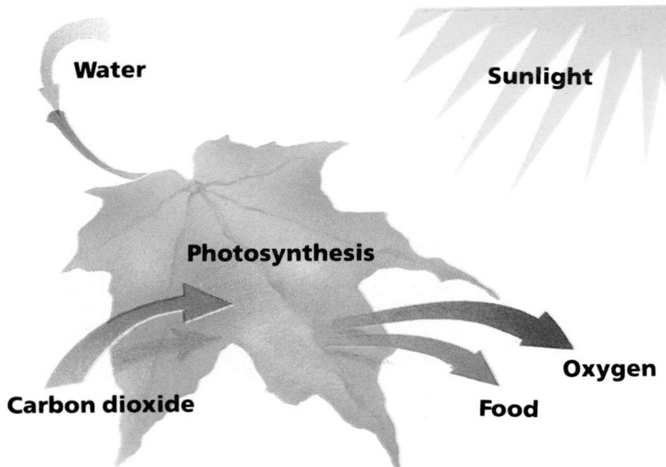

Photosynthesis Plants can make their own food. The food-making process in plants is called **photosynthesis** (foh-toh-SIN-thuh-sis). The plants take in carbon dioxide and water. Sunlight supplies the energy needed by plants to make food. Some of the food is used by the plants. The rest is stored. Stored food in plants is used by people and other animals when they eat the plants. During photosynthesis, oxygen is given off by plants. The oxygen goes into the air. People and other animals need oxygen to survive.

▶ *Define:* What is photosynthesis?

Fossil Fuels The sun is the source of most of Earth's energy resources. The most common energy resources on Earth are fossil fuels. Fuels are burned to supply energy. Coal and oil are examples of fossil fuels. Coal and oil are the remains of plants and animals that lived long ago. Those plants and animals needed sunlight to live.

▶ *Name:* What are Earth's most common energy resources?

Dangerous Sunlight Earth receives only a small part of the sun's energy. The atmosphere filters out most of the sun's energy. However, some of the energy that gets through can be harmful. You know that sunlight can tan your skin. Too much sunlight can cause a sunburn. Some kinds of skin cancer can be caused by over-exposure to the sun. The direct rays of the sun can damage your eyes. You should always take care to protect yourself from over-exposure to sunlight.

▶ *Name:* What prevents most of the sun's energy from reaching Earth?

LESSON SUMMARY

- The sun is the most important source of Earth's energy.
- Plants use the energy of sunlight to make food.
- The sun is the source of most of Earth's energy resources.
- Some of the energy in sunlight is harmful.

CHECK *Complete the following.*

1. The sun is the source of most of the earth's ______ .
2. The energy in sunlight causes water to ______ .
3. Plants need sunlight to make ______ .
4. The food-making process of green plants is ______ .
5. Plants take in ______ and water.
6. Plants produce food and ______ .
7. Most of the earth's energy resources are ______ fuels.
8. Two fossil fuels are ______ and oil.
9. Some kinds of ______ are caused by too much sunlight.

APPLY *Complete the following.*

10. **Interpret:** The process of photosynthesis can be shown in an equation, as follows:

    carbon dioxide + water + energy → glucose + oxygen

    What does the glucose represent in this equation?

State the Problem

What problem is shown in the picture?

Ideas in Action

IDEA: Some of the energy in sunlight can be harmful.

ACTION: List some ways in which you can protect yourself from the harmful rays of the sun.

SCIENCE CONNECTION

SUNSCREENS

The "healthy-looking" summer tan has become a hazard to your skin. More and more people are getting skin cancer from over-exposure to the sun. Your best bet is to avoid the sun as much as possible. However, there is another way to protect your skin from the sun, use a sunscreen. A sunscreen does exactly what its name states. It screens the sun's harmful rays.

With so many sunscreens on the market, how do you know which one is best for you. When buying a sunscreen, the first thing to look for is the SPF, or sun protection factor. You should look for a SPF of 15 or higher. The higher the SPF, the slower you will tan and burn your skin. You should also look for a sunscreen that is waterproof or at least water-resistant. By using a waterproof product, you will still get some protection while in water. A third item to check on a sunscreen label is that the sunscreen protects against both kinds of ultraviolet rays—UVA and UVB.

GUIDELINES AGAINST THE SUN
1. Stay out of the sun as much as possible during peak hours, 10 AM to 3 PM.
2. Apply sunscreen to your whole body at least thirty minutes before going into the sun.
3. After a year and a half, throw out sunscreen. The older the sunscreen is, the less effective it is.
4. Do not forget your eyes, ears, nose and lips when applying sunscreen. Many companies offer a special sunscreen for these areas.

18-10 What are constellations?

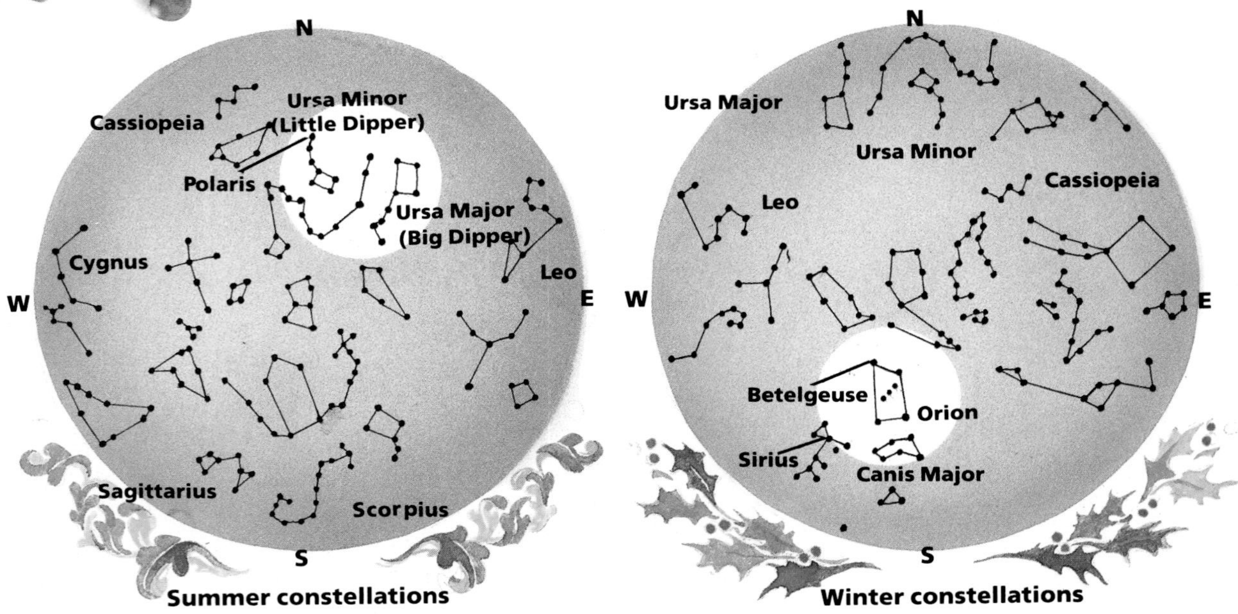

Objective ▶ Explain what constellations are and name some familiar constellations.

TechTerm

▶ **constellation** (kon-stuh-LAY-shun): grouping of stars that form a pattern in the sky

Star Patterns When you look at the night sky, you can see many stars. Some of these stars seem to form patterns. These patterns are **constellations** (kon-stuh-LAY-shuns). Ancient people imagined that they could see animals and people in these patterns. They gave the constellations names and made up stories about them. Today, astronomers recognize 88 constellations. The stars in a constellation appear to be close together. However, they may actually be very far apart. You can use the constellations to locate individual stars.

▶ ***Define:*** What is a constellation?

The Big Bear One of the easiest constellations to find is *Ursa Major.* Its name means "big bear." Ancient people thought they could see the shape of a large bear in the constellation. The Big Dipper is a part of *Ursa Major.* The Big Dipper is made up of seven stars. Three stars form the handle of the dipper. Four stars form the cup. The stars of the Big Dipper can easily be seen in the northern sky. Two bright stars in the cup of the Big Dipper are called the pointers. They point to *Polaris,* the North Star.

▶ ***Name:*** What does the name *Ursa Major* mean?

The Little Bear *Ursa Minor* is another constellation in the northern sky. The name *Ursa Minor* means "little bear." Ursa Minor is also called the Little Dipper. *Polaris* is the first star in the handle of the Little Dipper.

▶ ***Infer:*** Why do you think the constellation *Ursa Minor* was called the little bear?

The Hunter *Orion,* the Hunter, is a constellation in the southern sky. In the Northern Hemisphere, *Orion* can be seen low in the sky on clear winter nights. Three bright stars make up *Orion's* belt. Betelgeuse is a giant red star in *Orion.* Rigel is a very hot white star in this constellation.

▶ ***Locate:*** Where can *Orion* be seen?

LESSON SUMMARY

- Constellations are groupings of stars that form patterns in the sky.
- The Big Dipper is part of *Ursa Major,* the Big Bear.
- *Polaris* is the first star in the handle of the Little Dipper, *Ursa Minor.*
- *Orion,* the Hunter, can be seen in the southern sky.

CHECK *Complete the following.*

1. What are patterns of stars called?
2. How many constellations are there?
3. What does Ursa Major mean?
4. What is the Big Dipper?
5. What are the two bright stars in the cup of the Big Dipper called?
6. What is the name of the North Star?
7. What is another name for the Little Dipper?
8. Where is *Polaris* found?
9. What is the name of the red star in the constellation *Orion?*

APPLY *Complete the following.*

10. **Infer:** Why are the two bright stars in the cup of the Big Dipper called the pointers?

Skill Builder

Researching When you research, you gather information about a topic. Many constellations were named after real or imaginary animals, legendary heroes, or mythical characters. Using library references, look up the names of the following constellations: Sagittarius, Draco, Cygnus, Pegasus, Pisces, Cassiopeia, Hercules, Capricorn. Write a brief report about the history of each constellation. Tell what each name means.

LOOKING BACK IN SCIENCE

NAMING THE CONSTELLATIONS

Ancient people looked at the night sky and made up stories about the patterns of stars they saw there. The oldest astronomical texts were written by the ancient Sumerians. They record the names of constellations still known today as the lion, the bull, and the scorpion. The ancient Greeks and Chinese had different names for some of the same constellations. The Egyptians named about 25 constellations, including the crocodile and the hippopotamus. Astronomers continued naming the constellations right up until the 20th century. In 1930, a list of 88 constellations was established by the International Astronomical Union. Some of these constellations and their meanings are shown in the table.

CONSTELLATION	MEANING	CONSTELLATION	MEANING
Taurus	Bull	Cetus	Whale
Leo	Lion	Centaurus	Centaur
Scorpius	Scorpion	Aquila	Eagle
Auriga	Charioteer	Columba	Dove
Monoceros	Unicorn	Lacerta	Lizard

18-11 What is a galaxy?

Objective ▶ Describe the three main types of galaxies.

TechTerms

- ▶ **elliptical galaxy:** spherical or flattened disk-shaped galaxy
- ▶ **galaxy** (GAL-uhk-see): large group of stars
- ▶ **irregular galaxy:** galaxy with no definite shape
- ▶ **spiral galaxy:** galaxy with a thick center and flattened arms

Galaxies Stars appear as small points of light. Among these points of light, you can also see some fuzzy patches. Some of these patches are nebulas, or clouds of gas and dust. Others are **galaxies** (GAL-uhk-sees). A galaxy is made up of billions of stars. With telescopes, astronomers can see millions of galaxies. Galaxies are the main features of the universe.

Galaxies have different shapes. Astronomers classify, or group, galaxies based on shape. There are three kinds of galaxies.

▶ *Define:* What are galaxies?

Spiral Galaxies One kind of galaxy is a **spiral galaxy.** Spiral galaxies have a nucleus, or center, made up of bright stars. They also have two or more spiral arms that branch out from the center. Three out of four galaxies are spiral galaxies.

▶ *Describe:* What is the nucleus of a spiral galaxy made up of?

Elliptical Galaxies Some galaxies are almost perfectly round. They are called **elliptical galaxies.** Elliptical galaxies can also look like flattened disks. The stars in an elliptical galaxy are much older than the stars in other kinds of galaxies. Elliptical galaxies are much smaller than spiral galaxies.

▶ *Compare:* Which is larger, an elliptical galaxy or a spiral galaxy?

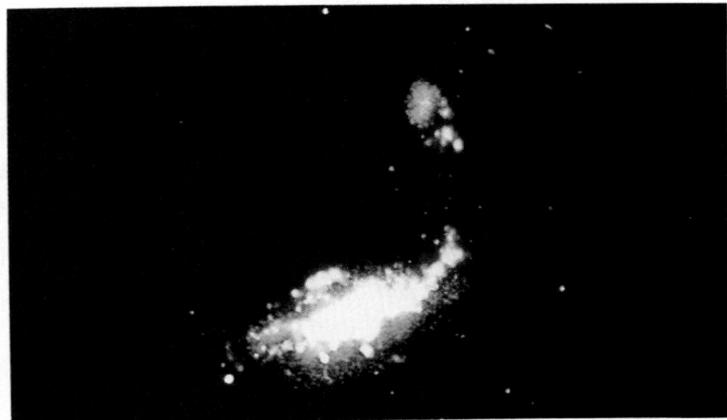

Irregular Galaxies Galaxies with no definite shape are called **irregular galaxies.** The stars in an irregular galaxy are not arranged evenly. Irregular galaxies are smaller and fainter than other kinds of galaxies. They are the least common kind of galaxy.

▶ *Infer:* Why do irregular galaxies have no definite shape?

LESSON SUMMARY

- A galaxy is a large group of stars.
- Galaxies can be classified according to shape.
- Spiral galaxies have a nucleus of bright stars and two or more spiral arms.
- Elliptical galaxies are spherical or flattened disks.
- Irregular galaxies do not have a definite shape.

CHECK *Complete the following.*

1. Galaxies are made up of billions of ______ .
2. Astronomers classify galaxies on the basis of their ______ .
3. There are ______ main types of galaxies.
4. Most galaxies are ______ galaxies.
5. Spiral galaxies have at least two ______ .
6. The oldest stars are found in ______ galaxies.
7. The smallest galaxies are ______ galaxies.

APPLY *Complete the following.*

8. **List:** What are the three main types of galaxies?
9. **Classify:** Classify each of the galaxies shown as spiral, elliptical, or irregular.

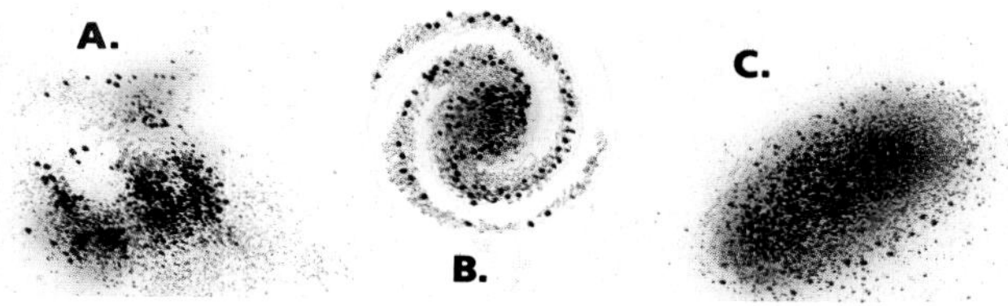

InfoSearch

Read the passage. Ask two questions about the topic that you cannot answer from the information in the passage.

Galactic Neighbors Most galaxies are billions of light years from Earth. For example, the great spiral galaxy in Andromeda is two billion light years away. The Andromeda galaxy is much larger than the galaxy to which the sun belongs. You can even see the Andromeda galaxy without a telescope. The closest galaxies to Earth are the Large Magellanic Cloud and the Small Magellanic Cloud. These galaxies are between 150,000 and 160,000 light years away. They are irregular galaxies.

SEARCH: Use library references to find answers to your questions.

ACTIVITY

MAKING A MODEL OF THE EXPANDING UNIVERSE

You will need a balloon, a marking pen, string, a rubber band, and a metric ruler.

1. Partially inflate a balloon. Close the opening with a rubber band.
2. With the marking pen, draw four dots on the surface of the partially inflated balloon. Label them A, B, C, and D.
3. Using the string, measure the distance between each of the four dots. Hold the string next to the ruler and record each measurement.
4. Inflate the balloon to its fullest and tie the end.
5. Repeat your measurements and record the distances.

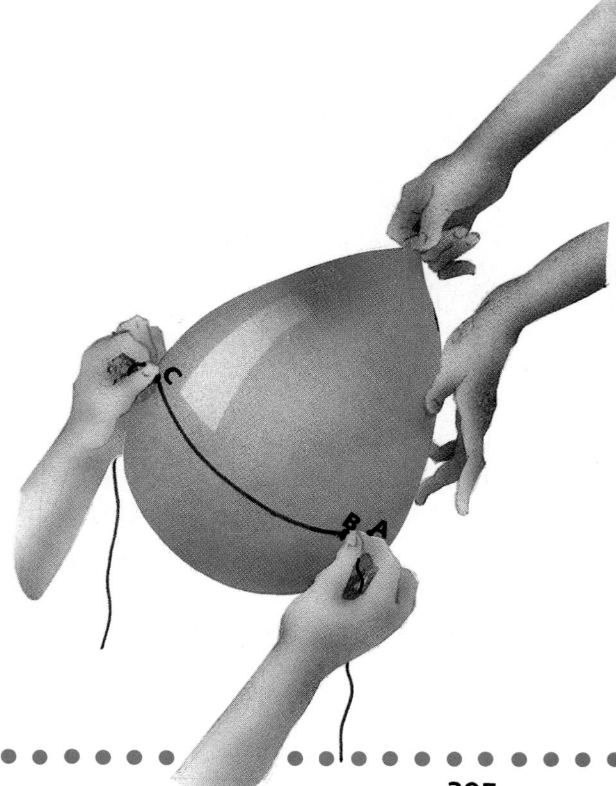

Questions

1. **a.** What does the balloon represent?
   b. What do the dots on the balloon represent?
2. **Observe:** What happened to the distances between dots as you inflated the balloon?
3. **Analyze:** How does this activity show what is happening to the universe and to the galaxies?

18-12 What is the Milky Way Galaxy?

Objective ▶ Describe the Milky Way Galaxy.

TechTerms

- ▶ **binary stars:** pairs of stars that revolve around each other
- ▶ **cluster:** large group of stars in a galaxy

The Milky Way Galaxy All the stars you can see in the night sky are part of the Milky Way Galaxy. The sun and all the planets in the solar system, including Earth, are in the Milky Way Galaxy. The Milky Way Galaxy is part of a group of 17 other galaxies. Together, these galaxies are called the Local Group.

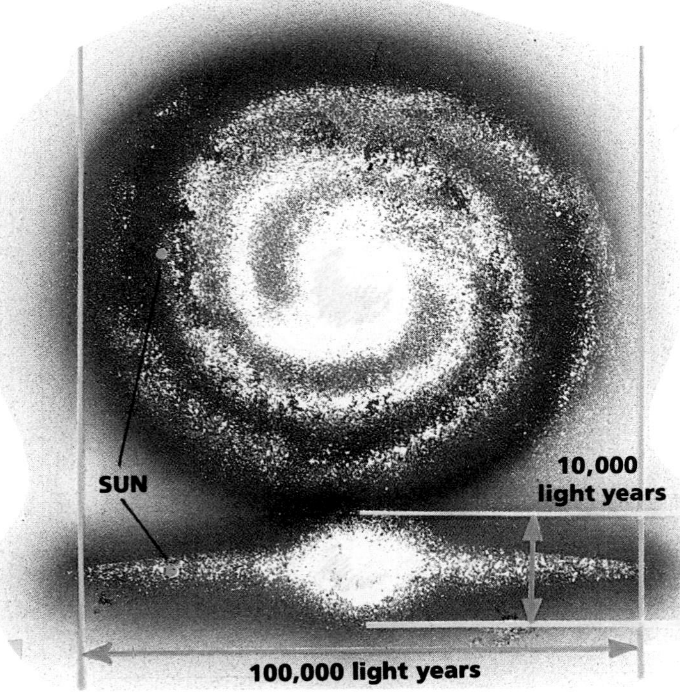

The Milky Way Galaxy is a spiral galaxy. About 20 billion stars make up the spiral arms of the Milky Way Galaxy. There are about 80 billion stars in the center of the galaxy. The distance from top to bottom of the nucleus is about 10,000 light years. The distance from edge to edge of the spiral arms is about 100,000 light years. The sun is in a spiral arm about two-thirds of the way from the center of the Milky Way Galaxy.

Classify: What kind of galaxy is the Milky Way Galaxy?

The Milky Way Have you ever looked at the sky on a dark, moonless night? If you have, you probably saw a band of stars stretching across the sky. Ancient people called this band of stars the Milky Way. They thought it looked like a river of milk. When you look at the Milky Way, you are seeing part of a spiral arm of the Milky Way Galaxy.

Identify: What is the Milky Way?

Clusters and Double Stars The sun is only one of billions of stars in the Milky Way Galaxy. Unlike the sun, most of the stars in the galaxy are double stars, or **binary stars.** These are pairs of stars that revolve around each other. Some stars belong to multiple-star systems with more than two stars.

Some stars in the Milky Way Galaxy are found in groups called **clusters.** There are two kinds of clusters. Some clusters are spherical, or round, in shape. Others are open, or loosely arranged.

Define: What are binary stars?

LESSON SUMMARY

- The sun and all the planets in the solar system belong to the Milky Way Galaxy.
- The Milky Way Galaxy is a spiral galaxy.
- The Milky Way is a band of stars that is part of a spiral arm of the Milky Way Galaxy.
- Most stars in the Milky Way Galaxy are binary stars.
- Some stars in the Milky Way Galaxy are found in clusters.

CHECK *Complete the following.*

1. What is the name of the galaxy to which the sun belongs?
2. What is the Local Group?
3. How far across is the Milky Way Galaxy?
4. Is the sun located in the nucleus or in a spiral arm of the galaxy?
5. What is the band of stars stretching across the sky called?
6. What is another name for binary stars?
7. What are clusters?

APPLY *Complete the following.*

8. **Calculate:** About how many stars make up the Milky Way Galaxy?
9. **Infer:** Why did ancient people call the band of stars stretching across the sky the "Milky Way"?

Skill Builder

Researching When you research, you gather information about a topic. Astronomers using large telescopes have identified and catalogued many different galaxies. Using an encyclopedia or other library references, look up the following galaxies: Andromeda, M 51 (Whirlpool), NGC 205, NGC 3193, Small Magellanic Cloud, Large Magellanic Cloud. Write the name of each galaxy on a piece of paper. Next to each name, identify the type of galaxy and its location. What do the letters "M" and "NGC" stand for?

TECHNOLOGY AND SOCIETY

HUBBLE TELESCOPE AND DISTANT GALAXIES

The Hubble Space Telescope was launched into earth's orbit in 1990. In orbit, the telescope is above the atmosphere, air pollution, and city lights that block out much starlight. Therefore, the Hubble telescope can see galaxies that cannot be seen from earth.

Like many other telescopes, the Hubble uses a camera to photograph the sky. Film or videotape can be exposed to faint starlight for minutes, hours, or even days. Over this time, faint starlight collects on the film or tape and shows stars that you could not see with your eyes alone. The Hubble telescope has photographed hundreds of galaxies never seen before. These galaxies are about 12 billion light years away. That means the light from them has taken about 12 billion years to reach earth. By observing these galaxies, scientists see how they looked 12 billion years ago.

Many of the newly discovered galaxies appear on one photograph called the Hubble Deep Field. This photograph was made by focusing the telescope on one small part of space for ten days. Over this period, the telescope collected enough light from the galaxies for them to become visible.

UNIT 18 Challenges

STUDY HINT Before you begin the Unit Challenges, review the TechTerms and Lesson Summary for each lesson in this unit.

TechTerms

binary stars (396)
chromosphere (384)
cluster (396)
constellation (392)
core (384)
corona (384)
elliptical galaxy (394)
fusion (388)
galaxy (394)
irregular galaxy (394)
magnitude (378)
main sequence stars (380)
nebula (374)
nova (382)
nucleus (388)
photosphere (384)
photosynthesis (390)
prominences (386)
protostar (374)
red giants (380)
solar flares (386)
spectroscope (376)
spectrum (376)
spiral galaxy (394)
star (374)
sunspots (386)
supergiants (380)
supernova (382)
white dwarfs (380)

TechTerm Challenges

Matching *Write the TechTerm that matches each description.*

1. inner layer of the sun's atmosphere
2. grouping of stars that form a pattern in the sky
3. spinning cloud of hot gases
4. measure of a star's brightness
5. dark, cool areas on the sun's surface
6. large group of stars in a galaxy
7. very small, hot stars
8. center, or core, of an atom
9. instrument that separates light into different colors
10. galaxy with no definite shape
11. star that has been blown apart in a violent explosion
12. process by which plants use light from the sun to make food
13. ball of gases that gives off light and heat
14. pairs of stars that revolve around each other
15. large, bright stars that are fairly cool

A.

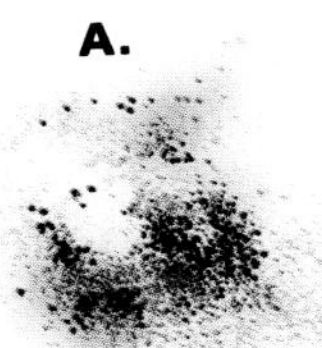

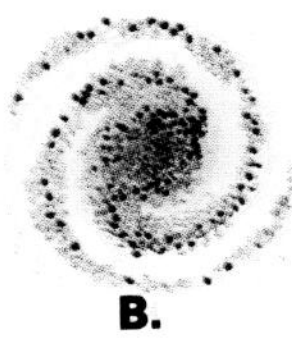

B.

C.

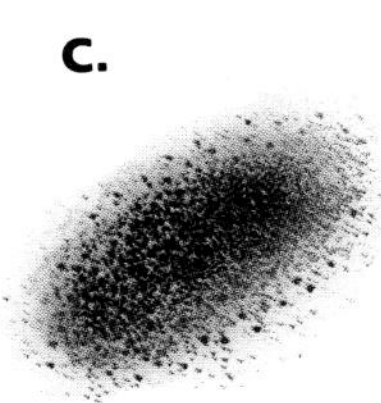

Fill-in *Write the TechTerm that best completes each statement.*

1. A galaxy with a thick center and flattened arms is a _______ .
2. When a white dwarf blows off its outer layers in an explosion a _______ is formed.
3. Material in the center of a nebula that becomes a star is a _______ .
4. Stars that fall within a band in the middle of the H-R diagram are _______ .
5. The outer layer of the sun's atmosphere is the _______ .
6. Bands of the different colors of light make up the _______ of light.
7. Streams of gases that shoot high above the sun's surface are called _______ .
8. A large group of stars is a _______ .
9. The layer of the sun's atmosphere above the photosphere is the _______ .
10. A reaction in which atomic nuclei combine to form larger nuclei is a _______ reaction.
11. Eruptions of electrically charged particles from the sun's surface are _______ .
12. A spherical or flattened disk-shaped galaxy is called an _______ .
13. Very large stars are called _______ .
14. The center part of the sun is the _______ .

Content Challenges

Multiple Choice *Write the letter of the term that best completes each statement.*

1. The sun is only one of billions of
   a. nebulas. **b.** stars. **c.** galaxies. **d.** constellations.
2. In Einstein's equation, $E = mc^2$, c is
   a. energy. **b.** mass. **c.** the speed of light. **d.** the amount of matter.
3. The Milky Way Galaxy is a
   a. spiral galaxy. **b.** elliptical galaxy. **c.** irregular galaxy. **d.** spherical galaxy.
4. The hottest stars are
   a. red. **b.** blue. **c.** yellow. **d.** orange.
5. The source of the sun's energy is the
   a. corona. **b.** photosphere. **c.** chromosphere. **d.** core.
6. Photosynthesis takes place in
   a. plants. **b.** animals. **c.** the corona. **d.** fossil fuels.
7. The actual brightness of a star is its
   a. apparent magnitude. **b.** first-magnitude. **c.** sixth-magnitude. **d.** absolute magnitude.
8. The spinning of the sun on its axis causes
   a. solar flares. **b.** sunspot movement. **c.** prominences. **d.** fusion.

True/False *Write true if the statement is true. If the statement is false, change the underlined term to make the statement true.*

1. The gravity of a black <u>dwarf</u> is so great that nothing can escape.
2. The main features of the universe are <u>galaxies</u>.
3. The most common element in most stars is <u>helium</u>.
4. During photosynthesis, <u>carbon dioxide</u> is given off by plants.
5. The brightness of most stars increases as the stars surface temperature <u>decreases</u>.
6. The sun and all the planets in the solar system are in the <u>Milky Way Galaxy</u>.
7. Each <u>element</u> gives off its own spectrum of light.

Understanding the Features

Reading Critically *Use the feature reading selections to answer the following. Page numbers for the features are shown in parentheses.*

1. What are two special features of the Keck Telescope? (375)
2. What is a Cepheid variable? (381)
3. What idea did Tycho Brahe's observations of a nova show not to be true? (383)
4. When are auroras formed? (387)
5. What conditions are needed for fusion reactions to take place? (389)
6. What three things should you check on a sunscreen label? (391)
7. Who wrote the oldest astronomical texts? (393)
8. What is the Hubble Deep Field? (397)

Concept Challenges

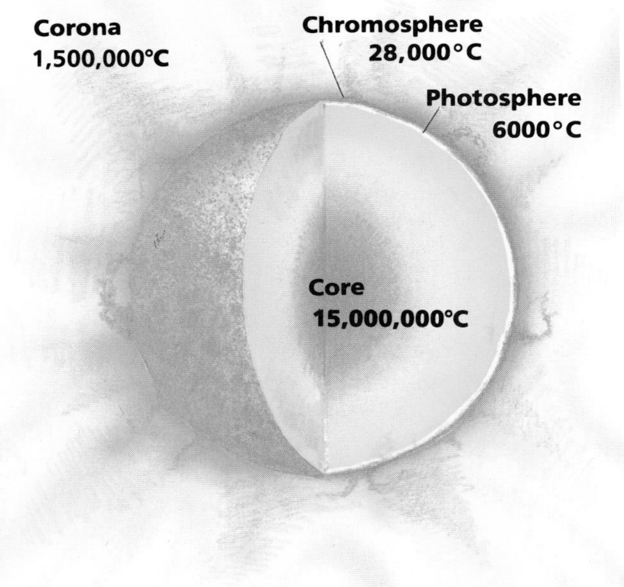

Interpreting a Diagram *Use the diagram to answer each of the following.*

1. What is the center part of the sun?
2. What three layers make up the sun's atmosphere?
3. What is the outermost layer of the sun's atmosphere?
4. What is the temperature of the core?
5. What is the temperature of the corona?
6. About how many degrees Celsius hotter is the chromosphere than the photosphere?

Critical Thinking *Answer each of the following in complete sentences.*

1. Why is the sun's density low?
2. How do astronomers find out the chemical makeup of a star?
3. What is meant by the "birth" and "death" of a star?
4. Why can fossil fuels be called "stored sunlight?"
5. Why is an old main sequence star made up of a larger percentage of helium than a young main sequence star?

Finding Out More

1. Observe the sky on the next clear night. Draw sketches of the constellations that you observe. Name the constellations, and label any star that you can identity.
2. On a posterboard, draw a diagram showing the activities that take place in the sun's atmosphere.
3. Quasars are the most distant objects that have been observed from the earth. Using library references, find out about the characteristics of quasars. Write your findings in a report.
4. Write to the America Cancer Society for information about skin cancer. Display any pamphlets you receive in the classroom. Summarize the information in an oral report.
5. Using library references, write a brief biography on Egvar Hertzsprung or Henry Russel.

Appendix A

THE METRIC SYSTEM AND SI UNITS

The metric system is an international system of measurement based on units of 10. More than 90 percent of the nations of the world use the metric system. In the United States, both the English or Imperial Measurement System and the metric system are used.

Systeme International, or SI, has been used as the international measurement system since 1960. SI is a modernized version of the metric system. Like the metric system, SI is a decimal system based on units of 10.

In both SI and the metric system, prefixes are added to base units to form larger or smaller units. Each unit is 10 times larger than the next smaller unit, and 10 times smaller than the next larger unit. For example, the meter is the basic unit of length. The next larger unit is a dekameter. A dekameter is 10 times larger than a meter. The next smaller unit is a decimeter. A decimeter is 10 times smaller than a meter. Ten decimeters is equal to one meter. How many meters equal one dekameter? 10

When you want to change from one unit in the metric system to another unit, you multiply or divide by a multiple of 10.

- When you change from a smaller unit to a larger unit, you divide.
- When you change from a larger unit to a smaller unit, you multiply.

SI UNITS

The basic unit is printed in capital letters.

Length	*Symbol*
kilometer	km
METER	m
centimeter	cm
millimeter	mm
Area	*Symbol*
square kilometer	km^2
SQUARE METER	m^2
square millimeter	mm^2
Volume	*Symbol*
CUBIC METER	m^3
cubic millimeter	mm^3
liter	L
milliliter	mL
Mass	*Symbol*
KILOGRAM	kg
gram	g
tonne	t
Temperature	*Symbol*
KELVIN	K
degree Celsius	°C

SOME COMMON METRIC PREFIXES

Prefix		*Meaning*
micro-	=	0.000001, or 1/1,000,000
milli-	=	0.001, or 1/1000
centi-	=	0.01, or 1/100
deci-	=	0.1, or 1/10
deka-	=	10
hecto-	=	100
kilo-	=	1000
mega-	=	1,000,000

SOME METRIC RELATIONSHIPS

Unit	*Relationship*
kilometer	1 km = 1000 m
meter	1 m = 100 cm
centimeter	1 cm = 10 mm
millimeter	1 mm = 0.1 cm
liter	1 L = 1000 mL
milliliter	1 mL = 0.001 L
tonne	1t = 1000 kg
kilogram	1 kg = 1000 g
gram	1 g = 1000 mg
centigram	1 cg = 10 mg
milligram	1 mg = 0.001 g

SI-ENGLISH EQUIVALENTS

	SI to English	*English to SI*
Length	1 kilometer = 0.621 mile (mi)	1 mi = 1.61 km
	1 meter = 0.914 yards (yd)	1 yd = 1.09 m
	1 meter = 3.28 feet (ft)	1 ft = 0.305 m
	1 centimeter = 0.394 inch (in)	1 in = 2.54 cm
	1 millimeter = 0.039 inch	1 in = 25.4 mm
Area	1 square kilometer = 0.3861 square mile	1 mi^2 = 2.590 km^2
	1 square meter = 1.1960 square yards	1 yd^2 = 0.8361 m^2
	1 square meter = 10.763 square feet	1 ft^2 = 0.0929 m^2
	1 square centimeter = 0.155 square inch	1 in^2 = 6.452 cm^2
Volume	1 cubic meter = 1.3080 cubic yards	1 yd^3 = 0.7646 m^3
	1 cubic meter = 35.315 cubic feet	1 ft^3 = 0.0283 m^3
	1 cubic centimeter = 0.0610 cubic inches	1 in^3 = 16.39 cm^3
	1 liter = .2642 gallon (gal)	1 gal = 3.79 L
	1 liter = 1.06 quart (qt)	1 qt = 0.94 L
	1 liter = 2.11 pint (pt)	1 pt = 0.47 L
	1 milliliter = 0.034 fluid ounce (fl oz)	1 fl oz = 29.57 mL
Mass	1 tonn = .984 ton	1 ton = 1.016 t
	1 kilogram = 2.205 pound (lb)	1 lb = 0.4536 kg
	1 gram = 0.0353 ounce (oz)	1 oz = 28.35 g
Temperature	Celsius = 5/9 (°F −32)	Fahrenheit = 9/5°C + 32
	0°C = 32°F (Freezing point of water)	72°F = 22°C (Room temperature)
	100°C = 212°F (Boiling point of water)	98.6=F = 37°C (Human body temperature)

Appendix B

SAFETY IN THE SCIENCE CLASSROOM

Safety is very important in the science classroom. Science classrooms and laboratories have equipment and chemicals that can be dangerous if not handled properly. To avoid accidents in the science laboratory, always follow proper safety rules. Listen carefully when your teacher explains precautions and safety rules that must be followed. You should never perform an activity without your teacher's direction. By following safety rules you can help insure the safety of yourself and your classmates. Safety rules that should be followed are listed below. Read over these safety rules carefully. Always look for caution statements before you perform an activity.

Clothing Protection • Wear your laboratory apron. • Confine loose clothing.

Eye Safety • Wear safety goggles in the laboratory. • If anything gets in your eyes, flush them with plenty of water. • Be sure you know how to use the emergency wash system in the laboratory.

Heat and Fire Safety • Be careful when handling hot objects. • Use proper procedures when lighting Bunsen burners. • Turn off all heat sources when they are not in use. • Tie back long hair when working near an open flame. • Confine loose clothing. • Turn off gas valves when not in use.

Electrical Safety • Keep all work areas clean and dry. • Never handle electrical equipment with wet hands. • Do not overload an electric circuit. • Do not use wires that are frayed.

Glassware Safety • Never use chipped or cracked glassware. • Never pick up broken glass with your bare hands. • Allow heated glass to cool before touching it. • Never force glassware into a rubber stopper.

Chemical Safety • Never taste chemicals as a means of identification. • Never transfer liquids with a mouth pipette. Use a suction bulb. • Be very careful when working with acids or bases. Both can cause serious burns. • Never pour water into an acid or base. Always pour an acid or base into water. • Inform your teacher immediately if you spill chemicals or get any chemicals on your skin. • Use a waving motion of your hand to observe the odor of a chemical. • Never put your nose near a chemical. • Never eat or drink in the laboratory.

Sharp Objects • Use knives, scissors, and other sharp instruments with care. • Cut in the direction away from your body.

Cleanup • Clean up your work area before leaving the laboratory. • Follow your teacher's instructions for disposal of materials. • Wash your hands after an activity.

Appendix C

MINERAL GUIDE

Mineral	*Chemical Formula*	*Color*	*Streak*
Apatite	$Ca_5\ (PO_4)_3F$	green, brown, red	white
Augite	$(Ca,Mg,Fe)\ (SiO_3)_2(Al,Fe)_2O_3$	dark green, black	green to grey
Biotite (Mica)	complex substance containing Fe, Mg, Si, O, and other elements	Black, brown, dark green	white to light brown
Calcite	$CaCO_3$	gray, white	white
Chalcopyrite	$CuFeS_2$	brass, yellow	greenish black
Copper	Cu	copper red to black	copper red
Corundum	Al_2O_3	usually brown	white
Dolomite	$CaMG(CO_3)_2$	pink, white, gray, green, brown, black	colorless
Feldspar	$(K,\ Na,\ Ca)\ (AlSi_3O_8)$	colorless, white, various colors	colorless, white
Fluorite	CaF_2	light green yellow, bluish green, other colors	colorless
Galena	PbS	lead gray	lead gray
Graphite	C	black to gray	black
Gypsum	$CaSO_4 + 2H_2O$	whitish gray	colorless
Hematite	Fe_2O_3	reddish brown to black	light to dark red
Hornblende	complex substance containing Fe, Mg, Si, O, and other elements	dark green, black, brown	gray to white
Magnetite	Fe_3O_4	iron black	black
Olivine	Mg_2SiO_4	olive green	white
Pyrite	FeS_2	brass, yellow	greenish, brownish, black
Quartz	SiO_2	colorless, white, any color when not pure	colorless, white
Serpentine	$Mg_3Si_2O_5(OH)_4$	green	white
Sphalerite	ZnS	brown to black	white, yellow, brown
Sulfur	S	yellow	white
Talc	$Mg_3(OH)_2Si_4O_{10}$	gray, white, greenish	white

Mineral	*Luster*	*Hardness*	*Specific Gravity*	*Fracture/Cleavage*
Apatite	Nonmetallic	5	3.15–3.2	cleavage
Augite	Nonmetallic	5–6		cleavage
Biotite (Mica)	Nonmetallic	2.5–6	2.8–3.2	cleavage
Calcite	Nonmetallic	2–3		cleavage
Chalcopyrite	Metallic	3.5–4	4.1–4.34	cleavage
Copper	Metallic	2.5–3	8.5–9	cleavage
Corundum	Nonmetallic	9	4.02	cleavage
Dolomite	Nonmetallic	3.5–4	2.85	fracture
Feldspar	Nonmetallic	6	2.55–2.75	cleavage
Fluorite	Nonmetallic	4	3.18	cleavage
Galena	Metallic	2.5	7.4–7.6	cleavage
Graphite	Metallic	1–2	2.3	cleavage
Gypsum	Nonmetallic	2		cleavage
Hematite	Metallic	5.5–6.6	5.26	cleavage
Hornblende	Nonmetallic	5–6	3.2	cleavage
Magnetite	Metallic	5–6	5.18	cleavage
Olivine	Nonmetallic	6.5–7		cleavage
Pyrite	Metallic	6–6.5	5.02	cleavage
Quartz	Nonmetallic	7.5–8	2.65	cleavage
Serpentine	Nonmetallic	2.5	2.2–2.65	cleavage
Sphalerite	Nonmetallic	3.5–4	3.9–4.1	cleavage
Sulfur	Nonmetallic	1.5–2.5	2.07	fracture
Talc	Nonmetallic	1	2.7–2.8	fracture

Appendix D

PREFIXES AND SUFFIXES

Prefixes and suffixes are words parts that can be helpful in determining the meaning of an unfamiliar term. Prefixes are found at the beginning of words. Suffixes are found at the end of words. Both prefixes and suffixes have meanings that mainly come from Latin and Greek words. Some meanings of prefixes and suffixes commonly used in earth science words are listed below.

Prefix	*Meaning*	*Example*
alti-, alto-	high	altitude
astr-, aster-	star	asteroid
atmo-	air	atmosphere
bar-, baro-	weight, pressure	barometer
batho-, bathy	depth	bathysphere
epi-	on	epicenter
ex-, exo-	outside of	extrusion
fore-	before	forecast
geo-	earth	geologist
hemi-	half	hemisphere
hydro-	water	hydrosphere
iso-	equal	isostasy
litho-	rock, stone	lithosphere
mar-	sea	marine
meso-	middle	Mesozoic
meta-	change	metamorphic
micro-	small	microclimate
nimbo-	rain	nimbostratus
paleo-	old	paleontology
ped-, pedo-	soil	pedocal
peri-	around	perihelion
petro-	rock, stone	petrologist
photo-	light	photosphere
proto-	first, original	protostar
seismo-	earthquake	seismograph
sol-	sun	solstice
sub-	under	subsoil
thermo-	heat	thermometer
top-, topo-	place	topography
trop-, tropo-	change, turn	troposphere

Suffix	*Meaning*	*Examples*
-cline	slope	syncline
-graph	write	seismograph
-logy	study of	meteorology
-meter	device for measuring	anemometer
-morph, -morphic	form	metamorphic
-sphere	ball, globe	hemisphere

Glossary

Pronunciation and syllabication have been derived from *Webster's New World Dictionary,* Second College Edition, Revised School Printing (Prentice Hall, 1985). Syllables printed in capital letters are given primary stress. (Numbers in parentheses indicate the page number, or page numbers, on which the term is defined.)

PRONUNCIATION KEY

Symbol	*Example*	*Respelling*	*Symbol*	*Example*	*Respelling*
ah	composite	(kum-PAHZ-it)	ks	axis	(AK-sis)
aw	atoll	(A-tawl)	oh	biome	(BY-ohm)
ay	abrasion	(uh-BRAY-zhun)	oo	altitude	(AL-tuh-tood)
ch	leaching	(LEECH-ing)	oy	asteroid	(AST-uh-royd)
e	chemical	(KEM-ih-kul)	s	satellite	(SAT-uh-lite)
ee	equinox	(EE-kwuh-nahks)	sh	specialization	(SPESH-uh-lih-zay-shun)
ew	nucleus	(NEW-klee-us)	uh	volcanism	(VAHL-kuh-niz-um)
f	hemisphere	(HEM-uh-sfeer)	y	elevation	(el-uh-VAY-shun)
g	galaxy	(GAL-ack-see)	yoo	cumulus	(KYOOM-yuh-lus)
ih	anticline	(AN-tih-klyn)	z	deposition	(dep-uh-ZISH-un)
j	geologic	(jee-uh-LAJ-ik)	zh	erosion	(eh-ROH-zhun)
k	current	(KUR-unt)			

A

abrasion (uh-BRAY-zhun): wearing away of rock or by particles carried by wind and water (104)

absolute age: specific age of a rock or a fossil (176)

acid rain: rain containing nitric acid and sulfuric acid (86, 282)

adaptations (ad-ap-TAY-shuns): features that let living things live and reproduce in their environments (274)

air current (KUR-unt): up-and-down movement of air (226)

air mass: large area of air that has the same temperature and amount of moisture (250)

altitude (AL-tuh-tood): height above sea level (266)

amber: hardened tree sap (168)

anemometer (an-uh-MOM-uh-tur): instrument used to measure wind speed (232)

anticline (AN-tih-klyn): upward fold in rock layers (126)

aphelion (af-FEEL-yun): point in a planet's orbit at which it is farthest from the sun (330)

apogee (AP-uh-jee): point of moon's orbit at which the moon is farthest from the earth (358)

asteroid (AST-uh-royd): large chunk of rock that orbits the sun (344)

astronomical (as-truh-NOM-ih-kul) **unit:** unit of measurement equal to about 150 million kilometers (314)

astronomy (uh-STRON-uh-mee): study of stars, planets, and other objects in space (304)

atmosphere (AT-muhs-feer): envelope of gases surrounding the earth (20, 212)

atoll (A-tawl): ring-shaped coral reef (206)

atom: smallest part of an element (40)

axis (AK-sis): imaginary line through the center of a planet on which the planet rotates (350)

B

barometer (buh-ROM-uh-ter): instrument used to measure air pressure (224)

bedrock: solid rock that lies beneath the soil (88)

benthos: organisms that live on the ocean floor (204)

binary stars: pairs of stars that revolve around each other (396)

biome (BY-ohm): large area of the earth that has certain kinds of living things (274)

C

capacity (kuh-PAS-ih-tee): amount of material something can hold (240)

carbonation (car-buh-NAY-shun): chemical reaction between carbonic acid and another substance (82)

cast: mold that has filled with sediments (166)
cavern: series of underground caves formed by groundwater erosion (84)
chemical formula (FOR-myoo-luh): shorthand way of writing the name of a compound (46)
chemical (KEM-ih-kul) **symbol:** shorthand way of writing the name of an element (40)
chemical (KEM-ih-kul) **weathering:** weathering in which the chemical makeup of a rock is changed (80)
chromosphere (KROH-muh-sfeer): layer of the sun's atmosphere above the photosphere (384)
cinder cone: volcanic cone made up of rock particles, dust, and ash (136)
cirrus (SIR-us): light, feathery clouds (246)
clastics (KLAS-tiks): sedimentary rocks made up of pieces of rock (68)
cleavage (KLEE-vij): splitting of a mineral into pieces with smooth, flat surfaces (52)
climate (KLY-mut): average weather conditions of an area over many years (264)
cluster: large group of stars in a galaxy (396)
cold front: forward edge of a cold air mass, formed when a cold air mass pushes under a warm air mass (252)
comet: body made up of rock, dust, gases, and ice that orbits the sun (344)
composite (kum-PAHZ-it) **cone:** volcanic cone made up of alternating layers of lava and rock particles (136)
compound (KOM-pownd): substance made up of two or more elements that are chemically combined (42)
concave mirror: mirror that curves inward (310)
condensation (kahn-dun-SAY-shun): changing of a gas to a liquid (184, 244)
conduction (kon-DUCK-shun): movement of heat through a solid (218)
conservation (kahn-sur-VAY-shun): wise use of natural resources (290)
constellation (kon-stuh-LAY-shun): grouping of stars that form a pattern in the sky (392)
continental (KAHNT-un-ent-ul) **drift:** idea that the continents were once a giant landmass that broke into pieces that moved to the positions they are in today (150)
continental shelf: part of a continent that slopes gently away from the shoreline (202)
continental slope: part of a continent between the continental shelf and the ocean floor (202)
contour interval (IN-tur-vul): difference in elevation between one contour line and the next (34)
contour (KON-toor) **line:** line on a map that connects all points having the same elevation (32)
convection (kon-VEK-shun): movement of heat through a liquid or a gas (218)
convection (kuhn-VEK-shun) **current:** movement of a liquid or gas caused by changes in temperature (158)
convex (kon-VEKS) **lens:** lens that is thicker in the middle than at the edges (308)
coral: small animals found in shallow ocean waters (206)
core: solid, inner, layer of the earth (22); center of the sun (384)
corona (kuh-ROH-nuh): outer layer of the sun's atmosphere (384)
crater (KRAY-tur): funnel-shaped pit at the top of a volcanic cone (134); round hole on the moon's surface (336)
crescent (KRES-ent) **phase:** phase when less than half the moon is visible (360)
crest: highest point of a wave (198)
crust: thin, solid, outer layer of the earth (22)
crustal plates: large pieces of the solid part of the earth (156)
crystal (KRIS-tul): a natural solid substance that has a definite shape (50)
cumulus (KYOOM-yuh-lus): big, puffy clouds (246)
currents (KUR-ents): streams of water flowing in the oceans (196)

D

data (DAY-tuh): information (6)
deflation (dih-FLAY-shun): removal of loose material from the earth's surface (104)
degree Celsius (SEL-see-us): metric unit of temperature (14)
delta: triangular-shaped deposit of sediment located at the mouth of a river (110)
density (DEN-sih-tee): amount of matter in a given volume (12, 50)
density currents: streams of water that move up and down in the oceans (196)
deposition (dep-uh-ZISH-un): process by which material carried by erosion is dropped in new places (100)
dew point: temperature to which water in the air must be cooled to reach saturation (244)
distortion (dis-TOHR-shun): error in shape, size, or distance (24)
drumlin: oval-shaped mound of till (116)

E

earthquake: sudden, strong movement of the earth's crust (138)
ebb tide: outgoing, or falling tide (366)
element (EL-uh-munt): substance made up of only one kind of atom (40)
elevation (el-uh-VAY-shun): distance above or below sea level (32, 128)
ellipse (uh-LIPS): flattened circle, or oval (330)

elliptical galaxy: spherical or flattened disk-shaped galaxy (394)
environment (in-VY-run-munt): everything that surrounds a living thing (280)
epicenter (EP-ih-sen-ter): place on the surface of the earth directly above the focus (138)
equinox (EE-kwuh-nahks): "equal night"; day on which the sun shines directly on the equator (354)
erosion (eh-ROH-zhun): process by which weathered material is moved from one place to another (100)
erratics (uh-RAT-iks): rocks left behind by a retreating glacier (114)
evaporation (ih-vap-uh-RAY-shun): changing of a liquid to a gas (184, 238)

F

fault: break in the earth's crust along which movement has occurred (126)
flood plain: flat area on the side of a river where sediments are deposited during floods (110)
flood tide: incoming, or rising tide (366)
focus (FOH-kus): place inside the earth where an earthquake starts (138)
foliated (FOH-lee-ay-ted): texture of a metamorphic rock that has mineral crystals arranged in bands (72)
fossil (FOSS-il): remain or trace of a living thing that lived long ago (166)
fossil fuels (FEWLS): natural fuels that come from the remains of living things (170)
fracture (FRAK-chur): splitting of a mineral into pieces with uneven surfaces (52); break in a rock (126)
front: surface between two different air masses (252)
frost: ice formed from condensation below the freezing point of water (244)
fusion (FYOO-zhun): reaction in which atomic nuclei combine to form larger nuclei (388)

G

galaxy (GAL-ack-see): large system of stars (306, 394)
gem: gemstone that has been cut and polished (54)
geologic (jee-uh-LAJ-ik) **time scale:** outline of the major events in the earth's history (178)
geothermal (jee-oh-THER-mul) **energy:** energy produced from heat inside the earth (298)
geyser (GY-zur): heated groundwater that erupts onto the earth's surface (188)
gibbous (GIB-us) **phase:** phase when more than half the moon is visible (360)
glacier (GLAY-shur): moving river of ice and snow (112)
global winds: large wind systems around the earth (228)
globe: spherical model of the earth (24)
gravity (GRAV-uh-tee): force of attraction that exists between all objects in the universe (332)
groundwater: water that collects in pores in the soil (186)
guyot (GEE-oh): flat-topped, underwater seamount (202)

H

half-life: length of time it takes for one-half the amount of a radioactive element to change into another element (176)
hanging valley: small glacial valley above a main valley (114)
hard water: water containing a lot of calcium and magnesium minerals (286)
hardness: physical property of a mineral to resist being scratched (48)
hemisphere (HEM-uh-sfeer): one-half of a sphere (28)
horizon (hor-Y-zun): soil layer (92)
hot spot: place where magma reaches the earth's surface within a crustal plate (160)
humidity: amount of water vapor in the air (240)
humus (HYOO-mus): part of soil made up of decaying remains of plants and animals (88)
hurricane (hur-uh-KAYN): tropical storm with very strong winds (254)
hydroelectric (HY-droh-ih-LEK-trik) **power:** electrical energy produced from moving water (296)
hydrolysis (hy-DRAHL-uh-sis): chemical reaction between water and another substance (82)
hydrosphere (HY-droh-sfeer): part of the earth that is water (20)
hypothesis (hy-PAHTH-uh-sis): suggested answer to a problem (4)

I

ice wedging: mechanical weathering caused by the freezing and melting of water (80)
igneous (IG-nee-us) **rock:** rock that forms from melted minerals (60)
index fossil: remains of an organism that lived only during a short part of the earth's history (174)
indicator (IN-dih-kay-tur): chemical used to identify the presence of other substances (94)
international date line: boundary formed where the first and twenty-fourth time zone meet (356)
ionosphere (Y-on-uh-sfeer): upper layer of the atmosphere (214)
irregular galaxy: galaxy with no definite shape (394)
isobar (Y-suh-bar): line on a weather map that connects points of equal air pressure (258)

J

jet stream: belt of high-speed wind (228)

K

kettle lake: lake formed by a retreating glacier (116)
kilogram (KIL-uh-gram): basic metric unit of mass (10)
kinetic (ki-NET-ik) **energy:** energy of motion (296)

L

L-waves: seismic waves that move along the earth's surface (140)
lagoon: shallow body of water between a reef and the mainland (206)
landform: physical feature of the earth's surface (132)
latitude (LAT-uh-tood): number of degrees by which a place is north or south of the equator (28, 266)
lava (LAH-vuh): magma that reaches the earth's surface (62, 134)
leaching (LEECH-ing): downward movement of minerals in soil (90, 272)
legend (LEJ-und): list of map symbols and their meanings (30)
light year: unit of measurement equal to about 10 trillion kilometers (314)
liter (LEE-tur): basic metric unit of volume (12)
lithosphere (LITH-oh-sfeer): solid part of the earth (20)
litter: materials that are thrown away on the ground (288)
loess (LESS): deposits of wind-blown dust (104)
longitude (LON-jih-tood): number of degrees by which a place is east or west of the prime meridian (28)
longshore current: movement of water parallel to a shoreline (120)
lunar eclipse (uh-CLIPS): passing of the moon through the earth's shadow (362)
luster: the way a mineral reflects light from its surface (48)

M

magma (MAG-muh): molten rock inside the earth (62)
magma chamber: underground pocket of molten rock (160)
magnetism (MAG-nuh-tiz-um): natural force that occurs when objects made out of iron and steel are attracted by a magnet (50)
magnitude (MAG-nuh-tood): measure of a star's brightness (378)
main sequence stars: stars that fall within a band in the middle of the H-R diagram (380)
mantle (MAN-tul): thick layer of the earth below the crust (22)
map: flat model of the earth (24)
map projection (pruh-JEK-shun): drawing of the earth, or part of the earth, on a flat surface (26)
maria (MẠHR-ee-uh): broad, flat plains on the moon (336)
mass: amount of matter in an object (10)
mass movement: downhill movement of weathered materials caused by gravity (102)
matter: anything that has mass and volume (212)
meanders (mee-AN-durs): loops in a mature river (108)
mechanical (muh-KAN-ih-kul) **weathering:** weathering in which the chemical makeup of rocks does not change (80)
meridian (muh-RID-ee-un): imaginary line running from the North Pole to the South Pole (28)
metamorphic (met-uh-MOR-fik) **rock:** rock that forms when existing rocks are changed by heat and pressure (60)
meteor (MEE-tee-or): piece of rock or metal that enters the earth's atmosphere (344)
meteorite (MEE-tee-or-ite): piece of rock or metal that hits the earth's surface (344)
meteoroid (MEE-tee-or-oyd): piece of rock or metal that orbits the sun (344)
meter (MEE-tur): basic SI and metric unit of length (8)
microclimate (MY-kroh-kly-mit): smallest climate zone (270)
mid-ocean ridge: underwater mountain chain (152)
middle-latitude zone: region between 30° and 60° north and south latitude (268)
millibar: unit of measurement for air pressure (256)
mineral (MIN-uh-rul): natural solid formed from elements and compounds in the earth's crust (46)
mold: cavity, or opening, in a rock that has the shape of an extinct organism (166)
molecule (MAHL-uh-kyool): smallest part of a substance that has all the properties of that substance (42)
molten (MOHL-tun) **rock:** melted minerals (62)
monsoon: wind that changes direction with the seasons (230)
moraine (moor-AYN): ridge of till deposited by a retreating glacier (116)

N

natural resource: material from the earth that is used by living things (290)
neap (NEEP) **tide:** tide that is not as high or as low as a normal tide (368)
nebula (NEB-yuh-luh): spinning cloud of hot gases (328, 374)
nekton (NEK-tun): free-swimming ocean animals (204)
newton: metric unit of force (220)
nodules (NAHJ-ools): mineral lumps found on the ocean floor (200)
nonclastics: sedimentary rocks made up of dissolved minerals, or the remains of living things (68)

nonrenewable resource: natural resource that is not replaced by nature (290)
nova: star in which the outer layer has been blown off in an explosion (382)
nuclear (NOO-klee-ar) **energy:** energy produced by breaking apart atoms (298)
nucleus (NEW-klee-us): center, or core, of an atom (388)

O

oceanography (oh-shun-OG-ruh-fee): study of the earth's oceans (190)
ooze: ocean sediment formed from volcanic dust and the remains of ocean organisms (200)
orbit: curved path of one object around another object in space (318, 328)
ore: mineral that is mined because it contains useful metals or nonmetals (54)
oxbow lake: lake formed when a meander is cut off from the rest of the river (108)
oxidation (ok-suh-DAY-shun): chemical change between oxygen and another substance (82)

P

P-waves: fastest earthquake waves (140)
parallel (PAR-uh-lel): imaginary line running horizontally around the earth (28)
penumbra (peh-NUM-bruh): light part of a shadow (362)
perigee (PER-uh-jee): point at which the moon is closest to the earth (358)
perihelion (per-uh-HEEL-yun): point in a planet's orbit at which it is closest to the sun (330)
pH scale: number scale used to measure acidity (94)
phases (FAYZ-uz): changing shapes of the moon (360)
photosphere (FOH-tuh-sfeer): inner layer of the sun's atmosphere (384)
photosynthesis (foh-toh-SIN-thuh-sis): process by which plants use light from the sun to make food (390)
plankton (PLANK-tun): floating organisms (204)
polar air mass: air mass that forms over cold regions (250)
polar zone: cold region above 60° north and 60° south latitude (268)
pollutants (puh-LOOT-ents): harmful substances in the environment (280)
pollution (puh-LOO-shun): anything that harms the environment (280)
pores: tiny holes or air spaces (190)
potential (puh-TEN-shul) **energy:** stored energy (296)
precipitation (prih-sip-uh-TAY-shun): water that falls to the earth from the atmosphere (184, 248)
pressure: amount of force on a unit of area (70, 220)
prominences (PRAHM-uh-nuns-ez): streams of gases that shoot high above the sun's surface (386)
properties (PRAHP-ur-teez): features that describe objects (42)
protostar: material in the center of a nebula that becomes a star (374)
psychrometer (sy-KRAHM-uh-tur): instrument used to find relative humidity (242)

R

radiant (RAY-dee-unt) **energy:** energy that can travel through empty space (216)
radiation (RAY-dee-AY-shun): movement of energy through empty space (216)
radio telescope: telescope that can receive radio waves from sources in space (312)
rain gauge (GAYJ): instrument used to measure precipitation (248)
recycling: using natural resources over and over again (292)
red giants: large, bright stars that are fairly cool (380)
reflecting (rih-FLEKT-ing) **telescope:** telescope that uses a concave mirror to collect light (310)
refracting (rih-FRAKT-ing) **telescope:** telescope that uses convex lenses to produce an enlarged image (308)
relative age: age of an object compared to the age of another object (174)
relative (REL-uh-tiv) **humidity:** amount of water vapor in the air compared to the amount of water vapor the air can hold at capacity (242)
renewable resource: natural resource that can be replaced or reused (290)
residual (rih-ZIJ-oo-ul) **soil:** soil that remains on top of the bedrock from which the soil was formed (90)
respiration (res-puh-RAY-shun): process by which living things combine oxygen with food to produce energy (212)
revolution (reh-vuh-LOO-shun): movement of a planet in its orbit (350)
Richter (RIK-ter) **scale:** scale that measures the energy released by an earthquake (142)
rift valley: deep crack running down the center of the mid-Atlantic ridge (152)
Ring of Fire: major earthquake and volcano zone that almost forms a circle around the Pacific Ocean (144)
rock cycle: series of natural processes by which rocks are slowly changed from one kind of rock to another kind of rock (74)
rotation (roh-TAY-shun): spinning of a planet on its axis (350)
runoff: rainwater that flows into streams and rivers (106)

S

S-waves: second earthquake waves to be recorded at a seismograph station (140)
salinity (suh-LIN-uh-tee): amount of dissolved salts in ocean water (194)
sand bar: long, underwater deposit of sand parallel to a shoreline (120)
satellite (SAT-uh-lite): natural or artificial object orbiting a body in space (318, 334)
saturated (sach-uh-RAYT-ed): filled to capacity (240)
scale: feature that relates distances on a map to actual distances on the earth (30)
scientific method: model, or guide, used to solve problems and to get information (6)
sea arch: gap formed when waves cut completely through a section of rock (118)
sea stack: column of rock remaining after the collapse of a sea arch (118)
sea-floor spreading: process that forms new sea floor (152)
seamount: volcanic mountain on the ocean floor (202)
sediment (SED-uh-munt): soil and rock particles that settle in a liquid (66, 110)
sedimentary (sed-uh-MEN-tuh-ree) **rock:** rock that forms from pieces of other rocks or the remains of once-living things (60)
seismic (SIZE-mik) **waves:** earthquake waves (138)
seismograph (SIZE-muh-graf): instrument that detects and measures earthquakes (138)
sewage: waste that usually is flushed away in water (284)
shield cone: volcanic cone made up of layers of hardened lava (136)
sinkhole: large hole in the ground formed when the roof of a cavern collapses (84)
smog: mixture of smoke, fog, and chemicals (282)
soft water: water containing few or no minerals (286)
soil profile (PRO-fyl): all the layers that make up the soil in an area (92)
solar cells: structures that change sunlight into electricity (298)
solar (SOH-ler) **eclipse:** passing of the moon between the earth and the sun (364)
solar flares: eruptions of electrically charged particles from the surface of the sun (386)
solar noon: time when the sun is highest in the sky (356)
solar system: sun and all the objects that orbit the sun (304, 328)
solstice (SAHL-stis): "sun stop"; day on which the North Pole points toward or away from the sun (354)
sonar: system that bounces sound waves off the ocean floor (192)
specialization (SPESH-uh-lih-zay-shun): studying or working in only one part of a subject (2)
specific humidity (hyoo-MID-uh-tee): actual amount of water in the air (240)
spectroscope (SPEK-truh-skohp): instrument that separates light into different colors (376)
spectrum: bands of the different colors of light (376)
spiral galaxy: galaxy with a thick center and flattened arms (394)
spit: long, narrow deposit of sand connected at one end to the shore (120)
spring tide: tide that is higher and lower than normal tides (368)
spring: natural flow of groundwater to the earth's surface (188)
star: ball of gases that gives off light and heat (374)
station model: record of weather information at a weather station (256)
stratosphere (STRAT-uh-sfeer): middle layer of the atmosphere (214)
stratus (STRAT-us): clouds that form layers across the sky (246)
streak: color of the powder left by a mineral (48)
subduction (sub-DUKT-shun) **zone:** place where old crust is pushed down into a trench (154)
submersible (sub-MUR-suh-bul): underwater research vessel (192)
subscripts (SUB-skriptz): numbers in a chemical formula that show the relative amounts of the elements in a compound (44)
sunspots: dark, cool areas on the sun's surface (386)
supergiants: very large stars (380)
supernova: star that has been blown apart in a violent explosion (382)
symbols: drawings on a map that represent real objects (30)
syncline (SIN-klyn): downward fold in rock layers (126)

T

talus: pile of rocks and rock particles that collects at the base of a slope (102)
temperature: measure of how hot or cold something is (14)
texture (TEKS-chur): size of crystals in an igneous rock (64); size of soil particles (90)
theory (THEE-uh-ree): statement of an idea supported by evidence over a period of time (156)
theory of plate tectonics (tek-TAHN-iks): theory that states the earth's crust is broken into plates that float on the lower mantle (156)
thermocline (THUR-muh-klyn): layer of ocean water in which temperature drops sharply (194)
thrust: force produced in a rocket engine (316)
thunderstorm: storm with thunder, lightning, heavy rain, and strong winds (254)

tide: daily change in the level of the earth's oceans (366)
till: rock material deposited by a glacier (114)
topography (tuh-PAGH-ruh-fee): surface features of the earth (32)
tornado (tohr-NAY-doh): small, very violent funnel-shaped storm (254)
transpiration (tran-spuh-RAY-shun): process by which plants give off water vapor into the air (238)
transported (trans-POR-tid) **soil:** soil that has been moved from above the bedrock from which the soil was formed (90)
trench: long, V-shaped valley on the ocean floor (154, 202)
tributary (TRIB-yoo-ter-ee): small stream that flows into the main stream of a river (106)
tropical (TRAHP-ih-kul) **air mass:** air mass that forms over warm regions (250)
tropical (TRAHP-ih-kul) zone: warm region near the equator (268)
tropopause (TROHP-oh-pawz): place where the troposphere ends (214)
troposphere (TROHP-uh-sfeer): lowest layer of the atmosphere (214)
trough (TROFF): lowest point of a wave (198)
tsunami (tsooh-NAHM-mee): ocean wave caused by an earthquake (142)

U

umbra (UM-bruh): dark part of a shadow (362)
unfoliated: texture of a metamorphic rock that does not have mineral crystals arranged in bands (72)
unit (YOU-nit): amount used to measure something (8)

V

vegetation (vej-ih-TAY-shun): plants (274)
vent: opening from which lava flows (134)
volcanism (VAHL-kuh-niz-um): movement of magma on or inside the earth (134)
volcano (vahl-KAY-noh): vent and the pile of volcanic material around the vent (134)
volume: amount of space something takes up (12)

W

warm front: forward edge of a warm air mass, formed when a warm air mass pushes over a cold air mass (252)
water cycle: repeated movement of water between the earth's surface and the atmosphere (184)
water table: upper layer of saturated rock (186)
wave: regular up-and-down movement of water (118, 198)
wave-cut terrace: flat section of rock formed by the erosion of a sea cliff (118)
weather: day-to-day conditions of the atmosphere (264)
weathering (WETH-ur-ing): breaking down of rocks and other materials on the earth's surface (80, 272)
weight: measure of the pull of gravity on an object (10)
well: hole dug below the water table that fills with groundwater (188)
white dwarfs: very small, hot stars (380)
wildlife: all the plant and animals that live in an area (294)
wind: horizontal movement of air (226)
wind vane: instrument used to measure wind direction (232)

Index

A

B

C

D

E

F

G

H

I

J

K

L

M

N

O

P

Q

R

S

T

U

V

W

Z

Photo Credits

Unit 1
p.1, Grant Heilman
p.3, Rhoda Sidney;
p.15, Culver Pictures

Unit 2
p.19, Grant Heilman;
p.24, Runk/Schoenberger/Heilman;
p.24, Rhoda Sidney;
p.25, NASA;
p.31, Rhoda Sidney;
p.33, B. Roberts/Photo Researchers;
p.33, SuperStock

Unit 3
p.39, Ward's Natural Science;
p.41, The Bettmann Archive;
p.42, Rhoda Sidney;
p.42, Rhoda Sidney;
p.47, AMNH;
p.48, Wolfgang Vogt;
p.49, Ward's Natural Science;
p.50, Ward's Natural Science;
p.52, J. Wilson/SPL Photo Researchers;
p.52, Ward's Natural Science;
p.52, Carolina Biological Supply;
p.52, Carolina Biological Supply;
p.53, Runk/Schoenberger/Grant Heilman;
p.53, AMNH;
p.53, R. Crandall/Stock, Boston

Unit 4
p.59, T. Knauer/Photo Researchers;
p.60, Grant Heilman;
p.60, USGS;
p.61, Hans Namuth/Photo Researchers;
p.63, NYPL Picture Collection;
p.64, Barry Runk/Grant Heilman;
p.64, Ward's Natural Science;
p.65, Ward's Natural Science;
p.65, Breck Kent/Earth Scenes;
p.65, Ward's Natural Science;
p.66, Ward's Natural Science;
p.66, Brent Kent/Earth Scenes;
p.67, Animals, Animals;
p.67, Earth Scenes/Animals, Animals;
p.68, Grant Heilman;
p.68, Wolfgang Vogt;
p.68, Grant Heilman;
p.68, Ward's Natural Science;
p.69, Grant Heilman;
p.71, Rhoda Sidney;
p.72, Ward's Natural Science;
p.72, Grant Heilman;
p.72, Ward's Natural Science;
p.73, Rhoda Sidney;
p.75, Rhoda Sidney

Unit 5
p.79, Grant Heilman
p.80, Barry Runk/Grant Heilman;
p.82, Tony Arruza/Coleman;
p.82, B. Littman;
p.84, Runk/Schoenberger/G. Heilman;
p.84, Biological Photo Service;
p.85, Timothy O'Keefe/Bruce Colman;
p.86, Runk/Schoenberger/Grant Heilman;
p.86, Runk/Schoenberger/Grant Heilman;
p.89, C. G. Maxwell/Photo Researchers;
p.91, Gary A. Connor, Photo Edit;
p.95, Catherine Ursillo/Photo Researchers

Unit 6
p.99, Grant Heilman;
p.100, Frank L. Mendonca/Photo Researchers;
p.101, Bob Daemmrich/Stock, Boston;
p.101, Runk/Schoenberger/Grant Heilman;
p.102, William Felger/Grant Heilman;
p.102, Tom McHugh/Photo Researchers;
p.103, Billy Barnes, Stock Boston;
p.104, Grant Heilman;
p.104, Tracy Knaver/Photo Researchers;
p.105, Photo Researchers;
p.106, Peter Menzel/Stock, Boston;
p.107, Tim McCabe/Soil Conservation;
p.108, Niagara Falls C&V Bureau;
p.109, Sylvie Chappaz/Photo Researchers;
p.110a, Photo Researchers;
p.110b, David Ulmer, Stock Boston;
p.112, Francisco Erize/Bruce Coleman;
p.112, Charlie Ott/Photo Researchers;
p.113, The Bettmann Archive;
p.114, William Felger/Grant Heilman;
p.114, Wardene Weisser/Bruce Coleman;
p.116, William Felger/Grant Heilman;
p.117, William Felger/Grant Heilman;
p.118, Grant Heilman;
p.118, Grant Heilman;
p.119, Jack Denmid/Photo Researchers;
p.121, McIntyre/Photo Researchers;
p.121, Fred Lyon/Photo Researchers

Unit 7
p.125, E. R. Degginger/B. Coleman;
p.126, E. R. Degginger/Earth Scenes;
p.129, Stuart Cohen/Stock, Boston;
p.130, Spencer Grant/Monkmeyer;
p.133, Peter B. Kaplan/Photo Researchers;
p.133, Grant Heilman;
p.135, USGS;
p.137, Rick Smolan/Stock, Boston;
p.139, Peter Menzel/Stock, Boston;
p.142, D. Weintraub/Photo Researchers;
p.145, Monkmeyer Press

Unit 8
p.149, J. Baum/SPL/Photo Researchers;
p.153, USGS Photo Library;
p.155, Scripps Institute of Oceanography

Unit 9
p.165, Runk/Schoenberger/G. Heilman;
p.166, Runk/Schoenberger/G. Heilman;
p.166, Runk/Schoenberger/G. Heilman;
p.167, Ward's Natural Science;
p.167, Ward's Natural Science;
p.167, Carolina Biological Supply;
p.168, J. Koivula/SS/Photo Researchers;
p.171, Bill Gallery, Stock Boston;
p.173, Bruce Coleman;
p.173, Ward's Natural Science;
p.177, GECO UK/SPL/Photo Researchers

Unit 10
p.183, A. Pitcairn/Grant Heilman;
p.188, J. McDonald/Earth Scenes;
p.189, P. Shambroom/Photo Researchers;
p.191, Laurence Gould/Earth Scenes;
p.192, Rod Catanach/ W.H.O.I.;
p.193, Mikki Ansin/Gamma-Liaison;
p.195, Chuck Place/The Image Bank;
p.199, NOAA;
p.200, Steinhart Acquarium/Photo Researchers;
p.200, Carolina Biological Supply;
p.202, Tom McHugh/Photo Researchers;
p.203, AP/Wide World;
p.205, John Colwell/Grant Heilman;
p.206, Tom McHugh/Photo Researchers
p.207, Tom Stack & Associates;

Unit 11
p.211, Photo Researchers;
p.213, F. Pedrick/The Image Works;
p.215, Goddard/NASA;
p.217, Image Bank;
p.221, B. Daemmrich/Stock, Boston;
p.224, Jeff Greenberg;
p.226, Bruck Henderson/Stock, Boston;
p.229, P. Menzel/Stock, Boston;
p.231, Coco McCoy/Rainbow;
p.232, Mark Antman/The Image Works;
p.232, Krasenann/Photo Researchers

Unit 12
p.237, P. Jude/SPL/Photo Researchers;
p.238, Four-By-Five;
p.241, L. Migdale/Photo Researchers;
p.244, B. L. Runk/Grant Heilman;
p.244, Jeff Lepore/Photo Researchers;
p.246, K. Van Den Berg/Photo Researchers;
p.246, R. Dollarhide/Monkmeyer;
p.246, D. Frazier/Photo Researchers;
p.247, N-CAR;
p.247, Grant Heilman;
p.250, Runk/Schoenberger/G. Heilman;
p.253, John Yurka, The Picture Cube;
p.254, D. Baumhefner/NOAA;
p.255, NOAA;
p.259, David Young-Wolff, Photo Edit

Unit 13
p.263, The Image Bank;
p.265, J. Holland/Stock, Boston;
p.269, AP/Wide World;
p.271, Everett C. Johnson, Folio;
p.273, Grant Heilman;
p.274, F. Prenzel/Animals, Animals

Unit 14
p.279, A. Pitcairn/Grant Heilman;
p.281, AP/Wide World;
p.282, T. McHugh/Photo Researchers;
p.284, H. Rogers/Monkmeyer;
p.284, Tom Myers;
p.287, M. Antman/The Image Works;
p.288, Eastcott/Momatiuk/The Image Works;
p.289, Tom Myers;
p.290, Runk/Schoenberger/G. Heilman;
p.291, P. Conklin/Monkmeyer;
p.292, Grant Heilman;
p.292, M. Antman/The Image Works;
p.294, Tom Myers;
p.294, R. S. Virdee/Grant Heilman;
p.295, Jerry Cooke/Photo Researchers;
p.296, Runk/Schoenberger/G. Heilman;
p.297, Barry L. Runk/Grant Heilman;
p.298, Larry Lefever/Grant Heilman
p.299, Rod Planck/Photo Researchers

Unit 15
p.303, NASA;
p.304, Runk/Schoenberger/G. Heilman;
p.304, G. Haling/Photo Researchers;
p.306, NASA;
p.311, Rhoda Sidney;
p.312, NRAO/AUI;
p.313, FPG;
p.316, W. Bocxe/Photo Researchers;
p.318, NASA;
p.320, NASA;
p.320, NASA;
p.320, NASA;
p.321, NASA;
p.322, NASA;
p.322, NASA;
p.323, NASA

Unit 16
p.327, J. Giannicchi/SS/Photo Researchers;
p.334, NASA;
p.334, NASA/JPL;
p.334, NASA/JPL;
p.335, NASA/JPL;
p.336, NASA;
p.336, NASA;
p.336, NASA;
p.338, NASA;
p.338, NASA/JPL;
p.338, NASA/JPL;
p.339, NASA/JPL;
p.340, NASA/JPL;
p.340, NASA/JPL;
p.340, NASA/JPL;
p.341, David A. Hardy/Science Photo Library, Photo Researchers;
p.342, NASA/JPL;
p.342, NASA;
p.342, Hale Observatories/Hansen Planetarium;
p.343, NASA;
p.344, NASA;
p.344, NASA;
p.345, John Stanford/SPL/Photo Researchers

Unit 17
p.349, NASA;
p.351, Bill Belknap, Photo Researchers;
p.355, Hugh Rogers/Monkmeyer;
p.357, R. Dollarhide/Monkmeyer;
p.358, G. K. Scott/Photo Researchers;
p.359, NASA;
p.360, Lick Observatory;
p.361, NASA;
p.362, G. East/Photo Researchers;
p.365, Dan McCoy/Rainbow;
p.366, Runk/Schoenberger/G. Heilman;
p.366, Runk/Schoenberger/G. Heilman;
p.367, R. Das/Monkmeyer;
p.369, Eastcott/Momatiuk/The Image Works

Unit 18
p.373, Science Source/Photo Researchers;
p.374, NASA;
p.375, Image Bank
p.378, Hansen Planetarium;
p.381, NYPL Picture Collection;
p.384, NASA;
p.386, NASA;
p.386, NOAO;
p.386, NASA;
p.387, NASA;
p.388, UPI/Bettmann Newsphotos;
p.389, Bruce Coleman, Inc.;
p.389, Science Source/Photo Researchers;
p.390, Bruce Coleman;
p.394, Bruce Coleman;
p.394, NASA;
p.394, NOAO;
p.394, NOAO;
p.396, NOAO;
p.397, NASA, Photo Researchers